The Journal of Midshipman Chaplin

BERINGIANA is a series of publications relating broadly to the explorer Vitus Bering. Its scope encompasses Danish-Russian relations, exploration of the North Pacific, Russian eighteenth-century culture and history, Siberian studies, and the history of Russian America.

Series editor: Peter Ulf Møller, Professor Emeritus, Department of East European Studies, Institute of History and Area Studies, Aarhus University.

The logo of the BERINGIANA series, designed by Lotte Bruun Rasmussen, is a free variation of Vitus Bering's coat-of-arms. Its "bear" (German: Bär) and "ring" components are drawn from the explorer's surname.

The Beringiana series:

Volume 1
Under Vitus Bering's Command
New Perspectives on the Russian Kamchatka Expeditions
Edited by
PETER ULF MØLLER AND NATASHA OKHOTINA LIND

Volume 2
Peder von Haven: Reise udi Rusland
Første udgave fra 1743
Annotated edition (in Danish) by
PETER ULF MØLLER AND JESPER OVERGAARD NIELSEN

Volume 3
Letters from the Governor's Wife
A View of Russian Alaska
1859-1862
Edited by
ANNIE CONSTANCE CHRISTENSEN

Volume 4
INGE MARIE LARSEN
Da smør var guld
Sibirisk smørproduktion og -eksport
1895-1905
In Danish, with summaries in English and in Russian

Russian State Naval Archives (RGAVMF)
Institute of History and Area Studies, Aarhus University

The Journal of Midshipman Chaplin

A RECORD OF BERING'S
FIRST KAMCHATKA EXPEDITION

Edited and translated from the Russian
by Tatiana S. Fedorova, Peter Ulf Møller,
Viktor G. Sedov, and Carol L. Urness

With a foreword by Vladimir S. Sobolev,
Director of the Russian State Naval Archives

Aarhus University Press |

The Journal of Midshipman Chaplin
A Record of Bering's First Kamchatka Expedition
(Beringiana, Volume 5)

© The editors and Aarhus University Press 2010

Cover: Lotte Bruun Rasmussen
Pen-and-ink drawing by Igor Pshenichnyi
Typeset and printed by Narayana Press

ISBN 978 87 7934 314 6

Aarhus University Press

Aarhus
Langelandsgade 177
DK-8200 Århus N

Copenhagen
Tuborgvej 164
2400 Copenhagen NV

www.unipress.dk

The publication has been supported by grants from
The Carlsberg Foundation and
The Aarhus University Research Foundation

Contents

Acknowledgements

The editors would like to thank

Dr. Elena Viktorovna Orlova, chief of the laboratory of digital cartography of the State Hydrological Institute in St. Petersburg and an outstanding expert on Geographical Information Systems (GIS), for her assistance in preparing the first digital layout of Chaplin's journal and the modern maps outlining the route of the First Kamchatka Expedition; James R. Gibson, historical geographer and professor emeritus at York University, Ontario, for reading and most helpfully commenting on an early version of our translation of Chaplin's journal; Artist Igor Pshenichnyi of St. Petersburg, for permitting us to use samples of his work in the genre of marine painting for cover and illustrations in this book; Photographer Nikolai Turkin of St. Petersburg for his valuable services and skilled work.

Finally and yet importantly, the editors wish to express their gratitude to The Carlsberg Foundation and The Aarhus University Research Foundation for generously funding this volume.

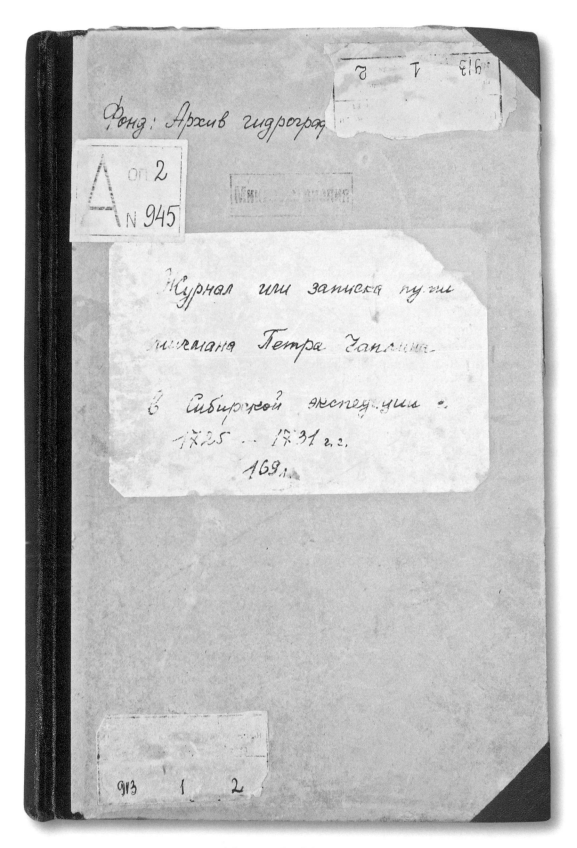

PLATE 1. Front cover of the journals of the First Kamchatka Expedition.
The label on the cover reads: "Journal or Travel Notebook of Midshipman Piotr Chaplin from the Siberian expedition 1725-1731". Fund 913, inventory 1, unit 2 of the Russian State Naval Archives in St. Petersburg (RGAVMF). 19 × 31,5 cm.

Courtesy RGAVMF. Photo by Nikolai Turkin.

Foreword

The Kamchatka expedition 1725-1730, dispatched by order of Peter the Great, was the first voyage of discovery ever to be undertaken by the Russian Navy. The expedition faced a complicated task – to proceed from the Kamchatka River to the north along the Asian shore in order to define the north-eastern borders of the Russian Empire and lay them down on a map. For this special expedition, a team of shipwrights from the St. Petersburg Admiralty constructed a single-masted vessel on Kamchatka, in the shortest possible time. The vessel was named the *Holy Archangel Gabriel*, and it became the first ship under the ensign of the Russian Navy to sail on the Pacific Ocean.

Historians are aware of the fact that the number of surviving, original documents passed down to us from the First Kamchatka Expedition is extremely small. Today each of these documents is considered a unique historical source. One document, however, that is outstandingly worthy of such appraisal is the journal of one of the expedition members, Midshipman Piotr Chaplin. This document is in the custody of the Russian State Naval Archives in St. Petersburg.

The journal reflects the course of the entire expedition as it proceeded under Captain Vitus Bering's command. Chaplin kept his journal from the moment of the expedition's departure from St. Petersburg in January 1725 and through to its return to the Russian capital in March 1730. He recorded, systematically and thoroughly, all events in the exhausting life of the expedition. His entries reflect the long and strenuous road of the expedition members with their heavy loads across Siberia all the way to Okhotsk, and further by sea across to Kamchatka and overland on to Lower Kamchatsk. Daily records also describe the historical voyage of the *Holy Gabriel*.

During the voyage, many important geographical discoveries were made. Numerous hydrographical investigations were carried out, and contacts were made to the indigenous population.

Throughout the expedition Chaplin usually found himself in the proximity of the commander, Bering, carrying out his orders and managing the expedition's cash box. For that reason, his journal entries have pre- served much information about the activities of Bering himself, the decisions made by him, and his methods for managing such a vast undertaking as the First Kamchatka Expedition.

The main task of the expedition was practically fulfilled. The *Holy Gabriel* succeeded in passing through the strait separating Asia from America.

Bering's expedition enriched the science of his day with precious information about the endless expanses of Siberia and its eastern coastline. In particular, the expedition's determination of the coordinates of many places on its long route through Siberia and along the Asian shore of the Strait was quite accurate for the time. Based on expedition records a "Catalogue" was made of towns and "conspicuous places" that had been mapped and, additionally, a "Table" with information about other settlements encountered by the expedition.

This information was presented to the Russian government and used when preparations for the Second Kamchatka Expedition began. The order to dispatch the new expedition was signed by Empress Anna Ioannovna in April 1732.

The present publication of the Journal of Midshipman Chaplin is the result of longstanding research cooperation between scholars from three countries: Denmark, Russia, and the United States of America. The publication was made possible by grants from The Carlsberg Foundation and The Aarhus University Research Foundation.

The present publication will be an important addition to the source material readily available to investigations into the history of the Kamchatka Expeditions and the opening up of Siberia.

In addition, it sets an example of contemporary significance: As an international project within the humanities, it serves the noble cause of mutual understanding and peaceful cooperation among nations.

V.S. Sobolev
Director of the Russian State Naval Archives,
Doctor of History

St. Petersburg, June 2008

12.

1

Книга платьности в начало
Интендуй миллона
Петра Еаттина

с 725 по 731 г

4 бумага одинакова содержанія

The Editors' Introduction

On Chaplin's journal and its author

The logbooks or "journals" of the *Holy Archangel Gabriel* (usually abbreviated to *Holy Gabriel,* in Russian: *Sviatoi Gavriil*) hold a special place among the documents of the First Kamchatka Expedition. They are the only official sources that preserve the history of the expedition in detail. Two logbooks were kept, by assistants to the leader of the expedition, Vitus Bering: Lieutenant Aleksei Chirikov and naval cadet, later midshipman, Piotr Chaplin both made daily or almost daily entries, each in his own volume. Their logbooks were later bound together in a single volume (shown in the adjacent illustration).

From the eighteenth century to the present this volume has been kept in the archives of the Russian navy. It makes up one separate unit in the Russian State Naval Archives in St. Petersburg (RGAVMF), among the papers of the Hydrographic Archives (RGAVMF, fund 913, inventory 1, unit 2).

Entries in the logbook by Chirikov were begun on 23 April 1725 and end abruptly on 9 November 1729. His journal was not signed, but the distinctive handwriting of Chirikov leaves no doubt about its authorship. The logbook by Chaplin starts with the departure from St. Petersburg on 24 January 1725 and continues until his return to the capital on 1 March 1730. It is in Chaplin's handwriting and signed by him.

For the present publication the logbook of Piotr Chaplin was chosen, since it covers the entire period of the First Kamchatka Expedition, and records it in detail. Besides, Chaplin was usually near the commander of the expedition, carrying out his instructions. He recorded when and where Bering went, and for what purpose, and thus offers the closest view of Bering as the head of the expedition and as a man whose character is still a topic of discussion among historians.

Records in the two journals differ from each other for the time when the expedition was traveling by land and preparing for the voyages. Chirikov and Chaplin were often in different places, fulfilling different tasks, and consequently their journal entries were different on the overland journey. For instance, in 1725 Bering sent Chaplin ahead with a few men to prepare the way for the main body of the expedition. Chirikov spent the winter 1726-1727 in Iakutsk, while Bering and Chaplin were already in Okhotsk. Differences in contents between the journals are often due to the different tasks performed by a midshipman and a lieutenant. Chaplin was working under Bering's immediate instructions. On behalf of the expedition's leader, he would submit requisitions to the chancelleries of local authorities and press for their fulfillment. He was in charge of practical household matters, such as paying wages and handing out provisions to the expedition members. Chirikov was responsible for transportation of the expedition's heavy and bulky equipment and food supplies. Differences in personality and intellectual curiosity of the two men are also reflected in their journals. However, during the voyages at sea in 1728-1729 Chaplin and Chirikov were together and took turns on watch. Each recorded his own watch in his logbook, and then copied the missing information from the logbook of the other. Usually these entries are therefore completely identical. It is our hope that Chirikov's logbook will also eventually be published. Until that happens, the reader may get a preliminary impression of it in our notes to Chaplin's journal, where we cite some passages from Chirikov for comparison.

The historiographer of the Russian Navy V.N. Berkh was the first scholar who came upon the logbooks and used them in his book on Bering's First Kamchatka Expedition (Berkh 1823). Shortly thereafter, the Russian explorer Count F.P. Litke studied the logbooks while preparing for his circumnavigation of the globe on the navy sloop *Seniavin* (1826-1829). At the end of

◄ PLATE 2. Fund 913, inventory 1, unit 2, folio 1. The title reads: "Journal of Midshipman Piotr Chaplin from the Kamchatka expedition from 1725 to 1731 + a journal of similar contents [i.e., Lieutenant Chirikov's journal]".

Courtesy Russian State Naval Archives (RGAVMF). Photo by Nikolai Turkin.

the nineteenth century, the American naturalist W.H. Dall gave a summary in English of Berkh's rendering of Chaplin's journal (Dall 1890). In the same year, the Russian naval historian V. Vakhtin published excerpts from the journals of both Chaplin (70 pp.) and Chirikov (12 pp.) (Vakhtin 1890). Internal archival records show that more recently researchers have consulted the logbooks in 1936, 1946, 1968, and 1971.[1] Some fragments from Chaplin's logbook were published in *Russkie ekspeditsii* 1984. The present edition of Chaplin's journal is the first complete one in any language.

Piotr Avraamovich Chaplin was born in 1699 "in his patrimony", the village Rozhestvennoe, in the Dmitrovsk District of the Moscow Province where his father, a retired major, owned five peasant households.[2] On 13 January 1715, he was admitted to the School of Mathematical and Navigational Sciences in Moscow.[3] By 1716, the number of peasant households belonging to his father had dropped to three. Young Piotr was therefore entitled to public "board money", 4 *den'ga* (2 kopecks) per day. At the end of 1716, he transferred to the Naval Academy in St. Peterburg, together with other pupils of the School.[4] In 1718, Chaplin entered military service in the navy. In 1718-1724, he sailed as a corporal on various ships in the Gulf of Finland and the Baltic Sea, getting practical marine experience. In 1724, he graduated from the Academy in the rank of naval cadet (*gardemarin*). His diploma states that he knows the arts of navigation and gunnery, soldiers' drill and seamen's work, and – "in part" – how to turn a ship and other practical sailing skills.[5]

In January 1725, Naval Cadet Chaplin was assigned to the crew of the First Kamchatka Expedition, and on 24 January he set out from St. Petersburg on his long journey. In accordance with the Navy Regulations (*Morskoi ustav*) of 1720, created under the personal supervision and participation of Peter the Great, he kept a travel diary from the very first day, and, when sailing, a logbook.

On 25 October 1727, expedition leader Bering promoted Chaplin midshipman for his "hard and diligent service, in anticipation of approval by the Admiralty College".[6] Bering's order was announced to the crew on 26 October.[7] The decree of the Admiralty College on the promotion of Chaplin followed on 25 June 1728.[8] With the expedition completed, nearly all participating officers received higher ranks, including Chaplin, who was promoted sublieutenant (*unter-leitenant*) on 23 October 1730.

Chaplin took part in the drawing up of the concluding map of the expedition. In 1731-1732, he was in

Moscow together with Bering, for the revision of the financial documents of the expedition. On 18 January 1733, in connection with the introduction of new staff categories in the navy, he was listed among "lieutenants in the rank of major". In 1734, he sailed on the ship *Peter II*. The following year he was sent to Kazan' to supervise the delivery of timber to the Admiralty in St. Petersburg, and returned to the capital only in September 1736. He then sailed on various ships in the Gulf of Finland and the Baltic Sea. In 1746, as commander of the frigate *No. 2*, he took this newly launched ship from the shipyard of Arkhangel'sk to Kronstadt. In 1749-1751, he was in command of the *Saint Nicholas* (*Sviatoi Nikolai*) and sailed to Danzig. On 5 September 1751, with the introduction of a new staff list, Chaplin was promoted captain of the third rank. In the years 1751-1755, he was in charge of the frigate *Selafail* and a squadron of training frigates under the Marine School for the Gentry (*Morskoi shliakhetnyi kadetskii korpus*). He went with the naval cadets on training voyages in the Baltic and the North Sea.

On 5 March 1756, Chaplin was promoted captain of the second rank. In 1757-1759, he commanded the *Saint Paul* (*Sviatoi Pavel*) and the *Archangel Michael* (*Arkhangel Mikhail*), and went with a fleet to Danzig and Copenhagen. In 1760 he commanded first the *Saint Clemens Romanus* (*Sviatoi Kliment papa rimskii*), and then again the *Saint Paul,* and took part in the blockade of Kolberg during the Seven Years' War. In 1760-1762, he was captain of the Port of Reval (present-day Tallinn).

On 21 December 1762, "due to old age and ill health", Chaplin was appointed captain of the Port of Arkhangel'sk. On 22 September 1763, he was promoted captain-commander. On 29 August 1765, he died in Arkhangel'sk.[9]

A cape in the Bering Sea has been named after Chaplin.

For biographical information on Chirikov, cf. note 6, pp. 291.

Editorial principles and notes on the translation
Chaplin wrote his journal in a tiny Cyrillic cursive (*skoropis'*), thus saving paper, but making reading quite difficult. For that reason, step one in the translation process was to produce an accurate typewritten transcription of the Russian manuscript. Tatiana Fedorova carried out this task. The transcription was then translated into English through the concerted efforts of Viktor Sedov, Carol L. Urness and Peter Ulf Møller. At the initial stage of this work, the late Janis Cers (of Minneapolis) made valuable contributions. Tatiana

Fedorova and Peter Ulf Møller annotated the text of the journal. Viktor Sedov made the modern maps.

In presenting the translated text, we have made scrupulous efforts to preserve the page layout of the original manuscript. As a rule, one printed page of the translation corresponds to one page – recto or verso – of a manuscript folio. However, in the parts of the journal that record the voyages of 1728 and 1729, we have had to divide the translation of one manuscript page over two or even three book pages. Still, we hope the continuous indication of manuscript folio numbers will help the reader preserve a sense of turning over pages in the original journal.

Dates are given in accordance with the Julian calendar, which in the eighteenth century was eleven days behind the Gregorian calendar. The Julian calendar was in official use in Russia from 1700 until 1918. We call attention to a peculiarity in the dating of navy documents of the time. In the eighteenth century, days at sea started at 12 o'clock noon, whereas days on land were reported according to the civil calendar. On the sea, the day began not from midnight but from noon. The first part of the "sea day" was the second half of the previous day of the civil calendar.

This explains why an event in Chaplin's logbook and the same event in a report from Bering could occur on different dates. On 9 June 1728, Chaplin wrote: "At 4 p.m. we prayed and began to launch the ship." (Cf. the present edition, folio 42). In Bering's report of 10 July 1728 to the Admiralty College, we read: "Today I humbly report: on 8 June the ship was launched…".[10] Under 14 July 1728 we read in Chaplin's logbook: "At 7 p.m. having weighed anchor, we left with God's help from the mouth of the Kamchatka River" (folio 43). In Bering's report of 10 March 1730 to the Admiralty College, it says: "…13 July 1728, with God's help, we put out from the mouth of the Kamchatka River…".[11] In such cases, the difference in dates is not a mistake or a slip of the pen by the authors. Chaplin's logbook used "sea days," Bering's reports used "civil days". More examples of differences in dates between the logbook and other expedition records are likely to exist.

The reader should also note that Chaplin starts out using civil days, but shifts to sea days when the expedition puts out from the Port of Okhotsk. As he explains, "dates are reckoned from midnight to midnight until August 22, 1727, and after that date, from midday to midday" (folio 2).

Chaplin and Chirikov both used astronomical symbols for the days of the week. For practical reasons, we have replaced the symbols with more familiar abbreviations: Sun., Mon., etc. To familiarize themselves with the symbols, readers are invited to compare the photograph of folio 2 of the original manuscript with the adjacent translation (pp. 18-19).

The expedition navigators measured *time of day* by sand glasses. Chaplin's logbook usually recorded events with reference to the hour during which they occurred, e.g., *at/ during the sixth hour*, in Russian *v 6-m chasu* (= between 5 and 6 o'clock). For readability, we usually translate these highly frequent indications of time as, e.g., *by 6 o'clock* or *at 6 o'clock*, even if this means abolishing in the translation the distinction between *during the sixth hour* and the less frequent indications of the precise hour, *at 6 o'clock* (sharp), in Russian *v 6 chasov*. In most cases, the context will make it clear which is meant. We annotate the more ambiguous cases.

When Chaplin records events that took place *at, from* or *until the beginning of an hour*, e.g., *the sixth hour*, in Russian *v nachale/ s/ do 6-go chasa,* we translate by reference to the previous hour: *(just) after/ from/ to 5 o'clock.*

In *transliterating Russian words*, mostly names, into Roman alphabet we use the Library of Congress system, with a few slight modifications: We omit ligatures, transliterate Russian *ë* as "io", and make no distinction between Russian *и* and *й*, rendering both as "i".

Russian names in the translation are usually direct transliterations of the form used by Chaplin. However, if a Russian name has a well-established anglicized form, we use it (*Moscow, St. Petersburg, Peter the Great*). Names of non-Russian origin are rendered in their original form, when possible, rather than in transliteration from the Cyrillic. For instance, we give the name of Bering's Danish-born lieutenant as *Spanberch*, which is the obvious German form behind the Russian *Shpanberkh* (Шпанберх) that Chaplin used consistently. In editorial text, however, we refer to the same person by his more usual Danish name Spangberg.[12]

Geographical names in the text have been verified as far as possible. *Iudomskii krest* and *Krest* will be rendered as *Iudoma Cross* and *the Cross. Verkhnii Kamchadal'skii ostrog* and its synonyms *Verkhnekamchatskii ostrog* and *Verkhnii* will appear as *the Upper Kamchatsk outpost*, or just *Upper Kamchatsk*. Correspondingly, *Nizhnekamchadal'skii / Nizhnekamchatskii ostrog* will be translated as *the Lower Kamchatsk outpost,* or just *Lower Kamchatsk*. Various spellings by Chaplin of the same name, we usually reduce to one (e.g. *Okhotsk* and *Akhotsk* in the document will both be *Okhotsk* in the translation).

Whenever we found there was a point to citing the precise Russian wording of a passage, we have done so in notes to the translated text.

Square brackets in the text of the journal indicate editorial interpolations or comments. Thus, a few missing lines and characters in Chaplin have been re-established by comparison with the logbook of Chirikov and inserted in square brackets, e.g., *NbE½[E]*. In addition, we annotate some of these cases.

Italics in the text of the journal indicate that the italicized word is explained in the glossary, p. 16. Italics are used only the first time the word occurs in the journal.

Small things betray that Chaplin did not always make his entries immediately. For example, there is an entry in the logbook for 3 July 1727: "I received an order to distribute provisions to the soldiers that had arrived from the Cross, and reported on the distribution. This order I received on the 5 [July]" (folio 27). Sometimes Chaplin would leave small gaps in his entries to be filled in with details later – and then forget to return to them. Such cases are also annotated.

The journal (*zhurnal*) was an official genre of writing defined by certain guidelines in the Russian Navy Regulations. In book three, chapter 12, on the obligations of the navigator and the second mate, it says: "[The navigator or second mate] must keep an accurate journal, writing down the course, the distance covered, the leeway, various occurrences, the increase and decrease of winds and sails, compass variation, sea currents and sea bottom". In addition, he must verify the compass, watch the sandglasses, keep track of coastlines and mark unknown shoals and submerged rocks on the map. At the end of a voyage, he had to submit it to his commanding captain for examination in a conference of senior officers.[13]

Following these guidelines, Chaplin wrote much of his journal in tabular form. At this time, ship's log entries on Russian navy vessels had not yet taken a definite, mandatory shape, and throughout his long journey, Chaplin tried in various ways to improve upon the layout of his tables and the order of presentation of the required information.

A considerable part of the journal is devoted to the description of weather conditions during the expedition. A universally recognized system for the recording of wind velocity, cloudiness, wave height etc. had not yet come into existence. Nevertheless, it is clear that Chaplin described *the force of the wind* in a systematic terminology that seems to make up a wind scale of 12 classes. His gradation of the 10 classes between *calm* (*tikho*) and *violent storm (shtorm velikoi)* relies on different adjectives to the same noun *wind* (*vetr*). A few times, *wind* is also used without an adjective (e.g., folios 12v, 33v). This presents a considerable challenge to the translation. Rather than recreating the entire range of adjectives in English, we have chosen to reduce the number of different adjectives by shifting some of the gradation to the noun. We have used the English terms for the first twelve classes of the modernized Beaufort wind force scale to render Chaplin's wind descriptions. Below, we have tabulated the corresponding Russian and English terms, and added, for comparison, the

TABLE No. 1 · WIND SCALE

In the journal	In our translation	The Beaufort Scale	Mph
Tikho, shtil', bezvetrie (тихо, штиль, безветрие)	Calm, still	0. Calm	0
Vetr tikhoi, vetr ves'ma mal, vetr samoi maloi (ветр тихой, ветр весьма мал, ветр самой малой)	Light air	1. Light air	2
Malyi vetr, vetr mal, vetr maloi (малый ветр, ветр мал, ветр малой)	Light breeze	2. Light breeze	5
Vetr nebol'shoi, vetr nebol'shei (ветр небольшой, ветр небольшей)	Gentle breeze	3. Gentle breeze	10
Vetr nevelikoi, vetr nevelik (ветр невеликой, ветр невелик)	Moderate breeze	4. Moderate breeze	15
Vetr umerennoi (ветр умеренной)	Fresh breeze	5. Fresh breeze	22
Vetr srednei, vetr iz srednikh, vetr posredstvennoi (ветр средней, ветр из средних, ветр посредственной)	Strong breeze	6. Strong breeze	27
Vetr nemaloi, vetr nemal (ветр немалой, ветр немал)	Moderate gale	7. Moderate gale	35
Vetr bol'shei, vetr izriadno velik (ветр большей, ветр изрядно велик)	Fresh gale	8. Fresh gale	42
Vetr velikoi (ветр великой)	Strong gale	9. Strong gale	50
Zhestokoi vetr (жестокой ветр)	Whole gale	10. Whole gale	60
Shtorm velikoi (шторм великой)	Violent storm	11. Violent storm	70

first twelve classes of the Beaufort scale, including the mean wind speeds that now define them, in miles per hour. The reader should, however, keep in mind that Chaplin's observations were made a century before the Beaufort scale became a standard for Great Britain's Royal Navy. They are likely to be much more subjective than the modern measurable figures for wind speed.

In a few cases, Chaplin describes the wind with reference to the spread of canvas on the ship, e.g., "the wind did not allow carrying the upper sails", in Russian *vetr rifmarsel'skut* (folio 31). Apart from the adjectives that graduate wind force, the wind may also be *gusty (poryvnyi)*, *changeable (nepostoianen)* (that is, of varying strength), *variable (peremennyi)* (that is, from shifting directions), *contrary/adverse (protivnyi)*, *fair (sposobnoi)* etc.

Chaplin's other meteorological observations also reflect his efforts towards a systematic description. Recording the *cloud coverage*, he used a terminology that seems to form a scale from bright to dark, in spite of some redoubling and overlapping. The basic terms are:

TABLE No. 2 · CLOUD COVERAGE

In the journal	In the translation
Svetlo (светло)	Bright, light
Iasno (ясно)	Fair weather, clear
Solntse (солнце)	Sun, sunny
Siianie (сияние)	Sunshine
Prosiianie (просияние)	Clearing up, sunny spells
Oblachno (облачно)	Cloudy, clouds
Pasmurno (пасмурно)	Gloomy, overcast
Primrachno (примрачно)	Dusky
Mrachno (мрачно)	Dark, murky

Each of these terms may be modified in several ways, to provide a more detailed description of the cloud ceiling. *Cloudy,* for instance, may form part of combinatory variants like *with few clouds (malooblachno)*, *lightly cloudy (svetlooblachno)* and *with dark clouds (temnooblachno)*, not to mention *cloudy with sunny spells/ cloudy with sun breaking through (oblachno s prosiianiem)* or even *cloudy with occasional breaks (oblachno s vremennym prosiianiem)*. *Fair weather (iasno)* may be *with small/ light clouds (s malymi oblakami)*, etc.

Rain may be described as a *downpour (dozhd' velikoi)* or a *drizzle (dozhd' maloi)*, and it may be *intermittent (dozhd' s peremeshkoiu)*. Snowfalls may be *heavy (sneg velikoi)* or *light (sneg maloi)* – or *not so big (sneg nebol'shei)*. Snow and wind may combine to

blowing snow of various degrees, from *heavy snow-storm (metel' velikaia)* to *drifting snow (metel')* and *snow-squalls (metel' vremenem, metel' malaia)*.

Frost *(moroz)* also has its gradation, from *light (maloi)* through *moderate (nebol'shei, nevelik)* to *hard (velikoi)*. Chaplin had no way of measuring temperatures. Thermometers were still at an experimental stage.

Glossary
Scholarly translations from Russian often abound in transliterations of culturally unique and presumably "untranslatable" Russian words, which the reader should subsequently look up in a special glossary. As a result, things Russian often appear stranger than they actually are. We try, as far as possible, to use English near-equivalents rather than transliterated Russian words. Rather than explaining in the glossary that a *iam* is a posting station, we prefer to translate the Russian word as *posting station*, and provide details on Russian posting stations in a note. *Ostrog*, the historical Russian word for a stronghold, wooden fortress or minor settlement in Siberia and Kamchatka, will be translated as *outpost*. Another frequent word in the journal is *iasak*, the fur tribute paid to the Russian state by the native peoples of Siberia. We translate it as *tribute*, with an annotation.

Consequently, our glossary below (table no. 3) is limited to a few recurring Russian terms that seem to lack a reasonably adequate English equivalent, and to some historical terminology.

Several of these terms, however, we render in existing anglicized versions rather than in direct transliteration, e.g., *verst*, plur. *versts* (rather than Russian *versta*, plur. *viorsty*); *sazhen*, plur. *sazhens* (rather than Russian *sazhen'*, plur. *sazheni*); *ruble* and *kopeck* (rather than *rubl'* and *kopeika*); *kvass* rather than *kvas*; *yurt* rather than *iurta*.

Some of the terms explained in the glossary are actually in English, but their use in the Russian cultural context may nevertheless require some explanation, e.g., *boyar's son, dugout, seafarer, servitor.*

The terms explained in the glossary are in italics the first time they occur in the text of the journal.

Indication of compass bearings
The logbooks of the *Holy Gabriel* recorded the directions of wind and sea currents, ship's courses and compass bearings of coastal objects in the system of the Dutch navy. Table No. 4 shows the Dutch system, its conversion into English (as used in the translation) and into the modern circular system.

Balagan	Native or Cossack summer dwelling in Kamchatka (for more details, see note XXX)
Boyar's son	in Russian *syn boiarskii*. "An impoverished member of Russian nobility; in Siberia such persons played a prominent role as middle-rank military commanders and civil administrators" (Kushnarev 1990, p. xxii)
Den'ga	Russian monetary unit, 0.5 kopeck
Doshchanik	Large, flat-bottomed river-boat
Dugout	In Russian *bat*. A small river and coastal boat, usually made by hollowing out a log
Guberniia	Literally, "governorship"; an administrative division equivalent to the province
Iar	A steep bank, as in the geographical name Beriozovyi Iar
Iukola	Dried fish, usually salmon
Kaiur	Dog-team driver, reindeer driver or ferryman, on Kamchatka
Karbus	A type of large rowboat, a small cargo boat (also with the spelling *karbas*)
Kopeck	Russian monetary unit, $\frac{1}{100}$ of a ruble
Kvass	Traditional staple beverage made from malt and rye flour
Lodka	A rowboat, a small vessel for river navigation
Pood	16.38 kg
Pound	In Russian *funt*, 0.4095 kg
Ruble	Russian monetary unit, 100 kopecks
Sailor	In Russian *matroz*. A trained seaman from the navy, as opposed to a *seafarer*
Sazhen	2.13 m
Seafarer	In Russian *morekhod*. A local seaman or navigator, usually without any formal training, as opposed to a *sailor*
Serviceman	In Russian *sluzhitel'*. A term used for workmen and common soldiers, i.e., people of no or low rank, in military or civil service. The word in its plural form will often be translated as "the men". Chaplin uses this term about the personnel of Bering's detachment, as distinct from local Siberian personnel that he refers to using the term *servitor* (see below)
Servitor	In Russian *sluzhilyi* or *sluzhivyi*. "State servitors […] were mainly military personnel (especially Cossacks) but also noblemen and others who owed civil or military service to the state in return for land" (Gibson 1969, p. xvii, n). Chaplin uses this term about local Siberian personnel, as distinct from the personnel of Bering's own detachment
Steward	In Russian *prikazchik*, a person empowered to work for somebody; in Siberia usually a low-ranking official, e.g., administrator of an outpost
Supervisor	In Russian *zakazchik*, in Siberia, the head of an outpost
Toion	Chief of aborigines
Uezd	District (administrative division)
Ulus	Nomad camp or other settlement or in Siberia
Verst	Russian measure of length, 1066.8 m = 500 sazhens
Voevoda	Military governor
Volost	Small administrative peasant division
Yurt	Nomads' tent, also used about natives' winter dwellings on Kamchatka

TABLE No. 4 · KEY TO BEARINGS

Dutch	English	in °	Dutch	English	in °	Dutch	English	in °
N	N	0°	ZOtO	SEbyE	123°8	WZW½W	WSW½W	253°1
N¼O	N¼E	2°8	ZO¾O	SEbyE¼S	126°6	WZW¾W	WSW¾W	255°9
N½O	N½E	5°6	ZO½O	SEbyE½S	129°4	WtZ	WbyS	258°8
N¾O	N¾E	8°4	ZO¼O	SEbyE¾S	132°2	WtZ¼W	WbyS¼W	261°6
NtO	NbyE	11°2	ZO	SE	135°0	WtZ½W	WbyS½W	264°4
NtO¼O	NbyE¼E	14°1	ZOtZ¾O	SE¼S	137°8	WtZ¾W	WbyS¾W	267°2
NtO½O	NbyE½E	16°9	ZOtZ¼O	SE¾S	143°4	WtN¾W	W¼N	272°8
NtO¾O	NbyE¾E	19°7	ZOtZ	SEbyS	146°2	WtN½W	W½N	275°6
NNO	NNE	22°5	ZZO¾O	SEbyS¼S	149°1	WtN¼W	W¾N	278°4
NNO¼O	NNE¼E	25°3	ZZO½O	SEbyS½S	151°9	WtN	WbyN	281°2
NNO½O	NNE½E	28°1	ZZO¾O	SEbyS¾S	154°7	WNW¾W	WbyN¼N	284°1
NNO¾O	NNE¾E	30°9	ZZO	SSE	157°5	WNW½W	WbyN½N	286°9
NOtN	NEbyN	33°8	ZtO¾O	SSE¼S	160°3	WNW¼W	WbyN¾N	289°7
NOtN¼O	NEbyN¼E	36°6	ZtO½O	SSE½S	163°1	WNW	WNW	292°5
NOtN½O	NEbyN½E	39°4	ZtO¼O	SSE¾S	165°9	NWtW¾W	WNW¼N	295°3
NOtN¾O	NEbyN¾E	42°2	ZtO	SbyE	168°8	NWtW½W	WNW½N	298°1
NO	NE	45°0	Z¾O	SbyE¼S	171°6	NWtW¼W	WNW¾N	300°9
NO¼O	NE¼E	47°8	Z½O	SbyE½S	174°4	NWtW	NWbyW	303°8
NO½O	NE½E	50°6	Z¼O	SbyE¾S	177°2	NW¾W	NWbyW¼N	306°6
NO¾O	NE¾E	53°4	Z	S	180°0	NW½W	NWbyW½N	309°4
NO¾O	NE¾E	53°4	Z¼W	S¼W	182°8	NW¼W	NWbyW¾N	312°2
NOtO	NEbyE	56°2	Z½W	S½W	185°6	NW	NW	315°0
NOtO¼O	NEbyE¼E	59°1	Z¾W	S¾W	188°4	NWtN¾W	NW¼N	317°8
NOtO½O	NEbyE½E	61°9	ZtW	SbyW	191°3	NWtN½W	NW½N	320°6
NOtO¾O	NEbyE¾E	64°7	ZtW¼W	SbyW¼W	194°1	NWtN¼W	NW¾N	323°4
ONO	ENE	67°5	ZtW½W	SbyW½W	196°9	NWtN	NWbyN	326°2
ONO¼O	ENE¼E	70°3	ZtW¾W	SbyW¾W	199°7	NNW¾W	NWbyN¼N	329°1
ONO½O	ENE½E	73°2	ZZW	SSW	202°5	NNW½W	NWbyN½N	331°9
ONO¾O	ENE¾E	75°9	ZZW¼W	SSW¼W	205°3	NNW¼W	NWbyN¾N	334°7
OtN	EbyN	78°8	ZZW½W	SSW½W	208°1	NNW	NNW	337°5
OtN¼O	EbN¼E	81°6	ZZW¾W	SSW¾W	210°9	NtW¾W	NNW¼N	340°3
OtN½O	EbyN½E	84°4	ZWtZ	SWbyS	213°8	NtW½W	NNW½N	343°1
OtN¾O	EbyN¾E	87°2	ZWtZ¼W	SWbyS¼W	216°6	NtW¼W	NNW¾N	345°9
O	E	90°0	ZWtZ½W	SWbyS½W	219°4	NtW	NbyW	348°8
OtZ¾O	E¼S	92°8	ZWtZ¾W	SWbyS¾W	222°2	N¾W	NbyW¼N	351°6
OtZ½O	E½S	95°6	ZW	SW	225°0	N½W	NbyW½N	354°4
OtZ¼O	E¾S	98°4	ZW¼W	SW¼W	227°8	N¼W	NbyW¾N	357°2
OtZ	EbyS	101°3	ZW½W	SW½W	230°6			
OZO¾O	EbyS¼S	104°1	ZW¾W	SW¾W	233°4			
OZO½O	EbyS½S	106°9	ZWtW	SWbyW	236°2			
OZO¼O	EbyS¾S	109°7	ZWtW¼W	SWbyW¼W	239°1			
OZO	ESE	112°5	ZWtW½W	SWbyW½W	241°9			
ZOtO¾O	ESE¼S	115°3	ZWtW¾W	SWbyW¾W	244°7			
ZOtO½O	ESE½S	118°1	WZW	WSW	247°5			
ZOtO¾O	ESE¾S	120°9	WZW¼W	WSW¼W	250°3			

2

ЖЮРНАЛъ= или записка пути Мічмана петра чаша
па будучі в сібірию Эчпезіці= о санктъ пітеъ букъ
довозвращеніа і повозаращені таки= до санкт петеъ
букъла=

адин чіслаі сполобноі дополобноъ= августа 20:22: дна 1721 года: або
паго чісла счіслаі сполоудна дополудна: всемъ ае серпалъ= вспа
ічтъ право: L: лето= R: рвіды: D: ораня: п:п:л:г впачітъ пополо
двні: пайн: впачітъ пополоуночи:

		Мцъ Генварб 1725: сличан	
☉	24	Пополуночи въ 11 часу взбібхали пса Тирадітетъ въ сібірю слобо дъ тутъ начевалі=	
☽	25	Побхали вLшЮ слободы нанимтъ поводъ Гдінъ літенатъ тирпнотъ Прикомандъ ето Ляна Рочезитъ да заделалн кокотъ остеиеъ Пісаръ матрозовъ 10 члпъ да алиноъ днінан вотодоан тиль почалата двлъ в синан матвопомоню гчені Поитча учемнкн Пубннй 3 чала Конопленй 2 Пабесипнъ 2 ХУ цб 1 да 25 поводъ сматриалами.	
		Мцъ Ѳеврал	
☉	7	Потрудъ недовъ зад дотологдъ за 20 вдстъ Полбили павіпие опочкнтъ ею пинрпатотію Велчестеа Петра вLкипаго уче посла ю пенитъ птотеъорха Ачипомъ лете на тъ Ткнкну сботпекн вачеръ Прибили в ологдъ вло го получаню Поштанъ опинеи пошъ дорое 620 вастъ неледнтъ: або мошаъ дотологдъ мечка 410 тетъ=	
♂	9	обхалъ з опдъ ншъ Писаръ:	
☉	14	павіверъ Прибилъ на тологрд Комадовшъ ншъ Тотилою Пета Вдінъ капктанъ обрхитъ і прише лете на тъ ди паубухъ 2: штотоиъ з чала Котамрозовъ=	
☽	15	вачеръ кппласа Писа вbоппаъ	
♂	16	Пополоночъ въ 5 часу Получа демина поводъ Побхаъ дволоцдъ Кполодди часу въ 10 Прислали влшію амъ Lетоко фолодъ воточенинъ 50 тетъ Переменили поводъ	
☿	17	Пополоночъ часу въ 5 Ддали о лчтаго чму тбннакъ стаа свбъ отетъ вхали гнодъ: сухонов	
♀	19	в подчнеъ Прибили в тотиу Городоъ Lотоф в тоточенна влдітанъ 160 тетъ Переменили поводъ і побхалю:	
☉	20	Пабторъ Прибили в борово квъ дотоф вотіюъ 130 влдтьтри і пременили поводъ Побхали	
☽	22	Поторъ часу въ 10 прислаъ Вустоду дании Которо оброитаъ 120 встъ тиди вобіне поводъ Понтже чму нкотбіъ і пошли в путъ вачеръ	
♂	23	Пополбочи часу въ 10 Прислаъ второ соръ вагвъліпдъ обпонъ га воточеннъ 50 встъ і преминіе поводъ в вачеръ вали.	
♃	25	в полночъ Прибили все дворъ воточенн восем 150 встъ нем ню мбхали пто до тетъ воточе нстъ	

Folio 2

Journal or Travel Notebook of Midshipman Piotr Chaplin during the Siberian Expedition from St. Petersburg to the Turnaround,[1] and from the Turnaround back to St. Petersburg.

Dates are reckoned from midnight to midnight until August 22, 1727, and after that date, from midday to midday.

In this journal P means right, L is left, R is river, D is village, a.m. – ante meridiem, p.m. – post meridiem.[2]

Day of the week	Day of the month	January 1725. Events	Which days which winds
Sun.	24	At 11 a.m. we left the Admiralty[3] for the posting station[4] and spent the night there.	
Mon.	25	We set out from the posting station by hired sleighs[5]: Lieutenant Chirikov,[6] and under his command a physician,[7] a geodesist,[8] a naval cadet,[9] a quartermaster,[10] a clerk and 10 *sailors*, and the following Admiralty men: an apprentice river craft and launch builder,[11] an apprentice mast maker,[12] a foreman of the carpenters, 3 carpenters, 2 caulkers, 2 sail makers, 1 blacksmith, and 25 sleighs with materiel.	
		February	
Sun.	7	In the morning, at a distance of 20 *versts* from Vologda, we received news of the death of His Imperial Majesty Peter the Great, from a messenger sent to Lieutenant General Chekin from St. Petersburg with this news. In the evening we arrived safely at Vologda. According to the inhabitants, the distance along this way is 620 estimated versts, and from Moscow to Vologda it is 410 measured versts.	
Tue.	9	Our crew clerk ran away.	
Sun.	14	In the evening our commander, Navy Captain Bering arrived at Vologda with Lieutenant Spanberch,[13] 2 navigators,[14] and 3 sailors.	
Mon.	15	In the evening the clerk reappeared.	
Tue.	16	At 5 a.m., having obtained sleighs from the posting station, we set out from Vologda, and at 10 p.m. we arrived at the Shuiskii posting station, which is situated at a distance of 50 versts from Vologda. Here we changed sleighs.	
Wed.	17	At 5 a.m. we left the Shuiskii posting station. There was a heavy snowstorm. We traveled on the Sukhona River.	
Fri.	19	At noon we arrived at the small town of Tot'ma, a distance of 160 versts from Shuiskii. We changed sleighs and went on.	
Sun.	21	In the morning we arrived at the Bobrovskii posting station, 130 versts from Tot'ma; we changed sleighs and went on.	
Mon.	22	At 10 a.m. we arrived at Ustiug Velikii, which is 120 versts from Bobrovskii, hired sleighs from the district authorities, since there was no posting station, and went on in the evening.	
Tue.	23	At 10 a.m. we arrived at the town of Sol'vychegodsk, which is 50 versts from Ustiug, and, having changed sleighs, left in the evening.	
Thu.	25	At midnight we arrived at the village of Kimra, a distance of 150 estimated versts from Sol'. For 90 versts we traveled through a forest where there was not a single dwelling.	

◄ PLATE 3. Folio 2 of Midshipman Chaplin's journal.

Courtesy Russian State Naval Archives (RGAVMF). Photo by Nikolai Turkin.

From Saint Petersburg to Tobol'sk

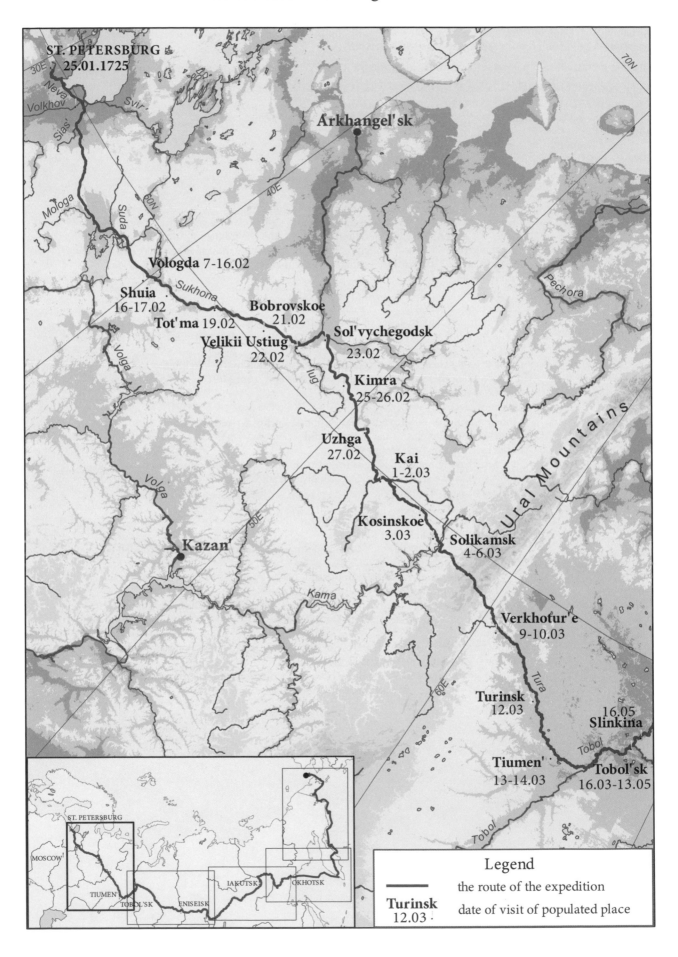

ST. PETERSBURG
25.01.1725

Arkhangel'sk

Vologda 7-16.02

Shuia
16-17.02

Bobrovskoe
21.02

Tot'ma 19.02

Velikii Ustiug
22.02

Sol'vychegodsk
23.02

Kimra
25-26.02

Uzhga
27.02

Kai
1-2.03

Kosinskoe
3.03

Solikamsk
4-6.03

Kazan'

Ural Mountains

Verkhotur'e
9-10.03

Turinsk
12.03

16.05
Slinkina

Tiumen'
13-14.03

Tobol'sk
16.03-13.05

Neva
Volkhov
Sias'
Svir'
Mologa
Suda
Sukhona
Iug
Volga
Volga
Kama
Pechora
Tura
Tobol
Tobol

30E
60N
40E
70N
30E
60E

ST. PETERSBURG
MOSCOW
TIUMEN'
TOBOL'SK
ENISEISK
IAKUTSK
OKHOTSK

Legend

——— the route of the expedition

Turinsk
12.03 — date of visit of populated place

Day of the week	Day of the month	February 1725. Events
Fri.	26	At noon, having got sleighs, we set off on our route.
Sat.	27	In the evening we arrived at the settlement of Uzhga, 100 estimated versts from Kimra, changed sleighs, and continued on our route.
		March
Mon.	1	In the evening we arrived at the small town of Kai-gorodok, a distance of 153 measured versts from Uzhga.
Tue.	2	In the morning, having obtained sleighs, we continued on our route.
Wed.	3	We arrived at the Kosinskii posting station, 135 measured versts from Kai-gorodok. We took posting station sleighs and set off.
Thu.	4	At 3 p.m. we arrived at Sol' Kamskaia [Solikamsk], a distance of 105 measured versts from the Kosinskii posting station.
Fri.	5	We were delayed due to the lack of sleighs.
Sat.	6	In the morning we obtained sleighs and left Sol' Kamskaia. The sleighs were from the area.
Tue.	9	We arrived at the town of Verkhotur'e, a distance of 276 versts from Sol' Kamskaia, where there are considerable mountains.
Wed.	10	We got posting station sleighs and left Verkhotur'e in the morning.
Fri.	12	In the morning we arrived at the small town, Turinsk, also named Epanchin; the distance from Verkhotur'e is 206 measured versts. We took posting station sleighs and left.
Sat.	13	We arrived at the town Tiumen', a distance of 150 measured versts from Turinsk.
Sun.	14	In the morning we got posting station sleighs and departed.
Tue.	16	We arrived at Tobol'sk. From Tiumen' to Tobol'sk the distance is 254 versts, and from St. Petersburg via Vologda by the above-mentioned road the distance to Tobol'sk is 2659 versts. Tobol'sk is situated at the latitude 58°05'N. The Irtysh River runs near it. The Irtysh has muddy water on the north side, into which the Tobol River flows, a little above the town from the western side (i.e., into the left side of the Irtysh). The width of the Irtysh near the town is about 300 *sazhens*. The town stands on a high and steep hill above the river.
		April
Fri.	23	The ice on the Irtysh River broke up, and in three days the river was clear.
Mon.	26	A considerable thunderstorm with lightning.
Tue.	27	We measured the altitude of the sun after noon: 42°27' and the azimuth from S to W 41°12', hence the compass declination 3°18' East was determined. The true declination of the Sun was taken.[15] We requisitioned four *doshchaniks* and seven *lodkas*.
		May
Sat.	8	Severe icy cold and snow.
Sun.	9	Icy cold, but no snow.
Mon.	10	Icy cold and snow.

◄ PLATE 4. Modern map 1: From Saint Petersburg to Tobol'sk. By Viktor Sedov.

Folio 3

Day of the week	Day of the month	May 725 [sic].[16] Events
Wed.	12	The chaplain[17] and commissary[18] arrived at our command; all *servicemen* moved aboard and loaded all the materiel into the doshchaniks.
Thu.	13	Fair weather, light breeze between N and W. At 4 p.m. we moved the doshchaniks from the town to the other bank of the river and cast anchors on the Irtysh.

In the journal entries from our river navigation after Tobol'sk, the distances are recorded in Russian versts (1 degree = 104½ versts), but the reckoned diurnal distances of the route are recorded in ordinary miles (1 degree = 60 miles). And dates are recorded from sunrise.

The letter P means right side of a river downstream, the letter L – left side, D – village, R – river.[19]

Hours[20]	Winds	Rhumbs	Versts	Right rhumbs	Fri. 14 May 725. Events and the weather
	WbS	NbE	5½	NbE¼E	Fair weather, gentle breeze. At 2 p.m. we moved
		NWbN	2½	NWbN¼N	from Tobol'sk downstream on the Irtysh River, and at 2½ versts to NWbN, came to the village of Sumgun,
		WbN	3	WbN¼N	which is on the right bank. A fresh wind, and here we stayed. At 8 o'clock calm air, we set off on our route and after 3 versts dropped anchor and spent the night near the village of Ryl'dina, which is on the right bank.
					Sat. 15 May 725. Events and the weather
½	SWbW	NEbE	2⅔	NEbE¼E	At 6 a.m. we went off on our route;
¼	SWbS	SEbS	1	SEbS¼S	fair weather, gentle breeze.
		NbE	1½	NbE¼E	On the turn from NbE to ENE we passed
½	-	ENE	2½	ENE¼E	the settlement of Kukaevskoe on the left bank, on the turn from NbE½[E] to EbN we passed
⅛	-	NbE	⅔	NbE¼E	on the right bank the settlement of Bronnikovo.
1	-	NbW	2½	NbW¼N	Having passed to ESE 2 versts, we stayed
½	-	NEbE	1½	NEbE¼E	for an hour and then went on. Strong breeze.
½	-	NbE½E	2	NbE¾E	Moving to NEbN 5 versts, we passed Mtsynskie *yurts*
½	-	EbN	3	EbN¼E	on the left bank.
⅓	WbS	ESE	2	ESE¼S	
⅜	-	ENE	3	ENE¼E	
⅛	-	NNE	2	NNE¼E	Direct distance via rhumb NNE 1°39'E,
1	-	NWbW	4	NWbW¼N	by Russian versts, is – 37.67, and corrected
⅝	-	NEbN	5	NEbN¼E	distance – 41.85 versts.[21]
¾	-	WbN	3	WbN¼N	
1⅛	-	N	8	N¼E	
¼	-	NE	2	NE¼ E	
¾	-	NW	3	NW¼N	
¼	-	NEbE	2	NEbE¼E	
1	-	SEbS	5	SEbS¼S	

Table of daily reckoning	Latitudes		Diff. of latitude	Departure	Rhumb	Distance of run	Distance added	Diff. of longitude	Compass declin.
	from	to	N	E					
Reckoned		58°24'73	19'73	8'84	NNE 1°39' by E	21.62			¼ R east
Corrected	58°05'	58°26'92	21'92	9'82		24.02	45.81	18.72	

Folio 3 verso

Hours	Winds	Rhumbs	Versts	Right rhumbs	Sun. 16 May 725. Events and the weather
½	SW	EbS	2	EbS¼S	Dense clouds, calm air.
1	-	NE	5	NE¼E	Going to NE, we passed the village Slinkina on the left.
1	-	W	6	W¼N	We proceeded under sail.
2	-	NNE	2	NNE¼E	We took in sail and drifted.
½	-	ENE	2	ENE¼E	
½	-	ENE½E	1½	ENE¼E	
⅛	-	NE	½	NE¼E	
1⅜	-	WbN	4	WbN¼N	We proceeded under oars.
½	-	N	2	N¼E	Going to N we passed the village Korytnikova,
¼	-	NEbE½E	1	NEbE¾E	which is on the left. In the afternoon
½	-	NbE	2	NbE¼E	fair weather, light breeze.
¼	-	E	1	E¼S	
¼	-	SEbE	1	SEbE¼S	
⅜	-	NbW	1	NbW¼N	
⅚	-	NWbW	2	NWbW¼N	
1	-	NWbN	2½	NWbW¼N	We passed Beriozovye yurts on the right, going to the NW 1 verst.
⅓	-	NW	1	NW¼N	We passed the stream Sora, which flows into the Irtysh from the left.
½	-	EbN	2	EbN¼E	
¾	-	SEbE	3	SEbE¼S	Turning from NbW to NW and proceeding 2½ versts,
½	-	NNE	2	NNE¼E	we remained for 2 hours, then went to N under oars.
½	-	NbW	2	NbW¼N	In the evening it rained. Going to N 2½ versts and turning to NE,
⅔	-	NW	2½	NW¼N	we passed on the left the Russian village Kupreianova.
1	-	N	2½	N¼E	Proceeding ½ verst, we turned to WNW,
1	-	N	2½	N¼E	passed the stream Turtas on the right and yurts of the
⅛	-	NE	½	NE¼E	same name. Proceeding in ½ hour 2¼ versts
¼	-	WNW	1	WNW¼N	to WNW, we passed the settlement of Uvat,
⅙	-	NbE	1	NbE¼E	on the left, and on the same side a Russian village,
⅓	-	E	1½	E¼S	the distance between them being ½ verst.
½	-	NEbN	2	NEbN¼E	Proceeding from the settlement of Uvat 7½ versts,
½	-	WNW	2½	WNW¼N	on the left is another hamlet of Uvat near a lake
½	-	SWbW	1½	SWbW¼W	of the same name, which extends from the river to SW
½	-	SWbW	1½	SWbW¼W	for about 8 versts, its width about 1 verst.
½	-	WbS	1½	WbS¼W	There is a village on the right side 5 versts from Lake Uvat.
½	-	WbS	1½	WbS¼W	Going to NEbE 3 versts, we turned to
1	-	NbW	4	NbW¼N	NE, and saw an island, 12 versts long, 3 versts wide.
¾	-	NE	3	NE¼E	
¾	NW	NW	3	NW¼N	We proceeded along the right side of the island.
¼	-	NbE	1½	NbE¼E	There are forests on the banks of the Irtysh River.
1	-	NNE	6	NNE¼E	
¾	-	NbW	3	NbW¼N	The distance calculated along curves was 98½ Russian versts and
¾	-	NEbE	3	NEbE¼E	the direct distance via rhumb N 7°38' by E was 55.43 versts, and
1½	-	NE	5	NE¼E	corrected 61.59 versts.
¾	-	NWbN	3½	NWbN¼N	
¼	-	NNW	1½	NNW¼N	
⅜	-	NWbW	2	NWbW¼N	

Table of daily reckoning	Latitudes		Diff. of latitude	Departure	Rhumb	Distance of run	Distance added	Diff. of longitude	Compass declin.
	from	to	N	E					
Reckoned	58°56'23		31'5	4'22	N7°38' by E	31.82			
Corrected	59°01'92		35'0	4'69		35.36	68.19	27.76	¼ R east

Folio 4

Hours	Winds	Rhumbs	Ver sts	Right rhumbs	Mon. 17 May 725. Events and the weather on the Irtysh River
½	-	NE	2	NE¼E	The morning was cloudy, calm air; we proceeded under oars. 10 versts from the island on the right is the settlement of Siurovoe to NbE½E.
⅜	SbW	EbN	1½	EbN¼E	
¾	-	SE	3	SE¼S	We proceeded 8 versts under sail by different rhumbs. And sailing from the settlement of Siurovoe 16 versts, we passed an island about 3 versts long and 1 verst wide.
⅜	-	ENE	2	ENE¼E	
¼	-	NEbN	1½	NEbN¼E	
1¼	-	NbE½E	8	NbE¾E	
½	-	NWbN	3	NWbN¼N	We proceeded along the left side of the island and, about 23 versts away from the settlement, we passed the stream Demianka, which flows into the Irtysh from the right side.
¼	-	NE	2	NE¼E	
1½	-	E	8	E¼S	
⅜	NWbN	NEbN	3	NEbN¼E	And sailing from the stream about 1 verst, we arrived at Demianskaia Sloboda, which stands on a high place above the Irtysh River on the right side, and stopped near it at 8 a.m. At 11 o'clock a strong gale rose with rain, and then snowfall and icy cold. At 8 p.m. the snowfall stopped and the snow cover remained on the ground until the 18th day. Direct distance via NE7°47'by E – 24.27 Russian versts, and corrected – 26.97 versts.

Table of daily reckoning	Latitudes		Diff. of latitude	Departure from mer.	Rhumb	Distance run	Distance added	Diff.of longitude	Compass declin.
	from	to	N	E					
Reckoned		59°04'66	8'43	11'10	NE 7°47' by E	13.93			¼R east
Corrected		59°11'29	9'37	12'33		15.48	30.13	51.77	

Hours	Winds	Rhumbs	Versts	Right rhumbs	Tue. 18 May 1725. Events and the weather. Irtysh River near Dem'iansk
					All day overcast, snow mixed with rain. In the afternoon the snow melted, and after 10 o'clock snow fell all night.

Hours	Winds	Rhumbs	Versts	Right rhumbs	Wed. 19 May. Events and the weather on the Irtysh River
1½	-	NbW	2	NbW¼N	Drifting clouds, fresh gale; the snow covered the ground until noon.
3¼	-	NEbN	4	NEbN¼E	
¾	-	NbW	2	NbW¼N	At 10 p.m. we set off on our route. Going to NbE 5 versts, we passed a village on the right, and going to EbN 2 versts, we passed Ostiak yurts on the left.[22]
¼	NNE	E	1	E¼S	
2	-	SSE	4½	SSE¼S	
½	-	EbS	1	EbS¼S	
2	-	NbE½E	5	NbE¾E	
⅜	-	EbN	2	EbN¼E	Turning from ENE to EbS, we passed the Russian village Vlasova on the left.
¼	-	ENE	1	ENE¼E	
1	-	EbS	2½	EbS¼S	
½	-	NbE	2	NbE¼E	The night was clear and calm. There are forests on the banks of the Irtysh River. The distance calculated along the curves was 45 Russian versts. Direct distance via rhumb NEbN 6°36' by East – 18.93, and corrected distance – 21.03 versts.
¾	-	NNW	2½	NNW¼N	
½	-	NEbN	2	NEbN¼E	
1	-	SE	4	SE¼S	
⅜	SW	NEbE	2	NEbE¼E	
¼	-	NbW	1½	NbW¼N	
1¼	-	NW	6	NW¼N	

Table of daily reckoning	Latitudes		Diff. of latitude	Departure	Rhumb	Distance of run	Distance added	Diff. of longitude from Tobol'sk	Compass declin.
	from	to	N	E					
Reckoned		59°12'94	8'28	7'039 [sic]	NEbN 6°36' E	10.87			¼ R east
Corrected		59°20'49	9'20	7'82		12.08	23.63	1°07'07	

Folio 4 verso

Hours	Winds	Rhumbs	Versts	Right rhumbs	Thu. 20 May 725. Events and the weather. Irtysh River
½	SbW	N	2	N¼E	In the morning sunshine, calm air, rime.
¾	-	NE	3	NE¼E	Going to NE 3 versts, we passed
½	-	NbE	2	NbE¼E	Ostiak yurts on the right, and 3 versts from
½	-	NWbW	2	NWbN¼N	these yurts, on the left we passed the Russian village
½	-	NWbN	2	NWbW¼N	of Denshchikova.
½	-	NbW	1½	NbW¼N	We turned to N and proceeded under sail, light breeze.
½	-	NEbE	2	NEbE¼E	And turning from N to NW, we passed Ostiak yurts
½	SWbW	N	1¼	N¼E	on the left, on the right the settlement of Vilino, which
1½	-	NW	4	NW¼N	stands on a steep mountain.
1	-	NbW	1½	NbW¼N	Going to NbW 7 versts, we took in sails and moved
¾	-	SSW	2½	SSW¼W	under oars. 39¾ versts from the village of
1	-	WbN	1½	WbN¼N	Denshchikova, on the right side of the Irtysh,
⅓	-	N	3	N¼E	there were 2 small islands, and we passed on the right
⅚	-	NEbN	5	NEbN¼E	Ostiak yurts called Sotnikovy. And having sailed
½	-	N	1½	N¼E	4 versts from the yurts, we moved in the channel
½	-	NEbE	3	NEbE¼E	on the right side of the island, while the big river
½	-	EbS	3	EbS¼S	was on the left.
½	-	NE	2	NE¼E	We moved along the channel to the NE 2 versts, ENE
1½	-	NbW	7	NbW¼N	2 versts, NE 2 versts and reached the big river.
½	-	NEbN	2	NEbN¼E	In the afternoon dense clouds and light breeze.
½	-	NE	2	NE¼E	13 versts from the channel we saw
½	-	ENE	2	ENE¼E	Ostiak yurts on the left.
½	-	NE	2	NE¼E	
¼	-	ENE	1	ENE¼E	Having moved from the Ostiak yurts 15 versts,
2	SbW	N	5	N¼E	we proceeded near islands located on the left
¾	-	WNW	7	WNW¼N	side. One of these islands was 8 versts long,
⅝	-	NE	4	NE¼E	and 2 versts wide. Passing this island
⅝	-	NbW	3	NbW¼N	on the left we saw the settlement of
½	-	WbN	2	WbN¼N	Repolovo.
½	-	NWbN	2	NWbN¼N	The night was cloudy and calm.
¾	-	NbE	4	NbE¼E	The distance, calculated on
¼	-	N	2	N¼E	different rhumbs is 93¾ Russian
⅜	-	NbW	2	NbW¼N	versts; the direct distance via rhumb N
½	-	NEbE	2	NEbE¼E	5°55' by East – 63.97, and the corrected
½	SbW	NbE	2	NbE¼E	one – 71.07 versts.

Table of daily reckoning	Latitudes		Diff. of latitude	Departure	Rhumb	Distance of run	Distance added	Diff. of longitude from Tobol'sk	Compass declin.
	from	to	N	E					
Reckoned		59°49'44	36'50	3'78	N 5°55' by E	36.73			
Corrected		60°01'05	40'55	4'20		40.81	80.83	1°15'4	¼ R east.

Hours	Winds	Rhumbs	Versts	Right rhumbs	Fri. 21 May 725. Events and the weather on the Irtysh River
¼	-	ENE	1	ENE¼E	In the morning, calm air, cloudy,
½	SbW	NbW	2	NbW¼N	and drizzle.
⅝	-	WbS	1½	WbS¼W	Traveling from the settlement of Repolovo
		SW	4	SW¼W	7 versts, on the right there were Ostiak yurts,
By channel					and we went by the channel on the right side
			2	NW¼N	of the river; this channel was called
		⌈NW			Repolova, and we came by this channel back
3		⟨W	2½	W¼N	to the Irtysh across from some Ostiak yurts
		⌊NWbN	2½	NWbN¾N	and proceeded on the river to NbE.
2		NbE	3	NbE¼E	13 versts from the Ostiak yurts we
¼		NW	1	NW¼N	passed the village of Kas'ianova on the right.

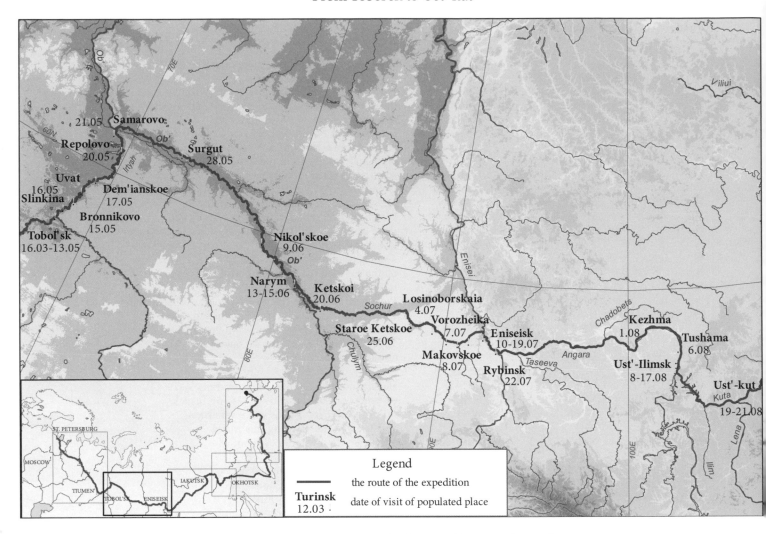

PLATE 5. Modern map 2: From Tobol'sk to Ust'-kut. By Viktor Sedov.

Folio 5

Hours	Winds	Rhumbs	Versts	Right rhumbs	On the same date
1	NW	WNW	4½	WNW¼N	Near noon dense clouds and drizzle, calm air.
¾	-	N	2	N½E	11 versts from the village Kas'ianovskaia we passed a Russian
1	-	WbN	5	WbN¼N	village on the left bank.
½	-	NWbN	2	NWbN¼N	The river banks there are forested.
½	-	NEbE	2	NEbE¼E	Going to WNW 5 versts, we hoisted sails.
1½	-	E	8	E¾S	And having moved 14 versts from the above-mentioned village,
⅜	NbE	NEbN	2	NEbN¾E	we proceeded near an island on the left side, and on the right
⅜	-	NWbW	2	NWbW¼N	side was a channel, which united with the Irtysh near the
¾	NNE	WbN	4	WbN¼N	Samarovskii posting station.
1½	-	WNW	5	WNW¼N	In the afternoon dense clouds, and at 5 o'clock strong gale and
½	-	WSW	1	WSW¼W	rain.
½	-	NNW	1	NNW¼N	At 6 p.m. we came to the Samarovskii posting station and put
½	NE	NW	2	WNW¼N	in to the bank.
⅜	-	WbS	3	WbS¼W	The calculated distance via NW 9°36 to W – 42.03, and the
¾	-	WbN	4	WbN¼N	corrected distance 46.70 Russian versts.
½	-	SWbW	3	SWbW¼W	
¼	ENE	WbN	2	WbN¼N	
¼	-	NNW	2	NNW¼N	

Table of daily reckoning	Latitudes		Diff. of latitude	Departure	Rhumb	Distance of run	Distance added	Diff. of long. from Tobol'sk	Compass declin.
	from	to	N	E					
Reckoned		60°03'42	13'98	19'67	NW 9°36' by W	24.13			
Corrected		60°16'58	15'53	21'85		26.81	54.49	00°30'57	¼ R east.

				Thu. [sic] 22 May 725.[23]
				In the morning murky, before noon intermittent sunshine, all day we made helms or rudders[24] for the vessels. The Captain ordered me to be ready to go ahead with a lodka.

Hours	Winds	Rhumbs	Versts	Sun. 23 May 725. Events and the weather.
½	-	NWbN	2	At 5 a.m. gloomy, at 10 the weather was calm with sunshine, at 12 o'clock
½	-	N	2	we went on from Samarovskii posting station; the Irtysh River downstream from Samarovskii has many islands and flows into the Ob' River. On the
½	NOtW	NbW	1½	way from Samarovskii we saw an island on the left side and, having moved from the posting station 2 versts, we turned N by a small channel on our
⅜	-	NbE½E	1½	left side.
				I received instructions from the Captain, by which I was ordered to go to Iakutsk, and also 7 decrees, namely for the Makovskii *outpost*, Eniseisk, Irkutsk, Verkholensk, Ilimsk, Iakutsk and 2 sealed decrees from the Tobol'sk Guberniia Chancellery.[25] I was given a lodka and servicemen, who had joined our command in Tobol'sk: a corporal and 9 soldiers. And I received from commissary Durasov 10 *rubles* for the necessary travel expenses and wages for 2 soldiers, who would be sent from Iakutsk to the Okhotsk outpost. At 3 p.m. I left the doshchaniks, took one of the coachmen of Samarovskii posting station as my guide, and moved upstream by the left channel to the Ob' River. In the evening it rained.

Day of the week	Day of the month			
Mon.	24			At 4 p.m. we came to the Ob' River and went upstream. Today intermittent rain.
Fri.	28			At 10 p.m. we arrived at the town of Surgut, which stands on the bank above a channel of the Ob' River. I was not satisfied with the accommodation. The distance from Samarovskii posting station to Surgut […] versts,[26] for which I paid the coachman who was my guide.

Folio 5 verso

Day of the week	Day of the month	May 725. Events
Sat.	29	At noon, having taken a *servitor* as a guide to Narym, we went off on our route.
		June
Tue.	1	Frost and snowfall to 8 a.m.
Thu.	2 [sic][27]	Sunshine. At 8 p.m. we passed the Vag River, which flows into the Ob' River from the right side. This is considered one-third of the distance from Surgut to Narym.
Fri.	4	Sunshine throughout. At 10 p.m. we passed the Rubashkino Reach.[28] Made one-half of the distance from Surgut to Narym.
Sat.	5	Sunshine with small clouds. At 10 a.m. a strong gale arose from the S and because of the wind we remained at the bank for about 2 hours, then went on [...][29]
Sun.	6	At 11 p.m. we came to Oslopovo Reach.[30]
Mon.	7	Gloomy. From 3 to 6 p.m. we proceeded under sail, with a fresh breeze; then it became calm and we proceeded under oars.
Tue.	8	At 1 a.m. a strong gale from the E. At 6 o'clock we tied up at the bank. Dark, cloudy, but with sunny spells. At 8 p.m. we went on our way.
Wed.	9	Sunshine. At 4 p.m. we passed a steep bank, called Veskov, on the left side of the river. It marks two-thirds of the route from Surgut to Narym. At 7 o'clock we passed the settlement of Nikol'skoe on the right bank of the river.
Fri.	11	Sunshine. At 6 p.m. we passed the Vasiugan River, which flows into the Ob' from the left between S and W. There were Ostiak yurts at the mouth of the Vasiugan River.
Sun.	13	At 11 a.m. we came to the town of Narym, which is situated ½ verst from the Ob' River on a low area. There are only a few dwellings, 25 or 30. Bright, cloudy. From Surgut to Narym residents count [...] versts.[31] I moved under oars mostly, as high water in the river made it impossible to move by towing and there was little fair wind.
Mon.	14	Thunder and heavy hail for about 2 hours. The men[32] baked bread. On my request a guide to Ketskoe was given to me.
Tue.	15	At 11 a.m. I set off on our route. Sunshine. We came to the Ket' River and went on. At 5 p.m. we passed a Russian village on the right bank.
Sun.	20	At 9 a.m. we came to the Ketskii outpost, which stands above a bay on the river at a distance of 2 versts. Having received a guide to Makovskii, at 12 o'clock we set off. It was very hot on the 18th, 19th and today. Ketskii is about one-fifth the distance from Narym to Makovskii. At 6 p.m. we passed a village on the right side of the river, 12 versts from Ketskii.
Wed.	23	At noon we passed Beriozovyi Iar, at 8 a.m. we passed the Lositsyna River, which flows into the Ket' between N and E.
Fri.	25	At 7 p.m. we passed Staroe Ketskoe, two-fifths of the way from Narym to Makovskii.

Folio 6

Day of the week	Day of the month	June 725. Events
Sun.	27	At 7 p.m. we passed on the right side of the river a steep bank, called Maksimkov. It is reckoned to be one-half of the way from Narym to Makovskii.
Wed.	30	At 8 p.m. we passed a place called Orliukovo Gorodishche.[33] All the river bottom was covered with gravel, and it is said to be ⅗ of the way from Narym.
		July
Sun.	4	At 6 a.m. we passed the Socher River, which flows from the right side into the Ket'. It was ⅘ of the way from Narym to Makovskii. At 8 p.m. we arrived at Losinoborskii Monastery, which stands on a low place by the river, on its left side. Sunshine.
Mon.	5	At 9 a.m. went off on our route.
Tue.	6	At 10 o'clock we passed on the same side a Russian village, Voroshilka. Sun shone through in the afternoon.
Wed.	7	At 2 p.m. we came to the village of Vorozheika, which stands on the high left bank of the river, and slept the night here.
Thu.	8	At 8 a.m., having got horses, we left for the Makovskii outpost. The boat and supplies[34] I gave to peasants for safekeeping. At 1 p.m. downpour and hail. At 4 o'clock we arrived at the Makovskii outpost, and I delivered a decree from the Tobol'sk District Office[35] to the local *steward* Prokopii Aleksandrov. I requested horses from him for [the] Makovskii [portage].[36] Sunshine. The Makovskii outpost stands above the Ket' River on a cheerful site. It is surrounded by a pine forest. Along the Ket' there are great forests.
Fri.	9	At 8 a.m., having received 11 riding horses, among them 1 pack horse, we went via the portage to Makovskii. I left 1 soldier in the ostrog to see that the steward assembled horses before the arrival of our commander, the Captain.
Sat.	10	At 6 p.m. we arrived at the town of Eniseisk. Since the *Voevoda* had died, I delivered a decree from the Tobol'sk District Office to commanding officer Tyzhnoi, about the dispatch of the Captain. I paid for 11 horses from Makovskii to Eniseisk, 4 rubles 40 *kopecks*, from the sum which had been given to me by the command. The town of Eniseisk stands on the bank of the Enisei River. The bank is steep. The town extends along the bank about one verst and there are plenty of wooden dwellings.[37]
Mon.	12	I requested, in accordance with the decree, in writing, the preparation of 4 doshchaniks with supplies; that 160 horses be sent to Makovskii for the transportation of materiel, and I also requested provisions for August and post-horses for one cart by land to Irkutsk and that the travel allowance be paid.
Wed.	14	We took provisions and prepared rusks. I requested from the office a post-horse order[38] and travel allowance for 2 vehicles with a guide[39] to Ilimsk.
Fri.	16	I sent a soldier with decrees to Irkutsk and Verkholensk. The office gave him a travel allowance and a post-horse order for 1 vehicle.

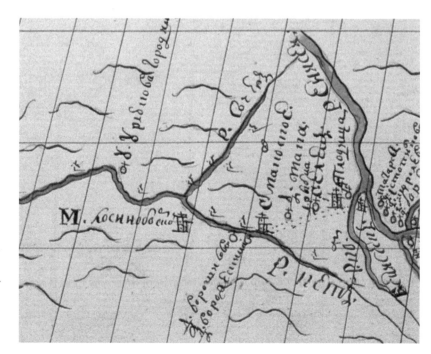

PLATE 6. The portage from Ket' River to the Enisei, between Makovskii outpost and the town of Eniseisk (marked with dotted lines). Detail from Chaplin's map of the itinerary through Siberia (p. 31).

Courtesy Russian State Archives of Military History, Moscow (RGVIA).

PLATE 7. Section of Luka Simanskii's copy of the original map of the First Kamchatka Expedition's itinerary through Siberia. The original has been attributed to P. Chaplin (Efimov 1964, No. 62). Total map size 105 × 35 cm. The left half of it, shown here, covers the river route from Tobol'sk to the Kashin Monastery.

Courtesy Russian State Archives of Military History, Moscow (RGVIA).

Folio 6 verso

Day of the week	Day of the month	July 725. Events
Sat.	17	On my request I received from the District Office an order for post-horses and a travel allowance to Ilimsk for 996 versts.
Sun.	18	I took a lodka with supplies.
Mon.	19	Rain. At 9 a.m. I went from Eniseisk up the Enisei River. To supervise the execution of the decrees delivered by me to the Eniseisk District Office,[40] I left a soldier there, and another man because of illness.
Tue.	20	At 1 p.m. we turned to the Tunguska River, which flows into the Enisei from the right side. On the left side of the Enisei River across from the Tunguska River there is a settlement named Streloshnoe. We passed the Streloshnoi rapids.[41]
Thu.	22	We passed the Rybinskii outpost at 4 p.m., at a distance of 100 old versts[42] from Eniseisk.
Sun.	25	We passed the village Belye Iarki.
Tue.	27	At 3 p.m. we passed the Mur rapids.[43] The Mur River flows into Tunguska from the left.
Thu.	29	At 4 p.m. we passed the stony Kashin shoal,[44] at 5 o'clock we passed Kashin Monastery on the right side of the Tunguska River.
Fri.	30	At 6 p.m. we passed the Aplinskii rapids. Between the monastery and the rapids there are 3 stony shoals.
		August
Sun.	1	At 4 a.m. we passed the village of Nizhnie Kezhmy, which is on the right side of the river.
Wed.	4	At 1 p.m. we passed the village of Sizykh, which is on the right side of the river.
Thu.	5	At 4 a.m. we came to the Ilim River. The Tunguska River, which is called Angara upstream to its source, was left on the right side, while we went up the Ilim River. From 6 to 9 o'clock we passed 2 rapids. Near the first rapid on the right side of the river, stands the village of Simakhina. At 12 o'clock we passed on the same side the village of Ziatei. Sunshine. At 2 p.m. we passed the third rapids.
Fri.	6	We passed the village of Tiushama on the left side of the river, and on the right side a small village. 2 versts before Tiushama on the same side, there is a high and steep bank, or hill, the sand of it is red in color. We passed the village of Tiushama at 7 p.m., and at 12 o'clock on the same side we passed the other village also.
Sun.	8	At 11 a.m. we came to the town of Ilimsk. I delivered the decree of Her Majesty from the Tobol'sk District Office to the administrator. Ilimsk stands on the Ilim River between high mountains, and the place is not very cheerful.[45]
Tue.	10	I requested from the chancellery, in writing, what my instructions allowed, and demanded a cart for travel by land to Ust'-Kuta. I left a soldier to enforce the decree I had issued, and I stayed here until the 17th day for the preparation of rusks.
Tue.	17	At 1 p.m. I received the order for post-horses to Iakutsk for 3 carts and the carts to travel to Ust'-Kuta, and left. At 10 o'clock we arrived at a winter outpost and slept the night here.

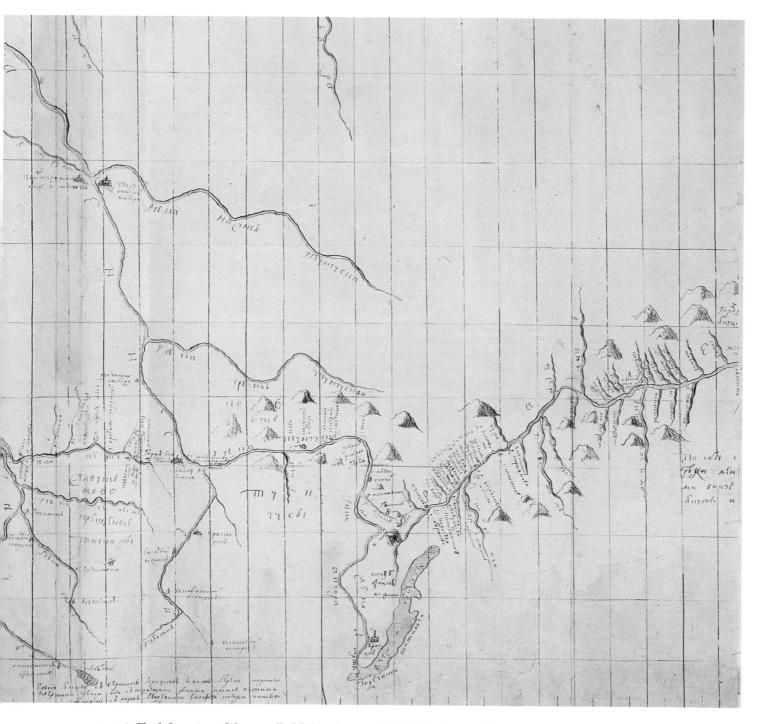

PLATE 8. The left section of the so-called "Khanykov copy" of the Final Map of the First Kamchatka Expedition.
It shows the expedition's route from Tobol'sk to the Lena River. Drawn by Midshipman Chaplin.
Copied from the original by land-surveyor Khanykov (Efimov 1964, No. 63). Total map size 56 × 135 cm.

Courtesy Library of the Academy of Sciences (BAN), St. Petersburg. Photo by Nikolai Turkin.

Folio 7

Day of the week	Day of the month	August 725. Events
Wed.	18	At 6 a.m. we set off along our route. At 12 o'clock we arrived at the rafting place[46] on the Muka River, where rafts and doshchaniks are made, and here we fed the horses for 2 hours, then left. Sunshine. I went for 20 versts towards Ust'-Kuta, then we slept the night.
Thu.	19	In the morning we went on, at 2 p.m. we arrived at Ust'-Kuta. The Ust'-Kutskii outpost stands at the mouth of the Kuta River, where it flows into the Lena River. Between Muka and Ust'-Kuta there are three small rivers: Muka, Kupa, Kuta.
Fri.	20	I was at Ust'-Kuta for the preparation of a lodka.
Sat.	21	At 8 a.m. I received 3 men as guides[47] and sailed down the Lena River. I left a soldier to supervise the building of vessels according to specifications of the decree. At 8 p.m. we passed the Taiura River, which flows into the Lena from the right side.
Mon.	23	At 4 p.m. we reached the Kirenskii outpost. Near the ostrog there is a monastery. Its location is very good. From Ust'-Kuta to Kirenga on both sides of the river there are a number of Russian villages, but they are small: 4 – 5 houses. At 7 o'clock we changed boats and sailed on. The Kirenga River flows into the Lena from the right side, the ostrog and monastery are on the right side of the Lena River and on the left side of the Kirenga River.
Tue.	24	At 8 a.m. we sailed past the Chechuiskii outpost on the left side. At 5 p.m. we reached the settlement Sploshnoe on the right side of the river. Russian villages are on both sides of the river from Kirenga to Sploshnoe. And having got boats to Oliokma, we took off at 7 o'clock.
Thu.	26	At 5 p.m. we sailed to the settlement of Vitim, which stands on the left side of the river. The Vitim River flows into the Lena from the right side. And here we changed one boat only, since we could not find more. At 8 o'clock we left Sploshnoe for Vitim. Only a few villages, deserted places.
Sun.	29	At 1 p.m. we sailed past the Niuia River, which flows into the Lena from the left side.
Mon.	30	At 6 p.m. we sailed to the Oliokminskii outpost and, having changed boats, we proceeded near this outpost. Russian villages are few. There were natives,[48] tribute-paying Iakuts and Tunguses. And after 15 versts we sailed past the Oliokma River, which flows into the Lena from the right side.
		September
Fri.	3	At 12 p.m. we sailed past the Pokrovskii Monastery, on the left, which is situated 50 versts from Iakutsk.
Sat.	4	At 8 p.m. we arrived at Iakutsk and slept the night about one verst downstream from the town, at a monastery.
Sun.	5	Sunshine. Living quarters were assigned for me and my men.

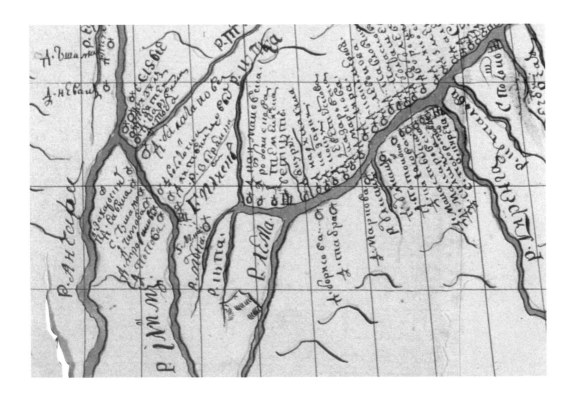

Folio 7 verso

Day of the week	Day of the month	September 725. Events
Mon.	6	At 10 a.m. I submitted 2 decrees of Her Imperial Majesty from the Tobol'sk District Office to Voevoda Poluektov. The town of Iakutsk stands about 300 sazhens from the Lena River and extends along the bank from S to N for a distance of 1½ versts. There are about 300 dwellings, situated on a plain. There are no Russian villages near the town, only natives – tribute-paying Iakuts, more than 30,000. Inhabitants of the town are mostly servitors, only a small number are merchants.[49]
Wed.	8	In accordance with the decree, I requested the Iakutsk chancellery to have supplies ready by the arrival of our Captain, and 5 carts for my dispatch of a corporal and a soldier to the Okhotsk outpost, to supervise the shipbuilding work; I also requested that official decrees be sent to the ostrog and provisions given to the departing men for the period 1 September to 1 January 1726.
Fri.	15 [sic][50]	I sent to the Okhotsk outpost a corporal and a soldier and ordered them to make their best efforts in the building of the vessels. A servitor was sent along with them as an interpreter.
Mon.	19 [sic][51]	I requested provisions for myself and for 2 soldiers for the period from 1 September to 1 January 1726.
		October
Thu.	6	I received provisions as requested and signed for them.
Sun.	17	Snowfall.
Tue.	19	I sent a report to the Captain with the servitor Iurkov. From 1 November to 1 December the frost was light; at times there were snowfalls. In December there was hard frost and no thaw in-between.
		1726
		In January there were hard frosts without thaw and frost fogs so thick that it was not possible to see a man 5 sazhens away. At times the sun shone through.
		February
Wed.	16	I sent a report to the Captain with Pezhemskii, a *boyar's son* of Irkutsk.
		March
Thu.	10	On my request 10 men and iron were sent to the Okhotsk outpost for the construction of the vessels. During this month there was sunshine, but no real warmth.

◄ PLATE 9. The transit from the Enisei river system to the Lena system, between Ilimsk and Ust'-Kut. Detail from Chaplin's map of the itinerary through Siberia (p. 44).

Courtesy Russian State Archives of Military History, Moscow (RGVIA).

Day of the week	Day of the month	April 726. Events
Sat.	9	I received information from the Corporal at the Okhotsk outpost. In accordance with it I submitted a request to the Iakutsk chancellery. This month was warmer.
		May
Sun.	1	The ice on the river broke.
Tue.	3	The ice was carried out and the river became clear.
Mon.	9	I received 3 orders in writing from the Captain: 1) from Ilimsk, of 2 December; 2) from Irkutsk, of 30 December; 3) from Irkutsk, of 8 January via Sobolev, a servitor of Iakutsk, in which the Captain ordered that I should request that 1000 pairs of leather bags be ready by his arrival, and other things.
Wed.	11	I submitted a request to the Iakutsk chancellery in accordance with the orders received.
Sun.	15	It became very hot and continued to be for the entire month, thick fog day and night. Rain and wind seldom occur.
		June 726
Wed.	1	At 10 a.m. the Captain arrived at Iakutsk with 8 doshchaniks, and with him Lieutenant Spanberch, a physician, 2 navigators, 2 geodesists, a commissary and other personnel: sailors, soldiers and a few workmen. Sunshine.
Thu.	2	I reported orally to the Captain that Sobolev, the servitor who was sent from Irkutsk with letters, had arrived at Iakutsk on 9 May. I asked in writing the chancellery to interrogate this servitor about where he has been loitering so long. Sunshine all day and very warm.
Fri.	3	Today quarters were obtained for the servicemen to bake bread, and they moved in.
Sat.	4	Very warm all day.
Sun.	5	Very hot all day.
Mon.	6	Very hot.
Tue.	7	Too hot. Coopers repaired containers for oil and wine flasks and were sent for hoops.
Wed.	8	I reported in writing to the Captain on the expenses and on the balance of cash received from commissary Durasov, and presented receipts for the lodkas left at Makovsk, at Ilimsk and at Iakutsk and passed the information I had received from the Iakutsk chancellery on the travel conditions to Lama [Okhotsk][52] from Iakutsk by land and by rivers. I received timber for masts from the chancellery and submitted an inquiry to the chancellery about the nobleman Aleksei Shestakov.[53]

Folio 8 verso

Day of the week	Day of the month	June 726. Events
Thu.	9	In the night thick fog; all day very warm. We began to make helms for vessels. Because of illness, a soldier was sent with an explanation from us to the chancellery of the Tobol'sk garrison.[54] I also submitted an application to the chancellery about the boyar's son L'vov.[55]
Fri.	10	In the morning heavy thunder and rain. From noon, sunshine. 6 helms were made.
Sat.	11	Very warm, a raft with flour from the contractor Zakharov arrived, with the soldiers of our command. 3 helms were completed. 860 pack bags were received from the chancellery.
Sun.	12	Very warm. I submitted to the chancellery 2 requests: 1. To appoint to us nobleman Ivan Shestakov,[56] to replace Aleksei Shestakov, and today it was done; 2. That a decree should be sent to the Lama that hay must be ready by the arrival of the Captain, and also concerning 10 horses with horsemen and one servitor.
Mon.	13	Warm. The Captain ordered the commissary to accept the flour from the contractor by weight. We hung helms on 8 vessels and began to make masts. I reported in writing to the Captain about the bread ration received during my stay at Iakutsk. I distributed provisions to the men.
Tue.	14	Very warm. I submitted an application for servitors to work on the vessels. 4 soldiers were sent from us to the nearby settlements to force the gathering of horses.
Wed.	15	Strong gale from N. I gave the commissary the remainder of the money for expenditure, as reported.
Thu.	16	Dense clouds, strong gale from N. At 1 p.m. Lieutenant Chirikov arrived at Iakutsk with 7 boats. I bought about 300 *poods* of flour on rafts. I submitted an application to the chancellery about gathering 600 horses for 3 detachments.
Fri.	17	In the morning fog and drizzle. We stood 10 masts on vessels. We took 670 poods of flour and loaded on the vessels.
Sat.	18	In the night a downpour, in the morning icy cold and fog; all day rain with intermittent sunshine. We received 851 poods of flour. On the order of the Captain I requested the Voevoda orally to send servitors immediately.
Sun.	19	Icy cold, little sunshine. We stood 4 masts and lifted helms on the rest of the vessels. We received 867 poods of flour. A soldier, who had to go to the Okhotsk outpost, was sent to the other side of the Lena River, and a servitor was sent with him.
Mon.	20	Dense clouds in the morning, then sunshine all day. We received 500 poods of flour, and loaded the vessels. I orally requested servitors from the Voevoda; he answered that at present there were few servitors in town, and all of them on duty, but those he could gather would be sent to the Captain immediately.
Tue.	21	Sunshine. We stuffed bags with flour. I submitted a request to the chancellery, to send a decree to the Okhotsk outpost on laying in hay and on clearing the road from [Iudoma] Cross[57] to Okhotsk. On the order of the Captain, I requested orally from the Voevoda 10 horses with horsemen and a guide. All of them would be sent ahead to Okhotsk. The Voevoda answered: a decree had been sent to [tribute] collector[58] Krivogornitsyn.
Wed.	22	Sunshine. I submitted an application to the chancellery, asking that wages be paid to the servitors, who had to leave by river and by land. 100 bags of floor were sent to the other side of the Lena River; 3 servitors were sent as guides. I asked the Voevoda orally, why he had not sent any servitors for so long, thus causing delay. He began to explain that 50 men would be sent tomorrow.

From Ust'-kut to Okhotsk

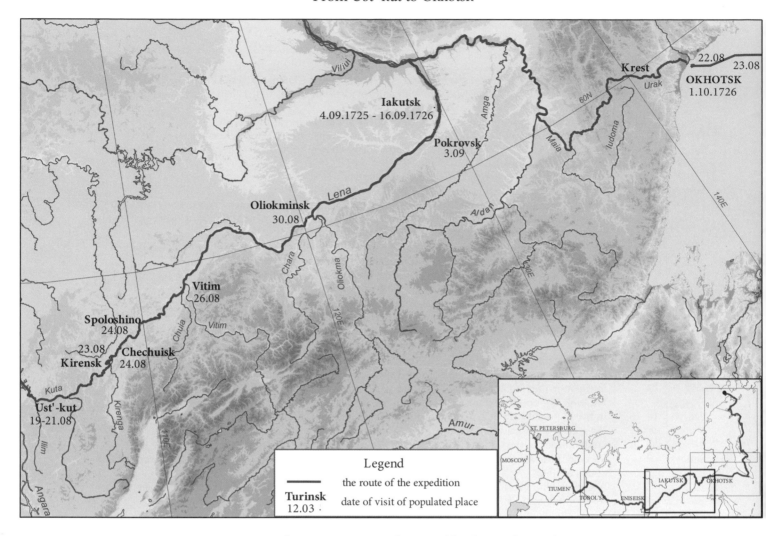

PLATE 10. Modern map 3: From Ust'-Kut to Okhotsk. By Viktor Sedov.

Folio 9

Day of the week	Day of the month	June 726, events
Thu.	23	Sunshine. We stuffed bags with flour. 50 servitors arrived from the chancellery.
Fri.	24	Sunshine and warm. I submitted 2 requests to the chancellery: 1. On servitors and a list of saddles, saddlecloths, and saddle-girths to be sent to us; 2. On the monk Kozyrevskii.[59] We stuffed bags with flour.
Sat.	25	Sunshine and warm. I asked the Voevoda orally, from where we would receive saddles, saddlecloths, saddle-girths. He answered that a decree would be sent to the bursar.[60] 174 bags were sent to the other side of the river.
Sun.	26	Clouds. We took from the chancellery 300 poods of rusks. 150 bags of flour were sent to the other side of the river.
Mon.	27	Sunshine and warm. I submitted a report to the chancellery about the boy, who ran away from the chaplain of our command. 136 bags of flour were sent to the other side of the river. 46 servitors were sent from the chancellery. I asked the Voevoda orally: 1) To order that wages were paid and bread rations issued to the arrived servitors;[61] 2) To order a place where materiel could be stored; 3) If there were letters to Tobol'sk, to get them ready to be sent, since on the 30th day of this month a soldier would be sent by us. He answered orally: on 1. I [the Voevoda] shall order the wages to be paid; on 2. We have no order to accept your materiel; on 3. If the Captain wants to send someone, this is his will; no letters will be sent by us.
Tue.	28	Sunshine and warm. I submitted an application to the chancellery to pay the wages to 46 servitors. The Captain with his officers chose to visit the chancellery to ask the chancellery to deliver what he had requested.
Wed.	29	Warm and fog.
Thu.	30	Fog and warm. The Captain together with the officers visited the chancellery, and requested that people and horses be sent. 10 servitors were sent. I requested the Voevoda to send 7 Iakuts to drive cattle to the Okhotsk outpost; and secondly, to send servitors, and if they were not sent soon, everything would be turned over to the chancellery. He answered orally: on 1. The Iakuts had been sent for, but they still had not arrived; on 2. We will immediately send as many as we are able to assemble.
		July
Fri.	1	Foggy and warm. 9 bulls were purchased as food for the sea voyage. 11 servitors were sent from the chancellery. 12 bulls were sent to the other side of the river. The iron was cut into small pieces that weighed less than 2½ poods, for packing into bags. I requested to the Voevoda orally: 1) To send servitors immediately; 2) If by tomorrow evening our request has not been fulfilled, all materiel would be transported to the town or a letter would be sent, which would be unpleasant for him. He replied orally: To 1) He will send as many servitors as will have been assembled. To 2) The Captain can do what he wishes, but now there are not many people. As soon as they arrive from the *uluses* [Iakut local settlements], they will be sent at once.
Sat.	2	Foggy and very warm. The Captain visited the chancellery and demanded execution of the requests. 8 servitors were sent. We received money from the chancellery for beer.

Day of the week	Day of the month	July 726. Events
Sun.	3	Foggy. The Captain reviewed the servitors and ordered all of them to be on the vessels. I went to the Voevoda and inquired if he wanted to send the men requested by us at once. If not, everything from the vessels would be unloaded at the storehouse today for sure. He replied orally: if the Captain says so, I will send even those who are on duty elsewhere, but then there will be no one to collect tribute[62] and no one to take it to the provincial center.[63] On behalf of the Captain I wrote to Lieutenant Spanberch, asking him to order the commissary to report in writing, how many bags have been received, how many have been filled and with which provisions, and how much has been distributed to the men; and also to make sure that the men sign for the bags they receive.
Mon.	4	Foggy. Soldier Karachintsov, a member of our command, arrived from Irkutsk with rafts, loaded with flour, groats, resin and hemp. I submitted to the chancellery a report about the money for beer, and asked the Voevoda how to get a vessel in which to transport the collected horses across the Lena River, also: has an individual been found to whom payment can be made for the horses? I also inquired about the Iakuts and workers who will tend the cattle.
Tue.	5	Foggy. I wrote to the chancellery to inquire if they could take over from us 2 remaining vessels with provisions. 14 head of cattle and 50 poods of iron were sent across the river. I submitted an inquiry if they would take over from us 800 poods of flour from the 2 vessels and send it to us overland.
Wed.	6	Foggy. I presented information on how much flour has been received from the contractor Zakharov. On the order of the Captain I received 100 rubles from the commissary.
Thu.	7	Sunshine and warm. Lieutenant Spanberch left Iakutsk with 13 vessels and 204 servicemen and servitors.[64]
Fri.	8	Light rain overnight, in the morning fog and warm. Reported to the chancellery about receiving hemp and pine resin from Irkutsk. Received from the bursar 50 pairs of soft dressed pack bags, 35 pairs of them used, and 552 sazhens pack rope.
Sat.	9	Warm and cloudy. Presented a request to take care of the sick sailmaker until he recovers. In the evening rain. Also today I asked the Voevoda: Who will be assigned to travel overland with Lieutenant Chirikov, and about the 7 Iakuts and the servitors who will tend the cattle.
Sun.	10	Overnight and till noon rain, in the afternoon cloudy. The Captain went to the other side of the river. 76 pairs of bags of flour were sent across the river. Proposed to the Voevoda that he should set the pay for the horses[65] judging from his own experience, since the Captain has no experience of how much to pay the natives.[66] In the evening rain.
Mon.	11	Overnight and in the morning rain. The Captain returned from the other side of the river and went to the chancellery, asked about the dispatch of the horses and paying the Iakuts. 922 sazhens of pack rope were sent across the river to the apprentice shipbuilder Kozlov.
Tue.	12	Sunshine throughout. I handed in a request to the chancellery for a translator and 6 servitors. 70 poods of flour were accepted from a raft. I reported that apprentice Kozlov will travel with commissary Makhnachevskii of Kamchatka.[67] I received a written order from the Captain to distribute the bread ration for September to the workers, 1¾ poods flour per man.
Wed.	13	Rain. I distributed provisions to the men and reported on it. Reported orally to the Voevoda that he should let us depart and if he would not permit it, then he will be responsible for refusal to honor the aforesaid request. The oral messages I conveyed to the Voevoda were based on instructions given by the Captain.
Thu.	14	Rain. With money received from the commissary, I paid for a bull and for the Iakuts who herd the cattle, according to an order received.

Day of the week	Day of the month	July 726. Events at Iakutsk
Fri.	15	Dense clouds and icy cold. On the order received I paid the nobleman Ivan Shestakov 44 rubles for 11 bulls.
Sat.	16	Sunshine and strong gale from NW. 4 servitors were sent from the chancellery.
Sun.	17	Sunshine.
Mon.	18	Sunshine. We received from a raft 97½ poods of flour and from the bursar's store[68] 280 sazhens of pack rope.
Tue.	19	Foggy, then sunshine. The sick sailmaker was sent to the monastery, since until today he had not been taken by the chancellery. We received 60 poods of flour from the raft.
Wed.	20	4 bundles of pack rope were sent to the other side of the river. I received an order to go to the other side of the river and pay 80 kopecks each to a guide and 7 Iakuts, who should be sent with the cattle to Okhotsk. I went on the same day.
Thu.	21	Light, dense clouds. I returned from the other side of the river and reported to the Captain orally, that I had paid the money to the Iakuts.
Fri.	22	Sunshine. I submitted a request to the chancellery [1.] for money to pay for the horses; 2. for a permission to the nobleman Ivan Shestakov to leave and [3.] for a list of the Iakuts and [4.] for saddlecloths and saddle-girths. Sergeant Liubimskii arrived on a barge with flour and with him 5 soldiers of our command. The Captain went to the other side of the river.
Sat.	23	Sunshine.
Sun.	24	Sunshine. The Captain arrived from the other side of the river in the evening.
Mon.	25	Sunshine. I submitted a request to the chancellery, to take the flour from the newly arrived barge into the storehouse. 2. I also reported that I would be leaving with the second convoy. The Captain ordered me orally that while dispensing money for horses I should keep a list together with the nobleman Shestakov. Following an order signed by the Captain, I was to pay money to the nobleman Dmitrii Kichkin for one head of cattle that had been given to the servicemen. Apprentice Kozlov was sent ahead on the route with 200 horses.
Tue.	26	Sunshine. The Captain went across the river. On receiving the order I distributed the bread ration for August and September to the arrived servicemen, a sergeant and the soldiers.
Wed.	27	Sunshine.
Thu.	28	Sunshine. I submitted a note to the chancellery on the urgency of our departure.
Fri.	29	Sunshine. 35 empty bags were brought over from the other side of the river.
Sat.	30	Dense clouds. I received 13 pairs of bags from the bursar's store and 46 poods of flour from the raft, and we filled bags.
Sun.	31	Sunshine. I reported to the Captain in writing on having given out the August and September bread ration to the men.

PLATE 11. Iakut with horse.
Ethnographical tablet from the Göttingen copy of Bering's Final Map (p. 190).

Courtesy Niedersächsische Staats- und Universitätsbibliothek Göttingen.

Day of the week	Day of the month	August 726. Events at the river Lena
Mon.	1	Sunshine. I submitted a request to the chancellery for official decrees to the outposts,[69] also for a man knowledgeable about rivers, to be sent with 120 horses to Lieutenant Spanberch.[70]
Tue.	2	Sunshine. I reported to the Captain in writing, what we had received from the bursar's store and for what I had signed. The Captain ordered me to transfer completely to the other side of the river. I did that on the same day.
Wed.	3	Dense clouds. I paid the Iakuts for horses: 2 rubles for each, and to the guides one ruble each.
Thu.	4	Dense clouds.
Fri.	5	Warm and sunshine. I paid for horses. At 5 p.m. the Captain arrived with his men on the other side of the river and brought 100 bags of flour. Lieutenant Chirikov was left with 6 servicemen in Iakutsk to send provisions to the Okhotsk outpost in the coming spring.
Sat.	6	Sunshine. An interpreter and a servitor were sent to us temporarily from the chancellery. The physician of our command was sent ahead on the route to the Okhotsk outpost and with him 3 carpenters, 84 horses, 32 bags of provisions and groats, 2½ poods each, and 112 bags of flour, 38 of them with 2½ poods each, and 74 bags with 2¼ poods each.
Sun.	7	Sunshine. The Voevoda visited our departure station today. On the order of the Captain I paid to the bursar Shangin 2 rubles for 10 baskets of charcoal.
Mon.	8	Sunshine and warm. We paid for more horses. On the order of the Captain 4 poods of flour were given to the Tunguses from the Lama.
Tue.	9	Sunshine. On the order of the Captain I took 2 rubles from soldier Trifonov. A sergeant went off on our route with 4 soldiers and 80 horses, 138 bags of flour, 6 of the Captain's flasks with lard and oil.
Wed.	10	Sunshine and warm. On the order of the Captain the apprentice mast maker Endogurov was given 3 poods 32 pounds of groats for the remaining servicemen and money for the transportation of the flour from the barge.
Thu.	11	Sunshine. On the order of the Captain a resident of Iakutsk was paid 60 kopecks. For the transportation of 110 bags of provisions from the Lena River to the station, 40 kopecks were paid to a group of Iakuts. We also paid the Iakuts for horses. A soldier was sent to the sergeant with 20 horses loaded with 38 bags of flour.
Fri.	12	Sunshine.
Sat.	13	Sunshine. The carpenters' foreman went on his route with 2 soldiers, another carpenter, 80 horses and 64 bags of flour loaded on 32 of the horses. The Captain's baggage was loaded on 35 horses. I was given 2 horses, the clerk and a sailor for their packs 2 horses. The remaining horses were given to the servicemen. One servitor went with them.
Sun.	14	Sunshine.
Mon.	15	Sunshine. The unloaded horses were let go with the boyar's son Antipin and 2 soldiers. He was told to wait for the Captain at the Amga River.

AKUTЪ.

PLATE 12. Iakut with horse. Ethnographical detail from the Stockholm copy of Bering's Final Map (p. 214).

Courtesy the National Library of Sweden (Kungl. biblioteket, Stockholm).

Folio 11

Day of the week	Day of the month	August 726. Events on our route from the Lena River to the Okhotsk outpost
Tue.	16	The Captain set off at 8 a.m., accompanied by myself, the clerk, a sailor, 3 soldiers, 1 carpenter, 1 cooper, 1 blacksmith, 2 servitors, 2 Tunguses from Lama, all on 26 horses. After about 15 versts, we rested the horses for about an hour, then went on. At 8 p.m., about 35 versts from the Lena River, we settled for the night. All day cloudy, with sun breaking through. 2 horses ran away from us, and we could not catch them.
Wed.	17	At 7 a.m. we went on, at 11 o'clock the horses had a rest; at 1 o'clock we went on and, at a distance of about 45 versts from the station, stopped for the night. All day sunshine and light clouds.
Thu.	18	At 8 a.m. we went off on our route. Sunshine and light clouds. At 12 o'clock we rested. At 3 p.m. we went on, and shortly thereafter a horse died. At 8 o'clock we settled for the night, having traveled some 30 versts from the outpost, where we spent the [previous] night. The weather light clouds, calm. We stayed for the night between 2 lakes, about 10 versts before the stream Tata.
Fri.	19	At 7 a.m. we went off on our route, at 10 o'clock came to the tribal princeling[71] Tortorgos, about 3 versts before Tata. Sun shining through light, small clouds, light breeze. From the Lena River to the Tata the land was dry; there were lakes and a great larch forest, and in some areas large grassland. By the evening a gentle breeze between S and W, and cold.
Sat.	20	Clouds. At 3 p.m. we went, at 5 o'clock crossed the stream Tata and, about 6 versts from Tata, slept the night at the stream Landra. Cloudy, light breeze, during the night light frost.
Sun.	21	At 7 a.m. we went and ascended a mountain and went along the mountains for about 10 versts, came down to a grassland and ate at noon. At 11 o'clock we received information from Lieutenant Spanberch that he had passed the Notora River on the 16th day of this month; and also from Okhotsk from the corporal. Strong breeze, clouds with sunny spells. At 7 p.m., having traveled 40 versts from the stream Landra, we settled for the night at a place called Torma, some 20 versts before the Amga River.
Mon.	22	At 7 a.m. cloudy and cold, we went off on our route. During the night there was a light frost. At 10 o'clock we came to the river Amga, to the distinguished princeling Nirgai,[72] and caught up with the sergeant and the foreman. They live in yurts covered with birch bark and have about 7,000 head of horned cattle and horses. Down the Amga River on the right side there are great mountains, and on the left – grasslands. Cold all day.
Tue.	23	The night was warm. From 7 till 8 o'clock drizzle, strong breeze between N and W. At 2 p.m. we crossed the Amga River and stayed on the bank. Overcast and cold.
Wed.	24	All night rain and snow. At 11 a.m. the rain stopped. Cloudy, gentle breeze between N and W. We paid for the horses.
Thu.	25	During the night frost. In the morning thick fog till 10 o'clock, then sun, light breeze from N. At 5 p.m. the foreman left with his baggage. He was also given 20 unloaded horses out of the 120 horses that were to be sent to Lieutenant Spanberch's ships.
Fri.	26	During the night hoar frost and thick fog. At 9 a.m. sunny. At 11 o'clock we left the Amga River. The sergeant stayed behind and was given 20 horses from the 120, and the other 80 horses went with us. At 3 o'clock we crossed the stream Kinesta and built a corduroy road.[73] At 6 o'clock, about 15 versts beyond the Amga, we stopped for the night.

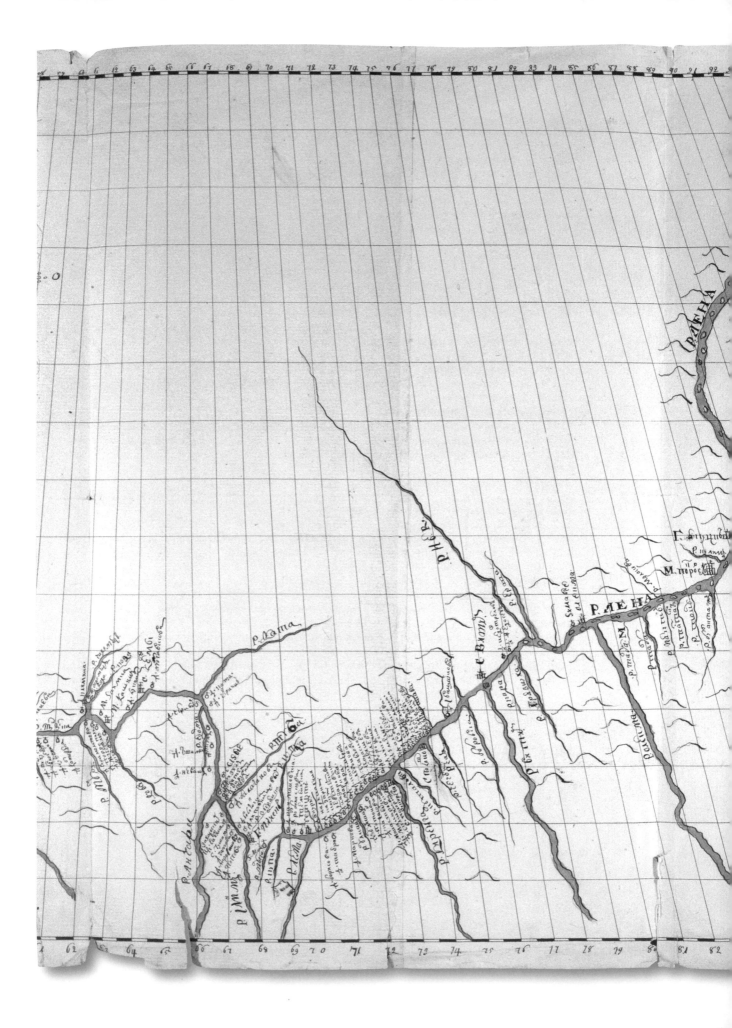

PLATE 13. Section of a map of the First Kamchatka Expedition's route through Siberia. Attributed to P. Chaplin, copied by Luka Simanskii (Efimov 1964, No. 62). Total map size 105 × 35 cm. The right half of it, shown here, covers the river route from the Kashin Monastery to Okhotsk.

Courtesy Russian State Archives of Military History, Moscow (RGVIA).

Folio 11 verso

Day of the week	Day of the month	August 726. Events on our route from the river Amga
Sat.	27	During the night, light frost. At 6 a.m. we went off on our route. Fair weather with light clouds. At 12 o'clock we ate lunch. Clouds with sun breaking through. At 1 p.m. we went on, at 2 o'clock crossed the stream Malaia Kolyma and built a corduroy road. At 7 o'clock we settled for the night, having traveled about 35 versts. Today there was mud and small marshes.
Sun.	28	Light frost. At 7 a.m. fair weather. We set off on our route and, after about 6 versts, came to the stream Bol'shaia Kolyma and made a bridge. It would have been possible to cross it without the bridge; the depth was about 3 feet. And we remained there for this reason about 3 hours and, having crossed the stream, we went up a high mountain and went about 2 versts, very muddy. And we came down to the stream Olbut, the place was marshy. And we ate there. At 2 p.m. we moved on and went along the marsh and small hills; at 7 o'clock we settled for the night. The distance passed today is about 20 versts, over the hills along the marsh.
Mon.	29	Light frost. At 7 a.m. we went on and, after about 7 versts crossed the marsh Chellen Tastoga. This took us about 2 hours. We passed the foreman with his baggage, and about 4 versts after the marsh we ate lunch at Lake Dzhebaka Birile. At 2 p.m. we moved on and went through marshes and mud; at 6 o'clock rain, at 7 o'clock we halted for the night at the stream Notora, having traveled about 25 versts today.
Tue.	30	Frost. At 9 o'clock we crossed the Notora River and went on. Fog, at 10 o'clock sun and light clouds. At 2 p.m. we ate, then crossed the same stream again and went on. At 6 o'clock we stopped for the night at the same stream. The distance passed today is 27 versts. Sun. There was little mud today.
Wed.	31	Frost. At 7 o'clock we went on, at 9 o'clock crossed the Notora River and, after 10 versts, crossed it once more. At 12 o'clock we ate lunch, then went on and, after about 7 versts, crossed the river again and, after about 5 versts, settled for the night, 15 versts before Aldan. At 7 o'clock drizzle.
		September
Thu.	1	Light frost. At 3 a.m. we went on. Cloudy, strong gale between S and E. At 10 o'clock we crossed a channel of the Aldan. At 12 o'clock we arrived at the Aldan River. Down the Aldan on the right side there are high stony mountains, and on the left side they are low. The source of the river is situated to the S. The river is about 150 sazhens wide. By the evening the foreman arrived.
Fri.	2	During the night rain, and all day gentle breeze between S and E. We ferried the horses by vessels left by Lieutenant Spanberch: 1 doshchanik, 2 *karbuses*, 1 small lodka. We also ferried bags. At 3 p.m. the sergeant arrived.
Sat.	3	In the night rain, and all day intermittent rain. We ferried horses and baggage.
Sun.	4	Rain. At 8 o'clock we and the foreman crossed the Aldan. At 11 o'clock we left the Aldan; we had 71 horses, and 5 spares, and all the others I gave the sergeant for assistance. At 7 or 8 p.m. we stopped for the night in a forest, on a marsh, about 25 versts from Aldan. Much mud.
Mon.	5	During the night, rain. At 7 a.m. we went on, the rain had stopped. At 11 o'clock we came to the Iunakan River, which is very swift and full-flowing. We covered a distance of 10 versts and spent the night at the stream. The source of the river lies between N and W. On both sides of the river there are high stony mountains. From noon sunshine.

Folio 12

Day of the week	Day of the month	September 726. Events on our route from the Aldan River
Tue.	6	Cloudy with sun breaking through. At 7 o'clock we went on. A horse was lost, which we could not find. We went along the left side of the river over a high mountain about 7 versts and then downstream and crossed the Iunakan. And some 8 versts after the ford, we ate. Sunshine with small clouds, light breeze from W. Then we went on, and after 13 versts, at 7 o'clock we settled for the night on an island. Today we went through mud.
Wed.	7	Light frost. At 7 a.m. we went on and, after 13 versts, at 12 o'clock we ate. Sunshine and warm. Then we went on and, having traveled 10 versts, at 5 p.m. stopped for the night in order to feed the horses. Today we went through muddy and dry places. We crossed the stream Iunakan 3 times, and walked mostly near the water on pebbles.
Thu.	8	Frost. At 7 a.m. we went on. Sunshine. And after 15 versts we ate at 12 o'clock. Then we went on and after 7 versts passed the night near the stream Iunakan. Around 5 o'clock it was very muddy, but otherwise there were more dry places today. 1 horse perished. The only food for the horses was a small horsetail[74] growing in the moss.
Fri.	9	Frost. At 8 o'clock we set off and went on all day, without stopping to eat. The road in the forest was dry; there was little mud. We crossed the stream Iunakan 6 times and, after about 30 versts, we halted for the night between high mountains; on some of them there was snow.
Sat.	10	Frost. At 7 a.m. we went on. Sunshine. After 20 versts, at 4 p.m., we halted for the night because ahead for about 30 versts there would be no food for the horses. Today we crossed the stream Iunakan 3 times. On the left side of the river there were high stony mountains, covered with snow, and near the stones in some low places there was ice, up to 7 feet thick. The place where we passed the night is named Iunakan Buskul, in Russian – icy lake.
Sun.	11	Frost. By 7 a.m. we started and after 30 versts, at 6 p.m. began to get ready for a night on the rock. The peak Iunakanskaia remained on the right side from us. Today the road was dry, very little mud. On both sides high stony mountains covered with snow. Sun shining through all day and warm. A horse stopped and we left it by the road. At that place spruce forests end.
Mon.	12	Frost. At 6 a.m. we started to cross the high ridge; the descent from it was very difficult, and at the half height a stream runs, on the right hand from us. And we went down along the stream about 6 versts, to where it flows into the stream Munakan. And we went up the Munakan, which flows into the Belaia, and the Belaia into the Aldan. At 2 p.m. we overtook the physician, and left him 10 unloaded horses for assistance. Having overtaken the physician, we crossed some rocks. At 6 o'clock we stopped for the night. We did a distance of about 30 versts today. In the morning, light snowfall and all day it was overcast and cold.
Tue.	13	Light frost, at 7 o'clock we went off on our route. Overcast and light snowfall. We overtook the Kamchadal commissary. We were going all day in mountains. In the afternoon bright, cloudy with a few sunny spells. We met a servitor from the Okhotsk outpost with a census list.[75] He had left Okhotsk 11 days ago. At 5 p.m., having traveled about 30 versts from the place where we slept, we settled for the night. This was 1½ versts before the Iuna River.

Folio 12 verso

Day of the week	Day of the month	September 726. Events on our route from the Aldan River
Wed.	14	In the morning it was cold. At 6 a.m. we went on, at 7 o'clock crossed the Iuna River and followed it to the E. At 12 o'clock we crossed the stream Amcha 2 times. It flows into the Iuna. Having covered about 35 versts, at 6 p.m. we stopped for the night by the same stream Amcha. Today there was plenty of mud. One horse died off.
Thu.	15	Frost. At 7 o'clock we went on and, after about 35 versts, halted for the night at the Tobe Ol'bud Ul'rug River. We crossed the stream Amcha 2 times; there was not much mud; all day sunshine. And we overtook apprentice Kozlov and his detail.
Fri.	16	Light frost, cloudy with a little sunshine coming through, light breeze from W. We gave 4 unloaded horses to apprentice Kozlov, and one horse with a lame leg, which could not walk, to the Iakuts for food. At 9 a.m. apprentice Kozlov left with his baggage, while we were resting our horses all day.
Sat.	17	Frost. At 7 a.m. we went off on our route. Sunshine. And after 30 versts we began at 6 p.m. to prepare for the night near the stream Eronda. Today there was not much mud, and we crossed some ice in 2 places.
Sun.	18	Light frost. At 7 a.m. we left. Clouds and light snowfall. Having traveled 35 versts, we passed the night at the stream Ukachan. At 5 p.m. today the road was dry. We crossed a large ice field, with ice about 7 feet thick. All day sunshine and cold, wind from N; the road was dry, 2 horses were exhausted.
Mon.	19	Frost. At 6 a.m. we left and, after traveling about 40 versts, rested for the night at the same stream. All day cloudy and cold. The road was dry. What mud there was froze. Feed for the horses was bad.
Tue.	20	Frost. Took off at 8 a.m., and after 40 versts put up for the night by the same stream at 6 p.m. Food for the horses passable. Today sunshine, the road dry. We went along the stream Ukachan 7 versts down on stones to where the stream Kol' flows into it from the N side. 4 horses gave out and were left lying by the road.
Wed.	21	Frost. At 10 a.m. we went on our route and left the boyar's son Antipin to round up the horses left along the road. He was instructed to feed the horses here up to the 23rd, and then move on to [Iudoma] Cross and stay there. After traveling for about 25 versts, we halted for the night at 4 p.m. The stream Ukachan, which flows into the Iudoma below the Cross, remained on the right hand from us. All day sunshine, road dry, remaining distance from this place to Iudoma about 20 versts.

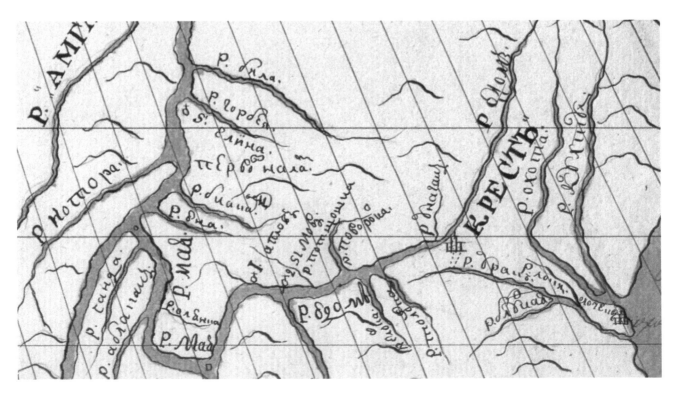

Folio 13

Day of the week	Day of the month	September 726. Events on our route from Iudoma to Okhotsk
Thu.	22	Frost. At 7 a.m. we went off and moved along marshes; there were few dry places. At 12 o'clock we came to the Iudoma River on the opposite side of the Cross. We left and went up the river about 1 verst, then crossed the river and overtook our cattle. We left 2 soldiers with 27 horses at the Cross. And they were instructed to stay there until an order came from Lieutenant Spanberch. And also, in case the latecomers of our command had tired horses, to put provisions into the storehouse and to guard it. We went on from Iudoma for about 10 versts, and at 5 o'clock put up for the night at the stream Iundra.
Fri.	23	Light frost. At 7 a.m. we moved on and went along marshes, and if they had not been frozen, there would have been horrible mud. At 3 o'clock we passed a lake, the way around it was about 5 versts long; having all day today covered 25 versts, we settled for the night at 4 o'clock, since there was no food nearby for the horses. All day overcast, but from 4 o'clock sunshine. A carpenter was punished; he was flogged with rods for his impoliteness.
Sat.	24	Light frost and in the morning thick fog. At 8 a.m. we departed and, after 5 versts, from the right side flows the stream Urak. And we went down the Urak. At 1 o'clock sun breaking through, at 3 p.m. we passed the stream Korshunovka, which flows into the Urak from the left side and, having done today 36 versts, at 6 o'clock we stopped for the night at the Urak River, where there was enough food for the horses.
Sun.	25	At 2 a.m. it rained and a strong gale arose from the N. At 8 o'clock we went on and, after 36 versts, we halted for the night by the same river. At 5 p.m. today sun breaking through, wind the same, and we saw places suitable for preparing hay in advance. The road was dry. At 8 o'clock calm and fair weather.
Mon.	26	At 4 a.m. overcast and icy cold. At 7 o'clock we went on and, after 36 versts, passed the night by the Urak River. At times light snowfall, at 6 o'clock and all night light snowfall.
Tue.	27	Overcast. At 8 o'clock we went on and crossed the Urak below the rapids. Bright, cloudy and light frost. We went up a mountain; the river remained on the left side and, after 36 versts we rested for the night at the stream Bludnaia, which flows into the Urak. It became overcast and calm, we moved through marshes and tundra, but they were frozen. One horse gave out and we left it. At 9 o'clock light snowfall.
Wed.	28	In the morning frost, at 8 o'clock we went downstream along the Bludnaia. In the afternoon we left the Bludnaia on the left and crossed the stream Kislaia that flows into Urak. Having covered 35 versts, we spent the night at Urak. Food for horses – willow branches, dry leaves, which they eat instead of grass. 2 horses gave out and we left them on the road. All day sun. We passed marshy places, and began to prepare for the night at 6 p.m.

◄ PLATE 14. The Iudoma Cross portage on the watershed between the Iudoma River (flowing westwards) and the Urak River (flowing eastwards). Segment of Chaplin's map of the itinerary through Siberia (p. 45).

Courtesy Russian State Archives of Military History, Moscow (RGVIA).

Day of the week	Day of the month	September 726. Events on our route from Iudoma to Okhotsk
Thu.	29	Hard frost. At 8 a.m. we moved 1½ versts near the Urak River and transferred to the left side of the river with great difficulties: its current is rapid, and there is drifting ice. And we went up a mountain. At 5 p.m. we came to the Okhota River and went down the river. After covering 34 versts from the Urak River, we passed the night on the right shore of the Okhota River. Today the road was dry, in places marshy and we crossed small rivers. 3 horses tired out, we left them with Tunguses to care for. From Aldan to this place we did not see any inhabited yurts. All day fair weather, light breeze from W. We left here 2 Tunguses, whom we had brought along from Iakutsk.
Fri.	30	Light frost. At 8 a.m. we went on. Light clouds with sun shining through. At 11 o'clock we crossed the stream Dzholokon, which flows into Okhota from the right side, went up a mountain and proceeded along the mountain for about 3 hours. There is a marshy place on the mountain. Today we did about 40 versts, and at 6 p.m. we halted for the night near Okhota. On the right side of the river there are good meadows and much grass. One horse tired out and was left on the road.
		October
Sat.	1	Light frost. At 8 o'clock we left and went along the bank of the Okhota River. At 1 p.m. we arrived at the Okhotsk outpost. Today we did about 15 versts. Sunshine, light breeze from W. The Captain looked over the storehouses in the outpost, in which different goods of Her Imperial Majesty are kept: gunpowder, linen and others. These storehouses were quite bad, and goods could go to waste. And I wrote to the Iakutsk chancellery requesting that new storehouses be built. A person of our command stationed at Okhotsk and responsible for speeding up the building of vessels reported to the Captain, orally, that one vessel was planked to the deck but still not completed because of shortage of resin. Also a small karbus or lodka was being built. A boyar's son of Iakutsk, 26 workers,[76] and 2 blacksmiths have been appointed to build the vessels. The outpost stands on the bank of the Okhota River; there are 11 houses. It is located 1½ versts from the sea and 5 versts upstream from the mouth of the Okhota River. The inhabitants are Russian, but they eat more fish and roots than bread. There are many tribute-paying natives, called Tunguses, in this outpost. They are also called "Lamutki", because they call the sea "Lamo".

PLATE 15. Tunguses mounted on reindeer. Ethnographical detail from the Prince of Liechtenstein copy of Bering's Final Map (p. 221).

Courtesy the James Ford Bell Library, Minneapolis, MN.

Folio 14

Day of the week	Day of the month	October 726. Events at the Okhotsk outpost
Sun.	2	Light frost, wind from N. The Captain ordered the sending of 10 servitors, of those working on the ship, to the forest for logs to build houses for our men; and 10 to make hay for the cattle. All day sunshine.
Mon.	3	Light frost, wind from N. Today the Captain went to the littoral locally called "koshka",[77] where a vessel was being built. Also here the local inhabitants have summer yurts for fishing. We examined 3 storehouses of Her Majesty, in which supplies for ship building are kept. And he ordered 2 of them cleaned for the provisions to be brought by us. All day sunshine.
Tue.	4	Frost and strong gale from N, sunshine.
Wed.	5	Hard frost, gentle breeze from N. 5 servitors were ordered to build a log house that had been bought by the Captain. 60 logs were rafted down the river. By 9 p.m. 15 more logs had been brought.
Thu.	6	Frost, light breeze. We laid the foundation for the second house and began to build. 10 servitors were building, and 10 more were in the forest cutting logs. At 7 p.m. a serviceman arrived and delivered 28 bags on 14 horses. All day sunshine.
Fri.	7	Frost and sunshine. All day the same work, at 2 p.m. 2 carpenters of our command arrived with 13 horses and 26 bags of provisions. At 5 o'clock 15 horses arrived, delivered 30 bags with flour.
Sat.	8	Considerable frost. At 1 p.m. 2 Admiralty carpenters arrived, with 27 horses, 54 bags with flour. At 4 o'clock apprentice Kozlov arrived, with 3 carpenters, horses and provisions: 45 horses with 90 bags of flour and 19 with 38 bags of groats. Same work. Apprentice Kozlov reported orally that out of the horses that went with him, 24 carrying 48 bags of provisions had been left by the Iudoma River near the Cross because of fatigue, under guard by soldiers of our command.
Sun.	9	Frost. On the order received, I distributed to the servicemen the bread ration for October: 1½ poods of flour and 5 pounds of groats to each. I shall report about this in writing late this month. In the afternoon 2 more carpenters that had been left behind by apprentice Kozlov arrived with 12 pack horses and 38 bags of flour. 2 rafts of logs arrived. All day sunshine.

PLATE 16. Walking Tungus woman.
Ethnographical detail from the Stockholm copy
of Bering's Final Map (p. 215).

Courtesy the National Library of Sweden
(Kungl. biblioteket, Stockholm).

Day of the week	Day of the month	October 726. Events at the Okhotsk outpost	Which days which winds
Mon.	10	Hard frost, gentle breeze, all day sunhine. We began to build a bathhouse; 15 men worked on it, and others were in the forest. A carpenter arrived with 3 horses and 6 bags of flour, and 27 head of cattle of Her Majesty were driven in.	E
Tue.	11	Frost and sunshine. The physician of our command arrived with 2 carpenters, 16 pack horses with 32 bags of groats, 29 horses with 58 bags of flour, and reported orally that he had left at the Cross 24 bags and near the outpost 1 carpenter with 30 bags, since the horses had tired out; the same day we sent 20 horses to this carpenter.	
Wed.	12	Frost and rime, all day sun shining through light clouds. A raft of logs was driven in; the Captain bought a storehouse which was transferred to the building site.	
Thu.	13	Light frost, overcast. The carpenter arrived with the provisions, for which horses had been sent.	
Fri.	14	Warm, all day sunshine. The Captain went to the place where the hay was being cut, people were sent to the forest.	
Sat.	15	Warm and sunhine. 213 logs were floated to the building site; work continued.	
Sun.	16	Sunshine. There was no work today. Iakuts who had driven the horses were let go home, but some were left to look after the horses, since some horses were still there.	
Mon.	17	Overcast and light snow, from noon sunshine. 50 logs were driven in.	
Tue.	18	Heavy snowfall. 50 logs were driven in. In the afternoon fair weather and strong gale.	N
Wed.	19	After midnight wind and snowfall. 26 men were sent to the forest. 4 *dugouts* with charcoal arrived. At 11 o'clock sergeant Liubimskii arrived with his group and with 92 pack horses with 174 bags of flour. 111 logs were driven in from the forest. The nobleman Shestakov arrived.[78]	N
Thu.	20	Fair weather. 20 men were sent to the forest to cut logs. At 12 o'clock sunshine, at 3 p.m. snowfall. 110 logs were driven in. Wind arose. One bull of the 27 was given to 8 carpenters.	S
Fri.	21	Overcast. 10 men were sent to the forest for logs and 4 Tunguses to build yurts. 50 logs were driven in. We began to build 2 cattle sheds.	
Sat.	22	Overcast and windy, all day snowfall. 10 servitors were sent to the forest for logs. Foreman Vavilov arrived. He brought the baggage of the Captain and reported that the bags with flour had been left after crossing the stream Dzholokon, since all the horses had tired out. A soldier and a carpenter had been left to look after them. 84 logs were driven in. After 8 p.m. the snowfall stopped.	N

Folio 15

Day of the week	Day of the month	October 726. Events at the Okhotsk outpost	Which days which winds
Sun.	23	From midnight heavy snowfall that lasted all day. 35 horses were taken from local inhabitants and sent for the flour that had been left behind. 17 horsemen who had arrived with the sergeant were let go.	
Mon.	24	Strong gale, at 8 o'clock light, cloudy and calm. All day the weather was the same and warm.	
Tue.	25	Light clouds and wind. The rest of the provisions arrived, for which horses had been sent.	NE
Wed.	26	Light frost, calm. The weather light, cloudy, and at times with sun breaking through. The carpenters of our command were at work.	
Thu.	27	Frost. I paid additional money for 45 horses: one ruble for each horse. To the Captain were given from Her Majesty's food supplies 64 bags, by weight about 130 poods. 1 bull from Her Majesty's cattle was given to the clerk, and all others were slaughtered.	
Fri.	28	Frost and calm, all day sunshine.	
Sat.	29	Frost. The Iakuts who grazed the horses reported that 13 had perished. All day sunshine and calm.	
Sun.	30	Frost and all day sunshine and calm.	
Mon.	31	Moonlit night. Frost. Light breeze. All day sunshine. The Iakuts reported that 23 horses had perished. Work was the same. 2 coopers were sent to the forest to fell and make staves for barrels.	N
		November	
Tue.	1	Moonlit night with small clouds, light breeze and frost, all day sunshine. A serviceman was sent with letters to Lieutenant Spanberch.	NNW
Wed.	2	Moonlit and frost, wind was the same. 10 horses perished.	NNW
Thu.	3	Hard frost and wind, all day sunshine, gentle breeze.	NW
Fri.	4	Hard frost and gentle breeze, all day sunshine. 1 horse perished.	W
Sat.	5	Hard frost, gentle breeze, all day sunshine.	N
Sun.	6	Frost, light breeze. The nobleman Shestakov was dismissed from our command, and left for Taui to take up the post of commissary there, as ordered by the Iakutsk chancellery. The horsemen who arrived with the foreman were let go also.	N

Folio 15 verso

Day of the week	Day of the month	November 726. Events at the Okhotsk outpost	
Mon.	7	Hard frost, gentle breeze, all day sunshine. The men were at work as before. One horse perished.	N
Tue.	8	Frost, light breeze, all day sunshine. A servitor was punished for absence without permission from the command.	N
Wed.	9	Frost, gentle breeze and sunshine.	N
Thu.	10	Frost and calm air, sunshine. By evening the wind arose.	N
Fri.	11	Frost and wind. To this date 121 horses have perished. All day sunshine. Today 30 horses were sent from the outpost to the Inia River 36 versts away for feeding.	N
Sat.	12	Hard frost, light breeze and all day sunshine.	NNE
Sun.	13	Light frost, at times strong breeze, sunshine all day.	N
Mon.	14	Light frost, at times strong gale, sunshine all day. 20 horses were sent to Inia.	N
Tue.	15	Few clouds and light frost, sunny spells, light breeze.	N
Wed.	16	Light frost and sunshine. The coopers returned from the forest and reported that they had prepared wood for about 30 barrels.	
Thu.	17	Overcast, light frost. Apprentice Kozlov was sent with the foreman and 3 Admiralty carpenters to the Arka River to look for timber suitable for building seagoing vessels. After 4 p.m. the wind arose. Light snowfall and drifting snow.	N
Fri.	18	Night clear, strong gale with light blowing snow, sun all day, but there was not much sunshine.	N
Sat.	19	After midnight calm and light frost, all day sunshine.	
Sun.	20	Night clear, frost, light breeze, all day overcast.	NNE
Mon.	21	Night clear, strong gale, light frost, all day overcast.	N
Tue.	22	Night overcast with breaks, gentle breeze with drifting snow, in the morning light snowfall and all day overcast and warm.	N
Wed.	23	Night clear with drifting clouds, wind and light frost and all day weather was the same.	N

PLATE 17. Okhotsk and surroundings.
Segment of the anonymous Copenhagen copy in Swedish of Bering's Final Map (p. 203).

Courtesy the Royal Library, Copenhagen.

Folio 16

Day of the week	Day of the month	November 726. Events at the Okhotsk outpost	
Thu.	24	Light frost. Strong breeze. Day was overcast with sun breaking through now and then. Today there was no work.	N
Fri.	25	Bitter cold, gusty wind, sunny day.	N
Sat.	26	Hard frost, light breeze. Apprentice Kozlov arrived and reported to the Captain that he had found timbers suitable for one vessel, but that the water in the mouth of the Arka River was only 4 inches. Sunshine.	N
Sun.	27	From 5 a.m. a strong gale arose and all day light frost and sunshine.	N
Mon.	28	Strong gale with blowing snow, cloudy. The Captain ordered all servitors living at the Okhotsk outpost to have skis and sleds, the same for the command of the Kamchadal commissary.[79]	N
Tue.	29	Strong gale with snowstorm. 2 servitors were sick. Today and yesterday there was a high tide from the sea, old residents did not remember the like of it for 20 years.	
Wed.	30	Overcast and light snowfall. In the morning light breeze, and at noon the wind changed, light snow all day.	SE N
		December	
Thu.	1	From midnight fresh wind arose with blowing snow all day.	NNE
Fri.	2	Strong gale with snowstorm till noon, and at noon the wind changed, the snowstorm stopped. Today on the order received, I distributed to the servicemen the bread ration for December: 1½ poods flour, 5 pounds groats per each man, and reported on it in writing. Today the Captain moved to live in the new-built house.	E NNE
Sat.	3	Cloudy, strong breeze, but all day some sun shining through, warm.	NNE
Sun.	4	In the night strong breeze, all day light, with clouds, gentle breeze and some sun shining through.	NE
Mon.	5	Overcast, gentle breeze and warm. From this day a guard with a gun was placed at the yard of the Captain.	NE
Tue.	6	Overcast and warm; light breeze.	NE

Folio 16 verso

Day of the week	Day of the month	December 726. Events at the Okhotsk outpost	
Wed.	7	Night overcast, a gentle breeze arose and light snowfall. At 10 a.m. fresh wind and heavy snowstorm. At noon the snowstorm changed to snow mixed with rain.	E
Thu.	8	Light frost, all day sunny and calm.	
Fri.	9	Frost and light breeze, sunshine.	N
Sat.	10	Light frost, light breeze, sun shining through.	N
Sun.	11	Light frost, all day sunshine with passing clouds, light breeze.	NNE
Mon.	12	Night clear, light breeze and frost, at day small clouds.	N
Tue.	13	Hard frost, light breeze. 3 servitors arrived from the town of Iakutsk, inhabitants of this outpost. All day small clouds.	N
Wed.	14	Hard frost, light air, sunny all day.	N
Thu.	15	Hard frost, calm air, sunny all day.	
Fri.	16	Bitter cold and sunny all day, calm air.	N
Sat.	17	Till midnight fair weather; from midnight overcast and snow, light breeze and light blowing snow. Today a commissary arrived at the outpost to collect tribute, and we received letters from Iakutsk from Lieutenant Chirikov. Also from him we received oral information on Lieutenant Spanberch, that he moved along the Iudoma River on sleds. All day overcast and snowstorm.	NNE NW
Sun.	18	Strong gale and snowstorm all day. The Captain ordered the corporal, 2 soldiers and 2 carpenters from our command, 6 of the local commissary's men, 11 of commissary Tarabukin's men, and 29 of the servitors who worked on the vessels, to get ready to go to the Cross.	
Mon.	19	Fair weather and bitter cold, strong breeze. On the order received I paid 6 rubles and […] kopecks[80] for kukliankas and parkas[81] that had been bought for the servicemen, and reported on it in writing.	

Folio 17

Day of the week	Day of the month	December 726. Events at the Okhotsk outpost	
Tue.	20	Strong gale and frost. All day sun.	NNW
Wed.	21	The night was bright, with strong gale. From 9 p.m. the wind dropped, light frost, all day sun. A serviceman arrived from Lieutenant Spanberch, and we received true information through his report that he was on his way to the Cross with all materiel on 90 sleds, and navigator Angel was left at the vessels, with 6 soldiers and 1 cooper for guard duty.[82]	
		I paid 50 kopecks each to 2 Tunguses, who are going to the Cross, and reported on it in writing.	NW
Thu.	22	Hard frost, light breeze. The corporal, 2 carpenters, and 7 servitors were sent to meet Lieutenant Spanberch on 10 sleds.	N
		With them were sent: 16 poods fresh beef, 100 dried fish, 1½ poods of fish flour.[83] Our 4 servicemen, who are going to the Cross, have been given 20 pounds of meat.	
		1 man sick.	
Fri.	23	Frost and gentle breeze. Today the following men were dispatched to meet Lieutenant Spanberch: 2 soldiers, 37 servitors with 36 sleds.	
		They brought with them 30 poods of meat, 3½ poods of fish flour and 400 dried fish for the servicemen accompanying the Lieutenant.	
		All day overcast, light breeze. 1 man sick.	N
Sat.	24	Frost, gentle breeze. On order of the Captain, I gave out 20 pounds to each of 23 servicemen. Today there was sunshine, but it was cold. 1 man sick.	N
Sun.	25	Night moonlit, gentle breeze and hard frost, sunshine with small clouds. 1 man sick	N
Mon.	26	Hard frost. This evening 2 servicemen who lived at the Captain's [house] were arrested for drunkenness. 1 man was sick.	N
Tue.	27	Hard frost, light breeze, all day sunshine. 1 man sick.	NNE
Wed.	28	Hard frost, light air. Those under arrest were punished and released. All day sunshine.	
Thu.	29	Night moonlit, with few clouds, light breeze, bitter cold.	
		All day overcast with a few sunny spells.	

Folio 17 verso

Day of the week	Day of the month	January 727. Events at the Okhotsk outpost	
Fri.	30	A night with bright clouds, strong gale and blowing snow, and the weather was the same all day.	N
Sat.	31	After midnight fair weather, the wind dropped, all day with sunny spells. Acting by received orders, I distributed among the servicemen of our command provisions for January, to each 1½ poods of flour, 5 pounds of groats, and reported on it in writing.	N
		January 727	
Sun.	1	A bright night, with light breeze and hard frost. All day sun. 1 man sick.	N
Mon.	2	A bright night, with light breeze, hard frost. All day sunshine.	NNE
		1 man sick. At 9 p.m. fresh wind arose with snowstorm.	NW
Tue.	3	Strong gale with drifting snow and snowfall all day, but from 7 p.m. the wind and snow subsided. Light frost. 1 man sick.	NW
Wed.	4	At night overcast, strong breeze with a light snowstorm.	NW
		In the daytime sun, a gentle breeze with blowing snow. 1 man sick.	
Thu.	5	A bright night, with a light breeze, frost, till noon bright with some clouds.	N
		In the afternoon strong gale arose with snowstorm.	NW
		1 man sick.	
Fri.	6	At night cloudy, strong gale with snowstorm and hard frost. In the daytime cloudy, strong breeze. At 1 p.m. Lieutenant Spanberch arrived at [Okhotsk] outpost on 7 sleds, together with 2 of his soldiers and some of the men we had sent – the carpenter and 2 servitors. 1 man in [our] command is sick. And he [Spanberch] gave an oral report on his detachment to the Captain, saying that his detachment was coming after him, and some because they were sick had been left at Iudoma Cross.	
Sat.	7	The night was cloudy and calm, with light snowfall till noon. From 6 o'clock strong breeze and light snowstorm.	S
		In the afternoon the wind changed, at 6 o'clock it was calm and snowed lightly. 1 man sick.	NW

Folio 18

Day of the week	Day of the month	January 727. Events at the Okhotsk outpost	
Sun.	8	The night was bright, cloudy and calm, in the daytime sunny spells, light, changeable breeze. 3 men sick.	
Mon.	9	A clear and calm night, hard frost, the day was sunny, with a light breeze. By order of the Captain I told commissary Paranchin of this outpost that the servitors under his command must have traveling clothes, and that they must be ready when requested, and should not make excuses for themselves. 3 men of our command are sick.	NNE
Tue.	10	Hard frost, all day sun, light breeze. A group from Lieutenant Spanberch's remaining detachment arrived at the outpost: 2 sailors, 2 drummers, 2 soldiers, together with 8 servitors, who had been sent out to meet them. They brought with them a medicine chest and some carpenter's tools. 3 men sick.	NNE
Wed.	11	The night was clear and calm. Hard frost. 3 carpenters, of Eniseisk, 1 servitor from Iakutsk arrived. All day sunshine. light breeze. Another 2 sailors and 2 more servitors of Iakutsk arrived. 3 men of our command are sick.	NNE
Thu.	12	A clear night, light breeze and frost. Tonight the geodesist and the corporal who had been sent to meet him arrived at the outpost. 2 soldiers brought the state monies.[84] At 10 p.m. the geodesist's instruments were brought in. Today sun and light snowfall at times. 10 carpenters arrived. 3 men of our command are sick. 2 sailors and 3 servitors of Iakutsk arrived.	NNE
Fri.	13	Frost, light breeze. 2 sailors, 2 soldiers, a caulker, a sail maker, a carpenter, 4 servitors arrived. Today sunshine. 3 men sick.	NNE
Sat.	14	Frost, light breeze. The following arrived at the outpost: the commissary, 3 carpenters, 3 blacksmiths. 11 men were sick. All day sunshine.	NNE
Sun.	15	Frost, light breeze. 2 carpenters arrived. Today overcast; light blowing snow. 11 men were sick.	NNE

Folio 18 verso

Day of the week	Day of the month	January 727. Events at the Okhotsk outpost	
Mon.	16	Frost, light breeze. Tonight 2 sick carpenters were brought in on sleds that had been sent to fetch them. All day sunshine. The following men of our command are sick: the geodesist, 4 sailors, 5 soldiers, 6 carpenters.	NNE
Tue.	17	From midnight the wind arose, all day overcast, strong breeze that later changed direction. Light blowing snow and snowfall. The number of sick is the same.	NWbN NE
Wed.	18	Light frost and moderate breeze. By order of the Captain I distributed the fish and fish flour that was left over from the ration that had been sent out to the arriving servicemen. All day clouds, from 1 to 7 p.m. wind that changed direction. 13 men sick.	NE E NE
Thu.	19	Moderate frost. All day cloudy, light breeze, at 7 p.m. there was a light snowfall. 16 men sick.	NE
Fri.	20	Moderate frost, calm, today sunshine. The following men of our command are sick: 1 geodesist, 1 drummer, 5 soldiers, 4 sailors, 6 carpenters, altogether 17.	
Sat.	21	Frost and calm, this morning sunshine, light breeze. 17 men sick.	NNE
Sun.	22	Frost and light breeze with blowing snow. All day sunshine. 17 men sick.	N
Mon.	23	Moderate frost, light breeze with blowing snow. By order of the Captain, I distributed entrails of cattle to 73 servicemen, that is heads, legs and other entrails. The [written] order to do so I received on the 27th of this month. 18 men sick.	N
Tue.	24	Frost, light breeze, all day sunshine. A cooper and 2 servitors on 3 sleds were sent out to bring staves for barrels. 18 men sick.	N
Wed.	25	A moonlit night, light breeze, in the daytime sunny. 16 men sick.	N

Folio 19

Day of the week	Day of the month	January 727. Events at the Okhotsk outpost	
Thu.	26	Frost and light breeze. The chaplain[85] of our command arrived from the Cross with 5 sleds, which had been sent from the river Urak by the Lieutenant, and with him: 1 sailor, 1 soldier, 5 servitors. I received an order from the Captain to hand out additional provisions for January to the men who arrived with the Lieutenant, and for the past months according to the list received from commissary Durasov. I did so and reported on the issue of rations. All day sunshine. 18 men sick.	NNE
Fri.	27	Frost and moderate breeze. 2 carpenters and 1 serviceman arrived from the Cross and reported that along the Urak 2 carpenters had died and 3 men had been left behind. They did not know if they were alive or not. 15 men were sick. Sunny all day.	NNE
Sat.	28	Wind with light blowing snow, sunshine. Lieutenant Spanberch inspected the servicemen of his own command and the servitors, and having selected the most able-bodied, ordered them to be ready to go to recover the materiel that had been left. 15 men sick.	N
Sun.	29	Light frost and wind, all day gloomy. A cooper arrived, bringing staves. I received an order on giving out of bread ration for February to all servicemen, gave it out and reported in writing. 2 of the Kamchadal commissary's servitors left for Iakutsk. 14 men sick. The Captain ordered me to get ready to go back for the rest of the materiel.	N
Mon.	30	Light frost, light breeze, with white clouds. The number of sick is the same.	N
Tue.	31	During the night light snowfall, sunny all day, light frost and light breeze. 15 men sick. The Lieutenant inspected the servitors who are going with commissary Tarabukin to Kamchatka and ordered some of them to get ready to leave. In the evening light snowfall.	N
		February	
Wed.	1	In the morning frost, strong breeze, all day cloudy and light snowstorm. 14 men sick.	NNW
Thu.	2	At night strong gale with blowing snow. Sunny day, light breeze. 14 men sick.	NNW

Folio 19 verso

Day of the week	Day of the month	February 727[86]. Events at the Okhotsk outpost	
Fri.	3	Light frost and sunshine, light breeze. I received an order on giving out rations to 42 servitors, who were being sent for materiel, 2 poods of flour and 1 pood of meat for each. And another order to issue the bread rations for February and March plus one pood of meat to each of the men of our command who are going out to recover the materiel. The Lieutenant reviewed all the men who are going out to recover the materiel. 14 men sick. And I reported on the issue of rations in accordance with the above-mentioned orders.	NW
Sat.	4	Light frost and wind, in the daytime sunshine and calm. 10 men sick.	NW
Sun.	5	Frost, light breeze and snowfall. In the morning and during the day sunshine. 10 men sick.	
Mon.	6	Sunshine, light breeze and frost. The following men of our command are sick: 2 sailors, 5 soldiers, 3 carpenters.	N
Tue.	7	White clouds, light frost, light air. I received an order to issue bread ration for the January third of the year to doctor Vilim Butskovskii for one orderly[87] and reported on the issue. 8 men sick.	N
Wed.	8	Frost and light snow in the morning, in the daytime gloomy, at times snowfall. By oral order of the Captain, I gave out flour and groats to commissary Durasov, and got a receipt. 8 men sick.	N
Thu.	9	Frost all day, cloudy with a little sun breaking through, light breeze. 9 men sick.	NE
Fri.	10	Frost, light breeze and all day sunshine. During the day the wind changed. 10 men sick.	NE N
Sat.	11	Light frost and wind, in the daytime sunshine and calm. The Lieutenant ordered the people who were to recover the materiel to be ready by 7 a.m. of the 13th day. 10 men sick.	
Sun.	12	All day frost, overcast and light snowfall, moderate breeze, from changing directions, but from 4 p.m. a wind blew from E. 10 men sick.	

▶ PLATE 18. Folio 122 of Lieutenant Chirikov's journal, with entries from Iakutsk in January and early February 1727.

Courtesy Russian State Naval Archives (RGAVMF). Photo by Nikolai Turkin.

Мѣсяца Генваря 1727 года ...

Мѣсяца Генваря 1727 Года ...

15 ...

16 ...

17 ...

18 ...

19 ...

20 ...

21 ...

22 ...

23 ...

24 ...

25 ...

26 ...

27 ...

28 ...

29 ...

30 ...

31 ...

Мѣсяцъ Февраль

1 ...

2 ...

3 ...

4 ...

5 ...

6 ...

7 ...

8 ...

9 ...

Day of the week	Day of the month	February 727. Events at the Okhotsk outpost	
Mon.	13	Warm, strong breeze with snowstorm, all day overcast and snowfall, at times snowstorm, from noon variable wind. 8 men sick.	ENE
Tue.	14	Frost, gentle breeze. At 10 a.m. we went off on our route from Okhotskii ostrog with 76 sleds to recover the materiel: Lieutenant Spanberch, and with him me, the corporal, 3 Admiralty carpenters, 9 soldiers, 5 carpenters of Eniseisk and Irkutsk, 42 servitors of Iakutsk, 30 Tunguses from Taui and Okhotsk. Having covered 2 versts, we stopped for the night. All day sunshine and light blowing snow. And it was warm.	N
Wed.	15	Frost and calm. At 5 a.m. we went off on our route and kept going all day. Having covered 20 versts, we settled for the night at the Okhota River, by the landmark Polovinnyi Kamen'. All day sunshine.	
Thu.	16	Frost. At 6 a.m. we went off on our route by the Okhota River, and having covered 10 versts, ate lunch, then pushed on and walked for a while up the stream Dzholokon and, having passed 10 versts after lunch, we slept in the tundra. All day sunshine.	
Fri.	17	Frost, light breeze. At 5 a.m. we took off. Light snowstorm. At 12 o'clock we had lunch. We let a servitor go back because of illness, and pushed on over the ridge and kept going up to 5 o'clock. Having reached the descent to the Urak River, we stopped for the night. The total distance from Dzholokon to Urak by the winter road is 30 versts. All day sunshine.	N
Sat.	18	Light frost, light breeze. At 6 o'clock we started going up the Urak River. At 8 o'clock we passed Shcheki, where we found a dead carpenter of our command. We carried him to the bank and buried him. At 12 o'clock we ate lunch, then continued. From Shcheki we walked about 15 versts on naked ice. At 6 p.m. we stopped for the night on the left side of the Urak River. Today we did 25 versts, all day sunshine. 8 carpenters and 3 servitors were left behind.	N
Sun.	19	Light frost and wind. From 3 a.m. snowfall, at 7 o'clock we set out on our route, and at 10 o'clock we had lunch. At 4 o'clock we passed the stream Lomki, which flows into the Urak from the left side. We stopped for the night, having covered today 15 versts. All day heavy snowfall.	N
Mon.	20	At night strong gale and snowstorm. Tonight if we had not been careful, many of us could have been choked to death by the snow. In the morning fair weather and blowing snow, frost. At 9 o'clock we set out, and having covered 5 versts, stopped for the night at 2 p.m., since we were wet through. In the afternoon sunshine and drifting snow.	E
Tue.	21	Hard frost. At 5 a.m. we set out, and after 5 versts we crossed the stream Bludnaia, which flows into the Urak from the right side. At 1 o'clock we had lunch, then pushed on, and at 6 o'clock we began to prepare for the night, having done today 20 versts. Sunshine and calm.	

Folio 20 verso

Day of the week	Day of the month	February 727. Events on our route from Okhotsk by the river Urak	
Wed.	22	Hard frost. At 5 o'clock we set out on our route, at 7 o'clock we passed the landmark Tomilovo Poboishche and walked all day. Having covered 15 versts, we stopped for the night near the rapids. All day sunshine with light clouds.	
Thu.	23	In the morning light snowfall. At 7 o'clock we departed and kept going all day. At 4 p.m. snowstorm. Having covered 15 versts, we settled for the night at 6 o'clock, beyond Kisloe Plioso. Later snowfall and calm.	
Fri.	24	Cloudy and calm, light snowfall. At 7 o'clock we set out and, having covered 20 versts and crossed big mountains, we stopped for the night at 6 p.m.	
Sat.	25	Sunshine and calm. At 7 o'clock we started and, having covered 20 versts, stopped for the night. Today 2 servitors fell behind.	
Sun.	26	Sunshine and warm. At 8 o'clock we departed. We left some provisions for our return and one carpenter who had frozen his feet to guard it. At 2 p.m. we passed the stream Korshunovka, at 6 o'clock we arrived at the ridge we had to cross in order to get to the Cross, and stopped for the night, having covered 20 versts.	
Mon.	27	At 7 a.m. we left and started up the ridge. At 7 p.m., having covered about 15 versts, we stopped for the night, 4 or 5 versts from the lake. Sunshine and light breeze.	W
Tue.	28	At 7 in the morning we set out. 1 soldier was sick, and we pulled him along on a sled. In the afternoon gentle breeze. At 6 p.m. we arrived at the Iudoma River, at the winter outpost of [Iudoma] Cross, but not with all our sleds. And the geodesist Luzhin reported that there were 7 servicemen at the winter outpost, and that navigator Morisen died on 2 February. Sunshine all day.	W
		March	
Wed.	1	Sunshine and frost. The rest of the sleds arrived, except for those left at Urak. The entire command was reviewed, and the Articles of War[88] were read. The Lieutenant divided up his men. I was ordered to go by the Iudoma River to Bol'shaia Elovka with 30 men; the corporal and a sailor had to go to the stream Povorotnaia with 42 men. By order of the Lieutenant I drew up an inventory of the dead navigator's belongings. And upon my return to the Okhotsk outpost, I reported on this and delivered the inventory in my own handwriting.	
Thu.	2	Hard frost and calm, sunshine all day. The men were allowed to rest today.	

Day of the week	Day of the month	March 727. Events on our route by the Iudoma River	
Fri.	3	At 8 a.m. we departed from the Cross and went down the Iudoma River. Having covered about 10 versts, we had lunch, then pushed on and kept going until 6 p.m. We stopped for the night having done about 30 versts from the Cross. All day sunshine, light breeze.	W
Sat.	4	At 6 in the morning we went on. At 10 o'clock we went over the mountain Krivaia Luka. By 12 o'clock we came to the equipment left there, and having had lunch went on and found a half-dead carpenter of our command, who was walking from Povorotnaia. We gave him some provisions and went on our way. Having covered today about 25 versts, we stopped for the night. All day sunshine. From the Cross to Krivaia Luka there are many islands in the river.	
Sun.	5	Hard frost. At 7 o'clock we went on. At 12 o'clock we arrived at the rapids and had lunch. Then we went on and passed the stream Podporozhnaia that flows from the right side. Having covered that day 25 versts, we stopped for the night. All day sunshine and calm.	
Mon.	6	Frost and calm. At 6 o'clock we set out, at 1 o'clock we had lunch, then went on and, having covered that day 25 versts, prepared for the night. Sunshine with few clouds and warm. We stopped for the night at 7 p.m.	
Tue.	7	Hard frost. At 7 o'clock we went and left behind 2 of our men and 1 from the corporal's detachment, because they were sick. Having covered about 10 versts, we ate lunch at the crosses of Bobrovskii and Shestakov,[89] then went on and, having covered about 13 versts, settled for the night across from the mouth of the stream Talovka, which flows into the Iudoma from the left side. It was sunshine and calm.	
Wed.	8	Hard frost. At 7 o'clock we set out. After 10 versts we had lunch and then pushed on. At 6 o'clock, having covered about 20 versts that day, we arrived at the stream Bol'shaia Elovka. Here was the materiel which I had been ordered to bring back. We found a dead servitor and committed his body to the earth following Christian custom.	
Thu.	9	Frost. At 7 o'clock the corporal and his command went on to Povorotnaia, which is only 1½ days away on foot. I and my command packed the sleds with materiel. All day white clouds with sun breaking through, at times also snowfall.	
Fri.	10	Tonight a servitor of Iakutsk ran away from my command. Overcast and light snowfall. At 10 o'clock, having packed the materiel, we headed towards the Cross. The materiel included: One 7-inch cable, another 6.6-inch cable, 6 anchors, 7 cannons. There was sunshine all day. And, having done 14 versts, we stopped for the night.	
Sat.	11	Light frost. At 7 o'clock we left and kept going all day (and came to the sick men, who had been left, and stayed there for the night).[90] All day sunshine and warm. Having done 4 versts after passing the stream Talovka, we stopped for the night.	

Day of the week	Day of the month	March 727. On our route by the Iudoma River	
Sun.	12	At 6 a.m. I received information from the corporal via a Tungus that 12 servitors of Iakutsk had run away from him at Povorotnaia on 10 March. And I set out on my route. At 12 o'clock we ate lunch. I dispatched the Tungus to the Lieutenant with a report on the runaway, and also to request the provisions left by us, since the men were running out of provisions. Sunshine and warm. Then we went on. At 5 p.m. wind and light snowfall. At 6 o'clock we came to the men who had been left by me because of illness, and here we spent the night.	
Mon.	13	At 7 o'clock I set out, taking my men with me. Light snowfall. At 10 o'clock sunshine. At 12 o'clock we had lunch, and then went on. Light breeze with drifting snow. Having covered 16 versts, we stopped for the night.	SW
Tue.	14	Frost. At 7 o'clock we went on and after 7 versts had lunch, then went on and kept going until 7 o'clock, then stopped for the night at a distance of 3 or 4 versts before the rapids. All day sunshine and warm.	
Wed.	15	Hard frost. At 7 o'clock we departed and came to the rapids at 9 o'clock. Because of the hard frost could not go any further and halted here until 12 o'clock, then went on and kept going up to 8 o'clock, when we arrived at the place where we had slept the second night on our way from the Cross. All day sunshine, in the afternoon it was warm.	
Thu.	16	Frost. At 7 o'clock we went on, and the Lieutenant came to meet us with his men. He dispatched 13 of them to Povorotnaia instead of the runaways and returned to the Cross with us. At 12 o'clock we ate. At 3 o'clock we crossed over the mountain at Krivaia Luka, and after about 1 more verst stopped for the night. The sun shone all day. On the river there was a little [melt] water.	
Fri.	17	Light frost. At 8 o'clock we left. At 12 o'clock we had lunch at the camp where we had slept the first night after the Cross. The Lieutenant moved ahead to the Cross. We went on too, walking through water. Having covered about 13 versts, we stopped for the night. All day sunshine and warm, light breeze.	W
Sat.	18	Warm. At 7 o'clock we set out and after about 5 versts had lunch, then went on again. At 5 p.m. we arrived safely at the Cross with all our materiel and people. The Lieutenant thought it proper to tell me that geodesist Luzhin had died on the 11th day of this month.[91]	
Sun.	19	Light frost. The servitors and Tunguses begged the Lieutenant for provisions, and he ordered me to give out some, as stated in my written report to the Captain. We buried the dead geodesist. All day sunshine and warm.	
Mon.	20	Light frost. At 10 o'clock I set out from the Cross with the same materiel, and the Lieutenant stayed to wait for the corporal's return from Povorotnaia. At 1 p.m. wind arose and the snow began to blow. Having done some 15 versts, we stopped for the night. The road was difficult, all blocked up by snow.	SW

Folio 22

Day of the week	Day of the month	March 727. Events on our route from the Cross to Okhotsk	
Tue.	21	Light breeze and warm. At 8 o'clock we set out on our route. By 9 o'clock a strong breeze arose with light blowing snow. Having done some 5 versts, we had lunch, and then pushed on. Towards the end of the 6th hour we stopped for the night, after about 6 versts. The road was very difficult. It was sunshine. 2 Tunguses ran away, leaving an anchor behind.	
Wed.	22	Light frost. At 6 o'clock we departed on our route, at 11 o'clock arrived at the lake and ate lunch. Then we went on and kept going until the second half of the 7th hour, when we stopped for the night. On the ridge the going was very difficult. 2 men sick. And it began to snow.	
Thu.	23	Snowfall all night. By 7 or 8 o'clock we set out and kept going, all the way with one man walking in front of us. By 7 o'clock we had descended from the ridge to the old camp, where we stayed for the night. It snowed all day.	
Fri.	24	Heavy snowfall. At 7 o'clock we continued down the Urak River, and at 12 arrived at the stream Korshunovka, where we ate lunch, then went on and had to walk a lot through water. We stopped for the night some 4 versts before the place where we had left some provisions. All day intermittent snowfall.	
Sat.	25	Snowfall. At 6 o'clock we departed, and at 9 we came to where we had left the provisions. I had the rations that belonged to the runaways and distributed half of them to the men, since they were dissatisfied with their provisions, and the Tunguses had none at all. Then I went on. In the afternoon sunshine. At 6 o'clock we stopped for the night.	
Sun.	26	Warm. At 7 o'clock we set out. At 1 we repaired sleds for about 2 hours, then went on. By 5 o'clock the Lieutenant overtook us, and I reported to him that the men did not have enough food. I fed many of them with my own provisions. Then he left us and continued towards the outpost. White clouds with sun breaking through.	
Mon.	27	Warm. At 7 o'clock we went on and walked through much water. At 11 o'clock we ate lunch, at 1 we went on. All day white clouds, light breeze. At 7 o'clock we stopped for the night, with 11 sleds; the 10 sleds that had fallen behind also stopped for the night.	SE
Tue.	28	At 8 in the morning we left without further waiting, and kept going all day. At 7 o'clock, having passed Kisloe Plioso, we stopped for the night. Sunshine, light breeze.	SE
Wed.	29	Light frost. At 7 o'clock we set out, at 2 p.m. we passed the rapids and, after another 4 versts, we began to prepare for the night at 6 o'clock. All day sunshine. 4 men sick.	

Folio 22 verso

Day of the week	Day of the month	April 727. Events on our route from the Cross to Okhotsk
Thu.	30	Frost. At 7 o'clock I let 12 sleds go to the outpost, while I, myself, waited for the last 8 sleds. At 3 p.m. the last sleds arrived and stopped for the night. The Tunguses who had run away on the 21st turned up again. At 7 o'clock a carpenter arrived from the outpost and said that some men were on their way to meet us.
Fri.	31	In the morning frost and dense clouds. At 3 p.m. the men from the outpost, 19 in all, arrived with provisions. I kept 4 of these men and sent the others on to the corporal. Then we set out on our route and, after some 5 versts, stopped for the night. All day sunshine and warm weather.
		April
Sat.	1	Frost. At 5 o'clock we left and walked on ice up to 1 o'clock, but then the road became very difficult. By 7 p.m. we began to settle for the night. At 10 a.m. we passed Tomilovo Poboishche, and on the left hand – the stream Torvochan, which flows into the Urak.
Sun.	2	Light frost. At 6 o'clock we set out. At 8 we passed the stream Bludnaia, at 11 had lunch, then went on and kept going until 6 p.m. For a considerable time we walked on ice and about 3 versts before the stream Lomki we stopped for the night.
Mon.	3	Light frost. At 6 o'clock we departed. Sunshine and warm weather. We kept going till 6 p.m. and, about 3 versts before Shcheki, put up for the night.
Tue.	4	Light frost, overcast. At 5 o'clock we set out, and by 11 o'clock we had climbed the ridge. I received an order from the Lieutenant via the Tungus Poteshnyi, in which he told us to go by the river to the sea, if it was too difficult to climb the ridge. At 1 o'clock we set out along the ridge and met 20 men who had been sent from the outpost with 1,000 fresh fish. I took 4 men for assistance and sent the rest to the corporal. Around 11 and 12 a.m. it snowed, but the afternoon was sunny. At 6 o'clock we stopped for the night, some 5 versts before the stream Dzholokon.
Wed.	5	Warm and overcast. I sent a report to the Lieutenant with the same Tungus. At 5 o'clock we, ourselves, set out on our route, at 7 we crossed the bridge over the stream Dzholokon, and at 10 crossed the Okhota River and kept going until 7 o'clock. About 5 versts beyond Polovinnyi Kamen' we stopped for the night. Moderate sunshine.

Folio 23

Day of the week	Day of the month	April 727. Events at the Okhotsk outpost	
Thu.	6	Warm weather. At 5 o'clock we set out, and at 3 or 4 p.m. we arrived at the Okhotsk outpost. I reported to the Lieutenant on the arrival of the materiel. All day sunshine and warm.	
Fri.	7	Light frost. At 4 p.m. the corporal arrived with his command on 27 sleds and brought the following materiel: 5 cables, 1 anchor, 1 cannon, sails and other things, as specified in the Lieutenant's report to the Captain.	
Sat.	8	Light frost. The materiel just brought in was taken down to the sea and deposited in the storehouse. The servicemen who had been living at the Cross while sick arrived. However, 2 soldiers had been left there as guards.	
Sun.	9	Light frost, all day sunshine and warm weather.	
Mon.	10	Light frost, overcast, light breeze.	
Tue.	11	Overcast, light breeze, at 5 p.m. light snowfall, and at 7 o'clock a strong gale arose.	SE
Wed.	12	Overcast, light breeze. Apprentice Kozlov was sent to the Cross to get the materiel still left there. He took 24 men with him. In the daytime changeable wind.	SW
Thu.	13	From morning to noon it was overcast, with light breeze, in the afternoon sunshine, and the wind changed. I received an order to audit Her Majesty's property.[92] Having assembled some tellers, I made out a report. 15 men from our command are sick.	SE SW
Fri.	14	Light frost and wind, sunshine all day. 15 men sick.	N
Sat.	15	Light frost, strong breeze, all day sunshine. 15 men sick.	N
Sun.	16	Frost and light breeze. By 9 o'clock the men who had been sent to Povorotnaia arrived, and they brought nothing. Another 3 men arrived who had been sent to fetch materiel remaining near the Cross, which they did. All day sunshine, light breeze. 15 men sick.	SE
Mon.	17	Light frost and sunshine, warm weather, gentle breeze in the afternoon. 1 sailor and 2 soldiers were sent down to the sea as guards. 15 men sick.	NW
Tue.	18	Frost, all day sunshine and wind. 16 men sick.	N

Folio 23 verso

Day of the week	Day of the month	April 727. Events at the Okhotsk outpost	
Wed.	19	Light frost. The Captain inspected the entire command and ordered the commissary to issue provisions for May and June. He addressed those of the men who were in good health and told them to be prepared to set out, when ordered to do so. Sunshine and warm weather, light breeze. In the afternoon the wind changed. 16 men sick.	N S
Thu.	20	Light frost. The Lieutenant inspected the entire command and selected 56 men of all ranks and ordered them to get ready to go to the Gorbeia winter quarters to fetch the remaining provisions. I received an order to take over state monies and provisions from commissary Durasov and to give the clerk Turchaninov money with which to pay the marine and Admiralty personnel their wages for the January third of the year. All day sunshine and light breeze. 17 men sick. Another order I received was on paying wages to the soldiers and carpenters for May and June. And I reported in writing on the execution of both orders.	
Fri.	21	Light frost. In the morning, when I came to report to the Lieutenant on the command, clerk Semion Turchaninov told the Lieutenant that he knew of a grave matter concerning the Captain, and handed him a denunciation. The Lieutenant gave orders to arrest him and keep him closely guarded.[93] In the afternoon the Lieutenant inspected the entire command and said that the expedition to the Gorbeia was called off for now. Sunshine, light breeze. 17 men sick.	S
Sat.	22	Light snowfall, at 10 o'clock sunshine with small clouds. The Lieutenant gave the Captain a report on sending the clerk to Petersburg. I received an order to give money to the 2 soldiers who were to go with the arrested clerk, and to the clerk himself, for living. And I reported on the payment in writing. 17 men are sick, 1 is under arrest.	
Sun.	23	Light frost, sunshine and warm weather, light breeze. Received an order to pay commissary Durasov his wages for the January third of the year, And I reported on the payment in writing. 15 men sick, 1 under arrest.	E SW
Mon.	24	Light frost and overcast. From 10 o'clock sunshine with clouds, cold wind. 14 men sick, 1 under arrest.	

Folio 24

Day of the week	Day of the month	April 727. Events at the Okhotsk outpost	
Tue.	25	Light frost and overcast, strong breeze and cold. 14 men sick, 1 under arrest.	
Wed.	26	Gloomy and cold, light breeze. The prisoner was sent off from the outpost with a guard of 2 soldiers. The following men of our command are sick: a commissary, a sailor, 4 soldiers, 9 carpenters.	
		By order of the Captain, a pood of meat was given to the soldiers who went with the prisoner.	
Thu.	27	Overcast until noon, light breeze, in the afternoon sunshine with small clouds.	E
		The wind changed. 15 men sick.	S
Fri.	28	Overcast, light breeze and warm, at times light snowfall. Same number of sick.	S
Sat.	29	Strong gale with snow. Same number of sick.	E
Sun.	30	Light breeze, heavy snowfall. In the afternoon the wind changed.	NE
		Light snowfall now and then. 15 men sick.	E
		May	
Mon.	1	Sunshine with white clouds. A Tungus from the detachment that had been sent to the Cross for materiel arrived to get food. 16 men sick.	
Tue.	2	White clouds, light breeze. At 5 p.m. a soldier, a drummer, a carpenter and 7 Tunguses arrived from the Cross with materiel, as specified in the report made out by apprentice Kozlov on his arrival.	SE
Wed.	3	Fair weather with small clouds. The delivered goods were sent down to the seaside. In the daytime sunshine and warm, before noon strong gale.15 men sick.	S
Thu.	4	Bright with some clouds, moderate breeze, sunshine now and then.	E
		In the afternoon the wind changed. 15 men sick.	S
Fri.	5	Bright with some clouds, and calm, from 11 o'clock sunshine, in the afternoon light breeze. 2 caulkers and 2 blacksmiths, all of them [state] servitors,[94] were sent to the seaside. It was warm all day. 12 men sick.	S
Sat.	6	In the morning light frost, light breeze now and then. 10 of our carpenters were sent down to the seaside, to the shipbuilding site. Sunshine, warm weather. 12 men sick.	SSW

Folio 24 verso

Day of the week	Day of the month	May 727. Events at the Okhotsk outpost	
Sun.	7	In the morning light frost and dense clouds, calm, from noon with some sunshine, light and changeable breeze. 12 men sick.	
Mon.	8	Light frost, changeable wind, sunshine. 3 dugouts with charcoal were sent down to the seaside. 11 men sick.	
Tue.	9	Frost and calm, sunshine. In the afternoon gentle breeze.	SSW
		The river has started to swell with water from upriver. 9 men sick.	
Wed.	10	Frost and calm, sunshine, high water level in the river, periodically with drifting ice. 8 men sick.	
Thu.	11	Calm and sunshine. The Captain and the Lieutenant went to the seaside, to the shipbuilding site. High water level. 8 men sick.	
Fri.	12	Sunshine, gentle breeze. The water level in the river began to go down. 7 men sick.	S
Sat.	13	Sunshine and warm weather, light breeze. The Lieutenant went down to the shipbuilding site by the sea, with a detachment consisting of a corporal, 5 seamen, 5 soldiers, and a drummer.	
		In the afternoon apprentice Kozlov arrived by water, on rafts, together with a soldier and a carpenter. He reported orally to the Captain that they had left some equipment on a mountain slope, with 2 carpenters to guard it.	
Sun.	14	Sunshine and warm, light breeze. 7 men sick.	SSW
Mon.	15	Sunshine and warm, in the afternoon strong gale that changed at 4 o'clock.	SE
		I received 2 orders: to distribute provisions and wages to the men who had arrived from the Cross. And I reported on doing so.	E
Tue.	16	Overcast and cold, strong gale. At 12 a.m. thunder and showers of hail, after 4 p.m. the wind dropped. 7 men sick.	E
Wed.	17	Gloomy and calm. A dugout with charcoal was sent to the seaside.	E
		From noon strong breeze, at 6 o'clock drizzle. 8 men sick.	
Thu.	18	Gloomy, strong breeze. A karbus with charcoal was sent to the seaside. Also 2 blacksmiths, 2 *seafarers,* and with them small Admiralty things were sent. At 5 p.m. drizzle. 8 men sick.	E

Folio 25

Day of the week	Day of the month	May 727. Events at the Okhotsk outpost	
Fri.	19	Gloomy, strong breeze and downpour all day. I received an order to issue to the servicemen the bread rations they had earned. I reported in writing on the issue.	E
Sat.	20	Overcast, light breeze, in the afternoon white clouds with spells of sunshine. The servitor and the carpenters that had been left to guard the materiel arrived. 8 men sick.	
Sun.	21	Sunshine, gentle breeze, in the afternoon the wind changed, and at 10 o'clock fog. 7 men sick.	SSW E
Mon.	22	In the morning gloomy, light breeze. The Captain was at the seaside, at the shipbuilding site, and, having gathered the entire command, they sold the belongings left by the deceased navigator Morrison. In the daytime sunshine. 7 men at the outpost are sick.	E
Tue.	23	Sunshine, strong breeze. 7 men sick.	SSW
Wed.	24	Sunshine and warm weather, strong breeze. All the men were given permission to leave the outpost and go to the seaside to catch fish for themselves. I received an order to pay out wages for April to the soldiers and carpenters who had arrived from the Cross. 9 men are sick.	SSW
Thu.	25	Sunshine, strong breeze. 4 carpenters arrived at the outpost, having received orders to go from the seaside to the Gorbeia. 7 men at the outpost are sick.	SE
Fri.	26	White clouds, in the afternoon overcast, gentle breeze, drizzle now and then. Same number of sick.	SE
Sat.	27	White clouds. 7 men sick.	
Sun.	28	Gloomy, light breeze and cold. Same number of sick.	SE
Mon.	29	Gloomy and calm, cold, from 4 a.m. rain, from 12 to 5 p.m. sunshine with small clouds, gentle breeze. 1 servitor and 6 Tunguses were dispatched in dugouts up the Urak River for the rest of the materiel. Same number of sick.	SE
Tue.	30	In the morning overcast, gentle breeze, at 12 a.m. sunshine, light breeze. 7 men were sick. I received an order to issue the bread ration to the physician for his orderly for the May third of the year and reported on the issue.	N S

Folio 25 verso

Day of the week	Day of the month	June 727. Events at the Okhotsk outpost	
Wed.	31	Sunshine, gentle breeze, in the afternoon the wind changed. Some servitors left the outpost for Iakutsk with Her Majesty's property from Tauisk.[95]	SW S
		June	
Thu.	1	Sunshine and calm, warm. In the afternoon strong breeze. 7 men are sick.	SSW
Fri.	2	Sunshine, strong breeze, warm weather. 2 carpenters of Irkutsk were sent back home for reasons of health. 4 men sick. I received an order to pay a servitor for a whetstone, and I reported on the expense.	SbW
Sat.	3	Sunshine, light breeze. On observation, the latitude of this place was found to be 59°13'. In the afternoon strong gale. A Tungus came from the mouth of the Urak River and said that some materiel had been brought there. However, because of the rough sea it was impossible to transport it by water to the mouth of the Okhota River. 4 men are sick. I received an order to send (to issue)[96] provisions and to have them sent with commissary Durasov, for distribution among them.[97]	SWbS S
Sun.	4	In the morning fog and calm, from 8 o'clock sunshine, light breeze. The horses which last fall were left at the Inia river were brought; but there were only 4 of them left.[98] All the others had perished and been eaten by the wolves. At 6 p.m. rain. I sent 3 horses to the Urak for the things that had arrived there. The rest was to be transported by sea.	
Mon.	5	Rain, light breeze. I received an order to pay a carpenter for the fish flour bought from him, and I reported on the expense.	E
Tue.	6	Sunshine, light breeze. I received an order to pay out wages to the commissary and 3 carpenters, who are being sent to the Gorbeia River, and reported on the payment.	E
Wed.	7	Sunshine, strong breeze. 5 sailors and 5 soldiers were sent to the seaside. The commissary was sent to the Gorbeia with 1 sailor and 3 carpenters. They took along with them 488 empty bags and were ordered to bring back from the Cross 242 saddle-girths, 100 pack ropes on 21 horses, and for the return of the horses one soldier was sent along. They were given for the road 1 reindeer. These horses were taken from local inhabitants.	SWbS
Thu.	8	Sunshine, strong breeze. Today the new-built vessel was launched and given the name "Fortuna". At the outpost 2 men are sick.	SEbS

Folio 26

Day of the week	Day of the month	June 727. Events at the Okhotsk outpost	
Fri.	9	Sunshine, light breeze and warm weather. In the afternoon the wind rose. From 8 o'clock and until midnight there was thunder. At the outpost 2 men are sick.	SSW
Sat.	10	Dense clouds and calm. From 10 a.m. to 5 p.m. sunshine, light breeze. 2 men sick.	SSW
Sun.	11	Dense clouds, drizzle and calm, by 9 o'clock bright with some clouds and sunny spells. The belongings of the deceased geodesist Luzhin were given, in accordance with his will, to our chaplain: A silver cross and a ring, 37 kopecks in cash and some other things, valued about 10 rubles. Her Majesty's instruments – a quadrant, an astrolabe, a set of drawing utensils, compasses – remain with the command.	
Mon.	12	Sunshine, light breeze. 2 men sick.	SSW
Tue.	13	Sunshine and warm weather. The Captain was at the shipbuilding site by the seaside, and they sold the rest of the baggage left by the deceased navigator.[99] At 8 p.m. rain. 2 men at the outpost were sick. The mast was erected on the vessel.	
Wed.	14	Sunshine, strong breeze, at times fresh wind. In the afternoon fresh wind. Same number of sick.	SW
Thu.	15	At night strong gale and drizzle, from noon sunshine, but at 10 o'clock rain. The Captain was at the seaside, by the vessel. Same number of sick.	SW
Fri.	16	Sun breaking through light fog. By order of the Captain, 377 saddlecloths, 582 saddle girths, 39 with straps, were handed over to the *supervisor*.[100] Strong breeze.	SSW
Sat.	17	In the morning fog, at 8 o'clock sunshine, light breeze. I was at the seaside. The vessel was equipped with galiotte rigging. Around 6 p.m. the wind changed. 3 men at the outpost are sick.	SSW E
Sun.	18	Fog, from 9 o'clock sunshine, light breeze.	SSW
Mon.	19	Sunshine and warm weather, light breeze, in the afternoon the wind changed. The Captain chose to be by the vessel. Same number of sick.	ESE SSW
Tue.	20	Clouds, strong gale. The men who had been ordered to go to the Gorbeia winter quarters arrived from the seaside. I received 4 orders: 1) to pay for 10 bundles of valerian.[101] 2) to pay out money to the geodesist for distribution among the marine and Admiralty servicemen. 3) to pay out wages to the soldiers and carpenters. 4) to issue provisions to the servicemen who are going to the [Gorbeia] winter quarters. And I reported in writing on the execution of the orders.	SSW

Folio 26 verso

Day of the week	Day of the month	June 727. Events at the Okhotsk outpost	
Wed.	21	Overcast, rain during the night, strong breeze. Tungus reindeer-breeders arrived at the outpost to change hostages.[102] I received an order to pay the Iakuts who were being sent with horses to the Cross and the servicemen, and reported completion.	
Thu.	22	Cloudy, gentle breeze, from 8 p.m. dark clouds with thunder. 2 men at the outpost are sick.	SSW
Fri.	23	White clouds, light breeze, from 8 o'clock sunshine and warm weather. The following men were dispatched to the Gorbeia winter quarters: 4 sailors, 1 corporal, 1 drummer, 9 soldiers, 13 carpenters of Eniseisk and Irkutsk, 1 blacksmith, 1 cooper, in total 30 men with 26 horses, taken from those that had been left by the Kamchadal commissaries and servitors.	SSW
Sat.	24	In the morning gloomy, gentle breeze, from 10 o'clock sunshine with some clouds. The Captain was at the vessel.	
Sun.	25	At night downpour and all day overcast, at times rain, strong gale. 2 men sick. High water level in the river.	E
Mon.	26	At night rain, in the morning sunshine and wind. I received an order to issue provisions to the servicemen for July and August. In the afternoon the wind changed. I reported on the issue of provisions. Another order arrived, to give out provisions to the seafarer.	NNW WSW
Tue.	27	Sunshine with clouds, strong breeze. An ailing carpenter of Eniseisk was let go. 2 men were sick. I was at the seaside.	
Wed.	28	Sunshine and wind, from noon the wind changed, became light. 1 man sick at the outpost.	N SWbS
Thu.	29	In the morning partly cloudy, light breeze between S and E. 2 soldiers arrived from the Cross, where they had been on guard, and reported that the soldier who had been sent with the commissary had run away. They brought with them the rest of the things from the Cross, and also church utensils. These things were sent to the vessel, except those of the church.	

Folio 27

Day of the week	Day of the month	July 727. Events at the Okhotsk outpost	
Fri.	30	Sunshine, light breeze. All materiel that had been brought was loaded onto the vessel and also sails, 23 bags of flour, 25 bags of groats, 31 poods 35 *pounds* of iron, 18 pounds of tool steel,[103] 18 poods of dry meat, 31 raw skins, 6 poods of pack ropes. At 6 p.m. a Iakut arrived from the corporal and reported that 3 carpenters of Irkutsk had run away and taken with them 3 horses from the Bludnaia River.	
		July	
Sat.	1	Sunshine, light breeze and warm weather. The Lieutenant stood out to sea under oars, with the following men: 1 geodesist, 6 seamen, 1 apprentice ship builder, 1 foreman, 3 Admiralty carpenters, 1 caulker, 1 blacksmith, 1 drummer, 6 soldiers, 12 carpenters and blacksmiths of Eniseisk and Irkutsk. Moreover, a commissary and 13 servitors were sent to their local outposts. In the afternoon wind. 2 men sick at the outpost.	E SSW
Sun.	2	Sunshine and warm. Calm. At 12 o'clock light breeze, at 8 p.m. cloudy. The sergeant was sent to live at the seaside.	SSW
Mon.	3	Sunshine, warm and calm. Lieutenant Chirikov arrived from Iakutsk with the apprentice mast maker, a soldier, and 2 servitors on 18 horses and reported orally what he had done to fulfill the given instructions. I received an order to distribute provisions to the soldiers who had arrived from the Cross, and reported on the distribution. This order was received on the 5th.[104]	
Tue.	4	Sunshine and wind. The Captain went to live at the seaside. Cloudy, the wind was the same. Soldier Trifonov arrived, driving 29 head of cattle and bringing 1 pair of bags of flour. 1 man sick.[105]	E
Wed.	5	Cloudy, with wind. 2 servitors who had arrived with the Lieutenant were sent back to Iakutsk. They were instructed to go by the Iudoma River to the Gorbeia winter quarters and bring carried letters for the navigator and the commissary.[106] Around 10 and 11 o'clock p.m. lightning, from noon with thunder.	E
Thu.	6	Overcast. Quartermaster Borisov arrived. He brought 200 bags of flour and had 110 horses with him. All day strong breeze.[107]	EbN
Fri.	7	In the morning gloomy, light breeze, at 12 o'clock sunshine, light breeze that changed. 2 men sick.	E SSW

Folio 27 verso

Day of the week	Day of the month	July 727. Events at the Okhotsk outpost	
Sat.	8	Sunshine, light breeze, from 10 a.m. the wind changed direction and increased.	N SWW[108]
Sun.	9	Sunshine, light breeze, in the afternoon clouds with sun breaking through.	SSE
Mon.	10	Overcast, strong breeze. 10 pairs of bags of flour arrived. At 6 p.m. rain. At 8 o'clock a vessel arrived from Kamchatka with the property of Her Imperial Majesty.[109] Onboard were 2 commissaries who had been sent out from Iakutsk in the year 725.[110] They reported that the vessel was in need of repair, and it was indeed an old vessel.[111] A Iakut arrived from the Cross with the horses which had been used by the servicemen.[112]	ESE
Tue.	11	Downpour and wind, in the afternoon the wind changed. 2 men were sick.	ESE N
Wed.	12	Downpour, strong gale, at 9 o'clock the wind, still strong, changed direction. Same number of sick.	N E
Thu.	13	Downpour and strong gale. A carpenter of Irkutsk was let go home because he was sick.	E
Fri.	14	Rain now and then, strong breeze. I received 2 orders: the first one to pay for horses, the second one to pay the sergeant a travel allowance, and I reported on the payments.	E
Sat.	15	Sunshine, light breeze, warm weather. 2 coopers were sent to the forest to make staves for barrels.	S
Sun.	16	Sunshine and warm weather, now and then a gentle breeze. 2 men were sick.	SW
Mon.	17	Sunshine and warm weather, in the afternoon gentle breeze, and at 8 o'clock the wind changed.	WSW E
Tue.	18	Sunshine and calm, at 10 o'clock wind and fog, at 4 p.m. rain.	SSW
Wed.	19	Rain and gentle breeze. A Cossack lieutenant[113] of Iakutsk arrived, with 207 bags of flour. The servitors were sent back to Iakutsk. They were given 63 horses, 63 saddle cloths, and 63 saddle-girths.	

Folio 28

Day of the week	Day of the month	July 727. Events at the mouth of the Okhota River	
Thu.	20	At night rain, light breeze and all day overcast. At 6 p.m. the sergeant was sent to St. Petersburg, with reports to the State Admiralty College.[114] He had orders to fetch the arrested clerk at the Gorbeia winter quarters and to convey him under guard. Soldier Vyrodov arrived, bringing 1 pair of bags of flour.[115] The vessel was beached for repairs.	
Fri.	21	Calm and light fog, at 10 o'clock sunhine, light breeze. The coopers returned from the forest with wood, and servitors floated wood blocks and butts[116] for the vessel. 1 man was sick.	SWbW
Sat.	22	Overnight rain, morning overcast till 11, then bright clouds, variable winds. We caulked the vessel. 3 servitors who had arrived on the 20th ran away and took 42 horses with them.	
Sun.	23	All day rain, strong gale. 14 horses arrived, bringing in 14 pairs of bags of flour, out of the 800 poods shipped by the chancellery to us.	E
Mon.	24	Rain and calm, in the afternoon white clouds, light breeze. Serviceman Karandashev arrived with 146 horses, bringing 146 pairs of bags of flour. 1 man was sick, 3 Iakuts ran away.	SE
Tue.	25	Overcast and calm, in the afternoon bright with some clouds, at times some sunshine. We tarred the left side of the vessel. 1 Iakut ran away.	
Wed.	26	At 2 a.m. with rising tide we tipped the vessel on the other side. Until 10 o'clock rain, and then bright with some clouds, light breeze. 1 man sick.	SSW
Thu.	27	Cloudy, light breeze. 1 man sick.	
Fri.	28	In the morning rain, at 8 o'clock cloudy, gentle breeze. 3 servitors were let go with 38 horses. With this party, we returned 100 pairs of saddle-girths and 100 saddlecloths.	SW
Sat.	29	Overcast and rain, gentle breeze. I received 2 orders: 1) to pay for 1 horse, 2) to give out groats to the servicemen.	S

Folio 28 verso

Day of the week	Day of the month	August 727. Events at the mouth of the Okhota River	
Sun. Mon.	30 31	In the morning rain, at 9 o'clock sun breaking through, in the afternoon light breeze from S. Soldier Shorokhov arrived, driving the rest of the cattle – 50 head – and bringing 1 pair of bags. In the morning rain, all day gloomy. I received 2 orders: 1) to receive and to give out money. 2) to pay wages to the soldiers. I reported on the receipt and the payment. The lodka that belongs with the vessel was repaired. I signed for the receipt of flour from Karandashev, 793 poods 20 pounds.	S
		August	
Tue. Wed.	1 2	Rain, gentle breeze. There was work going on around the vessel. In the morning cloudy and calm, from 9 a.m. sunshine lasting all day. At 6 p.m. light breeze, and at 9 strong gale. 9 servitors were let go to Iakutsk. With them, that is with Karandashev, we sent 275 saddlecloths, 310 pairs of saddle-girths, and 130 horses, and with Pakhomov 20 saddlecloths, 20 saddle-girths. A soldier went with Karandashev as far as to the Cross, to return the saddlecloths and saddle-girths.	SE NW
Thu. Fri. Sat.	3 4 5	In the morning sunshine, fresh wind, from 4 p.m. calm. Sunshine, light breeze and warm weather. I received an order to pay out money, and reported on this. Today we set the vessel afloat, and we expended 2½ poods of tallow and some felt on repairs. In the morning some sunshine, in the daytime overcast, with rain now and then. Apprentice mast maker Endogurov was dispatched with a soldier, 6 servitors, 9 Iakuts, and with 151 horses, carrying 135 saddlecloths and 135 pairs of saddle-girths. In addition, he received 3 head of cattle, 5 poods of fish flour, 2 poods of fat for the servicemen. He had orders to go with his horses to meet the men who were heading along the Iudoma River from Gorbeia to the vessels before the Talovka River. An ailing soldier was let go to the Tobol'sk garrison. I received an order to pay out money and reported on the payment.	NW S
Sun. Mon.	6 7	In the morning downpour and wind, in the afternoon bright with some clouds, changeable wind. Overcast, at times rain. On the vessel work went on until noon: We prepared for the cargo and attached a wale.[117] In the afternoon everyone went across the river to kill ducks, which are traditionally driven in from the sea in the following manner: In the evening they take 20 or more dugouts, and 5 or 6 men get into each of them. They set out, and pass the night on the coast 6 or 7 versts away. In the morning, at dawn, if the sea is calm, they stand out to sea, 4 or 5 versts.	

Folio 29

Day of the week	Day of the month	August 727. Events at the mouth of the Okhota River	
		At this time the ducks are moulting and do not have big wings. And they drive them on the rising tide to the mouth of the Okhota River and, as they are driven to the mouth and the water rushes into the river, the ducks are forcibly pulled into the river, and the men drive them on about 3 versts upstream, to a bay. Here, close to the bank they surround them with their boats and do not let them out of that spot. And when the water begins to fall, then all Russians and natives with wives and children gather here. They wait until the depth of the water in the place where the ducks are guarded has fallen to 1 foot or less. If there is more water, it is impossible to catch the ducks: they dive and can stay under water for nearly a quarter of an hour. And so, when the water is no longer deep, people go out and stab them with spears or catch them alive. In this way we killed about 3,000 today, and about 5,000 got away. This procedure is usually repeated 2 or 3 times, and they store them up for the winter.	
Tue.	8	Overcast and rain, at 9 o'clock sunshine, light breeze.	SWbS
Wed.	9	Sunshine, strong breeze, at 5 p.m. the wind changed direction.	N, E
Thu.	10	Sunshine, until noon gentle breeze, and in the afternoon it changed direction.	N
		At 3 p.m. we sighted a vessel that proceeded under sail from E and, 10 versts before the mouth the Okhota River, it anchored because of contrary wind.	SSW
		Today we loaded 200 bags of flour onto our vessel. At 6 o'clock thunder from NW, at 9 strong breeze and drizzle.	S
Fri.	11	In the morning overcast, light breeze. At 9 a.m., the vessel that we had sighted to E came to the mouth of the Okhota River under oars and in tow. It brought Lieutenant Spanberch back from Kamchatka, after he had been sent from Okhotsk to the Bol'shaia River with materiel.	N
Sat.	12	Sunshine, gentle breeze. One head of the newly arrived cattle was given to the geodesist Putilov. The Captain deigned to take 3 head of cattle in return for those he gave for distribution among the servicemen this past winter, and to give 2 head to Lieutenant Spanberch, in return for those he gave away. 29 servicemen received 4 head of cattle.	SW

Folio 29 verso

Day of the week	Day of the month	August 727. Events at the mouth of the Okhota River	
Sun.	13	Overcast, at 6 o'clock drizzle and calm. In the afternoon at times white clouds, strong breeze.	SE
Mon.	14	At night drizzle, and at 6 a.m. gloomy, light breeze.	W
		In the afternoon the wind changed. White clouds.	SE
		The carpenters and coopers made barrels.	
Tue.	15	Rain, strong gale. A soldier arrived from the Gorbeia winter quarters, and we received reports from the navigator on the runaway carpenters who had been sent off with the corporal on 23 June.	SE
Wed.	16	Rain and strong gale. We received information from the mast maker apprentice Endogurov that a servitor and the Iakuts had run off and driven away all the horses. From 5 p.m. variable wind.	SE
Thu.	17	Sunshine, strong gale, warm all day and variable winds. A servitor was sent to apprentice Endogurov to order him to come back. However, he had sent 3 men to the Talovka with 10 horses for the remaining materiel.	N
Fri.	18	Sunshine, at times fresh wind. Both vessels were loaded. The new one was loaded with 395 bags weighing 997½ poods, the old one with 405 bags weighing 1,195 poods. I received an order to give out to the servicemen groats for September and to the apprentice mast maker Endogurov 200 rubles cash for wages for the servicemen who went with him and for those at the Gorbeia, against a receipt. If he did not return before our departure, I was to leave this money with soldier Vorotnikov, against a receipt, and have him pass it on to Endogurov.	NW
		Distributed groats and money were reported in writing.	
Sat.	19	Sunshine, changeable wind. Today everyone moved on board the vessels. The Captain and Lieutenant Spanberch were on the new vessel, with [...][118] men. On the old one was Lieutenant Chirikov, with me, the chaplain, 15 servicemen and 4 seafarers.[119]	

Folio 30

Day of the week	Day of the month	August 727. Events at the mouth of the Okhota River
Sun.	20	White clouds, changeable wind, at times sunshine.
Mon.	21	Sunshine, strong gale. A report was sent with the boyar's son Krivogornitsyn to the [Admiralty] College, in a parcel addressed to the Iakutsk chancellery. A soldier was left at the mouth [of the Okhota River], with 50 bags of flour, 26 empty bags, a tent of double unbleached linen and he was ordered to give it all to apprentice mast maker Endogurov when he returned. And an instruction was left for him also.[120]

Hours	Winds	Rhumbs	Knots	Right rhumbs	Events on the sea route from the mouth of the Okhota River, and reckoned from midday to midday. Tue. 22 August 727
2					
4					
6					
8	NW				Sunshine, strong breeze.
9	do.				At the beginning [of the hour] the Captain with his vessel cast off
11	N				and dropped anchor in the middle of the Okhota River. At the end [of the hour] our vessel cast off.
12					At the beginning of the 11th hour we hoisted the sails and proceeded from the mouth of the Okhota River along the right side of the small island in the middle of the mouth. By 12 o'clock we stood offshore to SEbE.
1	NbE	ESE¼S	2.8	ESE¾S	
2	N	ESE½S	5.1	SEbE	We sighted the mouth of the Inia River 7 versts to NNE.
4	do.	SEbE	3¼	SEbE½S	At 4 o'clock Cape Shilkapskii was 15 versts from us to EbN.[121]
6	N	do.	2½	do.	
8	NbE	ESE¾S	2¼	SE¾ [122]	Sunshine, light breeze.
10	do.	SEbE	2¼	SEbE½S	From 10 o'clock sunshine and calm.
12	do.	do.	½	do.	Calm also by 12.

Table of daily reckoning	Latitudes		Diff. of latitude	Dep. from meridian	Rhumb	Distance right	Distance added	Differ. of long.	Compass declin.
	from	to	S	E					
Reckoned	59°13'3	58°56'42	17'42	23'01	SE 7°56' by E	28.9			
Corrected		58°51'45	21'55	28'46		35.75	69.51	55'34	5°37' E

Folio 30 verso

Hours	Winds	Rhumbs	Knots	Right rhumbs	Wed. 23 August 727. Different events
2	SW	SEbE	1½	SEbE½S	At the end of the 1st hour wind arose, and we ran.
4	do.[123]	do.	2.4	do.	
6	SWbS	SEbE	2⅛	SEbE½S	Sunshine, light breeze.
8	do.	do.	1.3	do.	By 8 o'clock Cape Shilkapskii was 30 versts from us to NNE.
10	SSW	ESE½S	2.1	SEbE	From 9 o'clock we ran to ESE.
		ESE	2.1	ESE½S	
		ESE	2.1	do.	
12	do.	ESE½S	4.4	SEbE	From 11 o'clock we ran to ESE½S
2	SbW	do.	4.4	do.	From 1 o'clock we ran to SEbE. Dusky. Strong breeze.
3	S	EbS¼S	2.1	ESE¼S	
4	ENE	ENE	3.2	ENE½E	At 4 o'clock we sighted a distinct cape on land, to NEbN.
5	SSE	do.	2¼	do.	We did not see our second vessel.
6	SEbS	NEbE	2¼	NEbE½E	
7	do.	do.	1¼	do.	Clouds, strong breeze and cold.
8	do.	NE	1.5	NE½E	Strong gale arose, we took in 1 reef.
10		do.	1	do.	In the 9th hour drizzle, and in the 10th downpour.
12	SEbS		1		Overcast.

Table of daily reckoning	Latitudes		Diff. of latitude	From meridian	Rhumb	Distance right	Distance added	Diff. of longitude	Compass declin.
	from	to	S	E					
Reckoned	58°56	58°44'	12'33	40'39	ESE 6°36' by E	42.23			
Corrected	58°51'45	58°36'2	15'25	49'95		52.23	100.7	2°31'64	5°37' eastern

Hours	Winds	Rhumbs	Knots	Right rhumbs	Thu. 24 August 727, different events
2	SEbS	NE½E	1.6	NEbE	Dark and rain, fresh breeze.
3	SE	NE	3.2	NE½E	At 3 o'clock we turned to SW.
4	variable	SW	1.6	SW½W	Light variable breeze.
6	do.	WSW	1.6	WSW½W	From the beginning of the 5th hour to the 8th we
7	do.	do.	1.6	do.	drifted.
8	NNE	SSE	2	SSE½S	In the beginning of the 8th hour strong gale arose from NNE.
		SE	2.5	SE½S	We had sail at half of the mast. Storm-clouds.[124]
10	N	SEbE	5	SEbE½S	From 8 o'clock to 12 wind N.
12	do.	do.	do.	do.	
2	NNW	SEbE	4	SEbE½S	From 12 o'clock strong breeze.
4	do.	do.	do.	do.	
6	NW	do.	do.	do.	
8			4.5		At 8 o'clock we let out a reef and
10			5		hoisted sail at full mast. Sunshine, fresh breeze.
12			5		At noon we took the Sun, declination N, from this was found the latitude 57°46'.

Table of daily reckoning	Latitudes		Diff. of latitude	From meridian	Rhumb	Distance right	Distance added	Diff. of longitude	Compass declin.
	from	to	S	E					
Reckoned	58°44'	57°56'	48'04	60'02	SE 6°13' by E	77.24			
Corrected	58°36'2	57°36'78	59'42	74'25		95.53	180.8	4°51'14	5°37' E

Folio 31

Hours	Winds	Rhumbs	Knots	Right rhumbs	Fri. 25 August 727. Different events
2	NWbW	SEbE	4.5	SEbE½S	Clear weather, fresh breeze.
4			4.5		
6			5.3		
8			5.6		We had sail at ⅔ of mast, the wind
10			5.2		did not allow carrying the upper sails.
12	NWbN		5.2		
2			5.8		We took in one reef.
4			5.3		
6			5.5		
8	NbE		4.5		Lightly cloudy, strong breeze, we let out
10			3.2		a reef and had sail at full mast.
12	NbW		5		We took the sun at noon 41°04', the sun declination 7°8'N, from this was found the latitude 56°04'.

Table of daily reckoning	Latitudes		Diff. of latitude	From meridian	Rhumb	Distance right	Distance added	Diff. of longitude	Compass declin.
	from	to	S	E					
Reckoned	57°56'	56°41'	75'	91'4	SEbE½E	118.2			
Corrected	57°36'78	56°04'	92'78	113'1		146.2	273.6	8°18'04	5°37' E

Hours	Winds	Rhumbs	Knots	Right rhumbs	Sat. 26 August 727. Events occurring[125]
2	NNW	SEbE	3	SEbE½S	Sunshine, at times drizzle, cold,
	NW				moderate breeze.
4			4.5		Fresh breeze.
6			4.5		
8	NbE		4.5		Fair weather with small clouds, gentle breeze.
10	N		2.8		
12			2.8		
2			2.2		Light breeze with drifting clouds.
4	NNE		2.2		
6			1.5		By 5:30 light breeze ENE and drizzle, from 6 o'clock on we drifted.[126]
8	SbW	calm	.5	SSW	
10		SSE	.8	SbE	Drifted, wind, sunshine.
12	SE	WbS	.4	W	We took the sun at noon 41°31', the sun declination 6°46'N, and found the latitude 55°15'.

Table of daily reckoning	Latitudes		Diff. of latitude	From meridian	Rhumb	Distance right	Distance added	Diff. of longitude	Compass declin.
	from	to	S	E					
Reckoned	56°41'	55°21'96	42'04	38'75	SEbS 8°55 by E	57.17			
Corrected	56°04'	55°15'	49'	45'16		66.64	118.2	9°38'13	1 R east.

Hours	Winds	Rhumbs	Knots	Right rhumbs	Sun. 27 August 727. Events occurring
2	ESE	SSW	.2	SWbS	Drifted. Cloudy weather, at times
4			.2		rain.
6	SE	NNE½E	.2	NEbN½E	At 5:30 we fixed one reef
			1		and ran to rhumb NNE½E.
8	SEbS	NEbN½E	2	NE½E	
10		NE½E	2.3	NEbE½E	
12			2.5		
2			3		Dark, with intermittent rain, strong gale.
4	SSE	NEbN½E	3	ENE½E	
6	SbE	ENE½E	3	EbN½E	Rain.
8			3		
10	S	E½S	3	EbS½S	
12			3		Overcast, very rough sea and strong gale.

Table of daily reckoning	Latitudes		Diff. of latitude	From meridian	Rhumb	Distance right	Distance added	Diff. of longitude	Compass declin.
	from	to	S	E					
Reckoned	55°21'96	55°25'44	10'44	46'05	ENE 9°44 by E	47.22			
Corrected	55°15'	55°30'44	15'44	68'14		69.86	123.1	11°38'23	1 R east.

Hours	Winds	Rhumbs	Knots	Right rhumbs	Mon. 28 August 727. Events occurring
2	S	E½S	2.6	EbS½S	Dark and rain, wind was the same.
4			2.6		
6			3		
8			3		Rain, strong gale.
10	SbE	EbN½E	2	E½S	
12		E	.5	EbS	Light variable breeze.
2	WNW	SEbS½S	1.5	SSE½S	Rain stopped.
4			1.5		
6	NE	SEbE	1.9	SE	
8			1.9		
10	still				After 9 o'clock[127] calm, very high sea, depths under the vessel 32 sazhens, bottom – fine sand.
12	SSW	ESE	2	SEbE	After 11 o'clock a light breeze arose and we ran.

Table of daily reckoning	Latitudes		Diff. of latitude	From meridian	Rhumb	Distance right	Distance added	Diff. of longitude	Compass declin.
	from	to	S	E					
Reckoned	55°25'44	55°05'01	20'43	36'85	SEbE 4°45' by E	42.13			
Corrected	55°30'44	55°15'68	14'76	26'62		30.44	53.62	12°25'12	1 R east.

From Okhotsk to Kamchatka River

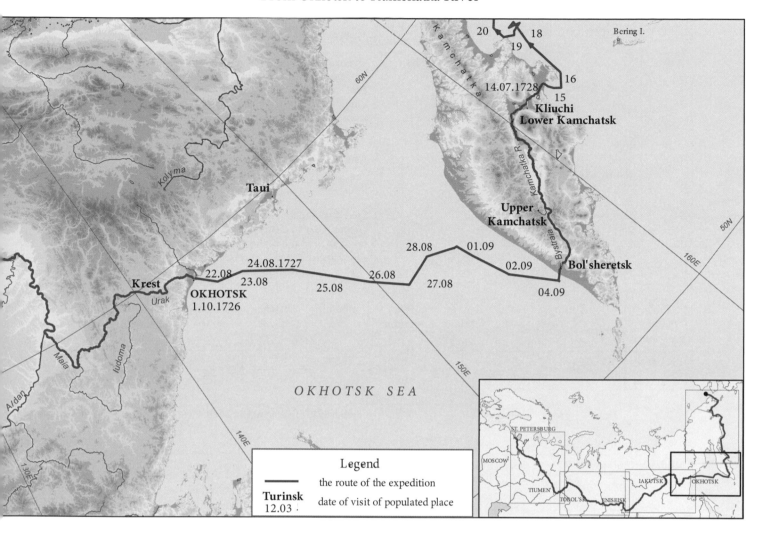

PLATE 19. Modern map 4: From Okhotsk to Kamchatka River. By Viktor Sedov.

Folio 32

Hours	Winds	Rhumbs	Knots	Right rhumbs	Tue. 29 August 727. Events occurring
2	S	E	1.4	EbS	Overcast and light rain, gentle breeze, we saw land.
3			.7		By 2:30 we reached Kamchatka and because of
					contrary wind lay at anchor, at a depth of 12 sazhens, bottom
					– fine sand, at a distance of 3 versts
					from land. The land extended, as far as we could see,
					to SEbS and NbE.
	still	6			
10	wind				Rain.
	changeable				
1	ESE				Rain.
6	E				
9	SE				Overcast, light variable breeze, rain. We raised
10	*do.*				anchor and ran closer the shore, and, in 1½ versts,
12	S				lay at anchor at 6 sazhens. A lodka was sent to the
					shore for fresh water. And in front of us was a
					stream called Krutogorova.

Table of daily reckoning	Latitudes		Diff. of latitude	From meridian	Rhumb	Distance right	Distance added	Diff. of longitude	Compass declin.
	from	to	S	E					
Reckoned	55°05'01				EbS				
Corrected	55°15'68	55°15'				3.5	6.3	12°30'71	1 R east.

Day of the week	Day of the month	Hour	Wind	August 727. Events at the anchorage
Wed.	30	2	SSE	Rain, light breeze.
		4	SbE	Rain stopped.
		10	*do.*	Fresh breeze.
		2	SSE	Cloudy, strong gale.
		8	*do.*	Lightly cloudy, strong gale.
		10	*do.*	Sunshine.
		12	S	Cloudy, strong gale and rough sea. We observed a high mountain in the upper reaches of the Ilcha River to the rhumb NEbE, which changes appearances. At first it looked white like snow, and then like the other mountains.
Thu.	31	1	SbE	Dark, with stars shining through at times, strong breeze.
		5	*do.*	The weather the same.
		12	*do.*	Cloudy.
		2	*do.*	Light breeze.
		5		Lightly cloudy, light variable breeze.
		11	S	From 10 o'clock sunshine. Having raised the anchor, we ran and sighted land, the N <) [point][128] to NbE, the eastern one to EbN.
		12	calm	At the beginning of the 12th hour the locations of these points from us were: the northern point to NE½E, the eastern one to E¼S. At noon we took the altitude of the sun 39°36', declination 4°51', giving the latitude 55°15'.

Folio 32 verso

Hours	Winds	Rhumbs	Knots	Right rhumbs	Fri. 1 September 727. Events occurring
1	still				At noon we took in sail and dropped anchor. Depths
3					15½ sazhens. Sunshine and warm. In the beginning [of the hour] we saw the [other] vessel to SSE½S, 20 versts or more away.
5	N				Light breeze arose.
7	*do.*	S	.3	SbW	In the beginning [of the hour], we raised anchor and ran. Light breeze.
8	NW		.5		
10	W	SbW	.7	SSW	The sky clear, to W near horizon dark clouds.
11			.3		
12	calm				By 11:30 we dropped anchor at a depth of 19 sazhens. Lightly cloudy.
2	EbN				
4	*do.*	SSE½S	.4	S½W	By 4 o'clock, raising anchor, we ran, the weather clear.
6			1.6		At 6 o'clock we saw to N a fairly high cape from the shore to N¾E, the middle of a high rock to NE¼E, a steep mountain on the shore to S, SEbE¾S.
8	NNE	SSE	3.1	SbE	
10	NEbN	SEbS¼S	3.2	SSE¼S	At 9 o'clock we saw a high mountain above the Bol'shaia River to SE, by 11:30 the mouth of Kolpakova River was left to EbN in 5 versts.
12	NWbN	SSE¼S	4.2	SbE¼S	We took the altitude of the sun at noon 39°59', the sun's declination 4°28 N, giving the latitude 54°29'.

Table of daily reckoning	Latitudes		Diff. of latitude	From meridian	Rhumb	Distance right	Distance added	Diff. of longitude	Compass declin.
	from	to	S	E					
Reckoned		54°48'85	26'15	6'35	SbE 2°24' by E	26.91			
Corrected	55°15'	54°29'	46'	11'17		47.34	82.24	12°50'11	1 R east.

Hours	Winds	Rhumbs	Knots	Right rhumbs	Sat. 2 September 727. Events occurring
2¾	NW	SSE	4.5	SbE	Fair weather, fresh breeze, at 2 o'clock the mouth of the stream Brumka was from us to NEbE.
4			4-5		By a quarter to 4 we ran SEbS.
6		SEbS	4	SSE	Sunshine, fresh breeze.
8		SEbS½S	3	SSE½S	By 8 we caught up with our other vessel, which we saw SSE½S.
10	ENE	SSE½S	2.2	SbE½S	Light breeze.
12		SW½W	1.8	SWbW½W	At midnight the wind changed clockwise to S.
2	S	WbN½N	1.5	WNW½N	Winds still.
4	NE	ESE	.5	SEbE	By 4 o'clock gentle breeze NE.
6	NNE		1.3		
8	N		3		Sunshine, fresh breeze, the Kykchik River remained to NE½E, 6 versts away, at 8 o'clock.
9	NNW	SE	2	SEbS	
10		SEbS	2.5	SSE	
12		SE	2	SEbS	By 12 o'clock calm and cloudy.

Table of daily reckoning	Latitudes		Diff. of latitude	From meridian	Rhumb	Distance right	Distance added	Diff. of longitude	Compass declin.
	from	to	S	E					
Reckoned	54°48'85	53°36'96	52'04	15'35	SbE 5°11' by E	54.26			
Corrected	54°29'	53°28'82	60'18	17'77		62.74	106.7	13°20'32	1 R east

Hours	Winds	Rhumbs	Knots	Right rhumbs	Sun. 3 September 727. Events occurring
2	still	S	.4	SbW	Drizzling. We towed.
4	N	SSE¾S	1.4	SbE¾S	After 2 o'clock light breeze.
6	ENE	SSE	.5	SbE	
8			.2		
10	EbN	SbE	1.3	S	
12			1.		Lightly cloudy, light variable breeze.
2	ENE	SSE	2.	SbE	
4		SEbS½S	1.6	SSE½S	
6			2.4		
8			3		By 7 o'clock strong gale.
10	ENE	SEbS½S	3		
11	E				After 10 violent storm, and we dropped anchor, depth 13 sazhens, land was to E from us, 6 versts away, and extended to S. Since 1 September we have had the land on our left not far away.
12	*do.*				Rain.

Hours	Winds	Rhumbs	Knots	Right rhumbs	Mon. 4 September 727. Events occurring
2	E				Cloudy, strong gale and rain.
4	*do.*				
6	*do.*				Light clouds, wind dropped.
8	ENE				The same weather, fresh breeze.
10	*do.*				
12	*do.*				
2	NNE				By 2 the Captain weighed anchor and left. At 2:30 we weighed anchor and ran to ESE.
4	*do.*	ESE	3	SEbE	Clouds and dark. By 5 we came closer to land and
6		SE	2	SEbS	ran along the shore to SE. Depth 3 sazhens. Light breeze, cloudy. By 6 o'clock we arrived at the mouth of the Bol'shaia River on ebb tide and dropped anchor. Depth 2½ sazhens. The weather lightly cloudy.
8	NE				By 9 o'clock our second vessel arrived, with the Captain, and dropped anchor before the mouth.
10	variable				Rain, light breeze.
12					Rain.

Table of 3-4 Sept. reckoning	Latitudes		Diff. of latitude	From meridian	Rhumb	Distance right	Distance added	Diff. of longitude	Compass declin.
	from	to	S	E					
Reckoned	53°36'96	52°56'47	40'49	12'18	SbE 5°30' by E	42.28			
Corrected	53°28'82	52°42'	46'82	14'09		48.89	81.45	13°43'79	11°15 eastern

Day of the week	Day of the month	September 727. Events at the mouth of the Bol'shaia River	
Tue.	5	On reckoning with correction, the difference of latitudes between the mouth of the Okhota River and the Bol'shaia 6°31', rhumb SE 4°38' by East, the distance run was 603.6 miles, in Russian versts 1,051.27, the departure 460 miles. Dark, winds quiet and rain. By 2 o'clock the water in the river began to rise and we towed our vessel to the river, by 3 o'clock we entered the river and tied up at the bank. At the river's mouth there are no dwellings, except balagans or thatched huts on piles, which they [the natives] use when they come to fish.[129] The upper reaches of the Bol'shaia River are situated to the rhumb ENE, and the outpost is 34 versts from its mouth. The high mountain called Opanskaia lies to E, and sometimes this mountain appears white, sometimes black. The Ozernaia River, which flows from a lake to SE, flows into the sea through the same mouth as the Bol'shaia River. By 4 o'clock fair weather, fresh gale. The rain stopped. By 6 o'clock the second vessel was brought in. By 7:30 o'clock it was high tide, 4 hours 54 minutes before the moon midnight culmination.	WbS NW
Wed.	6	At 1 a.m. strong gale and rain. At 6:30 it was high tide, 6 hours 18 minutes before the moon noon culmination. Dark. Strong gale, at 12 o'clock strong breeze and intermittent rain. Rain, strong variable breeze, during the night drizzle. By 6 a.m. lightly cloudy, light breeze. At 12 o'clock the Captain, Lieutenant Spanberch, and the physician left with their luggage for the [Bol'sheretsk] outpost in 21 dugouts, with the medicine chest and cash box. Light breeze, sunshine. We took the altitude of the sun at noon – 39°51', the sun declination – N 2°33', this gave the latitude of 52°42'.	W SW S
Thu.	7	At 2 o'clock lightly cloudy, at 5 o'clock rain, at 8:15 o'clock the high tide, at 12 o'clock and through the night strong gale with rain. At 8:30 a.m. it was high tide, sunshine, gentle breeze.	SSE SSE SE
Fri.	8	Intermittent light rain, sometimes strong, from 9 o'clock till midnight gentle breeze, by 10 a.m. lightly cloudy, at times drizzle, wind.	W E
Sat.	9	At 3 o'clock a sailor arrived from the outpost with 20 dugouts. Lightly cloudy, strong breeze. The chaplain was brought to the outpost in 3 dugouts, the luggage of the Captain on 6 dugouts, of Lieutenant Spanberch on 2 dugouts. Night clear, strong breeze. At 9 a.m. Lieutenant Chirikov went with his luggage and myself and one soldier on 10 dugouts. Sunshine, fresh breeze. We went up the Bol'shaia River.	N
Sun.	10	Sunshine. Having moved up from the mouth of the river Bol'shaia by 6 o'clock about 17 versts, we spent the night at natives' huts, and by 6 a.m. we went on. Gloomy. By 12 o'clock winds quiet and drizzle.	

PLATE 20. Kamchadal summer dwelling in the form of a thatched hut on piles, from the Prince of Liechtenstein copy of Bering's Final Map (p. 220).

Courtesy the James Ford Bell Library, Minneapolis, MN.

Day of the week	Day of the month	September 727. Events at the Bol'sheretsk outpost	
Mon.	11	At 2 o'clock we arrived at the Bol'sheretsk outpost, having just passed the Bystraia River that flows into the Bol'shaia from the right side, from NNW. The Bol'shaia River stretches from the mouth to the outpost, with its upper waters to ENE, and has many islands. Transportation up the river is by dugouts. Each dugout is manned with two native *kaiurs*, in Russian podvotchiki[130] – who shove the dugouts forward with poles. At 6 o'clock downpour and on till 4 a.m. At 10 a.m. 20 dugouts under the command of 1 sailor were sent down to the vessels. Light breeze, sunshine and warm weather. We took the altitude of the sun at noon – 37°51', the sun's declination 00°36'N, which gave the latitude 52°45'.	
Tue.	12	At 1:30 we took the sun's azimuth from S to W – 25°55', at the altitude 32°06' the azimuth was found from S to W – 36°23', from which the compass declination was found – 10°28'east. The upper waters of the river Bol'shaia are to EbS from the Bol'sheretsk outpost. In the evening fair weather, and after midnight cloudy and cold, from 9 o'clock fair weather, light breeze.	W
Wed.	13	From 4 o'clock overcast and at times drizzle, fresh breeze, all night rain, strong breeze. At 6 a.m. calm, lightly cloudy.	SW
Thu.	14	From 1 o'clock till 7 overcast and calm. At 3 o'clock 15 dugouts arrived from the vessels, brought 50 bags of flour, and 5 dugouts with officers' baggage, and 4 carpenters. During the night cloudy, wind variable, from 6 a.m. and to 12 variable wind, at times rain.	
Fri.	15	Lightly cloudy with sunny spells, light breeze, and from midnight till 6 p.m. intermittent rain.	NW
Sat.	16	In the morning frost, occluded with sun breaks, light breeze between N and E. Lieutenant Spanberch was sent to the vessels with 30 dugouts that were to bring materiel and provisions up the Bystraia River. I was sent with him to the seaside.	
Sun.	17	At 3 o'clock we arrived at the vessels and loaded the dugouts with equipment and took 107 bags of flour, and the Lieutenant took for himself 2 bags. At 6 o'clock we started our return trip to the outpost and having moved 4 versts, stopped for the night. At 3 a.m. we went on. Night clear and calm.	
Mon.	18	Fair weather, light breeze. At 6 o'clock we arrived at the Bystraia River and here, leaving the dugouts at a cove under guard, went the distance of ¾ versts to the outpost. Light frost in the morning.	N
Tue.	19	Fair weather, light breeze. At 6 a.m. the Lieutenant was ordered with loaded dugouts up the Bystraia River, with him 7 servants of our command. Frost in the morning.	NW

Folio 34 verso

Day of the week	Day of the month	September 727. Events at the Bol'sheretsk outpost	
Wed.	20	Fair weather, light breeze between S and W, during the night fair weather and light frost. In the morning drizzle. 2 dugouts were sent to the vessels to bring provisions.	
Thu.	21	Cloudy with sunny spells, fresh breeze, and at times strong gale.	SW
		Wind changed during the night.	SSE
		From 10 a.m. heavy showers of rain, wind changed again.	SE
Fri.	22	Cloudy, light breeze and rain, in the night downpour with hail, wind changed.	SW
		In the morning 7 dugouts were sent to the sea.	
		Moderate breeze, at times rain.	WSW
Sat.	23	Rain, at times sun breaking through, light breeze, during the night rain.	W
		In the morning the sailmaker arrived from the vessels, bringing 5 bags of flour.	
		Wind changed.	SW
Sun.	24	By 5 o'clock 10 dugouts with 3 servicemen of our command arrived from the vessels, bringing 70 bags of flour.	
		In the night drizzle and wind, in the morning cloudy.	E
		6 dugouts were sent to the sea with a sailor.	
Mon.	25	Cloudy, gusty wind.	E
		3 dugouts arrived from the vessels, bringing 17 bags of flour, 2 poods of lead, an anvil, 4 pincers, 4 mallets.	E
		In the night strong gale with rain.	
		By either 8 or 9 a.m. 8 dugouts arrived from the vessels, with a soldier of our command, bringing 60 bags of flour.	
		3 dugouts were sent to the vessels with soldiers.	
		Cloudy, wind was the same.	
Tue.	26	Cloudy, light breeze all night.	
		In the morning 8 dugouts were sent to the vessels with a sailor.	NE
		Strong breeze as before and cloudy.	
Wed.	27	Cloudy, at times strong gale.	
		8 dugouts arrived from the vessels with a soldier and brought 68 bags of flour.	NE
		During the night light drizzle and quiet, in the morning cloudy.	
Thu.	28	Clear and quiet, with a few clouds now and then.	
		The 8 dugouts that arrived yesterday with a carpenter of our command were returned to the vessels.	NEbN
		By 5 o'clock 3 dugouts arrived from the vessels with a seafarer, bringing 21 bags of flour.	
		Light rain, at night frost, light breeze, and by 12 noon the dugouts that had just arrived were sent back to the seaside with the same seafarer.	
Fri.	29	8 dugouts with a soldier arrived from the seaside, brought 61 bags of flour, and in the morning 7 of these dugouts were sent to the vessels again, with a soldier, who had arrived on 27 September.	SWbS½W
		Sunshine and cold.	

Folio 35

Day of the week	Day of the month	October 727. Events at the Bol'sheretsk outpost	
Sat.	30	At 1 p.m. the sailor and the carpenter who had been sent out with dugouts arrived in 7 dugouts, bringing 57 bags of flour. Drizzle and wind, and in the morning these dugouts were sent to the vessels again. Strong breeze and sunshine.	SE S
		October.	
Sun.	1	At 2 p.m. the quartermaster arrived from the vessels with 4 dugouts, brought 26 bags of flour. Sunshine, and in the morning light frost, calm and overcast.	
Mon.	2	At 2 p.m. the sailor arrived from the vessels with 7 dugouts, bringing 51 bags of flour. A light breeze arose, and during the night strong gale with rain. In the morning 2 soldiers arrived from the vessels in 7 dugouts, bringing 49 bags of flour. 9 dugouts were returned to the vessels with servitors.	SE
Tue.	3	Overcast, strong gale, intermittent rain, toward evening clearing, but at night strong gale with snowfall. In the morning sun breaking through now and then. 6 dugouts were sent to the sea with a servitor.	SW
Wed.	4	Gusty wind with rain, at times fair weather. During the night heavy snow till 7 a.m., then clearing and strong gale, some snow-squalls, sunshine.	W
Thu.	5	Sunshine, light breeze, by 5 o'clock drifting clouds. In the morning until 6 a.m. heavy snow, and after 6 intermittently rain and snow.	W
Fri.	6	Cloudy and quiet. A sailor and a caulker arrived from the vessels in 9 dugouts, bringing 60 bags of flour. Lieutenant Spanberch's dugouts also arrived with materiel and provisions. With them were also the seafarer and a guide. They reported that going up the Bystraia River they lost 2 anchors that were sunk and a 6 inch towing rope, 8 bags of flour and one kaiur. They had been unable to find these things. In the morning intermittent snow. 12 dugouts were sent to the seaside. Calm.	
Sat.	7	Light clouds, intermittent light snow. The caulker arrived from the vessels with 6 dugouts and brought 43 bags of flour. In the morning light frost, strong gale, intermittent light snow.	ENE
Sun.	8	Snow and cold, strong gale, in the morning snow, warm, then rain.	ENE

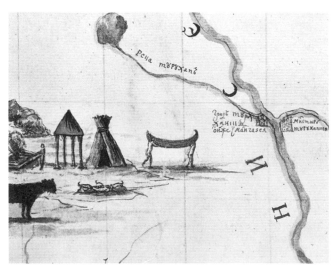

PLATE 21. Kamchadal kaiurs carrying a dugout. Ethnographical detail from the Stockholm copy of Bering's Final Map (p. 214).

Courtesy the National Library of Sweden (Kungl. biblioteket, Stockholm).

Day of the week	Day of the month	October 727. Events at Bol'sheretsk outpost	Winds
Mon.	9	Overcast, at times sun breaking through, light and changeable breeze. Dugouts arrived from the vessels, bringing all the servicemen, namely: 2 sailors, 2 soldiers and the rest of the supplies: 54 bags of flour, 6 cannons, 27 poods of iron. All the snow melted, warm morning sunshine, light breeze.	WNW
Tue.	10	Sunshine, light breeze, cold morning sunshine and calm.	WNW
Wed.	11	Sunshine and calm, in the night frost, morning overcast. At 11 o'clock up the Bystraia River to the habitation of Ga[na]lin[131] were sent 2 sailors, 1 soldier, 1 carpenter, and the following servitors: 1 interpreter and 1 guide, in 14 dugouts or lodkas,[132] and with them were sent 60 bags of flour, 6 poods 22 pounds of iron in 3 bags, 51 grenades, 3 big lanterns, 2 wick night-lights, 1 kettle for cooking and also the baggage of the Captain. And these dugouts were manned with 36 kaiurs. The weather dull and cold.	
Thu.	12	Overcast and cold. At 6 o'clock the seafarers arrived from the vessels together with the men who had been sent to repair them. And the seafarers reported orally that the vessels had not been repaired, since the high tide was not high enough. In the morning frost, fresh breeze. At 9 o'clock a seafarer and with him a sailor, 3 servitors, and 8 kaiurs were sent in 4 dugouts to look for the sunken anchors and rope, and also 2 servitors to look for the flour that also had sunk. The weather gloomy and cold. Wind was the same.	E
Fri.	13	Gloomy, fresh breeze, by the evening a few light clouds,[133] in the night clouds and drizzle, in the morning it rained briefly, warm.	E
Sat.	14	Gloomy, fresh breeze, at 5 o'clock light snow, night gloomy, in the morning light breeze. 4 carpenters and 8 servitors were sent to the forest to select timbers for runners and other parts for the building of sleds.	E / SE
Sun.	15	Overcast, wind was the same, by the evening it cleared up, night cold and snow fell, in the morning cloudy with sunny spells, light breeze.	SE / E
Mon.	16	The weather and wind were the same, at times rain, at 7 o'clock rain, then frost, in the morning lightly cloudy, by 9 o'clock overcast, light breeze.	E
Tue.	17	Gloomy. At 5 o'clock the sailor and the seafarer arrived with the men who had been sent to look for the anchors, rope and bags of flour. They brought the anchors, rope and 7 bags. During the night strong gale with rain. In the morning the wind changed.	SE / E
Wed.	18	Wind with rain, by the evening light clouds, moderate breeze, in the morning cloudy with sun shining through, then snow mixed with rain.	SE
Thu.	19	Rain and snow, gentle breeze, in the night lightly cloudy and calm. In the morning light breeze.	ESE / N
Fri.	20	Cloudy, wind the same, by 4 o'clock sunshine, night lightly cloudy and calm, in the morning cloudy with sunny spells, at times light snow.	N
Sat.	21	Cloudy with sunny spells, light breeze. Some dugouts returned from the upper waters of the Bystraia River with the kaiurs who had gone through the portage to the Kamchatka River with Lieutenant Spanberch. In the night rain, in the morning sunshine, wind.	WSW / W

Folio 36

Day of the week	Day of the month	October 727. Events at the Bol'sheretsk outpost	Winds
Sun.	22	Sunshine, light breeze, in the night clouds, in the morning rain, wind variable.	W E
Mon.	23	Rain, light breeze, by 6 o'clock rain stopped, night lightly cloudy, in the morning cloudy, fresh breeze the same. At 9 o'clock cloudy with sun breaking through, at times light snowfall, fresh breeze.	S WSW
Tue.	24	At times sun shining through, wind was the same, but at 8 o'clock strong gusty wind arose, in the night light snow. In the morning sunny spells and at times light snow and warm. Wind.	do. W
Wed.	25	Sunshine, at times snow and wind. At 6 o'clock gloomy and calm, night was warm, in the morning at times rain and warm, wind changed.	NW W
Thu.	26	Gloomy, wind the same, at 8 o'clock heavy rain. The Captain issued an order appointing me a midshipman of his crew, and his order was read out. In the morning rain, light breeze.	SW
Fri.	27	Weather and wind were the same. The carpenters and servitors returned from the forest, bringing runners for 48 sleds. Night was dull and in the morning light breeze.	WSW
Sat.	28	Gloomy, wind the same. The servitors who had gone with the sailors up the Bystraia River to the habitation of Ganalin arrived in dugouts. They brought 4 bags of flour that had sunk coming up the Bystraia, and going down now this flour was found. In the night light frost, in the morning cloudy, strong breeze and snow.	NE
Sun.	29	The weather and wind were the same, at 5 o'clock snowfall stopped, light air, during the night light snow, in the morning frost, about noon snow again.	NE
Mon.	30	Snow stopped before evening, light breeze and light clouds. By 7 o'clock lightning and thunder for about 3 minutes. The sound began from NW and finished on ESE. The weather cloudy, in the morning frost.	NW
Tue.	31	Fair weather with drifting clouds, cold. Ice floes drifted on the Bol'shaia River. Wind slightly variable to N and S.	W
		November	
Wed.	1	Dark, at times snow, strong breeze, in the morning light frost.	WSW
Thu.	2	Warm and rain, moderate breeze, by nightfall strong gale with hail and snow, in the morning cold, moderate breeze, occasional breaks in the skies.	SSE WSW
Fri.	3	The weather and wind were the same, during the night snow, in the morning cold and calm.	
Sat.	4	Intermittent snow and calm, in the night strong gale, snow and hail. In the morning light breeze from the same direction, sunshine, from 8 o'clock calm, light frost.	WSW
Sun.	5	Calm and sunshine, in the morning frost, fair weather, snow before noon.	
Mon.	6	Calm and snow, in the morning calm, light frost and cloudy.	
Tue.	7	The weather was the same, in the morning light frost, calm, sunshine, at times snow.	

Folio 36 verso

Day of the week	Day of the month	November 727. Events at Bol'sheretsk	Winds
Wed.	8	Sunshine and at times snow, clear night, in the morning occasional snow, light breeze.	W
Thu.	9	Light clouds, calm air, in the morning the weather the same, warm, light breeze. Sailors and soldiers were training with guns.	WSW
Fri.	10	Cloudy, at times snow, in the morning light frost, fresh breeze, warm, at times snow.	EbS
Sat.	11	Cloudy, strong gale and warm, in the night also strong gale with snow-squalls. In the morning the weather was the same, but the strong gale had shifted.	EbS / WSW
Sun.	12	The weather and wind were the same. At 1 o'clock the administrator of the outpost fell ill, and died at 8 o'clock.[134] In the morning strong gale and snowstorm. 1 man of the command was sick.	WNW
Mon.	13	The weather and wind were the same, in the morning gloomy, light air. 1 man of the command sick.	
Tue.	14	Overcast, light breeze, and in the morning became fresh. From about 8 o'clock snowstorm.[135] 1 man sick.	W / E
Wed.	15	Strong gale with drifting snow till 8 o'clock, then the wind decreased, and rain. In the morning strong gale with drifting snow. 1 man sick.	E
Thu.	16	The weather and wind were the same, from 7 o'clock lightly cloudy, calm air, in the morning light snow. 1 man was sick.	
Fri.	17	Murky, light frost, wind with snow-squalls, in the evening wind changed and it cleared up. In the morning lightly cloudy, calm air. 1 man sick.	SW / W
Sat.	18	Murky and cold. Night was lightly cloudy, and in the morning overcast, then snow and calm. 1 man sick.	
Sun.	19	The weather the same. Moonlit night, in the morning frost and calm and snowfall. 1 man sick.	
Mon.	20	Lightly cloudy, in the morning frost.	
Tue.	21	Murky, wind with blowing snow all night and in the morning.	W
Wed.	22	The weather and wind were the same, and in the morning snow-squalls.	W
Thu.	23	The weather and wind were the same, in the morning hard frost and sunshine.	do.
Fri.	24	Sunshine and calm, in the morning hard frost, light breeze. In honor of the name-day of Her Imperial Majesty the following salute was fired: 11 men from hand-guns 3 times, 7 cannons 3 times, once from 5 at the same time, and once from 3. 28 pounds of gunpowder were expended for the salute.	N
Sat.	25	Cloudy, wind was the same, in the morning hard frost, light breeze and light clouds.	NE
Sun.	26	Light clouds, calm air. In the morning frost, light breeze that changed later, and sunshine.	E / N
Mon.	27	Sunshine, light breeze, in the morning hard frost, light breeze that changed, sunshine.	N / NE
Tue.	28	Lightly cloudy, calm air, in the morning frost, wind changed, sunshine. A servitor was sent to the Upper Kamchatsk outpost with letters from the Captain.	N / ENE

Day of the week	Day of the month	December 1727. Events at the Bol'sheretsk outpost	Winds
Wed.	29	Fair weather, light breeze, in the morning again fair weather, light variable breeze.	N SW
Thu.	30	Fair weather, at times clouds and snow. Servicemen were learning to shoot from guns to a target. Gentle breeze. In the morning light frost, at times light snow.	W
		December	
Fri.	1	The weather and wind were the same. In the morning gloomy and calm. We received letters from Lieutenant Spanberch at the Lower Kamchatsk outpost via servitor Shipunov.	
Sat.	2	Gloomy, but in the morning lightly cloudy, occasional snow, calm air, changing.	
Sun.	3	Lightly cloudy. Servicemen were trained with hand-guns. In the morning cloudy, light breeze, frost. Today some servitors under the administrator's command were sent off along the rivers to collect tribute.	E
Mon.	4	The weather and wind were the same, in the morning clear and calm, at times light snow.	
Tue.	5	Bright and calm, in the morning cloudy, fresh breeze with snow-squalls.	W
Wed.	6	Sunshine, at times drifting clouds with snow, fresh breeze, in the morning lightly cloudy, light frost and calm.	WNW
Thu.	7	Intermittent sunshine, snow, calm and warm. In the morning hard frost, then snow, light breeze.	EbN
Fri.	8	Intermittent snow, calm air, in the morning light frost, overcast.	
Sat.	9	Gloomy, calm and warm, in the morning hard frost. Light clouds, gentle breeze.	NE
Sun.	10	The weather and wind were the same, in the morning wind with snow-squalls.	NE
Mon.	11	Strong gale and heavy snow. In the morning light frost, wind was the same, at times blowing snow.	NE
Tue.	12	Lightly cloudy, in the morning warm and cloudy, calm air.	W
Wed.	13	Lightly cloudy, calm air again. In the morning light breeze and frost.	EbN
Thu.	14	Lightly cloudy and calm. In the morning light frost, light breeze, and sunshine.	ESE
Fri.	15	Sunshine, wind as before. In the morning hard frost, fresh breeze. Overcast, then snow.	ESE
Sat.	16	Snow, wind was the same. Later on the snow stopped. Night clear, in the morning light frost, light breeze and sunshine, then wind changed. A seafarer was sent to the Opala River on 8 sleds for fish.	N ENE
Sun.	17	Fair weather, gentle breeze, in the morning cloudy, light breeze and warm.	N ENE
Mon.	18	Cloudy, wind was the same, in the morning the weather was the same and warm. Light breeze.	N
Tue.	19	The weather and wind were the same, in the morning light snowfall, calm. A soldier was sent to the sea for whale's blubber.	
Wed.	20	Snow and warm. In the morning the same weather, calm.	

Day of the week	Day of the month	December 1727. Events at the Bol'sheretsk outpost	Winds
Thu.	21	Snow and warm, light breeze. In the morning snow, light breeze.	WSW EbN
Fri.	22	Snow and warm, light breeze with blowing snow. In the morning fair weather and frost, light breeze and intermittent snow.	EbN ESE
Sat.	23	Strong gale arose, intermittent snow. In the morning wind changed, light breeze and at times snow.	ESE E
Sun.	24	Overcast, wind the same, in the morning light frost and calm.	
Mon.	25	Cloudy and calm. 9 sleds arrived with about 40 poods of whale's blubber from the seafarer.[136] In the morning frost, fair weather and calm.	
Tue.	26	Fair weather. The whale's blubber, for which a soldier had been sent, was brought in, about 120 poods of it. In the morning frost, sunshine and calm.	
Wed.	27	Sunshine, light breeze. In the morning hard frost, wind was the same. 20 more sleds were sent for blubber. The servitor that we had sent to the Upper Kamchatsk outpost returned.	E
Thu.	28	Sunshine, light breeze from the same direction. In the morning hard frost, wind.	E, SW
Fri.	29	Sunshine, light breeze, in the morning hard frost.	NE
Sat.	30	Cloudy, gentle breeze. Some servitors arrived with the tribute from the Vorovskaia River. In the morning frost, light breeze, clouds.	E N
Sun.	31	Sunshine and calm. In the morning hard frost, calm and snow. A soldier was sent to the Kolpakova and Khariusova rivers to assemble kaiurs.	
		January 1728	
Mon.	1	Sunshine and calm, hard frost. About 40 poods of whale's blubber were brought from the sea.	
Tue.	2	The weather lightly cloudy, light breeze, in the morning frost, light breeze.	SW EbN
Wed.	3	Lightly cloudy, light breeze, frost.	NE
Thu.	4	Cloudy. To the Upper Kamchatsk outpost were sent: caulker 1, carpenter 1, servitors 2, and with them 86 bags of flour, 23 poods of iron, 2 poods of lead, 2 baskets of bullets, other small things, and blacksmith's instruments: 1 anvil, 4 pincers, a whetstone – on 63 sleds, including the Captain's baggage on 10 sleds – and with 69 natives. In the morning light snow and wind.	EbS
Fri.	5	The weather cleared up, warm, in the morning strong gale and light blowing snow, cold.	E
Sat.	6	Cloudy, light breeze, in the morning fresh breeze, frost.	ENE SEbE
Sun.	7	Cloudy, light breeze. After midnight hard frost, calm and sunshine.	SEbE
Mon.	8	Sunshine. After midnight hard frost, light breeze and sunshine.	ENE
Tue.	9	Sunshine, and all night strong gale with blowing snow till 10 a.m., then the snow stopped, and the wind dropped.	N
Wed.	10	Cloudy and at times blowing snow. From midnight strong gale and snowstorm.	WNW
Thu.	11	Fresh breeze and snow-squalls. To the Upper Kamchatsk outpost were sent 21 sleds with the baggage of the Captain and 1 soldier and 1 carpenter. They carried the medicine chest.	
Fri.	12	Light clouds with sunny spells, light breeze and warm.	ENE
Sat.	13	At times light snow, from midnight clear, moderate breeze.	NE

Folio 38

Day of the week	Day of the month	January 1728. Events on our route from Bol'sheretsk to the Upper Kamchatsk outpost	Winds
Sun.	14	Cloudy, moderate breeze and light snow. At 3 p.m. the Captain left Bol'sheretsk for Upper Kamchatsk accompanied by the physician and myself, 1 soldier, 1 carpenter, 2 seafarers on 29 sleds and, having gone to SE 6 versts, we slept the night there. After midnight frost and calm. We went to ENE – 13 [versts], EbN – 7. Sunshine.	NE
Mon.	15	Sunshine. EbN – 20 versts, and came to the Apacha *toion*, that is in Russian – best man,[137] and slept the night there. Hard frost. We received letters from Lieutenant Spanberch at the Lower Kamchatsk outpost. At 10 a.m. we went on our way.	
Tue.	16	Sunshine all day. We went up the Bol'shaia River to rhumbs NE 15 versts, NEbN 13 versts, at 3 p.m. stopped for the night, in the morning went to NEbN – 17 and turned to N, and left the upper Bol'shaia behind us to the E.	
Wed.	17	Sunshine. We followed rhumbs N for 13 versts and slept the night. From midnight hard frost. We went by NbE – 10 [versts] and came to the Bystraia River and went upstream.	
Thu.	18	Sunshine with drifting clouds. [We went] NbE – 15 versts and slept the night.	
Fri.	19	Cloudy. Since morning we followed NbE – 20 [versts]. At 2 p.m. we came to the toion at Ganala. Here our materiel and provisions left by Lieutenant Spanberch were kept under guard. And here we slept the night. During the night a heavy snowstorm arose. Wind.	N
Sat.	20	Snowstorm, wind E. By 5 p.m. the snowstorm stopped. At 10 a.m. kaiurs with baggage were sent on their way. Warm.	Eb[138]

Dates	Rhumbs	Versts	Right rhumbs
14	SE	6	SEbS
	ENE	13	EbN
15	EbN	27	E
16	NE	15	NEbE

Dates	Rhumbs	Versts	Right rhumbs
17	NEbN	30	NE
18	N	13	NbE
19	NbE	25	NNE
in total 129			

	Latitudes		Diff. of latitude	Dep. from meridian	Direction	Distance	Difference of longitudes		Distance added	Compass declin.
	from	to	N	E			daily	total route		
	52°45'	53°21'14	36'14	51'02	NE 9°42' b E	62.51				1 R east
	52°45'	53°26'62	41'62	58'75		71.98	1°37'38 E		119.2	

Sun.	21	Gloomy and calm, in the morning clear weather with light clouds. At 11 a.m. we left. We received a report from Lieutenant Spanberch.	
Mon.	22	Light snowstorm. We went by rhumbs NNE – 10 versts, up the Bystraia River, at 5 p.m. we stopped for the night. In the morning overcast, at times light snow. At 7 o'clock we went by NNE – 10 versts, crossed the upper waters of the Kamchatka River and the Bystraia River. The upper waters were left behind us between N and E. The weather warm.	N
Tue.	23	NNE½E for 15 versts. At 4 p.m. we stopped for the night. In the morning fair weather. At 6:30 o'clock we went to NNE½E – 5 versts, crossed the stream Pushchina. Sunshine.	
Wed.	24	Sunshine and warm. NE – 20 versts, NNE½E – 6 versts, ENE – 2 versts. At 5 p.m. we stopped for the night. Today we overtook our servicemen, who had been sent from Bol'sheretsk on the 4th and 11th days of this month. In the morning overcast and calm. At 8 o'clock we crossed the river and proceeded to ENE – 5 versts.	

Folio 38 verso

Day of the week	Day of the month	
Thu.	25	Overcast, we moved by rhumbs NNE – 10 versts, NbW – 17 versts. At 5 p.m. we arrived at the Upper Kamchatsk outpost, and this outpost stands on the left side of the Kamchatka River. There were about 17 households. Servitors as well as tribute paying natives live there. They speak a language slightly different from that in Bol'sheretsk.[139] In some places the Kamchatka River had no ice cover. In the morning several servicemen arrived, all with provisions from the upper reaches of the Kamchatka River. And before the outpost we passed through a fairly large birch forest, but also some open country here and there.

Rhumbs	Versts	Right rhumbs
NbE	20	NNE
NNE	20	NEbN
NNE½E	20	NEbN½E
NE	20	NEbE

Rhumbs	Versts	Right rhumbs
NNE½E	6	NEbN½E
ENE	7	EbN
NNE	10	NEbN
NbW	17	N
in total 120 versts		

	Latitudes		Diff. of latitude	Dep. from meridian	Rhumb	Distance right	Difference of longitude		Distance added	Compass declin.
	from	to	N	E			daily	total route		
rec.	53°21'14	54°14'44	53'30	36'90	NEbN 1°47' E	64.82				1 R east.
cor.	53°26'62	54°28'	61'38	42'50		74.65	1°12'29	2°49'67	124.0	

Fri.	26	Overcast and calm. In the morning all natives who were in sleds were allowed to go home. A sailor was sent to Ganala on 29 sleds for equipment and for the rest of the provisions. The Kamchatka River below the outpost became clear, the ice has drifted away.	
Sat.	27	Frost, sunshine with small drifting clouds.	
Sun.	28	Frost and sunshine, light breeze.	
Mon.	29	Cloudy, light frost and calm.	
Tue.	30	A soldier with 16 sleds was sent to Ganala. Warm and light snow.	
Wed.	31	Light frost, sunshine and calm. We dried all the sails, but could not find one foresail. These sails had been sent with Lieutenant Spanberch.	S
		February	
Thu.	1	Frost, sunshine and calm. We dried sails.	
Fri.	2	Lightly cloudy, after midnight light breeze and snow.	ENE
Sat.	3	Heavy snow, calm and warm. A seafarer was sent to the Lower Kamchatsk outpost with letters to Lieutenant Spanberch.	
Sun.	4	Overcast, intermittent snow.	
Mon.	5	Overcast and calm, light breeze during the night, in the morning broken clouds. We dried sails.	E
Tue.	6	At times sunshine and calm.	
Wed.	7	The sailor arrived from Ganala, brought 30 bags of flour, 3 mainsails and various small things.	
Thu.	8	Fair weather and calm, after midnight light snow.	
Fri.	9	Lightly cloudy. After midnight sunshine,[140] warm and calm. Dried sails. A soldier arrived from Bol'sheretsk with reports from Lieutenant Chirikov. 2 carpenters of our command were sent to work in Lower Kamchatsk. With them were sent 8 new axes, 10 pounds of tool steel and some carpenter's instruments.	
Sat.	10	Sunshine, calm, light frost.	
Sun.	11	Cold and calm. From Ganala were brought 1 rope, 2 hawsers, ropes for shrouds, 1 pair of sail tackle and other things, 1 cannon. All these items as recorded in the list that Lieutenant Spanberch had with him.	

Day of the week	Day of the month	February 1728, events at the Upper Kamchatsk outpost	
Mon.	12	Cloudy and light snow. A soldier was sent to the Lower outpost, with 4 poods 7 pounds of iron in 2 bags.	
Tue.	13	Light clouds, warm and calm. We dried sails.	
Wed.	14	Warm and sunshine. The soldier who had been sent to Ganala for provisions and other things returned.	
Thu.	15	Sunshine and calm. At 7 p.m. light clouds. Moon eclipse that ended at 7:30. In the morning sunshine and calm.	
Fri.	16	Sunshine, calm and quite warm. Dried sails.	
Sat.	17	Sunshine and calm. In the morning frost and overcast.	
Sun.	18	Light clouds and calm. In the morning sunshine and warm.	
Mon.	19	Hard frost. Sunshine and warm. Dried sails.	
Tue.	20	After midnight snow and calm.	
Wed.	21	A soldier arrived with reports from Lieutenant Spanberch.	
Thu.	22	Strong gale with snow. After midnight light breeze and snow. 3 servitors arrived from Lower Kamchatsk with 81 sleds.	SSE N
Fri.	23	Strong gale with drifting snow. After midnight wind the same, only less. Sunshine. To Lower Kamchatsk were sent 48 sleds with 68 bags of flour, 19 bags of iron and hemp, an anvil, whetstone, medicine chest and other small items, and with them a caulker and 3 servitors.	SSE
Sat.	24	Sunshine, wind was the same, after midnight sunshine, wind. A soldier was sent to Lower Kamchatsk, and with him the cash box and the baggage of the Captain, in total on 19 sleds.	SE
Sun.	25	After midnight sunshine. A commissary arrived from Lower to Upper Kamchatsk. 1 physician and 2 soldiers were sent to Lower Kamchatsk and with them the Captain's baggage on 8 sleds. The physician was given 6 sleds.	
Mon.	26	Frost and sunshine.	
Tue.	27	Sunshine. 5 natives' sleds and 9 tradespeoples' sleds[141] arrived from Lower Kamchatsk. Light breeze and snow.	N
Wed.	28	Snow and warm. 1 soldier, 1 carpenter, 2 servitors arrived from Bol'sheretsk. They brought 92 bags of flour, iron in 4 bags. In the morning sunshine and frost.	
Thu.	29	Sunshine. The kaiurs who had arrived from Bol'sheretsk were allowed to go home, as well as the servitors.	
		March	
Fri.	1	Sunshine and warm. In the morning hard frost. From Ganala arrived the soldier and the carpenter who were on guard duty.	
Sat.	2	Sunshine. At 2 p.m. we left Upper Kamchatsk to go to Lower Kamchatsk: the Captain, myself, 2 soldiers, a carpenter, 2 servitors on 13 sleds. We went by these rhumbs: NNE – 15 versts, and slept the night. At 6 a.m. we went to NNE – 8 versts, crossed the stream Kyrganik. The weather was overcast.	
Sun.	3	Heavy snow and wind. Rhumbs N – 10 versts, ENE – 6 versts. At 5 p.m. we stopped for the night. All through the night heavy snow. In the morning – wind. At 6 o'clock we went to NE – 6 versts, ENE – 5 versts. Snowfall and warm.	NE SW
Mon.	4	Heavy snow. We went by the Kamchatka River E – 4 versts, NE – 2 versts. At 3 p.m. we arrived at a natives' outpost,[142] called Mashurni, and in this outpost the yurt of the toion was very big, with a depth of 3 sazhens. 250 men could be placed in it without difficulty.[143] And in this outpost we slept the night.	
Tue.	5	Light breeze. At 1 p.m. we went on our way to NW – 2 versts, NNE – 8 versts, NE – 10. At 7 o'clock we stopped for the night. Strong gale during the night, in the morning light clouds, then sunshine. At 6 o'clock we went to N – 5 versts and came to the upper reaches of the Kozyrevskaia River and went down this river NE – 2 versts and saw a mountain that glowed near Lower Kamchatsk, 8 versts to NE-NNE. Sunshine and warm.	NNE
Wed.	6	Rhumb NNE½E – 10 versts. At 6 p.m. we stopped for the night. In the morning frost. At 8 a.m. we went to NNE 15 versts, at 12 o'clock passed some yurts on the right side of the Kozyrevskaia River.	

Folio 39 verso

Day of the week	Day of the month	March 1728. On our way from Upper to Lower Kamchatsk
Thu.	7	Sunshine, partly cloudy, light breeze, rhumb NE – 10 versts. At 5 p.m. we stopped for the night. After midnight hard frost. At 5 o'clock we went to NNE – 5 versts, NE – 4 versts, ENE – 3 versts.

Rhumbs	Versts	Right rhumbs
NNE	23	NEbN
N	10	NbE
ENE	6	EbN
NE	6	NEbE
ENE	5	EbN
E	4	EbS
NE	2	NEbE
NW	2	NWbN
NNE	8	NEbN

Rhumbs	Versts	Right rhumbs
NE	10	NEbE
N	5	NbE
NE	2	NEbE
NNE	8	NEbN
NNE½E	10	NEbN½E
NNE	15	NEbN
NE	10	NEbE
NNE	5	NEbN
In total 131 versts, and 75.2 Italian miles		

	Latitudes		Diff. of latitude	Dep.from meridian	Direction	Distance	Difference of longitudes		Distance added	Compass declin.
	from	to	N	E			daily	total		
rec.	54°28'	55°20'27	52'27	45'52	NEbN 7°18' b E	69.32				1 R east.
cor.	54°28'	55°35'33	67'33	58'64		89.30	1°37'28 E		151.0	

Fri.	8	Lightly cloudy. NbE – 6 versts, NE½E – 5 versts. At 3 o'clock we arrived at some yurts on the right side of the Kozyrevskaia River, and on our way from the yurts which we visited yesterday to these, we crossed the Kozyrevskaia 30 times. At 8 o'clock a commissary came to us from Upper Kamchatsk. We slept the night here. After midnight gentle breeze with snowfall, at 9 o'clock we went from the yurts to NNE – 2 versts, N – 3 versts, NE – 5 versts, ENE – 6.	N
Sat.	9	Lightly cloudy, light air from N. Rhumb NNE – 3 versts, NE – 6 versts. At 3 p.m. we came to the Kamchatka River and went downstream along it. From the yurts, where we slept the night, to the mouth of the river we crossed Kozyrevskaia 10 times. Rhumbs NW – 3 versts, ENE – 2, NNE – 5. At 5 o'clock we stopped for the night. At 6 a.m. we went to NNE – 5 versts, N – 6 versts, NE – 3. We went by tundra. The weather was gloomy and calm.	
Sun.	10	Lightly cloudy. We came down the Kamchatka River and went to ENE – 4 versts, NNE – 6 versts. At 3 p.m. we arrived at the Ushki landmark, where workmen of our command are preparing different wood for building the ship, and here slept the night. After midnight hard frost. At 8 o'clock we left for the outpost, and the carpenter who was with us from Upper Kamchatsk was left at the building site. Rhumbs: NE – 20 versts, NEbE – 5 versts and N – 4 versts by the river. Sunshine, light breeze.	N
Mon.	11	ENE – 5 versts, E – 6 versts, ESE – 10 versts, SE – 5. At 4 p.m. we arrived at the Lower Kamchatsk outpost, which stands on the right bank of the Kamchatka River. There were 40 households spread out along the bank for about 1 verst. The mountain that glows lies on the rhumb S by compass, at a distance of 30 versts from the outpost.[144] After midnight hard frost and sunshine.	
Tue.	12	Sunshine. The Captain wished to go for an outing and I accompanied him. We visited Kliuchi, where there is a church and 15 households. Lieutenant Spanberch had his lodgings here and was ill. Rhumb from the outpost to Kliuchi SEbE – 7 versts. After midnight a caulker was sent to the building site, with him were sent in 10 bags 16 poods of iron, 9 poods of hemp, 4 mallets, 4 pincers, 8 bags of flour, 40 sazhens of white rope, which we had taken from the state store at the outpost.	

Rhumbs	Versts	Right rhumbs
NE	4	NEbE¼E
ENE	3	EbN¼E
NbE	6	NNE¼E
NE½E	5	NEbE¾E
NNE	2	NEbN¼E
N	3	NbE¼E
NE	5	NEbE¼E
ENE	6	EbN¼E
NNE	3	NEbN¼E
NE	6	NEbE¼E
NW	3	NWbN¼N
ENE	2	EbN¼E
NNE	10	NEbN¼E
N	6	NbE¼E
NE	3	NEbE¼E

Rhumbs	Versts	Right rhumbs
ENE	4	EbN¼E
NNE	6	NEbN¼E
NE	20	NEbE¼E
NEbE	5	ENE¼E
N	4	NbE¼E
ENE	5	EbN¼E
E	6	EbS¼S
ESE	10	SEbE¼S
SE	5	SEbS¼S
SEbE	7	SE¼S

In total 132 versts, or 75.7 Italian miles from the outpost to Kliuchi

	Latitudes		Diff. of latitude	Dep.from meridian	Rhumb	Distance of sailing	Difference of longitude		Distance added	Compass declination
	from	to	N	E			daily	total		
rec.	55°20'27	55°47'18	26'91	51'11	NEbE 8°01' b E	63.16				1¼ R E
cor.	55°35'33	56°10'	34'67	73'56		81.36		2°11'3	153.6	

Wed.	13	Lightly cloudy and calm.	
Thu.	14	From 6 p.m. strong gale arose with blowing snow. It blew all night. From 5 a.m. heavy snow and calm.	W
Fri.	15	Snow, then strong gale with blowing snow. After midnight light clouds and calm.	NW
Sat.	16	Drifting snow, strong gale and snowfall. From 7 p.m. calm, only snowfall.	SEbE
Sun.	17	Strong gale with blowing snow and light snowfall, from midnight cloudy, then sunshine. 1 drummer and 1 soldier were sent to the work site. With them were sent 5 bundles of iukola and 5 poods of cod-liver oil.	SE
Mon.	18	Sunshine. The Captain wished to review the servitors and selected 30 men for work.	SW
Tue.	19	Sunshine and warm, from midnight heavy snowstorm.	SE
Wed.	20	Strong gale with drifting snow. After midnight overcast and warm. 27 natives were sent to work instead of servitors.	SE
Thu.	21	Snowfall and calm, from midnight clear sky, strong breeze. A soldier was sent down the Kamchatka River to assemble workers for the building.	SW
Fri.	22	Sunshine, strong gale.	SW
Sat.	23	Sunshine, strong breeze, at times strong gale. After midnight the wind changed, sunshine. 3 barrels of salted fish were sent to the work site.	SWbW NW
Sun.	24	Sunshine, towards evening cloudy, light breeze, after midnight heavy snowfall and calm.	SE
Mon.	25	Snowfall, from midnight clear sky, fresh breeze, and at times drifting snow.	N
Tue.	26	Sunshine. 11 natives with dogs were sent to the work site, and also a servitor. With them were sent 3 bundles of iukola,[145] and 8 bundles of iukola for 8 servitors.	
Wed.	27	Sunshine and calm, after midnight snowfall and calm.	
Thu.	28	At times snowfall, light variable breeze, from midnight light snow. The physician was sent to the work site to examine the sick.	E NE N

Day of the week	Day of the month	April 1728. Events at the Lower Kamchatsk outpost	Winds
Fri.	29	Strong gale with drifting snow. After midnight the physician arrived from the work site.	W
Sat.	30	Sunshine and calm.	
Sun.	31	Sunshine. To the work site were sent 2 barrels of salted fish, 6 bundles of iukola, 5 poods of cod-liver oil,[146] 2 deer killed and 1 black tackle rope.	E
		April	
Mon.		Snowfall, light variable breeze, from midnight strong gale with drifting snow.	E
Tue.	2	Strong gale with drifting snow, in the morning sunshine. 6 bundles of iukola, 2 bags of flour were sent to the work site.	NW
Wed.	3	Sunshine, light breeze, at 8 a.m. the Captain and I went to the building site. Quiet and sunshine.	SW
Thu.	4	Sunshine, wind was the same. At 5 p.m. we arrived at the building site, and the apprentice shipbuilder, who was in charge, reported that all the wood to lay the ship's keel was ready. In the morning hard frost, fair weather. The glowing mountain on the Tolbachik is to rhumb SbE at a distance of 50 versts from the building site. At 9 a.m., having assembled all servicemen and artisans, and having prayed, we laid the ship's keel, and then the Captain entertained the people with plenty of vodka.[147] 7 natives were allowed to go home, and with them the greater part of the dogs.	
Fri.	5	Overcast, strong gale with blowing snow, then snowfall. The state treasury's fur tribute arrived from the outpost on its way to the Bol'shaia River.[148] From midnight calm, with light snow, at 10 o'clock sunshine. We went from the building site to the outpost.	NE
Sat.	6	At 8 a.m. light breeze and snowfall. At 10 o'clock we arrived at the outpost. From midnight cloudy and warm.	NE
Sun.	7	Light frost and wind, the weather cloudy with occasional breaks.	SW
Mon.	8	Frost and wind, sunshine with drifting clouds. To the work site at Ushki were sent 16 bags of flour, 9 poods of iron and, from the state store, 3 rope ends, white, 90 sazhens long. Furthermore, 4 poods of cod-liver oil and a flask of blubber, 4 skins of ringed seal for the preparation of blacksmith's bellows and 6 sled loads of stickleback[149] for the natives and the dogs were sent to the site.	
Tue.	9	Sunshine and warm, light breeze. 1 man of the command sick.	SE
Wed.	10	The same.	
Thu.	11	Light snow, strong breeze.	N
Fri.	12	Snow and rain, light variable breeze and. After midnight warm, light snow and wind.	ESE
Sat.	13	} Warm, wind ESE	
Sun.	14		
Mon.	15	Sunshine with small clouds, light breeze. 13 natives were sent to work on building the ship.	
Tue.	16	Sunshine. A commissary who was collecting fur tribute left Lower Kamchatsk for Bol'sheretsk.	
Wed.	17	Warm and calm.	
Thu.	18	Cold, light snow.	
Fri.	19	Cold, strong breeze. 6 sled loads of stickleback were sent to the building site, for the natives.	SE
Sat.	20	Strong gale [with] snow, then sunshine. Apprentice Kozlov arrived from the building site with a few workers to celebrate Easter.	SE
Sun.	21	Sunshine and calm.	
Mon.	22	In the afternoon the physician was sent with the medicine chest to the shipbuilding site. In the night strong gale and warm.	ESE
Tue.	23	After midnight clear sky, light breeze and warm.	NW
Wed.	24	Workmen who had come for the celebration were sent back to the building site. At 9 a.m. Lieutenant Spanberch was sent to the building site to take command, and with him were sent 4 servitors to work as carpenters, and 1 blacksmith. The physician returned from the building site and reported to the Captain that the sick men would like to see the chaplain.	
Thu.	25	Sunshine, light breeze. At 8 p.m. the chaplain was sent to the building site for the sick men, and after midnight cold, strong breeze and clear sky.	E
Fri.	26	Sunshine, wind was the same.	ESE
Sat.	27	The physician was sent to the building site and ordered to stay there with the command. For the skilled workers[150] the Captain sent 1 deer, 20 hares, and for the natives 2 sled loads of stickleback. A report from Lieutenant Spanberch was received, in which he wrote that on the 25th of this month the caulker had died.	
Sun.	28	Strong gale and warm.	
Mon.	29	Lightly cloudy, light breeze from the same direction and cold.	ESE
Tue.	30	Lightly cloudy, fresh breeze.	E

▶ PLATE 22. Folios 40 verso and 41 of Midshipman Chaplin's journal, with description of the shipbuilding on Kamchatka.

Courtesy Russian State Naval Archives (RGAVMF). Photo by Nikolai Turkin.

☿	29	
♄	30	
☉	31	

Маiй Аprѣль

☽	1	
♂	2	
☿	3	
♃	4	
♀	5	
♄	6	
☉	7	
☽	8	
♂	9	
☿	10	
♃	11	
♀	12	
♄	13	
☉	14	
☽	15	
♂	16	
☿	17	
♃	18	
♀	19	
♄	20	
☉	21	
☽	22	
♂	23	
☿	24	
♃	25	
♀	26	
♄	27	
☉	28	
☽	29	
♂	30	

Мцъ Маи 1728 году ...

	OZO
	ZO
	NW
	NW
	OZO O
	NW
	NW N
	NW
	NW
	WZW

Day of the week	Day of the month	May 1728. Events at the Lower Kamchatsk outpost	Winds
Wed.	1	Sunshine, the air fragrant, fresh breeze. After midnight the ice broke in the channel above which the outpost stands. Sunshine and warm. A sailor was sent down the Kamchatka River to assemble kaiurs for dugouts to be sent to the Upper Kamchatsk outpost for equipment and for provisions.	ESE
Thu.	2	Sunshine and calm, after midnight light frost, later also sunshine. From Lieutenant Chirikov in Bol'sheretsk we received news that had been written in March. We sent 6 dugouts with 12 men to Upper Kamchatsk, and to the building site 10 bags of flour, 1 bag of iron, 4 bundles of iukola.	
Fri.	3	Today the entire river became clear.	
Sat.	4	Sunshine, strong breeze. A soldier was sent out to order natives to go to the sea for fishing.	SE
Sun.	5	Sunshine and warm. Light air.	NW
Mon.	6	10 dugouts with 27 kaiurs were sent to Upper Kamchatsk and with them a servitor.	
Tue.	7	Sunshine.	
Wed.	8	Sunshine.	
Thu.	9	Sunshine. In the afternoon the chaplain of our command arrived from Upper Kamchatsk with a servitor, brought 6 bags of flour. After midnight fair weather and strong gale. The soldier who had been sent for kaiurs arrived, brought 13 men.	
Fri.	10	Sunshine and calm. To Upper Kamchatsk were sent 4 dugouts, 12 kaiurs and one servitor. To the building site were sent 150 ducks and 6 hares for the workmen, and for the natives 7 boilers of seal blubber and half a boat load of stickleback.	
Sat.	11	Sunshine, light breeze and warm.	ESE
Sun.	12	Sunshine, light breeze and warm.	E
Mon.	13	Cloudy, light breeze. In the night strong gale arose. After midnight wind decreased, the weather cloudy with sunny spells.	NW
Tue.	14	All provisions were brought from the outpost to Kliuchi.	NW
Wed.	15	Strong breeze, at times snowfall.	N
Thu.	16	Drizzle mixed with snow. At 10 a.m. the Captain and all servicemen who had lived at the outpost sailed to Kliuchi. A dugout with fresh fish was sent to the building site.	
Fri.	17	At 2 p.m. we arrived at Kliuchi and got our quarters. After midnight light frost, later sunshine and calm.	
Sat.	18	Sunshine, light breeze.	NW
Sun.	19	During the night strong gale, in the morning it dropped, and sunshine. At noon we took the sun's altitude – 55°38', the sun's declination on the local meridian – 21°48' N. From this the latitude of fix was found – 56°10'.	NW
Mon.	20	Sunshine by 2 o'clock. In the afternoon we went with the Captain to the seaside. At 5 o'clock we reached the natives' outpost Kamennyi, which stands on the left side of the Kamchatka River. At 11 o'clock we arrived at the natives' outpost Ktavachiu, which stands above the channel, and stayed here for the night. At 3 a.m. we sailed and reentered the big river, and on the left side of the Kamchatka River Cossacks or servitors have summer dwellings, where they fish. From the right side flows the stream Gachki, also called Kapicha. Below this stream flows another one – Nalchigach. And on this side there are plenty of summer dwellings of servitors. 5 versts below these dwellings we reached Shchioki. Between the outpost and Shchioki the Kamchatka River has many islands. The place is called Shchioki because there are high stone mountains on both sides of the Kamchatka River.[151] The distance between the stony banks is no more than 400 sazhens. At 9 a.m. we reached a place called Shantaly, with the same kind of dwellings as in Kapicha, and here we ate lunch. The weather was cloudy and calm.	
Tue.	21	At 6 p.m. we reached the sea. The very mouth of the Kamchatka River is, from the Cossack habitation that stands on the cape, to rhumb SW½W at a distance of 4 versts. Light breeze WSW. The sea was calm and there was no ice. We saw a mountain that glowed, to the rhumb SWbW¼W.	WSW
Wed.	22	Much ice was washed from the sea to the shore. At 6 o'clock a servitor brought reports from the Lieutenants, from Upper Kamchatsk and from the ship building site.[152] We observed Cape Kronovskii to SSW½W as far as we could see.[153]	

Day of the week	Day of the month	May 1728. Events at different places	Winds
		The cape that extends to E is on rhumb SEbE by compass. After midnight light breeze SW and sunshine. At noon we took the sun – 56°20', the sun's declination at the local meridian – 22°13', from this the latitude of fix was found 56°03'.	

From Kliuchi to the sea	Latitudes		Diff. of latitude	Dep.from meridian	Rhumb	Distance of sailing	Difference of longitude		Distance added	Compass declination
	from	to	S	E			daily	total		
cor.	56°10'	56°03'	7'	70'91	EbS 5°37' b E	71.31	2°07'6		128.4	1¼ R E

Thu.	23	Sunshine. From the mouth of the Kamchatka River we saw a glowing mountain to WSW½W, Cape Kronovskii to SbW, Cape Kamchatskii to ESE. From midnight thick fog till 5 o'clock, and then sunshine and warm. There was ice on the sea, as far as the eye could see.	
Fri.	24	Sunshine. At 1 p.m we headed back from the sea towards Kliuchi. Very warm. At 10 o'clock we came to Shantaly and slept the night here. At 4 a.m. we went on. Sunshine, calm air. At 9 o'clock at Shchioki a sailor met us with a report from Lieutenant Chirikov, in which he wrote that provisions and equipment had been sent from Upper Kamchatsk on 10 dugouts accompanied by a sailor and a soldier.	
Sat.	25	Sunshine and very warm. We were going all day and all night.	
Sun.	26	Sunshine and warm, calm air and changing. At 1 p.m. we arrived at Kliuchi. The soldier who had been sent to buy reindeer from Koriak reindeer-breeders arrived and reported that he was in good health. After midnight a sailor and a soldier were sent to assemble kaiurs that had to take dugouts to Upper Kamchatsk.	
Mon.	27	Cloudy, calm and warm. At 9 o'clock it rained. After midnight the sailor arrived, brought 17 kaiurs.	
Tue.	28	Overcast and calm, light breeze. At 10 o'clock the soldier arrived, brought [ ] kaiurs.[154] At 9 o'clock fresh breeze. To Upper Kamchatsk were sent 7 dugouts, and 21 kaiurs, and with them 1 servitor. 2 sailors were sent to the shipbuilding site.	ESE
Wed.	29	Sunshine and warm, in the morning overcast, light breeze. Today the water in the river began to rise.	W
Thu.	30	Gloomy, strong breeze. At 3 p.m. Lieutenant Chirikov arrived from Upper Kamchatsk, and with him the sick geodesist, 1 sailor, 1 sails master, 2 soldiers, on 6 dugouts. They brought 6 bags of flour. Toward evening drizzle, in the morning overcast, fresh breeze, then sunshine. At noon we took the sun – 56°45', the sun's declination 23°04', from this the latitude of fix was found – 56°.	E
Fri.	31	Sunshine with small clouds, from midnight overcast and calm.	
		June [1728]	
Sat.	1	White clouds, light air, by the evening drizzle and all through the night. At 10 a.m. sunshine, strong breeze. A soldier was sent to the sea to prepare fish supplies.	NW WNW
Sun.	2	Cloudy, strong gale. After midnight wind was the same and clear sky.	WNW
Mon.	3	Sunshine, strong breeze. At 3 p.m. the Captain and I went to the ship building site and were traveling all the day. At 10 o'clock we stopped for the night. After midnight it became calm. At 3 o'clock we went on, at 6 o'clock a drummer from the building site met us with a letter from Lieutenant Spanberch and was sent to Kliuchi. And the Captain ordered Lieutenant Chirikov to send 3 workers and 20 natives to the building site. Sunshine.	ESE
Tue.	4	Cloudy, from about 3 p.m. rain.[155] At 11 o'clock we stopped for the night. The weather dark, cloudy and rain. At 3 a.m. we went on. The weather lightly cloudy and calm, then sunshine, light breeze.	E
Wed.	5	Sunshine with drifting clouds. At 3 p.m. we arrived at the shipbuilding site, and Lieutenant Spanberch reported to the Captain that the ship was ready for launching. Ongoing work on it: planking the inside and caulking the upper chinks. The ship's boat was finished, but not yet caulked. Also he reported that a carpenter from Irkutsk ran away on [ ] May.[156] At 8 o'clock strong gale arose from W. At 2 a.m. the smithy caught fire that was put out only with great difficulty. Inside 2 drums and 2 blacksmith's bellows had burned. It started to rain, but by 10 o'clock the rain stopped. The Captain ordered the blacksmiths to make new bellows, since the work of the smithy had stopped. For this 3 raw tanned bags were spent, and a soldier was sent to the outpost with a request to Lieutenant Chirikov to send 2 blacksmith's bellows.	

Folio 42

Day of the week	Day of the month	June 1728. Different events	
Thu.	6	Gloomy. The Captain wished to go and see the place where pine resin was distilled and barrels made. The distance from the shipbuilding site was 4 versts. At the building site planks were hewn. Strong breeze, in the morning sunshine and warm. 3 servitors arrived from Upper Kamchatsk, 2 of them to work as carpenters, and one brought 18 bags of flour.	W
Fri.	7	1 sailor and 1 drummer arrived from Kliuchi, brought from the house of the Captain his own provisions: 20 pieces of salted meat, 50 salted fish, 100 ducks dressed to serve, and from the state stocks 1 pood 17 pounds of iukola, which on the order of the Captain were divided among the servitors and artisans.	
		The natives got 1 dugout load of stickleback, 2 packs of nerpa or seal blubber.[157]	
		Today the ship and boat were caulked and tarred. In the morning sunshine and calm. On the order of the Captain I went with the natives to the place where pine resin was distilled and barrels were made. The wood, which was prepared for barrels and for other needs, all was rafted. Pine resin and barrels that had been done, and small wood for various purposes was loaded on the rafts and sent to the seaside with 2 carpenters and 2 servitors.	
		At 5 a.m. the ship was tipped onto the left side for launching.	
Sat.	8	Sunshine. At 2 o'clock drizzle, then sunshine, light breeze.	E
		The ship was fully prepared for launching. At 5 a.m. the chaplain of our command arrived from the outpost. Workmen rafted all prepared wood for floating to the sea. Strong gale from the same direction and cloudy.	
Sun.	9	At 4 p.m. we prayed and began to launch the ship toward the water. Drizzle.	
		And we tried up to 7 o'clock, but could not lower her and two tackles were torn. But at 7 o'clock with the help of God she was launched on the water safely. And after the launching all the people present at the launching were given 2½ buckets of vodka.[158] Rain stopped, strong gale, same direction.	E
		After midnight it was reported that the ship did not take in water. At 10 o'clock work was resumed. We rafted things. The weather gloomy, strong gale.	
		At 12 o'clock the Captain, chaplain and myself sailed to the outpost.	
Mon.	10	Strong gale, at 9 p.m. wind dropped, night was calm.	E
		At 3 a.m. we reached Kliuchi. The weather cloudy.	
Tue.	11	Sunshine, light breeze. At 10 a.m. two rafts arrived from Ushki with barrels and pine tar, and 2 carpenters and 2 servitors onboard. One of these rafts remained at Kliuchi to build a new storehouse, while the other was sent to the seaside with the barrels and the tar. The carpenters and 1 servitor went on this raft. High water in the river and the outpost was completely flooded.	ESE
Wed.	12	Cloudy, at 8 o'clock drizzle. The new-built ship arrived with a few workmen onboard, and the rest of them on rafts. After midnight all rafts were sent to the seaside, except for 2 rafts and 6 servitors, for building the storehouse.	
		We loaded on the ship all rigging, anchors, cannons, ropes and various small equipment for the ship, and sails: 2 mainsails, 2 foresails, 4 jibs, 2 forestaysails, 2 topsails, tarpaulins and breechings [?],[159] and all ammunition, 200 bags of flour.	
Thu.	13	Gloomy, strong breeze. We began to build the storehouse. All night rain, in the morning the ship was sent to the seaside with all servicemen and artisans, at Kliuchi only the Captain, Lieutenant Chirikov, myself, 1 sailor, 4 soldiers remained.	ESE
Fri.	14	Overcast, light breeze. We built the storehouse. After midnight few clouds, sunny spells, light breeze.	E
Sat.	15	Toward evening wind increased. At 8 a.m. the quartermaster and one soldier arrived with 10 dugouts from Upper Kamchatsk. They brought the rest of the provisions, that is: 87 bags of flour, groats 25 bags, rusks 113 poods 35 pounds,	E
		5 flasks of vodka.	
Sun.	16	At 6 p.m. the arrived quartermaster and his dugouts were sent to the seaside with all the provisions, and with him 3 timbers for masts and 1 for spars.	
		At 11 a.m. sunshine, light breeze, the water in the river began to fall.	E
Mon.	17	Sunshine, light air.	E

Folio 42 verso

Day of the week	Day of the month	June 1728. Different events	Winds
Tue.	18	Cloudy and calm. A soldier was sent down the river to set afloat the raft, that had run aground. At night rain, after midnight clear sky and calm.	
Wed.	19	Half of our gunpowder was sent to the outpost to be given to the supervisor against a receipt. Sunshine, light breeze, in the morning cloudy, wind was the same, fresh breeze. The storehouse was completed and everything that was left was put in the storehouse, and listed in a protocol.	E
Thu.	20	Sunshine, strong gale, after midnight cloudy, strong breeze, then clear sky. The servitors who built the store house were allowed to go from the work.	E
Fri.	21	Sunshine, strong breeze. At 3 p.m. the Captain, Lieutenant Chirikov, the chaplain, myself, and 2 soldiers left Kliuchi for the seaside. At Kliuchi 1 sailor and 2 soldiers were left, who were ordered to sail to the seaside as soon as dugouts were available. 1 soldier was left to guard the storehouse. At 7 a.m. we arrived at Kapichenskii outpost.	E
Sat.	22	Sunshine, wind dropped. At 5 p.m. we went on, at 8 o'clock reached Shchioki. Night dull and calm. We sailed all night, in the morning fog and calm. At 8 a.m. we arrived at the seaside. All workmen were working on the ship, planked the deck and made cabins. Intermittent sunshine. One of our command was sick – the geodesist.	
Sun.	23	Sunshine and calm. After midnight strong gale. Today there was no work. Wages were distributed to the servicemen and artisans.	NE
Mon.	24	Thick fog was brought in from the sea, strong breeze. From midnight light breeze. A sailor and a soldier arrived from Kliuchi, brought gunpowder and rusks. A carpenter and a blacksmith arrived from Ushki on a raft with charcoal.	S
Tue.	25	Cloudy, strong breeze. We caulked the deck on the ship. In the morning sunshine.	S
Wed.	26	Some sunshine. Work as before. In the morning sunshine, strong breeze. 2 servitors were released from work.	SSE
Thu.	27	Sunshine, wind was the same. The work was as before. High tide was at 9 p.m. In the morning sunshine, fresh breeze. After a thanksgiving service at 10 o'clock, work continued all day.	SSE
Fri.	28	Sunshine, strong gale, in the morning sunshine and calm. At noon we took the sun – 56°21', the sun's declination 22°24', from this the latitude of fix was found 56°03'.	
Sat.	29	Sunshine, at times fog, calm air. We set the rudder on the vessel and built a trestle for erecting the masts. In the morning sunshine and calm. At 6 a.m. we raised the mast and continued the work. At 10 o'clock, after grace, vodka was given to all servicemen and artisans.	SE
Sun.	30	Sunshine, gentle breeze. Work. In the morning sunshine, strong breeze. We rigged the ship and did other work. 3 men sick.	SE SSE
		July	
Mon.	1	Cloudy, wind was the same, in the morning gloomy and calm, by noon some clearing.	
Tue.	2	Cloudy. We loaded the ship with flour, rusks, groats, meat. I was ordered by the Captain to go to Kliuchi to receive money and provisions. At 5 a.m. I went to Kliuchi with 4 dugouts. Sunshine and very warm.	
Wed.	3	Sunshine and warm. At 9 p.m. we came to Shchioki and slept the night. At 3 a.m. we left. At 6 o'clock sunshine, light breeze.	SW
Thu.	4	Sunshine, we were going all day and all night, strong breeze. At 8 a.m. we arrived at Kliuchi.[160]	N
Fri.	5	Cloudy, wind was the same. At 5 o'clock, having made 2 barges, I loaded 58 bags of flour, 3 kegs of gunpowder, 800 rubles for wages – and took with me 1 soldier from the guard. At 7 o'clock I took off to the sea and was sailing all night. In the morning overcast, light breeze.	E
Sat.	6	The weather and wind were the same. At 4 a.m. I reached the sea and reported to the Captain on what I had brought and loaded the flour on the ship.	
Sun.	7	At 1 p.m. a vessel arrived from Bol'sheretsk, under a sailor of our command,[161] and brought 67 bags of flour, 25 bags of rusks. In the morning overcast and calm. We loaded the ship with rusks from the arrived vessel, and with firewood.	
Mon.	8	Cloudy, light breeze. 1 sailor and 1 soldier arrived from Bol'sheretsk by land. In the morning sunshine, strong breeze.	S SE

▶ PLATE 23. Folios 42 verso and 43 of Midshipman Chaplin's journal, with the beginning of the voyage of the Holy Gabriel.

Courtesy Russian State Naval Archives (RGAVMF) . Photo by Nikolai Turkin.

☿	18	...
♀	19	...
♃	20	...
♂	21	...
♄	22	...
☉	23	...
☽	24	...
♂	25	...
☿	26	...
♃	27	...
♀	28	...
♄	29	...
☉	30	...
☽	1	... Мѣсяць Июнь ...
♂	2	...
☿	3	...
♃	4	...
♀	5	...
♄	6	...
☉	7	...
☽	8	...

№ 16. 1728 =

К: № 13 день

С: № 14 день

			N	Z	O		Румб				
	56·03	55·51 ½	—	11·68	00·8	—	Z: 3·55 Z: 0	11·	20·9	1·43	1 ½
	56·03	65·59 ½	—	12·30	00·84	—	—	12·33	21·96	1·43	

Folio 43

Day of the week	Day of the month	July 1728. Different events	Winds
Tue.	9	Sunshine, wind was the same. The Captain ordered all servicemen who had been told that they would go to sea to embark. In the morning rain, strong gale.	S
Wed.	10	Rain, in the morning sunshine, light breeze, then drizzling. All men embarked the ship definitively.	NE S
Thu.	11	Gloomy, gentle breeze and rain. In the morning murky.	SSE
Fri.	12	Sunny spells, in the evening cloudy, strong breeze. In the morning murky and calm.	SSE

Hours	Rhumbs	Miles	Winds	Right rhumbs	Sat. 13 July. Different events at the mouth of the Kamchatka River aboard the Archangel Gabriel
2	SW¾W	1.75			At 1:30, having prayed, we cast off from the bank and moved down the Kamchatka River. At 2:30 we reached the mouth of the river and dropped anchor due to a head wind. Aboard were: the Captain, 2 lieutenants, 1 physician, 1 midshipman, 1 quartermaster, 8 sailors, 1 shipbuilder apprentice, 1 foreman, 1 drummer, 9 soldiers, 1 sails master, 1 caulker, 5 carpenters, 2 blacksmiths, 1 seafarer, 2 interpreters from servitors, 6 officers' servants. In all – 44 men. Provisions: flour [ ] poods, rusks [ ] poods,[162] meat – 21 poods, salted fish – 22 barrels, fresh water – 20 barrels, iukola – 80 bundles, groats – 60 poods. The following servicemen were left at the outpost: 1 geodesist and 1 soldier – owing to ill-health, and 3 soldiers to guard the remaining provisions and money and other things. Fog with sun breaking through.
4	do.	1.75	SSE		
6					
8					
10					
12			calm		
2					
4					
6			SbE		
8					
10					
12			calm		

Hours	Rhumbs	Miles	Winds	Right rhumbs	Sun. 14 July. Different events at sea
1					Sunshine and calm.
2			calm		At 7 p.m. having weighed anchor, we left with God's help
3					from the mouth of the Kamchatka River, when the high
4					tide started to fall. And we moved with outgoing stream till
5			NE		7:30 o'clock.
6					
7					At 7:30 o'clock we dropped anchor.
8	SbW	3		SSW¼W	The depth [ ] sazhens,[163] bottom – fine sand.
9					Calm air. The balagans on the spit or tongue
10			calm		of land[34] are to the rhumb NEbN½E from us, the summer
11					dwellings at the mouth of the Kamchatka River are
12					to NNE½E.
1					At 2 a.m. light breeze. And having weighed
2	SbW				anchor, we sailed. We carried mainsail,
3	do.	0.8	N	SSW¼W	foresail, jib, topsail.
4	EbS	1.8		ESE¼S	
5	do.	1.4			
6	do.	1.4	NW		
7	do.	1.1			
8	SE	0.4		SEbS¼S	
9	do.	1.0	vari-able		
10	SEbS	1.0		SSE¼S	
11	E½S	1.5	S	EbS¾S	
12	do.	1.5			

in all[165]

Table of daily reckoning	Latitudes		Diff. of latitude		Departure		Rhumb	Distance		Diff. of longitude		Compass declin.
	from	to	N	S	E	W		right	added	daily	total	
Reckoned	56°03'	55°51'32		11'68	8'		S	11	20.9	1°43'E		1¼ R E
Corrected	56°03'	55°50'7		12'30	84'		3°55' by E	12.33	21.96	1°43'		

Conspicuous places	No. of these places	Time of observation	Directions			
			N – E	N – W	S – E	S – W
The cape we have to pass[166]	1	At 4h 44m a.m.			78°56'	

Folio 43 verso

Hours	Rhumbs	Miles	Winds	Right rhumbs	Leeway[167]	Mon. 15 July 1728. Different events at sea
1	EbN	2.9		EbN½E	¾	Sunshine, gentle breeze, we carried all sails.
2	do.	2.9	SEbS		do.	At 2 o'clock we turned windward.
3	SWbS	1.5	do.	SW¼W	do.	
4	do.	1.5			do.	At 4 o'clock we turned windward.
5	EbN	1.5		EbN½E	do.	
6	do.	1.5			do.	
7	SbE	2.5	ESE	SbE½S	do.	At 7 o'clock we turned windward and at sunset took amplitude of the sun from N by W 66°00'.
8	SWbS	2.0	SEbS	SWbW¼W	1R	At 8 o'clock we turned windward.[168]
9	EbN	0.6		E	¼R	At 11 o'clock we turned windward.
10	NEbE	0.4	do.	ENE	⎫	The weather clear, light breeze.
11	NNE	.3	ENE	NEbN	⎬ ¼R	
12	SE	.8		SEbS½S	⎭	
1	SbW	.6	SEbE	SWbS¼W	1	Clear weather, calm air.
2	do.	.6		do.		At 3 a.m. fog rose from the land.
3	EbS	2.2	SbE	EbS½S	¾	At sunrise the amplitude of the sun was
4	do.	2.2		do.		observed from N by E and from this
5	ENE½E	1.5	SE	ENE¾E	⎫	observed amplitude at sunset
6	NEbE	.6		ENE¼E	⎬ 1	the compass deviation 14°45'E was found.
7	do.	3.0	SEbS	do.		
8	do.	4.2		do.		Cloudy, fresh breeze. Gloomy,
9	NEbN¼E	4.6	SSE	NE½E		before noon strong breeze, we carried
10	do.	4.6		do.		all sails, except the forestaysail.
11	NNE	6.0	do.	NEbN¼E		
12	do.	6.0				

In all   54.5

Table of daily reckoning	Latitudes		Diff. of latitude		Departure		Rhumb	Distance		Diff. of longitude.[169]		Compass declin.
	from	to	N	S	E	W		right	added	daily	total	
Reckoned	55°51'32	56°03'41	12'099		33'02		ENE	35.16	62.7	58'9		1¼ R E
Corrected	55°50'7	56°03'43	12'73		34'77		2°24' by E	37.02	65.73	1°01'73	1°03'16	

Conspicuous places	No. of these places	Time of observation	Directions			
			N – E	N – W	S – E	S – W
The cape we have to pass	1	0:30 p.m.	69°04			
Newly emerged [cape][170]	2	9:30 a.m.		4°56'		
Again the same	2	10 a.m.		9°26'		
Another [cape] along the same land	3	at the same time		6°56'		
The same again	3	11:15 a.m.		16°56		

Folio 43 verso, continuation

Hours	Rhumbs	Miles	Wind	Right rhumbs	Leeway	Tue. 16 July 1728. Different events at sea
1	NNW	6	SSW	NbW¼N		Sunshine, fresh breeze.
2	do.	6		do.		At 2 o'clock we took in mainsail and foresail, and
3	do.	6	do.	do.		hoisted forestaysail.
4	NW½N	6.5		NWbN¾N		
5	NWbW	6.5	SSE	NW¼N		
6	do.	6.5		do.		
7	N	6.5		NbE¼E		
8	do.	6.5		do.		At sunset the sun amplitude 70°00' from N by W
9	NbE	6.3		NNE½E		was observed, and on reckoning by 8 numbers
10	do.	5.0		do.		we were at the latitude of fix 56°48' and from this
11	N¾E	4.6	S	NNE¼E		the compass deviation was found 16°59' east.
12	do.	4.6		do.		From 8 o'clock the weather cloudy, moderate
1	NbE	4.5	SSE	NNE½E		gale. At 10 o'clock we took in forestaysail and
2	do.	4.5		do.		proceeded with foresail and topsail.
3	do.	4.5		do.		At 3 o'clock we hoisted forestaysail and took in foresail.
4	NbW	4.2		N½E		From 4 o'clock murky, wind dropped.
5	do.	2.8		do.		
6	do.	2.8	SEbS	do.		
7	do.	2.8	do.			
8	do.	2.8		do.		From 8 o'clock light variable breeze between N and W, wet fog.
9	NE	1.3	NNW	ENE½E	1R	We carried mainsail, foresail and forestaysail.
10	do.	1.3		do.	1R	
11	EbS	2.	NEbN½E	SEbE¼S	1¼	
12	do.	2.		do.	1¼	

in all   93.5

Table of daily reckoning	Latitudes		Diff. of latitude		Departure		Rhumb	Distance		Diff. of longitude		Compass declin.
	from	to	N	S	E	W		right	added	daily	total	
Reckoned	56°03'41	57°34'08	90'67		9'08		N5°43' by E	91.15	166.6	16'6		1½ R E
Corrected	56°03'43	57°38'9	95'47		9'56		do.	95.98	175.7	17'49	1°20'65	

Conspicuous places	No. of these places	Time of observation	Directions			
			N – E	N – W	S – E	S – W
A newly appeared [cape][171]	4	1:15 p.m.		38°08'		
Another new one[172]	5	at the same time		48°08'		
The same one a second time	4	3 p.m.		53°08'		
Again the same one	5	at the same time				81°52'

Hours	Rhumbs	Miles	Winds	Right rhumbs	Leeway	Wed. 17 July 1728. Different events while at sea
1	NNW½N	2.8	NE	NNW	2	Foggy, light breeze. We carried
2	NWbN½N	2.9	NEbN	NW¾N	2¼	mainsail, foresail, topsail and jib.
3	NWbN	1.9	NNE	NW¼N	2¼	
4	NWbW	1.8	NbE	WNW¼N	do.	From 4 o'clock the weather and wind the
5	WNW½N	2.2		WNW	2	same. We carried the same sails.
6	NWbW	2.6		WNW½N	2	At 6 o'clock we saw something black
7	WNW	3.0		WbN½N		to SWbW 8 miles. Soon after it turned out to be land, extending to WNW.[173]
8	WbN	3.0		do.	1	From 8 o'clock cloudy, strong breeze.
9	NEbE	2.7	NbW	EbN½E	1	
10	do.	2.7	do.	EbN¾E	⎫	At 10:30 o'clock topsail was lowered.
11	do.	2.3	do.	do.	⎬1½	
12	NE	2.	NNW	EbN	⎭	
1	NNE	1.	NWbN	ENE½E	.3	From midnight gloomy, gentle breeze.
2	NEbN	1.	NNW	EbN½E	3	We carried mainsail, foresail and
3	WbN	2.		WbN	⎫	jib. Shore extends to WNW.
4	WNW	1.9	NbW	WNW	⎬1½	At 4 o'clock the coastline came
5	NE	1.5	NNW	EbN½E	⎭	into view to N 1°00' by W.
6	do.	1.5		do.	⎫2	
7	do.	2.5	EbN		⎭	
8	do.	2.3		do.	⎫1½	From 8 o'clock cloudy with rare sunshine.
9	NEbN	1.0		ENE	⎭	We carried mainsail, foresail, topsail, jib.
10	EbN	2.5	NNE	ESE	⎫1½	
11	do.	2.9	N	do.	⎬	At 10:30 o'clock topsail was lowered.
12	ENE	1.5		EbS	⎭	

In all   51.5

Table of daily reckoning	Latitudes		Diff. of lat.		Departure		Rhumb	Distance		Diff. of long.		Compass declination
	from	to	N	S	E	W		right	added	daily	total	
Reckoned	57° 34'08	57° 46'77	12'69		4'87		NbE 10°15' 26 by E	13. 59	25.4	9'1		1½ R
Corrected	57° 38'9	57° 52'26	13'36		5'13		the same	14. 31	26.89	9'64	1°30' 29 b E	eastern

Conspicuous places	No. of these places	Time of observation	directions			
			N – E	N – W	S – E	S – W
A mountain white with snow[174]	6	6:27 p.m.				51°52'
Again the same a second time	6	7:43 p.m.				36°52
Illustrious place on the shore[175]	7	3 a.m.				54°52
Again the same	7	4 a.m.				50°52
A hill, where the shore seems to end[176]	8	at the same time	12°52			
The same again	8	9:30 a.m.		2°08'		

Folio 44, continuation

Hours	Rhumbs	Miles	Winds	Right rhumbs	Leeway	Thu. 18 July 1728. Different events while at sea	
1	NW	2.5	NNE	NW	} 1½	Cloudy, at times sun breaking through, fresh breeze.	
2	do.	2.5		do.		We had mainsail, foresail, jib.	
3	do.	2.5		do.			
4	do.	2.0		NWbW½N	2		
5	NW	1.9		NWbW	} 2½		
6	do.	1.9		do.		The weather the same.	
7	NWbN	1.5	NEbN	NWbW½N	3		
8	do.	3.0		NW	2½	At sunset we sighted amplitude of the sun	
				NWbW½N	3	71°00' from N by W, and the reckoned	
9	EbN	1.5	NNE	SEbE	} 2½	latitude at 9 o'clock – 57°59'. From this	
10	do.	1.8		do.		the compass declination was found – 18°48'	
11	do.	1.9		ESE½E		east. At 10 o'clock the wind rose	
12	ENE	1.5		EbS½S	} 2	and it rained. Jib was lowered.	
1	E	1.5	NEbN	SEbE½S		Soon after 12 o'clock we took in 1 reef	
2	do.	2.		do.		of mainsail. Strong gale with rain.	
3	NNW	2.5		NWbN½N	} 2	At 2 o'clock the leeboard on the right side	
4	do.	2.5		do.		broke.	
5	NNW	1.5		NWbN		At 3 o'clock we wore the ship to port.	
6	do.	1.5		do.	} 2½		do.
7	do.	1.5		do.		Strong breeze with rain. We had	
8	EbS	1.6		SEbS		mainsail and foresail.	
9	ESE	2.		SSE			
10	do.	2.		do.		Strong breeze and at times rain.	
11	do.	2.5		do.	} 2½	We held the same sails.	
12	do.	2.5		do.			

In all   56.1

Table of daily reckoning	Latitudes		Diff. of latitude		Departure		Rhumb	Distance		Diff. of longitude		Compass declination
	from	to	N	S	E	W		right	added	daily	total	
Reckoned	57°46'77	57°52'33	5'56			6'22	NW 3°13' by W	8.34	15.7	11'69 W		1½ R
Corrected	57°52'26	57°58'11	5'85			6'55	the same	8.78	16.51	12'32	1°17' 97 E	eastern

Folio 44 verso

Hours	Rhumbs	Miles	Winds	Right rhumbs	Leeway	Wed. 19 July 1728. Different events while at sea aboard the Holy Archangel Gabriel
1	EbS	1.4	NE	SEbS½S	3	Dark and rainy, strong breeze, and
2	SEbE	1.4	ENE	SbE	2½	at times strong gale.
3	NNE	0.7	EbN	NbW½N	4	At 2 o'clock we turned down wind,
4		2.	E	NbE	2½	the mainsail halyard broke
5		2.		NbE½E	2	and until 3 o'clock we drifted,
6		3.		NNE	1½	then let out a reef of mainsail.
7		2.5		NbE½E	} 2	At 4 o'clock we hoisted jib.
8		3.1				We had mainsail, foresail, jib. The same weather.
9		2.0			2	At 9 o'clock jib was lowered. Fresh
10	SEbS½S	2.0		SbW½W	2½	breeze, heavy sea from NNE,
11		1.5			2½	the weather dark.
12	SSE	1.8			2	
1		1.		NbE½E	2	
2	NNE	0.8		NbE½E	2	At 2 o'clock we hoisted jib, turned
3		1.1			2	down the wind.
4	NE	1.3	ESE	NEbN½E	2	From 4 o'clock light breeze and
5	N	1.5	ENE	NbW½N	2	cloudy, subsiding sea.
6		1.5				
7		1.4		N	1½	At 8 o'clock we hoisted topsail.
8		1.3			do.	Cloudy with sunshine,
9	NEbE	1.0	SEbE	NE½E	} 2	light air.
10		1.7	SE	ENE½E		From 10 o'clock fog.
11	NE	3.6		NEbE½E		
12		2.2				

In all   41.8

Table of daily reckoning	Latitudes		Diff. of latitude		Departure		Rhumb	Distance		Diff. of longitude		Compass declination
	from	to	N	S	E	W		right	added	daily	total	
Reckoned	57°52'33	58°10'7	18'37		11'72		NNE 10°02' E	21.8	41.05	22'07		
Corrected	57°58'11	58°17'45	19'34		12'34		the same	22.96	43.34	23'29	1°41'26	1½ R eastern

Conspicuous places	No. of these places	time of observation	directions			
			N – E	N – W	S – E	S – W
A hill on the shore, which seems to divide the land[177]	9	9:58 a.m.	25°52			
The same place	9	11:25 a.m.	21°52			

Folio 44 verso, continuation

Hours	Rhumbs	Miles	Winds	Right rhumbs	Leeway	Sat. 20 July 1728. Different events while at sea
1	NE	2.1	SE	NEbE½E		The weather dull, fresh breeze,
2		2.2				we carried mainsail, foresail,
3		1.5				topsail and jib.
4		1.5				
5		3.1	NEbE½E			
6		3.1				
7		3.0				
8		3.0	SEbS			From 8 o'clock cloudy, fresh breeze.
9		5.2		NEbE½E		At 9 o'clock we took in mainsail and
10		3.1				jib and proceeded under topsail and
11		3.1				foresail. We ran in parallel of the shore,
						which extended to NE. At 9½ o'clock
12		3.7	SbE			[a cape], from which the shore bent
1		4.0		NEbE½E		by N and extended to NbE, was observed
2		4.5				to the NW of us, 13 miles away.[178]
3		4.0				At 2 o'clock we hoisted mainsail and
4		5.2				jib, fresh breeze, the weather
5		3.7				cloudy.
6		4.7				At 6 o'clock and 56 minutes the end of the
7	NEbN	4.3	SEbS	NE½E		eastern shore [of Karaginskii Island] was to the left
						of us, 86° S by W, 22 miles away.
8		4.7				From 8 o'clock the weather and wind
9		6.1				the same. We held mainsail,
10		4.5				foresail, topsail and jib.
11		5.7				
12		5.8				

In all   91.8

Table of daily reckoning	Latitudes		Diff. of latitude		Departure		Rhumb	Distance		Diff. of longitude		Compass declination
	from	to	N	S	E	W		right	added	daily	total	
Reckoned	58°10'7	58°59'05	48'35		77'54		NebE 1°50' by E	21.55	174.2	2°27'9		
Corrected	58°17'45	59°03'36	50'91		81'65		the same	96.19	185.3	2°37'3 E	4°18'56 E	1½ R eastern

Conspicuous places	No. of these places	Time of observation	Directions			
			N – E	N – W	S – E	S – W
A hill that stands out against the others[179]	10	3h 50m p.m.	27.52			
The same again	10	5 p.m.	21.52			
A corner of the land, jutting out into the sea[180]	11	2 a.m.		63.08		
The same again[181]	11	4 a.m.		76.08		
Once more rising ground[182]	12	7h 48m a.m.	8.52			
The same again	12	12 a.m.		49.08		

Hours	Rhumbs	Miles	Winds	Right rhumbs	Leeway	21 July 1728. Different events while at sea aboard the Holy Archangel Gabriel
1	NEbN	4.9	SWbS	NE½E		The weather dull, fresh breeze, the land was on
2		5.3				the left side at a distance of 13 miles, extending to
3		5.3				NNE.[183] We carried mainsail, foresail, topsail and jib.
4		5.1				From 4 o'clock the same weather
5	NNE½E	6.0	SW			and we held the same sails.
6	NNE½E	5.2		NE		At 7 o'clock the shore was to the NWbW of us.
7		5.2	SWbW			at a distance of 15 miles, extending to NbE½E.
8		5.2				From 8 o'clock the weather dull and at times
9	NE	5.	SW	NEbE½E		drizzling mostly from the wet fog. We carried topsail,
10		5.				foresail and jib.
11		5.				From midnight the weather dark and at times it was
12		5.				drizzling, fresh breeze.
1	NE	5.				We carried the same sails, and soon after 1 o'clock we
2	NEbN½E	5.4		NEbE		hoisted mainsail.
3	NE	8.2		NEbE½E		At 4 o'clock jib was lowered. The shore was on our
4	NEbE	4.8		ENE½E		left at a distance of 14 miles, extending to NNE.[184]
5	SEbS	4.5	WSW	SSE½S		At 5 o'clock topsail was lowered, since we ran
6		4.5				parallel to the shore, and we saw in
7	SEbE	5.		SE½S		front a land to ENE[185] and ran to SEbS.
8		5.				The sighted land was 15 miles away. At 7
9		5.				o'clock we again hoisted topsail.
10		5.				From 9 o'clock dark. Fresh breeze.
11		5.4				We carried mainsail, foresail,
12		6.7				topsail, jib. At 10 o'clock the land
						was 13 miles away to the NEbN of us.

In all   126.7

Table of daily reckoning	Latitudes		Diff. of latitude		Departure		Rhumb	Distance		Diff. of longitude		Compass declination
	from	to	N	S	E	W		right	added	daily	total	
Reckoned	58°59'05	59°17'	17'95		97'1		EbN 0°47' by E	98.76	192.6	3°94'		1½ R
Corrected	59°8'36	59°27'27	18'91		102'3		the same	104.0	203.5	3°20'2	7°38'76 b E	eastern

Conspicuous places	No. of these places	Time of observation	Directions			
			N – E	N – W	S – E	S – W
A mountain white with snow[186]	13	1h 40m p.m.		5.38		
Again the same	13	3h 03m p.m.		19.08		
An easily recognizable mountain[187]	14	4 p.m.	4.22			
The same again	14	7 p.m.		19.08		
A mountain distinctly different from the others[188]	15	1 a.m.	8.52			
The same once more	15	3h 05m a.m.		22.08		
A point of land jutting out into the sea[189]	16	at the same time	20.52			
The same once more	16	4 a.m.	13.22			
A small mountain beyond the bay[190]	17	at the same time	35.52			
The same a second time	17	6 a.m.	15.52			
A mountain on the very seashore[191]	18	at the same time			83.44	
The same a second time	18	8 a.m.	66.52			
A mountain with 3 peaks[192]	19	at the same time			73.08	
The same mountain once again	19	9:30 a.m.			89.08	

Hours	Rhumbs	Miles	Winds	Right rhumbs	Leeway	Mon. 22 July 1728. Different events while at sea
1	ENE	4.	WSW	EbN½E		The weather gloomy, moderate breeze.
2		4.				We carried mainsail, foresail, topsail and jib.
3		5.				At 1 o'clock one of the high stone mountains, the southernmost one (of those that are washed by the sea in the extreme W) was 12 miles to the
4		5.				NE¼E of us.[193] From 4 o'clock the sky was covered with light clouds, moderate wind.
5	ENE	6.	WSW	EbN½E		We carried the same sails. The shore was on our
6		6.				left side, at a distance of 15 miles, extending
		3.3				parallel to our route by sight.
7	NE	3.3		NEbE½E		At 7 o'clock the sky cleared, only the western side of the horizon remained in clouds. Jib was
8		6.6				lowered. At 8 o'clock we took in mainsail.
9	NE	6.	WSW	NEbE½E		From 8 o'clock clear. In the night moonlight and
10		6.				stars, clouds near the horizon only.
11		5.5				Strong breeze. We held foresail and topsail in one
12		5.2				third of topmast. After midnight wind the same
1	NE	5.5	WSW	NEbE½E		and we held the same sails.
2	NNE	5.6		NEbN½E		
3		5.3				At 3:30 o'clock we hoisted mainsail and
4		5.8				foresail. By 4 a.m. the sun broke through
5	NNE	4.2	WSW	NEbN½E		the darkness, in places the sky was cloudy,
6		3.				wind dropped. We carried the same sails.
7		2.5				At 10 a.m. the altitude of the sun was observed,
8		1.8				46°54' with correction, and the azimuth from S
9	NNE	1.5	WSW	NEbN½E		by E 32°00. We were then at latitude 60°15' N,
10		1.5				and from this the azimuth from S by E 15°04'
11		.6				was found. Compass declination was 16°56' east.
12		.6				At noon we sighted the altitude of the sun to S 47°34' with correction, sun declination by local meridian 17°50'N, from this latitude of fix 60°16'N.

in all   105.8

Table of daily reckoning	Latitudes		Diff. of latitude		Departure		Rhumb	Distance		Diff. of longitude		Compass declination
	from	to	N	S	E	W		right	added	daily	total	
Reckoned	59°17'	60°03'27	46'27		87'34		NEbE 5°50' by E	98.84				
Corrected	59°27'27	60°16'	48'73		92'01		the same	104.1	207.4	3°03'4 E	10°42'16 E	1½ R E

Conspicuous places	No. of these places	Time of observation	Directions			
			N – E	N – W	S – E	S – W
A point of land extending into the sea	20	5h 48m p.m.	1.52			
The same point once more	20	6½ p.m.		3.08		
A mountain with 6 peaks[194]	21	2h 24m a.m.		10.08		
The same once more[195]	21	4h a.m.		33.08		
A mountain with 2 peaks like a tent[196]	22	at the same time		21.08		
The same again	22	6h 17m a.m.		32.38		
A steep mountain[197]	23	at the same time		13.38		
The same again	23	12 a.m.		19.38		

PLATE 24. Modern map 5: From Kamchatka River to the Turnaround. By Viktor Sedov. ▶

From Kamchatka River to the Turnaround

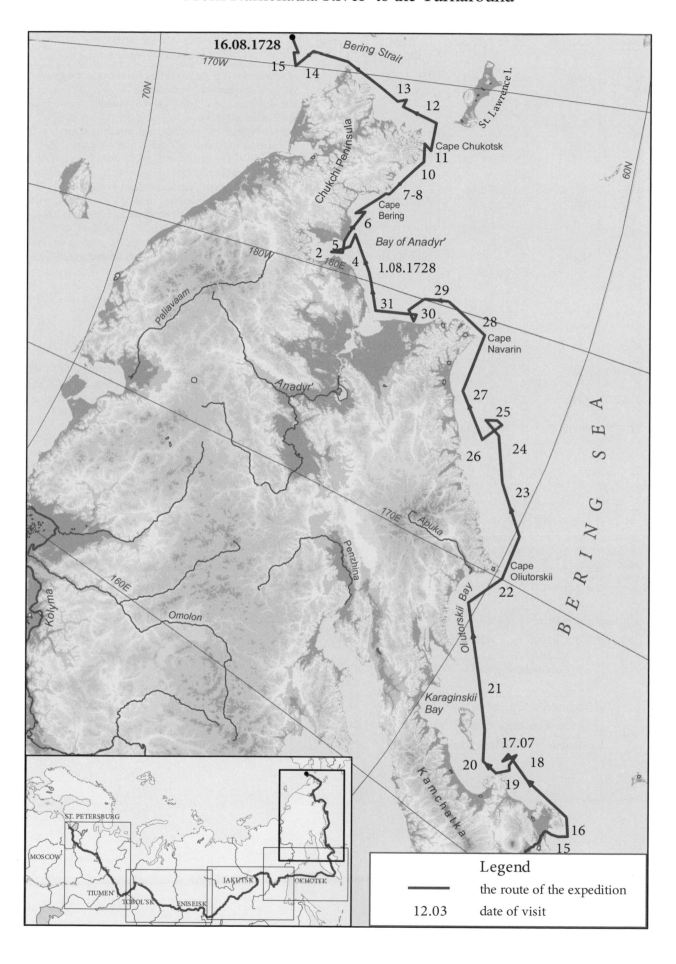

Legend

——— the route of the expedition

12.03 date of visit

Hours	Rhumbs	Miles	Winds	Right rhumbs	Leeway	Tuc. 23 July 1728. Different events while at sea
1	NNE	3.9	SW	NEbN½E		Moderate breeze and sunshine breaking through. We held mainsail, topsail and jib.
2		3.4				The shore on the left side extends parallel to our route
3		3.4				in 20 miles or more.
4		3.4				From 4 o'clock the weather and wind the same.
5	NNE	3.	SW	NEbN½E		We carried the same sails. At sunset we sighted the
6		2.8				amplitude of the sun from N by W 70°30', and at 8
7		2.7				o'clock the reckoned latitude was 60°26' and from this
8		3.2				was found the compass declination 19°37' east.
9	NNE	2.	SSE	NEbN¾E		From 9 o'clock the weather clear, wind calm. We took
10		2.				in mainsail and ran under topsail and forestaysail.
11		1.7	SSW			
12		1.7				From midnight the sky partly cloudy, wind calm. We
1	NNE	2.	S	NEbN¾E		carried the same sails, the shore extended parallel to
2		2.				our route in 13 miles distance.
3		2.				
4		2.				From 4 o'clock sunshine breaking through. The shore lies parallel to our route.
5	NNE	2.	S	NEbN¾E		Calm air. We carried the same sails.
6		1.8				At 9:30 a.m. we lowered forestaysail and hoisted foresail.
7		1.				At 8:45 a.m.,[198] when we were at the latitude of 61°03',
8		.5				the sighted azimuth of the sun from S by E 60°08' and
9	NNE	.5	WNW	NEbN¾E		the altitude of the sun center 42°46'.
10		.7				Sun declination by this meridian during sighting
11	NEbE	.4	calm	ENE¾E		17°35'N.
						From this the azimuth was found 34°44' from S by E and the compass declination 25°24' east.
12		1.				At noon against S we sighted the altitude of sun center with correction 48°31', the sun declination 17°34' N. From this latitude of fix 61°03' N. Sunshine and calm.

in all 49.1

Table of daily reckoning	Latitudes		Diff. of latitude		Departure		Rhumb	Distance		Diff. of longitude		Compass declination
	from	to	N	S	E	W		right	added	daily	total	
Reckoned	60°03'27	60°52'5	36'5		32'43		NEbN 7°52' by E	48.8				to 9h 1½ R
Corrected	60°16'	61°03'	47'		41'76		the same	62.84	125.5	1°23'43 E	12°05'59 b E	1¾ R eastern

Conspicuous places	No. of these places	Time of observation	Directions			
			N – E	N – W	S – E	S – W
A mountain, easy to recognize[199]	24	6 p.m.		6°44'		
The same once more	24	3:30 a.m.		69°19'		
A mountain patched with snow[200]	25	9:20 a.m.		26°19		

Folio 45, verso, continuation

Hours	Rhumbs	Miles	Winds	Right rhumbs	Leeway	Wed. 24 July 1728. Different events while at sea
1	NNE	1.9	SSE	NE		Sunshine and warm, winds calm.
2		2.1				We held mainsail, foresail, topsail.
3		2.1				From 4 o'clock the weather and wind
4		2.2				the same. We carried the same sails.
5	NNE	2.9	SSE	NE		The shore on the left side extends
6		3.3				parallel to our route 12 miles away.
7		3.5				At 7 o'clock forestaysail was hoisted.
8		3.5				From 8 o'clock the weather clear,
9	NNE	2.3	SE	NE		fresh breeze. We carried all sails
10		1.6				set. In the night fog, therefore
						land was not seen.
11		1.	calm			At 12 o'clock forestaysail was
12	NEbE	1.2	NbW	EbN		lowered. At 2 a.m. the wind began to
						rise, at 3 o'clock strong gale, with
1	ENE	4.	N	ESE	2R	gusts. Topsail was lowered, at 4
2		4.0			2	o'clock wet fog drifted in.
3	E	3.5	NNE	SE	2	From 4 o'clock the weather dark,
4		3.4			2	strong breeze. We held mainsail and
5	NWbN½N	1.9	NEbN	NWtN½W	3	foresail.
6	NNW½N	1.9	NE	NWbN½N	3	At 7 o'clock we took 1 reef of mainsail, at
						the same time the hank of the spanker gaff
						broke[201] and therefore at 8 o'clock
7	NbW	2.4		NNW½N	2½	the mainsail was lowered.
8	SE½S	2.5		SSE½S	0	From 8 o'clock the weather and wind
9	E	3.	NEbN½E	SE½S	2½	the same. We held mainsail and
10		3.			2½	foresail. At 12 o'clock the lift broke[202]
11		3.			2½	and therefore for about half an hour
12		3.			2½	the mainsail was down.

In all   63.1

Table of daily reckoning	Latitudes		Diff. of latitude		Departure		Rhumb	Distance		Diff. of longitude		Compass declination
	from	to	N	S	E	W		right	added	daily	total	
Reckoned	61°03'	61°7'74	4'74		37'63		EbN 3°34' by E	37.9				
Corrected	61°03'	61°7'74	the same		the same		the same	37.9	78.07	1°17'52 by E	13°23' 11 b E	2 R E

Conspicuous places	No. of these places	Time of observation	Directions			
			N – E	N – W	S – E	S – W
Same motley-looking mountain with snow[203]	25	4½ p.m.		45.30		

PLATE 25. "The Holy Gabriel", pen-and-ink drawing by Igor Pshenichnyi, on the basis of his study of Russian shipbuilding at the time.

Courtesy the artist and T. Fedorova. Photo by Nikolai Turkin.

Hours	Rhumbs	Miles	Winds	Right rhumbs	Leeway	Thu. 25 July 1728. Different events while at sea
1	NNW½N	3.2	NEbN½E	NNW	2½	Rain, moderate gale, we carried
2		3.2			2½	mainsail, unbending 1 reef, and
3		3.2			2½	foresail.
4		3.2			2½	From 5 o'clock the weather the same,
5	⌈ EbS	1.1	NEbN½E	SEbS½S	2½	wind decreased slightly.
	⌊	1.1				
6		2.1			2½	We carried the same sails.
7		1.1			2½	
8	ESE	1.6		SSE¾S	2¾	
9	EbS	1.	NEbN½E	EbS¾S	2¾	From 9 o'clock and to midnight dark, at
10		1.			2¾	times rain, moderate breeze but rough sea.
11		1.			2¾	We carried mainsail and foresail.
12		.5			2¾	
1	NWbN	1.9	NNE	NW½N	2½	
2		1.8			2½	
3		1.9		NWbN	2	From 5 a.m. sunshine, fresh breeze.
						We held mainsail, foresail, jib.
4		2.3			2	At 8 o'clock we hoisted topsail. At the
5	NW	3.5	NNE	NW½N	1½	same time land appeared ahead to N¼O.
6	NWbW	3.5	N½E	NWbW½N	1½	From 9 o'clock variable sunshine,
7	NW½N	2.5	NNE	NWbN½N	1	winds calm. We carried the same sails.
8		1.8			1	At 2½ hours before noon by sand
9	NNW	1.5	NEbN	NNW½N	1½	watch we took the altitude of the sun
						39°35' with correction and the azimuth
10		1.5			1½	from S by E 67°30', the azimuth found
11	NW½N	1.	calm	calm	0	43°30' and the compass declination
						24°00'E. At noon we sighted the
12	NbW	.6		NbE	0	meridian altitude of the sun by S
						45°31' with correction, and its
						declination on the local meridian
						17°03' N, from this the latitude of
						fix 61°32'.

In all   47.1

Table of daily reckoning	Latitudes		Diff. of latitude		Departure		Rhumb	Distance		Diff. of longitude		Compass declination
	from	to	N	S	E	W		right	added	daily	total	
Reckoned	61°07'74	61°31'56	23'82			14'07	NNW 8°4 by W	27.66				
Corrected	61°07'74	61°32'	24'26			14'07	the same	27.66	57.62	29'31 by W	12°53'80 E	2 R eastern

Conspicuous places	No. of these places	Time of observation	Direction			
			N – E	N – W	S – E	S – W
A mountain standing apart behind a lowland[204]	26	3¾ p.m.		23.30		
Another one, similar[205]	27	at the same time		6.30		
The mountain standing apart a second time	26	8 a.m.		16.30		
The similar one a second time	27	at the same time	7.30			

Folio 46, continuation

Hours	Rhumbs	Miles	Winds	Right rhumbs	Leeway	Fri. 26 July 1728. Different events while at sea
1	NNE	.2	⎫calm	NEbN¾E		The weather clear, winds calm. We held
2		.3	⎭			mainsail, foresail, topsail, jib.
						At 2 o'clock mainsail and
3		1.6	S			foresail were lowered, hoisted
4		2.8	SW			forestaysail. From noon
5	NNE	3.5		NEbN¾E		to 9 o'clock we ran parallel
6		3.5				to the shore, having it on the left
7		3.5				side, 12 miles away. At sunset we sighted
8		4.5				amplitude 73°00' from N by W, and at
						that time we were at the latitude
						61°46' N, and from this the compass
						declination 21°05' east was found.
9	NNE	4.	SWbS	NEbN¾E		In the night bright stars, gentle
10	NEbN	3.	SbW	NE¾E		breeze. We carried the same sails.
11	NE	4.6		NEbE¾E		The shore was at a distance of 13 miles
						from us. At 11 o'clock, there was
12		3.6	SWbS			a bay to the NW½N of us.[206] From midnight
1	NE	3.5	S	NEbE¾E		we carried forestaysail and topsail.
2		3.5				
3	⎡NNE	2.		NEbN¾E		
		2.				
4	⎣	4.2				
5	NNE	3.5	SW	NEbN¾E		
6		3.5				
7		3.1				At 8 a.m. we took the altitude of the
						sun center with correction 32°24'
8		3.4				and azimuth 83°30' from S by E, and
						the reckoned latitude at that time
9	NNE	4.3	SSW	NEbN¾E		61°59' N, from this compass
						declination was found – 21°10' east.
10		4.6				By 9 o'clock sun breaking through the
						dark, but above the shore thick fog.
11	NbE½E	5.		NEbN¾E		We carried topsail and forestaysail.
12		3.5				By 12 o'clock wind began to rise and to
						scatter the fog.

In all   80.9

Table of daily reckoning	Latitudes		Diff. of latitude		Departure		Rhumb	Distance		Diff. of longitude		Compass declination
	from	to	N	S	E	W		right	added	daily	total	
Reckoned	61°32'	62°27'57	54'57		57'26		NE 1°48 by E	79.59				
Corrected	61°32'53	62°26'58	55'58		59'03		the same	81.06	172.7	2°05'5 by E	14°59'6 E	1¾ R eastern

Conspicuous places	No. of these places	Time of observation	Directions			
			N – E	N – W	S – E	S – W
A high sharp-pointed mountain[207]	28	4 p.m.	26.41			
The same again	28	7¾ p.m.		7.00		

Folio 46 verso

Hours	Rhumbs	Miles	Winds	Right rhumbs	Leeway	Sat. 27 July 1728. Different events while at sea aboard the Archangel Gabriel
1	⎰NNE	2.5	SW	NEbN¼E		Intermittent sunshine, strong breeze, the land
	⎱NEbN	1.2		NE¾E		extends parallel to our route in a curve,
2	NE	1.2		NEbE¾E		at a distance of 15 miles.[208]
	ENE¼E	5.2		E		At 12:30 o'clock a bay was from us to NEbN.[209]
3	NEbE¼E	3.9		EbN		At 2 o'clock we saw land ahead on our course[210]
4	ENE	1.3		EbN¾E		and bore away to the recorded rhumbs [i.e., to the east].
5	ENE¼E	5.6	SW	E		We carried topsail and forestaysail and, when we saw land ahead of us, the forestaysail
6	EbN	4.5		E¾S		was lowered and mainsail and foresail hoisted.
7	⎰E	.4		EbS¾S		At 4 o'clock the weather the same.
	⎱EbS	2.2		EbS¾S		We carried mainsail, foresail, topsail.
8		4.6				At 5 o'clock we saw a bay to NWbN, where
9	E½S	4.3	SbW	SSE¼E		we believe a river flows into the sea, since sea water in this place is discolored.[211]
10		4.5				At 6:30 land was from us 7 miles to NbE.[212] Wind dropped. At 7 o'clock halyard of topsail
11		5.				broke, and we then lowered it and ran under mainsail, foresail and jib.
12		5.				From 9 o'clock dark, fresh breeze, at 11
1	E	4.5	WSW	EbS¾S		o'clock wind rose, we could see the shore,
2	ENE	6.1		EbN¾E		and ran parallel to it. We carried the same sails. From midnight dark weather, moderate gale.
3	⎰ENE	3.1				We had mainsail and foresail. The land was on
	⎪NE	1.1		NEbE¾E		our left, but how it extended we did not see
	⎪NNE	2.	SW	NEbN¾E		because of fog. At 3 o'clock we saw a land to
	⎱N	.9		NbE¾E		WNW, 12 miles away.[213]
4		5.8	WSW			
5	NNW½N	5.5		N¼E		From 5 o'clock the weather cloudy, fresh breeze. We ran near the land at a distance of 6 miles.
6	NNW	5.8		NbW¾N		At 6 o'clock we saw to WSW a bay, from
7		5.1				which, we think, a river flows into the sea.[214]
8		5				And we hoisted jib.
9	NNW	1.8	WSW	NbW¾N		At 8 o'clock the land was 3 miles away from
10	NbE	1.5		NNE¾E		us. From 9 o'clock to noon cloudy with sunny
11	N½E	1.		NNE¼E		spells, calm air. We held mainsail, foresail, jib. At 10 o'clock we hoisted topsail.
12	-	.2				At noon the shore was at a distance of 3½ miles from us.

In all   105.8

Table of daily reckoning	Latitudes		Diff. of latitude		Departure		Rhumb	Distance		Diff. of longitude		Compass declination
	from	to	N	S	E	W		right	added	daily	total	
Reckoned	62°26'57	62°32'79	26'22		70'38		ENE 2°04 by E	75.11				1⅓ R eastern
Corrected	62°27'58	62°54'28	26'70		71'69		the same	76.50	166.8	2°36'3	17°35' b E	

Conspicuous places	No. of these places	Time of observation	Direction			
			N – E	N – W	S – E	S – W
Conspicuous land[215]	29	5:23 p.m.	81.11			
The same a second time	29	7 p.m.	70.41			
A point jutting out into the sea, land behind it not visible[216]	30	7:10 p.m			80.19	
The same again	30	8 p.m.			85.19	
A new point of land[217]	31	9:12 a.m.		10.19		

Hours	Rhumbs	Miles	Winds	Right rhumbs	Leeway	Sun. 28 July 1728. Different events while at sea
1	NbW	.2	⎫	N¾E		Drizzling and calm. At 2 o'clock fog and rain.
2		.1	⎬ calm			
3		.1	⎪			At 3 o'clock rain stopped and it cleared up.
4		0	⎭			Soon after 4 o'clock wind dropped, the weather
5	NbW	1.2	SSW	N¾E		overcast. We carried mainsail, foresail, topsail and
6		1.				jib. The current in the sea was determined to be
7		.7				SEbS 1 mile per hour and then returns to NWbN.
8		.8				In this sea there are many animals: whales – a large
9	NbW½N	1.5	SWbS	NbE¼E		number that have variegated skins;[218] sealions,
10	NNW	2.3				walruses, porpoises.
11		2.8				The weather calm, clear starry night, near horizon fog. We carried
12		3.3				the same sails through the night.
1	NWbN½N	2.8	WSW	NbW¼N		Cloudy, light breeze. We carried
		1.4				mainsail, foresail, topsail, jib.
2	⎣NWbN	1.4		NNW¼N		
3		2.5				
4		2.2				
5	NNW	.6	⎫	NbW¾N		From 4 o'clock to 9 calm air,[219] the weather foggy. We carried the same
6		1.	⎬ calm			sails. Land was seen from us to
7	NbE	⎫.3	⎪	NNE¾E		WSW.[220]
8		⎭	⎭			
9	NbE	0		NNE¾E		From 8 o'clock till noon overcast and foggy, moderate breeze. We carried
10	W	2.	SbW	WbN¾N		mainsail, foresail, topsail and jib.
11		2.2				Through fog only a part of the land could be seen between SW and NW at a
12		2.5	SSE			distance of 15 miles.[221]

In all　32.9

Table of daily reckoning	Latitudes		Diff. of latitude		Departure		Rhumb	Distance		Diff. of longitude		Compass declination
	from	to	N	S	E	W		right	added	daily	total	
Reckoned	62°32'79	63°20'88	28'09			7'78	NbW 4°14 by W	29.14				
Corrected	62°27'58	63°22'89	28'61			7'92	the same	29.68	65.67	17'50 W	17°13' 32 b E	1 ¾ R eastern

Conspicuous places	No. of these places	Time of observation	Directions			
			N – E	N – W	S – E	S – W
Once more the same newly appeared point[222]	31	5 p.m.		26°19		
A high steep mountain by the sea[223]	32	the same time		25°19		

Hours	Rhumbs	Miles	Winds	Right rhumbs	Leeway	Mon. 29 July 1728. Different events while at sea aboard the Archangel Gabriel
1	WbN	2.7	SEbS	WNW¾N		The weather overcast and foggy, gentle breeze. We carried mainsail, foresail,
2		2.8				topsail from noon to 4 o'clock.
3		2.4				The shore was from us to NWbW
4		2.				and extended to SbW for 14 miles.
5	WbN	2.	SEbS	WNW¾N		From 4 o'clock a few sunny spells, fresh breeze.
6		3.2				We carried the same sails. At 5 o'clock the land
		.4				was from us to SbWn in 8 miles. From 8 o'clock
7	WNW	.8		NWbW¾N		on the weather the same. We carried mainsail,
	WbN	2.		WNW¾N		foresail, topsail and jib, at 11 o'clock mainsail
8		3.1				was taken in. At 12 drizzling.
9	WNW	4.2	SEbS	NWbW¾N		From midnight the weather the same,
10		4.2				fresh breeze. We carried foresail, topsail and jib.
11		4.2				At 12:30 o'clock the depth of the sea –
12	NWbW	3.2		NW¾N		10 sazhens, bottom – fine sand.
						And we saw land to NW 3 miles away.
1	NEbN	2.2	S	NE¾E		And the Captain ordered us to drift and
2	SEbE	2.0	SWbW	SE¾S		we drifted for 3 hours.
	SE	1.3		SEbS¾S		At 3:30 a.m. we proceeded near and
3		2.5				parallel to the land. The land was low near the
						shore, which we had on our
4	SE	1.2				left.[224] As far as this place there had been
	NE	1.3		NEbE¾E		high mountains along the shore.
	NNE	1.2		NEbN¾E		We carried mainsail and foresail.
5		1.3	WSW			From 4 o'clock intermittent drizzle,
	N	3.4		NbE¾E		strong breeze, at 6 o'clock we hoisted jib.
6		2.4	W			
	NWbN½N	2.2		N¼E		
7	NNE	2.2	NW	NEbE¾E	2	From 7 o'clock to noon overcast, strong breeze. We carried mainsail, foresail
8	WbS	2.5		WSW¾W	2	and jib.
9	WbS	2.3			2	At 11 o'clock we approached the land at a
10	WSW	2.4	NWbW	SWbW¼W	2½	distance of 1½ miles and had the depth
11		2.5				of water 9 sazhens. From this place
12	NEbN	2.5	NNW	EbN¼E	2¼	the seashore extends to NEbN, to the left from us.

In all   72.4

Table of daily reckoning	Latitudes		Diff. of latitude		Departure		Rhumb	Distance		Diff. of longitude		Compass declination
	from	to	N	S	E	W		right	added	daily	total	
Reckoned	63°20'88	63°46'67	25'79			23'3	NWbN 8°23 W	34.76				
Corrected	63°22'89	63°49'16	26'27			23'74	the same	35.00	78.74	53'41 W	16°24' 97 E	1 ¾ R eastern

Conspicuous places	No. of these places	Time of observation	Directions			
			N – E	N – W	S – E	S – W
The mountain by the sea a second time[225]	32	3 p.m.				44.41
A mountain ahead	33	the same time				84.41
A mountain like a haystack[226]	34	the same time		84.19		
Once more	33	6:30 p.m.				67.41
Once more	34	the same time				82.41

Folio 47, continuation

Hours	Rhumbs	Miles	Winds	Right rhumbs	Leeway	Tue. 30 July 1728. Different events while at sea
1	NNE	2.	NWbN½N	ENE	2½	The weather overcast, fresh breeze. At 2 o'clock, turned toward the land.
		.6				
2	W	.5	} vari-	WSW½W	3	Breeze light and variable.
	WbN	.9	able	WbS½W	3	At 4 o'clock sunshine. Soon after 4 o'clock we
3	WNW	2.	}	WbN½N	2	cast anchor at a distance of 1½ miles from the
4		2.	NWbN½N			land at the depth of 10 sazhens. The bottom – sand and pebbles.[227]
5			N			I was sent on shore with the boat and 4 men to look for fresh water and to search for a place where the ship could come
6						closer and stay safely.
7						On arrival, neither fresh water
8			SSE			nor a suitable place for the ship were found, except maybe for a small
9	NNE	1.1		NEbN½E		bay, where it might enter with difficulty, and only with inflow water. We did not see any people on shore. I returned to
10	N	2.1		NbE½E		the ship shortly before 8 o'clock and reported on carrying out the order. At 8:30 o'clock we lifted anchor
11	NbW	3.6		N½E		and ran at a short distance from land. We carried topsail and foresail.
12		4.7				Broken clouds, bright stars, calm air.
1	NbW	4.5	SE	N½E		At 12 o'clock wind rose. We held the
2		4.6				same sails.
3	NNW	6.5		NbW½N		Soon after 1 o'clock we hoisted jib.
		3.2				The weather cloudy, fresh breeze.
4	NW	3.3		NWbN½N		The depth 12 sazhens. Soon after 2
	WbN	1.8	SE	WNW½N		o'clock we hoisted forestaysail,
5	NWbW	3.7		NW½N		and foresail was lowered.
		2.7				
6	NW	2.8		NWbN½N		We ran parallel to the land, at a distance of 3 miles. The land was low, at 6:30
		4.1				o'clock a mountain appeared to WNW½N[228]
7	N	.9		NbE½E		and we ran to N. At 8 o'clock forestaysail
8		3.4				was lowered, mainsail hoisted.
	N	2.	SE	NbE½E		From 9 o'clock to noon cloudy, fresh
9	EbN	1.5		ENE½E	2	breeze and rain.[229] Depths 12 sazhens,
10	EbN	3.				at 8:30 o'clock topsail was lowered
11	EbN	1.5				and we ran close-hauled.[230]
	NE	2.5		NEbE½E	2	
12		5.0				

In all   76.5

Table of daily reckoning	Latitudes		Diff. of latitude		Departure		Rhumb	Distance		Diff. of longitude		Compass declination
	from	to	N	S	E	W		right	added	daily	total	
Reckoned	63°46'67	64°41'21	54'6		00'3		N 00°18' E	54.7				
Corrected	63°49'16	64°44'78	55'62		00'35		the same	55.71	128.4	00°00'87	16°25'84 E	1½ R eastern

Conspicuous places	No. of these places	Time of observation	Directions			
			N – E	N – W	S – E	S – W
A small hill on the lowland[231]	35	2 p.m.		63.08		
Another conspicuous place	36	the same time		53.08		
The small hill a second time	35	4 p.m.		41.08		
The conspicuous place again	36	the same time		32.08		

Hours	Rhumbs	Miles	Winds	Right rhumbs	Leeway	Wed. 31 July 1728. Different events while at sea aboard the Holy Archangel Gabriel
1	NE	3.1	SSE	NEbE½E		The weather overcast and intermittent fog, rain.
2		3.0				We had mainsail, foresail, jib.
3	N	3.9	SEbS	NbE½E		
4		3.9				At 4 o'clock sun breaking through clouds.
5	⎡NNW	1.8	SEbS	NbW½N	1½	From 4 o'clock the weather the same.
	⎣EbN	1.8		EbN	1½	We carried the same sails. At 4:30 o'clock
6		3.6				we saw low land in 4½ miles between NW and NE extending to NNE, and further
7		2.2				we could not see because of fog.
8	ENE	3.9		EbN¼E	¼R	The land was covered with thick snow.
9	ENE	3.6	SSE	EbN¼E	¼	From 8 o'clock to midnight rain, fresh
10		3.2				breeze. We carried mainsail and
11		3.8				foresail, 1 reef of mainsail was unbent.
12		3.8				
1	EbN	3.5	SEbS	ENE½E	2	From midnight to 4 o'clock rain and fog, strong gale, the land was not
2		3.5				seen. We held the same sails.
3		3.5				
4		3.5				
5	N	4.5	SE	NbE½E		From 4 to 8 o'clock the weather and
6		4.5				wind the same, rain.
7	NbE	5.6		NNE½E		
8		5.6				
9	NbE¼E	5.5	SE	NNE¾E		From 8 o'clock to noon the weather the same,
10		5.5				strong gale. We carried mainsail and foresail,
11	NbE	4.1		NNE½E		1 reef of mainsail was unbent. The land could not be seen through the fog.
		⎡2.				At 11 o'clock the water color changed, and therefore we knew that the shore
12	ENE	⎣1.8		NEbE	2½	was near.[232] The depth was 11 sazhens, and we ran close-hauled.

In all   94.3

Table of daily reckoning	Latitudes		Diff. of latitude		Departure		Rhumb	Distance	Diff. of longitude		Compass declination
	from	to	N	S	E	W		right	added	daily	total	
Reckoned	64°41'27	65°35'88	54'61		63'94		NE 4°30'	84.09				
Corrected	64°44'78	65°40'41	55'63		65'12		the same	85.64	217.5	2°45'4	19°11'24 b E	1½ R E

Hours	Rhumbs	Miles	Winds	Right rhumbs	Leeway	Thu. 1 August 1728. Different events while at sea
1	SbW	3.	ESE½E	SW½W	2	The weather dull and rainy, strong breeze. We carried mainsail, foresail, jib. Soon after 12
2		3.	SE			o'clock we saw land on the left side in 3 miles to NbW[233] and we
3		3.				turned bow to the wind.[234]
4		3.				At 4 o'clock wind rose and jib was
5	⎰SbW	1.	SE	SW½W	2	lowered. From 4 o'clock to 8
	⎱ENE	1.2		NEbE	2½	strong gale with rain.
						At 5 o'clock we took in 1 reef of
6		2.2				mainsail and foresail.
7	NEbE	2.	SEbE	NE	2½	
8		2.5				From 8 o'clock to midnight rain,
	⎰NEbE	.6	SEbE	NE		strong gale. We carried mainsail
9	⎱SbE½S	1.8	ESE	SWbS½W	2½	and foresail.
10		2.5				
11		3.				
12		2.8				From midnight the weather the same and
1	SbE½S	2.	ESE	SWbS½W	2½	cold. At 2 o'clock, when turning bow
2	NEbN½E	2.	E½S	NNE½E		to the wind, a line along which the iron sheet of mainsail moved broke
3		2.				in half.
4	NNE½E	2.	EbN	NbE½E		
5	NNE½E	2.2	EbN	NbE½E	2½	From 4 o'clock murky. Intermittent rain. We carried mainsail
6		1.9				and foresail. After 5 o'clock[235] the cloud
7	SE¾S	2.		S¾W	2½	cover slightly dissipated, and we saw between NbE and ENE a shore with high mountains, the nearest ones
8		1.7				to NEbN½E at a distance of 16 miles.[236]
9	SE¾S	2.2	EbN	S¾W	2½	From 8 o'clock to noon the same weather, we carried mainsail,
10	NNE½E	2.2		NbE½E	2½	foresail.
11		2.0				At 12 o'clock we unbent reefs of
	⎰	1.				mainsail and foresail.
12	⎱NbW½N	1.		NbW½N	1½	

In all   55.8

Table of daily reckoning	Latitudes		Diff. of latitude			Departure		Rhumb	Distance		Diff. of longitude		Compass declination
	from	to	N	S		E	W		right	added	daily	total	
Reckoned	65°35'88	65°33'30		2'58			7'00	WSW 2°16 W	7.46				
Corrected	65°40'41	65°37'78		2'63			7'13	the same	7.60	18.50	17'35 W	18°53'89 b E	1½ R east

Hours	Rhumbs	Miles	Winds	Right rhumbs	Leeway	Wed. 2 August 1728. Different events while at sea
1	NNE	⎫		NbE	2½	The weather dull and rainy.
2		⎪				By 2 o'clock rain stopped, and we saw land
3		⎪				on all sides.
4		⎬1.0	calm			From 12 o'clock to 7 calm, and we stood
5		⎪				at the same place.[237] Depth 50 sazhens,
6		⎪				bottom – silt.
7		⎭				By 8 o'clock a soft wind blew, and we ran from the bay. We held mainsail, foresail, topsail.
8	SEbS¼S	3.	NE	SSE¾S		Starry night, but to the W dark clouds.
9	SE	2.3	NE	SEbS½S		From 8 o'clock to midnight we held
10		2.5	-	-		1 foresail. By 11 o'clock wind increased.
11	ESE½E	3.3	-	SE		Land from us to ENE 5 miles away,
12	-	3.3	-	-	-	extending to E,[238] depths 10 and 12 sazhens, bottom – stone.
1	SE	1.8	NE	SEbS½S	-	From midnight to 4 o'clock the weather
2	SEbS½S	1.	-	SbE		was with drifting clouds, strong breeze.
		.5				We held only foresail. At 2:30 a.m.
3	SEbE¼S	1.4	-	SE¾S		we hoisted mainsail.
4		1.8				From 4 o'clock to 8 the weather and
5	E	2.5	NEbN½E	SEbE½S	2	wind the same. We carried mainsail
6		2.6				and foresail. From 2 o'clock we began
7		2.6				to run with wind on the bow.
8	NWbN[239]	3.0	NNE	NW½N	2	
9	NWbN	2.2	NNE	NW¼N	2¼	From 8 o'clock to noon the weather
10	NWbN¾N	2.2	NEbN	NWbN	2¼	cloudy, with a few sunny spells, fresh breeze.
11		1.7				We carried the same sails.
12	NW½N	2.5	NNE	NWbW½N	2½	At noon the latitude of fix was found – 65°25'N.

In all   41.2

Table of daily reckoning	Latitudes		Diff. of latitude		Departure		Rhumb	Distance		Diff. of longitude		Compass declination
	from	to	N	S	E	W		right	added	daily	total	
Reckoned	65°33'30	65°20'74		12'56	9'36		SEbS 2°57 by E	15.66				
Corrected	65°37'78	65°25'		12'78	9'53		the same	15.95	38.44	22'97	19°16'86 b E	1½ R eastern

Folio 48, continuation

Hours	Rhumbs	Miles	Winds	Right rhumbs	Leeway	Sat. 3 August 1728. Different events while at sea
1	NW½N	2.5	NNE	NWbW¾N	2½	Soon after 12 jib was lowered.
						The weather overcast, strong breeze and rain.
2		3.		NW¼N	2	We held mainsail and foresail.
3		3.				At 3 o'clock we hoisted the jib. Gentle breeze and rain.
4	EbN½E	2.6		SEbE¼S		Soon after 4 o'clock drizzle, wind decreased.
5	EbN½E	1.5	NNE	SE¼S	3	Land was seen on both sides, since we
6		1.2				were sailing back to the bay at which we called
7		1.				yesterday, in order to find a convenient
8	NEbN	.5	E	NbE¾E	3	place to get fresh water.
9	NNW	.4	calm	NbW¼N	½	At 7 o'clock jib was lowered.
10		0.0				From 8 o'clock calm, the weather overcast,
11	NWbN	1.2	NNE	NW¼N	2½	and until 10 o'clock, because of still, we had the mainsail at clewline.
12		1.6				From midnight the weather overcast with
1	NWbN	1.6	NNE	NW½N	2	rain, light breeze, we carried
2	⌠	.8				mainsail, foresail.
	⌊ENE	.8	NbE½E	EbS¼S	1½	
3		1.6				
4		1.				
5	⎫					From 4 o'clock till 8 rain and fog, very light breeze, and the ship drifted on the waves.
6	⎬SbE	.7		S¾W		
7	⎭					
8	WNW	.8	⌠the same ⌊S and W calm	NWbW¾N		From 8 o'clock to noon cloudy and calm.
9						From 8 to 10 we had mainsail at clewline.
10						By 11 o'clock gentle breeze blew from S. We
11	E	1.	SbE	EbS¾S		hoisted mainsail, foresail, topsail and ran
12	EbS	1.8		EbS¾S		from the bay.[240]
						By 12 o'clock a little sunshine broke through the fog.

In all   28.6

Table of daily reckoning	Latitudes		Diff. of latitude		Departure		Rhumb	Distance		Diff. of longitude		Compass declination
	from	to	N	S	E	W		right	added	daily	total	
Reckoned	65°25'	65°29'39	4'39			4'27	NWbN 10° 27' by W	6.13				
Corrected	65°25'	65°30'5	5'50			5'35	the same	7.68	18.63	12'84 W	19°04'02 b E	1¾ R eastern

128

Folio 48 verso

Hours	Rhumbs	Miles	Winds	Right rhumbs	Leeway	Sun. 4 August 1728. Different events while at sea aboard the Archangel Gabriel
1	ESE	2.1	SbE½S	SEbE¼S	½	The weather overcast, gentle breeze. We had all sails, except forestaysail.
2	SWbW	1.4	-	WbS¾W	1	At 1:30 o'clock we saw the land to E½S, which on the second day of this month we
3	WSW	1.4	S½W	W¾N	1	saw from the bay to 63° from S by E,[241]
4	SEbE	2.	-	SEbE½S	1¼	and turned bow to the wind to SWbW. At 2:30 o'clock the land, from which we
5	ESE	2.	S½W	ESE½E	1¼	turned at 1:30 o'clock, was on our left to
6		1.6				EbN¾E.
7		1.3				At 8 o'clock there was a considerable
8		.6				current from the shore to SbW.[242]
	SbW	.4		SSW¾W	E[243]	From 8 o'clock cloudy and very calm.[244]
9	SSW	.1		SWbS¾W		
10		.2	calm			At 11 o'clock gentle breeze blew from N.
11		.2				From midnight cloudy, calm air. We
12	ENE	2.2	NNW	EbN¾E		held mainsail and foresail.
1	E½S	2.8	NbW	SSE¼E		At 3 o'clock we hoisted topsail and jib.
2	E	3.4		EbS¾S		At 2 and 3 o'clock it was raining.
3	EbN	4.1		E¾S		A land with high mountains extends to NEbE from us at a distance of 8
4	ENE	3.1		EbN¾E		miles to NNW.[245] From 4 o'clock cloudy
5	NEbN	1.5		NEbE¼E	½	without rain, light breeze. We carried
	NE	1.8	NbW	ENE¼E	½	mainsail, foresail, topsail, jib.
6		3.3			½	The shore lies at a distance of 2 miles
7		2.5			½	from us. Low land extends to ENE and
8	ENE	2.2	NbE½E	E¼S	½	SSW, but there are stone mountains about 4 miles from the shore.[246] They are situated parallel to the shore.
9	EbN½E	2.2	NbE	ESE	¾	From 8 o'clock cloudy, moderate breeze. We ran parallel to the shore 2 miles away.
10	ENE½E	1.8	NbE	E¾S	½	Depth – 10 sazhens, the
11	EbN	1.0	NNE	SSE¼E	1½	bottom – small stones. At 11 o'clock rain, calm air. We carried
12	EbS½S	.9	NE	SE¾S		mainsail, foresail, topsail, jib.

In all   49.2

Table of daily reckoning	Latitudes		Diff. of latitude		Departure		Rhumb	Distance		Diff. of long.		Compass declination
	from	to	N	S	E	W		right	added	daily	total	
Reckoned	65°29'39	65°21'57		7'82	35'68		ESE 10°08 by E	36.53				
Corrected	65°30'5	65°20'7		9'80	44'71		the same	45.78	109.8	1°47'2 E	20°51'22 b E	1¾ R east

Folio 48 verso, continuation

Hours	Rhumbs	Miles	Winds	Right rhumbs	Leeway	Mon. 5 August 1728. Different events while at sea
1	EbS½S	1.5	NEbE	SE¼S	1	The weather gloomy and foggy with
2	EbN½E	2.	NEbN	ESE½E	1	continuous rain.
3	EbN	2.		SSE¼E	1½	
4		1.5				At 6 o'clock rain stopped, and the shore
5	ENE	1.8	NEbN	E¾S	1	appeared at a distance of 5 miles.
6	NEbE	2.	NbW½N	EbN¾E	1	We saw then in front of us a high
7	ENE½E	3.		E¼S	½	land to 75° from N by E.[247] At 7 o'clock land was seen to 85° from S by E.[248] From noon we carried mainsail, foresail, topsail, jib.
8	EbN	5.5	NNE½E	SSE¼E		
9	ENE	1.5	NNE½E	EbS	1¾	From 9 o'clock cloudy, gentle breeze. We carried mainsail and foresail.
10		1.9				At 10 o'clock drizzling, the shore is from us in 6 miles to NNW and extends
11		2.		EbS¼S	1½	to NE½E and forms a bay,[249] then returns to ESE and SE. We reckon the return of the shore to S is 12 miles away.[250]
12	EbN	1.6		ESE	1¾	
1	EbS	1.2	NE½E	SEbE¼S	0½	After midnight gloomy, light breeze, at 3 o'clock changeable wind.
2	⎰	.7	variab.			At 3 o'clock wind changeable, at the
	⎱ SE	.6		SSE¼S	do.	same time we hoisted topsail and jib. Then wind rose.
3	NNW	2.	NEbN	NNW¾N	1	
4	NNW½N	3.		NbW¼N	1	From 4 o'clock murky. We carried
5	NWbN½N	3.1	NEbN	NW¾N	2½	mainsail, foresail, topsail, jib.
6	NNW	3.4		NNW¼N	1½	At 6 o'clock heavy rain.
7	NWbN½N	1.3		NW¾N	2½	By 8 o'clock rain stopped and we saw
8		2.1				the shore, in front of which we
9	NNW½N	3.	NEbN	NNW¾N	1½	maneuvered yesterday.
10	NWbN½N	3.1	NNE	NWbN¾N		From 8 o'clock cloudy. We carried the
11	NWbN	3.2	NbE½E	NWbN	1¾	same sails. By 10 o'clock it cleared up.
12	ENE½E	2.0	NNE	ESE		

In all   55.0

Table of daily reckoning	Latitudes		Diff. of latitude		Departure		Rhumb	Distance		Diff. of longitude		Compass declination
	from	to	N	S	E	W		right	added	daily	total	
Reckoned	65°21'57	65°32'81	11'24		18'02		NEbE 2°42' by E	21.24				
Corrected	65°20'7	65°34'78	14'08		22'58		the same	36.62	63.91	54'21	21°45'43 b E	1¾ R eastern

Hours	Rhumbs	Miles	Winds	Right rhumbs	Leeway	Tue. 6 August 1728. Different events while at sea
1	E¼S	3.4	NEbN	SEbE	1R	Cloudy with intermittent sunshine, strong breeze,
2	NWbN½N	3.5		NNW¼N	⌈1R	and at times moderate gale. During both watches
3	⌈	4.3			⌊	we had all sails, except forestaysail, only at 6 o'clock
	⌊SEbE	.9	NE½E	SEbS¼S	½	jib was lowered because of gusty winds. Also, the
4	⌈	2.7		SSE¼S	1½	topsail halyard broke near the lower block, and until
	⌊NNW	2.7	NEbN	NbW¼N	1R	7 o'clock we carried no topsail while the halyard was
5	⌈NNW½N	2.9	NEbN	NbW¾N	1R	being spliced.
	⌊NbW	1.2				At 8 o'clock wind dropped. All the time from midnight to 8 o'clock we maneuvered by the
6	SEbE	2.1		SSE¾S	2	shore to take fresh water, since we had
7	ESE	2.9		SEbS¼S	1½	only one barrel of water.
8	⌈	3.0		SSE¼S	2½	From 8 o'clock cloudy, light breeze.
	⌊EbN	1.5		SEbE¼S	2½	We held mainsail, foresail, topsail.
9	EbN	2.5	NEbN	ESE½E	2	By 10 o'clock the wind began to rise.
10		2.5				By 11 o'clock topsail was lowered. At 12
11	ENE	3.	NNE	EbS¾S	2	o'clock strong gale, and we ran under mainsail
12	ENE½E	1.5		SE¼S	4	only. From midnight cloudy, moderate gale.
1	ENE	1.3	NbE	SE¾S	5	We held mainsail only.
2	EbN	4.5		EbS¾S	2	At 2 o'clock we hoisted foresail and jib. At the end of the same hour wind rose considerably,
3		6.1		EbS¾S	1	jib was lowered. The shore extended to ENE
4		6.5		EbS¼S	½	at a distance of 17 miles.
5	EbS	7.8	NW	EbS¾S		And at 5:30 o'clock we turned to SSE.
6	⌈ESE	4.0		SEbE¼S		From 5 o'clock cloudy, strong gale. We held
	⌊SE	3.4		SEbS¾S		mainsail, foresail, topsail. At 6 o'clock we drew near a point of rocky mountains at a distance of 200 sazhens,[251] and the mountains stretched to E by compass.[252] They were all very high and equally steep, like a wall, and variable winds blew from the ravines between the mountains.
7	SEbE	2.8		SE¾S		
8	⌈EbS	1.5		EbS¾S		From 8 a.m. cloudy with sunny spells, strong
	⌊E	1.5		EbS¾S		and variable gale from the valleys lying between mountains.
9	E	2.8				At 10 o'clock we went between the mountains into
10		4.0				a small inlet.[253] A drawing of it was made on the map.[254] Here we dropped anchor. The depth under
11						vessel 10 sazhens, the bottom – stones, not very
12						large, and broken slabs.[255] By 11 o'clock I was sent to the shore in the boat with 6 men for observing the position of the inlet and measuring the depth, and most of all to find fresh water.

In all   86.8

Table of daily reckoning	Latitudes		Diff. of latitude latitude		Departure		Rhumb	Distance		Diff. of long.		Compass declination
	from	to	N	S	E	W		right	added	daily	total	
Reckoned	65°32'81	65°06'06		26'75	51'04		SEbE 6°06' by E	57'62				
Corrected	65°34'78	65°01'26		33'52	63'93		the same	72'21	172.8	2°33'	24°18'43 18'433	1¾ R eastern

Folio 49, continuation

Hours	Rhumbs	Miles	Winds	Right rhumbs	Leeway	Wed. 7 August 1728. Different events while at sea[256]
						By 1 p.m., having gone about 3 versts from the ship along the shore, we found a place where natives had their dwelling that year and saw that many paths had been worn around the mountains. And I found fresh water: a stream of melted snow flows from the mountains. The weather gloomy, at times strong gale from N with turns by E and W, blowing from the lowlands between mountains. At 5 o'clock I arrived at the ship and reported what I had seen. On the way back to the ship we had found fresh water from the melting snow running from a high cliff only some 100 sazhens from the ship, and we sent men to fill barrels. At 6 o'clock drizzle, calm air. From midnight to 8 o'clock strong gale at times, and at others light breeze. From 8 to 11 o'clock gloomy, at 12 sunshine, light shifting breeze between N and E. From 11:30 wind from E. And at the end of that hour we raised anchor and went. We took 22 barrels of water.

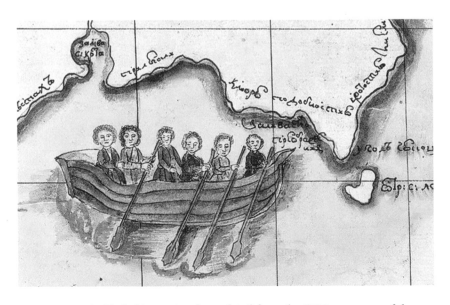

PLATE 26. Chukchi men in a boat, detail from the Göttingen copy of the ethnographic version of the Final Map from the Asch Collection (p. 191).

Courtesy Niedersächsische Staats- und Universitätsbibliothek Göttingen.

Folio 49 verso

Hours	Rhumbs	Miles	Winds	Right rhumbs	Leeway	Thu. 8 August 1728. Different events while at sea aboard the Archangel Gabriel
1	SSE¾S	2.7	SWbW	S½W		The weather cloudy, gentle breeze. We set off on our route, having all sails set, except the forestaysail. At 1:30 o'clock we observed that the shore extended to EbS,[257] and we proceeded parallel to the shore at a distance of 1½ miles. The shore was rocky and high like a wall.
2	[SE	1.8				
		1.1		SEbS¾S		
3	ESE	2.8	WNW	SEbE¾S		
4		1.2				
5	SSW	.6	NbE	SWbS¾W		At 7 o'clock we were in front of a bay 9 miles wide, which extended into the land to NNE.[258] From 4 o'clock to 8 we ran along the shore.
6	ESE	1.2		SEbE¾S		At 8 o'clock the shore was at a short distance to NbE, 5 miles away. From 7 o'clock clear weather, fresh breeze. We took in topsail, and carried mainsail, foresail and jib. From 1 a.m. cloudy, strong breeze. At 2:30 o'clock the shore was 3 miles from us to N.[259]
7	[	1.3				
	EbS	1.3		EbS¾S		
8		2.7				
9	EbS	6.0	N	EbS¾S		At 7 a.m. we saw a small craft paddling out from land toward us, in which 8 men were seated. When they had paddled up near our ship they asked where we had come from and why, and said about themselves that they were Chukchi. But when we invited them to come to the vessel, they for a long time did not dare to come alongside. Then they put one man on a bladder made of seal hide, and sent him to converse with us. And he told us that the Chukchi live along the shore and that there are many of them. They do not know how far the land extends to the east. And they had long ago heard about Russians. The Anadyr' River is far from them to the west. At first he did not mention anything about islands, but later he said that there is an island that can be seen from land on a clear day, if one moves not far from here to the east. Then he returned on the bladder to his boat and persuaded his friends to paddle over to the ship. And they pulled alongside for a very short time, but would not come aboard. And their little boat was made of the hide of sea lion and of other sea creatures. And our interpreters spoke with them in the Koriak tongue, but said that they could not understand each other much. For that reason we could not really obtain the necessary information from them.[260] From 6 o'clock and to 10 calm, and we had all sails taken in. By 11 o'clock we ran under mainsail and foresail, light variable breeze, the weather with sunshine through gloom.
10	E½S	5.0		SSE¼E		
11	E	3.5		EbS¾S		
12		4.0	NbE			
1	E	4.		EbS¾S		
2	E¼S	2.8		ESE		
3	[	1.5				
	SEbE	.5	NEbE	SSE¼S	1½	
4		.6	NNE	SE¾S		
5	E	.5	}vari-	EbS¾S		
6		.2	}able			
7		.1	}			
8						
9						
10						
11	EbS	.7		EbS¾S		
12						

in all 46.1

Table of daily reckoning	Latitudes		Diff. of latitudes		Departure		Rhumb	Distance		Diff. of long.		Compass declination
	from	to	N	S	E	W		right	added	daily	total	
Reckoned	65° 06'06	64° 41'47		24'59	34'59		SE 9°16' by E	42.44				
Corrected	65° 01'26	64° 30'45		30'81	43'35		the same	53.18	124.1	1° 51'2 E	26° 09'63 b E	1¾ R eastern

Conspicuous places	No. of these places	Time of observation	Directions			
			N – E	N – W	S – E	S – W
A mountain near the sea		2 p.m.			76.19	
The same a second time[261]		6:30 p.m.			83.29	
A cape stretching out into the sea[262]		at the same time			73.19	
The same a second time		8 p.m.			75.09	

PLATE 27. The encounter between the *Holy Gabriel* and eight Chukchis in a skin boat on 8 August 1728, painting by Igor Pshenichnyi.

Courtesy the artist. Photo by Nikolai Turkin.

Folio 49 verso, continuation

Hours	Rhumbs	Miles	Winds	Right rhumbs	Leeway	Fri. 9 August 1728. Different events while at sea
1			calm			The weather cloudy and calm.
2	EbS	.2	SSE	SEbE¾S	½	At 2:30 o'clock a thick fog came in.
3	E	1.		SSE¼E		
4	EbS	.8	variable	SEbE¼S		At 4 o'clock rain, and the fog was dispersed.
5	⎫ drif-					From 4 o'clock to 7 downpour. At
6	⎬ ted		calm	NNE¼E		8 o'clock gentle breeze. We
	⎭ to N					hoisted mainsail and foresail and ran.
						The rain stopped.
7						At 7:30 o'clock we had land to ENE, 3
8	SSE	1.6	ESE	SbE¼S	1	miles away.[263]
9	⎧ SEbE	.7	NEbE	SbE½S	2¼	From 8 o'clock gloomy, variable wind by
	⎨ E	.4	NbE	SE½S		N and S, heavy sea. At 9:30 o'clock 1 reef of
	⎩	.4	change-		2½	mainsail was made fast.[264]
10	⎩ ESE	.7	able	SbE¼S	3	
11	SEbE½S	1.8	ENE	S¼W	2½	At 11 o'clock wind rose.
12	ESE½E	2.4		SbE¼S		
1	ESE	1.8	NE	SbE¼S	3	From midnight moonlight, strong breeze,
2	⎧ EbS½S	1.		SSE¾S		at 3 o'clock clear.
	⎩ EbS	1.	NEbE	SSE¼S		
3	E½S	2.	NE½E	SEbS¾S		At 4 o'clock at sunrise we sighted
4	E	2.2	NEbN	SEbS¼S		amplitude of the sun from N by E –
5	EbS	2.3		SSE¼S	3	35°30'. From 5 o'clock the weather
6	E	2.4	NNE	SE¾S	2½	clear, moderate gale.
7	EbN	2.8		SEbE¼S	2	At 9 a.m. we sighted the altitude
	⎧	1.6				supplement of the sun center – 58°16'
8	⎩ NWtN½	1.5		NW¼N	2½	and azimuth from S by E 74°30', and
9	NW	3.5	NbE	NW¼N	2	then we were at the latitude of 64°07'N.[265]
10		2.5				The sun declination – 12°37' and the
						found azimuth – 47°52' from S by E,
11		1.5				compass declination 26°38' east.
12	SSE	.3		S¼W		At 11 o'clock, at the latitude of 64°09'N, we sighted
						the altitude of the sun center 38°09' and azimuth
						35°00' from S by E, sun declination 12°30' N and
						the azimuth found 8°6' from S by E, compass
						declination 26°54' east.
						The latitude of fix by noon observation was found to
						be 64°10'north.

in all   37.5

Table of daily reckoning	Latitudes		Diff. of latitude		Departure		Rhumb	Distance		Diff. of longitude		Compass declination
	from	to	N	S	E	W		right	added	daily	total	
Reckoned	64° 41'47	64° 25'15		16'32	5'34		SbE 6°52 by E	17.17				
Corrected	64° 30'45	64° 10'		20'45	6'69		the same	21.51	50.07	15'57 E	26° 25'20 b E	2¼ R eastern

Hours	Rhumbs	Miles	Winds	Right rhumbs	Leeway	Sat. 10 August 1728. Different events while at sea
1	⌈SSW	.4	NNE	SW¼W		Sunshine, gentle breeze. We carried
	⌊EbN	.9	-	SEbE½S	2¼	mainsail and foresail.
2		1.3	-			
3	ENE	2.4	-	ESE½E		At 3 o'clock wind rose. At 6 o'clock the sky
						covered with clouds.
4	EbN	2.5	-	SEbE½S		
5	NWbN½N	2.4	NNE	NWbN½N	2¼	
6		2.4				
7		2.7				From noon to 8 o'clock we maneuvered
8		3.				off the shore, the extension of which
9	NWbN	2.7	NNE½E	NWbN	2¼	finished by east, and went to NbW½N.[266]
10	E	2.7		SE½S	2¼	From 8 o'clock cloudy, fresh breeze.
11		3.1				We held mainsail and foresail.
12		3.1				
1	E	1.7	NNE½E	SE¾S	2½	From midnight the weather overcast,
2		1.9				wet haze, fresh breeze. We held
3		2.6				mainsail and foresail.
4	NWbN	2.6		NW¾N	2½	
5	NWbN	3.	NNE½E	NWbN¼N	2	From 4 o'clock the weather gloomy, we
6	⌈NW	1.5	⌉vari-	NW¼N		held mainsail and foresail.
	⌊NWbW	1.6	⌡able	NWbW¼N		
7	NWbN	3.0		NWbN¼N		From 8 o'clock the weather the same
8	NW	3.0	NbE	NW¼N		and we held the same sails.
9	NW½N	3.	NNE	NW½N	2¼	At 10 o'clock the shore was 5½ miles
10		3.				away from us to NWbN, from where
11	EbN	3.		SEbE¼S	2	it extended to NbE. At 10 o'clock
12		3.1				we hoisted jib.

in all   62.6

Table of daily reckoning	Latitudes		Diff. of latitude		Departure		Rhumb	Distance		Diff. of longitude		Compass declination
	from	to	N	S	E	W		right	added	daily	total	
Reckoned	64° 10'	64° 18'08	8'08		0'86		N 6°06' by E	8.1				
Corrected	64° 10'	64° 21'69	11'29		1'20		the same	11.32	26.17	2°78' E	26°25' 98 b E	2¼ R eastern

Conspicuous places	No. of these places	time of observation	directions			
			N – E	N – W	S – E	S – W
A point of land by N[267]		10 a.m.		8.26		
The same a second time		12 a.m.		36.01		

Folio 50, continuation

Hours	Rhumbs	Miles	Winds	Right rhumbs	Leeway	Sun. 11 August 1728. Different events while at sea
1	EbS	2.2	NE	SEbS¾S	2½	The weather cloudy with rare sunshine, light air.
2		2.2			2½	At 2 o'clock we saw a land on the right side to SSE, which we believed was an island.[268]
3	⌈	1.0				At 2:30 o'clock we ran toward the island that
	⌊ESE	.6			1½	had been sighted at 2 o'clock.
4	SEbE	2.5		SEbS¼S	1½	
5	SE	2.8	NE	SSE¼S	⌉	
6		2.5	NE		⎬1½	At 7:30 o'clock we saw a land to SEbE½S, and
7		3.2			⎪	the middle of the island, which had been seen
8	SEbE	4.5		SEbS¼S	⌋	previously, was at this time 4½ miles away from us to SbE. The depth 15 sazhens, bottom
9	⌈EbS½S	1.4		SEbS¾S	2	– sand with silt.
	⌊NNW	.4	NE	NWbN¾N		From 8 o'clock murky, and wet fog.[269]
10		.5			⎫2½	At 8:45 o'clock the depth 11 sazhens
11	NbW	1.2		NNW¾N	⎬	and the Captain gave orders to turn
12		0.8			⌋	the ship to the other side of the wind.
1	NNE	.8	variable	NbE¾E	2½	From 12 o'clock to 4 calm air and thick wet fog. The depths were 14 and 15 sazhens,
2	NbE	1.	ENE	N¾E	⎫2½	the bottom – sand. We carried mainsail and
3		1.			⌋	foresail.
4	NbE½E	1.		NbE¾E	2	From 4 o'clock to 8 thick fog, and temporary
5	N½E	1.5	ENE	NbW¾N	3	clearing, strong breeze, depth of
6	NbW	2.4	NE	NbW¼N	⌉	the sea 15 and 16 sazhens, at 8 o'clock
7	NbW½N	2.3	NE	NbW¾N	⎬2	18 sazhens.
8	NNW½N	2.4	NEbN	NNW¾N	⌋	From 8 o'clock to noon thick fog and
9	NNW	3.0	NEbN	NNW¼N	2	a few glimpses of sunshine, moderate gale.
10	NW½N	3.5	NbE	NWbN¼N	⎫	
11		3.5			⎬1½	We held mainsail and foresail.
12		3.5		NW¾N	2	

in all 52.7

Table of daily reckoning	Latitudes		D. of latitude		Departure		Rhumb	Distance		Diff. of longitude		Compass declination
	from	to	N	S	E	W		right	added	daily	total	
Reckoned	64° 18'08	64° 23'26	5'18		2'59		NNE 4°04 by E	5'79				
Corrected	64° 21'69	64° 28'53	7'24		3'62		the same	8'09	18.64	8'35 E	26°34'33 b E	2¼ R eastern

Conspicuous places	No. of these places	Time of observation	Directions			
			N – E	N – W	S – E	S – W
S point of the island		1h 54 min p.m.			2.41	
E point of the same island[270]		the same time			12.41	
Again S point		3½ p.m.				4.19
Again E point		the same time			5.41	

Folio 50 verso

Hours	Rhumbs	Miles	Winds	Right rhumbs	Leeway	Mon. 12 August 1728. Different events at sea aboard the Archangel Gabriel
1	NW½N	2.6	NNE	NW¾N	2	The weather foggy, rare sun breaking
	EbN	.4		SEbE¼S	2	through fog, strong gale. We held
						mainsail and foresail. At 1 o'clock[271]
2	EbN½E	3.		SE¼S	2½	we made fast 1 reef of mainsail.
3	E	1.5		SE¼S		
	E½S	1.5	NEbN	SE¾S	2R	At 5 o'clock wind rose, fog was
4	E	3.		SE¼S		dispersed and there was intermittent
5	EbN	2.5	NEbN	SEbE¼S	2	sunshine.
6	E	4.5		SEbE¾S		At 8 o'clock at sunset we sighted
7	NW¾N	2.3	NNE	NWbN½N	1½	the amplitude of the sun from N by W
8		4.7		NW¼N	2¾	87°30', and then we were at the
						latitude 64°23'N, and the sun
9	NW½N	2.	NNE	NWbW¾N		declination 11°43'N, amplitude was
						found 61°59' from N by W, compass
10		2.			3	declination 25°31' east.
11		2.				From 8 o'clock we ran under mainsail
12		2.				only. Strong gale.
1	EbS	2.2	NNE	SbE	3¾	After midnight the weather cloudy,
2	ESE	2.2		S		strong gale, we carried mainsail only.
3	ESE	.8				
	SE	.8		SbW¾W	3½	
4		.6				At 4 o'clock wind dropped and we
	NbE	.9	NEbE½E	N½E	2¾	hoisted foresail.
5	NbE	3.	NEbE½E	NbE¼E	2	From 4 o'clock cloudy, strong breeze,
						we carried mainsail, foresail, jib, and
6		3.		NbE½E	1¾	unbent one reef of mainsail.
7		3.				
8	NNE	3.	EbN	NNE½E	1¾	
9	NbE	2.8		NNE¼E		
10	N½E	2.8		NbE¾E	1	Weather cleared up, fresh breeze.
11		3.				We carried the same sails.
12	NbE	4.7		NNE¼E		At noon we observed the latitude of
	N½E	2.8		NbE½E	1¼	fix – N 64°59'.
	in all	69.6				

Table of daily reckoning	Latitudes		Diff. of latitude		Departure		Rhumb	Distance		Diff. of longitude		Compass declination
	from	to	N	S	E	W		right	added	daily	total	
Reckoned	64°23'26	64°45'06	21'8		10'16		NNE 2°29' by E	24.06				
Corrected	64°28'53	64°59'	30'47		14'20		the same	33.63	78.8	33'28 E	27°07'61 b E	2¼ R E

Conspicuous places	No. of these places	Time of observation	Rhumbs	Distance in miles
A black outline, probably of E shore		8 p.m.	NWbW	
Land behind us		10½ a.m.	SWbS½W	15

Folio 50 verso, continuation

Hours	Rhumbs	Miles	Winds	Right rhumbs	Leeway	Tue. 13 August 1728. Different events while at sea
1	NbE	5.2	E	NEbN¼E		The weather cloudy, strong breeze, we
2		5.2				held mainsail, foresail, topsail.
3	NbE½E	5.		NEbN¾E		At 1:45 o'clock topsail was lowered and we
						ran under mainsail and foresail.
4		5.				At 4 o'clock strong gale rose and
						a reef of mainsail was unbent.
5	NbE½E	3.		NNE¾E	1	From 4 o'clock wet fog came on, until
6	NbE	4.2	EbN	NEbN¼E		5 o'clock we carried mainsail only,
7		4.		NNE¼E	1	then hoisted foresail.
8		3.5		NNE	1¼	
9	NbE¼E	3.7	EbN	NEbN½E		From 8 o'clock the weather cloudy, fresh
						breeze. We held mainsail and foresail.
10		3.7				
11		3.7				
12	NEbN	2.7		NNE¼E	3	By 12 o'clock foresail was lowered.
1		1.8	EbN	NbE¾E		From midnight gloomy, fresh breeze. We ran
2		1.8			}3½	under mainsail only until 3 o'clock.
						At 3:15 o'clock we hoisted foresail and
3		2.4				jib. Wind rose and rough sea.
4	NbE½E	5.5		NEbN¾E		
5	NbE	4.7	ESE	NEbN¼E		From 5 o'clock gloomy, fresh breeze.
6		4.7				We carried mainsail, foresail and jib.
7		4.0				
8		4.1				
9	N	4.1	ESE	NNE¼E		From 8 o'clock to noon gloomy, at times drizzling.
10		4.5	SE			We carried mainsail, foresail, jib. At 10 o'clock topsail
						was hoisted.
11		4.5				
12		3.5	E			By 12 o'clock we unbent a reef of mainsail.

in all   94.5

Table of daily reckoning	Latitudes		Diff. of latitude		Departure		Rhumb	Distance		Diff. of longitude		Compass declination
	from	to	N	S	E	W		right	added	daily	total	
Reckoned	64°59'	66°17'14	78'14		50'41		NNE 10°20' by E	92.98				
Corrected	64°59'	66°17'14	78'14		50'41		the same	92.98	225.4	2°02'2 E	29°09'81 b E	2¼ R eastern

139

Folio 51

Hours	Rhumbs	Miles	Winds	Right rhumbs	Leeway	Wed. 14 August 1728. Different events while at sea aboard the Holy Archangel Gabriel
1	N	2.4	E	NNE¼E		The weather overcast, gentle breeze.
2		1.				We carried mainsail, foresail, topsail, jib. At 2 o'clock calm, and jib was lowered,
3	NWbN	.9	NEbN	NWbN¼N		mainsail was taken in at brails.
4		.9			2	From 4 o'clock to 8 the weather the same.
5	WbN	.3	calm	NWbW¼N		We held foresail and topsail.
6	WNW½N	1.	NbE	WNW¾N	2	The depth of the sea 25 sazhens.
7		.6		WNW	2¾	
8	WNW¼N	.4	calm	WNW¾N	2	From 8 o'clock to midnight calm air,
9	SW	.1	NbW	WSW¼W		the weather cloudy and very dark.
10		.2				We drifted without sails.
11		.1				From midnight to 2 o'clock we drifted without sails, then hoisted mainsail, foresail, jib.
12		.2				
1	SbW	.5		SWbS¼W		
2						
3	NbE	1.8	NWbW¼N	NE	¾	From 4 o'clock to 8 the weather cloudy, with fog. We carried the same sails.
4		1.8			do.	From 8 o'clock cloudy, fresh breeze.
5	N	1.8	NWbW	NE¾E		We held mainsail, foresail and jib.
6		2.				By 12 o'clock rain.
7		2.3			2½	In this place we took into account the sea current to NWbW by compass,
8	NbE	2.	NW	NEbE¾E		though sometimes there was an opposite
9		1.8		NEbE	1¾	current. However, during our sailing
10		1.8			do.	here the current was mostly in the shown direction. For that reason we entered
11	NbE½E	3.		NEbE¾E		into the reckoning for this day, 8¾ miles
12		3.			2	by the right compass, and the current
	In all	29.9				NNW 8°28' by W, because the compass declination was taken 2¼ R east without
Sea current	NWbW	8¾		NNW 8°28' by W		small minutes, but those did not affect the correction of other rhumbs.
	In all	38.65				

Table of daily reckoning	Latitudes		Diff. of latitude		Departure		Rhumb	Distance		Diff. of longitude		Compass declination
	from	to	N	S	E	W		right	added	daily	total	
Reckoned												
Corrected	66°17'14	66°41'34	24'20		10'63		NNE 1°13' by E	26.43	66.19	26'62	29° 36'43 b E	2¼ R eastern

Conspicuous places	No. of these places	Time of observation	Rhumbs	Distance in miles
A high land behind us[272]		3 p.m.	SbW	20
High mountains, probably on the big land[273]		6:30 p.m.	between WbS and WNW	15

Folio 51, continuation

Hours	Rhumbs	Miles	Winds	Right rhumbs	Leeway	Thu. 15 August 1728. Different events while at sea
1	WbS½W	2.8	NWbN	W	1¾	The weather cloudy, strong breeze,
2		2.8		WbS¾W	2	at times fog. We carried mainsail and
3		1.5		⎱		foresail until 8 p.m.
4		1.5		⎰2	2	
5	SWbW½W	2.7	NWbW	SWbW½W	2¼	
6		2.7		⎱		
	⎰	1.1		⎰SWbW¾W	2	
7	⎱SW	1.	WNW	SW¾W	1½	
8	⎡NbW	.9		NEbN¾E	2½	From 8 o'clock to midnight the weather
	⎣NNW	.9	WbN	NNE¾E		gloomy and intermittent rain.
9	NNW½N	2.2		NEbN¾E	⎱	We carried the same sails.
10		2.3			⎰2½	
11		2.2		NNE¾E	2	
12		3.		NNE¼E	1½	From midnight to 4 o'clock very wet
1	NNW	1.5	WbN	NEbN¾E	⎱	fog, gentle breeze. For 3½ hours we ran
2		1.5			⎰3½	under one mainsail only, then hoisted
3		1.5				foresail.
4		1.6		NEbN¼E	3	From 4 o'clock to 8 the same weather.
5	NNW	2.3	WbN	NNE½E	⎱	We carried the same sails. Today
6		2.2				we saw a considerable number of whales.
7		2.			⎰2¼	From the 12th of this month the sea
						water is white in color, depths 20, 25
8	NbW	1.9		NEbN½E		and 30 sazhens. From 8 o'clock to noon
9	NbW½N	1.9	WNW	NE	2¼	overcast with a little intermittent sunshine
						through the murk.
10		2.1		NEbN¾E	2	At 10 o'clock we hoisted jib.
						Sea current the same as it was
11		2.7		NEbN½E	⎱	recorded on the 14th [of August].
12		2.6			⎰1¾	
sea						In the table, the sailing of the
current	NWbW	8¾		NNW		16th [of August] has been reckoned till
				8°28'W		the Turnaround, that is until 3 o'clock p.m.[274]

in all   66.15 with addition.[275]

Table of daily reckoning	Latitudes		Diff. of latitude		Departure		Rhumb	Distance		Diff. of longitude		Compass declination
	from	to	N	S	E	W		right	added	daily	total	
Reckoned												
Corrected	66°41'34	67°18'48	37'14			15'68	NNE 1°7' by E	40.4	103.4	40'61	30°17'04 b E	2¼ R eastern

Hours	Rhumbs	Miles	Winds	Right rhumbs	Leeway	Fri. 16 August 1728. Different events while at sea aboard the Holy Archangel Gabriel
1	N	2.6	WNW	NE	1¾	The weather cloudy. Fresh breeze.
2	NbE	2.4	NWbW		¾	We had mainsail, foresail, jib.
3		2.			do.	At 3 o'clock the Captain announced that in accordance with the decree he must turn back, and, turning the ship, he gave
4	SbE	2.6		SbW¼W		orders to hold to SbE.[276]
5		2.7	NW			From 4 o'clock to 8 the weather and wind
6		3.5				the same.
7		3.5				We carried mainsail, foresail, topsail and jib.
8		5.3				From 8 o'clock to midnight cloudy with
9	SbE	4.7	NW	SbW¼W		moonlight and stars, strong breeze. We carried mainsail, foresail, topsail and jib.
10		4.7				
11		4.				
12		4.2				From midnight cloudy, fresh breeze.
1	SbE	5.3	NW			We carried the same sails. At 8 o'clock
2	SbE¼S	5.2		SbW½W		jib was lowered.
3	SbE	3.8		SbW¼W		From 3 o'clock to 8 the same weather.
4	S	4.6		SSW¼W		We carried the above-mentioned sails,
5	S	5.	NW	SSW¼W		at 7 o'clock jib was lowered.
6		6.3				
7		6.5				
8	SSW	7.5				From 8 o'clock to noon gloomy, moderate
9		7.	NW			gale. We carried mainsail and foresail.
10	SW	2.		WSW¼W		At 10 o'clock we hoisted jib.
	SSW	1.3		SW¼W		
		1.2				
	S	1.		SSW¼W		
11	SbE¾S	7.		SSW		At 12 o'clock the land was from us on
12		6.8				the right side, to S¼W, 13 miles distant, from where it extends to SSW and NW.[277]
Sea current	NWbW	8.75	NW	NNW 8°28' by W		The sea current was the same as on the previous 2 days.

In all   114.45   with subtraction of what was added to the 15th [of August].[278]

Table of daily reckoning	Latitudes		Diff. of latitude		Departure		Rhumb	Distance		Diff. of longitude		Compass declination
	from	to	N	S	E	W		right	added	daily	total	
Reckoned	67° 18'48	65° 51'79		86°69		46°52	SSW 5°43' by W	98.39				
Corrected	67° 18'48	66° 02'5		75°98		40°77	the same	86.23	217.9	1°43' by W		2¼ R east

Conspicuous places	No. of these places	Time of observation	Rhumbs	Distance in miles
A mountain, on which Chukchi live[279]	1	9 a.m.	SW½W	20
High mountains on the right side[280]	2	12 a.m.	S¼W	13
A land on left, presumed an island[281]	3	at the same time	between SEbE½S and EbS½S	16

Folio 51 verso, continuation

Hours	Rhumbs	Miles	Winds	Right rhumbs	Lee-way	Sat. 17 August 1728. Different events while at sea
1	SbE	8.	NNW	SbW¼W		The weather overcast, moderate gale. We held mainsail,
2	⎡SbW	5.5		SWbS¼W		foresail and jib. At 1:30 o'clock the shore was from us
	⎣SSW	2.5		SW¼W		to WbN, ⅓ miles distant. We ran parallel to the shore
3	⎡SSW½W	3.5		SW¾W		and saw on the shore a considerable number of people
	⎣SbW½W	3.		SWbS¾W		and in 2 places their dwellings.[282] When they saw us,
4	SbW½W	6.8				they ran to the high rocky mountain.
5	SbW¾W	7.5	NNW	SW		At 2 o'clock strong gale rose, therefore
6		7.5				we took in mainsail at brails, and jib
7	SbW½W	6.5		SWbS¾W		was lowered, and we made fast 1 reef of mainsail. Soon after 2 o'clock we hoisted mainsail. At 2:15 o'clock we passed a high land and the end of the mountains was 1 mile away from us to NbW.[283] After the mountains a
8	SSW	7.		SW¼W		lowland began, and from us its extent was
9	SWbS	6.	NNW	SWbW¼W		seen to NWbW in 5½ miles, and its further
10		4.5				extension was not seen because of fog.
11		3.1				At 3 o'clock a high land was seen to WbN,
12		4.	NWbW			5 miles distant and extending to SSW.[284]
1	SWbS	6.5		SWbW¼W		The weather cloudy with sunny spells, and at times fog came in.
2		6.7				At 6:30 o'clock there was a high mountain to WtN½W
3	SbW½W	6.8		SWbS¾W		from us, ½ miles away, with a small bay beneath.[285]
4	⎡SbW	3.2		SWbS¼W		From 9 o'clock cloudy, strong gale. We held
	⎣SbE	3.5		SbW¼W		mainsail and foresail ⅔ taken at brails. At
5	SE½S	5.3	NWbW	SSE¾S		10 o'clock wind dropped and mainsail was
6	SSE½S	7.		S¾W		hoisted. At midnight moonlight and stars.
7	S	6.7		SSW¼W		How far the land was we could not determine because
8	⎡	4.4				of darkness. At 2 o'clock we saw land to SbW, 1½ miles
	⎣SSE½S	1.4		S¾W		distant,[286] and ran in parallel to the shore.
9	⎡SE	2.6	N	SSE¼S		The shore was sloping, and steep by the sea.
	⎣ESE	2.8		SE¼S		From 4 o'clock slightly cloudy, moderate gale.
	⎡E	1.6		SSE¼E		At 6 o'clock we passed a point of land, on which there
10	⎢SSE	2.5		S¼W		was a dwelling, ½ miles from us to WbN, and we ran
	⎣SSW	2.		SW¼W		to another point that came into sight ahead of us, and
11	SWbS½W	4.		SWbW¾W		had a bay on the right hand.[287] At noon we sighted the
12		3.5				meridian altitude of sun center from zenith 54°36', and
Sea-current	EbyS¼ and 3'E			SEbE 3' by E		Sun declination 9°45'N and from this was found the latitude of fix 64°21'N.

in all   163.93

Table of daily reckoning	Latitudes		Diff. of latitude		Departure		Rhumb	Distance		Diff. of longitude		Compass declination
	from	to	N	S	E	W		right	added	daily	total	
Reckoned	65° 51'79	63° 56'03		115'76		63'81	SSW 6°22' by W	132.2				
Corrected	66° 02'5	64° 21'		101'50		55'93	the same	115.8	276.4	2°13' 58 E		2¼ R E

Conspicuous places	No. of these places	Time of observation	Rhumbs	Distance in miles
The shore, where we saw people[288]	4	1½ p.m.	WbN	⅓
A high rocky mountain[288]	5	6½ p.m.	W½N	¼
A point of land with dwelling[290]	6	6 a.m.	WbN	½

▶ PLATE 28. Folios 51 verso and 52 of Midshipman Chaplin's journal, with the record of the "turnaround".

Courtesy Russian State Naval Archives (RGAVMF) . Photo by Nikolai Turkin.

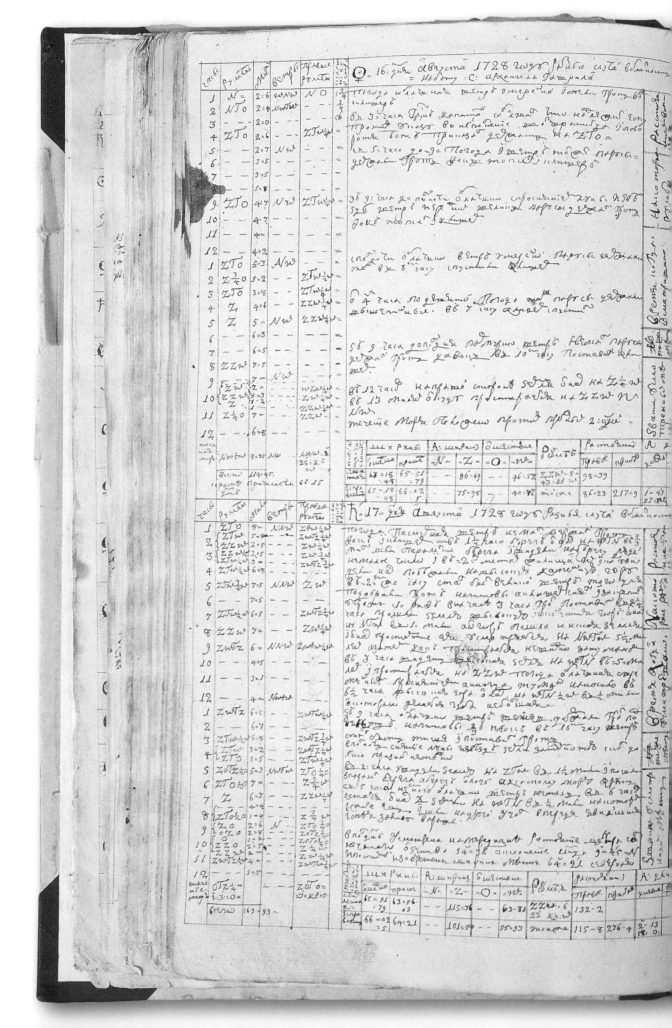

16 дня августа 1728 году

17 дня августа 1728 году

☉ = 18 = день Августа 1728 году ...

... по сю ... Архангела Гаврила =

[текст записи плохо читается]

© 19 = день Августа 1728 году ...

[текст записи плохо читается]

Hours	Rhumbs	Miles	Winds	Right rhumbs	Leeway	Sun. 18 August 1728. Different events while at sea aboard the Holy Archangel Gabriel
1	SWbS½	2.5	N	SWbW½W		Sunshine, gentle breeze. We held mainsail, foresail,
2	SSW	2.1		SW¼W		topsail, jib. We ran parallel to the shore at a short
3		2.5	E			distance from it. In this place there was a great
4		2.2				number[291] of whales in the sea. By 4 o'clock we had
						passed a bay or the mouth of a river, to NWbN,
						5 miles distant, and we believe that it would be
						possible to call at this bay for protection from violent
5	SSW	1.3	variable			weather.[292]
6	SWbW / EbS	.2 / .2	S / SWbS	WbS / SEbE		At 6 o'clock calm, then light breeze from S, and we ran with wind on the bow.
7	SE	1.8	SW	SSE		At 7:45 o'clock we sighted at sunset the sun
8		2.				amplitude from S by W 86°20'.
9	SE	2.8	SSW	SEbS¾S	¼	From 9 o'clock the weather the same, we
	WbS¾W	.6		WNW		carried the same sails.
10	W½N	1.8	variable	WNW¾N	¼	
	NW	.4		NNW¼N		
11	S	3.	SWbW	SbW½W		
						From midnight the weather clear,
12	S½W	3.8	WSW	SSW	½	moonlight and stars. To N side there were
1	SbW	3.3		SSW	1	columns of light in the air,[293] strong breeze.
2	SSW	2.4		SSW½W	1¾	We held mainsail and foresail.
3	SbW	2.3		SbW¼W	1¾	At 5 a.m. we saw the island that
4		2.7				we named St. Lawrence,[294] to
5	SbE¾S	2.6	SWbW	S¼W	1½	73°00' from N by E, 20 miles distant.
6		2.6		S	1¾	At sunrise we sighted amplitude of the sun
7		2.5				from N by E 46°40'.
8	WNW	1.5		NNW½N	2½	From 8 o'clock intermittent sunshine,
9	WbN	1.5	SW	NWbN		moderate gale. We held mainsail and foresail
10		1.6			2	from 4 o'clock to noon.
11	WNW	3.2	SWbW	NNW		At 10 o'clock we sighted altitude of the
12	WbN	3.7	SW	NWbN		sun 27°58' and azimuth from S by E
sea-current	N	15		NNE		75°00'. At 12 o'clock it became murky.

in all [72.1][295]

Table of daily reckoning	Latitudes		Diff. of latitude		Depart.		Rhumb	Distance		Diff. of long.		Compass declination
	from	to	N	S	E	W		right	added	daily	total	
Reckoned												
Corrected	64° 21'	64° 10'35		10'65		19'78	SWbW 5°27' by W	22.47	51.89	45'69 W	25°31'89 E	2 R E

Conspicuous places	No. of these places	Time of observation	Rhumbs	Distance in miles
A point of land extended by W to the sea[296]		at 3 p.m.	WbS½W	4½
W point of the same shore		at 8 p.m.	E½S	14
St. Lawrence Island		at 5 a.m.	ENE 5°30' E	20

Folio 52, continuation

Hours	Rhumbs	Miles	Winds	Right rhumbs	Leeway	Mon. 19 August 1728. Different events while at sea
1	WNW	2.5	SWbW	NWbW¾N	} 2	Gloomy, gentle breeze. We held mainsail and foresail.
2		2.5				
3	WbN½N	1.6		NWbN½N		
4	WbN	1.6		NWbN	} 2¼	From 4 o'clock light breeze and variable. We held the same sails.
5	[WNW	1.4	variab.	NNW¼N		At 8 o'clock the left side-keel[297]
	[NW	.2		N¼E	} 2½	was split. From 7 o'clock to midnight dark, at times drizzle, strong
6	SbE	1.5		SSE¼S		breeze. We carried mainsail and
	[	1.				foresail, and could not see land
7	[SSE	.5		SEbS¼S	}	through the fog.
8	SEbS¾S	2.4		SEbS¼S		
9		2.4	}		} 2	
10	SEbS¼S	2.4	vari-	SE½S		
11		2.4	able			
12		2.	}		}	From midnight the weather foggy, gentle breeze. We carried mainsail
1	[SSE	1.4	SWbS	SEbS¾S	} 2	and foresail, and could not see land
	[W	1.5		WNW¾N		through the fog.
2		2.9				From 3 o'clock, the weather the same
3		2.9		WNW¼N		with wet fog, strong breeze. We
4	WbS½W	3.		NWbW¼N	}	carried mainsail and foresail, and
5		2.6	SWbS	WNW½N		could not see land.
6	W½N	2.2		NWbW½N	} 1½	
7		1.9				
8		1.9	}		}	
9	WSW	2.5	vari-	WbN¼N		At 9 o'clock strong breeze. At 10
10	W½N	3.	able	NWbW¼N		o'clock we hoisted jib, at 11 o'clock
					} 1	it was lowered again. The weather
11		2.5		NWbW¾N		foggy and till noon we did not see
	[W½N	1.3				land through the fog.
12	[SbE	1.2		SbE¼S	}	
sea current	N	15		NbE¾E		

In all   [70.2][298]

Table of daily reckoning	Latitudes		Diff. of latitude				Rhumb	Distance		Diff. of longitude		Compass declination
	from	to	N	S	E	W		right	added	daily	total	
Reckoned												
Corrected	64° 10'35	64° 35'78	25'34			19'16	NWbN 3°15' b W	31.81	73.74	44'38 by W	24°48'51 by E	1 ¾ R E

Hours	Rhumbs	Miles	Winds	Right rhumbs	Leeway	Tue. 20 August 1728. Different events while at sea aboard the Holy Archangel Gabriel
1	SSE½S	2.	SW	SSE¼S	⎫	The weather overcast, moderate breeze. We
2		2.3			⎬ 2½	carried mainsail, foresail until 8 p.m.
						and could not see land through the fog.
3		2.1				From 8 o'clock dark and calm. At 10
4		2.			⎭	o'clock dead still. We then took in sails.
5	WbN	2.3	SW	NW¼N	1½	From midnight to 4 o'clock the same weather
6	WbN½N	2.4			1	with wet fog. We lay to without sails because of still air.
						At 2 o'clock we measured depth
7	W½N	2.		NWbW¾N	⎫	– 17 sazhens, at 4 o'clock – 15 sazhens,
8	WbS½W	3.2		WNW¼N	⎬ 1	on a rocky bottom.
9	SSE½S	2.5	SW	SSE½S	⎫	From 5 o'clock to 7:30 the weather the
10	SSE	1.5		SSE	⎬ 1¾	same. We lay to without sails.
11	⎫					At 6 o'clock the depth – 18 sazhens. At 8
	⎬ NEbN	.5				o'clock it cleared slightly and we saw the
12			⎫			shore ½ mile distant. Gentle breeze rose from
1	⎬		⎬ calm	NE¾E		N and we hoisted mainsail, foresail. At
2	⎭					10 o'clock we hoisted topsail. At the same
3	⎫ NEbN	1.2				time we observed how the shore extended,
4	⎬		⎭			and saw that behind us it extended to E,
5	⎭					and ahead to WbN. At the same time we saw
6						4 boats,[299] rowing from the shore toward us,
7						and we began to drift awaiting the boats.
8	SbW	.2	N	SSW¾W		In these boats some Chukchi came to visit us.
						They told us that the Anadyr' River was
						at a considerable distance to the south from here.
						And, said they, we have known Russian people for a
						long time. One of them said that he had
9		.2	NE			visited the Anadyrsk outpost. To the Kolyma River,
						they said, we travel by reindeer, not by sea, and along
						the seashore people of our
10	S½W	2.		SSW¼W		kin[300] live for a long distance. They
11	SSE	1.5		SbE¾S		do not know people of another kin.
12	SSW¾W	9.4		SW½W		They brought us meat, fish, water, skins of
						foxes, polar foxes – in all about 15 pieces
						and also 4 walrus teeth, which were
						bought by our men.[301]

in all   37.0

Table of daily reckoning	Latitudes		Diff. of latitude		Departure		Rhumb	Distance		Diff. of longitude		Compass declination
	from	to	N	S	E	W		right	added	daily	total	
Reckoned	64° 35'78	64° 21'54		14°24		10°03	SWbS 1°24' by W	17.42	40.49	23.37 W	24°25'14 by E	1¾ R E
Corrected	the same as reckoned											

Folio 52 verso, continuation

Hours	Rhumbs	Miles	Winds	Right rhumbs	Leeway	Wed. 21 August 1728. Different events while at sea
1	SWbS	7.1	NE	SW¾W		The weather overcast, at times fog came
2	SSW¾W	7.3		SW½W		in, moderate gale. We had
3		7.3				mainsail, topsail, forestaysail.
4	SWbS	7.5	NE	SW¾W		From 4 o'clock cloudy, wind rising.
5		7.6	NE			We carried the same sails, except for topsail.
6		7.6				
7		7.7				
8		8.				
9	SWbS	7.0	NE	SW¾W		From 8 o'clock the weather the same.
10		5.6				We carried only forestaysail.
11		6.6				
12		6.4				From midnight the weather cloudy, moderate
1	SSW½W	7.	NE	SW¼W		gale. We held only forestaysail, at 4
2		7.				o'clock we hoisted mainsail.
3		7.				
4		7.				
5	SWbS	1.6	NEbN	SW¾W		From 5 o'clock to 7 the weather cloudy,
		4.8				fresh breeze. We held the same sails.
						By 7 o'clock the weather began to clear up,
6		6.6				wind dropped. At 6:45 o'clock we hoisted topsail.
7		6.5				
8		5.5	NEbE			
9	SWbS	5.5	NE	SW¾W		From 8 o'clock cloudy, with only few glimpses of sun.
10		5.2				At 10 and 11 o'clock rain, variable
11		4.				wind. During all watch we held
12		6.				mainsail, topsail, forestaysail.

in all 159.4

Table of daily reckoning	Latitudes		Diff. of latitude		Departure		Rhumb	Distance		Diff. of longitude		Compass declination
	from	to	N	S	E	W		right	added	daily	total	
Reckoned	64° 21'54	62° 43'83		97'71		125'74	SW 7°10' by W	159.1	357.2	4°42'3 by W	19°42'84 b E	1¾ R E
Corrected	the same as reckoned											

Conspicuous places	No. of these places	Time of observation	Rhumbs	Distance in miles
The Bay of the Transfiguration of our Lord, where we took water on 6 August[302]		1½ p.m.	NbW	7

From the Turnaround to Kamchatka River

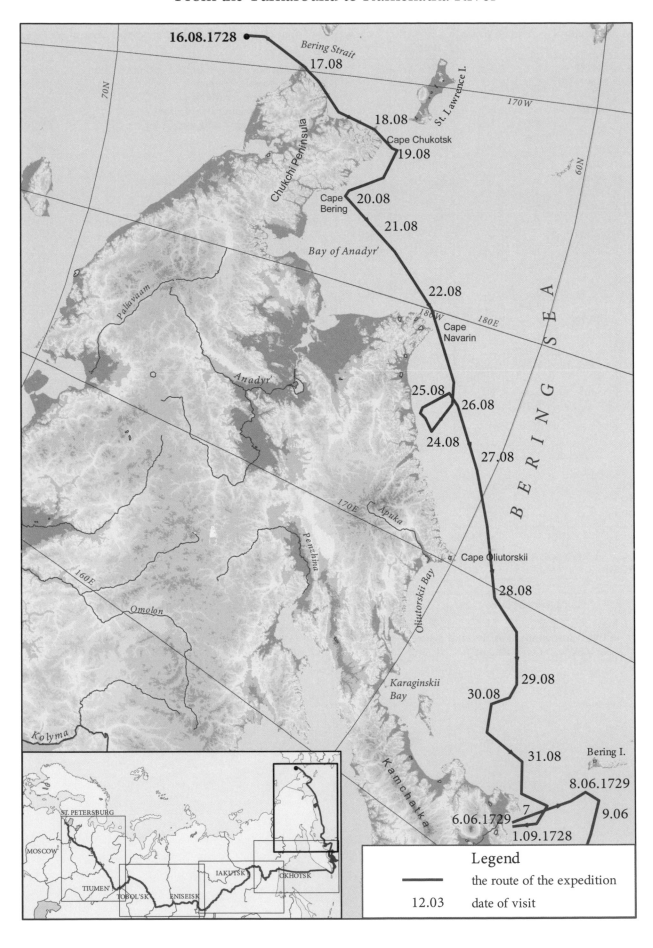

Hours	Rhumbs	Miles	Winds	Right rhumbs	Leeway	Thu. 22 August 1728. Different events while at sea aboard the Holy Archangel Gabriel
1	SWbS	7.	N	SW¾W		The weather cloudy, strong breeze. We held mainsail, foresail and forestaysail.
2		6.5				From 2 o'clock intermittent sunshine.
3	SWbS¼W	6.		SWbW		From 4 o'clock the weather the same, wind rose. Topsail was lowered.
4		6.2				
		1.6				At 8 o'clock mainsail was taken in at
5	SW	4.5	NbE	SWbW¾W		brails. At the same time forestaysail was struck
6		6.2				to change bad gaskets[303] and hoisted again.
		3.5				
7	SWbS	3.6		SW¾W		From 8 o'clock to midnight we held only
8		11.2				forestaysail. The weather cloudy, with starry spells, moderate gale. From midnight to 4 o'clock we held one forestaysail. The weather cloudy. At 2 o'clock it rained, and the wind dropped.
9	SWbS¼W	6.8	NNW	SWbW		From 3 o'clock the weather the same. We
10		6.8				held mainsail and forestaysail, at 5:30 o'clock hoisted topsail.
11		6.7				From 8 o'clock sunshine with some
12		6.7				obstruction from clouds, strong breeze.
1	SWbS¼W	6.5	NNW			We carried mainsail, topsail and forestaysail.
2	SWbS	5.5		SW¾W		At 11 o'clock it became calmer.
3		4.				At 10 o'clock the altitude of the sun center was sighted – 29°29' and azimuth
4	SWbS¼W	5.		SWbW		from S by E – 64°45', and then we were
5		5.	NW			at the latitude 61°36'N, azimuth found
6		5.5				from S by E – 44°38', and from this the
7	SWbS	6.		SW¾W		compass declination – 20°00' east.
8		5.5				At noon we sighted the meridian altitude
9	SWbS¼W	4.5		SWbW		of the sun center with correction –
10	SWbS½W	4.2		SWbW¼W		36°22', its declination on local meridian
11	SWbS¼W	3.3	NNW	SWbW		– 7°56'N and from this was found the
12		3.9				latitude of fix – 61°34'N.

in all 142.2

Table of daily reckoning	Latitudes		Diff. of latitude		Departure		Rhumb	Distance		Diff. of longitude		Compass declination
	from	to	N	S	E	W		right	added	daily	total	
Reckoned	62°43'83	61°34'		69'89		123'14	SWbW 4°10' by W	141.5	302.9	4°23'6 W	15°29'24 b E	1¾ R E
Corrected				the	same	as	reckoned					

Conspicuous places	No. of these places	Time of observation	Rhumbs	Distance in miles
Cape of the Holy Apostle Faddei[304]		4 p.m.	WbS	25
Ahead a steep corner of land[305]		8 p.m.	SWbW½W	22
Behind, as far as the sight could reach[306]		at the same time	NW	30

◄ PLATE 29. Modern map 6: From the Turnaround to Kamchatka River. By Viktor Sedov.

Folio 53, continuation

Hours	Rhumbs	Miles	Winds	Right rhumbs	Leeway drift	Fri. 23 August 728. Different events while at sea
1	SWbS½W	2.3	NbW	SWbW¼W		Sunshine, light air, at 2 o'clock it became calm. Very high sea from NNE. We had mainsail, topsail, forestaysail.
2		1.				
3		.8				From 5 o'clock the weather the same, mainsail was struck, at 7 o'clock topsail and forestaysail were lowered due to still air. At sunset we sighted amplitude of the sun [by our clock at 6:15 p.m.] – 88°00' from S by W, and then we were at the latitude – 61°31'N, the sun declination – 7°52'N, amplitude accounted – 16°40' from W by N, and the compass declination – 18°40' east. From 9 o'clock the weather clear, calm. We drifted without sails. At 12 o'clock light breeze began to blow and we hoisted mainsail and foresail and ran with wind on the bow to N. There were columns of light [aurora borealis] in the air.
4		.5	calm			
5		.3				
6		.2				
7		.1				
8		.1				
9	SWbS	3.		SW¾W		
10						
11	NWbN	.9	SbW	NNW¾N		
12	WbS	.9		W¾N		
1	WSW¼W	1.9		W¼N	¼	From midnight to 5 o'clock moderate breeze and clear. We carried mainsail and foresail. From 5 o'clock sunshine with clouds impeding, strong breeze. We carried mainsail and foresail, at 12 o'clock wind dropped. At noon the altitude of sun center was sighted at meridian to S 35°50' with correction, and its declination – 7°34'N. From this was found the latitude of fix – 61°44' N. The disparateness of the latitude of fix is thought to be due to the sea current to NEbE while we have been here, and a correction was therefore made.
2		1.9				
3	WSW¾W	1.5	variable	W¾N		
4		1.5				
5	WSW	2.		WbN¼N	1½	
6		2.3				
7		2.7		WbN½N		
8		3.3				
9	WSW½W	3.	SbW½W	WNW	1¾	
10		3.				
11		2.9				
12	W	1.4	variable			
		1.0		NWbW½N		

in all   35.1

Table of daily reckoning	Latitudes		Diff. of latitudes			Departure		Rhumb	Distance		Diff. of long.		Compass declination
	from	to	N	S	E		W		right	added	daily	total	
Reckoned	61°34	61°40'	5'47				32'70	WbN 1°45' b W	33.16				
Corrected	61°34'	61°44'	10'00				25'86	WNW 1°20' by W	27.73	58.51	54'57 W	14°24'67 b E	1 ¾ R E

152

Hours	Rhumbs	Miles	Winds	Right rhumbs	Leeway	Sat. 24 August 1728. Different events while at sea aboard the Holy Archangel Gabriel
1	WbS	1.5	SSW	NWbW½N	2¾	Sunshine, strong breeze,
2	WbN	1.7	SW	NW½N		the sky partly cloudy. We carried mainsail and foresail.
3		1.5			}2	
4	WNW	1.9	SW½W	NWbN¾N		From 4 o'clock the weather the same.
5	WbN	2.		NW¾N	2	
6		2.5	SW	NW¼N	2½	At 6 o'clock we turned down the wind and sailed close-hauled.
7	SSE	2.	SWbS	SE¾S	}3	
8	SEbS	3.	SSW	SEbE¾S		From 8 o'clock to midnight the weather clear. We carried mainsail and foresail. Variable gentle breeze.
9		1.8	}vari-		}3	
10	SE½S	1.8	}able	SEbE¼S		
11	SEbS½S	1.5		SE¼S		From midnight to 4 o'clock the weather was fine, light breeze.
12		1.4				
1	SEbS	1.5	}SSW	SE		We carried the same sails.
2		1.7	}with		}2¾	From 3 o'clock to 8 the same weather.
3		2.1	}small			We held mainsail and foresail,
4	SE	2.	}changes	SEbE		at 5 o'clock [braced] the yards307 and hoisted topsail and jib.
5	[SEbS	.9	SW	SE	2¾	From 8 o'clock to noon the sky was
	[W	1.5	with	NWbW¾N	2	clear with short impediment from
6	W¼N	3.5	changes by S		1½	clouds, strong breeze. We carried mainsail, foresail, topsail and jib.
7		2.8	and by W	NWbW½N	}1½	At 10 by our clock we sighted
8	WbS½W	3.		WNW¾N		azimuth of the Sun 46°00' from S by E
9	WbS	3.5	SSW	WbN¼N		altitude of the Sun with correction –
10	W	3.5	SWbS	WNW¼N	}½	33°07'. At 11:30 o'clock the sky
11	WbS	3.5	SSW	WbN¼N		covered with clouds, and strong gale
12	WbN	3.2	SW	WNW½N		rose. Therefore topsail and
	SSE	.6		SbE¼S		jib were lowered.

in all   [55.9]308

Table of daily reckoning	Latitudes		Diff. of latitude		Departure		Rhumb	Distance		Diff. of longitude		Compass declination
	from	to	N	S	E	W		right	added	daily	total	
Reckoned	61° 44'	61°51'36	7'36			14'34	NWbW 6°35' b W	16. 12				
Corrected	61° 44'	61°53'77	9'77			19'04		21. 40	45.34 W	40'34 W	13°44'33 b E	1 ¾ R E

Conspicuous places	No. of these places	Time of observation	Rhumbs	Distance in miles
We saw the shore309		at 1:30 p.m.	WNW	20
The nearest distance after turning from the shore		at 6 p.m.	NWbW½N	15
Again we saw the shore310		at 6:30 a.m.	WbN	15

153

Hours	Rhumbs	Miles	Winds	Right rhumbs	Leeway	Sun. 25 August 1728. Different events while at sea
1	SbE	1.2	SW	SE¾S	4	Soon after 12 o'clock strong gale rose,
2		1.		SE¼S	4½	and the halyard of foresail broke.
						Foresail was lowered, one reef
3	SSE½S	1.		SEbE¾S	}	of mainsail was unbent and until 5 o'clock we
4		1.4			} 4½	ran under mainsail only.
5	SSE½S	1.1	SW	SEbE¾S	}	The weather unstable, sunshine, from 5
6		1.1			} 4½	o'clock to 8 overcast and whole gale
7		1.1				with high sea.
8		1.1			}	From 8 o'clock to midnight murky,
9	SSE½S	1.9	SW	SEbE¼S		strong gale. We ran under mainsail
10		1.7				only, unbending one reef.
11		1.9			} 5	At 11 o'clock rain.
12		1.7			}	From midnight to 4 o'clock the weather
1	SbE½S	1.8	SW	SE¼S	}	and wind the same.
2		1.9				From 4 o'clock to 6 gloomy and rain,
3		1.7			} 5	moderate gale. We ran under mainsail
4		1.7			}	only. At 7 o'clock wind dropped
5	SSW	.9	WbS	SSE½S	}	and rain stopped, and we hoisted
6		1.			} 5¼	foresail. By 8 o'clock it began to clear
7	{	.5				up. From 7 o'clock to 10 cloudy with a
	{ NE	.5		NEbE¾E	E	short sunny spell. We held mainsail
8	SbE	1.8		SSE¼S	2½	and foresail.
9	SbE	1.5	} WbS	SSE¼S	2½	From 10 o'clock to noon sunshine, light
10	S	1.5	} vari-	SbE¾S	}	and variable breeze. We unbent
11	SbW	1.5	} able	S¾W	} 2	one reef of mainsail and hoisted jib.
12	SSW	1.7	}	SbW¾W	2½	At noon we sighted the distance of the sun center from
						zenith – 54°30', its declination – 6°50'N, from this the
						latitude of fix – 61°20'N.

in all   33.9

Table of daily reckoning	Latitudes		Diff. of latitude		Departure		Rhumb	Distance		Diff. of longitude		Compass declination
	from	to	N	S	E	W		right	added	daily	total	
Reckoned	61° 51'36	61° 25'93		25'43	18'44		SEbS 2°12' b E	31.41				
Corrected	61° 53'77	61° 20'		33'77	24'50			41.71	86.56	52'02 by E	14°36'35 b E	

Conspicuous places		No. of these places	Time of observation	Rhumbs	Distance in miles
The land was too far away to be seen					

Hours	Rhumbs	Miles	Winds	Right rhumbs	Leeway	Mon. 26 August 1728. Different events while at sea aboard the Holy Archangel Gabriel
1	SSW½W	1.8	W	SSW½W	2	Sunshine, moderate breeze. Till 2 o'clock we held mainsail, foresail, jib.
2	SWbS	2.8			2½	
3		3.	NWbW	SWbW		At 3 o'clock we hoisted topsail. At 4 o'clock
4	SWbS¼W	3.7		SWbW¼W		wind rose, and jib was lowered.
5	SWbS¼W	3.	NWbW	SWbW¼W		From 4 o'clock to 8 the same weather. We
6	SWbS½W	3.		SWbW½W		held the same sails. From 7 o'clock to midnight starlight with impediment
7		3.7				from drifting clouds. Fresh breeze, we carried mainsail, foresail, topsail.
8		3.5				
9	SWbS¼W	4.0	NW	SWbW¼W		From midnight to 4 o'clock cloudy with starry intervals, fresh breeze.
10		5.8				We held the same sails.
11		6.3	NNW			From 4 to 8 o'clock clear,
12		4.8				fresh breeze. We carried mainsail, topsail, forestaysail. At 5:15
1	SWbS¼W	4.7	NW	SWbW		o'clock by sand clock,[311] at sunrise we sighted amplitude of the sun
2		4.8				from N by E – 58°00', and then we were
3	SWbS½W	5.	NWbN	SWbW¼W		at the latitude of 60°36', the sun declination – 6°34'N, and from this
4		5.				the amplitude 76°32' from N by E was found, and the compass declination 18°32'
5	SWbS¼W	4.5	NNW	SWbW		east. From 7 o'clock to noon sunshine,
6		5.3				moderate breeze. We carried
7		5.5	N			mainsail, topsail, forestaysail.
8		5.2				At 10 o'clock by sand clock we sighted
9	SWbS	5.1	N	SW¾W		the altitude of the sun center 31°17' and azimuth from S by E 55°30', and
10		5.3	NEbN			then we were at the latitude 60°22'N, the sun declination 6°29'N, and from
11	SWbS¼W	5.	NNE	SWbW		this the azimuth 36°40' from S by E was found, compass declination 18°50'E.
12		4.1				At noon the supplement of the sun altitude was sighted – 53°50' with correction, its declination – 6°28'N, the latitude – 60°18'N.

in all   104.9

Table of daily reckoning	Latitudes		Diff. of latitude		Departure		Rhumb	Distance		Diff. of longitude		Compass declination
	from	to	N	S	E	W		right	added	daily	total	
Reckoned	61° 20'	60° 22'21		57'79		85'76	SW 11°13' b E	103.4				2 R E and after midnight 1¾ R E
Corrected	61° 20'	60° 18'		62'00		92'01		110.9	227.8	3°08'9	11°28'26 b E	

Conspicuous places	No. of these places	Time of observation	Rhumbs	Distance in miles
The land was too far away to be seen				

Folio 54, continuation

Hours	Rhumbs	Miles	Winds	Right rhumbs	Leeway	Tue. 27 August 1728. Different events while at sea
1	SWbS¼W	6.	NNE	SW¾W		Sunshine, fresh breeze, at times strong
2		4.6				gale, and sometimes more.
3		5.				
4		5.3				Until 8 o'clock we carried mainsail, topsail and forestaysail.
5	SWbS	5.5	N	SW½W		
6		6.8				At 7 o'clock cloudy.
7		7.3				From 7 o'clock the weather murky,
8		5.0				fresh breeze abating. We carried
9	SWbS½W	5.1	NbW	SWbW		the same sails.
10		6.6				At 10 and 11 o'clock it rained.
11		6.6				Soon after 11 o'clock mainsail was pulled up to clewlines and topsail was
12		7.3				lowered to half topmast for rising wind.
1	SWbS¼W	6.8		SW¾W		From midnight to 4 o'clock the weather
2		6.5	ENE			cloudy, with stars briefly shining through,
3		6.2				but from the middle of the watch it rained. We held topsail at half topmast
4		9.				and forestaysail. Moderate gale.
5	SWbS½W	7.	NEbN	SWbW		From 4 o'clock to 8 cloudy, at times
6		6.6				rain, wind with gusts. We carried
7		6.	NE			the same sails.
8		5.5				
9	SWbS¼W	6.5	NEbN	SW¾W		From 8 o'clock to noon the weather and
10		6.5				wind were the same and we carried the
11	SWbS	5.7		SW½W		same sails.
12		6.5				

in all   149.9

Table of daily reckoning	Latitudes		Diff. of latitude		Departure		Rhumb	Distance		Diff. of longitude		Compass declination
	from	to	N	S	E	W		right	added	daily	total	
Reckoned	60° 18'	58° 49'31		88'69		120'72	SW 8°42' by W	149.8				
Corrected	60° 18'	the same as reckoned							295.9	3°57'8 W	7°30' 70 E	1½ R E

The land was too far away to be seen

Folio 54 verso

Hours	Rhumbs	Miles	Winds	Right rhumbs	Leeway	Wed. 28 August 1728. Different events while at sea aboard the Holy Archangel Gabriel
1	SWbS¼W	6.	NEbN	SW¾W		The weather cloudy, rain alternating
2		6.				with sunny spells, strong breeze
						abating. We ran under topsail and
3		4.5				forestaysail until 8 o'clock. From 8
4		6.				o'clock to midnight the weather cloudy,
5	SWbS½W	3.9		SWbW		gentle breeze and a little starlight.
						We carried the same sails.
6		4.4	NbE			From midnight to 4 o'clock the weather
7		5.8				cloudy, moderate breeze. We ran under
8	SWbS¼W	5.2		SW¾W		topsail and forestaysail. From 4
9	SWbS¼W	4.8		SW¾W		o'clock to 8 cloudy with sun breaking through,
						light air. We carried mainsail, topsail
10		5.5	N			and forestaysail. Soon after 5
						o'clock forestaysail was lowered and
11	SWbS	5.		SW½W		foresail and jib were hoisted From 8
12		5.				o'clock to noon sunshine, gentle
						variable breeze and occasional drifting
						clouds. We carried all sails,
1	SWbS	4.	N	SW½W		except forestaysail.
2	SWbS¼W	4.		SW¾W		At 10:30 o'clock by sand clock we
3		3.5				sighted supplement of latitude of the
						sun center – 55°54', sun declination –
4		3.6				5°44', azimuth sighted from S by E –
5	SW	3.8	NW	SWbW½W		50°00', and then we were at the
						latitude 57°44', azimuth found from S
6		2.7				by E 32°10', compass declination 17°50'
7		2.4	vari-			east.
8		2.2	able			At noon we sighted at meridian
						supplement of the altitude of the sun
9	SWbS	1.6	W	SW	½	center – 51°57' with correction, its
						declination – 5°43'N. From this
10	SbW½W	2.2	WbS	SSW		the latitude of fix – 57°40'N.
11		2.8			1	In this place the sea current to SEbE¼S
						by corrected compass was taken into
12	S	3.4	SWbW	SbW	½	account for thc time we have been here, and the
						latitude of fix was corrected accordingly.

in all 98.3

Table of daily reckoning	Latitudes		Diff. of latitude		Departure		Rhumb	Distance		Diff. of longitude		Compass declination
	from	to	N	S	E	W		right	added	daily	total	
Reckoned	58°49'31	57°49'03		60'28		75'47	SW 6°23' b W	96.60				
Corrected		57°40'		69'28		63'33	SWbW 8°41' b W	93.86	176.0	1°58'7 W	5°31' 76 E	1½ R E

Conspicuous places	No. of these places	Time of observation	Rhumbs	Distance in miles
The land was too far away to be seen				

Folio 54 verso, continuation

Hours	Rhumbs	Miles	Winds	Right rhumbs	Lee-way	Thu. 29 August 1728. Different events while at sea
1	SbW¼W	3.	WbS	SSW¼W	⎫	Sunshine, light breeze, at times variable.
2		2.9			⎪	We carried mainsail, foresail, topsail, jib.
3	S	3.1	SWbW	SbW	⎬ ½	At 5 o'clock yards.[312]
4	SbE½S	2.8		S½W	⎭	At 7 o'clock by sand clock, at sunset, we
5	SbE	1.5	SW	S	½	sighted amplitude of the sun from S by W
6	⎡NWbW	1.5	⎫	NWbN¼N		84°00', we were then at the latitude 57°32',
	⎣WbN½N	1.2	⎬ vari-	NWbW¾N	⎫ ¾	sun declination – 5°35'N and from this
7	W½N	2.2	⎭ able	WNW¾N	⎭	amplitude was found from N by W 79°33',
8	W¼N	2.5	SWbS	WNW½N	⎫	compass declination 16°27' east.
9	WNW½N	2.2	SWbW	NWbN	⎪	From 7 o'clock to midnight the weather clear,
10	WbN½N	1.9		NW	⎬ 1	gentle breeze. We carried mainsail, foresail,
11	WbN	1.7	SW	NWbW¼N	⎪	topsail, jib.
12		1.1			⎭ ¾	From midnight to 4 o'clock stars, light breeze,
1	W½N	2.	SWbS½W	WNW½N		at times changeable. We held the same sails.
2	W¼N	2.		WNW¼N		
3	⎡WSW¾W	1.	⎫ vari-	W¾N	⎬ ½	From 3 o'clock to 8 the weather clear
	⎣WbS	.9	⎭ able			with few clouds, moderate
4		2.3	SSW½W	WbN	⎫	breeze. We held the same sails.
5	WbS	2.4	SSW	WbN¼N	⎬	
6	W½N	1.2	SWbS½W	WNW¾N	⎭ ¾	From 8 o'clock to noon sunshine,
7	WbS	2.	SSW	WbN¼N		gentle breeze.
8	WSW	2.2	SbW	W¼N	⎫	At noon we sighted the supplement of
9	WSW¼W	2.5	SbW	W½N	⎬	altitude of the sun center – 52°14',
10	WSW	2.5		W¼N	⎭	declination of the sun N 5°21',
					⎫ ¾	latitude of fix – 57°35'N.
	⎡	1.5			⎪	During this day the sea current to SbE
11	⎣WSW¼W	1.		W½N	⎬	by right compass brought us from
12		2.6			⎭	reckoned to observed latitude.

in all   53.7

Table of daily reckoning	Latitudes		Diff. of latitude		Departure		Rhumb	Distance		Diff. of longitude		Compass decli-nation
	from	to	N	S	E	W		right	added	daily	total	
Reckoned	57°40'	57°41'8	1°8			38'08	WbN 6°37' by W	35.12				
Corrected	57°40'	57°35'		5'00		37'73	WbS 3°42' by W	38.06	71.10	1°10' 48 W	4°21' 28 E	1½ R E

Conspicuous places	No. of these places	Time of observation	Rhumbs	Distance in miles
The land was too far away to be seen				

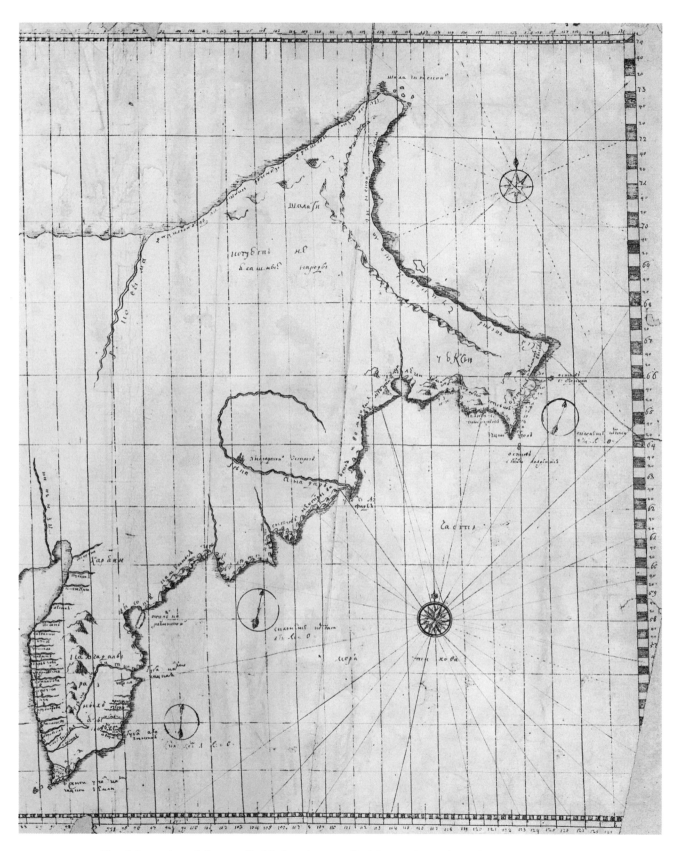

PLATE 30. The right section of the so-called "Khanykov copy" of the Final Map from the First Kamchatka Expedition, copied by land-surveyor Ivan Khanykov from the original (Efimov 1964, No. 63). The Final Map gave the outline of Kamchatka and northeastern Asia with far greater precision than any previous one. It was to exert great influence on international map-making. Total map size 56 × 135 cm.

Courtesy Library of the Academy of Sciences (BAN), St. Petersburg. Photo by Nikolai Turkin.

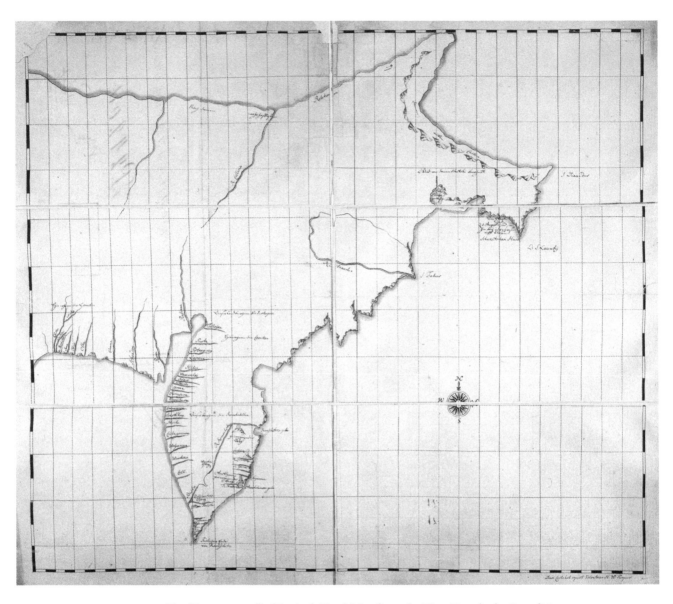

PLATE 31. The "Purpur copy" of Bering's Final Map from the First Kamchatka Expedition.
Map size 65 × 56 cm. Place names are in German. The inscription in the lower right corner reads
"Diese Carte hat copiert Volonteur H.W. Purpur" (Efimov 1964, No. 67).

Courtesy Russian State Archives of Military History, Moscow (RGVIA).

Folio 55

Hours	Rhumbs	Miles	Winds	Right rhumbs	Leeway	Fri. 30 August 1728. Different events while at sea aboard the Holy Archangel Gabriel
1	SWbW	2.	S	WbS¼W	¾	Sunshine, gentle breeze. We held
2	SW½W	2.	SbE½S	WSW¾W	¾	mainsail, foresail, topsail, jib.
3	SWbS	2.8	SSE	SWbW	}½	At 2 p.m. we sighted the supplement of
4		2.8				the altitude of the sun center to zenith
						57°43' and azimuth by compass 21°30'
5	SWbS	3.2		SW¾W	¼	from S by W, and then we were at
6	SWbS½W	3.2	SE	SWbW		the latitude – 57°34', sun declination 5°19'N,
7	SW¼W	4.	SE½S	SWbW¾W		azimuth found 37°50' from S by W,
8	SWbS¾W	3.8		SWbW¼W		compass declination 16°20' east.
9	SWbS½W	2.9	SE½S	SWbW½W	}½	At 6 o'clock clouds appeared and wind rose.
10		3.4				From 8 o'clock to midnight the sky was clear,
11		3.9	SE	SWbW		but at 12 o'clock the sky in places got covered by
						clouds, fresh breeze. We held mainsail,
12	SWbS	4.2		SW½W		foresail, topsail. From midnight to 4 o'clock
1	SWbS¼W	5.2	SE	SW¾W		cloudy, moderate gale. We carried
2	SSW½W	3.5		SW		mainsail and foresail. From 4 o'clock
3	SSW¼W	4.		SWbS¾W		to 8 the weather cloudy, strong breeze,
4	SSW	5.2	ESE	SWbS½W		We carried mainsail, foresail, jib.
5	SWbS	6.6		SW½W		
6		6.5				At 6 o'clock forestaysail was set,
7	SWbS½W	5.5		SWbW		and foresail was lowered. From 7
8	SWbS	7.	E	SW½W		o'clock to noon the weather murky,
9	SSW¾W	6.2		SW¼W		strong gale. We ran under mainsail and
10	SWbS¾W	7.5	ENE	SWbW¼W		forestaysail. At 11 o'clock wind rose
11	SW	7.		SWbW		and we reefed mainsail for precaution
12	SW¼W	7.5		SWbW¾W		and took in at brails.

in all   109.9

Table of daily reckoning	Latitudes		Diff. of latitude		Departure		Rhumb	Distance		Diff. of longitude		Compass declination
	from	to	N	S	E	W		right	added	daily	total	
Reckoned	57°35'	56°33'4		61'60		88'46	SW 10°9' by W	107.8				
Corrected	57°35'	the same as reckoned							198.3	2°42' 7 W	1°38' 68 b E	1½ R E

Conspicuous places	No. of these places	Time of observation	Rhumbs	Distance in miles
The land could not be seen through the fog				

161

Folio 55, continuation

Hours	Rhumbs	Miles	Winds	Right rhumbs	Leeway	Sat. 31 August 1728. Different events while at sea
1	SW	7.2	ENE	SWbW½W		The weather dark, strong gale.
2	SWbW	7.		WSW½W		We ran under forestaysail only.
3		7.				At 4 o'clock a part of the land (which extends
4		7.5				to the sea on the eastern side of the bay,
						to which flows the Kamchatka River)
5	NbE	3.		NbE	1½	appeared through fog to WSW
6	SE	3.		SSE¼S	1¾	3 minutes away or less, and because of fog
7		3.				we did not discern soon that the land
8	SEbE½S	3.	NEbE	SEbS¾S	⎫	extends in an arch from SEbS to NbW.[313]
9	SEbE	3.		SEbS½S	⎬ 1¾	Then forestaysail was lowered, and
						mainsail and foresail were hoisted.
10		3.			⎭	Due to the strong gale and rough sea, this
11						was difficult to do and took time, and during
						this time we were carried to the shore
12						at a distance of half a minute. The shore
						was stony and steep as a wall, very high,
						and the same everywhere.
1			ENE			And we worked to run away from the
2						shore against adverse wind till 10 p.m.[314]
3						At 10 o'clock the halyards of mainsail
4						and foresail ripped. Then the sails
5			ENE			crashed down and all the rigging got
6						tangled up. And it was impossible to
7						straighten it out in such high seas. Therefore we
						dropped anchor at a depth of 18 sazhens at a
						distance of 1 mile or less from the shore,
8						close to 11 p.m. We struggled to put the sails
9						and other rigging in order for navigation, but it
						took us until noon, although everyone worked
						incessantly, for even though the wind dropped a
						little, it did not change its direction, and heavy sea
						increased. In addition, all this time it rained, with
						small interruption, and there was
10			NE			considerable gloom.
11						
12						

in all 46.7

Table of daily reckoning	Latitudes		Diff. of latitude		Departure		Rhumb	Distance		Diff. of longitude		Compass declination
	from	to	N	S	E	W		right	added	daily	total	
Reckoned	56°33'4	56°32'21		21'19		22'72	SW 2°00' by W	31.07				
Corrected	the same as reckoned								56.15	41'06 by W	00°57' 62 b E	1½ R E

Conspicuous places	No. of these places	Time of observation	Rhumbs	Distance in miles
A land of the Kamchatka		at 4 p.m.	WSW	3

Hours	Rhumbs	Miles	Winds	Right rhumbs	Leeway	Sun. 1 September 1728. Different events while at sea
1	SEbE	3.5	NE	SE½S		The weather murky with rain, wind dropped.
2		4.2				We began to weigh anchor to continue our voyage, when it was torn away as the
3		4.9				cable broke near the anchor, having been damaged by rocks.
4	SE	4.3		SEbS½S		
5	SE	4.	NE			We carried mainsail, foresail, jib. We unbent a reef of mainsail. Jib and foresail were taken in and we drifted under mainsail alone.
6		4.1				
7	ESE	2.3		S		
8	EbS	1.5		SbE	4½	At 8 o'clock we did not reach the bottom by lead. From 7 o'clock to midnight the
9	E½S	1.8	NE	SEbS½S		weather murky with rain, strong breeze.
10		1.8			3½	
11		1.5		SEbS		We ran under mainsail only.
12		1.5			3	From midnight to 4 o'clock dark,
1	NWbN	1.5	NNE	W½N		at times with stars, and it rained.
2		2.			4	We ran under mainsail only.
3	NW½N	2.	NbE	W		From 4 o'clock to 8 the same weather.
4		1.7				We held mainsail and foresail.
5	NWbW / WSW	1. / 2.	NNE / variable	NW½N / WbS½W		From 8 to noon the weather cloudy, with little sun shining through,
6		2.4	able			variable light air from N. We carried
7		2.				mainsail, foresail, topsail and jib.
8		1.5	between N – NW			
9	WSW	1.8	variable	WbS½W		
10		2.1	able			
11	WbN	2.2	between	WNW	½	
12		1.9	NE – NW	WNW½N		

in all   59.5

Table of daily reckoning	Latitudes		Diff. of latitude		Departure		Rhumb	Distance		Diff. of longitude		Compass declination
	from	to	N	S	E	W		right	added	daily	total	
Reckoned	56°12'21	55°44'26		28'95		14'00	SSW 3°19' by W	32.15				
Corrected	the same as reckoned								57.63	25'10 W	00°32'5 E	1½ R E

Conspicuous places	No. of these places	Time of observation	Rhumbs	Distance in miles
A point of land of the eastern shore of the Kamchatka Bay[315]		10 a.m.	NWbN	

Folio 55 verso, continuation

Hours	Rhumbs	Miles	Winds	Right rhumbs	Mon. 2 September 1728. Different events while at sea
1	NW	2.	NE	NWbN¼N	From noon to 8 o'clock the weather gloomy, light
2		2.5			and variable breeze between NE and SE.
3		4.	⌠vari-		At 6 o'clock wind rose. We held mainsail, foresail,
4	NWbN	3.5	⌡able	NNW¼N	topsail, jib.
5			3.		At 7 o'clock topsail and jib were lowered, and foresail shortly after.
6		3.5	SEbE		At 8 o'clock mainsail was reefed and we drifted
7		3.5			in the Kamchatsk Bay. We did not run to the mouth
8	NWbN	2.9		NNW¼N	of the river because it was night and foggy.
	ENE	0.5		NEbN¼E	From 8 o'clock to midnight dark, gentle
9				drift of the	breeze, at 10 o'clock rain and calm.
10				ship to ENE	We drifted under mainsail only.
11				4R	From midnight to 2 o'clock gentle breeze,
12					from 2 to 4 calm, and during all the watch it
1					rained.
2					From 4 o'clock to 6:30 calm, then light breeze rose
3					from NW, and we hoisted foresail and ran with
4					wind on the bow. During the same time fog was dissipated,
5					and the land appeared on the western side of
6					Kamchatsk Bay, 3 minutes distant.
7					At 7:45 a.m. we saw a dwelling, built at the mouth of the
8					Kamchatka River to NNW¼N, 8 minutes distant, and we
9					maneuvered by the mouth under full sail.
10					The weather became clear. Fresh breeze.
11					Sea current from the Kamchatka River SbW¼W
12					and by right compass SSW½W 10 minutes per day.

in all   24.9

Table of daily reckoning	Latitudes		Diff. of latitude		Departure		Rhumb	Distance		Diff. of longitude		Compass declination
	from	to	N	S	E	W		right	added	daily	total	
Reckoned	55°43'26	55°56'65	13'49			13'98	NW 1°14' by W	19.36				
Corrected	as reckoned								37.7 by W	25'06	0°06' 92 b E	1¼ R E

Conspicuous places	No. of places	Time of observation	Rhumbs	Distance in miles
A dwelling at the mouth of the Kamchatka River		7h 45m a.m.	NNW¼N	8

D.W.	D.M.	September 1728. Events by the sea	Winds
Tue.	3	Sunshine, fresh breeze. We ran under full sail by the Kamchatka River mouth. At 2 o'clock we came to the mouth. The channel is situated close to the western bank of the river's mouth. And from the shore a shoal extends for 300 sazhens. It is situated between the sea and the river. In the most shallow place its depth is 2 sazhens. The tide was rising from the sea, and the channel is situated W to SSE¾S from the outermost huts or balagans. At 3 p.m. we arrived by the river at the summer dwellings of the servitors of [Lower]Kamchatsk outpost, at which we had stood before the sea campaign,[316]and came to anchor. While at sea we consumed: 8 bags of flour, rusks [ ], meat 23 poods, barley groats [ ],[317] salted fish 4 barrels.	SW
Wed.	4	Gloomy, strong breeze between SE and E, from 4 o'clock rain. In the morning gloomy, light breeze. The physician was allowed to go to the outpost. By noon sun shining through. A sailor was sent up the Kamchatka River to make soundings of small rivers, where the ship could pass the winter.	N
Thu.	5	Cloudy with intermittent sunshine and calm. We dried sails. At 8 o'clock drizzle. In the morning gloomy, light breeze. Lieutenant Spanberch was allowed to go to the outpost because of illness. At 11 o'clock the Captain left for the outpost, with him 1 soldier. The sailor who had been sent to sound rivers arrived [and reported] that it was impossible for the ship to pass the winter in the small rivers, since they are shallow.	N
Fri.	6	The weather overcast, moderate gale with rain and all night heavy rain. At 7 a.m. rain stopped, moderate variable breeze, cloudy. The quartermaster was sent to the mouth near the bay.	N
Sat.	7	Cloudy, light breeze, at night rain and calm. In the morning overcast, temporary drizzle, light breeze. The quartermaster arrived and reported that the places [examined] were inconvenient.	SSE SW
Sun.	8	Overcast, light air, at times rain, in the morning sunshine, light breeze.	WSW
Mon.	9	Sunshine, gentle breeze. We dried sails. A sailor was sent to the Captain with a report and the sick geodesist was sent with him and 1 carpenter to take care of the geodesist. At 7 a.m. we brought the ship into a channel behind an island to pass the winter. Sunshine, light breeze.	SW
Tue.	10	Sunshine, the rigging of the ship was taken down and put into cabins on board, and also the sails. 210 bags of flour, by weight 546 poods, were given to the servitors for safe keeping. At 6 o'clock strong gale, in the night drizzle and strong gale, in the morning gloomy, wind the same.	S
Wed.	11	Overcast, strong gale. 38 more bags of flour, 100 poods, were given [to the servitors]. Until midnight rain, from midnight calm, at 8 o'clock sunshine, light breeze.	S SW
Thu.	12	Sunshine, fresh breeze. A soldier was sent to the outpost with 6 dugouts, and with him 78 bags of rusks, 4 bags of groats, and another soldier with the Captain's baggage. 57 more bags of flour, 154 poods, were handed over. In all 305 bags 790 poods of flour[318] and 16 bags 47 poods of groats were handed over. At night strong gale, after midnight wind dropped, at 8 o'clock sunshine.	WNW WNW
Fri.	13	Sunshine, light breeze. We tarred all the ship with resin. At 3 o'clock calm. The other vessel that had come from the Bol'shaia River [on 7 July][319] was brought by the ship for the winter. At night strong gale with gusts, in the morning sunshine, wind the same.	WNW
Sat.	14	Sunshine, strong gale, from 5 o'clock wind dropped and became variable. Night calm and clear, light frost, in the morning sunshine, light air. 50 empty bags were handed over.	WNW
Sun.	15	Some small artillery and ship supplies and other things left from the campaign were sent to Kliuchi on 5 dugouts accompanied by a sailor and a soldier. By the evening some sunshine broke through the gloom. Light breeze. The sailor who had been sent with a report arrived from the Captain with 3 dugouts. He brought from the Captain 3 deer for the men. In the morning sunshine.	SSE S
Mon.	16	Sunshine. We positioned the ship and the [other] vessel in the channel on the right side downstream, and anchored them. At night and in the morning fine intermittent rain, light breeze.	SSE
Tue.	17	Overcast, gentle breeze, at times drizzle. All night heavy intermittent rain. In the morning the same weather and wind.	NE
Wed.	18	Strong breeze and rain. In the morning a soldier arrived from the Captain with empty dugouts. Our ship was given, with all her rigging and sails, to the manager of the Lower Kamchatsk outpost for safe keeping during the winter. Fresh breeze with sunshine.	N N
Thu.	19	We left for Kliuchi and the outpost: Lieutenant Chirikov, myself, the quartermaster, the apprentice boat and sloop maker, 5 sailors, the carpenter foreman, a caulker, a sailmaker, 2 carpenters, a drummer, 5 soldiers in 9 dugouts. And for supervision during the winter 2 sailors were left at the ship. We went till 7 o'clock and then stopped for the night. At night strong gale rose with rain.	NE

D.W.	D.M.	September 1728. Events at Kliuchi	Winds
Fri.	20	Strong gale with rain. We stopped all day due to the wind. After midnight light air, but heavy rain. At 6 o'clock we set off on our route. Light breeze, at times rain.	NE
Sat.	21	Cloudy and calm, rain. At 7 o'clock we stopped for the night. Heavy rain. At 6 a.m. rain ceased, and we set off on our route. The weather cloudy with intermittent sunshine.	
Sun.	22	Cloudy with sunny spells. At 7 or 8 o'clock we settled for the night. Night clear, considerable frost. At 6 a.m. we set off on our route. Sunshine and calm.	
Mon.	23	Sunshine, gentle breeze. At 7 o'clock we arrived at Kliuchi and took up our quarters. In the morning sunshine, moderate gale. At Kliuchi 2 men were sick, namely the geodesist who had gone mad, and 1 soldier with headache.	NW N
Tue.	24	Sunshine, moderate gale. The kaiurs who had come with us were allowed to go. In the morning frost and strong gale, the weather with intermittent sunshine.	N NW
Wed.	25	The weather and wind the same, in the morning sunshine and frost, light air.	NW
Thu.	26	The servicemen staying at Kliuchi trained soldiers' drill. In the morning frost and sunshine with small clouds.	
Fri.	27	Sunshine, light air, in the morning frost and sun shining through, light breeze. The Captain wished to move from Kliuchi to the outpost for the winter and ordered [some of] the men to go to the outpost, where quarters were assigned to them.	SW
Sat.	28	A soldier arrived from the seaside with the Captain's fish provisions and 2 seafarers, who were sent to the outpost. From midnight heavy rain, light breeze.	E
Sun.	29	Rain, light breeze.	NW
Mon.	30	Rain, light breeze, in the morning cloudy with sunny spells. From Kliuchi the quartermaster, 4 sailors, a carpenter foreman, 2 Admiralty carpenters, a caulker, a sailmaker, a blacksmith, a drummer, 6 soldiers, and a carpenter of Eniseisk were sent to their quarters at the outpost. 2 men at the command were sick. The following remained at the quarters in Kliuchi: 2 lieutenants, 2 sailors, 1 geodesist, 1 apprentice boat and sloop maker, 1 Admiralty carpenter, 5 soldiers, a carpenter of Eniseisk.	W
		October	Winds
Tue.	1	The weather cloudy, light air and little sunshine through.	
Wed.	2	The weather cloudy with sunshine. In the night strong gale rose from W. In the morning we received information that servicemen of our command had arrived at Bol'sheretsk outpost from Okhotsk on the old vessel.	
Thu.	3	Intermittent sunshine, strong gale between N and W. In the morning the Captain arrived at Kliuchi with all servicemen of his command and ordered the men who arrived with him and those staying at Kliuchi to assemble at God's church. When the men had assembled, a manifesto, accompanied by a decree of His Imperial Majesty Peter the Second, Autocrat of All-Russia, from the Admiralty, was read out. It announced the decease of the Great Sovereign Empress Catherine I and the accession to the Russian Throne by His Imperial Majesty Peter II, and requested all servicemen to take an oath of faithful service to His Majesty.[320] After the manifesto had been read, all men of our command made the oath. The decree and manifesto were brought by the sailor of our command Ganiukov, who had arrived from Okhotsk at Bol'sheretsk outpost aboard the old vessel with navigator Angel.	
Fri.	4	Cloudy with a short spell of sunshine, strong gale. In the night calm, in the morning snowfall, and it snowed till noon; wind changed to	W E
Sat.	5	Wind the same and it was snowing incessantly. By the evening the wind changed and the snowfall stopped. In the night moonlight and stars now and then, in the morning snowfall. Before noon it cleared up.	W
Sun.	6	Sunshine with drifting clouds, light breeze. By the evening the wind rose, night clear, strong gale. In the morning frost. On the river ice. The weather cloudy with a few sunny spells.	W NW
Mon.	7	The weather and wind the same. Night moonlit, light breeze. In the morning cloudy, light air and warm.	NW
Tue.	8	A few sunny spells, light frost. In the morning sunshine with drifting clouds. 2 men at the command were sick. By noon strong gale rose.	N
Wed.	9	Strong gale with gusts from NW, warm and snowfall. At night moonlight and stars, by the morning gloomy, light breeze and small snowfall with rain.	NW NE

D.W.	D.M.	October 1728	Winds
Thu.	10	The weather gloomy, calm and warm. From the evening moderate gale rose, at night light snowfall, in the morning sunshine, light breeze.	W
Fri.	11	At 2 p.m. strong gale rose and gloomy. In the night and till noon the same wind, sunshine.	W
Sat.	12	Cloudy with sunny spells, strong gale. At night moonlight and stars, wind dropped, in the morning cloudy and light frost.	W
Sun.	13	The weather and wind the same, in the night snowfall, in the morning some sunshine and strong gale.	W
Mon.	14	The weather and wind the same, in the morning sunshine and light frost and small clouds. Today a commissary from Iakutsk arrived at Lower Kamchatsk outpost to collect tribute.	W
Tue.	15	The weather and wind the same, in the morning light frost, light breeze, on the river drifting ice. By noon strong gale rose, sunshine through clouds.	W
Wed.	16	The weather and wind the same, in the morning cloudy.	
Thu.	17	The weather and wind the same, in the morning sunshine with drifting clouds.	
Fri.	18	The weather clear. I left Kliuchi to winter at the outpost. In the morning overcast.	
Sat.	19	The weather the same, in the morning rain at times.	
Sun.	20	The weather the same, at night and in the morning snowfall and calm, warm.	
Mon.	21	Snowfall, calm and warm. In the morning strong gale with temporary humidity.	E
Tue.	22	Gloomy and calm. By the evening heavy snowfall, in the morning light frost, sunshine and calm.	
Wed.	23	The weather and wind the same, by the morning frost, sunshine and calm. The Kamchatka River in places was covered with ice.	
Thu.	24	Sunshine. By evening cloudy and moderate gale. At night heavy snowstorm, in the morning sunshine, calm and frost.	E
Fri.	25	The weather and wind the same. In the morning moderate gale from ………	E W
Sat.	26	The weather clear, strong gale with slight snowstorm. In the morning (cloudy)[321] sunshine.	
Sun.	27	Sunshine. Wind the same, and rising towards evening. In the morning moderate gale. By noon heavy snowfall.	SW
Mon.	28	Snowfall, then sunshine through, light breeze between S and W. In the morning hard frost, calm and sunshine.	
Tue.	29	Sunshine and warm. By the evening small clouds. In the morning light snowfall and calm.	
Wed.	30	Cloudy and calm. In the morning intermittent light snowfall and light breeze from ………	NW
Thu.	31	With intermittent light snowfall. In the morning hard frost and calm.	

D.W.	D.M.	November 1728	Winds
Fri.	1	Cloudy and calm. By the evening light snowfall and warm. In the morning sunshine with drifting clouds and frost and light snowstorm, moderate gale.	W
Sat.	2	The weather and wind the same. In the morning sunshine and strong gale with snowstorm and hard frost.	W
Sun.	3	The weather and wind the same. In the morning sunshine, moderate breeze, frost.	
Mon.	4	The weather and wind the same, night moonlit and hard frost. In the morning cloudy and calm, at times sun shining through and light snowfall at times.	
Tue.	5	The weather and wind the same. In the morning hard frost.	
Wed.	6	The same.	
Thu.	7	The weather the same, but frost. In the morning light frost and sunshine.	
Fri.	8	The same.	
Sat.	9	Sunshine with drifting clouds. By the evening windy and cloudy, by the morning strong gale with snowfall.	E
Sun.	10	The same. In the morning wind was the same with snowfall, then sunshine.	
Mon.	11	The same weather and calm. In the morning heavy snowfall.	
Tue.	12	Cloudy with sunshine through, light breeze. 2 sailors and 1 soldier were sent to the seaside to guard the ship. In the morning snowfall.	
Wed.	13	The weather the same.	
Thu.	14	The weather the same, in the morning snowfall and frost.	
Wed.	15	Snowfall and calm.	
Sat.	16	Cloudy, light breeze. In the morning light frost, the weather lightly cloudy.	
Sun.	17	The weather the same.	
Mon.	18	The weather the same. In the morning frost with rime and slight sunshine.	
Tue.	19	The weather the same. In the morning cloudy, calm and rime.	
Wed.	20	The same. In the morning warm and at times heavy snowfall.	
Thu.	21	Strong gale with snowstorm from W. In the morning strong gale with snowstorm from …..	E
Fri.	22	The weather and wind the same.	

Sat.	23	Wind the same, warm with wet snowfall, at times during the night whole gale, by the morning it dropped. Sailor Selivanov was sent to the Bol'shaia River with letters for navigator Angel.	NE
Sun.	24	The weather gloomy, light breeze and warm. In the morning cloudy, gentle breeze and intermittent light snowfall.	NE
Mon.	25	⎫ The weather and wind the same.	
Tue.	26	⎭	
Wed.	27	The weather and wind the same. Night moonlit, calm. In the morning hard frost and sunshine.	
Thu.	28	The same weather.	
Wed.	29	The same weather. In the morning cloudy and calm and light frost. At times a little sunshine.	
Sat.	30	The same weather. In the morning hard frost, then sunshine and calm.	

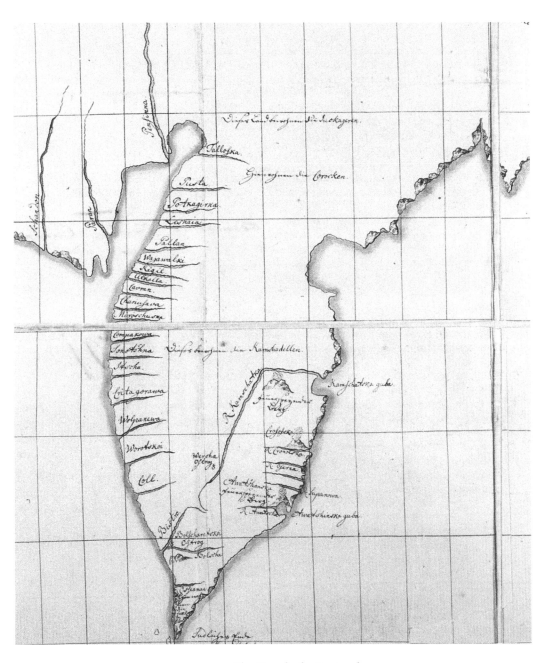

PLATE 32. The Kamchatka Peninsula.
Segment of the "Purpur copy" of Bering's Final Map (p. 160).
Courtesy Russian State Archives of Military History, Moscow (RGVIA).

Folio 57 verso

D.W.	D.M.	December 1728	Winds
Sun.	1	Sunshine and calm. In the morning hard frost and gloomy.	
Mon.	2	Gloomy. In the morning hard frost.	
Tue.	3	Sunshine. In the morning frost and overcast. At night snowfall.	
Wed.	4	Gloomy, gentle breeze from SE. In the morning the weather and wind the same.	
Thu.	5	The same weather.	
Fri.	6	Cloudy, light breeze. In the morning the same weather.	E
Sat.	7	The weather and wind the same. In the morning 1 sailor and 1 soldier were sent to the seaside to relieve the guard at the ship.	
Sun.	8	The same weather, in the morning light frost with sun breaking through.	
Mon.	9	The same weather, in the morning cloudy and calm.	
Tue.	10	The same weather, in the morning frost and sunny spells.	
Wed.	11	Sunny spells and calm. In the morning hard frost, the weather clear.	
Thu.	12	The same weather. 1 sailor and 2 soldiers arrived from the seaside. The weather in the morning clear, with hard frost, wind	NW
Fri.	13	Sunshine, a little rime and calm. Snowfall at night and in the morning.	
Sat.	14	Light snowfall. In the morning heavy snowfall and calm. A soldier was allowed to go to the Kigil River for his own needs.[322]	
Sun.	15	Heavy snowfall. In the morning sunshine, light frost.	
Mon.	16	Sunshine, light breeze, by the morning hard frost.	W
Tue.	17	Sunshine. In the morning cloudy with sunny spells and hard frost.	
Wed.	18	The same weather. In the morning wind with snowstorm.	E
Thu.	19	Wind the same, but no snowstorm. By evening wind rose from .... In the morning strong gale with blowing snow and warm with sunny spells.	W
Fri.	20	The weather and wind the same. In the morning great snow storm from	E
Sat.	21	Light variable breeze and drizzle. In the morning strong gale with snowstorm	SW
Sun.	22	Strong gale with snowstorm. In the morning sunshine, light breeze.	SW
Mon.	23	Sunshine and calm. In the morning overcast.	
Tue.	24	Sunshine. By the evening light breeze rose. In the morning strong gale with variable snowstorm.	E
Wed.	25	The weather and wind the same.	
Thu.	26	Sunshine with small drifting clouds. Light breeze. In the morning sunshine and calm.	
Fri.	27	Sunshine. 1 sailor and the sick apprentice mast maker arrived from Bol'sheretsk. In the morning sunshine.	
Sat.	28	The same weather. In the morning strong gale with snowstorm.	E
Sun.	29	The weather and wind the same. In the morning snowfall.	
Mon.	30	Wet snowfall. In the morning light breeze variable and small snowfall.	
Tue.	31	Gloomy and calm. In the morning sunshine, light breeze. This month at the command a geodesist and a soldier were sick. A sailor was allowed to go to Upper Kamchatsk for his own needs.	
		January 1729	
Wed.	1	Sunshine, light breeze. In the morning gloomy, light breeze. 2 men were sent to the seaside to relieve the guard.	NW / E
Thu.	2	Snowfall and calm. In the morning strong breeze with small snowstorm.	E
Fri.	3	The weather and wind the same. At night and in the morning calm, but heavy snowfall.	
Sat.	4	The same weather. In the morning strong breeze with gusts and with snowstorm from	E
Sun.	5	The weather and wind the same.	
Mon.	6	The weather and wind the same. In the morning wind dropped and snowstorm stopped.	ESE
Tue.	7	The weather and wind the same. In the morning frost and sunshine.	
Wed.	8	Sunshine and calm. In the morning frost.	
Thu.	9	The same.	
Fri.	10	The same. A sailor arrived from the seaside.	
Sat.	11	Sunshine and calm. In the morning frost.	
Sun.	12	The same.	
Mon.	13	The same.	
Tue.	14	The same.	
Wed.	15	The same.	

Folio 58

D.W.	D.W.	January 1729	Winds
Thu.	16	Snowfall and calm.	
Fri.	17	Light snowfall and calm. A sailor was sent to Bol'sheretsk outpost for materiel and other things. In the morning light breeze.	E
Sat.	18	Snowfall, light breeze.	
Sun.	19	Gloomy and calm. The sailor who had been allowed to go to Upper Kamchatsk arrived at the command. In the morning sunshine and frost.	
Mon.	20	Sunshine and calm. In the morning light frost.	
Tue.	21	Fresh breeze and light snowstorm.	
Wed.	22	The weather and wind the same.	
Thu.	23	Gloomy and calm. In the morning temporary sunshine through.	
Fri.	24	At times wind with small snowstorm. In the morning light frost and sunshine.	
Sat.	25	Sunshine and calm. By the evening cloudy, in the morning sunshine.	
Sun.	26	The same weather.	
Mon.	27	At night small snowfall and calm.	
Tue.	28	At times small snowstorm, wind.	W
Wed.	29	Sunshine, light frost.	
Thu.	30	Frost, the weather clear with rare clouds.	
Fri.	31	Frost. This month at the command were sick: 1 geodesist, 1 apprentice mast maker, 1 soldier.	
		February	
Sat.	1	Sunshine, light breeze. 2 men were sent to the ship to relieve the guard.	SW
Sun.	2	Sunshine and calm. Hard frost. The soldier who had been allowed to go in December arrived at the command.	
Mon.	3	Sunshine, in the morning hard frost. From 5 a.m. an eclipse of the moon began, and before sunrise the moon was all dark, as one could see with the naked eye; after sunrise it could no longer be seen. Today, on the name day of Her Sovereign Majesty,[323] the sailors and soldiers took up formation with guns and shot 3 times from 17 guns.	
Tue.	4	Sunshine and hard frost. A soldier was allowed to go for his own needs till 15 April.	
Wed.	5	Sunshine and calm. In the morning cloudy.	
Thu.	6	Cloudy with intermittent sunshine.	
Fri.	7	The same weather and calm.	
Sat.	8	Sunshine, light frost. 1 sailor and 1 soldier who were on guard at the ship arrived from the seaside.	
Sun.	9	Sunshine and warm. In the morning snowfall and calm.	
Mon.	10	Snowfall, in the morning spells of sunshine.	
Tue.	11	Sunshine, warm and calm.	
Wed.	12	Sunshine, in the morning gloomy.	
Thu.	13	Gloomy.	
Fri.	14	Fresh breeze with light snowstorm.	W
Sat.	15	The same, in the morning sunshine.	
Sun.	16	Sunshine, light breeze from ….	W
Mon.	17	Strong gale with snowstorm and sunshine.	W
Tue.	18	Sunshine, fresh breeze.	
Wed.	19	Sunshine and calm, considerable frost.	
Thu.	20	⎫	
Fri.	21	⎪	
Sat.	22	⎬ Sunshine and frost.	
Sun.	23	⎭	
Mon.	24	Fresh breeze and cold, sunshine.	N,W
Tue.	25	The weather and wind the same. Navigator Angel arrived from Bol'sheretsk with 1 corporal and 1 soldier. In the morning moderate gale and cold.	W
Wed.	26	The weather cloudy, wind the same and light snowstorm. In the morning sunshine and calm. The same as in January.[324]	
Thu.	27	Sunshine and calm. 3 men at the command were sick.	
Fri.	28	Light breeze and blowing snow. 2 sailors and 1 soldier arrived at the command from Bol'sheretsk. In the morning wind and heavy snowfall.	E

D.W.	D.M.	March 1729	Winds
Sat.	1	Heavy snowfall and calm, from midnight strong gale with blowing snow and sunshine.	E
Sun.	2	Strong gale with blowing snow and sunshine. In the morning sunshine and calm.	E
Mon.	3	Sunshine and calm.	
Tue.	4	Light snowfall. At night fresh breeze. In the morning heavy snowfall.	W
Wed.	5	The weather and wind the same. In the morning sunshine and calm.	
Thu.	6	Sunshine and calm.	
Fri.	7	The same.	
Sat.	8	Sunshine with small clouds. A soldier was punished for his offence and sent to the seaside as a guard.	
Sun.	9	By the evening moderate gale rose with snowstorm, continuing night.	W
Mon.	10	Light blowing snow, in the morning light breeze, snowfall, wind from the same direction.	
Tue.	11	The weather and wind the same.	
Wed.	12	The weather and wind the same. 2 men who were on guard arrived from the seaside.	
Thu.	13	The weather and wind the same. In the morning sunshine and calm.	
Fri.	14	Sunshine, light breeze.	
Sat.	15	Sunshine and calm. In the night fire was seen on the mountain that has been smoking incessantly. A sailor was sent to the seaside for flour.	
Sun.	16	At night snowfall, in the morning light breeze, sunshine with small drifting clouds. A corporal and a soldier who had orders to be at Bol'sheretsk outpost were sent there.	W
Mon.	17	The weather and wind the same.	
Tue.	18	Sunshine and calm.	
Wed.	19	The same.	
Thu.	20	Sunshine. 1 foreman, 3 sailors, 4 soldiers, 2 carpenters were sent to the forest to burn charcoal and prepare planks for side-keels and firewood.	
Fri.	21	Sunshine and calm. A soldier was sent to Bol'sheretsk on an errand for Lieutenant Spanberch.	
Sat.	22	Sunshine. The sailor arrived from the seaside and brought 20 bags of flour. Wind with light drifting snow, and at times strong gale.	W
Sun.	23	Sunshine, moderate breeze with light snowstorm, at night calm.	
Mon.	24	Gloomy, fresh breeze. In the morning sunshine and calm.	E
Tue.	25	Sunshine and calm.	
Wed.	26	Sunshine and calm. 8 men were sent to the forest in addition to those sent earlier.	
Thu.	27	Sunshine, light breeze between N and W.	
Fri.	28	Sunshine and calm.	
Sat.	29	The soldier who had been allowed to go for his own needs [on 31 December] arrived from Upper.	
Sun.	30	Sunshine and warm, moderate gale from ….	SW
Mon.	31	The weather and wind the same. This month the following were sick at the command: the geodesist, the apprentice mast maker, the soldier.	
		April	
Tue.	1	Moderate gale and warm. 2 soldiers were sent to the Bol'shaia River with the officers' baggage. 2 men were sent to the seaside to relieve the guards.	
Wed.	2	Sunshine and warm. The servicemen who burned charcoal and laid in wood arrived from the forest.	
Thu.	3	Sunshine and warm.	
Fri.	4	Sunshine, light air.	
Sat.	5	The sailor [Selivanov] who had been sent to Bol'sheretsk in November returned, and so did 3 men who had been on guard at the seaside.	
Sun.	6	Sunshine and warm, in the morning gloomy and calm.	
Mon.	7	Gloomy, at times moderate gale from ….	SW
Tue.	8	Gloomy, in the evening strong gale rose from ….	E
Wed.	9	Gloomy, strong gale, in the morning sunshine, wind the same.	SW

D.W.	D.M.	April 1729	Winds
Thu.	10	Gloomy. Strong gale, at times snowfall, then sunshine. Owing to his illness, Lieutenant Spanberch was allowed to go to Bol'sheretsk outpost, because he could not go by sea, and 1 soldier was sent with him. In the morning sunshine and calm. 19 men were sent to the forest to burn charcoal and to move out planks and firewood from the forest by the river. In the morning sunshine.	
Fri.	11	Sunshine, light breeze. In the morning overcast and light snowfall.	E
Sat.	12	Sunshine, wind N.	N
Sun.	13	Sunshine and calm, gloomy, light breeze and warm.	N
Mon.	14	The weather and wind the same. In the morning wind from W with light snowstorm.	W
Tue.	15	Sunshine and warm. The men arrived from the forest and reported that the planks were ready and one pit of charcoal had been burned. In the morning sunshine and calm. A sailor was sent to the seaside for flour.	
Wed.	16	Sunshine and calm.	
Thu.	17	Sunshine, light breeze. In the morning a soldier of our command, from the Tobol'sk garrison, died. He had been sick for 9½ months.	
Fri.	18	Overcast, light air, in the morning light sunshine, fresh breeze and warm.	W E
Sat.	19	The weather and wind the same, in the morning sunshine.	
Sun.	20	Sunshine, in the morning gloomy, strong gale rose.	
Mon.	21	Strong gale and warm. In the morning, wind the same and sunshine. 2 sailors and a caulker were sent to the seaside to protect the ship from ice, and they were ordered to caulk her.	ENE
Tue.	22	Sunshine, strong gale. In the morning a foreman was sent to the forest. He had orders to prepare wood for a main-boom.	ENE
Wed.	23	Overcast, wind the same. In the morning sunshine, calm and warm.	
Thu.	24	Sunshine and warm. A sailor arrived from the seaside bringing 20 bags of flour. The foreman arrived from the seaside and reported that the timber for the boom had been prepared and carried to the river. 400 empty rawhide bags were given to commissary Petrov at the Lower outpost.	
Fri.	25	Sunshine, moderate breeze. In the morning wind the same and gloomy.	NE
Sat.	26	Short spell of sunshine, wind, warm, in the morning dark.	E
Sun.	27	Dark, light breeze.	
Mon.	28	Snowfall, light breeze.	
Tue.	29	Sunshine and warm, light breeze. In the morning strong gale and a little sunshine breaking through.	W, E
Wed.	30	Gloomy, strong gale, and at times light wet snowfall. In the morning sunshine, wind the same. This month there was the same number of sick at the command as in March.	E
		May	
Thu.	1	Sunshine, fresh breeze, in the night snowfall, in the morning sunshine and warm, this night calm.	E
Fri.	2	The same weather, by the evening light breeze, in the night snowfall. The Captain ordered the commissary to request to cut 10 rafts of firewood at Kapichi and to float them to the seaside.	NW
Sat.	3	The weather and wind the same. Tonight the ice on Kamchatka River, in front of the outpost, has begun to break.	
Sun.	4	Sunshine, in the morning moderate gale and at times snowfall.	
Mon.	5	Moderate gale with snowfall. In the morning a foreman and with him 5 men of our command, 10 natives in 5 boats were sent to float the cut wood and charcoal to the seaside.	
Tue.	6	Gloomy, fresh breeze. In the morning a short sunny spell, light air, and at times strong breeze. The Captain ordered empty barrels and other things to be transported to Kliuchi.	W
Wed.	7	Gloomy, wind the same, in the morning sunshine.	
Thu.	8	With intermittent sunshine.	
Fri.	9	The weather quite clear, wind the same. The sailor Belyi arrived from the Upper outpost and with him 1 sailor and 4 soldiers in 8 dugouts. They brought rigging according to their orders, and provisions. Today the Captain moved from the outpost to Kliuchi. 5 carpenters arrived with wood and charcoal. In the morning sunshine, warm and calm.	N and W

D.W.	D.M.	May	Winds
Sat.	10	Sunshine and calm. All servicemen moved from the outpost to Kliuchi. In the morning sunshine and calm, warm. Rafts with wood and charcoal were sent to the seaside, with 11 servicemen, namely: 2 sailors, 1 foreman, a soldier, 5 carpenters, 1 blacksmith, and a soldier was sent separately for fishing. On the same rafts were sent 36 empty barrels and 6 flasks.	
Sun.	11	Warm, dark with sunny spells, light breeze between S and W. In the morning sunshine, warm and calm.	
Mon.	12	Sunshine. A navigator was sent to the seaside and with him 6 sailors, the apprentice boat maker, and 3 soldiers on 12 dugouts, and with them rigging and provisions brought from Upper Ostrog, also different small things, left from the last campaign. The Captain ordered them to make side-keels, boom, spanker gaff and other things in need of repair, and to rig up the ship. By the evening strong breeze rose from …. In the morning sunshine, wind the same. The following items were handed over to the commissary of the local outpost: the sails of the ship – mainsail, topsail, forestaysail, 2 jibs; 20 new empty bags, 10 raw skins, scrap-iron 3 poods 10 pounds, 5 old reindeer beddings,[325] a speaking-trumpet and some broken tin lanterns, 79 sazhens of old sweep-net, some geodesist's instruments: a quadrant with accessories, besides a balance-weight and a base for an astrolabe with its sights and with legs, a brass semicircle; a big padlock for a storehouse; canon powder […] pood […] pounds;[326] fine [gunpowder] 1 pood 34 pounds, and 35 pounds of fuse.	E
Tue.	13	Sunshine, moderate breeze, in the morning sunshine.	
Wed.	14	Sunshine, light breeze. In the night strong gale rose from NW and blew till noon, but the sun kept shining.	
Thu.	15	Sunshine and calm. The quartermaster was sent to the seaside with 2 soldiers on 3 ferries[327] and with them 116 poods 20 pounds of rusks and other small things and gunpowder. By the evening gentle breeze from E. In the morning sunshine, wind the same.	

D.W.	D.M.	May 1729	Winds
Fri.	16	Overcast, strong gale, at night and in the morning drizzling.	
Sat.	17	Overcast, light air. The seafarer who had been allowed to go in November arrived from Dol'sheretsk.	
Sun.	18	Sunshine, fresh breeze.	E
Mon.	19	Sunshine, light air. A sailor arrived from the seaside and brought 10 dugouts. In the morning, a soldier was sent along the stream Elovka to collect larch resin.	
Tue.	20	Sunshine. The sick geodesist was sent by the seaside with a drummer, 2 soldiers, a seafarer.	
Wed.	21	Sunshine, light breeze. Lieutenant Chirikov, together with the midshipman, an apprentice mast maker, a sailor, a soldier, a seafarer left for the seaside on 2 ferries. At Kliuchi were left: the Captain with the physician, 2 sailors, a soldier.	
Thu.	22	Sunshine, at times gentle breeze. By 7 o'clock we were close to the mouth. Due to the heavy adverse wind we halted for the night. At 6 a.m. we proceeded and arrived near the sea, where the ship was moored. The men were all at work, making side-keels, boom, wooden sweep and rigging the ship. The weather gloomy, moderate gale.	SSE
Fri.	23	Gloomy, fresh breeze and fog.	SEbS
Sat.	24	Gloomy, moderate gale, at times the fog drifted. In the morning gloomy and drizzle, light breeze.	SSE
Sun.	25	The weather and wind the same. The Captain with the physician, 2 sailors, 1 soldier arrived on 6 dugouts. In the morning thin fog, light breeze.	SSE
Mon.	26	Overcast, light breeze the same. At night rain, in the morning calm and rain.	
Tue.	27	Gloomy, moderate gale. In the morning strong breeze with a short spell of rain.	S
Wed.	28	The weather and wind the same.	NE
Thu.	29	Cloudy, wind from S, light breeze. The soldier who had been sent for resin arrived. In the morning sunny spells, fresh breeze.	NE

D.W	D.M		Winds
Fri.	30	The same weather, fresh breeze. In the morning sunshine with drifting clouds. A navigator was sent to the river mouth to sound the channel.	S
Sat.	31	The weather and wind the same. In the morning strong gale. The servicemen moved aboard altogether.	
		June	
Sun.	1	The weather cloudy, moderate gale. In the morning strong breeze and clear. Nobleman Chemesov of Irkutsk arrived from Iakutsk. From this date the Captain ordered giving sea provisions to all the men who were aboard the ship for the cruise. And the men aboard the ship[328] were: 1 The Captain,[329] 1 lieutenant, 1 physician, 1 navigator, 1 midshipman, 1 quartermaster, 13 sailors, 1 drummer, 6 soldiers, 1 carpenter foreman, 4 carpenters, 1 caulker, 1 sailmaker, 2 interpreters, in all 35 men, 6 officers' servants. Provisions aboard: flour – 458 poods 29 pounds, rusks – 116 poods 25 pounds, groats – 57 poods, meat – 70 poods, salted fish – 10 barrels, iukola – 21 bunches, cod-liver oil – 2 barrels, salt – 2 poods, suet – 7 poods 20 pounds, gunpowder – 7 poods 29 pounds, fresh water – 35 barrels, kvass – 2 barrels, peas – 2 poods, firewood about 5 or 6 sazhens. Aboard the other vessel:[330] 1 apprentice boat maker, 1 apprentice mast maker – sick, 1 geodesist – sick, 1 Admiralty blacksmith, 7 soldiers, 1 carpenter of Eniseisk. The weather clear, light air. At noon we took the altitude of the sun on meridian 57°07', its declination 23°10'N, from this the latitude of fix 56°03'N. The Captain deigned to announce sailor Belyi as assistant skipper[331] at the command.	S NEbN
Mon.	2	Clear, wind from S. In the morning wind from NNE, by 10 o'clock it blew from S.	N NNE
Tue.	3	Cloudy with sunny spells, moderate gale. In the evening strong gale and rain. In the morning cloudy with sun breaking through. Moderate breeze.	SSW SbE
Wed.	4	Clear with few clouds. After midnight light air and variable. At 7 o'clock we ran from the summer dwellings of the servitors to the mouth and dropped anchor. The other vessel followed us.	
Thu.	5	Sunshine and warm, light breeze, the high tide was at 8 p.m. In the morning sunshine, light breeze and variable between N and NW. At 5½ a.m. we raised the anchor and proceeded from the mouth of the Kamchatka River, and the river stream carried us near the shore over the submerged shoal head, from this shoal head between the sea and the river to the direction SWbS, at the most shallow place the depth was 3 sazhens, but the water was rising, and when we reached the deep water, the last 2 balagans were standing from us to NEbN¼E. Before us the vessel "Fortuna" put out to sea, higher than us, between the shoal head and a small submerged island, but we believe it is more shallow there. And proceeding from this place we carried all sails, except the forestaysail. But it was very calm, and for that reason we were carried only by the stream from the mouth of the river to SWbS¾W by compass. At 9:30 o'clock a strong current to WbS began from the eastern side of the bay towards the western shore, and there was hardly any wind. Due to this, we dropped anchor at a depth of 12 sazhens, on a bottom of fine sand. And from this place we observed the summer dwellings of the servitors, where the ship had been fitted for campaign, to NE½E, 6.5 miles away. From 8 o'clock (a strong current began)[332] and until noon it was cloudy with a little sunshine breaking through. At 11:30 o'clock we lifted anchor and proceeded. Light breeze. We towed the ship and then anchored.	

Folio 60 verso

Hours	Rhumbs	Winds	Miles	Right rhumbs	Leeway	Fri. 6 June 1729. Events on the route from Kamchatka River to Bol'shaia River
1		SbW				The weather cloudy with sunshine, gentle breeze.
2		SbE				At 1 o'clock we weighed anchor and went on, but were carried by the current. At 2 o'clock we dropped the anchor again near the same place.
3						At 3 o'clock we weighed anchor and began to
4						maneuver out from Kamchatsk Bay with all sails set, except the forestaysail. The vessel "Fortuna"
5						was left at anchor in the bay.
6						At 7:25 the balagan at the mouth was seen
7						to 47°00' from N by W. Having proceeded
8						to SW½W 1.3 miles, we observed the same balagan to 37°00' from N by W at a distance of 7.4 miles.
9	WSW	S	1.5	W	1R	From 7 o'clock to midnight rain.
10						At 9 o'clock light air and variable. And therefore all sails were lowered and we carried only topsail.
11						The weather gloomy, after midnight with rain.
12						
1	SEbE	NW	.5	SE		At 1 o'clock calm, we carried foresail and topsail.
2	EbS½S	NbE	3.2	ESE½E		At 2 o'clock we hoisted mainsail. Fresh breeze.
3			2.5			By 4 o'clock the shore extends to ESE.
4	EbS		4.0	ESE		From 3 o'clock to 6:30 calm. The weather cloudy
5	calm					with a little sunshine breaking through.
6	WSW	-	0.5	WbS		At 6:30 light breeze with rain.
7	E	WNW	2.0	EbS		By 8 o'clock the shore extends to NEbN.
8	-	N	3.5			We carried all sails, except the forestaysail.
9	E	-	3.0			From 7 o'clock to noon the weather murky
10	SSE½S	}calm	2.5	SbE½S		with rain, we carried mainsail, foresail,
11		}and				topsail.
12		}variable				From 9 o'clock we held only foresail.

Table of daily reckoning	Latitudes		Diff. of latitude		Departure		Rhumb	Distance		Diff. of long.		Compass declination
	from	to	N	S	E	W		right	added	daily	total	
Reckoned	56°03'	55°47'		16'	17'47		SE 2°31' E	23.69				
Corrected	56°03'	55°43'42		19'58	21'64			29.35	52.46	38'69		1 R E

Hours	Rhumbs	Wind	Miles	Right rhumbs	Leeway drift	Sat. 7 June 1729
1	ESE	NNE	.7	SWbS¼W	} 8	Sunny spells, light air and rough sea from NNE.
2			.7			We took in mainsail at brails. Soon after 2 o'clock we set mainsail, and wind rose, at 3:30 we
3	E		1.5	SEbE¼S	2	hoisted jib. The weather murky and rain.
4			3.5	SSE¼E	} 1	We carried mainsail, foresail, jib.
5	ENE	N	3.5	E¼S		At 4:30 o'clock jib was lowered until the 9th hour.
6			2.5	EbS¼S	2	The weather murky, fresh breeze, only high sea
7	NE	NNW	2.5	EbN¼E		from N.
8			3.		} 2	At 8 o'clock the eastern point of Kamchatka land[333] was to NWbW.
9	NE	NNW	3.	EbN¼E	2	At 9:30 o'clock we fixed a reef of mainsail, heavy
10			3.	EbN¾E	2½	wind rose. Soon after 10 we fixed a reef of foresail.
11			3.5	E		From 7 o'clock to midnight the weather murky
12			3.		} 2¾	with rain, strong gale. We carried mainsail and
1	NE	NNW	3.	E		foresail.
2			3.		} 2¾	At 2 a.m. the foresail was torn by strong gale,
3	NEbN		1.5	E¼S		therefore it was lowered and we ran under
4			1.5		} 4	mainsail only.
5	NEbN	NNW	1.5	E¾S		From midnight to 5 o'clock the weather
6			1.5		} 4½	murky with rain, strong gale.
7			1.7			From 5 o'clock to 9 and from 9 o'clock to
8			1.7			noon the weather murky and drizzling.
9	NE	NbW	1.5	EbS¾S		Strong gale.
10			1.5		} 4½	We ran under mainsail only.
11			1.5			
12			1.5			

Table of daily reckoning	Latitudes		Diff. of latitude		Departure		Rhumb	Distance		Diff. of long.		Compass declination
	from	to	N	S	E	W		right	added	daily	total	
Reckoned	55°47'	55°42'		5'05	46'96		EbS 5°07'E	47.23				
Corrected	55°43'42	55°37'40		6'02	58'18			58.51	103.0	1°42'4 E	2°21' 09 E	1¼ R
											09 E	

Folio 61

Hours	Rhumbs		Miles	Right rhumbs	Leeway	Sun. 8 June 1729. Events on the sea route from Kamchatka River to the mouth of Bol'shaia River
1	NE	NbW	1.5	EbS¾S	⎫	From noon to 4 o'clock strong gale,
2			1.5		4½	the weather murky with fog.
3	-	-	1.5		⎬	
4			1.5		⎭	Soon after 4 we hoisted foresail
5	NEbE	NbW	3.3	EbN¼E	⎫	with fixed reef. From 4 o'clock
6			3.3			to 8 the weather murky, strong gale and fog.
7			3.		1	We carried mainsail and foresail with fixed reefs.
8			3.		⎭	From 8 o'clock to 10 we held
9	NEbE	NbW	3.	EbN¼E	1	mainsail and foresail.
10			4.			
11	NEbN	NNW	1.5	EbS¼S	5	At 10 o'clock wind rose, and foresail
12			1.5		⎭	was lowered. Until midnight we ran under
1	NEbN	NNW	1.5	EbS¼S	⎫	mainsail only.
2			1.5		5	From midnight to noon we ran under
3			1.5			mainsail only. The weather murky, strong gale
4			1.5		⎭	with fog and very cold.
5	NEbN	NNW	1.5	EbS¼S	⎫	High sea from N.
6			1.5		5	
7			1.5			
8			1.5		⎭	
9	NEbN	NNW	1.7	EbS¼S	⎫	
10			1.7			
11			1.7		5	
12			1.7		⎭	

	Latitudes		Diff. of lat.		Departure		Rhumb	Distance		Diff. of long.		Compass declination
	from	to	N	S	E	W		right	added	daily	total	
Reckoned	55°42'	55°38'		4'4	46'37		EbS 5°50' E	46.58				
Corrected	55°37'40	55°32'32		5'08	57'44			57.10	106.8	1°46'3 E	4°07' 09 E 39 b E	1¼ R

PLATE 33. A Kamchadal (autoethnonym Ïtelmen) riding a dog sled,
ethnographical tablet from the Göttingen copy of Bering's Final Map (p. 191).

Courtesy Niedersächsische Staats- und Universitätsbibliothek Göttingen.

Hours	Rhumbs	Winds	Miles	Right rhumbs	Leeway	Mon. 9 June 1729
1	NEbN	NNW	1.5	EbS¼S	5	The weather murky, strong gale.
2	⌈		.8			At 1:30 o'clock we hoisted foresail,
	⌊SWbW		3.0	WSW¼W		turned to port and ran to SWbW.
3			6.			
4			6.			
5	SWbW	NNW	6.	WSW¼W		From 1 o'clock to 8 we held mainsail and
6			6.			foresail with fixed reefs. The weather
7			6.			gloomy, strong gale.
8			6.5			
9	SWbW	NNW	6.5	WSW¼W		
10			6.5			At 10 o'clock foresail was lowered and we
11	WNW	NbW	1.5	WSW¼W		began to drift under one mainsail and held
12			1.5			the sail on the left side.
1			1.5	WSW	⎫	
2			1.5		⎬5	Soon after 2 we hoisted foresail
3	SWbW	NNW	6.5	WSW	⎭	and proceeded.
4			6.5			At 10 o'clock we saw a land to WNW, 10
5			6.5			minutes distant.[334] This land was to the S of
6	SWbW¾W	NNW	6.5			Kamchatka. At noon the nearest distance
7	SWbW		7.	WSW		from the land was 9 minutes to WNW,[335]
8			7.			and the land extends back as far as sight
9			7.			can follow to the NNE, and ahead to W.[336]
10			7.			We took the altitude of the sun center on
11			6.			meridian 58°17', declination of the sun by
12			6.			local meridian 23°27'.
						From this the latitude of fix – 54°40'.

	Latitudes		Diff. of lat.		Departure		Rhumb	Distance		Diff. of long.		Compass
	from	to	N	S	E	W		right	added	daily	total	declination
Reckoned	55°38'	54°55'58		42'42		113'7	WSW 2°02' W	121.4				1¼ R to midnight, then 1 R
Corrected	55°32'32	54°40'		52'32		140'8		150.4	262.7	4°06' W	00°01' 39 b E	

Folio 61 verso

Hours	Rhumbs	Winds	Miles	Right rhumbs	Leeway[337]	Tue. 10 June 1729. Events on the sea route from Kamchatka River to the mouth of Bol'shaia River
1	SW½W	N	5.5	SWbW½W		The weather lightly cloudy with sunshine, fresh breeze. Soon after 1 o'clock we hoisted forestaysail. Foresail was lowered, and until 4 o'clock we held mainsail and forestaysail. The shore extended parallel to our route, high rocks.[338] Soon after 4 o'clock mainsail was lowered because spanker gaff was broken, and we repaired it.
2	SW	NE	5.5	SWbW		
3			5.8			
4			3.5			
5	SW	variable	2.	SWbW		
6		⎫	1.5			Light air and variable between NE and E.
7		⎬calm	.8			By 7 o'clock calm. Soon after 7 o'clock forestaysail was lowered and we drifted without sails.
8		⎭	.3			
9	calm					At 8 o'clock we saw a high mountain to NWbN 20' distant.[339] Soon after 10 o'clock we turned to port. From 9 o'clock to midnight the weather clear, light breeze.
10	WSW	S	1.5	WbS		
11	SE	SWbS	2.5	SE¾S		
12	SEbS		2.5	SEbS¾S	⎫¼R	
1			2.		⎭	
2	SSE		1.5	SSE	1	At 1:30 we hoisted topsail. At 2:30 o'clock at sunrise we observed amplitude from N by E 35°00', sun declination N 23°27', and the reckoned latitude was 54°20'N, from this compass declination was found 11°50' eastern.
3	S	WSW	2.5	S¾W	¼	
4	SSW	W	2.5	SSW½W	½	
5			3.			At 4 o'clock the land was behind us to NEbN½E. We carried mainsail, foresail, topsail, jib. From 4 o'clock to 8 we had mainsail, foresail, topsail, and forestaysail. From 8 o'clock to noon, sunshine through gloom and calm. We drifted without sails.
6			3.			
7			3.			
8	⎫					
9	⎪					
10	⎬calm					At noon we sighted the altitude of the sun with correction 59°21', sun declination N 23°28' from this the latitude of fix – 54°07'N. At 12 o'clock the shortest distance from the land to us was to NW – 24 minutes.
11	⎪					
12	⎭					

	Latitudes		Diff. of lat.		Departure		Rhumb	Distance		Diff. of long.		Compass declin. E
	from	to	N	S	E	W		right	added	daily	total	
Reckoned	54°40'	54°66'78 8⁸⁸										
Corrected	54°40'	54°07'		33'22		12'25	SbW 9°23 by W	35.50	62.54	22'04 W	20'65 W	1 R

179

Hours	Rhumbs	Winds	Miles	Right rhumbs	Leeway	Wed. 11 June 1729
1						The weather clear with sunshine through gloom.
2	S	WSW	1.0	S¾W	¼	Light breeze. From noon to 4 we carried mainsail, foresail, topsail, jib.
3			3.5			
4			4.0			From 3 o'clock to 8 fresh breeze and sunshine breaking through the dark.
5	S	WSW	4.	S	1	At 8 o'clock at sunset we sighted amplitude of the
6			4.			sun from N by W – 56°30', its declination – N 23°29', and the reckoned latitude was – N 53°40', from this
7			3.			compass declination was found – 8°31'east. Land
8			3.			from us to W, 20 minutes distant, and extending by WSW½W.[340]
9	SbW½W	WbS	2.2	SbW	1½	At 9 o'clock a point of land was ahead to SWbW.
10	SSW		3.			From 8 o'clock to midnight the weather clear, fresh
11	SWbS	W	2.5	SSW	2	breeze, we carried the same sails. At 12:30 topsail was
12	SSW½W		2.7	SbW½W	2	lowered, at 2 o'clock we set forestaysail, topsail, and took in mainsail.
1	SWbS	between N&W	1.8	SW		At 3 o'clock at sunrise we observed amplitude of the
2	SW		1.5	SWbW		sun from N by E 36°30', its declination – N 23°29',
3		NW	2.5			and the reckoned latitude was – N 53°27', from this
4			3			compass declination 8°46' east. At 4 o'clock the land was from us NWbW in 6 minutes.
5	SW	N	2.			From 3 to 8 o'clock clear, light air. We held
6	SSW	⎡calm	1.	SWbS		forestaysail, topsail. At 6 o'clock we lowered
7		⎢& va-				forestaysail and set mainsail.
8		⎢ri- ⎣able				From 8 o'clock to noon sunshine, variable light air. We carried mainsail, foresail, topsail, jib. At 12
9	SbW	WSW	1.5	SSW		o'clock the land was from us NWbW½N, 5 minutes
10		with	1.5			distant.[341] At noon the altitude of the sun was sighted
		turn				with correction 6°16', its declination – N 23°23', from
		by W				this the latitude of fix – 53°13'N.
11	S		1.	SbW		From the end of this day to the 20th of this month it was determined that the sea current, which usually
						flowed along the shore, as a result of prevailing winds
12	SbW½W	WbS	.8	SSW½W		between S and W, changed direction towards the open sea between S and E.

	Latitudes		Diff. of lat.		Departure		Rhumb	Distance		Diff. of long.		Compass declin. E
	from	to	N	S	E	W		right	added	daily	total	
Reckoned		53°24'07		43'93		15'	SbW 7°36' W	46.43				
Corrected	54°07'	53°13'		54'00		18'84		58.31	98.60	31'79 W	52'44 W	1 R

Conspicuous places	No. of these places	Time of observation	directions			
			N – E	N – W	S – E	S – W
A mountain in Kronoki[342]	1	5:30 p.m.		14.15		
A mountain on Zhupanova with 2 peaks[343]	2	the same time		79.15		
The mountain in Kronoki again	1	7 p.m.		13.25		
The mountain on Zhupanova again	2	the same time		72.45		
A mountain on Avacha that glows[344]	3	the same time		87.45		
The same again	3	9:30 p.m.		82.45		

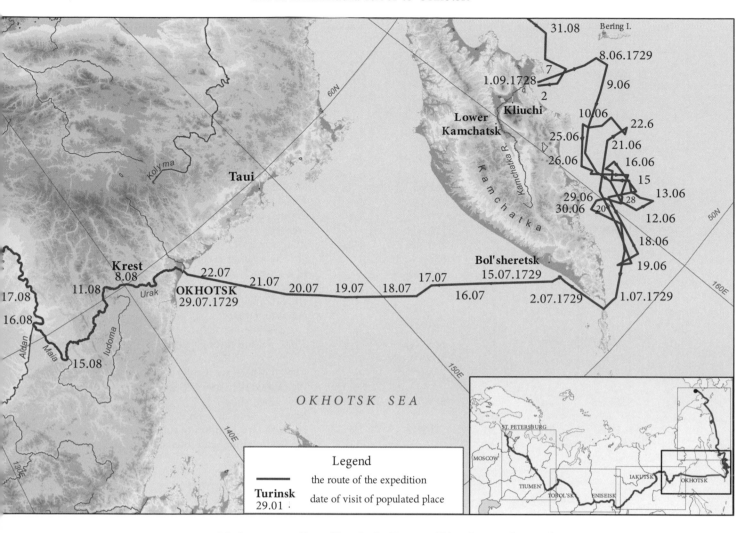

PLATE 34. Modern map 7: From Kamchatka River to Okhotsk. By Viktor Sedov.

Hours	Rhumbs	Winds	Miles	Right rhumbs	Leeway	Thu. 12 June 1729. Events on the sea route from Kamchatka River to the mouth of Bol'shaia River
1	SSW½W	W	1.	SSE¼S	1½	The weather clear, light air, at times
2	SbW½W		1.2		½	strong breeze. We held all sails and ran
3	S	SWbW	3.5	S¼W		along the shore described above, beyond the
						bay.³⁴⁵
4	SbW	WSW	3.5	SbW¼W		
5			3.3	S¾W	1	
6	S	SWbW	1.8	S¼W	½	
7	SbE		1.8	SSE½S	1¼	At 8 o'clock the Avacha Volcano was from us to
8			3.2	SSE¼S	⎱1½	NWbW¾N, ahead a high mountain to WbS¼W.³⁴⁶
9	SSE		2.3	SEbS¾S		At 8:30 o'clock we turned to starboard and
	NWbW	⎰WSW	2.2	NW¾N	1½	lowered topsail. The weather clear, fresh
10	WNW½N		4.0	NW¼N	1	breeze.
		⎱	1.8	NW¾N	⎱1½	At 10:30 o'clock we turned to port and lowered
11	SbE	⎰SW	1.7	SSE¼S		jib. The weather clear, strong breeze.
12			2.5	SEbS¾S	2	At 12 o'clock strong gale and wet fog.
1			2.2	SEbS¼S	2½	The weather murky with wet fog. The land
2			2.0			was out of sight due to fog. We carried
3			2.5			mainsail, foresail.
	⎧		1.3			
4	⎩WNW	SW	1.2	NWbN¼N		Thick wet fog, strong breeze.
5	W½N		2.5	NWbW¾N	2½	
6	WbN		2.	NW¼N		At 6:30 o'clock we turned to port.
			1.5			We carried the same sails as
7	⎩SSE½S		1.5	SE¾S	2½	mentioned above.
8			3.5			From 8 o'clock to noon the weather the same,
9	SSE¾S	SW	3.1	SEbS¼S	2¼	but with rare glimpses of sun through the dark.³⁴⁷
10			3.2			We held mainsail and foresail.
11			2.5			
12			2.5			

Sea current per day – 12   ESE½E

	Latitudes		Diff. of lat.		Departure		Rhumb	Distance		Diff. of long.		Compass declin. E
	from	to	N	S	E	W		right	added	daily	total	
Reckoned		52°39'4		33'6	4'86		SbE 10°14' b E	33.9				¾ R
Corrected	53°13'	52°33'74		39'26	15'44			42.19	69.96	25'6 E	26°84' W	

Folio 62, continuation

Hours	Rhumbs	Winds	Miles	Right rhumbs	Leeway	Wed. 13 June 1729[348]
1	WbN	SW	2.	NWbW¾N	} 2	From noon to 7 o'clock fresh breeze
2	W½N		2.	NWbW¼N		and thick fog. We carried mainsail and
3	WNW	SWbW	3.2	NW¾N		foresail.
4	WbN	SW	3.	NW¼N	1½	
5	W½N		2.5	WNW¾N		
6	W	SWbS	3.	WNW¼N	} 1½	
7			2.			
8			3.		}	By 8 o'clock the fog was slightly
9	WbS½W	SSW	3.5	WbN¾N		dissipated. We hoisted jib. The land was
10			3.		} 1½	out of sight. From 8 o'clock to midnight
11	SE	SbW	2.5	SEbE¼S		gentle breeze. We carried mainsail
12	SEbE	S	3.3		½	and foresail. The weather cloudy. At 10
1	SE½S	SSW	1.8	SEbE¾S	1½	o'clock we turned to port.
2			2.5		1½	
3			2.1	SEbE½S	} 1¾	From midnight to 4 o'clock the weather cloudy.
						Gentle breeze. We carried the same sails.
4	SEbS		2.3	SE	}	At 4 o'clock we turned to starboard.
5	WbN	SW	3.9	WNW¾N	} 1	From 4 a.m. to 8 moderate gale,
6			3.7			the weather murky with glimpses of sun.
7			3.7	NWbW	} 1¼	We carried mainsail and foresail.
8			3.6			
9	WbN		4.1	NWbW½N	}	From 8 o'clock to noon wind and
10			4.			weather the same. We carried the same
11			4.1		} 1¾	sails, the land was out of sight due to the
12			4.5			long distance.

Sea current per day   12.0   ESE½E

	Latitudes		Diff. of lat.		Departure		Rhumb	Distance		Diff. of long.		Compass declin. E
	from	to	N	S	E	W		right	added	daily	total	
Reckoned	52°39'4	53°02'29	22'89			37'08		43.31				
Corrected	52°33'74	52°50'97	17'23			26'23	NWbW 10°43' W	34.61	52.10	43'68 W	1°10' 51 W	¾ R

Hours	Rhumbs	Winds	Miles	Right rhumbs	Leeway	Sat. 14 June 1729. Events on the sea route from Kamchatka River to the mouth of Bol'shaia River
1	SEbS½S	SWbS	2.3	SE	⎫	The weather overcast, at times rain, moderate gale.
2	SSE½S		2.1	SEbS	⎬2¼	We carried mainsail and foresail.
3			2.		⎭	
4	SbE	SW	2.8	SEbS½S	⎫	
5	WbN		3.5	NWbW¼N	⎬1½	
6			3.4		⎭	After 8 o'clock[349] we saw a mountain to NWbW.
7			3.	NWbW½N	⎫1¾	From 8 o'clock to midnight fresh breeze,
8			3.2		⎭	the weather clear with starlight.
9	W½N	SW	3.3	NWbW¼N	⎫2	From midnight to 4 o'clock the
10			3.3		⎭	weather the same. We carried mainsail,
11	SbE		2.5	SEbS½S	⎫2¼	foresail. From 4 o'clock to 8 sunshine,
12			2.5		⎭	gentle breeze, roughness of the sea abated.
1	SbE	SW	1.9	SEbS¼S	⎫2½	
2			1.9		⎭	
3	WbN		2.3	NW	⎫2¼	From 7 o'clock to noon sun breaking through
4			2.4		⎭	the gloom, and at times thick fog. Moderate
5	WbN	SWbW	2.5	NWbW½N	¾	gale. We carried the same sails, except
6			2.5			that in the 10th hour we carried jib,
7			2.5	NWbW¼N	⎫1½	and in the 12th hour only mainsail.
8			2.5		⎭	
9	WbN	SW	1.9	NWbW¾N	2	
10			3.9	WNW¾N	⎫1	
11			3.7		⎭	
12			1.8	NNW¼N	4½	

Sea current per day   12.0   ESE½E

	Latitudes		Diff. of lat.		Departure		Rhumb	Distance		Diff. of long.		Compass declination E
	from	to	N	S	E	W		right	added	daily	total	
Reckoned		53°15'15	12'86			25'84		28.86				
Corrected	52°50' 97	52°58'17	7'20			15'26	NWbW 3°03' W bW	17.75	29.59	25'44 by W	1°35'96 W	¾ R

Folio 62 verso, continuation

Hours	Rhumbs	Winds	Miles	Right rhumbs	Leeway	Sun. 15 June 1729
1	SEbS½S	SWbS	3.3	SE¾S	} 1½	From noon to 4 o'clock the weather
2	SE½S	SSW	3.3	SEbE¾S		murky and thick fog, strong breeze.
3	SEbS½S	SWbS	2.7	SEbS¼S	} 1	We held mainsail, foresail and jib.
4			2.7			
5	W		2.7	WNW¼N		From 4 and to 8 o'clock and until midnight
6			2.5		} 1½	the weather and the wind the same.
7	WbS½W	SSW	2.	WbN¾N		We carried mainsail and foresail.
8	WSW½W	SbW	2.	W¾N		Land was out of sight.
9	SEbS	SSW½W	3.7	SEbE¾S	2	From midnight and until 4 o'clock the
10			2.5	SEbE¼S	2½	weather cloudy, fresh breeze rising at
11			2.5	SEbE¾S	} 2	times to strong gale. We carried mainsail
12			3.7			and foresail.
1	SE	SbW½W	2.5	ESE½E		From 12 o'clock to 3 one reef of
2			3.0		} 2¼	mainsail was fixed.
3			3.			
4	WbS		2.6	WbN	1¼	
5		SSW	3.2			From 5 a.m. rain. At 7 o'clock
6	W	SWbS	2.7	WNW	} 1¼	we hoisted jib.
7			2.8			
8			3.1			From 8 o'clock to noon the weather
9	WbS	SSW	3.1	WbN		murky with fog, gentle breeze.
10			3.1		} 1¼	We carried the same sails. Land could
11			3.			not be seen through the fog.
12	SEbS		2.2	SEbE½S		

Sea current per day   12   ESE½E

| | Latitudes | | Diff. of lat. | | Departure | | Rhumb | Distance | | Diff. of long. | | Compass |
	from	to	N	S	E	W		right	added	daily	total	declination E
Reckoned		53°00'82		14'32		5'49						
Corrected	52°58'17	52°38'19		19'98	5'09		SbE3°03'	20.61	34'1	8'49 E	1°27'47 W	¾ R

PLATE 35. A Kuril (Ainu), ethnographical tablet from the
Göttingen copy of Bering's Final Map (p. 191).

Courtesy Niedersächsische Staats- und Universitätsbibliothek Göttingen.

Folio 63

Hours	Rhumbs	Winds	Miles	Right rhumbs	Leeway	Mon. 16 June 1729. Events on the sea route from Kamchatka River to the mouth of Bol'shaia River
1	SEbE	SSW	2.3	SE		Murky weather, gentle breeze,
2			2.3		⎫1¾	at times slight glimpses of sun, we
3			2.4			held mainsail, foresail, jib.
4			2.8			At 3 o'clock we hoisted topsail, at 6
5	SEbS½S		2.8	SE¾S	1¾	o'clock jib was lowered. Land
6	SEbS	⎱vari-	2.3	SE¼S		was out of sight because of the fog.
7	WbN	⎰able	1.6	NWbW¼N	⎱1½	
8	WNW	betw.	1.7	NW¼N		
9	WbN	N & W	1.0	NWbW¼N		
10						From 10 o'clock light variable air and then calm.
11		⎰calm				We drifted to midnight without sails. The weather
12						gloomy and dark. From midnight murky and fog,
1						light variable air. First hour we drifted without
2	S	NE	0.8	S¾W		sails. At 2 o'clock we hoisted topsail and foresail.
3			1.7			
4	SSW		2.0	SSW¾W		From 4 o'clock to 8 light breeze and wet fog.
5	SbW½W	⎰NE	2.5	SSW¼W		
6		with	3.			At 6 o'clock we hoisted mainsail. At 7:30 o'clock
7		turn	3.5			we hoisted forestaysail, and foresail was lowered.
8		by E	3.			From 7 o'clock to noon gentle breeze with fog, in
9	SbW¾W	NE	3.2	SSW½W		the 11th hour glimpses of sun through the fog.
10	SSW		3.5	SSW¾W		We carried mainsail, topsail, forestaysail.
11			3.8			The land could not be seen through the fog.
12			3.5			

Sea current per day   8.0   ESE½E

	Latitudes		Diff. of lat.		Departure		Rhumb	Distance		Diff. of long.		Compass declina-tion E
	from	to	N	S	E	W		right	added	daily	total	
Reckoned		52°25'65		35'17		6'68						
Corrected	52° 38'19	51° 59'25		38'91	0'37		S 00°05' bW by E	38.95	63'72	0°0'6 E	1° 26'87 W	¾ R

Folio 63, continuation

Hours	Rhumbs	Winds	Miles	Right rhumbs	Leeway	Tue. 17 June 1729
1	SSW	⎫	3.5	SSW¾W		Murky weather, light breeze and fog.
2		⎪	3.5			From noon to 5 o'clock we carried mainsail,
3		⎬ NE with	3.			topsail, forestaysail.
4		⎪ turn	1.7			At 4 o'clock mainsail was brailed up.
5	SWbS	⎪ by E	1.5	SWbS¾W		At 5 o'clock the fog lifted, but it was still
		⎪	1.			cloudy. From 4 to 8 o'clock light breeze and
6	WSW	⎪	1.	WSW¾W		cloudy, and the land was out of sight.
7		⎪	1.5			From 7 o'clock to midnight the weather gloomy,
8		⎭	3.0			light air.
9	WSW	⎫ variable	2.8			At 9:30 o'clock forestaysail was lowered.
10		⎬ and	2.2			
11	SWbW	⎪ calm	0.5	SWbW¾W		From midnight to 4 o'clock the weather
12		⎭ from E	1.3			murky, light air, at 3 o'clock topsail
1	WSW		.5	WSW¾W		was lowered, wind variable from S by
2			.5			E and by W. At 5 o'clock we carried
3			.2			mainsail, foresail, jib. At 6 and
4			0.0			7 o'clock we drifted without sails
5	WNW	SbW	0.5	NW¼N	1½	because of stillness. At 8 o'clock we
6	⎫	calm and				carried mainsail, foresail, topsail,
7	⎬	variable	0.0			jib. From 8 o'clock to noon the weather
		by W				and wind the same. We carried the same
8	S½W		1.0	S	1¼	sails, and the land was out of sight.
9	⎫ SWbS		0.3	SWbS¾W		
	⎭ SE		0.2	SE¼S		
10	WbN	SW	3.0	WbN¾N		
11	WNW	SWbW	3.5	NWbW	¼	
12			3.8			

Sea current per day   8.0   ESE½E

	Latitudes		Diff. of lat.		Departure		Rhumb	Distance		Diff. of long.		Compass
	from	to	N	S	E	W		right	added	daily	total	declination E
Reckoned												
Corrected	51° 59'25	51° 42'50		16'75		22'1	SW7°50' by W	27. 74	44.88	35'76	2°02'63 W	¾ R

Hours	Rhumbs	Winds	Miles	Right rhumbs	Leeway	Wed. 18 June 1729. Events on the sea route from Kamchatka River to the mouth of Bol'shaia River
1	WbN¼N	SW	2.7	WNW¾N	¼	The weather cloudy, fresh breeze,
2			3.3			at times wet fog came in, and at times
3	WbN	SSW	3.2	WbN¾N		the sun was shining.
4	⌠		1.8			Until 8 o'clock we carried mainsail,
	⌊ W	SbW	2.2	W¾N		foresail, topsail and jib. Land was
5			4.0			not seen to any side.[350]
6			3.5			At 9 o'clock topsail and jib were
7	WbN		4.0	WbN¾N		lowered. At 10 o'clock we turned to
8	NWbW		3.5	NWbW¾N		port and lowered foresail, and we
9	W	SbW	4.5	W¾N		ran under mainsail only. From 8
10			3.2			o'clock to midnight the weather murky,
11	SEbS	SSW	0.8	E¾S	5	wet fog, fresh breeze.
12			0.8		do.	From midnight the weather with thick
1	SE½S		0.7	SbW	5½	wet fog, light air. At 2 o'clock
2			0.5			we drifted. At 3 o'clock we set
3	WbN½N		0.7			foresail and topsail and ran.
4			1.2			
5	WbN	SSW	3.			From 4 o'clock and to noon murky,
6		SSE	4.			at times wet fog, fresh breeze.
7			4.5			At 6:30 o'clock we set forestaysail,
8			5.5			and foresail was lowered. At 7:30
9						o'clock drizzle, and jib was
10						lowered.
11						
12						

Sea current per day –   9.0   ESE½E

	Latitudes		Diff. of lat.		Departure		Rhumb	Distance		Diff. of long.		Compass declination E
	from	to	N	S	E	W		right	added	daily	total	
Reckoned												¾ R
Corrected	51°42'50	52°14'29	31'79			46'5	NW 10° 38' by W	56.33	91.26	1°15'33 W	3°17'96 W	

Folio 63 verso, continuation

						Thu. 19 June 1729
1	NNW	SSW	5.5	NNW¾N		At 2 o'clock forestaysail and topsail were
2	NE	SSE	5.	NE¾E		lowered, and foresail was set.
3			5.			At 4 o'clock mainsail and foresail were lowered,
4		SSW	5.			and forestaysail set.
5	NW		3.5	NW¾N		From noon and until 4 o'clock rain, fresh breeze,
	NE	S	3.5	NE¾E		and at times fresh gale.
6			6.5			From 4 o'clock to 8 strong breeze with rain.
7	N		2.0	N¾E		We held one forestaysail. At 8 o'clock
	NE		4.5	NE¾E		forestaysail was lowered and
8			7.			mainsail was set, a reef was fixed
9	ESE	SbE	2.	NEbE¾E	}	and we drifted. From midnight to 4
10			1.5		} 5	o'clock fresh gale, the weather gloomy
11			2.			with rain. At 2:30 o'clock we took in
12			1.5		}	mainsail and set foresail and ran. At
1	ESE	SbE	1.5	ENE	}	3 o'clock we set forestaysail, and
2			1.5		} 5	foresail was lowered. From 4 o'clock
			0.6		}	to 8 the weather the same, but no
3	NE	SSW	3.0	NEbE		rain, fresh breeze. At 7 o'clock we
4			6.			set topsail. From 8 o'clock to noon
5	NE		6.	NEbE		moderate gale, from 10 o'clock it
6			6.			began to drop and the sky to clear.
7			5.			The Kamchatka shore appeared between W
8			5.			and NNE, extending to NEbN and SWbS.[351]
9	NE	SSW	6.5	NEbE		At 12 o'clock the glowing mountain on
10			6.0			the Avacha to WNW, and the shore to NW,
11			5.5			25 minutes distant.[352]
12			5.0			

Sea current per day –   9   ESE½E

	Latitudes		Diff. of lat.		Departure		Rhumb	Distance		Diff. of long.		Compass declination E
	from	to	N	S	E	W		right	added	daily	total	
Reckoned												¾ R to mid-night, then 1 R
Corrected	52° 14'29	53° 16'29	62'0		88'68		NE 10°03' by E	108.2	179.0	2°26'7 E	0°51'26 by W	

189

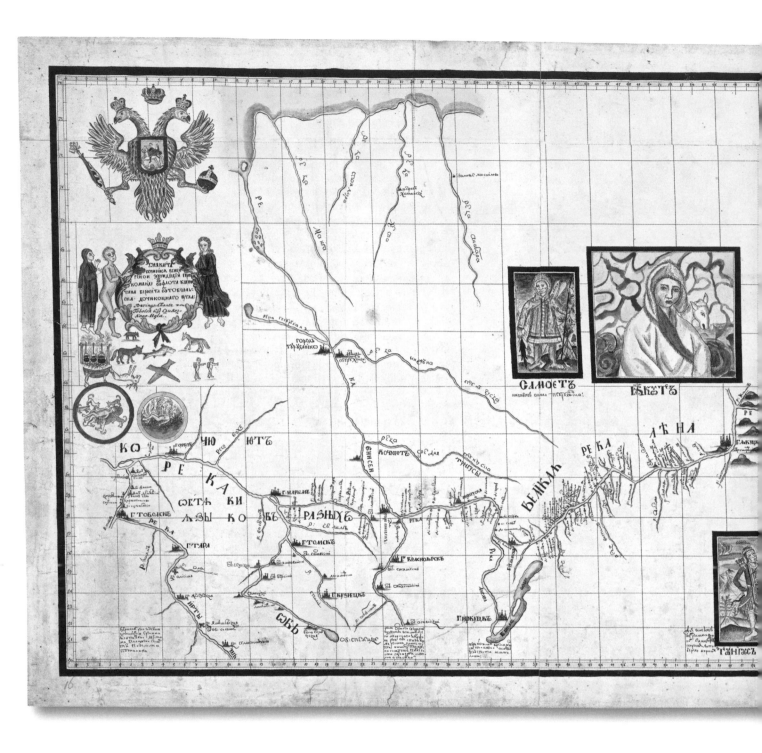

PLATE 36. Map of the route of the First Kamchatka Expedition, based on Bering's Final Map, and with ten ethnographical tablets. From the Asch Collection at the Göttingen State and University Library. The legend reads: "This map was compiled during the Siberian expedition under Navy Captain Bering, from Tobol'sk to Cape Chukchi". Map size 137 × 59.5 cm.

Courtesy Niedersächsische Staats- und Universitätsbibliothek Göttingen.

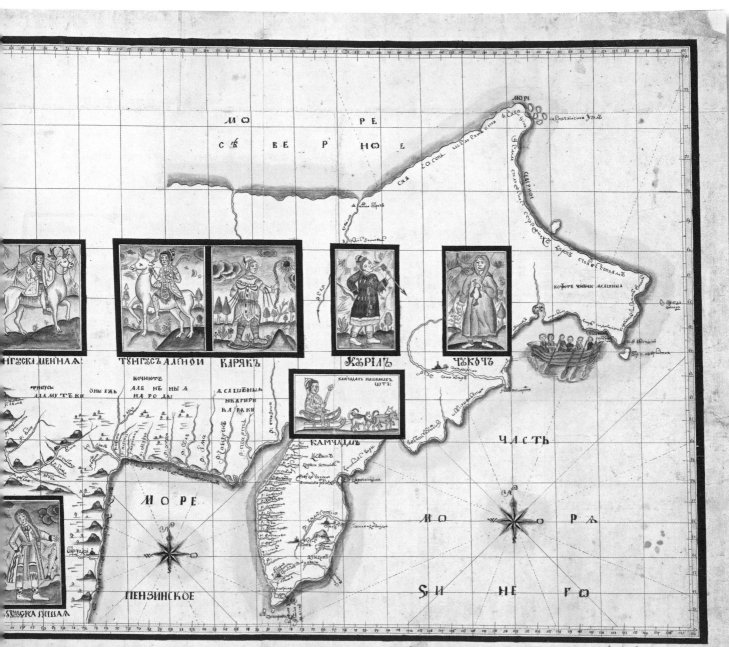

Folio 64

Hours	Rhumbs	Winds	Miles	Right rhumbs	Leeway	Fri. 20 June 1729. Events on the sea route from the Kamchatka to the mouth of Bol'shaia River
1	NE	SSW	5.2	NEbE		At 2 p.m. we hoisted mainsail.
2			4.8			The weather cloudy, moderate breeze.
3			7.			At 3 o'clock wind rose and topsail was lowered.
4			7.			At 4 o'clock rain.
5	NE	S	5.5	NEbE		From 4 o'clock to 8 the weather murky with rain, fresh breeze.
6			5.5			The land was out of sight due to fog.
7			3.5			We carried mainsail, forestaysail.
8			4.			At 8 o'clock mainsail and forestaysail were lowered, and foresail hoisted.
9	NEbE	S	2.	ENE		From 8 o'clock to midnight rain, light breeze.
10			1.5			
11			1.5			
12			1.5			From midnight to 4 o'clock rain, light air.
1	NEbE		1.5	ENE		
2			1.5			
3		SSE	1.5			From 4 to 8 rain, at 6:30 o'clock foresail was lowered and we hoisted mainsail and forestaysail.
4			1.5			
5	NEbE		1.5	ENE		The land could not be seen through the gloom.
6			1.5			Until noon rain. We carried the same sails and could not see the shore.
			1.5			
7	NE		3.	NEbE		
8			5.5			
9	NE½E	SSE	5.7	NEbE½E		
10			5.0			
11			5.0			
12			5.5			

	Latitudes		Diff. of lat.		Departure		Rhumb	Distance		Diff. of long.		Compass declination E
	from	to	N	S	E	W		right	added	daily	total	
Reckoned												
Corrected	53° 16'29	54° 04'72	26'7		46'89		NEbE 3° bW 15' by E	52'98	149.8	2°09'61 E	1°18'34 by E	1 R

Folio 64, continuation

Hours	Rhumbs	Winds	Miles	Right rhumbs	Leeway	Sat. 21 June 1729
1	NE¼E	SSE	5.5	NEbE¼E		The weather murky and rain. We held
2			5.5			mainsail and forestaysail to 8 o'clock,
3			4.5			and from 8 o'clock we drifted
4			3.			without sails.
5	NE¼E	SSE	2.	NEbE¼E		From 8 o'clock to midnight and from midnight to 4
						we drifted without sails, light air and
6			2.			variable, but rather rough sea from SSE.
7			1.5			
8		calm				
9	NNW		2.	NbW		
10						From 4 to 8 a.m. light air and variable,
11		calm				the weather murky.
12						We drifted without sails. Soon after 10
1		NNW				o'clock we hoisted foresail and
2		with				mainsail and ran. At the end of
3	NbW	turn by	0.5	N		this hour the sails were lowered and
4		NE & W				till noon we drifted without sails.
5		betw.				The weather murky and wet. Calm.
		NE				
6		and NW				We could not see land through
7	NbW		0.5	N		the gloom.
8						
9						
10						
11	SW		0.5	SWbW		
12						

Sea current per day   8.   W

	Latitudes		Diff. of lat.		Departure		Rhumb	Distance		Diff. of long.		Compass declination E
	from	to	N	S	E	W		right	added	daily	total	
Reckoned												
Corrected	54° 04'72	54° 16'05	15'02		11'79		NEbN 4° bW 21'by E	19'09	25.84	20'08 E	1°38'42 by E	1 R E

Hours	Rhumbs	Winds	Miles	Right rhumbs	Leeway	Sun. 22 June 1729. Events on the sea route from the Kamchatka to the mouth of Bol'shaia River
1	WSW	S	4.	WbS¾W	¾	The weather murky, light air and variable.
2	W	SSW	3.7	WbN¾N	¾	We carried mainsail, foresail, jib.
3	WbN		3.5	NWbW		
	⎡NWbW		1.5	NWbN	⎤1R	At 5 and 6 o'clock sunshine, then it darkened.
4	⎣SbE	W	0.8	SEbS	3	At 6 o'clock we hoisted topsail.
5	SEbS		2.5	SSE		
6	S		1.5			At 7 o'clock jib was lowered.
7	SbE½S		1.5	SEbS½S	⎤3	From noon and until 8 o'clock the land was
8	SSE	SW	1.3	SE½S	2½	not seen because of the long distance.
9	⎤					From 8 o'clock to midnight the weather
10	⎟					dark with clouds, variable light air and
11	⎬N	variable	2.	NbE		waves from S side. And we drifted
12	⎦					without sails. Drizzle.
1	⎤	calm and				From midnight to 4 o'clock the weather dark, with
	⎟					wet fog. Light air,
2	⎟	variable				high sea from SW.
3	⎬NE		2.	NEbE		We drifted without sails.
4	⎦					At 4:30 o'clock light breeze rose from W
5	SSW	WNW	.3	SWbS		and we set mainsail and foresail, but by 5
6	⎤	calm and				light air and variable, and we drifted without sails.
7	⎬N	variable	1.	NbE		At 8 o'clock it cleared up, and calm.
8	W		.1	WbN		From 8 o'clock to noon the weather cloudy, light air
						and variable. And we drifted without sails.
9	⎤	calm and				Rather rough sea from SWbS, at times sunshine.
10	⎬NEbN	variable	1.5	NE		The land was out of sight because of the long
11	⎟					distance.
12	⎦					

Sea current per day –   4   W

	Latitudes		Diff. of lat.		Departure		Rhumb	Distance		Diff. of long.		Compass declination E
	from	to	N	S	E	W		right	added	daily	total	
Reckoned												
Corrected	54° 16'05	54° 17'93	1'88			8'65	WNW bW 10°14'bW	8.73		15'64 W	1°22'78 by E	1 R

Hours	Rhumbs	Winds	Miles	Right rhumbs	Leeway	Mon. 23 June 1729.
1	}	Calm and				At 1 o'clock we hoisted topsail and foresail,
2		variable				at 2:30 o'clock we hoisted forestaysail and foresail
		between				was lowered.
3	}SWbW	N & E	1.5	WSW		From 12 o'clock to 4 sunshine, light air and
4						variable between N and E, rough sea from SSW.
5	SWbW	SE	1.	WSW		From 4 o'clock to 8 sunshine,
6			1.5			light breeze, at 6:30 o'clock we hoisted mainsail.
7	SW		2.0	SWbW		At 8 o'clock Kronovskaia mountain was
8			2.0			from us to WNW, 30 minutes distant.[353]
9	WSW	SE	0.5	WbS		At sunset we observed the amplitude of the sun
						from N by W – 59°00', its declination
10			1.7			N 23°01', and the reckoned latitude – 54°54',
11	WbS		1.5	W		amplitude was found – 47°09', from
12			1.0			this the compass declination – 11°50'E.
1	SWbW					From 8 o'clock the weather clear,
2		}SSE				light air and starlight.
3		}light	1.5	WSW		We carried all sails, except the forestaysail.
4	SW		1.5	SWbW		From midnight to 4 o'clock and until noon the
5	SWbW½W	S	1.4	WbS½W		weather clear, light air. We carried mainsail,
6	WSW		2.	W	}1	foresail, topsail and jib. At 2 and 3 o'clock we lay
						under topsail only, because of still.
7	WSW½W	SbW	1.	W½N		At 3 o'clock at sunrise we sighted the amplitude
8			1.			of the sun from N by E – 36°30', its declination –
9	WbN		1.5	WNW½N		N 22°58', and the reckoned latitude was N 54°53'.
10	WSW		2.5	WbS½W	½	The amplitude was found from N by E
11			2.5			47°58', from this the compass
12	WSW½W	SSW	1.5	W½N	1	declination – 10°47'E.
						At 8 o'clock the shore was from us to NWbN, 7
						minutes distant.
						At noon the shortest distance from us
						to the shore was 13 minutes to NWbN½N.
						And we shot the sun with correction
						– 58°46', its declination – N 22°58', from this the
						latitude of fix 54°12'.

Table of daily reckoning	Latitudes		Diff. of lat.		Departure		Rhumb	Distance		Diff. of long.		Compass declination E
	from	to	N	S	E	W		right	added	daily	total	
Reckoned												
Corrected	54° 17'93	54° 12'		5'09		28'29	WbS 1°03' W	28.75	56.65	55'75	27'03 by E	1 R

PLATE 37. Conical projection of Bering's Final Map. "Accurate Delineation des Oberhalb Siberiens ney gefundenen und Entdeckten Landes. Kamtschatka genannt, sambt deme was noch weiter daran gräntzet.". Hand-drawing by A. R. Witken in Frederik V's Atlas, 1740. (Bagrow 1948, no. 10). 74 × 43.5 cm.

Courtesy the Royal Library, Copenhagen.

Folio 65

Hours	Rhumbs	Winds	Miles	Right rhumbs	Leeway	Tue. 24 June 1729. Events on the sea route from the Kamchatka to the mouth of Bol'shaia River
1	WbN	SW	3.0	NWbW	}1	The weather clear, fresh breeze.
2			2.4			We held mainsail, foresail, topsail, jib.
3	WSW	SbW	1.3	W½N	1½	From 12 o'clock and until 8 we had the
4			2.7	WbN	2	land on our right side, extending
5	WbS	SSW	2.7		}	to WbN, then it turned to SW and
6			3.		}1	[got] higher.[354]
7			3.1	W½N	}	From 8 o'clock and until midnight the
8			3.1		}½	weather was clear, though cloudy in a northerly direction. Fresh breeze.
9	WbS	SSW	4.0	WbN	}	
10	WSW¼W	SbW	3.5	W¼N	}1	At 10 o'clock we turned to port. And
11	SEbE½S		2.5	SEbE¼S	}1¼	at 10:30 o'clock jib was lowered.
12			2.5		}	From midnight to 4 o'clock the sky
1	SE½S	SSW	2.6	SE	1½	was clear, though the northern
2			2.6	SEbE	}2½	horizon remained cloudy. At 1 a.m. we
3	SEbS		1.9	SEbE½S	}	hoisted jib.
4			2.5		}	From 4 o'clock to 8 sunshine,
5	W½N	SWbS	2.5	NWbW½N	}	strong breeze, but at 8 o'clock wind
6			3.0		}2	slackened a little. From 8 o'clock to
7	W¼N		3.3	NWbW¼N	}	noon intermittent sunshine, gentle
8	WSW	SbW	2.5	WbN	}	breeze. We carried mainsail and
9	WbS	SSW	1.4	WNW	}	foresail. At 9 o'clock we hoisted jib,
10	WSW		1.5	WbN	}2	and at 10 o'clock topsail. We had
11	SWbW	S	1.5	WbS	}1	the land on our right side, 18 minutes
12	SW	SbE	0.5	SWbW	}	away.[355] By 12 o'clock it misted over.

	Latitudes		Diff. of lat.		Departure		Rhumb	Distance		Diff. of long.		Compass declination E
	from	to	N	S	E	W		right	added	daily	total	
Reckoned												
Corrected	54° 12'	54° 15'47	3'47			30'11	WbN 4°40'b W	30.31	52.5	52'2 W	00°25'17 by W	1 R

Folio 65, continuation

Hours	Rhumbs	Winds	Miles	Right rhumbs	Leeway	Wed. 25 June 1729
1	SWbS	SE	2	SW		From 12 o'clock to 8 heavy rain, light air.
2			2			We carried mainsail, foresail, topsail and jib.
3			2.5			Land was not seen through the downpour.
4			1.0			From 8 o'clock to midnight the weather murky,
5	SWbS	SE	1.2	SW		at 9 o'clock the rain stopped.
6			1.5			At 12 o'clock we lay without sails because of still.
7			2.3			From midnight to 4 o'clock murky weather.
8			2.0			We held one foresail, light air.
9	SW	SE	1.2	SWbW		At 2 o'clock wind rose, and we hoisted mainsail,
10	W	SbW	1.3	WbN		topsail, jib.
11	WNW	variable	0.7	NWbW		At 3 o'clock we set forestaysail.
12						At 4 o'clock the wind started to drop.
1		calm				The land, visible to us at a distance
2	SSW	NW	3.5	SWbS		of 8 minutes, extended to SSW and NEbN.[356]
3	SWbS	NNW	4.5	SW		From 4 o'clock to 8 sunshine, the sky
4	S¾W		2.5	SbW¾W		partly cloudy, light air and variable.
5	SSE	variable	1.0	SbE		We carried mainsail, foresail, topsail, forestaysail
6	SE		0.5	SEbS		and jib.
7		SbW	1.5			At 5 o'clock forestaysail was lowered, at 8 o'clock we saw the land by S, which
8			1.2	ESE	3	disappeared by SSW½W.[357]
9	EbS¾S	SbE	1.5	ESE½E	¼	From 8 o'clock to noon sunshine,
10	SEbE½S	} vari-able	2.5	SEbE	} 1½	light and variable breeze.
11	EbS½S		2	EbS		We carried mainsail, foresail, topsail and jib.
12	E		1.8	EbN	2	At 12 o'clock the land was to SW½W, 12 minutes distant.[358] At noon we sighted the altitude of the sun with correction – 58°54', its declination – N 22°47', from this the latitude of fix – 53°53' north.

	Latitudes		Diff. of lat.		Departure		Rhumb	Distance		Diff. of long.		Compass declination E
	from	to	N	S	E	W		right	added	daily	total	
Reckoned												
Corrected	54° 15'47	53° 53'		24'45		9'79	SbW 10° 35' b W	26.33	44.79	16'66 W	41'83 b W	1 R

Folio 65 verso

Hours	Rhumbs	Winds	Miles	Right rhumbs	Leeway	Thu. 26 June 1729. Events on the sea route from the Kamchatka to the mouth of Bol'shaia River
1	SWbS	SSE	2.6	SW¼W	} ¼	Sunshine through gloom. At 3 o'clock
2			3.0			thick fog, at 5 o'clock rain,
3	SSW	SEbS	3.3	SW	1	at 8 o'clock the land was out of sight
4	SWbS	SSE½S	3.2	WSW	2	because of fog. From noon to 8
			1.5	SW¼W	¼	o'clock we carried mainsail,
5	WSW	SbW	0.7	W	1	foresail, topsail and jib.
			0.7		1	From 8 to 11 o'clock we lay under
6	EbS		0.8	EbN½E	2½	topsail only. Light air, variable, the
7	EbN		1.4	ENE½E	1½	weather – wet fog. Soon after 11
8	ENE		1.0	NE½E	2½	o'clock topsail was lowered and we set
9	NEbE	calm and				mainsail and foresail, since moderate
10		variable	1.5	NEbN	3	gale rose. But the wind dropped again, and it
11						started to rain. From midnight to 4 o'clock
12	SbW		0.5	SSW		cloudy, light variable air. We held
1		calm				1 foresail.
2		and va-				At 4 o'clock land in sight and
3	ESE	riable	1.2	E¾S	2	disappearing to SSW½W.[359]
4						
5	SbE½S		1.	SbE¾S	}	From 4 to 8 o'clock cloudy with sunny spells.
6	S	vari-	1.5	S¼W		From 8 to noon the sky was clear, except
7	SSE½S	able	1.0	SSE¾S	} ½	for clouds in a westerly direction.
8			1.0			We held mainsail, foresail, topsail, jib.
9	SEbS	SSW	1.7	SEbE¾S	2	At 9 o'clock fresh gale rose, therefore topsail and
10	SbE	SW	3.0	SSE¾S	}	jib were lowered.
11	SbE		4.0		} 1	The high Avacha Volcano was to WbS¼W,
12	SbE½S	SWbW	4.1	SbE¼S	}	20 minutes away from us.

Sea current per day   31.0   WSW¼W

	Latitudes		Diff. of lat.		Departure		Rhumb	Distance		Diff. of long.		Compass declination E
	from	to	N	S	E	W		right	added	daily	total	
Reckoned												1R to midnight and then ¾ R
Corrected	53° 53'	53° 19'51		33'49		32'37	SWbS10° 14' b W	46.57	48.54	52'78 W	1°34' 61 W	

200

Folio 65 verso, continuation

Hours	Rhumbs	Winds	Miles	Right rhumbs	Leeway	Fri. 27 June 1729
1	S	WSW	3.	SSE¾S	} 2	From noon and until 4 o'clock sunshine
2	S½W		3.	SbE¼S		with few drifting clouds,
3	SbW½W	WSW½W	3.	SbE¾S		strong breeze. At 4 o'clock wind
4	SSW½W	WbS	2.5	S¾W	} 2½	dropped. We carried mainsail
5	SSW		2.8	S¼W		and foresail. From 4 to 8 o'clock
6	SWbS	W	2.	SbW¼W		sunshine, fresh breeze, high sea.
7			3.	SbW¾W	} 2	
8			3.			At 8 o'clock fresh gale rose.
	{ S		1.	SEbS¼S	3½	We carried mainsail and foresail.
9	{ SWbS		2.2	SSW½W		From 8 o'clock to midnight the weather clear,
10			3.7		} 1¼	but NW part of the sky was cloudy.
11	SW		3.5	SWbS½W		We carried mainsail and foresail, unbending
12			4.0			one reef of each. Land was not in sight because of the dark.
1	SWbS	WbN	3.0	SSW		From midnight to 4 o'clock
2			3.0		} 1¾	the weather and wind the same. We carried
3			3.0			the same sails. At 4 o'clock we saw a
4			2.5			mountain and another one near it to NWbW.[360]
5	SWbS	W	2.5	SbW¼W		From 4 to 8 o'clock the weather cloudy with
6			3.5		} 2½	sunny spells, moderate gale with abating wind.
7			2.1			We carried mainsail and foresail.
8			2.7			The aforementioned mountains from us to
9	SSW	WbS	2.0	SbW¼W		NWbW½N.[361] From 9 o'clock to noon
10			3.0		} 1½	the weather clear, fresh breeze.
11	SbW½W		4.0	S¾W		We carried mainsail and foresail.
12			2.5			At noon we sighted altitude of the sun with correction 60°31' and its declination N 22°34', by the local meridian, from this the latitude of fix 52°03'N.

	Latitudes		Diff. of lat.		Departure		Rhumb	Distance		Diff. of long.		Compass declination E
	from	to	N	S	E	W		right	added	daily	total	
Reckoned												
Corrected	53° 19'	52° 03'		76'37		47'29	SSW 9° 10' b W	89.83	148.6	1°18'21 by W[362]	2°52'82 W	¾ R

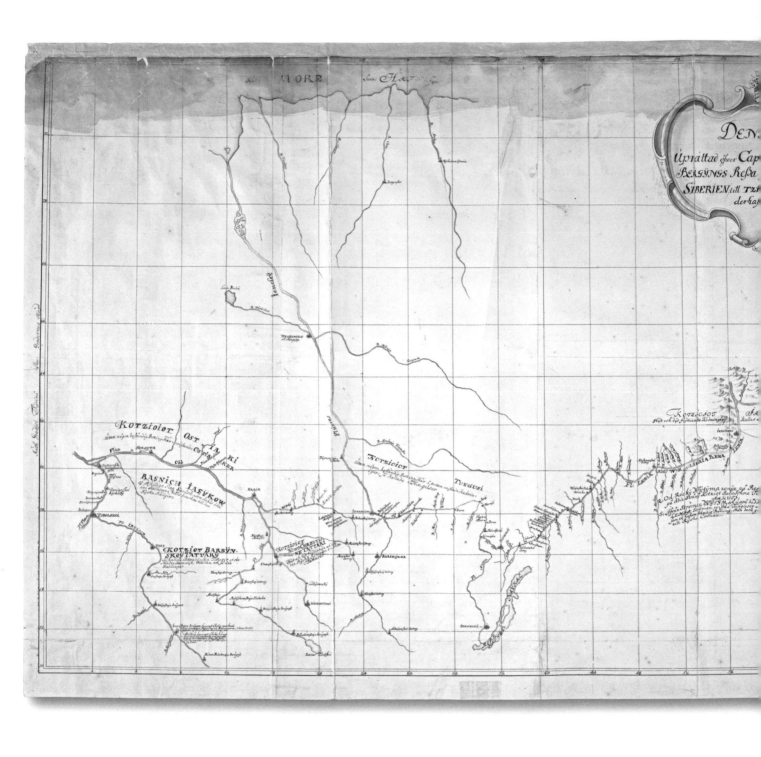

PLATE 38. Anonymous hand-drawn Swedish version of Bering's Final Map. With ethnographical annotations in Russian and Swedish. (Kejlbo 1993, no. 14). 56 × 133 cm.

Courtesy the Royal Library, Copenhagen.

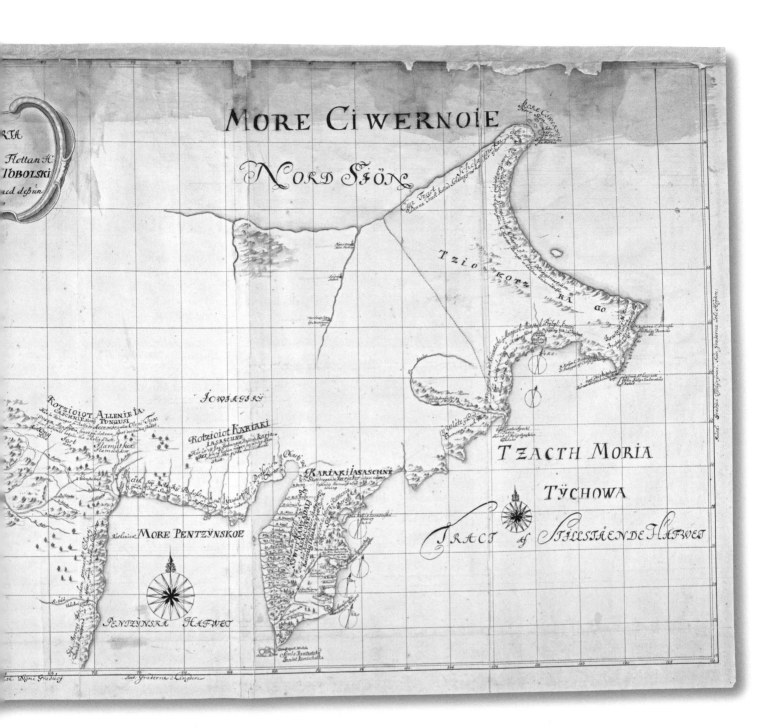

MORE CIWERNOIE

NORD SIÖN

TZIO KOTZ KA GO

JOWSAGSKY

Kotzioiot ALLENIE IA TUNGUSI

Kotzioiot KARIAKI IASASCILNE

KARIAKI IASASCHNI

MORE PENTZYNSKOE

PENTZYNSKA HAFWET

TZACTH MORIA

TYCHOWA

TRACT af STILLSTÄENDE HAFWET

Hours	Rhumbs	Winds	Miles	Right rhumbs	Leeway	Sat. 28 June 1729. Events on the sea route from the Kamchatka to the mouth of Bol'shaia River[363]
1	SWbS	W	2.	SbW¾W	} 2	The weather clear with small clouds,
2			2.8			strong breeze with abating wind. We
3	SSW	WbS	1.5	SbW	} 1¾	held mainsail and foresail. At 1 p.m.
4			1.3			we let out the reefs.
5	SbW	WSW	1.5	S¼W	} 1½	At 5 o'clock the wind dropped and
6			2.8			clouds appeared. By 9 o'clock the
7			2.4	S	} 1¾	land was no longer in sight because of the
8			2.7			distance. From 8 o'clock to midnight
9	NWbW	WSW	3.3	NWbN	}	cloudy and wet. Fresh breeze.
10	WNW	SWbW	3.3	NW	} 1¼	We carried mainsail and foresail.
11	WbN	SW	3.5	NWbW	}	From midnight to 5 o'clock the weather
12			3.0		}	murky with rain, gentle breeze.
1	W	SWbS	2.1	WNW¼N	1½	We carried mainsail, foresail and
2	WbS½W		3.2	WbN¾N	1½	jib. From 4 o'clock to 8 the weather
3		SSW	3.8	WbN¼N	} 1	the same, light and variable air. At
4			2.8		}	5 o'clock mainsail and jib were lowered,
5	WNW	} calm &	1.0	NWbN¼N	} 2½	and at 8 o'clock also the foresail.
6		} vari-	1.0		}	At 10 o'clock by sand clock we took the altitude
7	NNW	} able	0.5	NbE¾E	} 3	of the sun with correction – 56°37', its declination
						22°, and the reckoned latitude – N 52°00'. Azimuth,
						observed from S by E – 44°00',
8			0.5		}	and computed – 36°12', from this the compass
9	}	calm &				declination – 7°42' east.
10	} NE½E	vari-	1.2	NEbE¼E		At the same time the land was to WbS½W,
11	}	able				50 minutes distant.[364] At noon we took the sun
12	}					with correction – 60°26', its declination 22°27',
						from this the latitude of fix – 52°01' north.

	Latitudes		Diff. of lat.		Departure		Rhumb	Distance		Diff. of long.		Compass declination E
	from	to	N	S	E	W		right	added	daily	total	
Corrected	52°03'	52°01'		1'15		22'93	WbS 9°23' bW	22.96	37'32	37'27bW	3°30'09 W	¾ R

Folio 66, continuation

Hours	Rhumbs	Winds	Miles	Right rhumbs	Leeway	Sun. 29 June 1729
1		⎱calm				First and second hour we lay without
2		⎰				sails. At 2:30 o'clock light
3	SbE		0.5	SbE¾S		breeze rose, and we hoisted sails and
4	NWbW½N	WSW½W	3.5	NW½N	⎱¼	ran. From 2 o'clock to 8 the weather
5	NW	WbS	3.6	NWbN		clear, fresh breeze. We carried
6			4.5			mainsail, foresail, topsail and jib.
7			4.5		⎱¼	We ran towards land. At 8 o'clock the
8			4.5			land, which had gone out of sight to
9	SbE	SW	2.4	SSE¾S		WSW, extended to SSW – great rocky
10			1.3		⎰1	mountains. From 8 o'clock to midnight
11	SSE½S		2.0	SEbS¼S	2	the weather clear, light air, at 12
12	SEbS	SSW	2.9	SE¾S	1	o'clock wind increased. We carried the same
						sails. The land was in sight on our
1			2.8	SEbE¼S		right side.[365] From midnight to 4
2			2.5		⎱½	o'clock the weather and wind the same.
3	WNW	SW	2.0	NWbW¼N		We carried the same sails. At 1:45
4	WbN½N		2.0	NWbW	¾	o'clock we turned to starboard.
5	W½N		1.0	WNW¼N		From 4 to 8 clear with few clouds.
6	WNW	⎱calm &	1.5	NWbW¾N		We carried the same sails. The land
7	⎡NWbW	⎰vari-	0.7	NWbN¾N	⎱1	was 15 minutes away from us to NWbW.
	⎣SSW	⎰able	0.8	SbW¾W		
8	SW		1.5	SW¾W		At 8 o'clock the land extended from
9		⎱	1.8			Avacha Bay to SWbS.[366] From 8 o'clock to
10	⎱	⎰calm &				noon clear except for a few clouds, light
11	⎰SSW	⎰vari-	1.0	SSW¾W		and variable air. The land was at the same
12		⎰able				distance from us.

	Latitudes		Diff. of lat.		Departure		Rhumb	Distance		Diff. of long.		Compass
	from	to	N	S	E	W		right	added	daily	total	declination E
Corrected	52°01'	52°06'94	5'94			14'07	NWbW 10°52' W	17.27	27'36	22'77 W	3°52'86 W	¾ R

Conspicuous places	No. of these places	time of observation	directions			
			N – E	N – W	S – E	S – W
Flat mountain with small mountain on top[367]	4	at 6½ p.m.		59.34		
The same a second time	4	at 8 p.m.		63.34		

Hours	Rhumbs	Winds	Miles	Right rhumbs	Leeway	Mon. 30 June 1729. Events on the sea route from the Kamchatka to the mouth of Bol'shaia River
1	S	WNW	1.6	S¾W		Sunshine with thin fog, light variable air
2	SE½S	SSW	3.0	SE¾S	½	from S by E and by W.
3	SEbS		1.3	SE½S	⎫1¼	We carried mainsail, foresail,
4			2.5		⎬	topsail, jib.
5	SSE	SW	0.8	SEbS¾S	⎭	At 2 o'clock jib was lowered.
6	SEbS		1.5	SE¾S	⎫1	A high land, which had at noon been to
7		⎫vari-	0.7		⎬	SW½W, was at 8:15 o'clock to 65°30′
8	SbW½W	⎭able	1.8	SbW¼W	⎭	from S by W.[368]
9	SWbS	WbN	3.5	SWbS¾W		From 8 o'clock to midnight moonlight and
10			3.0			shining stars, light air, and at times
11	SW	NWbN	3.0	SW¾W		a fresh breeze. At 10 o'clock
12		NW	3.0			topsail and jib were lowered. The land
1	SWbW	NWbN	4.0	SWbW¾W		was on our right side, but could not
2	SWbW½W		3.1	WSW¼W		be seen through the fog. From midnight to
3	WSW	NW	2.0	WSW¾W		4 o'clock the weather clear, fresh
4			3.0			breeze abating. We carried
5	SWbW		2.0	SWbW¾W		mainsail, foresail, topsail, jib. From 4
6	SW		2.0	SW¾W		o'clock to noon sunshine breaking through
7		⎫calm	1.5			fog. At 12 o'clock the land was, judged by
8		⎬&	1.			eye,[369] 13 minutes distant to WbN,
9	SbE	⎬vari-	0.6	SEbE¼S		extending to SWbS and disappearing
10		⎭able				out of sight to SWbW¼W.[370]
11	⎫	⎫				We carried mainsail, foresail,
12	⎭SWbW	⎭	1.4	SWbW¾W		topsail, jib. Light air, variable.

	Latitudes		Diff. of lat.		Departure		Rhumb	Distance		Diff. of long.		Compass declination E
	from	to	N	S	E	W		right	added	daily	total	
Corrected	52° 06′94	51° 38′86		28′08		22′11	SWbW 4°28′ bW	35.74	57′6	35′8 W	4°28′66 W	¾ R

Conspicuous places	No. of places	Time of observation	Directions			
			N – E	N – W	S – E	S – W
A high mountain by S[371]	5	8¼ p.m.				81.56
Another mountain, small[372]	6	same time				73.56
The high mountain a second time	5	4¼ p.m.		86.34		
The other mountain a second time	6	same time				82.56

Folio 66 verso, continuation

Hours	Rhumbs	Winds	Miles	Right rhumbs	Leeway	Tue. 1 July 1729
1	SWbW	calm & variable	0.8	SWbW¾W		From noon to 3 o'clock sunshine, light air. From 3 o'clock fog and the land was out of sight.
2	WSW		1.0	WSW¾W		To 8 o'clock we carried mainsail, forestaysail,
3			1.5			topsail. Gentle breeze. From 8 o'clock to midnight
4			2.0			the weather wet with fog, gentle breeze. We carried
5	WSW	ENE	2.5			mainsail, topsail.
6			2.7			At 9 o'clock mainsail was clewed up.
7	SWbW		3.5	SWbW¾W		At 10 o'clock wind rose. The land could not be seen
8			3.0			through the fog.
9	SWbW	NEbE	3.6			From midnight to 4 o'clock wet fog, gentle breeze.
10			2.5			Before 2 o'clock we lay under topsail. After 2 o'clock
11	SW	NE	3.1	SW¾W		we lay without sails, after 3 o'clock we lay under
12			3.3			topsail and foresail.
1	SW	NE	3.0			The land was not seen through the fog. From 4 to 8
2			3.5			o'clock the weather the same.
3		NNE	1.0			At 5:30 o'clock we hoisted mainsail, at 6:30 we
4	W		4.0	W¼N		saw land between W and NW at a distance of 6½
5		NE	4.0			minutes and ran parallel to it. On the land there
6			2.0			were rather low stone mountains, and the seashore
	WNW	NEbN	2.2	WNW¾N		was steep.[373]
7			2.2			From 8 to noon weather and wind the same.
	SWbS½W		2.2	SW¼W		We ran parallel to the shore at a distance of 2 and
8	SSW½W		3.9	SWbS¼W		1½ minutes. The land was low, in places sloping
9	SW	ENE	5.5	SW¾W		down to the sea.[374]
10	SSW		4.5	SSW¾W		At 12 o'clock the S point of the land of Kamchatka
11	WSW		4.5	WSW¾W		was from us to NWbW, 1½ minutes distant, with
12	SWbS		3.5	SWbS¾W		sand stretching out from it into the sea for about 1 verst.[375] We carried mainsail, foresail, topsail and jib.

	Latitudes		Diff. of lat.		Departure		Rhumb	Distance		Diff. long.		Compass declination E
	from	to	N	S	E	W		right	added	daily	total	
Corrected	51°38'86	51°10'80		28'06		63'73	SWbW 9°59' bW	69.64	113'9	1°44'3W	6°12'96 W	¾ R

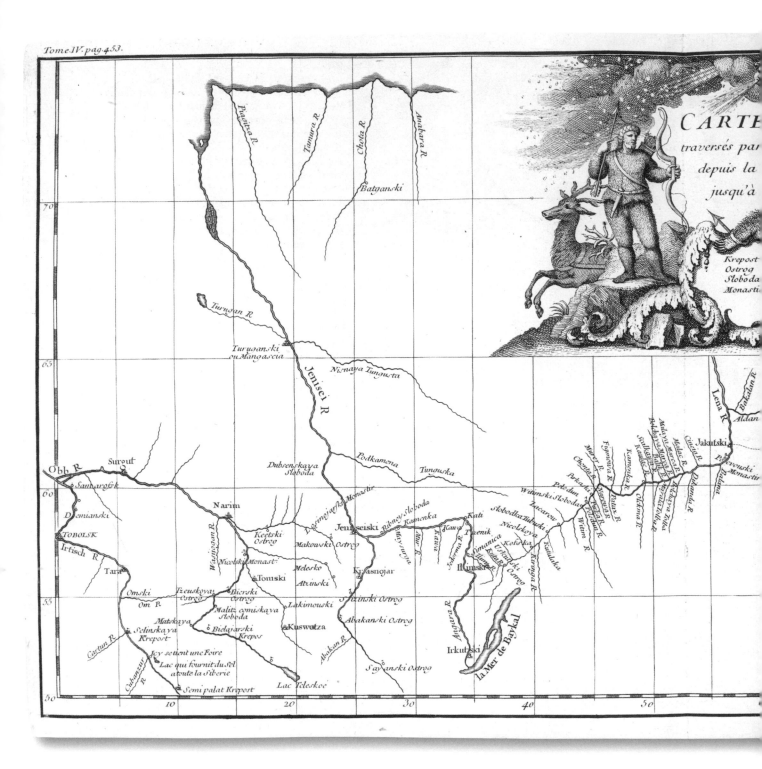

Map labels (within the engraving):

Tome IV. pag. 453.

Piazitza R.

Tianura R.

Chota R.

Anabara R.

Batganski

CART...

traversés par

depuis la

jusqu'à

Krepost
Ostrog
Sloboda
Monasti...

Turugan R.

Turuganski
ou Mangascia

Jenisei R.

Nisnaya Tungusta

Lena R.

Bakalan R.

Aldan

Jakutski

Podkamena

Dubsenskaya
Sloboda

Tungouska

Witimski Sloboda

Mayer R.

Fgonova R.

Maloe R.

Kamenka R.

Pevouski
Monastir

Obb R.

Surgut

Samarofsk

Demianski

TOBOLSK

Irtisch R.

Tara

Narim

Wasugan R.

Keetski
Ostrog

Makowski Ostrog

Nicolski Monast.

Meleske

Tomski

Atzinski

Krasnojar

Jegingjarski Monastir

Rabnov Sloboda

Kamenka

Kati

Kawa

Tzenik

Simanica

Slobodka Tulbuki

Nicolskoya

Kotska

Zacarov

Witim R.

Pete dun

Perkadai

Chenka R.

Tulbuki R.

Turuga R.

Kunilaka

Omski

Om R.

Tzeuskoya
Ostrog

Bicrski
Ostrog

Malitz comiskaya
Sloboda

Lakimowski

Jetzinski Ostrog

Abakanski Ostrog

Illimski

Urlutski
Ostrog

Matskaya

Selinskaya
Krepost

Bielaiarski
Krepos

Kuswetza

Abakan R.

Sayanski Ostrog

Angara R.

Irkutski

la Mer de Baykal

Cartun R.

Cibacziur R.

Icy se tient une Foire

Lac qui fournit du Sel
a toute la Siberie

Semi palat Krepost

Lac Teleskée

Coordinates: 70, 65, 60, 55, 50 (left); 10, 20, 30, 40, 50 (bottom)

PLATE 39. Engraved map of Bering's route on the First Kamchatka Expedition 1725-1730. From Du Halde (1735) *Description
[…] de la Chine et de la Tartarie chinoise*, vol. IV. Map size 23.4 × 53 cm.

Courtesy the Royal Library, Copenhagen.

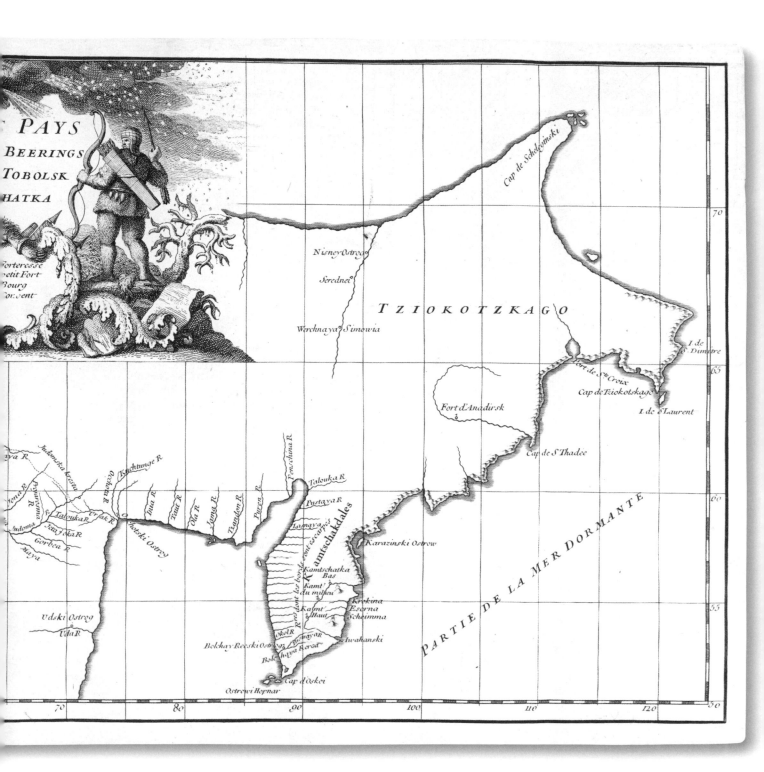

PAYS
BEERINGS
TOBOLSK
HATKA

Forteresse
petit Fort
Bourg
doivent

Cap de Scheloinski

70

Nisney Ostrog

Serednei

TZIOKOTZKAGO

I. de S. Dimitre

Werchnaya Simowia

65

Fort de Ste Croix

Fort d'Anadirsk

Cap de Tziokotskago

I. de S. Laurent

Cap de S. Thadée

60

Judomska Kresta

Kuchtunge R.

Tenschina R.

Talouka R.

Fona R.

Ochota R.

Inua R.

Taut R.

Ola R.

Jama R.

Tzandon R.

Puren R.

Pustaya R.

Indoma

Talouka R.

Indoma

Crak R.

Tiutski Ostrog

Lasnaya

Kamtschatka
Bas

Karazinski Ostrow

Jena Joka R.

Gorbea R.

R. dont les bords sont escarpés

Kamt'
du milieu

Krokina
Eserna
Scheimma

PARTIE DE LA MER DORMANTE

55

Udski Ostrog

Uda R.

Kamt'
Haut

Okol R.

Awahanski

Bolshay Reeski Ostrog

Awoy ar

Bolshaya Reroa

Cap d'Oskoi

Ostrowi Hopnar

70   80   90   100   110   120   50

Hours	Rhumbs	Winds	Miles	Right rhumbs	Leeway	Wed. 2 July 1729. Events on the sea route from the Kamchatka to the mouth of Bol'shaia River
1	⎰WSW	NEbE	2.0	WSW¾W		The weather gloomy, fresh breeze, we held
	⎱NWbN½N		2.3	NNW¼N		mainsail, foresail, topsail, jib. At 12:30 o'clock
2	NNW	ESE	4.8	NNW¾N		we saw an island to SbW, 1½ minutes distant,
3			5.5			extending from its middle to SSE and NNW,
4	NNW	SEbS	4.5			5 minutes to both sides, and then coming to
5	NNW		2.3	NNW¾N		an end at W to SWbW from us, 10 minutes
6		calm	2.0			away.[376] The W low shore of the land of
7		ESE	1.5			Kamchatka extends for 15 minutes from the S
8			1.0			point to N½E, and having reached some high
9	NNW	SSE	1.5	NNW¾N		mountains, it turns to NW, until crossing NNW.
10		calm	0.5			At 1:15 o'clock we saw another island.[377]
11						We lowered foresail, jib and hoisted forestaysail.
12			1.0			Until 5 o'clock sunny spells, then thick fog
1	NNW	ESE	1.5	NbW		descended. By 7 o'clock calm, and sails were
2			2.1			taken in. From 8 to 9:30 o'clock we carried
3			4.0			mainsail, foresail, topsail, and then until
4			4.0			midnight lay ahull. Thick wet fog. At 2 a.m. it
5	NNW	ESE	3.5	NbW		cleared and a land appeared, extending parallel
6			4.5			to our route, and on the 3rd island we saw a
7	N		4.3	NbE		high mountain to SSW¾W, 24 minutes distant.
8	NbE		5.5	NNE		From 4 o'clock to noon sunshine, fresh breeze.
9	NEbN	SE	5.2	NE		At 9 o'clock by sand clock we took the sun –
			2.0			with correction 44°40', azimuth from S by E –
10	⎱NbE		2.1	NNE		76°30', and the reckoned latitude was N 52°06',
11	NbW¾N		4.7	N¾E		it's declination – 21°56', azimuth observed
12	NNW½N	SWbS	3.9	NbW½N		– 65°30' from S by E, from this compass
						declination – 11°00' east. At noon we took the
						sun – with correction 59°37', its declination –
						21°55'N, from this latitude of fix 52°18'N.

	Latitudes		Diff. of lat.		Departure		Rhumb	Distance		Diff. of long.		Compass declination E
	from	to	N	S	E	W		right	added	daily	total	
Corrected	51°10'80	52° 20'	69'62			3'55	N 2°55' by W	69.8	122'6	6'24 W	6°19'20 W	¾ R to midnight, then 1R

Conspicuous places	No. of places	time of observation	directions			
			N – E	N – W	S – E	S – W
S point of the land of Kamchatka	7	1¼ p.m.			76°04'	
A snow-capped mountain N of this point[378]	8	same time	50°56'			
S point again	7	2¼ p.m.			47°34	
The snow-capped mountain again	8	same time	77°26'			
A cape at the mouth of Ozernaia River, low on left side	9	10 a.m.			48°45'	
Mount Opal'skaia near the Bol'shaia River	10	same time	56°15'			
The cape at the Ozernaia River again	9	at noon			32°45	
Mount Opal'skaia again	10	at noon	70°15			
Middle of the 1st island[379]	11	1¼ p.m.				20°41'
Middle of the 2nd island[380]	12	same time				82°56'
W point of the 1st island[381]	13	same time				68°26'
The same again:						
Middle of the 1st island	11	2¼ p. m.			4°04'	
Middle of the 2nd island	12	same time				77°26'
W point of the 1st island	13	same time				54°26'

Folio 67, continuation

Hours	Rhumbs	Winds	Miles	Right rhumbs	Leeway	Thu. 3 July 1729
1	NNW	SSW	4.8	NbW		From noon to 5 p.m. the weather clear, fresh
2			6.0			breeze. At 2 o'clock topsail was lowered,
3			5.5			at 3 o'clock forestaysail was lowered and we lay
	NW		1.5	NWbN		under mainsail and foresail, wind rose.
4			6.0			Soon after 4 we reached the mouth of the Bol'shaia
5						River and lay at anchor at a depth of 7 sazhens. Bottom –
6	ENE					fine sand, 1½ minutes from the shore.
7	ENE	S	1.5	EbN		We sent a boat to examine the mouth
8						of the river and find a channel where we could
9						enter, since the mouth changes every year.
10						The upper habitation at the mouth – to NbE,
11						the middle one – to NNE, the lower – to ENE,
12						Mount Opal'skaia – to E¼S.
						At 6 o'clock we began to raise the anchor, but when it was
						aweigh, fresh gale rose. The rope broke near the ring-bolt,
						and the anchor was lost.
						It weighed 10 poods.
						We proceeded to the mouth of the Bol'shaia River with
						rising water and dropped anchor at a depth of 3½ sazhens,
						in front of the middle balagans.
						It was not possible to find and to lift the lost anchor, since
						there were no such vessels in this place. On our arrival
						at the mouth of the Bol'shaia there were 2 other vessels
						here, one – the "Fortuna", which had been sent by us from
						Kamchatka, and the other one – the old vessel, which was
						used for transporting the fur tribute from Kamchatka.
						The weather cloudy, strong breeze.
						At 9 a.m. the first mate[382] was sent to the Bol'sheretsk
						outpost and with him a sailor. They were to surrender to
						the commissary our remaining things, which had been
						left at the outpost, and to bring the servicemen of our
						command back to the seaside.
						The weather cloudy, moderate gale.

	Latitudes		Diff. of lat.		Departure		Rhumb	Distance		Diff. of long.		Compass declination E
	from	in	N	S	E	W		right	added	daily	total	
Corrected	52°20'	52°42'	22'44			5'88	NbW 2°26' bW	23.2	38'04	9'64 W	6°27'00 W	1 R

Day of the month	Day of the week	July 1729, while lying at anchor in the mouth of Bol'shaia River	Winds
Fri.	4	The weather murky, with rain, strong breeze, and at times strong gale. From 6 a.m. sunny spells. We dried sails aboard. The physician was allowed to go to the outpost.	SWbW
Sat.	5	The weather cloudy with sunny spells, light breeze. After midnight light breeze, the same weather. We saw Mount Opal'skaia[383] to 83°30' from S by E, and, behind a lake, a high mountain to 62°30' from S by E.[384]	NW SSE
Sun.	6	The weather gloomy, moderate gale. 2 servitors who were aboard as interpreters were allowed to go to Lower Kamchatsk. At 3 o'clock wet fog descended. A sailor of our command who had been sent with the first mate arrived from Bol'sheretsk outpost, and so did 3 soldiers. After midnight the weather and wind the same. A drummer and 6 soldiers arrived from the outpost.	S
Mon.	7	The weather and wind the same. The physician arrived from the outpost. In the morning we surrendered to the commissary of the Kamchadal outposts[385]: flour – 338 poods in 130 bags, groats of barley – 24 poods in 8 bags.	SSE
Tue.	8	The first mate arrived from the outpost, having surrendered the following to the commissary: gunpowder – 6 poods 10 pounds, fine powder – 1 pood 11 pounds, grenades – 50, skins of Russia leather[386] – 5. The corporal arrived from the outpost with 2 soldiers. In the morning moderate gale, at times heavy rain.	
Wed.	9	The weather murky with intermittent rain, moderate gale. The chaplain, who had been at our command and had been allowed to go from the command 10 July [1]728, arrived at our ship.	
Thu.	10	The weather gloomy, fresh breeze. We dried sails. 8 servicemen were taken from the vessel "Fortuna" aboard the ship.	
Fri.	11	The weather clear, light breeze, the sky in places cloudy. Later calm.	WNW
Sat.	12	The weather cloudy with sunny spells. We dried sails. Light breeze. By the evening overcast. The Captain ordered a search for the anchor from the old vessel, which had fallen last autumn at time of high tide and strong winds and been covered with small stones. We looked for it all day, but could not find it.	S
Sun.	13	The weather murky, fresh breeze.	

Hours	Rhumbs	Winds	Miles	Right rhumbs	Leeway	Mon. 14 July 1729. Events on the sea route from Bol'shaia River to the mouth of Okhota River
1		NWbN				The weather clear, though in places the sky was cloudy.
2						Light air. At 5:30 o'clock, having raised the anchor,
3						we ran from the mouth of the Bol'shaia River to the
4						Okhota mouth (and from our arrival at the mouth
5		NWbN				of the Bol'shaia we worked to find the lost anchor,
6						only we had no vessel from which to search for it, as
7	} from the					mentioned above, and we could not look for it from
	} balagans					our ship because of the unceasing murky weather
8	} SSW		3.5	SWbS		during our anchorage at the Bol'shaia River, as
9	WNW	NbW½N	1.3	WbN	2	recorded in the log book).
10			1.6	WbN½N	}	The following men were aboard:
11	NWbW	N½E	1.3	WNW½N	} 1½	the Captain, 2 lieutenants, the chaplain, the physician,
12			1.0		}	the navigator, the midshipman, the first mate, the
1	WNW½N	} calm &	1.2	NWbW½N		quartermaster, 12 sailors, the apprentice boat maker,
2	NNW	} vari-	0.8	NbW		the foreman of the carpenters, 9 carpenters, the
3	} SW	} able				sailmaker, the caulker, the blacksmith, 2 drummers, 13
4	}	}	1.2	SWbW		soldiers, 1 seafarer, – and the sick: the geodesist, the
5	NWbW	}	1.0	NW		apprentice mast maker.
6		} calm	0.8			In all 78 men of all ranks, including officers' servants.
7		}	0.7			To avoid crowding, 1 corporal and 11 soldiers
8		}	0.5			remained aboard the vessel Fortuna.
9	NWbW	}	1.0	NW		At 6:45 o'clock we put out from the mouth with high
10		} calm	1.0			tide, at 8 o'clock the middle balagans at the mouth
11			0.8			were left from us to NNE, 3½ miles or minutes distant.
12		}	0.7			We carried mainsail and foresail. At 9:30 o'clock we
						hoisted topsail, from 8 a.m. to midnight light breeze
		In all	18.4			and starlight, then the sky was covered with clouds. From midnight the weather with wet fog, light air, at 1 o'clock mainsail was clewed up. From 4 to 8 o'clock the weather and wind the same. We had mainsail, topsail, forestaysail, at 7 o'clock we took in mainsail and forestaysail. From 8 o'clock the weather cloudy, light air, at times light breeze. We carried topsail and forestaysail. We reckoned the difference of longitude to the Okhotsk outpost from Bol'shaia River.

	Latitudes		Diff. of lat.		Departure		Rhumb	Distance		Diff. of long.		Compass declination E
	from	to	N	S	E	W		right	added	daily	total route from the Bol'shaia	
Corrected	52°42'	52°46'16	4'16			12'03	WNW 3°26' bW	12.72	21'10	19'96		1 R

PLATE 41. A Russian version of Bering's Final Map, with ethnographical illustrations, in the National Library in Stockholm (Efimov 1964, No. 65). The legend reads, in translation: "This map was drawn in the Siberian expedition under the command of Navy Captain Bering, from Tobol'sk to Cape Chuckchi." Map size 135 × 58 cm.

Courtesy the National Library of Sweden (Kungl. biblioteket, Stockholm). Photo by Jens Östman.

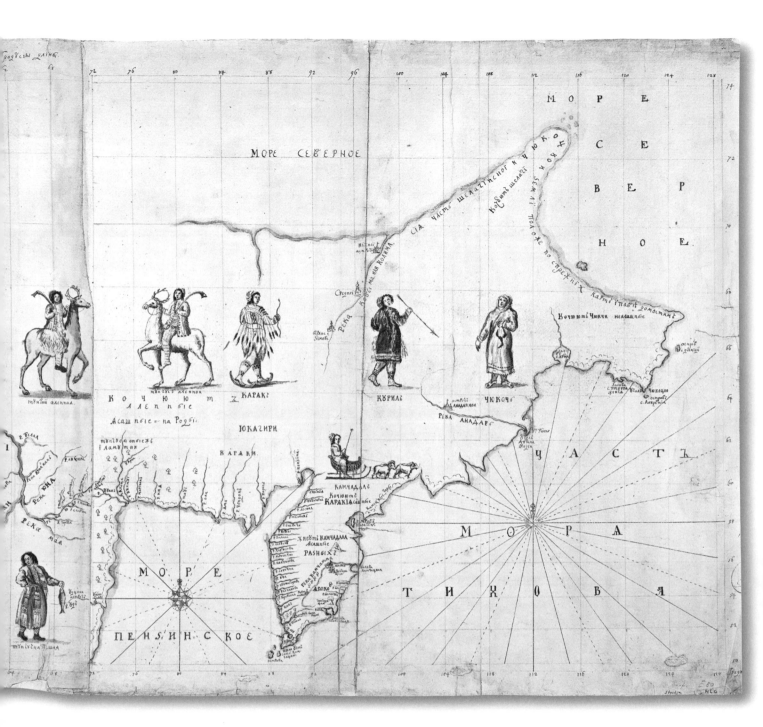

Hours	Rhumbs	Winds	Miles	Right rhumbs	Tue. 15 July 1729. Events on the sea route from Bol'shaia River to the mouth of Okhota River
1	NWbW	light	1.2	NW	The weather cloudy, from noon to 4 o'clock
2		air	1.4		we carried topsail and forestaysail.
3		with	1.4		At 4 o'clock Mount Opal'skaia was left
4		change	1.6		behind to 84°00' from S by E, at a
5	NWbW	from S	2.5	NW	distance of 50 minutes.
6		by E	2.5		From 4 to 8 o'clock the same weather,
7			3.0		gentle breeze. We carried mainsail,
8			2.5		topsail and forestaysail.
9	NWbW	SSE	3.5	NW	From 8 to midnight wind rose,
10			3.8		at 12 o'clock rain.
11			5.0		From midnight to 4 o'clock rain, moderate
12			5.5		gale.
1	NWbW	SSE	5.5	NW	We carried mainsail, topsail and
2			5.5		forestaysail.
3			5.0		
4			5.5		
5	NWbW	SSE	7.5	NW	From 4 o'clock to noon wind the same
6			6.5		and at times heavy rain. At 5
7			8.0		o'clock topsail was lowered.
8			7.0		
9	NWbW	SSE	7.5	NW	
10			7.5		
11			7.3		
12			7.0		

in all   113.7

	Latitudes		Diff. of lat.		Departure		Rhumb	Distance		Diff. of long.		Compass declination eastern
	from	to	N	S	E	W		right	added	daily	total from R Bol'shaia	
							NW					
Corrected	52°46' 16	54°07' 53	77'03			77'03		108.9	183'4	2°09'7 W	2°29'66	1 R

Folio 68, continuation

Hours	Rhumbs	Winds	Miles	Right rhumbs	Leeway	Wed. 16 July 1729
1	NWbW	SW	6.5	NW		From noon to 4 o'clock wet fog,
2			6.0			fresh breeze. At 1 p.m. forestaysail
3			5.5			was lowered, and topsail, foresail and
4			4.5			jib were hoisted.
5	NWbW	SW	5.0	NW		From 4 o'clock and until midnight the
6		with	4.5			weather and wind the same. We carried
7		change	3.8			the same sails, and at 9 o'clock jib
8		by W	4.5			was lowered.
9	NWbW	SWbS	5.0	NW		
10		SSW	5.			
11			5			From midnight to 7 o'clock the weather
12			4.5			murky and wet fog, light air. We
1	NWbW	SSW	3.	NW		carried the same sails, and from 7 to 8
2			2.			o'clock we drifted without sails.[387]
3			2.			From 8 o'clock to noon gentle breeze.
4			2.5			We carried mainsail, foresail,
5	NWbW	SSW	1.3	NW		topsail.
6		SEbE	0.7			At 11:30 o'clock we turned to
7	NNW	⎤between	0.4	NbW		starboard.
8	NNE	⎬N & E	0.6	NEbN		
9		⎦calm				
10	WSW	NW	2.	WSW	1	
11	SWbW	WbN½N	1.5	SW½W	⎤1½	
			1.0		⎦	
12	⎣NbE		1.	NEbN	1	

in all   77.8

	Latitudes		Diff. of lat.		Departure		Rhumb	Distance		Diff. of long.		Compass declination E
	from	to	N	S	E	W		right	added	daily	total	
Corrected	54°07' 53	54°55' 23	47'70			51'10	NW 2° 01' by W	69.94	120'3	1°27'87 W	3°57'53	1 R

Folio 68 verso

Hours	Rhumbs	Winds	Miles	Right rhumbs	Leeway	Thu. 17 July 1729. Events on the sea route from Bol'shaia River to the mouth of Okhota River
1	NEbN	NWbN½N	4.2	NEbE½E	1½	From noon to 8 o'clock sunshine.
2	WbN		2.5	W¼N	1¾	At 1 and 2 o'clock light breeze,
3	W		1.2	WbS		at times light fog. At 1 o'clock we
4	WbS½W	NWbN	2.8	WSW¾W	}2	lowered the topsail, turning to port,
5	WbS	NW	2.5	WSW¼W	1¾	then wind rose.
6			3.6			At 8 o'clock, at sunset, we sighted
7	W	NWbN	3.0	WbS½W	1½	amplitude of the sun from N by W
8	WbS		2.5	WSW	2	62°00', and then we were in the
9	W	NWbN	1.2			latitude N 54°55', the sun declination
10	WbN		1.2	WbS		N 15°11', the amplitude found from N
11	W		1.0	WSW	}2¾	by W 55°08', from this compass
12			1.0			declination 6°52' east. From 8 o'clock
1	W½N	}calm &	0.8	WbS	}2¼	to midnight starlight. Light air. We
2		}vari-	0.4	WbS		carried mainsail and foresail.
3		}able	0.4	W¼N	1	From midnight to 4 o'clock the sky was
4	WSW	}	0.2	WSW¾W		clear, though cloudy in places.
5	WNW	ENE	0.5	WNW¾N		We carried the same sails. From 3 to 4 o'clock
						we drifted without sails, because of stillness.
6	NWbW		0.5	NWbW¾N		From 4 o'clock to noon light air,
7			1.0			at 5 o'clock we hoisted mainsail,
8			1.5			topsail and forestaysail.
9	NWbW	}calm &	2.2	NWbW¾N		
10		}variable	2.7			The weather murky, by 12 o'clock rain.
11		}between	2.5			
12		}N & E	2.0			

in all 41.4

Latitudes		Dist. of lat.		Departure		Rhumb	Distance		Dist. of long.		Compass declin. E
from	to	N	S	E	W		right	added	daily	total	
54°55'23	54°59'89	4' 66			28' 03	WbN 1°54'bW	28.40	49.9	49'3 83 W	4°46' 83	1 R before 8 p.m. then ¾ R

Folio 68 verso, continuation

Hours	Rhumbs	Winds	Miles	Right rhumbs	Fri. 18 July 1729
1	NWbW	calm &	1.6	NWbW¾N	From noon to midnight the weather
2		vari-	4.2		murky, at times rain. We carried
3		able	5.4		forestaysail and topsail. At 2 p.m.
4			4.3		hoisted mainsail. Fresh breeze.
5	NWbW	NE	5.5	NWbW¾N	From midnight to 5 o'clock fresh breeze
6			6.5		the weather cloudy. We carried
7			5.7		mainsail, topsail and forestaysail.
8			5.3		From 5 o'clock to 9 the weather and wind
9	NWbW	NE	5.8	NWbW¾N	the same. We carried full set of sails,
10			5.8		except the foresail. From 9 o'clock to noon
11			5.3		the weather cloudy with a short sunny
12			5.3		spell, gentle breeze.
1	NWbW	NE	5.0	NWbW¾N	At noon we sighted altitude of the sun in S
2			5.5		direction with correction – 52°38', its
3			5.5		declination by local meridian –
4			6.0		18°52'N, from this latitude of fix –
5	NWbW	NE	5.0	NWbW¾N	56°14'N.
6			5.0		
7			5.0		
8			5.7		
9	NWbW	NE	5.8	NWbW¾N	
10			4.5		
11			4.2		
12			4.1		

in all   122.0

Latitudes		Diff. of lat.		Departure		Rhumb	Distance		Diff. of long.		Compass declin. E
from	to	N	S	E	W		right	added	daily	total	
54°59'89	56°14'	78' 50			86' 62	NW 2°49'bW	115.0	192.4	2°24'9 W	7°11' 73	¾ R

219

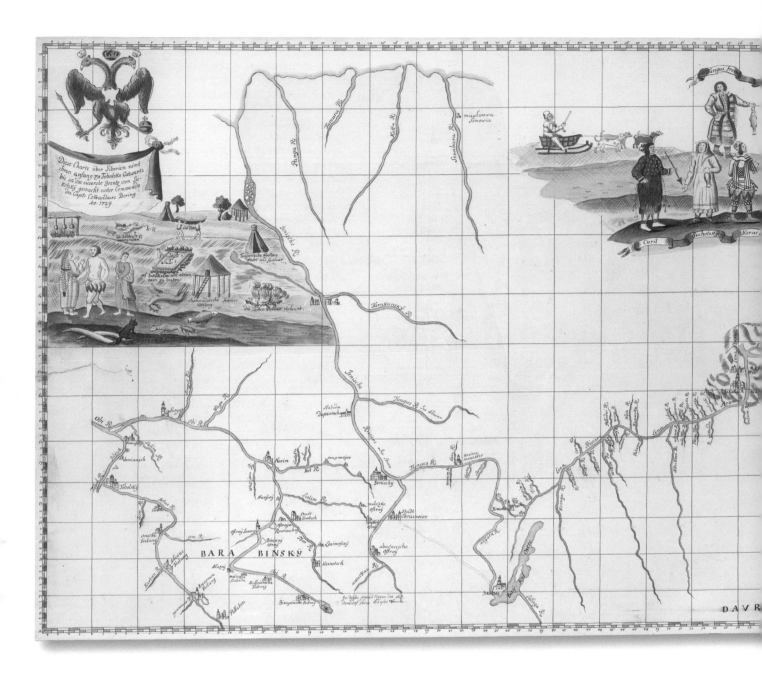

PLATE 42. The so-called "Prince of Liechtenstein copy" of Bering's Final Map. With ethnographical illustrations. The legend reads: "Diese Charte über Siberien nimt ihren Anfang zu Tobolsk ostwerts bis an die euserste Grentz von Sukotsky gemacht unter Commendo des Capt. Commandeurs Bering Ao: 1729." Map size 51 × 130 cm.

Courtesy the James Ford Bell Library, Minneapolis, MN.

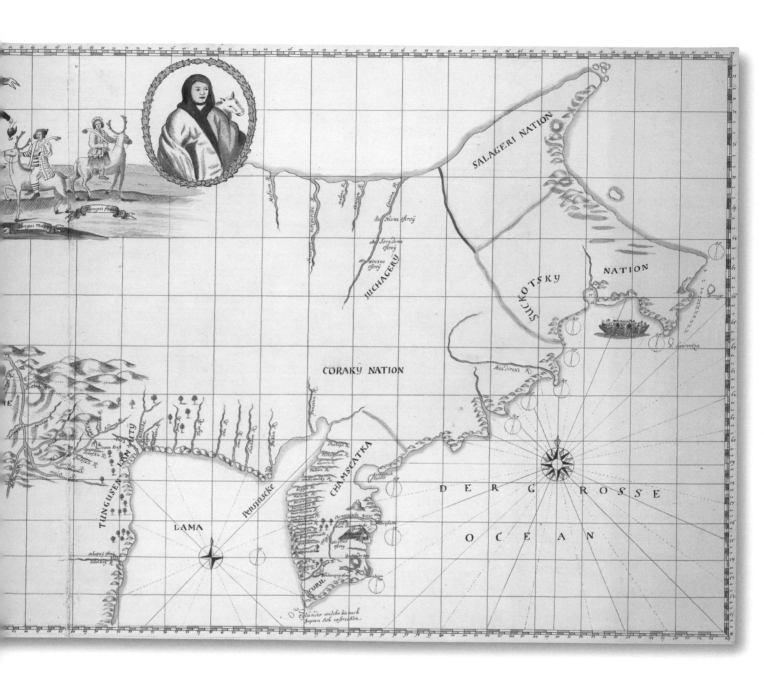

PLATE 43. The so-called Baron Klinckowström manuscript map of the route of Bering's First Kamchatka Expedition. It is a Swedish copy of a draft version of Bering's Final Map of 1729. (Bagrow 1948, no. 7). 51 × 131 cm.

Courtesy the James Ford Bell Library, Minneapolis, MN.

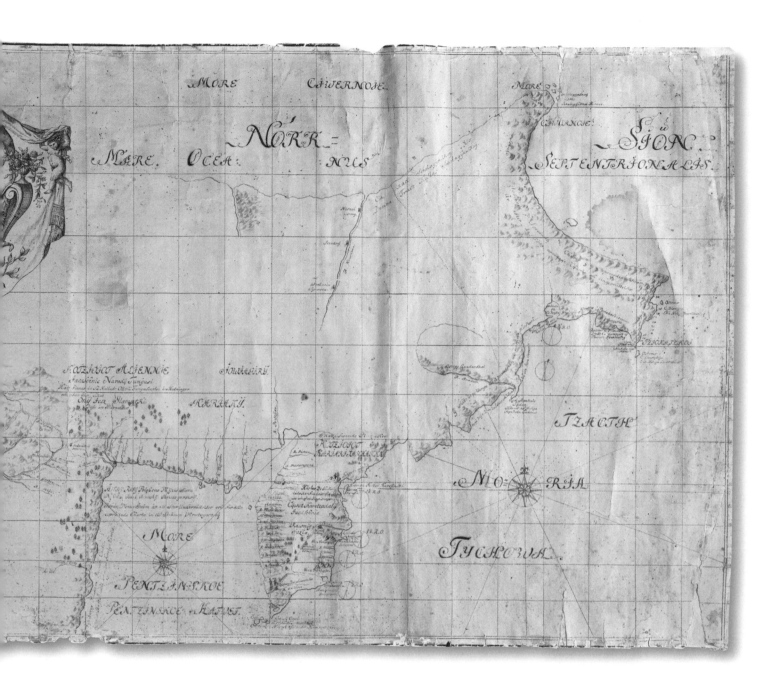

Hours	Rhumbs	Winds	Miles	Right rhumbs	Leeway	Sat. 19 July 1729. Events on the sea route from Bol'shaia River to the mouth of Okhota River
1	NW	NNE	4.0	NW¾N		From noon to 4 o'clock the weather
2			4.0			clear, fresh breeze. We carried
3			4.0			mainsail, foresail, topsail and jib.
4			4.0			At 4 o'clock the fog came in.
5	NW	NNE	3.0	NW¾N		From 4 o'clock to midnight the weather
6			3.0			gloomy and foggy, but at times the fog
7			2.8	NW¼N	½	was dissipated. We carried the same
8			1.7			sails. From midnight to 4 o'clock gloomy
9	NW	NNE	2.0			and wet fog. We carried mainsail,
10	NWbW	NbE	1.5	NWbW¼N	½	foresail, topsail and jib.
11			1.5			From 4 to 9 the weather gloomy and
12			1.0			because of stillness we drifted without
1	WNW	calm &	1.3	WNW½N		sails. At 10 o'clock we set mainsail,
2	W	variable	1.4	W½N	¼	foresail, topsail and jib. Sunshine breaking
3		between	2.0			through fog.
4	WbS	N &W	1.0	WbS½W		
5	WbN¾N		0.3	WNW½N		
6						
7		still				
8						
9						
10	NW	calm &	1.0	NWbN		
11		variable	2.2		¼	
12		between	1.5			
		SW&W				

in all   43.2

Latitudes		Diff. of lat.		Departure		Rhumb	Distance		Diff. of long.		Compass declin. E
from	to	N	S	E	W		right	added	daily	total	
56°14'	56°43'65	29'65			29' 07	NWbN 10°41'bW	41.52	75.2	52'61 W	8°04' 34	¾ R

Folio 69, continuation

Hours	Rhumbs	Winds	Miles	Right rhumbs	Sun. 20 July 1729
1	NW	calm &	1.7	NW¾N	From noon to 4 o'clock fog with a few glimpses
2		variable	1.5		of sunshine.
3		between	1.0		We carried mainsail, foresail, topsail and jib.
4		SW & W	0.8		From 4 to 9 the weather gloomy with
5	NW		1.0	NW¾N	fog, and at times sunshine.
6		calm	1.6		We carried the same sails. At 7 o'clock
7			2.5		hoisted forestaysail and foresail and
8		SSW	2.5		topsail were taken in.
9	NW	SW	4.0	NW¾N	From 8 o'clock to midnight cloudy,
10			4.3		at times a few stars could be seen,
11		SW	4.2		light breeze. We carried mainsail, topsail, forestaysail.
12			4.0		From midnight to 4 o'clock the weather cloudy,
1	NW		3.0	NW½N	at times rain. Light air.
2			1.5		We carried the aforementioned sails.
3		SW	2.0		From 4 to 8 o'clock cloudy, light air.
4			1.6		At 8 o'clock rain. We carried mainsail, topsail, forestaysail and jib.
5	NW	SW	3.0	NW½N	
6			2.0		From 8 o'clock to noon cloudy with sunny spells,
7			1.0		light breeze. We held the aforementioned sails.
8			1.5		At 11 o'clock by sand clock we took the azimuth
9	NW	SWbW	2.0	NW½N	altitude of the sun with correction 50°32', by compass 16°15' from S by E, then we were at the latitude N
10			1.5		57°24', the sun declination N 18°22', azimuth
11		SW	2.5		was found – 11°46' from S by E. From this
12			2.5		compass declination – 3°59' east. At noon the altitude of the sun was sighted with correction – 50°56', its declination by local meridian – 18°22'N, from this latitude of fix – N 57°26'.

In all   54. 2

Latitudes		Diff. of lat.		Departure		Rhumb	Distance		Diff. of long.		Compass declin. E
from	to	N	S	E	W		right	added	daily	total	
56° 43'65	57° 26'46	42'81			33' 21	NWbN 3°53'bW	54.18	99.74	1° 01'13 W	9°54'7	¾ to midnight, then ½ R

Hours	Rhumbs	Winds	Miles	Right rhumbs	Mon. 21 July 1729. Events on the sea route from Bol'shaia River to the mouth of Okhota River
1	NW	SW	1.7	NW½N	From noon to 4 o'clock the weather clear,
2			2.2		the sky in places cloudy, light air.
3			2.1		We carried mainsail, topsail,
4			2.0		forestaysail, jib.
5	NW	SW	2.5	NW½N	From 4 to 6 o'clock cloudy with sunny
6	NWbW		3.0		spells, light air. At 5:30 o'clock
7			2.5		forestaysail was lowered. From 6 to 8
8			2.0		o'clock cloudy, light air. We carried
9	NWbW	SW	1.3	NW½N	mainsail, foresail, topsail, jib.
10	⎫	⎫ calm	1.0		From 8 o'clock to midnight starlight,
11	⎬	⎬ then	0.7		the sky near horizon cloudy, light air.
12	⎭	⎩ light breeze S			We carried the aforementioned sails.
1	NWbW	S	1.0	NW½N	From midnight to 4 o'clock the sky was
2			2.0		clear, light air. We carried mainsail,
3			3.0		topsail, forestaysail and jib.
4			3.5		From 4 o'clock to 7 fog. Fresh breeze,
5	NWbW	S	4.5	NW½N	at times only light.
6			3.6		At 8 o'clock cloudy. We carried
7			4.5		mainsail, topsail and forestaysail.
8	NWbW		4.4		From 9 o'clock to noon the weather cloudy
9	NWbW	SSE	4.4	NW½N	with short sunny spells, fresh breeze.
10			4.6		We carried the aforementioned sails.
11			4.8		During all these days we took into account the sea current by right
12			4.5		compass to SWbW½W – 18 minutes.

Sea current per day[388] –   18.0   SWbW½W

Latitudes		Diff. of lat.		Departure		Rhumb	Distance		Diff. of long.		Compass declin. E
from	to	N	S	E	W		right	added	daily	total	
57°26'	58°01' 15	34'15			65'28	NWbW 5°46'bW	73.92	147.6	2°05' W	11°11' 37	½ R

Folio 69 verso, continuation

Hours	Rhumbs	Winds	Miles	Right rhumbs	Tue. 22 July 1729
1	NWbW	SE	5.3	NWbW½N	From noon to 4 o'clock the weather gloomy,
2			5.2		fresh breeze. We carried
3			5.7		mainsail, topsail, forestaysail. From 4
4			5.8		o'clock to 8 the weather and wind the same.
5	NW	SEbE	6.7	NW½N	We carried the aforementioned sails.
6			6.0		From 8 o'clock to midnight murky and
7			5.2		drizzle, fresh breeze. At 11 o'clock
8			5.0		we took in mainsail and topsail
9	NW	E	4.5	NW½N	and ran under one forestaysail, cast the
10			4.5		lead, but could not reach the bottom.
11			5.0		From midnight to 4 o'clock drizzle, fresh breeze, from 3 to
12			3.0		4 o'clock we ran under forestaysail, and at 4 o'clock hoisted
1	NW	E	5.0	NW½N	mainsail.
2			5.0		From 4 to 8 o'clock the weather murky, at times rain, land was
3			2.5		seen to E and WbN from us. We carried mainsail, foresail,
4	⎰ NW½N		4.0	NWbN	topsail and jib.
	⎱ NbW		1.5	NbW½N	At 7 o'clock the mouth of Okhota River and the store house at
5	NbE	EbN	5.2	NbE½E	the mouth stood from us to the rhumb N, 8 minutes distant.
6	N¾E		4.5	NbE¼E	From 9 o'clock to noon gloomy, light breeze, we maneuvered
7			3.6		towards the mouth of Okhota River. At 10 o'clock the
8	N		8.0	N½E	navigator[389] was sent in a boat to sound the mouth and find out
9					where to enter, since the river flows into the sea by 2 mouths. At
10					11:30 o'clock we lay at anchor at the depth of 8 sazhens because
11					of light air. Bottom – fine sand. The storehouse at the mouth
12					stood to NNE from us, 2 minutes away.

Sea current per day –   18.0   SWbW½W

Latitudes		Diff. of lat.		Departure		Rhumb	Distance		Diff. of long.		Compass declin.
from	to	N	S	E	W		right	added	daily	total	E
58°01'15	59°13'	71' 76			64' 04	NWbN 8°00'bW	96.18	84.7	2°03'0 W	13°14' 37	½ R

Folio 70

D. of week	D. of month	July 1729. Events at the Okhotsk outpost	Winds
Wed.	23	At 2 p.m. we waved a flag[390] and fired 2 cannons to call a boat from the shore. Soon after 2 o'clock light breeze arose, and having raised anchor, we ran closer to the mouth of the river. At 3 o'clock we lay at anchor at a depth of 5 sazhens and fired another cannon shot to call a boat. Light air, the weather clear. At 4 o'clock the navigator came on a boat and reported that the water in the river was falling and that it was impossible to enter the mouth. At 5 o'clock we raised the anchor and ran from the shore, then lay at anchor, and at 7 a.m. raised the anchor and maneuvered by the mouth of Okhota River. The weather sunny, with gentle breeze.	ESE
Thu.	24	At […] p.m.[391] we came into the river mouth with the rising tide, fired 5 cannons, and put the ship at the bank. The Captain ordered us to take the cordage off the ship.	
Fri.	25	Sunshine and warm. Light air. We unloaded provisions, artillery and ship equipment from the ship onto the shore. The ship was completely unrigged.	
Sat.	26	Murky and wind. After midnight clear. All men moved from the ship to the outpost, only the first mate and 5 sailors were left to be on guard and to hand the ship and various things over to the chief of Okhotsk.	ESE
Sun.	27	Clear, moderate breeze, at 10 a.m. the navigator with 1 sailor, 1 drummer and 3 soldiers were sent to Iakutsk to arrange for horses[392] to meet us at the Bel'skaia crossing on the Aldan River, and also for vessels to take us from Iakutsk up the Lena River.	S
Mon.	28	Gloomy and wind. We sent the sick geodesist and apprentice mast maker off on the route, and with them 3 soldiers, 1 carpenter.	SW
Tue.	29	The same weather, light air. We went on our route to Iakutsk: the Captain and with him Lieutenant Chirikov, the physician, the midshipman, the first mate, the quartermaster, 7 sailors, the apprentice boat maker, the drummer, the blacksmith, 5 soldiers, the sailmaker, 5 carpenters. Lieutenant Spanberch was left at the outpost for his own needs, and with him the chaplain, 4 sailors, 1 foreman of carpenters, 3 Admiralty carpenters, 1 caulker, 4 soldiers. In all for all the command 78 horses were hired, for 1 rouble per each horse from Okhotsk to Iudoma Cross. The horses were shared in the following way: The Captain – 8, 2 Lieutenants – 8 horses, the chaplain – 3, the physician – 3, the navigator – 2, the midshipman – 2, the geodesist – 2, the apprentice boat maker – 2, the apprentice mast maker – 2, the first mate and the quartermaster – 3, for geodetic instruments – 1, and the other servicemen – 1 horse each.	

D. of week	D. of month	July, on the route from Okhotsk to Iakutsk by land	
Wed.	30	Sunshine and warm. At 7 o'clock we put up for the night, and in the morning set out on our route. The weather gloomy and at times drizzling. We were met by a Cossack chief of Iakutsk, who had been sent to our party.[393]	
Thu.	31	The weather murky, in the morning overcast, and about 9 a.m. we crossed the Urak River to the right side of its stream.	

		August	
Fri.	1	Heavy rain, by the evening we overtook the sick geodesist and apprentice mast maker. In the morning overcast.	
Sat.	2	At 10 p.m. we came to the Urak River, where we crossed to the left side and spent the night. In the morning the water in the river was high from rain, and it was impossible to cross. Sunshine and very warm.	
Sun.	3	Sunshine and warm, we stood still because of high water.	
Mon.	4	Men were sent to find a ford where we could cross the river, and they found one. In the morning we crossed and continued our journey. The weather cloudy.	
Tue.	5	Rain. We crossed to the right bank of the Urak. In the morning it cleared up. In the morning, passing 15 or 20 versts, we came by a stream and stopped because of high water. Even if we had crossed here with difficulty, it would have been impossible to cross at the next place.	
Wed.	6	Sunshine, we remained at the same place.	
Thu.	7	Sunshine. We went off on our route and crossed to the left bank of the Urak. Towards evening we crossed again to the right bank. In the morning considerable frost and sunshine. We crossed to the left side of the Urak and went up a ridge,[394] or what we would call a mountain,[395] which adjoined the Iudoma River.	

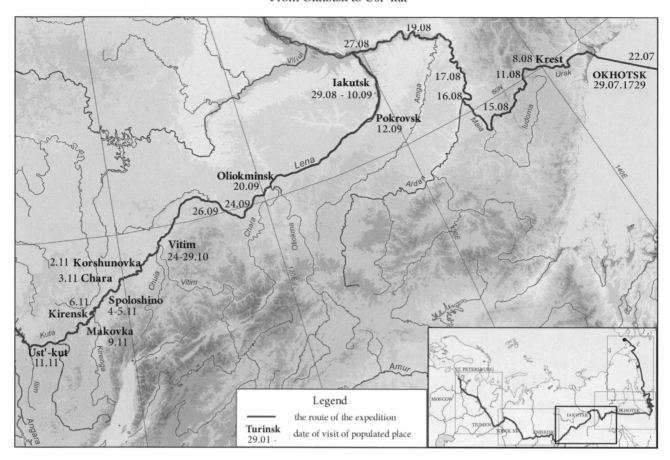

PLATE 44. Modern map 8. From Okhotsk to Ust'-kut. By Viktor Sedov.

▶ PLATE 45. Ivan Kirilov's General Map of Russia from 1733. Kirilov was first secretary of the Governing Senate. His map reflects the recent results of the First Kamchatka Expedition. (Efimov 1964, No. 72). Map size 54 × 87 cm.

Courtesy Library of the Academy of Sciences (BAN), St. Petersburg. Photo by Nikolai Turkin.

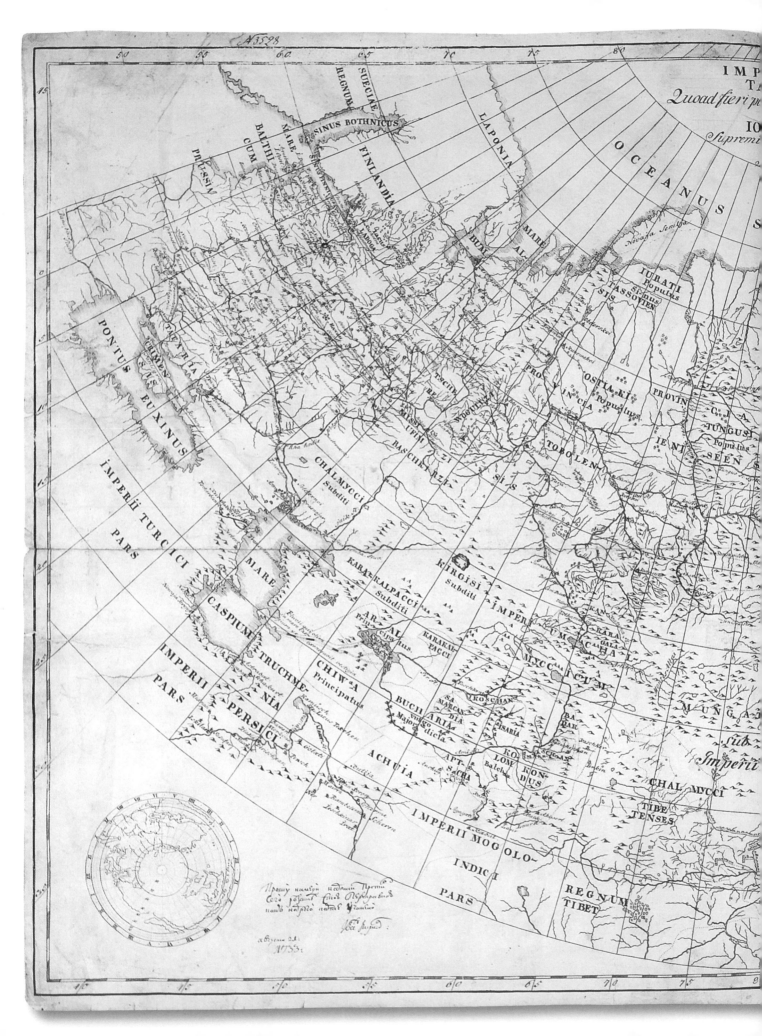

D. of week	D. of month	August 1729. On the route by the rivers Iudoma, Maia and Aldan
Fri.	8	Sunshine and warm, there was much mud on the mountain. At 9 or 10 a.m. we arrived at the Iudoma River by Krest and sent servicemen and carpenters to make rafts[396] for navigation on the rivers.
Sat.	9	Sunshine. We surrendered all the horses on which we had arrived. The water in the river began to fall.
Sun.	10	2 rafts were floated here, and one more raft was made at Krest. And the Captain took a rowboat[397] from Shestakov's command. In the morning we loaded the rafts and the boat and proceeded down the Iudoma River. Murky weather.
Mon.	11	Murky and rain. After passing Krivaia Luka, we made one more raft. Having stayed the night, we sailed on and passed the rapids safely.
Tue.	12	Considerable rain and in the morning murky, then it cleared up.
Wed.	13	Sunny spells and at times strong gale between the mountains. Towards evening we found a rowboat on the bank, left by the party sent ahead, and took possession of it. In the morning Lieutenant Chirikov, the midshipman, the apprentice boat maker, 2 sailors, 2 soldiers, 1 carpenter moved to this boat, and we sailed on, leaving one raft behind. Sunshine, adverse moderate gale, at times from the side.
Thu.	14	Sunny spells. In the morning we passed the upper and lower winter quarters, built by our men on their way up the river on the vessels. Sunny spells and calm.
Fri.	15	Cloudy and calm. At 3 p.m. we entered the Maia River, proceeded downstream and slept the night near the stream Oslianka. In the morning sunshine.
Sat.	16	Sunshine. At 6 p.m. we passed on the right side of the river some high white stone mountains on the very bank, just like a man-made wall,[398] in total extension about 10 versts. In the morning we sailed up the river Aldan and proceeded downstream.
Sun.	17	Short sunny spells, at 6 p.m. we arrived at the Notorskaia crossing place and slept the night. In the morning, 2 of our rafts caught up. They were sent on to the Bel'skaia crossing.
Mon.	18	We remained at the Notorskaia crossing, waiting for the raft with the sick, and with them the quartermaster, a sailor, 3 soldiers. In the morning we sailed on towards the Bel'skaia crossing, since the raft with the sick had not come. Sunshine and calm.

D. of week	D. of month	August. On the route to Iakutsk from Okhotsk
Tue.	19	Clear and calm. At 8 p.m. we reached the Bel'skaia crossing. In the morning we sent a raft with 7 men to the mouth of the Tata. And while we were sailing by the rivers, during the nights we stayed at the banks.
Wed.	20	Clear, at times cloudy, then there was rain. We found that the Iakut who lives here had 6 horses [of his own] and 10 horses that had come from Okhotsk outpost. On these horses the Captain left for Iakutsk in the morning, accompanied by myself – the midshipman – and 2 soldiers, 1 carpenter. The horses that the navigator had been ordered to assemble had not arrived. Intermittent rain.
Thu.	21	Towards the evening it cleared up, in the morning sunshine and calm.
Fri.	22	We arrived by the Mga River. 2 soldiers of our command, who had been sent with the navigator to collect horses, arrived and reported that 90 horses were sent to Bel'skaia crossing on 20 August. Having slept the night here, we went on. The weather clear with sunshine.
Sat.	23	Sunshine, at 10 a.m. we came to the best Iakut,[399] and the Captain gave orders to assemble 16 horses for changing.
Sun.	24	Cloudy. Towards the evening Lieutenant Chirikov arrived with the rest of the men and reported that he had left 1 soldier at the crossing and with him 46 horses for the rest of the men behind us. And here we slept the night. In the morning, having changed horses and paid money by account, we went on our route.
Mon.	25	Cloudy. At night it rained. We slept the night at a lake. In the morning gloomy.
Tue.	26	Gloomy. Today we passed a considerable number of lakes with plenty of fish, and slept the night at a deserted place.
Wed.	27	Clear, in places the sky cloudy. We slept the night at a great lake and today we have passed a considerable number of lakes. In the morning cloudy. At noon we came to the Lena River, a little below the town of Iakutsk, and sent a soldier to look for vessels on which to cross the river.
Thu.	28	Cloudy. The apprentice boat maker Speshnev, who had been sent to our party, came over to us and brought a decree from the State's Admiralty College, that I had been promoted midshipman on 25 June [1]728, ahead of schedule.[400]

D. of week	D. of month	August. Events at Iakutsk	
Fri.	29	Clear weather. 2 vessels sailed up and took us across the river to the town of Iakutsk, where we took up our quarters. From this day, we worked on preparing the vessels to use for going on the Lena River.	
Sat.	30	Murky and cold. The physician arrived and with him 1 blacksmith and 5 carpenters.	
Sun.	31	Sunshine. The quartermaster arrived with the sick men and had a sailor and a soldier with him. He reported that on the Iudoma River the raft on which they sailed had dashed against an island and capsized. They saved themselves with great difficulty, but much of the ammunition that was with them, and also their baggage, were sunk. They left 2 soldiers to salvage what little of the sunken materiel could be found.	
		September	
Mon.	1	Sunshine, though in places the sky was cloudy.	
Tue.	2	The same weather and warm.	
Wed.	3	The weather clear, towards evening Lieutenant Spanberch arrived and with him 2 sailors, 1 carpenters' foreman, 2 Admiralty carpenters, 3 soldiers, including the soldier who had been left at the Bel'skaia crossing with the horses from Bel'skaia and Notorskaia crossings and from the mouth of the Tata River. We paid the account for horses, and got a receipt from the Iakutsk chancellery for the things handed in by us.	
Thu.	4	Clear. The provisions for the future 3 months were given out to the servicemen.	
Fri.	5	The same weather.	
Sat.	6	The weather clear. 2 soldiers arrived who had been left at the Maia River to look for the sunken baggage and ammunition. They reported that none of the ammunition had been found, and only a small portion of their baggage had been recovered.	
Sun.	7	Intermittent sunshine and warm. In the morning the Captain and all his men moved onto the vessel.	
Mon.	8	Gloomy.	
Tue.	9	The same weather and calm.	
Wed.	10	The weather murky and warm, at times rain, and at times sunshine. And at 8 p.m. we set out from Iakutsk on 2 doshchaniks. The Captain was on the first one, and with him Lieutenant Chirikov, the midshipman, the apprentice boat maker, the first mate, 7 sailors, 5 soldiers, 1 drummer, 1 sailmaker, 1 carpenter of Eniseisk, 15 hired workers, 2 merchants, who paid for themselves to the servicemen of our command. On the second doshchanik were Lieutenant Spanberch, with the physician, the navigator, the geodesist, the quartermaster, the carpenters' foreman, 3 sailors, 9 soldiers, 1 drummer, 2 Admiralty carpenters, 1 interpreter, 12 workers, and 1 merchant, who paid to the servicemen, as did the other [merchants]. The apprentice mast maker Endogurov was left at Iakutsk owing to ill-health. The chaplain, 2 sailors, 1 Admiralty carpenter, 1 caulker, 2 soldiers had not arrived in Iakutsk from Okhotsk in time for our departure. In addition, we had left the following at the Bol'shaia River on the old vessel: 1 corporal and 11 soldiers, about whom it was known that they had arrived at the Okhotsk outpost.	
D. of week	D. of month	September. Events on the route from Iakutsk up the Lena River	
Thu.	11	The weather gloomy, variable light air. In the morning clear sky, but thick fog [early] in the morning.	
Fri.	12	Clear. At 7 p.m. we passed the Pokrovskii monastery. In the morning sunshine, by noon we ran under sail.	
Sat.	13	Sunshine, fresh breeze, from the morning to noon it rained.	N
Sun.	14	Sunny spells. Night clear with frost. All night we lay behind a shoal. In the morning sunshine. At 5 a.m. we proceeded on our route. At 10 o'clock we ran under sail and by towing. Fresh breeze between N and E.	
Mon.	15	Sunshine, wind the same. We ran by towing and held sail, and for about 2 hours we ran only under sail without towing. In the morning frost and sunshine.	
Tue.	16	Sunshine for a while, fresh breeze between N and E. We ran till the very evening, at times under sail without towing. In the morning frost. At times we ran under sail.	
Wed.	17	Sunshine, and in the morning frost. Before noon we met a doshchanik that was carrying government tobacco[86] from Irkutsk to Iakutsk.	
Thu.	18	It was clear and warm, adverse light breeze from W. We met a kaiuk,[402] sailing downstream with merchants on their way to Iakutsk. In the morning frost and murky.	W
Wed.	19	Murky and calm.	

D. of week	D. of month	September 1729. On the route up the Lena River from Iakutsk
Sat.	20	Gloomy and cold. At 8 p.m. we passed the mouth of the Oliokma River, and before the mouth we rowed from the right to the left side of the Lena River. At 4 a.m. we came to the Oliokminskii outpost. Considerable frost and sunshine. At noon we set off on our route.
Sun.	21	Sunshine and calm, warm, and at 8 p.m. we rowed to the right side of the Lena River. The weather gloomy, adverse moderate gale.
Mon.	22	It was clear, the night was moonlit. Hard frost. In the morning we met some boats with merchants bound for Iakutsk. The weather was sunny and calm.
Tue.	23	Clear and calm, all day it was warm, but at night hard frost.
Wed.	24	Clear weather, at times we ran under sail. At 10 a.m. we passed the Patama River. There was hard frost and a fair amount of ice drifting near the bank. This ice came from the small rivers, but not yet from the Lena.
Thu.	25	It was clear and warm. At times we ran under sail. At night it was light frost, in the morning sunshine, fair moderate breeze, and we ran under sail till noon.
Fri.	26	It was clear, in places the sky became overcast. At 3 p.m. we passed the Niuia River. From the evening a head wind blew from the west, and it was very cold. In the morning gloomy, wind the same and icy cold.
Sat.	27	The weather and wind the same. We met 2 boats that were sailing downstream on the Lena, near the left bank. In the morning gloomy, light breeze from west and snowfall. We passed the streams called Griaznukhi.
Sun.	28	The weather and wind the same. In the morning hard frost and head wind. At 5 a.m. a doshchanik came downstream with a boyar's son of Irkutsk and his recruits on their way to Iakutsk. At the same time we passed the hamlet of Fedosova and crossed from the right to the left side of the Lena.
Mon.	29	The sun began to shine a little. At 1 p.m. we passed the village of Nedostrela. In the morning hard frost and adverse strong gale. It was clearing up.
Tue.	30	The weather and wind the same and icy cold. By the evening ice began to drift down the Lena River. We ran all night, breaking the ice, and at 2 a.m. we reached the village of Peledui and took up autumn quarters.[403] The doshchaniks with all supplies we surrendered to the chief of Vitim. The workers[404] on the vessels were paid and allowed to go. From Iakutsk to Peledui we had run day and night, except when some impediment forced us to stop for the night.

D. of week	D. of month	October 1729. Events at the village of Peledui
Wed.	1	Gloomy and light snowfall. During the night moderate gale between N and W. In the morning frost. The weather murky.
Thu.	2	The weather murky and cold, in the morning frost.
Fri.	3	The weather and wind the same, at night snowfall, and in the morning warm.
Sat.	4	Murky, light breeze between N and W. In the morning sunshine and light frost. 2 carpenters of Eniseisk were allowed to go from our command to their former commands. Thick ice drifted down the Lena River.
Sun.	5	Sunshine and calm. At night strong, strong [sic] gale between N and W with snowfall. In the morning calm, only snowfall. Lieutenant Chirikov was sent to Irkutsk to receive money for current needs of the command on the route. With him 1 soldier and 1 officer's servant on 5 saddle-horses. And navigator Angel was allowed to go for his own needs, also to Irkutsk.
Mon.	6	Murky, at times snowfall and rare sunshine. At night the wind between S and W with snowfall. In the morning calm and light snowfall.
Tue.	7	Murky, in the morning hard frost.
Wed.	8	Snowfall and light snowstorm. In the morning gloomy and frost.
Thu.	9	Sunny spells. In the morning gloomy and light snowfall, only cold.
Fri.	10	The same weather. Captain-Lieutenant Kazantsov,[405] who was lagging behind our command, arrived from Iakutsk in the morning. He had been admitted to our command without sword[406] by decree of the Tobol'sk Guberniia Chancellery on 30 August.
Sat.	11	After noon sunny spells, but in the morning
Sun.	12	gloomy and light frost.
Mon.	13	
Tue.	14	Sunny spells, and in the morning gloomy.
Wed.	15	Wind between S and W, then sunshine.
Thu.	16	
Fri.	17	Frost, calm, sunshine.
Sat.	18	
Sun.	19	Sunshine, at night moderate gale with snowfall from W, in the morning gloomy and warm.
Mon.	20	Gloomy and warm.
Tue.	21	Gloomy and calm, in the morning considerable frost and clear.

D. of week	D. of month	October 1729. Events at the village of Peledui
Wed.	22	Clear, in the morning moderate breeze with light snowfall.
Thu.	23	Snowfall, in the morning cloudy and light frost. The Captain left the village of Peledui for the settlement of Vitim and with him the midshipman, the apprentice boat maker, the first mate, 7 sailors, 3 soldiers, and 1 blacksmith, on 13 sledges.[407]
Fri.	24	Gloomy. Having gone about 12 versts, we slept the night at a deserted spot. In the morning clear, and hard frost. At 12 a.m. we arrived at the settlement of Vitim.
Sat.	25	Clear and frost.
Sun.	26	Gloomy, at times light snowfall, in the morning considerable frost.
Mon.	27	Sun breaking through, light breeze from W. Lieutenant Spanberch arrived from Peledui with all the rest of the command. At 4 a.m. the first mate with 13 sailors and soldiers on 7 sledges were sent ahead to arrange for sledges for the command. The weather clear, with hard frost.
Tue.	28	The same weather.
Wed.	29	Sunshine. The Captain left the settlement of Vitim with all of his command on 24 sledges, namely: the Captain – 5, Captain-Lieutenant Kazantsov – 1, Lieutenant Spanberch – 3, the physician – 1, the navigator – 1, the midshipman – 1, the geodesist – 1, the apprentice boat maker – 1, and the other servicemen – 1 sledge for every 2 men, in all 31 sledges including those that had been sent ahead. The weather gloomy, in the morning considerable frost.
Thu.	30	Gloomy, in the morning clear and frost.
Fri.	31	The same weather. We came to the squatter's holding[408] of Kureiskaia and here slept the night. In the morning the weather gloomy and light snowfall.

D. of week	D. of month	November 729. On the route to Ilimsk
Sat.	1	Gloomy and light snowfall, cold.
Sun.	2	Clear. At 5 p.m. we came to the squatter's holding Ivanushkina and here slept the night. In the morning hard frost. At 8 o'clock we came to the village of Korshunovka and here paid for horses from Vitim to this squatter's holding, 202 versts.
Mon.	3	Clear. Having gone 30 versts, we slept the night at the village of Chara. In the morning considerable frost. Having gone 25 versts, we fed the horses at the village of Dal'nie. The weather clear.
Tue.	4	The same weather. At 7 p.m. we came to the settlement of Sploshennoe. Having paid for the transportation, we let the sledges go. Having slept the night, we hired sledges in the morning. Considerable frost, and murky. The distance from the village of Korshunovka 93 versts in all.
Wed.	5	The same weather. We moved on, and after 22 versts stopped for the night. In the morning frost and light snowfall.
Thu.	6	The weather gloomy, light breeze from NE. Today, having gone about 40 versts, we slept the night. In the morning frost, at 10 a.m. we arrived at Kirenskii outpost, changed sledges,[409] and went on. From Sploshnoe to Kirenga 87 versts.
Fri.	7	The weather gloomy, in the morning considerable frost.
Sat.	8	Gloomy and snowfall at times. We slept the night at the village of Krivaia Luka. In the morning light snowfall, but cold.
Sun.	9	Gloomy and snowfall. We slept the night at the village of Tirskaia. In the morning light snowfall. We came to the village of Markova. The distance from Kirenskii outpost to this village is 122 versts. Changed sledges, and went on.
Mon.	10	Light snowfall, in the morning hard frost.
Tue.	11	The same weather. In the morning hard frost. At 9 a.m. we arrived at Ust'-Kutskii outpost. From the village of Markova to this outpost 122 versts. We changed sledges and went on.
Wed.	12	Murky, in the morning light snowfall and warm.
Thu.	13	The same weather.
Fri.	14	Murky. At 3 p.m. we arrived at the town of Ilimsk. From Ust'-Kuta to Ilimsk 135 versts. In the morning gloomy, calm and warm.
Sat.	15	The same weather.
Sun.	16	The same weather, in the morning considerable frost.
Mon.	17	Hard frost.
Tue.	18	Hard frost. 4 men were sent ahead to arrange for sledges at the stations.
Wed.	19	Hard frost.
Thu.	20	Hard frost. We set off on our route from Ilimsk on 27 sledges. Geodesist Putilov was left at Ilimsk because of ill-health, and 2 soldiers were left to care for him. We instructed the office to send them on by waterway in the spring. His instruments and baggage were given to the Ilimsk Office with an instruction to look after them. The carpenters' foreman and 2 carpenters of Irkutsk were left till the arrival of Lieutenant Chirikov.

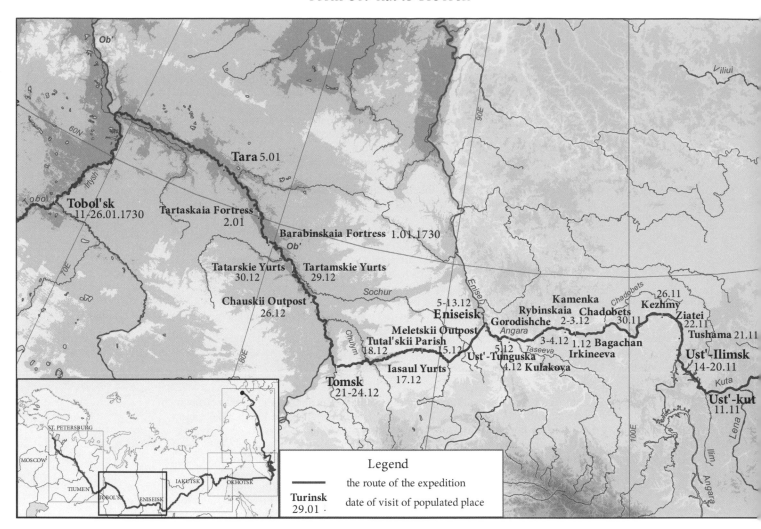

PLATE 46. Modern map 9: From Ust'-Kut to Tobol'sk. By Viktor Sedov.

Folio 72 verso

D. of week	D. of month	November 729. Events on the route from Ilimsk to Eniseisk
Fri.	21	Hard frost. Going in all 39 versts, we changed sledges. By the morning we came to the settlement of Tiushama. Here we changed sledges.
Sat.	22	The weather clear. In the morning hard frost. At 6 o'clock we came to the village of Ziatei. From Ilimsk to this village 130 versts 400 sazhens. The weather clear.
Sun.	23	The weather clear. We changed sledges, and Lieutenant Spanberch was sent forward with 11 men to fill up the quarters along the route ahead,[410] since villages were small, 1 – 2 homesteads in each. In the morning hard frost and sunshine. At 9 a.m. we went on our route.
Mon.	24	Frost. We were moving by the Tunguska River. The ice on the river was very rough, and we proceeded with great difficulty.
Tue.	25	Frost. About 9 a.m. we arrived at the village of Tiushamskaia and, having changed sledges, went on. From the village of Ziatei to this one – 88 versts.
Wed.	26	Gloomy and small snowfall, warm. At 10 p.m. we came to the village of Kata and, changing sledges, went on. From Tiushamskaia to Kata – 48 versts. In the morning warm and small snowfall. About 8 o'clock we came to the village of Panskaia, changed sledges, and went on.
Thu.	27	The same weather. At 5 p.m. we came to the settlement of Kezhmy and, changing sledges, went on. In the morning warm. From Panskaia to Kezhmy – 48 versts.
Fri.	28	Gloomy and light snowfall. In the morning cold.
Sat.	29	Gloomy, in the morning hard frost.
Sun.	30	Frost. At 3 p.m. we came to the village of Chadomets and, changing sledges, went on. From Kezhmy to Chadomets 203 versts. In the morning gloomy and warm.

D. of week	D. of month	December 729. Events on the route from Ilimsk to Eniseisk
Mon.	1	Gloomy. At 5 p.m. we came to the village of Bagachan and, changing sledges, moved on. From Chadomets to Bagachan – 88 versts. In the morning the weather gloomy and calm. At 4 a.m. we came to the village of Irkineeva. From Bagachan to Irkineeva – 44 versts. Changing sledges, we went on.
Tue.	2	Gloomy, wind with snowstorm. At 10 p.m. came to the village of Kamenka. From Irkineeva to Kamenka – 50 versts. In the morning gloomy and light snowstorm.
Wed.	3	The same weather. About 8 o'clock Lieutenant Chirikov arrived at the command from Irkutsk, and so did the navigator Angel, who had been allowed to go for his own needs. In the morning gloomy. About 9 o'clock we came to the sloboda of Rybinskaia and changed sledges. From Kamenka to this sloboda – 98 versts.
Thu.	4	The same weather. We started, and about 11 o'clock we came to the village of Kulakova and, changing some part of sledges, went. From Rybinskaia to this village 44 versts. In the morning gloomy.
Fri.	5	Gloomy and small snowfall. At 5 p.m. we came to the settlement of Ust'-Tunguska and, changing sledges, went on. From Kulakova to this settlement – 52 versts. And at 3 a.m. we came to the sloboda of Gorodishche and, changing sledges, went on. From Ust'-Tunguska to Gorodishche – 36 versts. The weather gloomy, light breeze. About 9 o'clock we came to the town of Eniseisk. From Gorodishche to Eniseisk – 24 versts, in all from Ilimsk to Eniseisk – 996 versts.
Sat.	6	The weather gloomy and calm.
Sun.	7	⎫
Mon.	8	⎬ Gloomy with a little sunshine breaking through.
Tue.	9	Light snowfall, and in the morning the sun began to shine a little. The members of our command from Tobol'sk garrison – 2 drummers and 12 soldiers – were sent to the Eniseisk office with a request to send them on to Tobol'sk next spring by waterway.
Wed.	10	⎫
Thu.	11	⎬ Gloomy and light snowfall.
Fri.	12	⎭
Sat.	13	We left Eniseisk on 26 sledges and, having gone 22 versts, changed sledges.
Sun.	14	Gloomy, light breeze and snowfall.

D. of week	D. of month	December 729. On the route from Eniseisk to Tomsk
Mon.	15	Heavy snowfall around 3 o'clock, then it began to clear up. About 9 a.m. we came to the Meletskii outpost, which stands on the Chulym River. The Captain moved ahead on 12 sledges. From Eniseisk to this outpost – 255 versts, and there was frequent changing of horses.[411]
Tue.	16	Light snowfall and wind with snowstorm. At 3 p.m. Lieutenant Chirikov and I went on 8 sledges, leaving behind us Captain-Lieutenant Kazantsov, the physician and some men, on 6 sledges. In the morning frost and a little sunshine.
Wed.	17	We came to the yurts of the Cossack captain[412] at 9 p.m., changed sledges, and went on. From Meletskii to these yurts – 41 [versts]. In the morning frost, with a little sunshine breaking through.
Thu.	18	The weather clear at night, in the morning light snowstorm. At 11 a.m. we came to the parish[413] of Tutal'skii. From the Cossack captain's yurts to the parish – 106 versts.
Fri.	19	Snowstorm. We changed horses and went on. In the morning sunny spells and light snowstorm.
Sat.	20	Sunny spells and light blowing snow. About 7 o'clock we arrived at the parish of Chardomskii, changed sledges, and went on. From Meletskii outpost to this parish all inhabitants are baptized Tatars. At midnight we came to the village of Zyrianskaia, changed sledges, and went on. From Meletskii to this place we followed the Chulym River. The Chulym is very meandering. We left this river behind us on our right. At 9 a.m. we arrived at the settlement of Spasskoe, changed sledges, and went on.
Sun.	21	Murky and snowstorm, at night calm and light snowfall. About 8 a.m. we came to the town of Tomsk. The distance from Eniseisk to Tomsk totals 627 measured versts and 217 sazhens. Tomsk was founded on the right bank of the Toma River, on a high hill, but the major part of the town is below the hill. The location is very cheerful.
Mon.	22	Murky. At 7 p.m. all the men of our command who travelled behind us arrived. In the morning considerable frost and all day gloomy. We delayed due to the lack of sledges.

D. of week	D. of month	December 729. On the route from Tomsk to Tara
Tue.	23	Gloomy and snowstorm. In the morning, having received sledges, the Captain went off on his route at 10 o'clock. The weather gloomy and light snowstorm.
Wed.	24	The same weather. About 1 o'clock all the command went from Tomsk on 26 sledges. In the morning gloomy.
Thu.	25	Murky and calm. About 6 o'clock we came to the Ob' River and went up this river. In the morning lightly cloudy.
Fri.	26	Cloudy, then strong gale with snowstorm. At 9 p.m. we came to Chauskii outpost, which is situated on the Chausa River, 221½ versts from Tomsk. We left the Ob' River behind us to our left. All night strong gale with snowstorm. In the morning cloudy, light breeze. Having taken sledges, we went off on our route and took for convoy 20 servitors for protection against the Kazakh Horde.[414]
Sat.	27	Gloomy and snowfall. In the morning and during all the day strong gale with snowstorm from SW.
Sun.	28	The weather and wind the same. In the morning it cleared slightly, then gloomy and snowstorm.
Mon.	29	Cloudy and very cold. About 9 o'clock we came to the yurts of Tartamsk. For 150 versts before these yurts there were only 3 winter dwellings, otherwise nothing but steppe, and the only forest was a little birch grove. In the morning heavy snowstorm, yet not very cold.
Tue.	30	The weather and wind the same. About 8 o'clock we came to some Tatar yurts, and near these yurts 50 servitors are stationed to protect tribute-paying Tatars and travelers from the Kazakh Horde. The distance from Chauskii outpost to these yurts – 220 versts. In the morning considerable frost. The Captain and with him the midshipman, the first mate, 6 sailors, on 10 sledges in all went ahead, and the others were ordered to go behind to distribute the sledges among the yurts.
Wed.	31	Clear. Considerable frost, light breeze with light blowing snow from SW, in the morning frost.

Folio 73 verso

D. of week	D. of month	January 1730. Events on the route from Tomsk to Tara
Thu.	1	Clear weather. At 10 p.m. we came to the Kamskaia and Barabinskaia fortress, where 1 Cossack chief with 150 equestrian servitors from Tomsk are stationed each year to protect travelers across the Barabinsk steppe and tribute-paying Tatars from the Kazakh Horde. Having changed sledges, we set out from here at 5 a.m. with [an escort of] servitors. The distance from Chauskii outpost to this fortress – 302 versts. In the morning sunshine and frost.
Fri.	2	The same weather. At 12 a.m. we came to Tartaskaia fortress, where 50 servitors from Tara were stationed. We changed sledges and went on. From Kamskaia to this fortress – 100 versts.
Sat.	3	Sunshine and calm, in the morning frost and light snowstorm.
Sun.	4	The weather and wind the same, at night snowfall and snowstorm. In the morning we came to some Russian villages and, having changed sledges, went on. The same weather.
Mon.	5	Gloomy and warm. About 5 a.m. we arrived at the town of Tara, and about 2 hours after our arrival the remaining people of our command came. In all from Tomsk to Tara 853 versts. And we submitted an application to the Tara office, asking them to give us a list of the distance to Tobol'sk in versts, and from one village to the next. But the voevoda Rukin refused not only to give us the list, but also to accept our application.
Tue.	6	The weather and wind the same, in the morning clear and considerable frost.
Wed.	7	Sunshine. At 1 p.m. we went from Tara toward Tobol'sk. In the morning sunshine.
Thu.	8	⎤
Fri.	9	⎦ Cloudy.
Sat.	10	Cloudy, at night light snowstorm and cold.

D. of week	D. of month	January 730. Events at Tobol'sk
Sun.	11	The same weather. At 2 p.m. we arrived at the town of Tobol'sk. The distance from Tara to Tobol'sk is 430 versts, based on our payments for horses, always to a Tatar.[415] And changing horses was very frequent. From the beginning of our winter route, that is from the village of Peledui to Tobol'sk, there were no posting stations, only compulsory horse service,[416] and we paid 1 den'ga [½ kopeck] per 1 verst for each sledge. On our arrival at Tobol'sk, the customs department sent a soldier and some tax-collectors for us, to escort us to the customs. And while we were at the customs, they reviewed all our belongings, made an inventory and then took customs taxes.[417]
Mon.	12	Cloudy.
Tue.	13	Sunny spells.
Wed.	14	Today we handed in our request for a post-horse order[418] and sledges.
Thu.	15	⎤
Fri.	16	⎬ Sunny spells, and on the 17th at times snowfall.
Sat.	17	⎦
Sun.	18	Strong frost.
Mon.	19	Cloudy.
Tue.	20	⎤
Wed.	21	⎬ Cloudy with sunny spells.
Thu.	22	⎦
Fri.	23	Frost, then sunshine and warm. According to a note we received from the [Tobol'sk] Guberniia Chancellery, Captain-Lieutenant Kazantsov has been transferred from our command to the [Tobol'sk] Garrison Chancellery. We received the post-horse order.
Sat.	24	Warm, in the morning gloomy and hard frost, then sunshine.
Sun.	25	Sunshine and warm, in the morning frost.
Mon.	26	Sunshine. At 1 p.m., having received the sledges, we left Tobol'sk on 24 sledges, that is to say: the Captain – 5, Lieutenant Spanberch – 3, Lieutenant Chirikov – 2, the physician and the navigator – 3, the midshipman – 1, the first mate and with him the cash box and the medicine chest – 1, the apprentice – 1, the other servicemen – 1 for every 2 men. In the morning sunshine.
Tue.	27	Sunshine. In the morning gloomy and hard frost.
Wed.	28	Gloomy. At 3 p.m. we came to the town of Tiumen', and at midnight, having received sledges, we went on. In the morning gloomy and cold.
Thu.	29	Gloomy. At 4 a.m. we arrived in the town of Turinsk, also called Epanchin. The weather foggy, and hard frost. We changed sledges and left at 8 a.m.

From Tobol'sk to Saint Petersburg

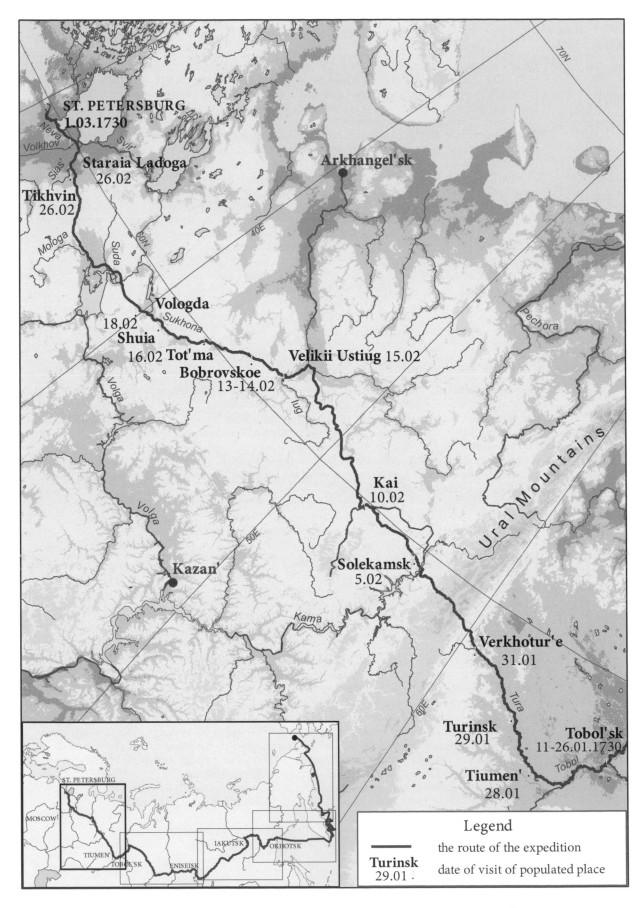

PLATE 47. Modern map 10: From Tobol'sk to Saint Petersburg. By Viktor Sedov.

Folio 74

D. of week	D. of month	February 730. Events on the route from Tobol'sk to St. Petersburg
Fri.	30	Sunshine and frost. In the morning cloudy, light frost.
Sat.	31	Warm and gloomy. In the morning we arrived at Verkhotur'e, and the customs servitors came to inspect our belongings.
		February
Sun.	1	Sunshine, in the morning considerable frost.
Mon.	2	Sunshine. At 6 p.m., having gotten sledges, we went on. The delay in our departure was due to customs formalities. In the morning frost.
Tue.	3	Sunshine.
Wed.	4	
Thu.	5	Murky. At 4 p.m. we arrived at Sol' Kamskaia.
Fri.	6	Murky.
Sat.	7	Murky. At 1 p.m. we departed from Sol' Kamskaia, having taken sledges.
Sun.	8	The same weather.
Mon.	9	Sunny spells. At 8 p.m. we arrived at the small town of Kam. In the morning cloudy. We took sledges and went on.
Tue.	10	Cloudy. At 10 a.m. we came to the settlement of Kai-gorodok, changed sledges, and went on.
Wed.	11	Cloudy. At 9 a.m. we came to the village of Ob"iachi, changed sledges, and went on.
Thu.	12	Sunshine. Light breeze. At 4 p.m. we came to the district of Loiomskaia volost', changed sledges, and went on. In the morning gloomy and small snowfall. At 10 a.m. we came to Lanskaia Sloboda.
Fri.	13	Cloudy, at 5 p.m. we went on. In the morning cloudy. At 10 a.m. we arrived at the town of Velikii Ustiug and were informed of the demise from this world to eternal bliss of His Imperial Majesty Peter II.
Sat.	14	Short sunny spells and warm. At 8 p.m. we took sledges and went off. In the morning light blowing snow.
Sun.	15	The weather and wind the same. At 6 p.m. we arrived at the settlement of Bobrovskoe. Formerly, when we started out on the expedition, one could get post-horses here. But today these [the coachmen] pay poll-tax like other peasants. Having changed sledges here, we went on, and at 11 a.m. came to the settlement of Brusenitsy, changed sledges, and went on.
Mon.	16	Light snowstorm. At 6 a.m. we arrived at the town of Tot'ma, changed sledges, went on. The weather clear, and light breeze with light snowstorm.
Tue.	17	The weather and wind the same.
Wed.	18	The weather cloudy. At 1 p.m. we arrived at the Shuiskii posting station, changed sledges, and went on. From Ustiug Velikii and until 20 versts before the posting station, we went by the Sukhona River and, leaving it on our right, we proceeded to the left. The weather clear. At 8 o'clock we arrived at the town of Vologda. In the morning cloudy.
Thu.	19	The weather and wind the same. In the morning sunny spells and warm.
Fri.	20	The weather and wind the same. At 2 a.m. we left Vologda for St. Petersburg on 19 hired sledges, distributed in the following way: one sledge for every 3 servicemen, for the Captain – 4, for the 2 lieutenants – 4 sledges, for the physician, the navigator, the midshipman, and the apprentice boat maker – 1 sledge each.
Sat.	21	Sunshine and warm. In the morning cloudy, light breeze.
Sun.	22	The weather and wind the same. In the morning the weather clear and calm.
Mon.	23	The same weather. In the morning frost and shine. The Captain moved ahead with 4 men.
Tue.	24	Sunshine and warm.
Wed.	25	Warm, cloudy and light snowstorm. In the morning heavy snowfall.
Thu.	26	Snowfall. At 8 a.m. we arrived at Tikhvin, and at 12 o'clock we went on.
Fri.	27	A little sunshine. At 3 p.m. we passed Staraia Ladoga. In the morning sunshine.
Sat.	28	Cloudy and cold. In the morning cloudy and cold.
		March
Sun.	1	Cloudy and warm. At 5 p.m. we passed Schlüsselburg.[419] In the morning hard frost and clear. At 8 a.m. we arrived at St. Petersburg and reported to the Captain.

And in finishing this, I sign,
Navy midshipman Piotr Chaplin
In the year 1730

Vitus Jonassen Bering
and the First Kamchatka Expedition

T.S. Fedorova

Vitus (in Russian also Vitez', or Ivan Ivanovich) Bering, a Dane by birth, rose to the rank of a captain-commander of the Russian Navy. He also became known in Russian and world history as the leader of the Kamchatka expeditions. Books and articles have been written, and movies have been made about Bering and his achievements. In recent years, contributions by Natasha Lind and Peter Ulf Møller have added important new information to our knowledge about Bering and his family.[1] Nevertheless, what we know about him is still far from sufficient, and this is particularly true with regard to the years of the First Kamchatka Expedition. In many ways, the personality of this extraordinary explorer still remains a mystery and continues to attract scholarly interest.

Vitus Bering was born between 30 July and 5 August 1681 in Horsens, a small town in the eastern part of the Jutland peninsula. His exact birth date is not known. There is information that he was christened on 5 August and that christening ceremonies took place only on Sundays. Vitus's father Jonas Svendsen had 5 sons and 4 daughters from two marriages. The family was modest but educated and pious. Bering's mother's sister, Margrethe Pedersdatter Bering, was married twice to burgomasters of Horsens, so by marriage the Berings were tied with the top strata of the town's society.

In April 1696 Vitus's brother Sven Jonassen put out to sea for the coasts of the East Indies. He was sent as a sailor as punishment for unpaid debts. Fourteen-year-old Vitus Bering sailed with him on this voyage, as a ship's boy. Vitus later made another voyage to the East Indies. He learned practical geography, cartography, navigation and other marine sciences. At that time, it was difficult to imagine that these voyages would play a decisive role in his future life and his appointment as the leader of the Kamchatka expeditions. What maritime school Bering attended and graduated from, if any, is still not known.

In 1703 in Amsterdam, Bering met Admiral Cornelius Cruys, a Norwegian in the Russian service, who was recruiting foreign seamen in Holland for the growing Russian Navy on instructions from Tsar Peter I. On his recommendation, Bering was hired for the Russian Navy with the rank of second lieutenant, and was appointed to the Baltic fleet. In 1704, Bering arrived in Russia via Arkhangel'sk, not realizing that Russia would become his second mother country, that most of his life would be devoted to its service, and that he would be buried on an island discovered by him and named after him.

In 1705, during the Northern War, Bering was in command of a small scoot[2] in the squadron of Admiral Cruys, and for the first time saw military operation when Swedish troops landing to attack Kotlin Island were repelled. Bering did not take direct part in the battle; his small vessel only carried firewood.

The young officer fulfilled his duties conscientiously and in 1707 he was promoted to the rank of lieutenant. On 1 May 1710 he was sent to watch for enemy vessels along the southern coast of the Gulf of Finland, a very important and responsible task. In April the town of Vyborg was besieged by Russian troops, and in early May a considerable number of transports were sent to supply them with food and ammunition. Ships and galleys under the command of Peter I protected the transports. In autumn 1710, during the war with Turkey, Bering was transferred to the Sea of Azov, where he was in command of various small vessels that were armed with few cannons, and carried crews of 24 – 40 men. In November 1710 he was promoted to the rank of captain-lieutenant.

The unsuccessful war with Turkey ended in 1711 with the Peace Treaty of Prut, under which Russia lost all its newly-built fortresses, including Azov, and access to the Black Sea. Peter I had hoped that Turkey would permit a few ships to pass from the Black Sea to Russia and assigned two ships and two snows[3] for this voyage. Captain-lieutenant Bering was appointed the commander of the snow *Munker*. Most likely Bering

PLATE 49. Epitaph over Bering's maternal aunt Margrethe
Pedersdatter Bering (d. 1732) and her two husbands, both of
them burgomasters of Horsens, J.C. Blimester (d. 1697) and
M.D. Cordsen (d. 1727), in Klosterkirken (the Monastery
Chapel), Horsens, Denmark.

Courtesy Eigil Holm.

had proved to be a disciplined and energetic officer;
otherwise he would not have received such an appointment. The special instruction to officers of ships who
had to go through "Tsargrad" forbade "while in Con-
stantinople loud banquets, cannon firing aboard the
ships, except with permission of the attending minis-
ters of His Majesty". The crews were to "act peacefully
and not commit any offence against the Turks that
could impede the passing of the squadron through the
straits."[4]

However, the Turkish authorities did not permit
the Russian vessels to pass through the straits, and the
ships were sold. Bering returned to St. Petersburg by
land and for the following twelve years served in the
Baltic Sea.

From December 1713 to January 1714 Bering was a
member of the naval court, presided over by the President of Admiralty College, Admiral F.M. Apraksin.
Another member was Peter I. The court examined the
case of Vice-Admiral Cruys, who was accused of los-
ing his ship, and permitting the enemy to escape, and
breaking off the pursuit. The Vice-Admiral not only
once, but on two occasions had failed to defend the
interests of the monarchy when in the line of duty,
said the indictment.[5] In July 1712, during the Northern War, Cruys had deliberately broken off the pursuit
of Swedish ships and allowed them to escape. In July
1713, while in pursuit of three Swedish ships, he had
run two Russian ships aground. Having seen that the
Vice-Admiral's ship *Riga* had run aground, the rest of
the ships stopped the pursuit, although exceeding the
Swedes in number and armaments. One of the ships
was later refloated, the other – *Vyborg* – had to be
burned.

Vice-Admiral Cruys was sentenced to death. A
similar punishment awaited Captain-Commander A.
Reys. Bering knew Cruys from his early youth, and
Reys was also his comrade in arms for a long time.
However, during the oral vote Bering did not hesitate
to speak out in favour of a death penalty. The sentence
was not carried out. Cruys was sent to Kazan' and in
1715 returned again to serve in the Navy, while Reys
was sent to Tobol'sk.

On 28 January 1715 Bering was promoted to captain
of the fourth rank and sent to Arkhangel'sk, where he
took command of a newly built 50-cannon ship called
Selafail. Being an experienced and efficient officer, he
led his vessel to Copenhagen. Of the four ships that
sailed from Arkhangel'sk to Copenhagen under the
command of I.D. Siniavin, only two reached Copenhagen. Bering's was one of them, and he was sent to
inspect the damage to one of the ships and its causes.

In 1716, as captain of the 50-cannon ship the *Pearl*, Bering took part in the voyage to Bornholm of a united fleet, consisting of Russian, English and Danish ships. For nine days the allied fleet cruised around under the banner of Peter I. Bering's wife, Anna Christina, née Pülse, joined him on this voyage. The couple visited Copenhagen, and here she gave birth to their son named Vitus. He was christened on 27 June 1716 in the church of St. Nicholas in Copenhagen.[6]

In May 1717, because of the abolition in the Russian Navy of the rank of Captain of Fourth Rank, Bering was reclassified as a Captain of Third Rank. On 1 March 1720 he was promoted to Captain of the Second Rank. In 1719-1723 he consecutively commanded the ships *Selafail*, *Marl'burg* and *Lesnoe* and took part in voyages of various squadrons in the Baltic Sea until February 1724.

On 20 January 1724 Bering suddenly handed in his resignation. In it, he complained that for 20 years he had served in the Russian Navy, 10 years of this time as a captain, but without an increase in salary that other officers had received.[7] The increase of salary had to be preceded by a promotion. In other words, Bering thought that he deserved promotion to Captain of the First Rank.

At that time the established custom of navy service and promotion was governed by the Navy Regulations, adopted in 1720, and by the Table of Ranks (1722). In accordance with these documents, promotions to captains of Second and First Rank were implemented by the Admiralty College taking into account the period of service in the preceding rank. This is why Bering wrote that he had already been a captain for ten years. While serving at Kronstadt he had found himself in a lower rank than some of his fellows, who had served for a shorter period, some of them under his command.[8] Such an injustice wounded Bering painfully. Feeling "a deep regret," he appealed to Admiralty College, "but had not received a reply. And that is why I am in a great turmoil, and do not expect for myself any better application,"[9] wrote the captain. The sense of offence that his faithful service had not been appreciated forced Bering to request a permission to retire and to return to his fatherland.

On 24 February 1724 his request was granted. By the decision of the Admiralty College Bering received his passport and his salary for 2 months. However, he continued to live in Kronstadt.

On 5 August 1724, during a night service at the Church of Holy Trinity in the Galley Harbor of St. Petersburg, Peter I "ordered... General-Admiral and President of the Admiralty College, Count Apraksin to reinstate Captain Bering in the service of His Majesty's Navy as a Captain of First Rank."[10] It would seem that the emperor already had plans for Bering's future, but the intercession of friends may also have helped. An order was sent to Bering in Kronstadt. He was told to arrive in St. Petersburg and report to Admiralty College.

On 18 August he confirmed that he had received his majesty's decree. He was grateful and ready to serve his majesty, "... the only thing I humbly ask is that there will be no offence regarding seniority".[11]

A month later, 18 September 1724, Bering was back in service. On October 3 he took the oath of allegiance, and on 9 October was promoted to Captain of the First Rank. He took command of the 90-cannon ship *Lesnoe*, which he had commanded before he had applied for retirement. Soon, however, a new appointment followed – as leader of the First Kamchatka Expedition.

The idea of creating a maritime expedition to ascertain whether Asia was joined with America had occupied Peter I for quite some time. By this time, a few other projects also existed regarding navigation by the North Sea Route to the Pacific Ocean leading to organized commerce with Japan and China. But charts compiled in Europe did not give an exact answer to the question of a passage between Asia and America. The beginning of the Russian settlement of Kamchatka and Chukotka demanded exploration of the Pacific coast. When Peter I signed the decree about the Siberian expedition, he also signed a decree about the need to compile maps for all provinces (*gubernii*) of Russia quickly.

Previously the opening up of Siberia and Kamchatka was managed by the efforts of local authorities. The 20 years of the Northern War did not permit Peter I to focus on Pacific Ocean affairs, but neither did he forget them entirely. During the war, the geodesists I.M. Evreinov and F.F. Luzhin were sent by imperial decree to Okhotsk to sail to the northern Kuril Islands, but they could not answer the question about a passage between Asia and America. In 1722, in Kazan', Evreinov handed Peter I a report about their voyage.

On 23 December 1724 Peter I signed a decree to the Admiralty College on the organizing of a "Siberian expedition".[12] The selection of expedition personnel was in the hands of Vice-Admiral P.I. Sivers, compatriot of Bering, and Rear Admiral N.A. Siniavin. Among other officers they recommended for the expedition were Lieutenant Martin Spangberg and Second Lieutenant Aleksei I. Chirikov. Sivers and Siniavin thought that the expedition should have "a leader with the rank of captain, either Bering or von Werd. Bering has been in the East Indies and knows conditions, and von Werd has had experience as a navigator".[13]

Vitus Bering was 43 years old, and had served in the Russian Navy for twenty years. He had not taken part in a single battle of the Northern War (1700-1721), but had always distinguished himself as an energetic officer, well organized, self-controlled, honest and conscientious. He was of mature age, fully developed, with a talent for organization, and could be trusted with an undertaking of national importance. Peter I knew Bering personally, and knew that he could be trusted with the leadership of the expedition. The trust of the Emperor was a great honor for Bering, but it also imposed on him a heavy burden of responsibility.

We do not know what the Captain thought about the appointment. Certainly, he could not envision the difficulties that lay ahead. No one could. The expedition was headed for the unknown. A new and most important phase in Bering's life was beginning. With his own hand, Peter I wrote the instructions for the leader of the expedition. They still give rise to variances of opinion and even disputes. To Bering, however, everything in them was clear. As he was carrying out his mission, he always emphasized that Peter I himself had written the instructions given to him. In all probability, there had also been some conversation between them to elucidate and supplement the written instructions.

The selection of personnel began early in January and was finished by 8 January 1725. Assembling the expedition's equipment was done on the whole by Chirikov, because Bering, in accordance with a decision of the Admiralty College of 23 December 1724, was at home on leave in Vyborg, with his family, until 7 January 1725.[14] Efforts to collect all the necessary equipment were prolonged into late January. Chirikov received details of the hull and masts and spars of the future ship, equipment of the galley and cabins, rigging, sets of sails, cannon, navigator's instruments, small arms, anchors, flags and lanterns, medicaments, uniforms and so on.

On 24 January most of the participants, under the command of Lieutenant A. Chirikov, left St. Petersburg on 25 sleighs. On 7 February they arrived at Vologda. Bering remained in the capital until 5 February, because of the death and funeral of Peter I. On 30 January 1725 a decree of the Senate was issued, and on 3 February in execution of the last will of the late Emperor the *Instructions* were signed for the expedition by the Admiralty College.

Bering also had to arrange for his family. On 8 October 1713 Bering had married Anna Christina Pülse, daughter of Vyborg merchant Matthias Pülse. By the start of the First Kamchatka Expedition they had two sons, Jonas and Thomas. Vitus, born in Copenhagen, had died soon after his birth.

Setting off for the unknown, Bering left his wife and their small children in Vyborg and asked Admiralty College to pay his wife 300 rubles from his salary per year from 1726 until his return from the expedition.[15]

By 14 February all the personnel of the First Kamchatka Expedition had assembled in Vologda, and after 2 days they set off on the long journey. Thirty-four men left from St. Petersburg – Navy and Admiralty personnel, privates, commissioned and non-commissioned officers. Only 28 of them returned, six were buried in Siberia.[16] The rest of the personnel of the expedition had to be recruited from the soldiers of the Siberian garrison and the resident population as the expedition traveled eastward.

The participants of the expedition moved by posting station sleighs via Sol'vychegodsk, Solikamsk, Verkhotur'e, and Tiumen' and on 16 March 1725 reached Tobol'sk, where they remained until May. Further on the travelers had to follow the rivers, but for this it was necessary to build vessels and to provide provisions.

In Tobol'sk Bering presented to the Siberian Governor, Prince M.V. Dolgorukov, the decree of Senate and the letter by Admiral F.M. Apraksin requesting assistance for the First Kamchatka Expedition. The governor was to give to Bering, on his demand, soldiers for guard duty, timber, iron, tar and caulk and other materials for building ships, as well as carpenters and blacksmiths, and sea provisions. Money for 1726 and bread rations were to come from local receipts on the account of the Admiralty.[17] The governor was to give Bering any other kind of assistance requested because the expedition was a very important state affair.[18]

At the time Siberia was governed from the district chancellery at Tobol'sk; towns by voevodas and regional chancelleries; outposts by local administrators, etc. Everything depended on them: to give or not to give horses, to deliver provisions on time, to assemble laborers as needed. In Siberia, unlike the European part of Russia, serfdom was never introduced. The people were free, but were subject to numerous exactions. Though being fully independent, they bore a heavy burden under the power of various officials. Additional exactions for the needs of the expedition increased this burden. Besides, the settling of Siberia was in an early stage, and the expedition demanded a huge numbers of horses, workers and provisions. It was even more difficult for the Iakuts, Tunguses and other inhabitants of Siberia. They had to pay *iasak* (a tribute in pelts) to the state. Collectors of tribute ruthlessly exploited them, not forgetting to enrich themselves.

Already in Tobol'sk, Bering worried about the conditions the expedition would face in Kamchatka and tried to gather information from everyone who had been there. He obtained much valuable information from Lieutenant Safonov of the St. Petersburg infantry regiment. To a considerable degree, his demands from the Tobol'sk guberniia chancellery were based on tales of Safonov. After finding out that the local inhabitants were sometimes hostile, Bering demanded soldiers with officers for protection. Intending to build two ships in Kamchatka, and taking into account that there were not enough sailors for two ships, he requested 24 more soldiers, who would have to serve on the sea voyage. He was told that there were no forests near the coasts and the Kamchatka River, and no hope for assistance from the local inhabitants. Besides, there was also a need to build storehouses, sheds and barracks, because the local inhabitants lived in earth houses. In addition, among the carpenters many were ill, so Bering demanded from the Tobol'sk chancellery 60 healthy carpenters and as many good workers as could be found. Considering that the voyage would take not less than one year, Bering requested for the expedition a supply of food for the sea voyage for one year, and food for the expedition on land for two years.[19]

On 19 April he sent to Tobol'sk guberniia chancellery a request to send to the expedition the soldier Boris Vyrodov of Tobol'sk regiment, with three of his friends, because these men had participated in the Kamchatka Expedition of geodesists I.M. Evreinov and F.F. Luzhin (1719-1721).

Lieutenant Safonov had told Bering that the vessel known to be in Okhotsk was in very bad condition (she was the lodiia *Vostok*), and that there were no vessels on the Lena River. Therefore, on 10 May, Bering asked the Tobol'sk authorities to send a directive to build on the Lama River (also named Okhota) two vessels for sailing to Kamchatka, and other boats for the Lena River as well.[20]

It would seem that Bering had thought of everything. However, in spite of the Senate decree regarding assistance for the First Kamchatka Expedition, it took constant attention and much effort, patience and perseverance to get the enterprise on its way.

On 14 May 1725 the expedition continued along the rivers Irtysh, Ob' and Ket'. On June 5 Bering sent a letter to the geodesist F.F. Luzhin, inviting him to come to Ilimsk and to join the expedition. The leader of the expedition referred to the Instruction of the Admiralty, according to which he had permission to take two geodesists with him from the Siberian guberniia.[21]

To ensure that more of the expedition could move faster, Bering would send Naval Cadet Piotr Chaplin ahead to collect horses, workers and provisions in good time, but it did not help much. In Surgut, for example, the administrator did not provide guides; and at the Makovskii outpost the horses needed for portage to Eniseisk were not ready. Because of this, it took fourteen days instead of four. In Eniseisk, where Bering arrived on 23 June, nothing was prepared except flat-bottomed boats without rigging: no workers had been sent, sails were not ready, and carpenters and other necessities for the expedition had still not been sent by 10 August. Bering complained that the head of Eniseisk district office, Ivan Tyzhnoi, was putting obstacles in the way of the expedition, because many times the appointed carpenters had been taken from ploughing their fields and only a few were fit – many of them were blind, lame or had another illness, confirmed by the physician.[22]

In Eniseisk Bering met with the German scientist Daniel Gottlieb Messerschmidt, who was returning from Siberia. Messerschmidt left short, but important records about their meeting. The travelers spoke repeatedly and Bering made a very pleasant impression upon Messerschmidt, who considered it his "Christian duty" to inform Bering about a reliable portage. "Other than information picked up from charts, and some not always reliable information obtained from Russians, there was no information about the route".[23] Messerschmidt acquainted Bering with charts of the north-eastern part of the Asian continent and with the chart by N. Witsen. Bering, in his turn, sent Messerschmidt a German translation of Louis le Comte's *Nouveaux mémoires sur l'état présent de la Chine*. The book made a great impression on Messerschmidt. He noted in his diary, "this work is surely one of the finest on this matter that has fallen into my hands so far".[24]

As Messerschmidt observed, Bering was quite a conversationalist. On 29 July he found the seafarer in an excellent mood and all alone, except for a steady flow of Russians coming to see him. He dealt with them briefly through his clerk, making sure, however, that every visit was duly recorded. This did not disturb their lively conversation in German. "The time [three hours], spent in various discourses, flashed by so quickly that I could not discuss with him even half of what I had intended" – such were the concluding words in Messerschmidt's diary entry that day.[25]

Recording their meeting of 8 August, Messerschmidt noted that the Dane had a hope of finding at the Kamchatka coast "Sperma Ceti e cerebro Balaenarum", – that is, spermaceti, a substance extracted from the head cavity of cachalots, which was used in perfumery and dermatology. Messerschmidt believed that the spermaceti was a mineral substance, but did not try to dissuade Bering, "as I knew in advance that Bering would not believe me […] or anybody else".[26] Most likely, Bering had become acquainted with spermaceti during his voyages to East India and, knowing its value, hoped to find it at the shores of Kamchatka.

Before the departure of the expedition, Bering sent with Messerschmidt a present to his wife in St. Petersburg – three lengths of China silk. Evincing enviable possession of knowledge, he warned the scientist that his diary with information about his route would be taken away without fail, but not his private records. He strongly advised Messerschmidt to make copies of all materials collected during his journey. "Without flattery, he assured me that many at court would wish to get the same thorough presentation of my travel and scientific work as he had had, and for which he was infinitely grateful", noted the scholar in his diary.[27]

At 7 p.m. on 12 August 1725 the First Kamchatka Expedition left Eniseisk on four flat-bottomed boats, accompanied by a drum-roll. They went on the Enisei River 40 versts to Tunguska, then by the Tunguska River 804 versts to the mouth of the Ilim River "with considerable difficulties, and passing some of the rapids not without fear."[28] For transportation of cargoes across the rapids 12 small and 4 large boats had been sent from Ilimsk. The cargoes were carried across rapids by hand and the reloaded boats were pulled by horses to Ilimsk, where they arrived on 29 September and remained there until the start of the winter roads.

At Ilimsk, Bering continued to study possible variants of the further route for the expedition and other preparations continued as well. Spangberg was sent to the mouth of the river Kuta to procure timber for shipbuilding and for transportation of cargoes. On 10 October the expedition watched a lunar eclipse and with the help of mathematical calculations established the distance between St. Petersburg and Ilimsk in degrees and versts.

However, most of all Bering was uneasy about the further road to Kamchatka. On 27 November he received from land-surveyor Luzhin, who had joined the expedition as far back as 2 August 1725 in Eniseisk, an account of his expedition to Kamchatka and the Kuril Islands (his colleague I.M. Evreinov had died in 1724). Apparently, it was written at Bering's request. In the report, only one sentence described the voyage to the Kuril Islands. Bering only wanted to know how to get to Kamchatka and across Kamchatka with the heavy and bulky equipment that the expedition had: cannons, anchors, ropes, rigging, provisions etc. In his mind, Bering kept returning to the idea of an overland route. A result of these considerations was the well-known "Location of the route", an appendix to his report to the Admiralty College of 30 November 1725.[29] In it Bering described in detail the possible means and time required to transport the people and loads of the expedition from Ilimsk to Kamchatka: by the Lena River to Iakutsk, then by shallow rivers down to Okhotsk, across the Sea of Okhotsk to Bol'sheretsk. From here, part of the cargo was to be transported overland to the mouth of the Kamchatka River, while the heaviest part was to go by ship around "Kamchatskii Nos", the southernmost point of the Kamchatka Peninsula.[30]

Discussing the difficulties on the poorly organized forthcoming route, Bering noted: "If, when I was sent out from St. Petersburg, I had been definitely ordered to go by an overland route from the mouth of the Kolyma River to the mouth of the Anadyr' River, which I believe to be entirely possible, which the new Asiatic maps indicate, and which many local people say they have been accustomed to using, then I am confident the desired goal could have been achieved at much less expense".[31] In the middle of the 19th century A.S. Polonskii drew attention to this extract for the first time, omitting, however, the most important words "by land.[32] Because of the omission, it looked as if Bering, foreseeing difficulties on the further route, proposed to sail to the strait from the mouth of the river Kolyma, not the Kamchatka River. This misreading of the extract from Bering's report remained accepted for 100 years by numerous historians of different generations (A.P. Sokolov, L.S. Berg, A.I. Andreev, V.I. Grekov, V.A. Divin, B.P. Polevoi). Some concluded on the basis of the unverified extract that Bering had misunderstood the instructions given to him by Peter I. E.G. Kushnarev was the first to notice and correct this mistake.[33]

Obviously, there was no doubt in Bering's mind that he had to reach Okhotsk and from there sail across to Kamchatka. He was constantly occupied with practical questions concerning this route. A number of these questions appeared in his request to the chancellery of the Iakutsk voevoda of 1 December 1725, one day after Bering's report to the Admiralty College with the above-mentioned "Location of the route".[34] Bering wanted to know, e.g., the distance in versts between Iakutsk and Okhotsk; how many poods of supplies a packhorse could carry on this route; if Okhotsk could be reached all year round; if it was at all possible to get to Iudoma Cross with such a heavy load; how long it took to get to Okhotsk from Iudoma Cross; the distance from Bol'sheretsk to Upper Kamchatsk, and how to travel to the latter place.

At that time, there were 140 men and about 10,000 poods of supplies in the expedition. Such numbers of people and loads had never traveled from Iakutsk to Okhotsk before. Bering was the first to try. The route led from Iakutsk down the Lena, then up the Aldan, Maia and Iudoma to Iudoma Cross, then by portage to the Urak River, and finally down the Urak to Okhotsk. It had been opened and tested recently by an expedition known as the Great Kamchatka Command (1716-1719), dispatched by Siberian Governor M.P. Gagarin following a decree of Peter I, and led by the voevoda of Iakutsk Ia.A. El'chin. One of the expedition's tasks was to verify information received from Cossack explorers about the geography and resources of the region, so rich in furs.[35] Due to a number of circumstances the expedition did not fulfill its tasks, but the road from Iakutsk to Okhotsk by rivers was not only tested, but also mapped, as was the one used previously: from Iakutsk via Verkhoiansk, Indigirsk, Alazeisk and the forts on the Kolyma.

The resulting "Chart of Iakutsk and Kamchatka and the previous route to Kamchatka as well as the new route" were presented to the Senate.[36] The new route was shorter and safer than the former, as it did not cross lands where natives were hostile. I.M. Evreinov and F.F. Luzhin, A.F. Shestakov and Lieutenant Safonov had all traveled on this route, but they did not have such large numbers of people, horses, and heavy, bulky loads. The route had not been equipped with necessary facilities. Over the entire length of it there were no storehouses for the cargo, no provisions reserved for the men or feed for the horses, and no winter quarters for the people to rest. Practically, the development of the new, difficult road fell on the shoulders of the First Kamchatka Expedition. However, thoughts of changing the route did not enter the mind of its commander. His focus was on how to proceed along this route as comfortably and cheaply as possible. That was his constant concern.

On 16 December 1725 Bering left for Irkutsk with the physician, geodesist and a few soldiers, and already on 30 December sent an instruction to Chaplin, based on information from local residents who had been to Kamchatka before. They told him that from Krest to the Urak River there are low mountains, and travelers sail down the Urak to the Okhota River on rafts and boats. Bering also learned that it would be much cheaper to hire Iakutsk natives with horses than residents of Iakutsk. It should be possible to hire about 140 or 150 men, Russians or natives, for work on the

vessels. Chaplin was to inquire about all this, including prices, and send the information to Bering immediately, possibly using a courier soldier for this purpose.[37]

At the same time, vessels for river transportation were being built in the settlement Ust'-Kut, under the supervision of Spangberg. The work also demanded close attention from the head of the expedition. Supplies were sent there from Ilimsk on 33 sleighs under the supervision of a navigator, a sergeant, 3 sailors and 8 soldiers. On 18 March 1726 the servicemen, the pharmacy and the cash box followed under Lieutenant Chirikov's command.[38] Finally Bering himself left Irkutsk. On 1 June 1726, he arrived at Iakutsk, which became the central base for further preparations for the expedition. Throughout his stay there, Bering would send urgent demands to the office of the Iakutsk voevoda or visit in person to press for supplies for the expedition. From here the heaviest loads had to be floated on the rivers, the rest were to be delivered by packhorses from Aldan to the Iudoma River. This required guides who knew "native customs". On 8 June Bering asked the voevoda to transfer the Iakutsk nobleman Aleksei Shestakov to the expedition. He was not available, and his relative, Afanasii Shestakov, was at the time in St. Petersburg to organize another expedition, a supplement to the First Kamchatka Expedition.[39] Instead, his nephew, Ivan Shestakov, was sent to Bering as a replacement.[40]

One had to be a strong-willed individual to obtain from the local administration the horses, flour, men, etc. requested. At last, on 7 July 1726 Lieutenant Spangberg left Iakutsk with 83 men of the expedition, 119 servitors from Iakutsk and 3 guides, on 13 flat-bottomed boats. They had loaded materiel that had been brought all the way from St. Petersburg, or acquired in Tobol'sk and Irkutsk, and 4,200 poods of provisions. For travel by land Bering had planned to hire 400 packhorses. However, in Iakutsk it became evident that 400 were not enough, and he demanded 600 instead. Every horse could be loaded with 5 poods. By 1 August 287 horses had arrived. On 27 July 200 of these were loaded with 178 pairs of bags with flour and cereals and 50 poods of iron. Apprentice shipbuilder Fiodor Fedotovich Kozlov and 10 carpenters accompanied them. Bering had hoped to send 200 more horses with provisions before 10 August, but the dispatch of materials and provisions became so difficult that Bering sometimes fell into despair. He had applied to the Iakutsk chancellery 37 times with different requests, but the work still moved extremely slowly. On 28 July he wrote to the chancellery that he still had not received any reply to his requests for resin, hemp, and everything else that was necessary for building the ships. His demands were not fulfilled, fewer horses were sent, and therefore it was highly probable that winter would meet them on the road and that they would not make it across to Kamchatka. The shortage of deliveries had caused much delay, and if the horses did not arrive this month, he would, in accordance with his instructions, have to report to the proper authorities, and the Iakutsk chancellery would be held accountable.[41] Apparently, the patience of the leader of the expedition was running out and he, as an extreme measure, resorted to threats.

After much pressure, Bering received the 600 horses. From Irkutsk province a wooden barge delivered 2,000 poods of flour that were stored at Iakutsk.[42] On 16 August 1726 Bering left for Okhotsk with 26 horses, leaving Chirikov in charge till the next summer. Bering informed the Iakutsk voevoda chancellery that Chirikov was to send the rest of the provisions from Iakutsk to Lama, and should be provided with all the necessary means to do that without delays, as ordered by Her Imperial Majesty.[43]

On 1 October 1726, having overcome, with great difficulties, a distance of 800 versts, Bering arrived at Okhotsk. "I am unable to describe with what difficulty I traversed this road, and if God had not granted frost and little snow, not a single horse would have survived".[44]

The Okhotsk outpost had only eleven homesteads and induced a feeling of oppression. On the very day of his arrival he wrote to the chancellery of the Iakutsk voevoda, describing the appalling condition of "Her Majesty's storehouses", which were badly covered and all wet from rain, and summoning Iakutsk authorities to build new storehouses for the protection of state property.[45]

Bering went to work. On 5 October five servitors were "ordered to erect a house, which the leader had bought for himself in advance. The next day one more house was laid out, and on 12 October he bought a storehouse which was moved to the building site.[46]

During October Bering looked over the outpost, sent 10 men to the forest for timber for building dwellings and vessels, made a trip to the spit where a vessel was being built, and to the yurts of the natives, and inspected the government storehouses and the environs of the outpost. On 26 October 1726 he sent a new report to the office of the Iakutsk voevoda giving his observations on the state of the outposts, in which he wrote: "Although the outpost of Okhotsk and the comments below do not refer to my business, in accordance with my oath to Her Imperial Majesty

I have to inform you of the state of this outpost. For example, Iakutsk shacks and huts are a better fortress than this fort". On the route between Aldan and Iudomskii Krest and along the Urak River there were good pastures, where it was possible to breed horses and cattle, in some places even to sow grain, if there were peasants. In these places, servitors and peasants could settle and become permanent residents, then raise cattle and horses. However, they should be protected from non-resident *prikazchiks* taxing their cattle and feed without paying for them. "In that case, I trust the people would have enough food".[47]

On 25 October provisions arrived at Okhotsk. Of the 600 horses, 267 had perished on the way. No hay had been prepared at the outpost in advance and therefore the rest of the horses had to be killed "because of the lack of feed and the deep snow that has just fallen", wrote Bering in his report to the Admiralty College. Again, he discussed alternatives to the route to Kamchatka chosen by him, and described the land routes from Okhotsk and from Iakutsk that, according to the residents' tales, were used by collectors of *iasak*. "If one were to go by land in winter to Kamchatka and go from here [Okhotsk] via Penzhinskoe, it would take 10-14 days from here to the Tauiskii outpost with dog teams, from the experience of *prikazchiks* that each year go from here to Taui for collection of *iasak*. Further, between Taui and Penzhinskaia Guba live hostile people, Koriaks, who every year make war on *iasak*-paying natives and Russians. From Iakutsk by land one goes to Zashiverskii by horses, from Zashiverskii along the Indigirka River across ridges to the Kolyma River by reindeer, and from Kolyma to Anadyrskii by dog-sled, from Anadyrskii to Penzhinskaia Guba and to Oliutorskii by reindeer, from Oliutorskii to Kamchatka by dogs. And there are no other land routes to Kamchatka".[48] In the opinion of Bering these routes were not easier than the one by which his command proceeded – in fact they were more dangerous. It should be noted that in this report Bering did not propose investigating the bay of Anadyr'.

While preparations were made in Okhotsk for the next stage of the expedition, the heaviest cargo, sent with Spangberg by flat-bottomed boats, was still only on its way to Okhotsk. The cargo included anchors, ropes, sails, cannons, church things, state vodka, possessions of servicemen, provisions, etc. Winter weather had caught the loads en route, and it was necessary to build temporary winter quarters and storehouses and store part of them along the road. They left the river Gorbeia on 4 November, after having constructed 100 sleds for the journey overland. On the way, the men suffered from starvation and cold. Some ran away, or died. Some of the sleds had to be left on the road. Only on 17 December did Bering receive the news that Spangberg was proceeding on sleds by the river Iudoma. On 22 December provisions consisting of 16 poods of meat, 100 dried fish, and 1.5 poods of fish flour were sent to Spangberg on 10 sleds from Okhotsk. On the evening of the same day 36 more sleds were sent with 30 poods of meat, 400 dried fish, and 3.5 poods of fish flour.[49] This assistance reached the worn-out, hungry and frozen people on 31 December 1726 and 1 January 1727. The entire command was finally assembled at Okhotsk by 16 January 1727. Of 203 servicemen and servitors only 59 reached Okhotsk in healthy condition – 26 were frost-bitten and ill, the rest had run away or died on the route. This was the high cost paid by members of the expedition and the Siberian residents for the route to Okhotsk. Bering sent a letter to Tobol'sk Guberniia Chancellery, pointing out that he had demanded that the Irkutsk Office clear the road from Iakutsk to Okhotsk, prepare hay in advance, and build winter quarters or yurts. A special decree about clearing the road had been sent to Iakutsk, but nothing was done.

In Bering's opinion, it would have been possible to hire more Iakuts to supervise the transportation and thus accomplish the task faster and for less expense, with fewer men and horses. Now they had used 600 horses, and all of them were dead. Besides, by the water route, the people hired had suffered heavily, and vessels with materiel and provisions had made it less than half way up the Iudoma River.[50] It became necessary to build winter huts and continue by land.

The winter had turned out to be more severe than expected, with snowdrifts and temperatures colder than the residents could recall. Bering reported to Admiralty College that "this winter deep snow and cruel frosts and snowstorms happen here and, as residents tell, who lived here more than 20 years, they do not remember such a severe winter."[51]

Since all the horses had died, the loads that had been left on the road had to be carried to Okhotsk on sleds pulled by men of the expedition helped by Tunguses. The leader of the expedition insisted that the Tunguses be paid promptly for reindeer taken, for fish brought in, and for work, recording these payments as traveling expenses with a receipt.

Bering ordered his subordinates: by all means, not to harm the natives. And if any prikazchik [steward] or one of his men would commit an offence to anybody, to report it to him and if it was repeated, report it to the Iakutsk office.[52]

Tunguses, in their turn, believing Bering, appealed to him for help against extortion and Bering responded by sending messages to local offices. He understood that it was important not to embitter the natives on whom he had to depend.

On 8 June 1727 the Fortuna, the vessel built at Okhotsk, was launched. Already on 30 June this vessel, under the command of Lieutenant Spangberg, was sent to Kamchatka with materials and provisions. Apprentice shipbuilder Kozlov, a carpenter and the blacksmiths went with him, to look for timber for the second sea-going vessel that was to complete the voyage ordered by Peter the Great.[53] Spangberg returned on the Fortuna on 11 August.

On 21 August 1727 the First Kamchatka Expedition left Okhotsk for Kamchatka. Bering and Spangberg sailed on the Fortuna, Chirikov and Chaplin on the old lodia. On 4 September they reached the mouth of the Bol'shaia River. They decided that "since it was late in the year by local conditions, and the place unknown, nobody had been there before with such vessels."[54] It appeared safer not to go around the southern point of Kamchatka, but to proceed across the peninsula by river. On 6 September, Bering, Spangberg and the physician, with their luggage, left on 18 boats for the Bol'sheretsk outpost, where there were 17 Russian homesteads and a chapel.

Taking into account that the expedition had about 3,000 poods of different cargoes, on 11 September 1727 Bering requested from the superintendent (zakazchik) of Bol'sheretsk information in writing about the easiest and quickest way to move these cargoes from the mouth of the Bol'shaia River to the mouth of the Kamchatka River across the Kamchatka peninsula. Proceeding by water, how many poods could each boat carry, how much time would it take to get there by land and by water, how many residents were in the local outpost, had anyone been around the cape by kayak or by land, and how much time did it take.[55]

On 13 September he received a comprehensive reply in writing and decided to go to the Lower Kamchatsk outpost by the Bystraia River, then to portage to the Kamchatka River and then go down that river to the outpost. On 18 September Spangberg was sent ahead with 30 boats. On 13 January 1728 Bering left for the Upper Kamchatsk outpost with 29 teams of dog sleds, and Chirikov was left in Bol'sheretsk to arrange the dispatch of the rest of the cargo. The transportation was only completed by May. Bering reported to Admiralty College that the transportation of materiel and provisions would not place a heavy burden on the natives, since they had already paid iasak (tribute) and were helped with sustenance by whale blubber prepared in Bol'sheretsk, as well as with tobacco.[56]

In reality, the First Kamchatka Expedition placed a heavy burden on the shoulders of the Kamchatka residents. To transport Spangberg's load, 30 boats with workers were required with a guide and an interpreter.[57] On 22 September Bering mobilized 40 kaiurs from Avacha.[58] On 14 October he sent two sailors with 14 boats and 36 kaiurs, who had to unload these and return back.[59] On 26 November he demanded from the commissar of the Kamchatka outposts, Tarabukin, 100 native men from Upper and Lower Kamchatsk with sleds, dogs and feed for the transportation of a cargo from Bol'sheretsk by 15 February 1728. It is true he requested that the natives be treated kindly, so that they would not run away.[60] A similar request was sent to the superintendent of Upper Kamchatsk, Petukhov: By 15 February he had to send 100 native men, and by 1 March another 80.[61] On 20 December 1727 Bering ordered the superintendent of Bol'sheretsk to collect *iukola* from the nearest places and to send 60 kaiurs by 10 January, and by 1 February 60 more for transportation of materiel. On 30 December he reminded Petukhov that he had to send, by 15 February and 1 March, kaiurs who had good overcoats and footwear. That "the poor would not be offended, and the rich would not shirk".[62] Bering had a continuous correspondence with administrators of the outposts and demanded, demanded, demanded relentlessly and persistently. Bering did not accept the explanations that the people were on hunting trips, considering that an excuse. He had his own tasks to fulfill: To secure the necessary deliveries in time for the voyage. As the people had still not arrived by 2 February 1728, Bering asked Tarabukin to come to the Upper Kamchatsk outpost. He had to bring with him "information about how much fish food had been collected for hostages and for our succor, and a list of all servitors in all the outposts, and also to assemble in Lower Kamchatsk kaiurs with sleds, dogs, and feed, as much as possible".[63]

By this time the inhabitants at both outposts, Upper and Lower Kamchatsk, were starving because in summer very little fish had been caught and preserved for winter. This complicated Bering's demands. On 14 January 1728 he received a letter from residents of Lower Kamchatsk, in which they wrote that they could not feed the men of the expedition, because they did not have enough for themselves.[64] Lower Kamchatsk was the largest outpost on Kamchatka at that time. According to Chaplin, there were about 40 homesteads and a monastery there. Bering ordered Spangberg to give to the members of the expedition fish from the government supply, and also to try to buy 3 or 4 barrels of salted fish from the monks in the monastery, at a reasonable price, and to distribute it among the servicemen.[65]

Meanwhile in the locality of Ushki, timber for the ship was being prepared. On 2 March Bering left Upper Kamchatsk, from where he had supervised all the activities of the expedition. On the way to the outpost he stopped at Ushki and visited the settlement of Kliuchi, where there was a church and where Spangberg lived. From this time on he became directly involved in the building of the ship. On 4 April, having all the servicemen and workers assembled, a prayer was said, and the ship's keel laid. Then the captain entertained all the people with plenty of vodka, as recorded by Chaplin.[66] He also recorded the procedure of the shipbuilding in his book. On 9 June the ship was launched and named the *Holy Archangel Gabriel* (*Sviatoi Arkhangel Gavriil*).

On 5 July Bering discussed with Chaplin and Chirikov some of the problems of the upcoming journey. How much salted fish to take along, whether to take the vessel that was to arrive from Bol'sheretsk, whether to take the chaplain along because space was limited on the *Gavriil*, what to do with the church utensils. Should the crew be paid before the journey, where to send the sick geodesist for care, how much flour to load, etc.[67] The question of where to sail was not discussed.

On 9 July the Captain ordered all the crew to move in aboard the ship. The next day he wrote a report to the Admiralty College, and on 11 July a request to the commissars and administrators of the Kamchatka outposts, not to cause any offence to the local inhabitants.[68] A number of other necessary instructions were issued, and on 13 July at 1:30 p.m. the *Holy Gabriel* sailed down the Kamchatka River on her historic voyage.

The ship, built under the guidance of apprentice shipbuilder Kozlov, was 60 feet long, 20 feet wide, and her hold was 7.5 feet deep. To build her 150 planks 25-30 feet long, with a thickness of 2-3 inches, 300 planks up to 36 feet long with a 1 to 3 inch thickness, and 60 poods of different sizes of nails were used.[69]

Internal space was divided into three parts: in the bow, the crew quarters; in the middle, cargo; at the stern, officers' quarters. Every inch of the vessel was used for storing provisions, armaments, reserve rigging, supplies belonging to the boatswain and navigator and other things. The ship had one mast with a topmast, and 5 sails: mainsail, foresail, jib, forestaysail and topsail. She had seven 3-pound cannons. On the

20.03 91

PLATE 50. The decked boat "The Holy Gabriel". Pen-and-ink drawing by Igor Pshenichnyi.

Courtesy the artist and T. Fedorova. Photo by Nikolai Turkin.

topmast, the long, three-colored captain's pennant with the blue St. Andrew's cross on a white field was hoisted – the first flag of the Russian Navy in the Pacific Ocean. In the holds were loaded 1,000 poods of provisions, 23 barrels of salted fish, 20 barrels of fresh water, etc.[70] The crew consisted of the 38 men of the ship's complement and 6 orderlies of the officers. Both lieutenants, the doctor Butskovskii, Midshipman Chaplin, apprentice shipbuilder Kozlov, seafarer Moshkov and others put to sea. The navigators, however, and the geodesist did not take part in the voyage. Navigator Morisen died in 1728 and the second navigator – Angel – was at Iakutsk. The sick geodesist Putilov was left at the Lower Kamchatsk outpost.

The voyage was thoroughly prepared, planned for a long time, and the captain and the officers had no doubts about the course of the vessel. Just as Bering had had no ideas about a route to Kamchatka other than by sea from Okhotsk, so he had no hesitations also in relation to the vessel's course for the voyage: from the mouth of the Kamchatka River to the north. Scholars are still debating about the purposes and tasks which Peter I set before the First Kamchatka Expedition. The contemporaries of Bering, G.F. Müller and I.K. Kirilov, shared his version. Later A.S. Polonskii, L.S. Berg, E.G. Kushnarev, V.M. Pasetskii and other Russian scholars had the same understanding of the expedition's task.[71] In the opinion of M.I. Belov, the participants of the expedition, in addition to searching for the strait, had to find a route from Arkhangel'sk to the Pacific Ocean and America.[72] V.I. Grekov believed that the expedition was not to look for the strait between Asia and America, but "to find a road to America, which bordered upon Asia, and to ascertain who the neighbour of Russia is at this continent".[73] There were other points of view.[74] B.P. Polevoi considered that Bering was ordered to sail south-east to the coasts of the mythical Juan da Gama Land and to determine whether it was a part of America.[75]

Bering set a northerly course with confidence. He carried out the instructions of the deceased emperor literally: "You are to build one or two boats, with decks, either in Kamchatka or in some other place" – these were built; "You are to proceed in those boats along the land that lies to the north" and to find "where it is joined to America,"[76] and Bering proceeded north. Obviously he had no doubts, as he knew what he was ordered to do much better than we do. Possibly, he had time to discuss the instructions with Peter I. Besides, while the expedition was traveling east through Siberia, Bering would ask Cossacks, trappers, natives of Iakutsk, Okhotsk and Kamchatka questions about

the Big Land that the Chukchis had ostensibly seen. The most valuable information he received from the steward of the Anadyrsk outpost, Captain P. Tatarinov. Chukchis, visiting Anadyrsk in 1718, had told him that not far from Cape Chukotsk there was an island, and behind this island across the sea there was a Big Land that could be seen from the island. During calm weather, the Chukchis could row in kayaks from the island to the Big Land in one day. There were great forests over there, and "sharp-toothed" (*zubatye*) people.[77] This information was supported by an earlier report by a servitor from Iakutsk, P.I. Popov, who had collected tribute on Chukotka Peninsula and reported to the Anadyrsk outpost in 1711. The natives told him that Russians had visited them, the Chukchis, earlier, arriving by sea in small wooden vessels. From the Makachkin Chukchis who lived on "the promontory" (*nos*), he learned that opposite "the Promontory of Anadyrsk, on both sides, over the Kolymskoe as well as the Anadyrskoe Sea, there was an island that they called Big Land [*Bol'shaia zemlia*]". It was rich in forests and diverse animals, but the residents, they said, "had sharp teeth, and their faith and customs and language were different from Chukchi".[78] G.F. Müller found the information of Popov and the Chukchis in the archives of Iakutsk Chancellery in 1736.[79] Consequently, the information was actually there, and Bering knew about it.

Following the regulations of the Russian Navy, Bering never made important decisions all by himself. He would most certainly have discussed changes in the route of the voyage with both lieutenants and reported any such changes to Admiralty College. However, as we have seen, no such reports were submitted, which means that he did not deviate from the instructions he had received.

On 14 July 1728 the *Holy Gabriel* sailed into the Pacific Ocean, which met the navigators with a storm. In only three days the waves caused some damage, but the ship continued on with confidence.

On 16 July she went round Cape Kamchatka and set a northerly course, keeping within 10 miles of the shore. Dangers always threatened the expedition, as no navigation charts existed for the area of navigation. With the assistance of Midshipman Chaplin, Lieutenant Chirikov began map-making as soon as the ship weighed anchor. The *Holy Gabriel*, performing geographical discoveries, steadily proceeded north along the Asian coast of Siberia.

On 8 August 1728 the first meeting with Chukchis took place. It supported the reports by Popov and Tatarinov and had considerable influence on the course of the voyage. The records of this conversation with Chukchis in Chaplin's logbook and the "Journal of incoming documents" are slightly different. In Chaplin's logbook: "They do not know how far the land extends to the east. And they had long ago heard about Russians. The Anadyr' River is far from them to the west". At first the Chukchis said nothing about islands, but later they said "that there is an island that can be seen from land on a clear day, if one moves not far from here to the east."[80]

In the "Journal of incoming documents": "You have passed the Anadyr' River and it is far behind […] We do not know the Kolyma River, but we have heard from the reindeer Chukchi that they go by land to a river and they say that Russian people live on this river, but we do not know if this river is the Kolyma or some other […] Almost from here our land turns to the left and extends far […] There is no promontory that extends from our land into the sea, all our land is level […] There is an island not far from land and when it is not foggy, one can see it […]"[81]

And so, in one record the land "extends" to the east, and in another – "almost from here" turns left. However, there is nothing about the Big Land mentioned by Chukchis in 1711 and 1718 and reported by Tatarinov.

On 10 August they maneuvered in front of the coast, which ended to the East, and turned to NbW½N.[82] Chaplin recorded that as the navigators rounded present-day Cape Chukotskii and proceeded a little further, they saw the island that the Chukchis had told them about during the meeting, and named it St. Lawrence. Almost all the time there was a thick wet fog, with the sun only rarely breaking through. Land they did not see.

On 13 August, when the ship was at 65° northern latitude, off the east coast of present-day Chukotka Peninsula, Bering invited both lieutenants and ordered them to express their opinion whether to continue the voyage or to return to Kamchatka. The reason for his seeking their advice was that "the indicated promontory [referred to as Chukotskii nos], which was supposed to be joined with America, was actually separated from it by the sea".[83]

Chirikov argued: "Since we do not know to which degree of northern latitude people known to Europeans have been, from the North Sea and along the east coast of Asia, we cannot know for certain whether the sea separates Asia from America unless we proceed as far as the mouth of the Kolyma River or as far as the ice. For this reason we should, based on the decree given to Your Excellency from His Imperial Majesty of Worthy and Blessed Memory, proceed along land […]

to the places indicated in His Imperial Majesty's decree. If the land still turns to the north, then by 25 August we should look for a wintering place […]" Referring to the information received from Chukchis via P. Tatarinov, Chirikov insisted on continuing the search.[84]

Spangberg noted that they had already reached 65°30' northern latitude, and there was not a single harbor for wintering on the Chukotka land. Therefore they should continue sailing north until 16 August, and then turn back "in time to search for a harbor and safe place on the Kamchatka River".[85]

On 15 August 1728 Bering concluded: "Having considered the given opinions, I have made my decision. If we remain here any longer, in these northern regions, there will be the danger that on some dark night in the fog we will become beached on some shore, from which we will not be able to extricate ourselves because of contrary winds. Considering the condition of the ship, the fact that leeboards and the keelboard are broken, it is difficult for us to search in these regions for suitable places to spend the winter. No other land is known around here, besides Chukotka where the natives are hostile and there is no forest. In my judgment it is better to return and search for a harbor on Kamchatka, where we will stay through the winter".[86]

The decision had been made. On 16 August at 15 o'clock at 67°19' northern latitude, Bering ordered the crew to turn the ship around and to steer S by E.[87] He had no doubt that in this place Asia and America did not join. Therefore, the task had been executed. He had no idea how close they were to America, and that just four years later other navigators would be here and see it from the same ship, the *Holy Gabriel*. Bering had no research streak. The credo of his life was that "everyone had to do his duties and to follow His Imperial Majesty's decrees and instructions, not his own will".[88] He expressed this credo later in his life, but probably acted in accordance with it always.

However, in this case he did violate the instructions given by Peter the Great, who had ordered him to sail "along the land that lies to the north." These instructions were carried out faithfully up to the SE point of Chukotka. Then, twice (near the capes Chaplin and Dezhnev) Bering moved away from the shore, ordering the ship to proceed NE. By 16 August, they had not seen land for two days, because they had deviated from it and not followed further NW. Bering did not try to go round the Diomede Island to verify the information from Tatarinov about the Big Land.

For more than three and a half years, the expedition prepared and transported to Kamchatka a huge amount of provisions and materiel, built 15 riverboats and one ship for sailing in the Pacific, and now they had finally reached 67°18'48"N. However, Bering had no desire to linger for as much as a few days longer, to ascertain that Asia was not joined with America near the Chukotka peninsula, and to search for the Big Land. The ice did not obstruct the movement of the ship, in fact they had seen no sign of ice. Obviously, the season permitted further sailing. But Bering turned back.

Returning by the same route, on 20 August they met some Chukchis again. This time there was a *toion* among them who could speak the Koriak language, but the navigators did not receive any new information. Evidently, this convinced Bering even more that he had made the right decision. On 3 September, having overcome many dangers, the *Holy Gabriel* arrived at the Kamchatka River and lay at anchor. On the Captain's order, the ship rigging was removed and put in storage, and the crew left for winter quarters at The Lower Kamchatsk outpost and the Kliuchi settlement.

In spring 1729 the vessel was re-equipped for sailing, and on 5 June the *Holy Gabriel* with a crew of 35 and 6 orderlies for the officers put out to sea again. The officers were Bering, Chirikov, Chaplin, Dr. Butskovskii, Navigator Angel and others. Spangberg, because of illness, could not travel by sea, and left for Bol'sheretsk by land.[89] The rest of the crew proceeded aboard the *Fortuna* around present-day Cape Lopatka.

This time, the expedition was sailing east in search of land they had heard about from natives of Kamchatka, lying in front of the mouth of the Kamchatka River.[90] The talk was, as it later turned out, about the Commander Islands. On 7 June the navigators were 30 miles from the islands, but they could not see them because of heavy fog. The following days were also gloomy, with strong gales, fog and very cold.[91] The weather was not favorable for the voyage. Bering quickly lost interest and gave up the search for the islands. Nothing suggested to him how important it could have been to wait for better weather and determine the position of the Commander Islands, where he was to suffer shipwreck in 1741.

The search for the islands was over, and on 8 June 1729 they returned to Kamchatka and sailed near the shore around the southern point of Kamchatka,[92] now moving off to sea, now returning to the shoreline. The purpose of these maneuvers was hardly, as some believe, to search for the legendary Juan da Gama Land, since such a task was never given to the First Kamchatka Expedition. In all probability, fog forced them to move away from the shore.

On 3 July 1729 they came to the Bol'shaia River,

and on 23 July to the mouth of the Okhota River. On 29 July they left Okhotsk on 78 horses on the already well-known route through Siberia to Petersburg, without lingering anywhere in particular. On 23 February 1730, after Vologda, the captain moved ahead with four men. His family was waiting for him in the capital. The rest of the expedition arrived at St. Petersburg on 1 March 1730 at 8 a.m. and reported to the captain.[93]

The First Kamchatka Expedition was over. On 10 March Bering presented a report and a chart to the Admiralty College about the voyages of 1728-1729, and to the Empress Anna Ioannovna a report about the expedition. During five years, an enormous amount of work had been completed. The geographical positions of towns and outposts through which the expedition passed were established. The distances between them were determined, as well as the number of settlements and villages, and the number of local residents. This incredibly difficult route was tested, the course to the Pacific Ocean was plotted. The unique voyage was performed along the eastern coast of Asia, where much geographical mapping was made, and charts of the voyage were compiled.

As already pointed out, Bering himself was sincerely convinced that he had fulfilled the task he had been given. In the report to the Admiralty College of 10 March 1730 he wrote that "on the 15 day of August we reached the latitude 67°19' north and longitude from the mouth of the Kamchatka River 30°14', and to the right of our course from the island [that the Chukchis had spoken about] he had seen no land. The land no longer extended north but to the west, and therefore I considered that I had fulfilled the order given to me, and turned back".[94] Considering his conscientiousness and attitude towards the performance of his duties (and the trial of admiral C. Cruys) it could not be any other way. All the more so, because he would never have allowed himself not to fulfill Peter I's orders. It is quite another matter that he did not have the mind-set of an explorer, and did not even try to make his return voyage by a different route.

On 16 March 1730 the *St. Petersburg News* No 22 (*Sankt-Peterburgskie vedomosti*) had already printed a notice that Bering "had reached the 67th parallel 19th minute of north latitude, whereupon he found that in this region there is in fact a northeast passage so that it should be possible, if the ice does not stand in the way in the northern area, to go by water from the Lena to Kamchatka and farther to Japan, China and the East Indies."[95] This was the first published information about the existence of a strait between Asia and America based on established facts. The same year the first news about Bering's expedition was also published abroad, when one of the newspapers in Copenhagen printed information similar to that in the *St. Petersburg News*.[96]

The Russian government, however, was not satisfied with the results of the First Kamchatka Expedition, since the expedition members had not seen America.

On 4 December 1730 the Governing Senate ordered Bering "to present a report on what might benefit state interests in Eastern Siberia".[97] In response, Bering gave to the Senate his proposals for improving the mode of life of the populations of Siberia and Kamchatka, but did not propose a new expedition, as many researchers have suggested. He never expressed a personal wish to reach the North American continent. He only fulfilled the order of the Senate by giving his views, showing his intellect, power of observation, sympathy to the population of Siberia and his understanding. Bering's proposals were: to open schools for Iakut children; to organize the production of iron for building ships since the Iakuts already knew how to melt and use iron; to establish in Okhotsk and at Kamchatka livestock production and agriculture (already during Bering's stay at Kamchatka they tried to sow rye and grow vegetables); to distill resin at Iudoma, Uda and Kamchatka, so that they would not have to transport it from Iakutsk to Okhotsk; to repair the vessels, and to teach Cossack children seamanship; to prevent hostile acts between Koriaks, Iukagirs and Chukchis by settling hunters and servitors at the former Oliutorskii outpost; to appoint an administrator at Kamchatka for the regulation of tribute collection; and to send to Kamchatka more people skilled in trade. Vessels with a draft of 8-9 feet should be built at the Kamchatka River. In Bol'sheretsk, Bering found out about the wreck of a Japanese vessel. He ordered that survivors of the disaster should be found – and "sent aboard our vessel to their country in order that we may learn the route, and find out possibilities of trading with them or look after other benefits for our state, since there are islands all the way from Cape Kamchatka to Japan, and these islands lie at a short distance from one another".[98] This information Bering had undoubtedly received from I. Kozyrevskii. Nevertheless, he had categorically refused to include him in the expedition.

To these considerations, Bering added another document under the heading "A most humble plan, not on command [i.e., unsolicited], should the intention begin to take form to send out an expedition especially from Kamchatka to the east".[99]

This text makes it clear that he was not proposing the immediate planning of a new expedition, but only referring to this possibility at some point, and certainly not expressing any desire to be in charge of it. In the new "plan", Bering wrote that in his opinion America was "not very far from Kamchatka, perhaps 150 or 200 miles". For finding it, a cargo-vessel of 45-50 lasts [80 or 100 tons] was necessary. It ought to be built in Kamchatka because the necessary timber could be obtained there, and because more help would come from Kamchatka natives than from the inhabitants at Okhotsk. Furthermore, the Kamchatka River was deeper than the Okhota.

Bering also proposed to investigate the coast of Asia to the Amur River, and further to discover a route to Japan, in order to open trade with the Japanese, and also to explore the coast between the Siberian rivers, proceeding by ships or by land starting from the Ob' all the way to Kamchatka.

Most of Bering's proposals were taken into account while preparing for the new expedition, but he did not participate directly in the preparations. Instead, in 1731 he was summoned to Moscow, to the Finance College (*Kamer-kollegiia*), to report on the financial affairs of the first expedition. Checking the expenses of the First Kamchatka Expedition dragged on for a long time and depressed Bering very much. In a letter to Count A.I. Osterman written on 15 February 1734, at the beginning of the Second Kamchatka Expedition, he shares his bitter thoughts: According to the expedition's books of expenditure, 4,400 rubles had been given out, and other expenses for the First Expedition amounted to less that 18,000 rubles, but the accounting was still not finished. "I have no hope that there will be an end to it, since this is now continuing for the fourth year. In this connection please kindly consider, Your Excellency, how much desire I have for this today, quite apart from the great danger ahead of a similar fuss over long-drawn accounting".[100] Moreover, during the expedition Bering had spent 379 rubles of his own money. The Admiralty College had promised to reimburse that amount, but had still not done so. "I am truly committed to serving the interest of the state, with all my zeal, and to the best of my ability, but I do fear another such long-drawn submission of accounts."[101]

Bering felt wounded by the lack of confidence and understanding of his activities. What he and the other participants of the First Kamchatka Expedition did could reasonably be called a heroic deed. To organize the expedition in an extremely short period, to cross all of Siberia with enormous loads, without adequate roads and means of conveyance, to build the ship at Okhotsk, to reach Kamchatka, to transport the massive load from the west to the east by land, to perform a voyage that had never been tried before, and to demonstrate the existence of the strait between Asia and America, could only be done by a man of great abilities, organizational skills, and strong will. Bering was in the highest degree honorable, confident in his judgment, and courageous. And everything that he accomplished was done for the first time in Russian history.

On 14 August 1730 by order of the Highest Authority, Bering was promoted out of turn to the rank of captain-commander, an intermediate rank between captain of the first rank and rear-admiral (*shautbenakht*). On 22 March 1732 the Admiralty College discussed the question of an award for his service in the Siberian expedition. Since a similar mission had never been performed, the size of the award was calculated on the basis of awards given to former commanders of the port of Astrakhan'. The Admiralty proposed to reward Captain-Commander Bering for his far-off expedition double the amount paid for stationing in Astrakhan' and to pay him 1,000 rubles.[102] The proposal was presented to the Senate, which approved the award. However, the 1,000 rubles did not help the Captain-Commander much in settling the financial problems of his family. In January 1733 he sent a petition to the Admiralty College, explaining that he "had been in the service for 29 years and had different extremely difficult commands, and had always carried out all his duties zealously and without fault". Although he was promoted to the rank of captain-commander, he did not receive a salary according to his rank. And while he was on the expedition he had to maintain two households. He had to leave his wife and children in St. Petersburg, and got into heavy debts, which he had been unable to pay back. Therefore, he requested promotion to the rank of rear-admiral with the proper salary and payment of the remaining salary of captain-commander so that he could pay his debts.[103] At that time, the Captain-Commander had three sons (Thomas, Ionas and Anton) and a daughter (Anna). He had no properties and lived on his salary alone.

The Admiralty College sent a report to Anna Ioannovna, who decided: that from the time of his promotion to the rank of captain-commander to 1733 Bering should be paid a salary in accordance with his rank, and during the Second Kamchatka Expedition he would be paid a double salary.[104] But he was never promoted to the rank of rear-admiral.

On 17 April 1732 Anna Ioannovna signed the decree concerning the organization of the Second Kamchatka Expedition. Bering was again appointed head.

Evidently upon his request, Chirikov and Spangberg were kept as his assistants, and Butskovskii, who later became Spangberg's son-in-law, was appointed as physician.

The new expedition was prepared thoroughly and carefully. This was a grandiose project with varied tasks that included the exploration of Siberia, Kamchatka and the northern Pacific, from the coast of the Arctic Ocean to Japan and America. The expedition also included a group of scholars from the St. Petersburg Academy of Sciences. The basic purpose of the expedition remained the same – the search for America.

Bering, already familiar with Siberia and Kamchatka and the Pacific Ocean, again left for the Far East. He was 50 years old and not a young man anymore. During the following nine years (1732-1741) he did his best to execute the instructions received.

During the Second Kamchatka Expedition the humane traits of his character appeared again: justice and kindness. Already during the First Kamchatka Expedition his caring attitude to sick members of his command and the natives was evident, and in the Second Expedition even more so. He protected abused people. If justice demanded punishment, it should never be so cruel that it oppressed the dignity of man. Not without reason the head of the port of Okhotsk, G.G. Skorniakov-Pisarev, complained that if someone were guilty and expected to be punished, they should run away to Bering, just as in the old days they had fled to the Don and Zaporozh'e.[105] The two locations, the Don River and Zaporozh'e (on the Dnepr), were renowned for being the homes of the free Cossacks.

Bering's activity during the Second Kamchatka Expedition allows us to speak about him as an outstanding personality, who did very much for the exploration and opening of Siberia and the Pacific coast. He was ill, and much of his energy was spent in quarrels with the Okhotsk administration, usually because he got tangled up in the disagreements of others. Although he tried to avoid this as much as possible, he could never escape it entirely because of his "sworn duty", as he wrote to Count Osterman on 20 April 1741.[106] Still, Bering followed through with the assigned tasks.

The Second Kamchatka Expedition completed almost all the many tasks assigned to it. Considerable investigation of Siberia was carried out; a route to Japan was opened. For the first time the Kuril Islands were mapped; the Kamchatka coast from the Bol'shaia River to Avachinskaia Bay was described; a part of the coast of the Arctic Ocean and the deltas of the Siberian rivers were described and mapped. The northernmost point of Russia was discovered, and later named Cape Cheliuskin after the navigator of the expedition. Finally, the myth of Juan da Gama Land was exposed at last, the voyage to the coast of America performed and the north-west coast of America and the entire route were mapped. Geographical discoveries by the First and the Second Kamchatka Expeditions laid the foundation for the exploration of the northern Pacific Ocean. These explorations were performed at great material expense and the cost of the lives of many of the participants, including Captain-Commander Bering himself, who died 8 December 1741. He found his last rest on the island he passed in 1729, without seeing it through the fog. The island was named after him.

The Russian Navy and Mapping

Carol L. Urness

The Russian navy played the principal role in the First Kamchatka Expedition, not Bering, Chirikov, Spangberg, Chaplin, and not even Peter the Great, the founder of the navy. The accomplishments of the expedition of 1725-30 are awesome: it traveled across Siberia, mapping in detail the route from Tobol'sk eastward to the Pacific. It built ships to sail from Okhotsk to Kamchatka and to explore and to map the coasts of Kamchatka and the Chukchi Peninsula (*Poluostrov Chukotskii*). To carry out their work the expedition members transported the instruments, ship equipment (anchors, ropes, sails, ironwork and cables, etc.), medicines, clothing, food, arms, ammunition and everything else that was needed and could not be obtained in Siberia. The navy had undertaken difficult tasks previously. Ships had been built, battles fought, supplies carried, routes mapped. But the First Kamchatka Expedition was a much larger undertaking, moving across an immense landscape before making an epic voyage to explore and map unknown coasts. What preparation did the Russian navy have for such an ambitious expedition? What kind of a navy was it?

Navy officers knew each other well and many who had foreign origins had been in Russian service for decades. Although they originated in various countries—Denmark, England, Germany, Holland, Norway, and Sweden, for example, they were united in their work for Russia. Being in a multi-national navy was not always easy. John Deane, an Englishman who was an officer in Peter the Great's navy noted the "…unavoidable difficulties…through want of languages wherein all officers in his service are obliged to command, viz. Russ, English, Hollands…"[1]

Peter founded the navy in 1696 but was not the first tsar interested in ships. He was not the first to hire foreigners for maritime endeavors, either. His grandfather, Mikhail Fedorovich, had obtained rights to carry Indian and Persian trade goods from Astrakhan' to Arkhangel'sk, and the tsar needed ships to protect the trade.[2] In 1634 Holsteiners agreed to build ships in Russia using their workers and Russian carpenters, who would learn shipbuilding from the Germans. Work began in the spring of 1635 at Nizhnii Novgorod. The Holsteiners built only one ship, the *Frederick*. Launched in July 1636, the flat-bottomed vessel was designed for use on the Volga River and the Caspian Sea. The ship struck bottom many times during its voyage down the river, which weakened it. The *Frederick* sank in a storm on the Caspian Sea, and with it the tsar's plans for a fleet.

Tsar Aleksei Mikhailovich, Peter's father, also wanted trade on the Volga River and the Caspian Sea. He sought help from the Dutch to build ships. The shipyard at Dedinovo, near Moscow on the Oka River, produced one large warship, the *Eagle*, a yacht and two smaller sloops in 1667-68. David Butler, a Dutchman, arrived at the shipyard on 20 November 1668 and with him came Karsten Brandt (or Brand), later an important teacher for Peter the Great.[3] The *Eagle* reached Astrakhan' in August 1669, but remained anchored for months because of the uprising led by Stenka Razin. Butler, Brandt, and three other crewmembers went to Astrakhan'. While they were gone the *Eagle* was abandoned and Razin's forces wrecked it. Butler and two others escaped when Astrakhan' surrendered. Like his father, Tsar Aleksei Mikhailovich had no luck with ships.

After his father's death in 1676, young Peter (b. 1672) lived at Preobrazhenskoe, a village on the outskirts of Moscow, with his mother, Natalia. Tsar Fedor, his half-brother, ruled until his death in 1682. Though Peter became "junior tsar" and his sixteen-year-old mentally retarded half-brother Ivan became "senior-tsar", the regent Sophia ruled for the next seven years.[4] As the Miloslavskiis and the Naryshkins (his family) vied for power, Peter grew up surrounded by interesting companions, including Patrick Gordon, a Scot, and Franz Lefort, a Swiss, whose tales of Western Europe made Peter want to travel there. General Gordon (1635-99) had joined the Russian army in 1661 and was a particularly influential supporter of the young tsar in the 1690s. Peter assumed power in 1689 but his mother Natalia and her friends ruled the country for several more years.

Young Peter's passion for ships was ignited in 1688 with the discovery of an astrolabe and a nearly wrecked boat. Inquiries about the astrolabe led him to Franz Timmerman, a Dutchman who taught him to use the instrument (a forerunner of the sextant). Peter's curiosity about the boat was fueled by Timmerman's assertion that it could sail into the wind. Peter wanted it repaired. He was referred to Karsten Brandt, who fixed the boat and made a mast and sails for it. Brandt taught Peter to sail. Brandt supervised the building of various vessels for Peter. During this time Peter visited the foreign quarter of Moscow, and he probably studied Dutch with Andrei Vinius, a government official of Dutch descent.[5]

Peter transferred his shipbuilding from the Iauza River to Lake Pleshcheevo, north of Moscow. By the time of Brandt's death in 1692, the fleet consisted of two small frigates, three yachts, two Preobrazhenskoe-built ships brought overland to the lake, plus many *strugi* (longboats used for freight) and other small boats built in Moscow. On 19 August 1692 F. Iu. Romodanovskii, Franz Lefort (Peter was a crew member in his command), and Patrick Gordon led the fleet on a voyage across the lake.[6] Peter last visited Lake Plescheevo, the site of his first large-scale maritime endeavors, in the spring of 1693.

That summer Peter visited Arkhangel'sk on the White Sea with a retinue of 100 men, remaining there nearly two months. Peter saw large ships, mostly Dutch. He sailed a yacht (the *St. Peter*) in the open sea. Peter decided that he wanted to sail the Arctic Ocean the next year, and ordered the governor of Arkhangel'sk, F.M. Apraksin, to construct a new ship. He ordered Lefort to purchase a second ship from the Dutch, which was done with the assistance of Nicolaas Witsen, burgomaster of Amsterdam.[7]

In May 1694 Peter returned to Arkhangel'sk to launch the new ship. The *St. Peter* and the *Holy Prophecy* (the Dutch ship) sailed the Arctic Ocean for three weeks. Peter was the "skipper" of the *Holy Prophecy*, with Admiral Romodanovskii in command. Peter remained in Arkhangel'sk until early September. Then he gave up playing with ships, since his mother had died and he had to take responsibility for governing.

Like his father and grandfather, Peter wanted a port. He planned to attack Azov, where the Don River meets the Sea of Azov and the Black Sea. Arkhangel'sk was unsatisfactory for trade because it was open too few months of the year. Attempts to take Azov in 1695 failed because Turkish galleys brought supplies to the city. Peter began to construct galleys for Russia. The largest were built at Voronezh, on the Don River.

Carpenters were recruited, including some sent from Arkhangel'sk by Apraksin. In January and February 1696 the carpenters, assisted by soldiers of the Preobrazhenskii and Semenovskii regiments, quickly cut parts for 22 galleys, using green and sometimes frozen timber, which had a detrimental effect on their quality.[8]

In May the vessels started down the Don River to attack Azov. The Russians assumed the Turkish fleet would be small; instead twenty galleys plus many small ships were present. The Russians retreated north. However, Cossacks in *strugi* attacked the Turkish fleet, setting fire to ships and capturing one, driving the rest away. When the Turks were beaten, writes Edward J. Phillips in *The Founding of Russia's Navy*, "It was not the presence of a technologically and militarily comparable naval force but the audacity of the primitively equipped Cossacks that cleared the Azov harbor of Turks."[9] The Russian fleet blocked the Don River so supplies could not reach Azov, which surrendered on 18 July 1696. At the triumphal march into Moscow Peter walked with the naval forces, as a "Great Captain."

But Azov was not a good port for Russian trade. The Turkish presence was too strong; the distance from Moscow to Azov too great; the river was not deep enough. About the ships, John Deane wrote: "In a word, little is to be said in favour of the ships built before the Tsar's return from his travels; to pass them by in silence is the highest compliment."[10] Deane is referring to travels begun in March 1697, when Peter's Grand Embassy (250 men) left Russia intending to visit Holland, England, and Venice, the three important shipbuilding centers in Europe. Rather than inviting foreigners to Russia as teachers, Peter had begun sending young Russians to Western Europe to learn naval skills. In 1697 twenty-eight Russians were sent to Italy; twenty two to England and Holland. During the period from 1700 to 1720, about 150 Russians were sent abroad for study.[11] The results were mixed. Few learned maritime skills, as Peter had hoped. However, the young men gained knowledge and experience.

Peter's travels lasted for sixteen months. While abroad he hired men for the navy, including officers, navigators, and shipbuilders. Supplies, armaments, material for uniforms, navigation instruments, and ship tools and equipment were purchased as well. Peter traveled incognito (or as much as he could, at nearly 6 foot 7 inches in height) and stopped first at the Dutch shipyards at Zaandam, to work as a ship's carpenter. Crowds followed him everywhere, and Peter remained only from 18 August to 25 August. He fled to Amsterdam, where he met Nicolaas Witsen, who had a deep interest in maps and in Siberia. Witsen published a large wall map of Siberia in six sheets in 1687. His large book, *Noord en oost Tartarije*, (Northern and Eastern Tartary) was published first in 1693 and then in a revised edition in 1705. For its second edition Witsen received information and maps from Peter. Witsen may have seen the large manuscript map of Siberia made in 1667 by U. M. Remezov, the first Russian map to show all of Siberia.[12] Peter gave the printer Johann van Thessing rights to publish books for Russia in dual language editions—Latin and Russian or Russian and Dutch. The subjects were to be geography, mathematics, architecture and other sciences.[13] Unfortunately, Russia offered only a tiny market for books. Thessing printed maps of Russia, including the S.U. Remezov *Book of Maps of Siberia*, published in 1701 with twenty-three maps, all but three of which portrayed towns.[14]

Through Witsen, Peter met Norwegian-born Cornelis Cruys (1657-1727), who was "inspector of naval equipment of the Amsterdam admiralty," an expert in shipbuilding, and possibly in cartography as well.[15] Peter hired Cruys as vice-admiral of his new navy, assigning him to oversee the construction of ships for the Russian fleet. Peter worked in the Amsterdam shipyard from late August to mid-November, when the ship he helped build was launched. Peter was frustrated because the Dutch did not have a "science" of shipbuilding. Rather, they learned their skills in ship design through years of experience.

Peter traveled next to England to study the technology of English shipbuilders, assuming they would have a more scientific approach to it.[16] The historian John Kendrick writes: "Shipbuilding in 1700 was based on the practices and prejudices of builders who guarded their knowledge from those not admitted to the craft. That knowledge was based on the slow accretion of experience. If something worked, it was repeated. If it did not work, there might be no one alive to tell what went wrong. Under these circumstances, the acceptance of new ideas was understandably slow and grudging, both on the part of builders and of the mariners whose lives depended on the soundness of their ships."[17] Little had been published in Europe about shipbuilding at the time.

Peter sailed on the *Yorke*, a Royal Navy vessel. Its captain, David Mitchell, spoke Dutch. Peter was delighted with the four-day voyage and asked questions constantly about the ship. At Peter's request Mitchell was assigned to the Russian embassy as a translator. Mitchell taught Peter basic navigation. Peter's visit to the Royal Observatory no doubt influenced his decision to have an observatory built in Russia. When he became aware of the Royal Mathematical School of Christ's Hospital for teaching navigation, he decided to establish a similar school in Russia. (See the chapter on Navigation for more commentary on this school).

After England, Peter visited Vienna, and was planning to travel to Venice when he received news of an uprising in Moscow. He returned home to end it. Men and supplies for the navy he was building followed in his wake. During his travels Peter had found no enthusiasm for war against the Ottoman Empire but support from the rulers of Saxony and Denmark for a war against Charles XII. On 19 August 1700 Russia proclaimed a thirty-year truce with Turkey. On 20 August Peter declared war on Sweden. As his price for participating in the war, Peter obtained the promise of a Russian port on the Baltic.[18] Although the Russians were soundly defeated in their first battle against Sweden, Peter persisted. In May of 1703 the Russians took the small town of Nyenskans from the Swedes, who, unaware of the capture, sent a snow (small armed ship with 12 guns) and a longboat (4 guns) up the Neva River toward the town. When the Swedes saw Russian land troops along the river they did not worry since Russia had no naval forces. Peter ordered the gathering of many *lotkeys* (small boats used on the river) to prevent the Swedish ships from escaping back through the mouth of the river, which was narrow and shallow. The Swedes came down the river, hindered by winds and the shoals. The Russians captured both vessels, and the master of the larger one, Charles van Werden, joined the Russian naval service.

The founding of St. Petersburg followed. A fort was built to protect the city; a shipyard was established nearby at Olonets. In England Peter had hired John Perry as an engineer to work on canals in Russia. Perry and a Russian named Korchmin searched for possible sites for canals to connect the Volga to the Gulf of Finland.[19] Perry was also involved in a plan for a canal connecting the Volga and Don rivers. The Russians made manuscript maps of the two rivers; in 1704 Henrik Donker of Amsterdam printed these maps in an atlas. The title page includes a portrait of Peter the Great; the dedication is to Peter from the author of the atlas, "Cornelis Cruys, Vice-Admiral van zijn Majesteits Zee-Magten." The text on the maps is printed in Russian and Dutch. The atlas demonstrates Russian mapping skills; there is a grid on the maps, with rhumb lines connecting the points of the circle. The maps include soundings of the river bottoms and as well as features along the shores.

In February 1716 Peter began his second journey to Western Europe. From April to June 1717 Peter was in Paris. He attended a meeting of the Académie des Sciences and was elected a special member of it. He enjoyed this honor.[20] Peter decided to found a similar academy in Russia. A friend, Vasilii Tatischev, told him that it was a waste of money because Russia was not yet ready for such an institution. Peter replied that he knew it but believed that the academy would be like a watermill without water. He was beginning something that his successors would be forced to complete, by bringing in the water.[21]

In Paris Peter met the famous French geographer Guillaume Delisle. They discussed Delisle's 1706 map of Russia, and Peter no doubt was pleased to be able to point out to Delisle that the latitude of St. Petersburg was wrong on it![22] They viewed a globe together and Peter changed the position and shape of the Caspian Sea on it. Peter invited Delisle to come to Russia. Delisle declined the invitation but later his brother, Joseph Nicolas Delisle, became an initial member of the Russian academy of sciences, serving there as an astronomer and geographer for more than twenty years.

Peter had a strong interest in mapping. From a practical standpoint, accurate maps aided in governing, something that other European rulers acknowledged. In France, Jean-Baptiste Colbert recognized that the available maps of France were inadequate. By 1679 Louis XIV had given his approval for a national map survey, initially under the direction of Jean-Dominique Cassini, who came to Paris in 1669. Maps of the accuracy that was desired depended on the measurements of length, breadth, and shape of lands and seas. Cassini had developed tables of the movements of the satellites of Jupiter that were invaluable to determine longitude by recoding the times of their movements in different places. One important part of French mapping was making a series of triangles along the length of France in the meridian of Paris.[23] Preparing an accurate map of France also depended on knowing the length of a degree at any latitude and knowing the shape of the earth, whether it was round or bulged at the equator and was flattened in the north. Expeditions were later made to determine these measurements. Louis XIV reportedly said that surveyors had lost him more land than his armies had won.[24]

Peter the Great wanted accurate maps of Russia, and to obtain them meant conducting geographical explorations to make careful measurements. He authorized several expeditions prior to the First Kamchatka Expedition. In 1697-99 Vladimir Atlasov collected information on Kamchatka and nearby islands. In 1716 a group of 200 men were sent to explore islands in the Pacific Ocean. The governor of Siberia drew up the

PLATE 51. Peter the Great as portrayed on the title page of Vice-Admiral C. Cruys's Atlas of the Don, printed in Amsterdam in 1704 by Henrik Donker.

Courtesy the James Ford Bell Library, Minneapolis, MN. Photo by Carol Urness.

orders; the Iakutsk voevoda Ia. A. El'chin, who had previously made a sketch map of northeastern Asia, executed them. The goal was to search for islands and a "mainland" opposite the Chukchi Peninsula. The expedition was a failure, poorly organized and badly executed.[25]

In 1719 Ivan M. Evreinov and Fedor F. Luzhin, geodesists (land surveyors) who had been trained at the Moscow School of Mathematics and Navigation, were sent to Kamchatka. Their assignment was to go to Tobol'sk and taking guides, go to Kamchatka and farther, "…and describe the local places [where or whether] America is joined with Asia, which must be done very carefully, not only in the south and north, but in the east and west, and place everything correctly on a map…"[26] The "flimsy" vessel of the expedition explored the Kuril Islands in search of precious metals, according to Evgenii Kushnarev, author of a major

Russian study of the First Kamchatka Expedition.[27] At an interview with Peter in Kazan' in May 1722, Evreinov presented the results of the exploration and Peter "with much interest engaged [Evreinov] several times in conversation and examined with satisfaction the map of Kamchatka and the islands mentioned, made by him and his associate Luzhin, and the description of their entire voyage."[28] Luzhin joined the First Kamchatka Expedition in Siberia, but died in March 1727, en route to Okhotsk.

In 1720 Peter sent Daniel Messerschmidt, a physician from Danzig, to explore Siberia. Messerschmidt remained in Siberia for seven years. His researches in geography, natural history, and history were so extensive that he may be considered the founder of Siberian studies. Bering met with Messerschmidt in Eniseisk. They discussed maps of Siberia.

In 1717 Captain-Lieutenant Charles van Werden and others journeyed to Astrakhan' to explore the Caspian Sea. He returned in 1720, after he had "perfected

PLATE 52. Homann sheet of two maps, on the left the Caspian Sea, on the right, NE Siberia.

Courtesy the Rare Book Division. Princeton University Library.

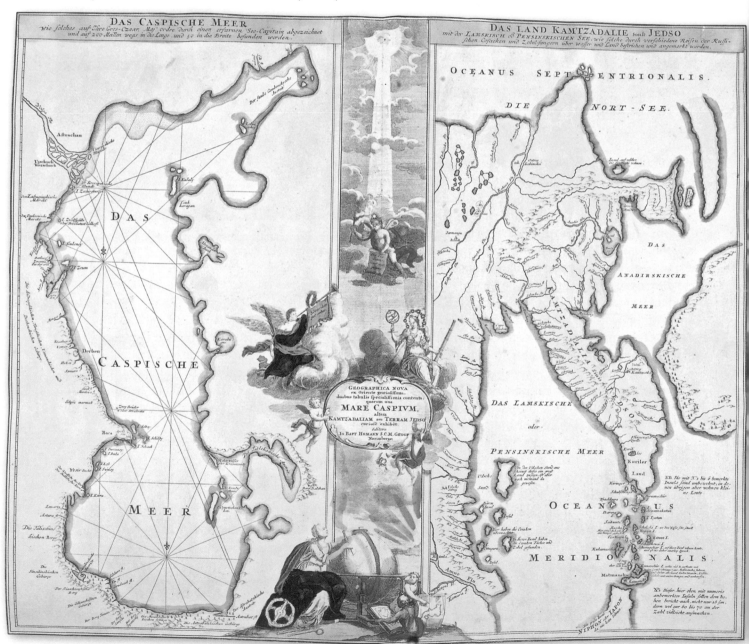

PLATE 53. Johann Baptist Homann, *Generalis totius Imperii Russorum, novissima tabula* ... Nuremberg, Johannis Baptistae Homanni [between 1721 and 1723]. Map size: 48 × 56 cm.

Courtesy the James Ford Bell Library, Minneapolis, MN.

an accurate chart, the best now extant..."[29] The map is a detailed rendering of the coasts, and in addition includes rivers, roads, and harbors. Mapping the Caspian Sea, the largest enclosed body of water on earth, was a major project. About 130 rivers flow into the Caspian, of which the largest is the Volga River. The Caspian's surface is over 140,000 square miles. The work took three years but resulted in a fine map, which Peter shared with Guillaume Delisle and other mapmakers in Western Europe.

Johann Baptist Homann of Nuremberg received a manuscript map of the Caspian Sea map together with an interesting manuscript map of northeastern Siberia. Bruce commissioned Homann to print these maps for Peter. The two maps reproduced here are the maps that Homann printed for Peter, on the left-hand side the Caspian; on the right, northeastern Siberia. Homann copied the manuscript maps onto copperplates that were then printed with black ink. Coloring was added to individual maps after they had been printed. Notice that there is no grid of longitude and latitude on either map. On later maps he made for Peter, Homann added scales of distance, grids of longitude and latitude, and geographical features. The two maps reproduced here are printed on one sheet. The maps are not dated, but clearly the Caspian map reflects the mapping done by Van Werden, which would date it after 1720. The map of northeastern Siberia does not reflect the Evreinov/Luzhin expedition, but is based on other Russian maps of the region.

Historians Boris P. Polevoi and Raymond H. Fisher assumed that this map of northeastern Siberia was the one given as a guide for the First Kamchatka Expedition. In their view, Peter's intention was that the route of the *Holy Gabriel* from Kamchatka would be along the southern border of the large land east of Kamchatka, in order to reach America.[30] This is a difficult thesis because since the ship sailed north, the officers would have had to either misunderstand their instructions from Peter the Great, or disobey them.

Before his death in December 1724, Homann made much better maps for Peter of the same area, with grids of latitude and longitude on them. Some confusion about the Homann maps may have arisen because they are undated. Without knowing that the

maps were printed at Peter's order before Homann's death in 1724, the assumption could be that the maps were not available to the Russians until they appeared in the atlas published as *Grosser Atlas über die gantze Welt*, Nuremberg, J.E. Adelbulner, 1725. However, the individual maps were sent to Russia as soon as they were printed, long before they were gathered together and printed for an atlas. The maps were printed copies of Russian original maps.

Russians had made maps while expanding eastward across Siberia in their search for furs. Examples of some of these maps are reproduced in Aleksei V. Efimov, editor, *Atlas geograficheskikh otkrytii v Sibiri i v sever-zapadnoi Amerike XVII-XVIII vv,* Moscow: Nauka, 1964. Homann used maps like these in printing the maps that were commissioned by the Russians. In a letter that he wrote on 17 June 1723 Homann said that "his great patron" [Bruce] had asked him to change "Moscowitisch" to "Russisch" in the title of his general map of Russia.[31] Other alterations included a new shape for the Caspian Sea and several changes in northeastern Siberia, including the addition of a land with an open-ended northern border, as "incognita". It is this newer map (among others, probably) that was given as a guide for the First Kamchatka Expedition.

PLATE 54. J.B. Homann's maps of the continents projected by Christian Sandler on a modern map for comparison.

Reproduced from *Mitteilungen des Vereins für Erdkunde,* Leipzig, 1894-95.

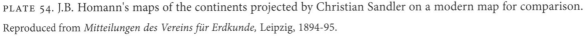
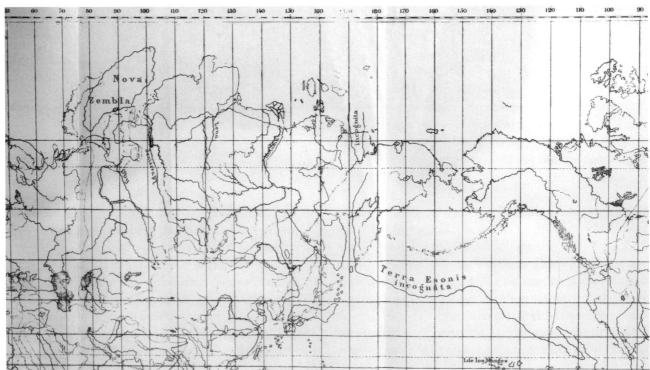

I have discussed these maps in relation to the voyages made by the expedition in *Under Vitus Bering's Command: New Perspectives on the Russian Kamchatka Expeditions*, edited by Peter Ulf Møller and Natasha Okhotina Lind (Aarhus University Press, 2003, pages 17-31), a previous volume in the Beringiana series, to which the reader is referred. A summary of that commentary follows:

First, the brief instructions for the expedition, in the translation in Kushnarev, *Bering's Search for the Strait*, are as follows:

1. You are to build one or two boats, with decks, either in Kamchatka or in some other place.

2. You are to proceed in those boats along the land that lies to the north, and according to the expectations (since the end is not known), it appears that land [is] part of America.

3. You are to search for the place where it is joined to America, and proceed to some settlement that belongs to a European power; or if you sight some European ship, find out from it what the coast is called, and write it down; go ashore yourself and obtain accurate information; locate it on the map and return here.[32]

These instructions have been translated into several languages. They can and have been interpreted in different ways. One major problem with them is the identity of "the land that lies to the north." In the Polevoi/Fisher view this land is the one shown to the east on the map, which indeed appears as though it might be attached to America. In my view "the land that lies to the north" is the one at the top of the map that looks like a finger. The end of it is not closed (unknown) and might very easily extend toward America. In the second Homann map this land is labeled "Incognita." Differences of the interpretation of the instructions persist. In any case, certainly the brief instructions given by Peter were supplemented by discussions between Peter and the officers.

The *Holy Gabriel* began its voyage to the north from the Kamchatka River. With the Homann maps and similar maps as guides, the route would apparently have been almost straight north. This proved to be impossible. Instead, the ship sailed to the northeast, and still more to the northeast. The maps were wrong; the coasts the ship followed and mapped led farther and farther to the east. The geography of northeastern Siberia forced the *Holy Gabriel* much more to the east than had been expected. (See maps). The expedition had a specific charge concerning the land that went to the north and "whose end was unknown." Comparing the route of the *Holy Gabriel* with their maps, the officers could only assume that they had sailed to the north and east of the land on the map, and that it was part of Siberia.

At 65° 35' north latitude, the *Holy Gabriel* was out of sight of land and Bering asked Chirikov and Spanberg for their opinions, in writing, about the future course of the expedition. This is discussed in Fisher's *Bering's Voyages*, pp. 82-97. The statement from Bering to them includes the following: "…we have arrived opposite the extreme end and have passed east of the land, what more needs to be done?"[33] Bering believed that they had sailed to the east and north of the unknown land on the map. They had found that the land was not connected to America. They had completed their assignment and had mapped northeastern Siberia in detail.

Bering wrote his decision: "If we remain here any longer, in these northern regions, there will be the danger that on some dark night in the fog we will become beached on some shore from which we will not be able to extricate ourselves because of contrary winds. Considering the condition of the ship, the fact that leeboards and keel board are broken, it is difficult for us to search in these regions for suitable places to spend the winter… In my judgment it is better to return and search for a harbor on Kamchatka where we will stay through the winter."[34] He ordered the turnaround at 67° 24' north latitude. Should he have done more? In his opinion he had finished the assignment he had been given. See the journal for August 15. In the words of Orcutt Frost, in his recent biography of Bering, "It was a good decision."[35] Critics who believe that the purpose of the voyage was to determine if it was possible to sail around Siberia in the far northeast rightly point out that the expedition had not proved that the voyage was possible. Given the time of the year (remember that the Russian calendar was 11 days later than the calendar of Western Europe) and the distance, attempting to sail all the way to the Kolyma River on the arctic coast would have been foolhardy in the extreme. Other critics have held that Bering should have been more daring and should have searched for America. In my opinion, Bering made the decision to turnaround because he believed, with very good reason, that he had completed his specific assignment.

When Bering returned to St. Petersburg in March 1730, everything had changed. Since Peter the Great died just before the expedition started, his widow and successor Catherine I sent the expedition on its way. She died in 1727. Her successor Peter II reigned only three years. When Bering arrived in St. Petersburg, preparations were in progress in Moscow for the coronation of Anna Ioannovna, Duchess of Courland. She was chosen to rule Russia under a set of conditions limiting her authority. Once in power, she rejected the conditions. Of the officers of the navy, the men who knew the background of the expedition best—Apraksin and Menshikov—were dead. The navy was in decline.

During Bering's absence a new organization had made its presence felt in Russia—the academy of sciences. Peter had planned it but was not able to bring it into existence prior to his death. Peter wanted an academy in Russia similar to the Royal Society of London, the Académie des Sciences in Paris, and the academy of sciences in Berlin. The academy envisaged by Peter would concern itself with three areas: 1. mathematics and related sciences (astronomy, geography, navigation); 2. physics, including anatomy, chemistry, and botany; 3. the humanities: economics, history, law, politics, etc.[36]

The initial sixteen members of the new St. Petersburg Academy met in November of 1725. Thirteen members were German; two were Swiss; the lone Frenchman was Joseph Nicolas Delisle, the astronomer and geographer. A fine observatory had been built in St. Petersburg, and for it Delisle brought the instruments purchased in Paris by Peter. Although no Russians were initial members of the academy, in December, Catherine I named Lavrentii Blumentrost to be its president. Blumentrost had been Peter's physician. Blumentrost, born in Moscow, was the son of a German immigrant to Russia and had studied in Halle, Oxford, and Leyden. Peter's plan for the academy stressed two missions: to search for new knowledge in the fields of its members and to disseminate that knowledge.[37]

Within Russia, therefore, a group of foreign scholars were impatient to learn about the discoveries made by the expedition. Soon after his return Bering met with Joseph Nicolas Delisle, the geographer, and the historian Gerhard Friedrich Müller. In the meeting, the twenty-five year old Müller served as the interpreter between Bering, aged forty-nine, and Delisle, who was fifty. Bering spoke no French; Delisle spoke no German or Russian. What a wonderful conversation it must have been! The academicians had already heard rumors that Bering was exploring the eastern end of a potential northeast passage from Europe to the East. That was a major interest of Europeans, who hoped to send ships along the northern arctic coasts on a shorter route for trade with China, Japan, and the East Indies.

Müller, as editor of the recently established St. Petersburg newspaper, published in Russian and German,

was anxious to make public what this famous man had to say about his five-year exploring expedition. It is difficult to know the questions that Delisle and Müller asked Bering. From the content of the article, it is not hard to see how Bering's answers, whatever they were, were interpreted. The newspaper report in the *Sanktpeterburgskiia Vedomosti* (16 March 1730) and the *St. Peterburgische Zeitung* (March 16 1730) is translated as follows:

"On the 28th of last month Captain Bering of the navy returned here from Kamchatka. He had been dispatched there on 5 February 1725 by the Admiralty College on the handwritten order of His Imperial Majesty Peter the Great, of glorious memory, and on the confirming instructions of the late Empress Catherine, with a rather extensive retinue of officers, geodesists, as well as seamen and soldiers, and in the spring of 1727 had the first vessel built at Okhotsk, in the farthest reaches of Siberia. With this he sailed across the Penzhina Sea to Kamchatka and, in the spring of 1728, had a second vessel built in Kamchatka on the river of the same name. As his precise orders were to investigate the northeastern limits of this region and to see whether, as according to some opinions, the land was connected with the northern part of America, or whether an open water passage was to be found between them, he, in the same year, set his course with the aforementioned vessels toward the northeast, and continued to the latitude of 67 degrees, 19 minutes north, where he then judged the northeast passage was actually there, so that one could, if not hindered by ice in the north, travel by ship from the Lena to Kamchatka, and farther to Japan, China and the East Indies—just as he had been told by the local inhabitants, how 50 to 60 years ago a vessel had come to Kamchatka from the Lena. Moreover he confirmed the previous report about this land, that it is connected to Siberia towards the north, and also, in addition to his map dispatched in 1728, which extends from Tobolsk to Okhotsk, had another completely accurate map drawn of the land of Kamchatka and his sea route from which it is seen that it begins at the south at 51 degrees north latitude and runs to 67 degrees north. He gives the geographical longitude of the west coast, reckoning from the meridian of Tobolsk, as 85 degrees, which, if converted to the more common meridian of the Canary Islands, makes 173 degrees of the one side, and 214 degrees of the other. More about these new discoveries will be reported at a future occasion. Captain Bering set out on his return journey from Okhotsk at the end of the month of August in the previous year, 1729, and was thus six months under way.[38]

PLATE 55. Manuscript map of
Delisle/ Müller/ Bering accompanying
conversation.

From Delisle's manuscripts in the Bibliothèque
nationale, Paris. Reproduced from F.A. Golder
(1914) *Russian Expansion on the Pacific, 1641-
1850.* Cleveland, Ohio.

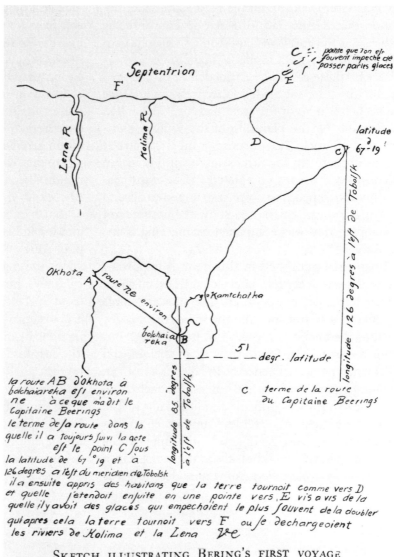

la route AB d'okhota à
bokhaiareka est environ
ne   à ce que m'a dit le
Capitaine Beerings
le terme de la route dans la
quelle il a toujours suivi la acte
       est le point C sous
la latitude de 67°19 et à
126 degres a l'est du meridien de Tobolsk
il a ensuite appris des habitans que la terre tournoit comme vers D
et quelle   s'etendoit ensuite en une pointe vers E vis a vis de la
quelle il y avoit des glaces qui empechoient le plus souvent de la doubler
qui apres cela la terre tournoit vers F ou se dechargeoient
les rivieres de Kolima et la Lena &e

SKETCH ILLUSTRATING BERING'S FIRST VOYAGE
Made by J. N. Delisle and based on his conversation with Bering
[*Delisle Manuscripts, xxv, 6*]

This newspaper article was reprinted in several newspapers, including one in Denmark. In the newspaper article, the emphasis is on the search for a northeast passage. Bering's answers to questions are put in the context of the search for a northeast passage, making the identity of "the land that goes to the north" the mainland of Siberia. Without a connection between it and America, a northeast passage would be possible if the ice did not prevent ships from sailing it. That the map was made at the time of the article is certain, since the figures of longitude and latitude correspond to those on the map. Frank A. Golder reproduced this map as the frontispiece of his book, *Russian Expan-sion on the Pacific, 1641-1850*, originally published in 1914, from the Delisle manuscripts in the Bibliothèque nationale. The caption for the map reads: "Sketch illustrating Bering's first voyage. Made by J.N. Delisle and based on his conversation with Bering".[39] In the official reports on the expedition, the term "northeast passage" is never used. Nor is any search for America mentioned. Perhaps because the article stressed the potential for the northern passage, which was the question of most interest to Western Europeans, a decision was made to withhold further information about the expedition, at least temporarily. Russians did not want Western European ships exploring their arctic coasts.

Müller later wrote about the First Kamchatka Expedition that Bering had "directed his course to the northeast, as the coasts of Kamchatka (which he generally had in view) led him. His main endeavor was to describe these coast as accurately as possible on a map, in which he succeeded fairly well—at least we have no better map of the area than his."[40] He noted also that during the planning of the Second Kamchatka Expedition, "The purpose of the first journey was not brought up for discussion again because it was considered already completed."[41] The maps produced by the expedition were distributed to several Western European rulers and show the accuracy of the mapping that was completed by the First Kamchatka Expedition.

The journal published in this book is important because it is one of the few official records extant about the First Kamchatka Expedition. The journal records the difficulties of transporting the many supplies for the ship—the anchors, ropes, sails, instruments, etc. and for the men—the food, clothing, medicines, and instruments that were needed.[42] The distance from St. Petersburg to Tobol'sk was 1,763 miles. The route from Tobol'sk eastward was difficult and little known. The terrain was almost impassable. Immense effort was required for the transport of goods and supplies. The route from Iakutsk to Okhotsk was the worst. On it men and many horses died. Some men deserted. The men and supplies reached Okhotsk in stages, with the able men going back to help those who could not keep up or were sick. The next stage of the journey, by sea from Okhotsk to the west coast of Kamchakta, was easier. Crossing overland from the west to the east coast was grueling, and caused great hardships for the Kamchadals, whose dogs were used to transport the expedition. Finally, after almost three years, the expedition arrived at the mouth of the Kamchatka River, where they would build a ship for the voyage of exploration. The river mouth was about 6,000 miles from where they had started.[43]

Much of the journal records the calculations of longitudes and latitudes that were essential for the mapping done by the expedition. These are the subject of a separate chapter. Mapping begins with Tobol'sk and continues through the Kamchatka voyages, as the route from St. Petersburg to Tobol'sk was already known. The distance eastward across Siberia to Okhotsk was found to be much greater than had been known earlier. The eastward extent of the northern coasts was striking: the earlier maps had shown the coasts leading directly north. In reality the *Holy Gabriel* had to sail far to the east to follow these coasts. Some 1,000 miles further to the east, in fact! The map that resulted from the expedition is very accurate and is a fine product of the Russian Navy and its men.

Navigation and Surveying

Carol L. Urness and Gary Davis

Chaplin's journal includes much navigational information which is puzzling to today's reader, who is accustomed to clocks and watches and to small hand-held devices that provide latitude and longitude readings, compass direction, altitude, humidity, wind speed and direction, the course and speed of movement, maps and more. It is not easy to think back to a time when such equipment was not available. In those earlier centuries navigators recorded the progress of their travels based on their experience and on readings made with the simple instruments available to them. This commentary is intended to help the reader understand the navigational information, since it is a significant part of Chaplin's journal.

Of the members of the First Kamchatka Expedition, Chirikov was the best and most highly trained navigator. His journal is discussed in the preliminary materials of this book. Others, including Chaplin and Bering, as well as geodesists (land surveyors), assisted Chirikov. The calculations made by the expedition on its journey from Tobol'sk eastward were made on land as well as on rivers and at sea. The navigators used essentially the same methods for recording their positions throughout their journey—dead reckoning, latitude measurements, compass readings with provision for magnetic declination.[1] The records kept were used to prepare a map of Russia. The maps that the expedition made were major contributions, not just somewhat better than earlier maps but immeasurably better than any map of eastern Russia available before the expedition. As Evgenii G. Kushnarev, a Russian scholar of the expedition, put it: "Only through the use of instruments, the observation of lunar eclipses, the systematic determination of geographical coordinates, and the strict calculation of distances could the expedition produce this first correct assessment of the length and breadth of Siberia. Furthermore, the members of the expedition, in contrast to many earlier cartographers, personally traveled the entire country from St. Petersburg, covering in all an extent of more than 160°, or almost half the globe."[2] The final general map of Russia made by the expedition showed that Siberia extended **30 degrees** further to the east than had been believed earlier!

The famous Captain James Cook, whose voyages into the North Pacific mapped some of the same regions that had been mapped earlier by the First Kamchatka Expedition, wrote that: "In justice to the memory of Beering [sic], I must say that he has delineated the coast very well, and fixed the latitude and longitude of the points better than could be expected from the methods he had to go by."[3] How did the expedition keep the records of their journey across Siberia?

The underlying principles by which astronomical observations were used to determine geographical position were essentially the same on land and at sea. A local measurement of the position of a celestial object and the local time of the measurement, together with knowledge of the object's position with respect to a fixed reference and time could be used to deduce local position. As Bertrand Imbert discusses in his "Bering and Chirikov: Pioneers of Siberian and North Pacific Geography," during the half-century following the expedition several scientific and technical advances combined to provide navigators and explorers with portable yet reasonably accurate tools for estimating geographical position. These included the invention of the reflecting quadrant, the predecessor of the modern sextant, around 1730; John Harrison's invention of a practical sea-going chronometer (tested in the 1760s); James Bradley's discovery of the effects of aberration (1729) and nutation (1748) on measured star positions[4]; and in the 1750s, the incorporation of perturbation solutions to improve the predicted positions of the sun and the moon, by Lacaille and Mayer, respectively.[5] The net effect of these advances was that by the last quarter of the eighteenth century navigators could use astronomical observations to reliably estimate latitude to within a few minutes of arc, and longitude to within about half of a degree.

Nonetheless, the late 18th century methods were for the most part improvements on earlier methods. Estimates of latitude were based on measurements of the angular altitude of celestial objects together with tabulated predictions of the objects' positions. The most accurate measurements were made using the fixed instruments of large radius found at observatories. In the field, carefully leveled stand-mounted quadrants, preferably with telescopic sights, were generally more accurate than the hand-held instruments used at sea. The difference in longitude between two observatories could be determined by comparing the local times of mutually observable astronomical events, such as an eclipse of the moon, an eclipse of one of Jupiter's Galilean moons, or the occultation of a star by the moon, using a high-magnification telescope (i.e. 40x or better) and a well-regulated pendulum clock.[6] The best results were obtained by comparing the observed times at the different locations, which usually meant that the longitude estimate would not be available until months or years after the fact. A more timely estimate could be made by comparing the observed time to the predicted time for a standard location, the accuracy of this being dependent on the accuracy of the prediction. Lacking a good clock, local noon could of course be found by identifying the time of the sun's highest altitude, while an estimate of a time other than noon could be made by first observing the altitude of the sun or star, obtaining that object's position from a table, and solving a spherical trigonometry problem.

Thus in the early eighteenth century, when a stable observing platform could be provided for a suitable length of time the best estimates of position were obtained from observations using a telescope and a pendulum clock. For example, members of the 1736-1737 expedition to Scandinavia, which measured the length of a degree of latitude near the Arctic Circle, determined the latitudes of the northern and southern ends of the measured arc by constructing temporary observatories and spending at least one week at each timing the transits of stars, using telescopic zenith sectors and pendulum clocks.[7] Given the more primitive conditions experienced in Siberia, the observations made by the expedition with the instruments they had were excellent. The expedition carried a telescope, though what kind it was is unknown. So far as is known, the expedition did not have a pendulum clock, but did have sundials and sandglasses. Throughout the course of the journey, the sandglasses were corrected at noon by observations of the sun, and noon sights of the sun were used to estimate latitude.

During the journey Chirikov also observed three eclipses of the moon. The first one took place on 10 October 1725, at Ilimsk. He had the information that the eclipse began in St. Petersburg at 7:03:31 p.m. and observed that it began at Ilimsk at 11:31:01 p.m, from which he calculated that the difference in longitude between the two places was 66°57' (4 hours, 27 minutes, 48 seconds). However, as Chirikov noted, "… the observation does not seem to produce the proper results…"[8] Chirikov made some separate comments about the problems with this observation of the lunar eclipse of the moon that have not survived.

Chirikov made a far more important and useful observation of a lunar eclipse at Bol'sheretsk that began at sunset on 14 February 1728. Although clouds caused some difficulties for him, Chirikov was able to use the bright star Sirius to calculate the time, as he had no clock. This eclipse, of course, was not visible in St. Petersburg or elsewhere in western Europe, so in immediate terms the observations were not useful. However, Joseph N. Delisle, the astronomer and geographer of the Russian academy of sciences, later learned that the same eclipse had been observed by J. de Herrera in Carthagena and Father Bonaventura Suarez in Paraguay. The longitude of these places had been established. Consequently, in November, 1733, Delisle reported to the Russian academy that the calculated longitude of Bol'sheretsk using these other sightings of the lunar eclipse was 154° 05' E, compared to 156° 37' longitude today.[9] The third eclipse took place before sunrise on 3 February 1729, when the moon "was all dark." (See the commentary on Chirikov's journal, p. 11).

We have firsthand information about the kind of education and training the navigators and geodesists (land surveyors) for the Russian navy received. When Peter the Great visited London in 1697 he became aware of the Royal Mathematical School of Christ's Hospital. The mathematician Jonas Moore and the diarist Samuel Pepys founded the school to train boys in navigation so that they could serve in the British navy. Peter hired two young men, Richard Grice (age 17) and Stephen Gwyn (age 15) from that school for the similar school he had decided to establish in Russia. He employed Henry Farquharson, who taught at Marischall College, Aberdeen, as head of the school.[10] The three traveled to Russia together. When Peter left England, his friend James Daniel Bruce (1669-1735), born in Moscow of Scottish heritage, remained there for a few further months, studying, meeting Newton, Halley and other scholars, and collecting books and scientific instruments. Bruce purchased quadrants, clocks, hourglasses, magnets, telescopes, and mathematical and other scientific instruments to be used for teaching in Russia.[11]

The teachers arrived in Russia in 1699. For a year they were ignored, and lived with Henry Crevett, an

Englishman who worked as a Russian translator. Presumably during this time they had the opportunity to learn some Russian. Once Peter turned his attention to the school, matters moved quickly. In 1701 the Moscow School of Mathematics and Navigation opened at the personal order of Peter the Great. It had 180 students the first year. James D. Bruce had set up a small astronomical observatory in the Sukharev Tower. The school was located in the tower so that the students would be able to make astronomical measurements. Peter and Farquharson set the syllabus for the school. Like its model in London, the top students from the lower school continued their study in the higher school, which prepared future naval officers and teachers. The courses included astronomy, navigation, and geodesy, plus geometry, trigonometry and other areas of mathematics.[12] In 1702 the school had 200 students. The advanced students took courses in arithmetic, geometry, trigonometry, plane navigation, Mercatorian navigation, diurnals (astrolabe), spherics, astronomy (celestial navigation), geography (naval cartography), and Great Circle navigation. In addition to problems with language, the students were handicapped because "Sectors, drawing instruments, books of charts, as well as more mundane materials like slates and slate pencils, were in short supply."[13] Farquharson translated textbooks and supervised the translations made by others. Between 1701 and 1716 a total of 1,200 graduates of the Moscow school served in the Russian navy. In 1715 the school moved to St. Petersburg and became known as the Naval Academy. Richard Grice had been killed by a gang of thieves in Moscow in 1709. Gwyn and Farquharson moved to St. Petersburg with the school. Both remained there until their deaths, Gwyn in 1720 and Farquharson in 1739. The School of Mathematics and its successor, the Naval Academy, had a profound influence, not only by producing the first generation of Russian explorers, surveyors, cartographers, astronomers and the like, but also in the area of secondary education.[14]

As noted in the chapter on the Russian navy and mapping, at the time of Peter's visit there were no books on shipbuilding published. Books on navigation, however, were available. Over a century earlier, William Bourne wrote *A Regiment for the Sea: Conteyning most profitable Rules, Mathematical Experiences, and Perfect Knowledge of Navigation, for all Coasts and Countreys*, published in London, 1574, by Thomas Hacket. This book went through several editions and was a new type of textbook for a new type of reader.[15] Bourne's book was not directed to learned readers, he explained, but rather to the skilled artisans and craftsmen who

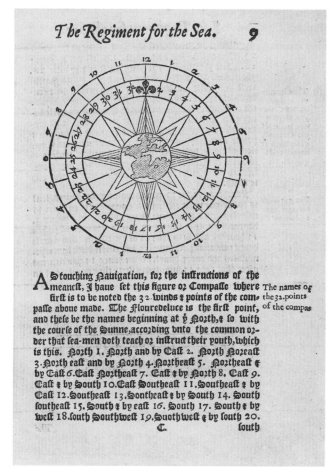

PLATE 56. Compass showing 32 winds, from William Bourne, *A Regiment for the Sea,* 1596 edition.

Courtesy the James Ford Bell Library, Minneapolis, MN. Photo by Carol Urness.

needed the practical knowledge it contained. Bourne writes: "As touching those persons who are meete to take charge, that is to say, to be as maister of ships in Navigation, he ought to be sober and wise, and not to be light or rash headed, nor to be so fumish or hasty, but such a one as can wel govern himselfe, for else it is not possible for him to governe his company well…"[16] Bourne also notes that the navigator should not gamble. In addition to being a "good coaster" the navigator must have knowledge of charts and maps for long voyages, and must be able to make astronomical measurements, especially of the sun's altitude. Bourne was writing at a time when the general practice of English seamen, to make their way at sea using the lead and line and the compass, was ending. Ships were making longer voyages over unknown seas. Near home the large continental shelf gave warnings to sailors using the lead and line. The composition of the bottom of the sea was revealed on a lump of tallow at the end of the lead; and that plus the depth gave sailors the information they needed to sail along the coasts.[17] In his text Bourne is teaching the "new navigation," based on astronomy and mathematics. He demonstrates the use of the sea astrolabe and the compass (for telling time as well as direction) and the log and line. The latter was the first original contribution that the English made to the mariner's art. The navigator tied a log of wood to a card, threw it overboard, and measured the amount of line that was let out during a stated time, usually half a minute. At times some phrases of known length were spoken as the line was played out. Knowing the elapsed time and the length of line expended, the speed of the ship could be calculated. For example, if the time is 120th part of an hour (½ minute); the line let out is 25 fathoms, then the ship goes 120×2.5 fathoms or 3,000 fathoms in an hour. As the English league is 2,500 fathoms, the ship is traveling at 1 ⅕ leagues per hour.[18] Bourne, in the edition of the *Regiment* of 1596, adds a commentary on five possible routes from England to Cathay, including one going over the North Pole.

Two textbooks that were new at the time of Peter's visit offer insight into the intellectual and practical training being offered at the Royal School of Mathematics at Christ's Hospital. Samuel Newton's *An Idea of Geography and Navigation*, published in London by Christopher Hussey in 1695, is dedicated to John Moore, President, and Nathaniel Haws, Treasurer, of Christ's Hospital. The book has many illustrations accompanying the text, intended to aid the student in learning the concepts of geography and navigation. Some broad definitions are included, for example: "Geographers for the clearer understanding of the Position of Places, have invented two terms of Art call'd Latitude and Longitude."[19] Newton points out that zero meridian in the Azores has been chosen by some geographers because no magnetic declination to the north or south is found there. But English geographers may choose zero meridian at London, and French geographers may choose Paris for zero meridian. Many foldout engraved plates illustrate the topics of Newton's book. Instructions on observing eclipses of the moon and the satellites of Jupiter are included. About using eclipses of the moon to determine longitude Newton writes: "This way would be of very great use if we could see an Eclipse every night…"[20] Newton gives a good description of the use of the log and line and the ½ minute glass at sea, as well as instructions on determining the variation of the compass.[21]

Another textbook, John Seller's *Practical Navigator*, was first published in 1669. Peter the Great may well have seen and purchased the 7th edition of this book, published in 1694 by "J.D. for the Author and Richard Mount". Like Bourne, Seller recognizes two types of navigation. He writes: "First, that which may be called the Domestick, or more common Navigation, (I mean Coasting or Sailing along the Shore). This Part employs the Mariner's Compass and Lead, as the chief Instruments."[22] Seller refers the reader to other books he has written for information on this subject. On the other hand: "the Art of Navigation, is that part which guides the Ship in her Course through the Immense Ocean, to any part of the known World; which cannot be done, unless it be determined in what place the Ship is at all times, both in respect of Latitude and Longitude; this being the principal Care of the Navigator, and the Master-piece of Nautical Science."[23] One feature of this book is a series of "Memorial Verses" to help the student learn important concepts in navigation.

PLATE 57. On the use of the log-line, from Samuel Newton's *An Idea of Geography and Navigation*, 1695.

Courtesy the James Ford Bell Library, Minneapolis, MN. Photo by Carol Urness.

The figure of the Azimuth Com=pas

The Use of the Azimuth-Compass.

First, You must rectify the Brass Limb on the Edg of the Box (by the Needle and Fly within the Box) according as the nature of the Observation doth require: For if the Observation be in the Forenoon, then you must put the Center of the Index upon the West Point of the Card or Fly within the Box; and so, that the four Lines on the Edg of the Card, and the four Lines by the inside of the Box, do always concur.

The Instrument being thus rectified, turn the Index towards the Sun, until the shadow of the Hypotenusal Thread fall directly into the very slit of the Sight that is on the Index, and also upon a Line that is in the

PLATE 58. The azimuth compass, from John Seller, *Practical Navigation*, 1694.

Courtesy the James Ford Bell Library, Minneapolis, MN. Photo by Carol Urness.

The many illustrations in the book must have intrigued Peter the Great, just as they do us today. The engraving of each instrument is accompanied by commentary on its use. Some of these are as follows:[24]

The mariner's compass. This compass, especially in the early period of navigation, was divided into 32 rhumbs or directions rather than being divided into degrees. The magnetized needle pointed to magnetic north.

The azimuth compass, used at first by astronomers rather than navigators, had its face divided into 360 degrees. A circular plate attached to the top of the compass had a vertical sight to fix an observation of a celestial object, primarily the sun.

Ring-dial. A hand-held instrument of two circles, used to tell time whenever the sun was shining. The first requirement was to know the latitude. The next

step was to turn the other ring to the day of the year. Then the time could be read. A sort of sophisticated sundial.

Cross-staff. A very old measuring device sometimes called Jacob's staff. The cross-staff was used to read the altitude of the sun, the Pole Star, or any other celestial body. In the high northern latitudes it could be difficult to use, since one end of the sliding indicator had to be fixed on the horizon and the other on the object being measured. It was difficult to look at the sun to get a sighting of it, so that a piece of smoked glass was often affixed to one end of the sliding indicator.

The backstaff is an offshoot of the cross-staff, more convenient to operate. Because of its design the user could stand with his back to the sun, adjusting the instrument so that a beam of light passed through the two sights of the backstaff. Seller notes that the invention has been ascribed to John "David", and indeed this is the Davis backstaff. Seller states that it is: "at present the best approved, and most general Instrument that is in use, for observing the sun's Meridian Altitude at Sea." (Seller, p. 168).

Nocturnal. This instrument was used for telling the time at night. Astronomers and navigators were well aware of the fact that the North Pole was not due north, so that some adjustments had to be made in reading the sightings obtained by it. The nocturnal gave the viewer a way to adjust for the observations of Polaris and the "guards" of the Big and Little Dipper that were used to make adjustments for readings using Polaris.

Seller provides instruction on keeping a journal at sea. It is in six columns, as follows:

1. Hour of day
2. Knots
3. ½ knots
4. Fathoms—that the ship runs upon any course in the space of half a minute, measured by the Log-line (Seller, p. 227).
5. Course… leaving the leeway to the discretion of the calculator
6. Point of the Compass the Wind direction

John Seller, the author, also includes in his book an advertisement telling the reader that he sells navigational instruments, logboards, sea charts, both plain and Mercator's, leads and lines, books and instruments… "or any other things belonging to the Art of navigation…."[25] From reading the textbook it is clear that book instruction was not enough; any successful navigator must have had many hours of experience to become proficient in the practice of navigation. These men learned their trade at sea as well as in school.

PLATE 59. Use of the common sea quadrant or back-staff, from Sir Jonas Moore, *A New Systeme of the Mathematicks*. London: A. Godbid, 1681 (between pp. 248-249).

Courtesy the Royal Library, Copenhagen.

As E.G.R. Taylor wrote: "For every master and pilot prided himself on knowing exactly how much way his ship was making. He knew the ship, he considered the wind, he watched the sails, he watched the water. In fact, it was a matter which just could not be explained to the landsman. A good sailor knew his ship, and that was all."[26]

Aleksei Chirikov (1703-1748), the primary navigator of the expedition, entered the School of Mathematics and Navigation in 1715. The following year, 1716, he was one of twenty students selected for transfer to the newly founded Naval Academy at St. Petersburg. Students at the Naval Academy learned the subjects noted above in the Moscow school, plus geodesy (land surveying), keeping a log book, drawing, rigging, artillery, etc. Seven foreign languages (English, French, German, Swedish, Danish, Italian, and Latin) were offered at the Naval Academy.[27] Chirikov graduated in 1721 with a fine record as a student, especially in geography. In recognition of his academic achievements Chirikov was raised to the rank of sub-lieutenant He served at sea briefly; in the fall of 1722 he was appointed to be an instructor in navigation at the Naval Academy. He was still in this position when Peter the Great assigned him to the First Kamchatka Expedition as one of the two lieutenants serving under Bering.[28]

No list of instruments carried by the expedition is known, though the journal entry for 12 May 1729 indicates that the expedition left in storage the "geodesist's instruments: a quadrant with its equipment, except for a weight and an astrolabe base with its targets and with legs, a copper semicircle" were given to the local commissary. Bertrand Imbert writes that "Bering and Chirikov… had only very limited tools to fix their position and the places they were surveying at sea as well as ashore."[29] On land the two-foot stand-mounted quadrants were used. On board ship sandglasses were employed for keeping time; the magnetic compass for the course (corrected for declination periodically) and the log line for speed. The hand-held "English" quadrant was the best-available tool at that time for measuring angles when at sea.

The navigator's job was to plot the course of the journey on land and at sea. In both cases, the daily progress was calculated from a known point, the "fix" and calculated from that point for the travel made that day. The progress was recorded on Mercator charts, which were later combined into large maps. The first map prepared by the expedition showed the journey from Tobol'sk to Ohkotsk. It was received with great pleasure in 1728 by the Academy of Sciences in St. Petersburg.

Much of the navigational material in Chaplin's journal is in the format that a sea-going navigator would use for keeping a reckoning of a ship's location. A log in which directions and distances traveled were recorded was used to produce dead-reckoning estimates of position, with these being supplemented when possible by astronomical observations. Chaplin recorded two types of astronomical observations: altitudes of the sun made at local noon, which were used to estimate latitude, and observations made to estimate compass variation, or magnetic declination. In what follows we will illustrate the methods that were probably used to produce some of Chaplin's navigational results.

Using the sun to determine local noon, and hence the start of the nautical day, was a traditional sea-faring practice. If at the same time the navigator could measure the angle between the sun and the horizon, and was able to determine the sun's astronomical declination (i.e. its angle with respect to the equator), usually from a printed table called an ephemeris, then an estimate of the ship's latitude could be computed using the relation

$$l = 90^o - h + d \qquad (1)$$

l = latitude, in degrees
h = sun's altitude, in degrees
d = sun's declination, in degrees

For example, at local noon on July 23, 1728, while aboard the *Holy Gabriel*, Chaplin recorded a measured sun's altitude of 47º34' and that the sun's declination was taken to be 17º50' north, which led to an estimated latitude of 60º16' north. The accuracy of these estimates depended on the ability of the available instrument to accurately measure angles, the ability of the observer to correct for the refractive nature of the earth's atmosphere and for the effect of observing from the deck of a ship rather than from the surface of the sea, and the accuracy of the solar tables. As Bertrand Imbert has emphasized, in the early eighteenth century the state of each of these components was markedly inferior to what was available 50 years later.[30]

Compass variation, or magnetic declination, is the difference between true north and the direction indicated by the compass needle, and this varies over the surface of the earth. Since compass variation was used to correct compass-determined courses in dead-reckoning navigation, it was important to estimate this value periodically while traveling. This could be done by comparing the sun's azimuth (i.e. the angle between the local meridian and the sun's position, measured along the horizon) as measured using a compass to the corresponding astronomical azimuth computed from a measurement of the sun's altitude, its astronomical declination at the time of measurement, and the latitude of the place where the measurement was taken. We do not know what procedure Bering's party used to compute astronomical azimuths, but the following formula from spherical trigonometry relates the quantities Chaplin recorded in his journal[3]

$$\cos^2(a/2) - \frac{\sin(k)\sin(k-\Delta)}{\sin(z)\sin(\lambda)} \qquad (2)$$

$a = azimuth$

$$k = \frac{z + \Delta + \lambda}{2}$$

$$z = 90^o - h$$

$$\Delta = 90^o - d$$

$$\lambda = 90^0 - l$$

For example, at about 8:45 a.m. local time on 24 July 1728 Chaplin recorded a successful effort to estimate compass declination, or variation. According to the compass the sun's azimuth was 60º8' east of south, while the ship's estimated latitude was 61º03' north and the sun's astronomical declination was taken to be 17º35' north. Chaplin reported an astronomical azimuth of 34º44' east of south, which led to an estimated magnetic declination of 24º24' east. Substituting Chaplin's recorded values for latitude, declination and altitude into equation (2) gives us an astronomical azimuth 34º43.3' east of south, which is close to the value recorded by Chaplin.

In the above examples Chaplin recorded all quantities needed for computation, including the sun's astronomical declination, which to some extent disguises the actual complexity of the process. In an ephemeris the sun's predicted position was tabulated against local time at some standard meridian (usually Greenwich or Paris), and to use the ephemeris effectively one had to have at least a rough idea of local time and one's longitude relative to the standard meridian. A reconstruction of the determination of compass variation made at the start of the journey from Tobol'sk illustrates this.

In his journal entry for 16 March 1725 Chaplin recorded that the presumed latitude for Tobol'sk was 58º05' north. On April 27, sometime after noon, he recorded a sun's altitude of 42º27', and a compass azimuth for the sun of 41º12' west of south. This gives two of the quantities needed to use equation (2), the third being the sun's astronomical declination. We do not have the astronomical tables used by Bering's party, but a table of positions for 17 April 1725 can be constructed using Bretagnan's and Simon's solar theory,[32] listed in Table 1. This table gives the astronomical declination and right ascension of the sun at each hour of Greenwich meantime, so to determine which declination value should be used one needs to know the Greenwich time corresponding to the local time of observation. An inspection of Table 1 reveals that the sun's declination was changing at about .011

degrees/hour, so knowing the time to within a couple of hours would be sufficient to find the astronomical declination within 2 arc-minutes. Now at that time of year and that location the sun would have achieved an altitude of 42°27' at about two hours after local noon, so the time of the observation was about 2 p.m. local time. Next, Tobol'sk is about 68° east of Greenwich, which means that local time at Tobol'sk is about 4 ½ hours ahead of that at Greenwich. 2 p.m. Tobol'sk local time would then correspond to about 9:30 a.m. Greenwich local time. Ignoring the difference between mean time and apparent time, the sun's declination at about 9:30 a.m. Greenwich time on 27 April 1725 would have been about 17.12° north. Substituting this value together with Chaplin's altitude measurement and latitude into equation (2) gives us an astronomical azimuth of 44°26.3 west of south. Chaplin's recorded compass variation was 3°18' east, which implies that Chaplin's party computed an astronomical azimuth for the sun of 44°30' west of south. Our azimuth and Chaplin's are probably closer than we have a right to expect, but hopefully this example shows how astronomical observations could be used to improve rough estimates of position, but not generally to produce an estimate from scratch.

As the above example illustrates, to effectively use astronomical tables to determine latitude or compass variation, one needs to have at least a rough idea of one's position. Much of the material in Chaplin's journal can be interpreted as a navigator's reckoning, or running estimate, of position. The format used changes somewhat over the years as the expedition proceeds, and we have found the later material, recorded while aboard the *Holy Gabriel*, somewhat easier to reconstruct. To illustrate this we will describe the entry made for 23 July 1728. This consists of two tables, the first being a list of 24 entries, one for each hour beginning at local noon on the 23rd and ending at noon the following day. The second table is the "Table of daily reckoning." In the first table, in the column labeled "rhumbs" Chaplin recorded the ship's course as indicated by its compass, while in the column labeled "miles" Chaplin recorded the distance traveled during that hour, in nautical miles. The column "winds" presumably gives the wind direction during that hour, while the column "right rhumbs" gives the estimate of the ship's course, obtained after correcting the compass course for the effects of magnetic variation, leeway, current and tide effects, or other influences which cause a ship's actual course to differ from that indicated by the compass. On this day the only correction applied was for magnetic declination, and the corrections used are listed in the

Hour	Declination(degrees)	Right Ascension(hours)
0	17,010	2,9851
1	17,021	2,9878
2	17,033	2,9905
3	17,044	2,9932
4	17,055	2,9959
5	17,067	2,9986
6	17,078	3,0012
7	17,089	3,0039
8	17,101	3,0066
9	17,112	3,0093
10	17,123	3,0120
11	17,135	3,0147
12	17,146	3,0174
13	17,157	3,0201
14	17,168	3,0228
15	17,180	3,0255
16	17,191	3,0282
17	17,202	3,0309
18	17,213	3,0336
19	17,225	3,0363
20	17,236	3,0390
21	17,247	3,0417
22	17,258	3,0444
23	17,269	3,0470
24	17,281	3,0497

Table 1. Declination and Right Ascension of sun for April 27, 1725, Julian Calendar.

"Table of daily reckoning" in the column "Compass declination." At sunset that day an observation of the sun's amplitude (i.e. the angle of the sun's center when setting with respect to due west) was made using the compass and this was compared to an estimate of the astronomical amplitude, yielding an estimate of magnetic declination of 19°37', or about 1 ¾ points, east. So prior to 9 p.m. a correction of 1 ½ points east was used but after 9 p.m. a correction of 1 ¾ points east was used.

The main reason for recording these data was to allow the navigator to compute an updated estimate of the ship's position, which is contained in the Table of daily reckoning. Basically, the navigator would use the hourly record of courses and distances to estimate the total distance traveled north, south, east and west, and then use these distances to compute the corresponding dead reckoning changes in latitude and longitude. If astronomical measurements of latitude were not available, the dead reckoning estimate of position was used as the best estimate. If a latitude fix were available, however, this would usually be taken as giving the ship's latitude, and the longitude estimate would then be adjusted for consistency. Not listed in Chaplin's journal are intermediate calculations where the day's run is decomposed into total distances traveled north, south, east and west. For this example, we converted the right rhumb entries into their corresponding bearings and then used these to decompose each hour's run into the distance traveled in each of the four cardinal directions. For this we used sine and cosine functions in a computerized spreadsheet, but navigators in Bering's party would probably have constructed the day's course graphically by plotting each hour's run using dividers and a ruler. Our calculations indicated that during that 24-hour period the ship traveled about 36.5 miles north and about 32.4 miles east from its position at noon on the 23rd, with a straight line direction of about 41° 38.8' east of north. By comparison, in the Rhumb column of the Table of daily reckoning Chaplin gives the ship's overall course as NEbN 7°52' by E, or about 41°37' east of north. In the entry Reckoned-D. latitudes, Chaplin gives a total northerly distance of 36'5, which we think safe to interpret as 36.5 miles, and in the entry Reckoned-Depart he gives total easterly distance of 32'43, which corresponds nicely to our 32.43 miles. The total north and east distances then give a total straight-line distance of 48.83 miles, close to Chaplin's entry Reckoned-Distance-right, 48.8 miles.

Chaplin indicated that at noon on the 23rd the sun's altitude was measured, producing the estimated latitude of 60°16' north, and at noon on the 24th a similar measurement gave a latitude of 61°03' north. The Corrected row of the Table of daily reckoning then takes these as given, uses them to re-estimate the distance traveled, and then to estimate the corresponding change in longitude. The difference between these latitude fixes is listed in the entry Corrected-D.latitudes, 47'. Since a one minute change of latitude along a meridian is approximately equal to one nautical mile, the latitude observations imply that the ship traveled 47 miles north, as opposed to the dead-reckoning estimate of 36.5 miles. Multiplying 47' by the cosine of the course (Rhumb) gives the easterly distance traveled, 41.75', which is close to Chaplin's entry for Corrected-Depart. The next step is to compute the change in longitude corresponding to this easting. Because the meridians converge at the north and south poles, the angle subtended by one nautical mile due east or west varies from about one arc-minute at the equator to essentially infinity at the poles. On a sphere the change in longitude corresponding to a given distance traveled along a parallel varies with the secant of the parallel's latitude. Choosing the latitude halfway between the initial and final values for this correction leads to what was called Middle Latitude Sailing. Alternatively, eighteenth century navigators often used a technique called Mercator Sailing, in which a Table of Meridional Parts allowed them to relate change in longitude to east/west distance. We do not know what table might have been used by the Bering party, but using Table III in Moore (1799) we find that the meridional part for latitude 60°16' is 4559 and that for 61°3' is 4655, for a difference of 96. Multiplying this by the tangent of the course then gives a change of longitude of 85.283 arc-minutes, or about 1°25'17", which is not too dissimilar from Chaplin's D.long- daily 1°23'43". Adding Chaplin's daily change to the previous day's longitude, 10°42'16" gives the new D.long-total 12°05'59". That is, at noon of the 24th the estimated position of the *Holy Gabriel* was latitude 61°03' north, and longitude 12°05'59" east of the original departure point.

During the course of the expedition, the eastward extension of Siberia, from Tobol'sk to Okhotsk, was found to be much greater than had been shown on earlier maps. The delineation of the coasts lying to the north of the Kamchatka peninsula was striking; earlier maps showed the coasts heading straight north. The reality was totally different: the *Holy Gabriel* had to sail far to the east to follow these coasts. Some 1,000 miles further to the east, in fact! The maps that resulted from the great labor of the First Kamchatka Expedition are very accurate and are a lasting memorial to the work of this expedition of the Russian navy.

A Survey of Literature
on the First Kamchatka Expedition

Peter Ulf Møller

*Early Russian and English reproductions
of Chaplin's Journal*

The present book is the first complete publication in any language of Midshipman Chaplin's journal. As explained in the editors' introduction, his journal is one of a pair that together make up the official diaries and logbooks of Vitus Bering's First Kamchatka Expedition. They are the original records of the expedition that culminated in the historic voyage of the decked boat *Holy Archangel Gabriel* in 1728 through the Bering Strait into the Arctic Ocean. While the journal kept by Lieutenant Aleksei Chirikov begins on 23 April 1725 and ends on 9 November 1729, Chaplin's journal comprises the entire duration of the First Kamchatka Expedition, from its departure from St. Petersburg on 24 January 1725 to its return on 1 March 1730. This makes it a particularly valuable source.

Though previously never published in complete form, the journals of Chaplin and Chirikov have long been known to students of Bering's explorations. Naval officer and historian Vasilii Nikolaevich Berkh (1781-1834) came across the journals in the navy archives, but rather than publishing them, he wrote a short account of the First Kamchatka Expedition based on them. He saw Bering's voyage as the Russian navy's first serious experience in sailing the open sea, hence the title of his book from 1823, *Pervoe morskoe puteshestvie Rossiian* (The first sea voyage by the Russians).

In his preface, Berkh explains how he found the manuscript. "Having, upon the recommendation of His Excellency, Vice-Admiral Gavriil Andreevich Sarychev, received permission to examine the archives of the State Admiralty Department, I set about this task with delight, hoping to discover many interesting manuscripts – and my expectations were not disappointed. Browsing through various old documents together with A.E. Kolodkin, head of the draughtsmen's office, we came across a notebook with the following heading, 'Journal of Midshipman Piotr Chaplin during the Kamchatka Expedition, 1725 to 1731'. At first glance, we decided that Chaplin was probably someone who had sailed with the geodesist Gvozdiov, the first Russian to sight America's coast. However, upon more careful examination, we realized that this was the most complete and detailed journal of Bering's First Expedition. The journal was bound together with an incomplete journal written by Lieutenant Chirikov, which was almost identical with the former. Rejoicing at this important discovery […] I composed the present narrative of Captain Bering's voyage."[1]

Among the new information that the journal revealed to Berkh was the fact that the expedition set out from St. Petersburg just *before* the death of Peter the Great, and not just after, as the historian G.F. Müller had written. In addition, Berkh learned that "during all their sailing on the Irtysh and the other rivers [that is onward from Tobol'sk], they worked out the reckoning" as if at sea. For the benefit of "the curious reader", he reproduced the table of daily reckoning for May 21, 1725 (folio 5 of the journal), adding, however, the latitude of Tobol'sk as calculated by the expedition (58°05′ N).[2] New, of course, were also the day-to-day records of events, the names of many expedition members, the detailed information on the route of the voyage, and the positions of newly discovered coastal landmarks. Berkh's narrative followed the progress of the expedition chronologically, as he turned page after page of the journals. He was deeply impressed by the detailed account of the hardships suffered by the expedition members, especially on the route from Iakutsk to Okhotsk, and found consolation in the historical perspective. "Since Captain Bering's expedition is the first sea voyage undertaken by Russians, all its minute details will please those who cherish the antiquities of our fatherland. Even if many of them will seem strange nowadays, they are still worthy of respect, because they demonstrate the gradual development of things from their first beginnings to their present state of perfection".[3]

One thing that surprised Berkh was Bering's decision, in September 1727, to sail from Okhotsk across to Bol'sheretsk on the west coast of Kamchatka. Because of this decision, Bering had to transport his heavy materiel and provisions overland from Bol'sheretsk to his ultimate destination on Kamchatka, the Lower Kamchatsk outpost on the east coast of the peninsula, near the mouth of the Kamchatka River. Why did he not just double the southernmost tip of Kamchatka and sail directly all the way to Lower Kamchatsk? If the threat of stormy autumn weather was the cause, Bering could have wintered in Okhotsk and sailed to Lower Kamchatsk in the spring of 1728, reasoned Berkh. "One must assume that the immortal navigator had his special reasons that remain completely unknown to us".[4]

Berkh was also surprised that Bering, sailing along the east coast of Asia, abstained from naming the numerous capes sighted from the *Holy Gabriel*. Chaplin's journal usually records them only as conspicuous places, designated as "a mountain white with snow" or "a mountain distinctly different from the others", for instance (folio 45). Today's navigators would certainly seize a similar opportunity "to remember their benefactors and several superiors". When Bering did accord a name to newfound bays, islands, and capes, he followed the customs of his day and took it from the orthodox calendar, wrote Berkh.[5]

The degree of precision in the journal's determination of the position of various geographical objects was a matter of great interest to Berkh. He noted, for instance, that the longitude of Cape Faddei (Mys Faddeia), 17°35' E of Lower Kamchatsk (folio 46 verso in the journal), was very close to the calculation by Captain Cook's third expedition – 179°13' E of Greenwich, since the longitude of Lower Kamchatsk was 161°38' E of Greenwich. Moreover, he took pride in quoting Cook's praise of Bering.[6] As for Bering's decision to turn around on August 16, at 67°18' N, Berkh deplored the fact that Bering did not say if he had seen ice or not. According to later navigators, the strait seemed to be free of ice in August and September.[7] As we shall see, Bering's turnaround became a recurring topic for discussion in the historiography of the First Kamchatka Expedition, especially after the emergence of new documentary evidence some thirty years after Berkh's book.

Furthermore, Berkh found it strange that in the voyage of 1729, from Lower Kamchatsk to Bol'sheretsk,

Bering chose to proceed close to the coast of southern Kamchatka, when he could have found better winds farther out to sea.[8] Berkh may have believed that the rounding of Kamchatka's southern part was a routine matter by 1729, which it was not, and that Bering had already completed his task with the voyage of 1728. He seems unaware that on its way to Bol'sheretsk the expedition was mapping the shores of southern Kamchatka.

In 1890 excerpts of Chaplin's and Chirikov's journals were published by V. Vakhtin, in his book *Russkie truzheniki moria* (Russian toilers of the sea), along with what amounts to a nearly complete reprint of Berkh's biographical information on Bering, Spangberg, Chirikov and Chaplin. In fact, Vakhtin's work may be seen as an enlarged second edition of the Berkh volume, but with extensive direct quotations from the original journals, instead of Berkh's paraphrase.

Almost a century after Vakhtin, in 1984, Tatiana Fedorova published a section of Chaplin's journal for the period 5-20 August 1728, that is, the records of the passage of the *Holy Gabriel* into the Arctic Ocean and back. This publication, in a Russian anthology of early eighteenth-century navy documents, was the first to present a sequence of Chaplin's pages in a tabular form similar to that of the original journal.[9]

In the United States, an English translation of Berkh's summary of Chaplin's journal appeared in 1890.[10] The translator was William Healey Dall, a naturalist and a former leader of the Western Union Telegraph Expedition, whose mission was to examine if a cable could be laid down between Alaska and Asia. Having sailed in the same waters as Bering, he took a profound interest in the Kamchatka Expeditions. Dall was aware of the importance of Berkh's book as a source of information about Bering's voyage through the strait, and complained that it had taken him so long to get hold of a copy of it. In fact, his English translation appeared the same year as the more complete Russian rendering of Chaplin's journal by Vakhtin.

Bering's own accounts of his first expedition
Although Berkh was the first to make mention of Chaplin's journal, he was not the first to write about Bering's first expedition. It seems logical to regard Bering's own report, submitted to Empress Anna Ioannovna shortly after his return in 1730, as the beginning of the literature on the First Kamchatka Expedition, even if it was not published in the original Russian until 1847, in an official journal of the Ministry of War.[11] In English, this report is often referred to as Bering's "Short Account". It is, undoubtedly, an im-

portant source for the discussion of the purpose of the expedition and its degree of success or failure. Bering starts out by quoting the instructions given by Peter the Great, and later offers his own explicit statement of why he believed the expedition had carried out these instructions. "On August 15 we were in a latitude of 67°18′ where I reached the decision that on the basis of everything we had observed, we had fulfilled the instructions given us by His Imperial Majesty of eternally blessed and deserving memory, because the land does not extend farther to the north, and there is nothing beyond Chukotka or the eastern extremity. And so I turned back".[12]

Bering's account is a chronologically arranged itinerary of his expedition. It has two appended schedules, "Catalogue of towns and notable places in Siberia that we passed through on our route and put on the chart, with their latitude and longitude, the latter computed from Tobol'sk", and "Table showing distances in Russian versts to the towns and notable places that we passed through during the Expedition as far as to the turnaround [...]".[13] Along with this material, Bering also submitted his concluding "Final Map" based on it.

As we know, Bering did not realize that he was passing through the narrow strait later named after him. Fog and bad luck prevented him from sighting the American coast. In presenting the achievements of the expedition, he focused on its measuring of the length of Siberia and its determination of the geographical position of the northeastern coastline of Asia from Kamchatka to its easternmost point. This information was summarized in the "Catalogue" and the "Table" mentioned above. The appendices also registered how the expedition traversed the various sections of its route (over land, by rivers, or by sea), which native peoples they met on their way, and the size of Russian settlements. Bering's own account of the laborious journey across Siberia with heavy cargoes had, for all its brevity, several memorable passages. Reporting on the arrival in Okhotsk of Lieutenant Spangberg's detachment on foot in January 1727, he wrote, "[...] on their journey they were all so starved that they ate the horses that died, leather saddlebags and any bit of hide, including their clothing and leather boots".[14] This record of the dearly bought experience in Siberian travel was potentially useful for the authorities.

The geographical results of the expedition were summarized and visualized in the form of two maps. The first one, attributed to Chaplin, showed the itinerary of the expedition from Tobol'sk to Okhotsk. It was made in Okhotsk and sent to the Admiralty College in St. Petersburg together with a report in the summer of 1727, before the expedition left for Kamchatka.[15] A contemporary manuscript copy of it, the so-called "Simanskii copy", now in the Russian State Archives of Military History in Moscow, is printed as plates 7 and 13 in the present volume. The second one, usually called the "Final Map" (in Russian *itogovaia karta*), was brought to the College by the returning expedition members in March 1730. It showed not only the expedition's route through Siberia, but also Kamchatka and the northeastern coast of Asia. It was probably compiled in 1729, in Lower Kamchatsk and during the homeward journey. Two original manuscript copies, both signed by Chaplin, have been identified in Russian archives.[16]

Bering's "Short Account" remained unknown to the reading public in Russia for more than a century after it had been submitted to the Empress, whereas it swiftly found its way to the learned world of Western Europe. While Bering had been away, the St. Petersburg Academy of Sciences had emerged, and Russia's new membership of the European republic of letters implied not only a steady import of information, but an export as well. When Bering arrived in the capital, he met foreign scholars at the Academy who were eager to interpret and disseminate the geographical results of his expeditions. Within the following couple of decades, the "Short Account" was translated and paraphrased into French, English and German, being printed several times.[17] Several manuscript copies of the "Final Map" also found their way to the West.

The account and the map were first printed in Paris in 1735, in the fourth volume of the French Jesuit J.B. Du Halde's *Description [...] de l'empire de la Chine* (cf. plate 39). There is circumstantial evidence that the St. Petersburg Academy's French astronomer and geographer, Joseph Nicolas Delisle, was the one who exported the manuscript copies used by Du Halde.[18] The map reappeared in later editions of Du Halde and in translations of his work into English and German. A somewhat smaller version of the map appeared in J. Harris, *Navigantium atque Itinerantium Bibliotheca, or, a Complete Collection of Voyages and Travels,* Vol. II, London 1748 and later editions (cf. plate 60). As Bering's map gradually became incorporated in new maps, it changed the image of the world: Siberia grew longer, and Kamchatka and the Pacific coast of northern Asia came closer to their modern outlines.

Bering himself contributed discreetly to the spreading of news about his discoveries. In April 1733, just before his departure on the Second Kamchatka Expedition, he paid a visit to the Dutch envoy in St. Pe-

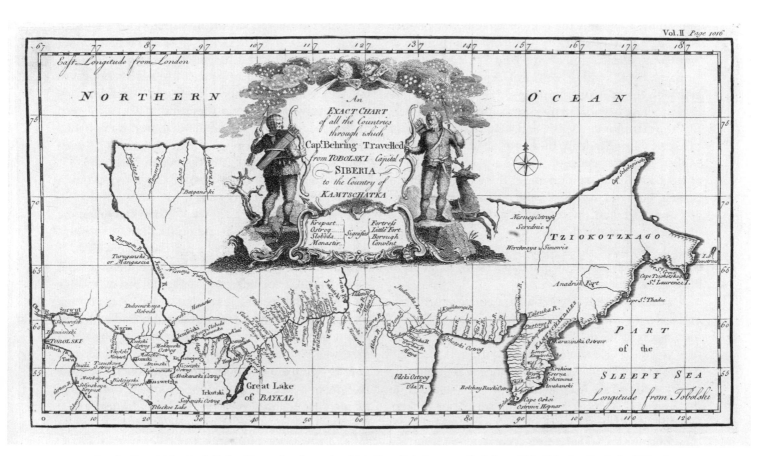

PLATE 60. An Exact Chart of all the Countries through which Cap. Behring travelled from Tobol'sk, the Capital of Siberia, to the Country of Kamtschatka. From John Harris, *Navigantium atque Itinerantium Bibliotheca, or, a Complete Collection of Voyages and Travels,* Vol. II, London 1764 (between pp. 1016-1017).

Courtesy the Royal Library, Copenhagen.

tersburg, M. De Swart, and gave him a copy of the "Final Map". De Swart's encoded report about the incident has recently been published.[19] Nearly twenty manuscript copies of the "Final Map" are known to have been preserved in libraries and other public collections in Russia, Sweden, France, the United States, Denmark, Germany, and Great Britain.[20] The present volume displays several of them.

Initially, there was hardly any consistent policy from the Russian side of keeping secret the information brought back by the expedition. Two weeks after Bering's return to St. Petersburg, a notice in the government newspaper *Sanktpeterburgskie vedomosti* from 16 March 1730, and in its German language counterpart *St. Peterburgische Zeitung*, announced to the world that Bering "reached the 67th parallel 19th minute of north latitude, whereupon he found that in this region there is indeed a northeast passage so that it should be possible, if the ice does not stand in the way in the northern area, to go by water from the Lena to Kamchatka, and farther to Japan, China, and the East Indies". The

notice mentions the two maps produced by Bering's expedition, "the map of his [land] journey, which extended from Tobol'sk to Okhotsk, sent here in 1728", and "another original map, of Kamchatka and his ocean route, from which it can be seen that this land begins in the south at the 51st degree north latitude and extends to the 67th degree in the north". It also gave away the exciting news about the many longitudes across Siberia. "Regarding the geographical distance, he [Bering] stated that 85 degrees of longitude are counted from the west coast [of Kamchatka] to Tobol'sk, but from the northeastern limit to this same meridian 126". It is safe to say that the notice had disclosed the very essence of the expedition's geographical results. It even made the promise that more details "will be given at the proper time".[21] This never happened, at least not in the form of an extended official report. However, the notice itself appeared in several newspapers abroad, in translation or paraphrase. A Danish version came out in a Copenhagen newspaper as early as 20 April 1730.[22]

Peter Lauridsen, author of the first sizeable Bering

biography, knew only the Danish version of the notice and assumed it "originated either with him [Bering] or with some of his immediate friends".[23] However, Bering was not the author. As Carol Urness argues in her article in the present volume (pp. 268-269), it is more likely to have originated in conversation between Bering, the astronomer Delisle and a German member of the Petersburg Academy, the historian Georg Friedrich Müller. The latter was probably the author. He got most of his factual information about the expedition from Bering, but the emphasis in the notice on the discovery of a northeast passage reflected Delisle's and his own preoccupation with this problem, an interest they shared with many other western scholars. However, it was hardly Bering's principal concern, to judge from his own writings.

Raymond Fisher devotes an appendix in his influential *Bering's Voyages: Whither and Why* (1977) to a discussion of what he calls "Bering's accounts of his first voyage".[24] He states, "Bering authored three accounts of his first voyage". The first one was the already mentioned "Short Account". Originally submitted to the Empress Anna, it became the source of French, English and German versions in the eighteenth century. Bering's second account, according to Fisher, is a report of his voyage which he submitted to the Admiralty College on March 10, 1730. Fisher regretted the fact that it remained unpublished. However, Tatiana Fedorova has since published it in Russian, along with another report from Bering to the College, submitted two days later.[25] Both reports are much shorter than the "Short Account". The first one outlines the voyages of 1728 and 1729, including the near-wreck of the *Holy Gabriel* on the east coast of Kamchatka on 31 August 1728 (not mentioned in the "Short Account") and the return journey as far as to Ilimsk. In the second report, Bering recommends 29 members of his command for promotion.

Bering's third account, according to Fisher, is the journal some believe he kept during his voyage. Fisher takes the reader into the discussion around this elusive text, which is wrapped in mystery and misunderstandings. Today there is a wide consensus among scholars that Bering kept no journal and that, consequently, there is no reason to lament the loss of it or hope for it to turn up. References in the literature to "Bering's journal" usually turn out to be to the journals of Chaplin and Chirikov, or to the "Short Account".

Bering, however, did write a more personal report about the expedition. In one of his only three surviving letters in Danish, a personal letter to his maternal aunt, presumably from the first half of 1731, he gave his family version of the expedition.[26] Though much shorter, it is in essence close to his "Short Account" to the Empress. Bering makes no mention of the Northeast Passage or America. What he chooses to tell Auntie Margrethe about his route is the following: "I have traversed several thousand miles of Eastern Tartary, as far as the land extended, past Kamchatka; and several hundred miles farther than can be seen from the maps, specifically the Asian part, which is otherwise available from Nuremberg. Having had a passion for travel in my youth, I must admit that so far I have had my share, for this journey has taken me beyond China and Japan, and no East Indian journey, whether over land or by sea, can compare with it."[27] This is not only a remarkably clear statement of what Bering himself considered his essential discovery. It is also the most direct reference that we have from Bering to a specific map he knew and possibly had with him on the expedition. The Nuremberg map of "the Asian part" was in all likelihood the Asia map from Homann's *Grosser Atlas*, either the first version of the map, *Asiae recentissima delineatio* by Johann Baptist Homann, or its second version, *Recentissima Asiae delineatio [...] unacum novissimis russorum detectionibus*, by his son Johann Christoph Homann. The latter version incorporated the so-called "newest" geographical information from Russia. Bering's discoveries rendered both versions antiquated.

Bering's discoveries as seen by the Academy professors
Delisle gave the first scholarly assessment of the results of the expedition. On 10 November 1730 he presented a report to the Academy staff conference, in which he discussed the longitudes of Kamchatka, Ilimsk, and Tobol'sk, as determined by Bering and "his lieutenant" (that is, Chirikov). Although most of Delisle's report was about uncertainties and sources of errors in the measurements, the news about the increased length of Siberia did come across to the learned audience. The protocol of the meeting stated, in clear Latin, that Kamchatka "must lie much further east [*multo orientaliorem esse debere*] than shown on the maps of present-day geographers".[28]

By Senate decree of 19 June 1732, the Academy of Sciences was instructed to take part in the Second Kamchatka Expedition.[29] Delisle and Müller, who had discussed the geographical results of the expedition with Bering immediately after his return in March 1730, were both to play important roles in the planning and execution of the Second Kamchatka Expedition (1733-43). For both of them, Bering's expeditions became major events in their lives and scholarly work, and the later controversy between them holds a significant place in the eighteenth-century literature on both expeditions.

Delisle was entrusted with the task of writing instructions for the "astronomical, geographical and physical observations" to be carried out by the travelling scientists.[30] He also drew a map for the new expedition. The purpose of the map was to combine the outline of Northeastern Asia from Bering's "Final Map" with earlier cartographical information from western sources on the Northern Pacific and Northwestern America, and thus serve as tool for helping the expedition's navy detachments find the shortest route to America. The map was good for its time and reflected the contemporary state of knowledge. Still, it was far from the geographical realities and included some lands that proved purely fictitious. Delisle presented it to the St. Petersburg Academy on 6 October 1732, together with a commentary entitled *Memoires sur la nouvelle Carte de la mer Orientale dressée pour montrer le plus court chemin de l'Asie à l'Amerique* (Explanation of the map of the eastern sea which was prepared for the purpose of showing the nearest way from Asia to America).[31]

Delisle's half-brother, the astronomer Louis Delisle de la Croyère, was appointed to the academic detachment of the expedition. He sailed to Alaska in 1741, on Chirikov's ship *Saint Paul*, and died on the home voyage to Kamchatka, as did Bering himself and many others. The expense in human lives was later to evoke criticism of Delisle's map. His memoir contained an indirect recommendation to sail south from Kamchatka and to search for the so-called Juan da Gama Land. Following this advice, the expedition lost precious time in the summer of 1741.

For a while, the Russian authorities had better luck with keeping secret the detailed information about the voyages of the Second Kamchatka Expedition. When it did leak out, Delisle was once again a source of indiscretions. Retiring from the Petersburg Academy in 1747, he had moved back to Paris, where he soon set about the publication of geographical materials that reflected the latest Russian discoveries. On 8 April 1750 he presented a map of "the new discoveries in the Northern Pacific" to a public meeting of the Paris Academy of Science. It was followed in 1752 by a printed memoir entitled *Explication de la Carte des nouvelles découvertes au Nord de la Mer du Sud* (Explanatory memoir on the map of new discoveries northward of the South Sea). The memoir exaggerated the roles played by Delisle and his half-brother in the Second Kamchatka Expedition, at the expense of Ber-

ing and Chirikov. According to Delisle, Bering had not reached the American coast but was shipwrecked on the island now bearing his name at the very beginning of the voyage.[32] As for Chirikov, commander of the second ship of the Alaska expedition, the *Saint Paul*, he is repeatedly mentioned in the same breath as "my brother", and his voyage is referred to as the "voyage of Captain Tschirikow and my brother".[33] In addition, Delisle boldly took credit for having suggested and planned the Second Kamchatka Expedition. He claimed he had presented his map of the North Pacific to the Empress Anna and the Senate in 1731, "in order to animate the *Russians* to undertake these discoveries". After this, the Empress ordered a second voyage to be made "according to the plan which I had drawn up for it [...] This expedition having been ordered according to my plan, Mr. Beerings [sic] was commissioned to go to the east of Kamtschatka".[34]

As Carol Urness points out, "Delisle annoyed readers in Russia by stating that his map had been the impetus for the Second Kamchatka Expedition", and a response was not long in coming.[35] Although it appeared in the form of an anonymous letter from a Russian sea-officer to "a person of distinction" at the Russian court, it was clear to insiders that its author was Delisle's former colleague at the St. Petersburg Academy, G.F. Müller, disguised for the occasion as an officer from Bering's command. As an expedition member for ten years, until 1743, Müller had every qualification to play this part. In addition, he was the commissioned historiographer of the expedition, and his rebuttal to Delisle was, if not on behalf of, then at least with the consent of the St. Petersburg Academy. The *Letter* appeared in French and German editions in 1753, in Berlin, and in English the following year, in London. Müller "carefully and politely discredited Delisle, and devastated the *Explication*".[36] Regarding the Frenchman's claim to have provided the impetus for the expedition, Müller concluded that "the real truth is that so far was Mr. de l'Isle from inciting the Russians to fresh discoveries, or setting Mr. Beerings's second voyage on foot, that he did no more than work as he had been bid; and then, whether this performance of his did more good or harm to the expedition is another question".[37]

Delisle's new indiscretion prompted the Russian authorities to reduce the secrecy around the Kamchatka Expeditions, and in 1758 Müller was able to publish a sizable historical account of the Russian discoveries in the Arctic and Pacific oceans, in German and in Russian.[38] It appeared in English in 1761, in French in 1766, and in Danish in 1784.[39] Although most of

PLATE 61. G.F. Müller's map relating to Bering's voyages, republished in London 1761 by Thomas Jefferys, geographer to his Majesty. The map was originally printed in 1754 by the Academy of Sciences at St. Petersburg, to accompany Müller's account of the Bering expeditions. Jefferys's version accompanied the first English translation of Müller's account, entitled *Voyages from Asia to America*.

Courtesy the Royal Library, Copenhagen.

the account was devoted to the Second Kamchatka Expedition, it also comprised an important discussion of the First Expedition. Bering's main endeavour, Müller explains, was to map the coastline northward of the mouth of the Kamchatka River, in which he succeeded fairly well ("welches auch so ziemlich gelung"). However, the Captain did not reach the northeast corner of Asia, as he thought, but only a promontory called "Serdze Kamen" by the Russians. The real northeast corner, "das eigentliche Tschuktschische Noss", is several degrees further to the north. Müller adds indulgently that no-one on board the ship could have known this since it only became clear later, thanks to the author's own geographical research in the archives of Iakutsk in

1736 and 1737.[40] Still, Müller's idea of the northeastern corner was a rather theoretical one. It was reflected in his map first printed in St. Petersburg in 1754 and again in 1758. A remake of the map appeared in the English edition of his account (Müller 1761), from which it has been reproduced for the present volume (plate 61).

Explorers in the wake of the Holy Gabriel
After the Kamchatka Expeditions, the next major effort to explore the strait and the high latitudes of the north-west coast of America was carried out by the British, as part of Captain James Cook's third voyage, on the *Resolution* and *Discovery*. Cook's comments on

Bering and the Russians form a tiny, but authoritative and much quoted portion of the literature on the First Kamchatka Expedition. They are found throughout his journal, usually as attempts to compare his own observations with those of his predecessor. During the spring and summer of 1778, Cook proceeded up the west coast of North America, reaching its western limit on 9 August. Two days later, he found himself in the middle of the strait, in crystal-clear weather, and was able to see the coastlines of both Asia and America. On his way back from the Arctic Ocean, on 4 September, he saw the island of St. Lawrence, "discovered by Captain Behring", and the southernmost point of the Chukchi Peninsula "which Capt. Behring calls [...] Cape Tchuktschi". The entry in his journal continues, "In justice to *Behring's Memory*, I must say he has delineated this Coast very well and fixed the latitude and longitude of the points better than could be expected from the Methods he had to go by. This judgement is not formed from Mr Mullers account of the Voyage or his Chart, but from the account of it in Harris's Collection of Voyages and a Map thereto annexed Vol. II. pag. [...] which is both more circumstantial and accurate than that of Mr Mullers".[41]

"Mr Mullers account", referred to by Cook as one of his sources for information on the Russian Kamchatka Expeditions, is, of course, the English edition of G.F. Müller's account mentioned above.[42] The other source, "Harris's Collection", was a popular anthology of travel writing first published by John Harris in 1705 and from 1748 republished in several enlarged editions by John Campbell. Vol. II included Campbell's paraphrase of Bering's "Short Account" and an English version of his "Final Map" (plate 60). Campbell claimed his version of Bering's text had been "compared with a Copy of Captain Behring's original journal".[43]

After Cook, the next important efforts towards specification of geographical knowledge about the Bering Strait and the Asian coast of the Bering Sea were made by the Russian expeditions of J. Billings and G. Sarychev (1785-1794), O. Kotzebue (1815-1819) and F. Litke (1826-1829). In the context of the present volume, Litke's reports are particularly relevant, since he devotes a special section of his geographical and nautical description of the western part of the Bering Sea to a comparison of Bering's observations, as recorded in Chaplin's journal from 27 July to 22 August 1728, with those of his own.[44]

A much later sailor in the wake of Bering was Arkadii Aleksandrovich Sopotsko. In 1976 and 1977 he carried out an experimental voyage with two yachts, the *Rodina* and the *Rossiia*, to repeat as closely as possible the voyage of the *Holy Gabriel*. Sopotsko reported on the investigation in a book in Russian, published in 1983. Its title translates as "The History of Bering's voyage on the decked boat *Holy Gabriel* into the Arctic Ocean." His remake of the original voyage allowed him to identify a great many of the unnamed points on the coast that Bering had observed. Based on this model voyage, Sopotsko compiled a table of 155 "territorial discoveries" made from aboard the *Holy Gabriel* in 1728. Another table registered 66 "geographical objects" that had been put on a map for the first time during the *Holy Gabriel's* voyage in 1729. A final table listed 87 "territorial discoveries" made by the *Holy Gabriel* during both voyages and confirmed by Sopotsko's yachts.[45] It is a most impressive report, in spite of occasional misreading of Chaplin's manuscript. It projects Bering's voyage along an unknown and unnamed coast onto a modern map in a most detailed and convincing way.

Sopotsko is also polemical. He believes strongly that the First Kamchatka Expedition was a great achievement and an unquestionable success. In spite of the relatively short duration of its two voyages, it produced more geographical results than many realize. Among Russian navigators of the first half of the eighteenth century that brought glory to Russia, Bering distinguished himself as the great seafarer who gave his life to the exploration of the northeastern Pacific Ocean.[46] Such praise of Bering cannot be taken for granted in the literature on his voyages. There, a critical attitude to Bering as a leader and as an explorer came to the fore already in the late eighteenth century, in the German naturalist G.W. Steller's portrayal of him.[47]

The issue of Bering versus Chirikov

As for Bering's role specifically in the First Kamchatka Expedition, there was an upsurge of criticism in the middle of the nineteenth century, in connection with the emergence of new archival material. In 1850 naval historian A.S. Polonskii published an article on the expedition that marked a leap forward in available information and degree of detail. It first appeared in an official naval periodical with limited circulation, but was republished the following year in a more popular journal.[48] Through Polonskii's presentation, the logistical problems and human sufferings in the course of the expedition became more tangible. Regrettably, from a scholarly point of view, the author did not provide references to the majority of his sources. But most of them were documents in the Russian navy archives, as evidenced by Evgenii Kushnarev's extensive account more than a century later.[49]

Polonskii's scoop was a copy of the written opinions submitted by Spangberg, Chirikov and Bering following the ship's council of 13 August 1728, shortly after the expedition had sailed through the strait. The council was convened to decide what to do next. Spangberg's advice was to return to Kamchatka and lay up for the winter, Chirikov's advice was for further exploration, even if it might mean wintering in the far north. Bering decided to play safe and turn around. In a footnote, Polonskii suggests that Bering tried to hide "the lucid proposals of his clever, but modest fellow traveler", since they are not mentioned in the journals of Chaplin and Chirikov, nor in any of Bering's reports.[50] If Polonskii is right, one wonders how he was still able to find the proposals in the navy archives.

Polonskii's article appeared shortly after a learned debate over Bering had made its way to the newspaper columns in St. Petersburg. On 14 January 1848 Karl Ber (K.E. von Baer), an esteemed Estonian member of the St. Petersburg Academy, gave a lecture to the Russian Geographical Society on Peter the Great's contributions to the growth of geographical knowledge about Russia and the lands bordering her to the east. He set out to prove that "the most important of all geographical expeditions" – by which he meant the Second Kamchatka Expedition – sprang from Peter's vision and foresight, as laid down in the three paragraphs of his short instruction for the First Kamchatka Expedition. As Ber saw it, Bering had been unjustly forgotten for nearly half a century, from the moment of his death until the noble Captain Cook revived his memory by naming the strait between Asia and America after him. In conclusion, he called on the Geographical Society and the Russian-American Company to join forces to erect a monument to Bering in the Russian capital. "In Kamchatka there is a small monument to Bering. Will European Russia ever recognize his services?"[51]

Ber's lecture, with its proposal of a Bering memorial, appeared in the journal of the Geographical Society in 1849.[52] Even before publication it provoked a sharp response from a reader who fully shared Ber's enthusiasm for the Second Kamchatka Expedition, but not for its foreign leader. Ber's adversary was Aleksandr Sokolov, a naval lieutenant employed by the Ministry of Shipping. He was working on what was to become a very significant account of this expedition.[53] His article, entitled "Bering and Chirikov", appeared in May 1849 over two issues of the newspaper *Severnaia pchela* (The Northern Bee). Sokolov argued that if any Russian explorer had been truly forgotten, it was not Bering but "his comrade Chirikov", captain of the *St. Paul* during the American voyage. He set out to demonstrate, by comparison of their performances, that Chirikov was superior to Bering, both morally and as a sailor.[54] His line of argument inflicted considerable damage on the idea of a Bering memorial, in spite of a rebuttal from Ber.[55] Polonskii's article provided strong and timely support for Sokolov's presentation of Chirikov as the true hero of the expeditions. The small Bering monument in Petropavlovsk on Kamchatka, erected in 1822 using limited means donated by a group of naval officers in the town, remained unique.

As the "cold war" set in after World War 2, the Soviet party line, expressed in the so-called Zhdanov Doctrine, required artists and scholars to assert national pride and stop "kowtowing to the West". For scholars studying the Kamchatka Expeditions, the import of this was plain. They had to find and develop a truly Russian protagonist. Fortunately, this was easy. Sokolov and Polonskii had already discovered him a century ago. For Soviet historiography a new heyday of the Bering versus Chirikov theme began. It became politically incorrect to mention Bering without pointing out that Chirikov, a Russian by birth, was the more important of the two, in spite of the formality of his lower rank. The authority of the eighteenth-century academician Lomonosov was evoked to back Chirikov's leading role. While reading the first edition of Voltaire's *Histoire de la Russie sous Pierre le Grand* in 1758, Lomonosov jotted down that the author had not mentioned Chirikov as a member of the American expedition, "although he was the more important and sailed further".[56] Now this statement became a guideline.

More guidelines were laid down in 1950, in a lecture by the navy historian Lieutenant-Colonel V.A. Divin, entitled *Chirikov – an outstanding Russian navigator and scientist*. 72,000 copies of this lecture were printed. Divin's political message was that Chirikov's name had been suppressed in spite of his great merits, and that the same thing was true of many other Russian mariners. "This is a manifestation of the disbelief of the nobility and the bourgeoisie in the creative powers of the Russian people, and the ruling classes' kowtowing to everything foreign. Unimportant voyages by foreign mariners, who often just take credit for the discoveries by Russian seamen, have been praised to the skies. At the same time huge discoveries by native mariners have been hushed up". Divin promised that "progressive scholars" would defend "the people, the honor, and the dignity of Russia", and fight "distortions of historical truth" such as the belittling of Russian sailors' role in geographical discoveries. Improving on the original quotation, Divin claimed that Lomonosov considered

Chirikov "the more important leader of the Second Kamchatka Expedition".[57]

Like reflexes from the spinal cord, Russian post-Stalin studies of the Kamchatka expeditions still occasionally show purely patriotic efforts to promote Chirikov. However, in the last decades of the Soviet period this emotional approach lost ground. Characteristically, by the early 1990's, American historian Raymond Fisher found that the time had come to bring the old Chirikov/Bering issue to a fair settlement. In his article "To give Chirikov his due", he offered a middle of the road view that ought to please everyone. With regard to the First Expedition, he gave Chirikov credit for organizing the rapid transport of flour from Iakutsk to Okhotsk in the early summer of 1727, for instance, and (together with Chaplin) for the accuracy of the nautical data later commended by Cook. On the other hand, he admitted that Chirikov's written proposal on what to do after 13 August 1728 would have been suicidal.[58] Still, it is surprising to see a historian completely ignoring the compulsory political context of the Soviet upgrading of Chirikov, and accepting a standard list of undocumented conjectures about the special contributions of the lieutenant, such as his status as the "scientist" of the expedition and the supervisor of its map-making, who just "left the drawing to Chaplin".[59]

However, by then Fisher had already made a major contribution to directing the study of the First Kamchatka Expedition in a different direction.

The meaning of Peter the Great's instructions

Academician Ber had set out to demonstrate the merits of Peter the Great in widening geographical knowledge about Russia and the lands bordering her to the east. Although the emperor certainly had a sustained interest in geography, maps, and expeditions, he had breathtaking political projects as well, and Ber saw Peter's geographical interest in the context of his overall ambition for securing a central position for Russia in world trade. The Kamchatka expeditions were part of his far-reaching imperial dreams, and Bering did his share in fulfilling them, at the cost of his life. He delivered to the Russian Empire not only new geographical insight, but also geographical material substance: the Bering Sea and the northwest coast of America.[60]

On this background, it would seem quite reasonable to scrutinize the emperor's instructions given to Bering for his First Kamchatka Expedition not only for their geographical contents, but also with an eye to a possible further political purpose. In other words, to ask the double question of "whither and why", which is the subtitle Fisher chose for his book *Bering's voyages*

from 1977. Nevertheless, ever since Müller and later Berkh, it had become a commonly accepted and largely unquestioned truth that the First Kamchatka Expedition was scientific, dispatched in order to determine the geographical relationship of Asia to America, and the feasibility of a northeast passage from Europe to the Far East. Fisher defied two centuries of scholarly tradition to point out that this view was not derived from explicit statements by Peter. "It is based, rather, on indirect evidence and on the statements and opinions of several of his close associates and certain contemporaries. Once established, the view became widespread [...]".[61]

Fisher credits the Soviet historian Aleksandr Pokrovskii with having first questioned the traditional interpretation of Peter's instruction. Pokrovskii was the editor of an anthology of archival documents related to Bering's expeditions and published to mark the bicentenary of the explorer's death in 1941. His introduction comprised a discussion of the three short paragraphs that made up the instructions (they are quoted in full by C. Urness on p. 267 of the present volume). Pokrovskii found that the traditionally accepted geographical task of the expedition was indeed expressed in the rather elusive instructions, but that its most important task was to sail along the American coast as far as the Spanish possessions in Mexico. This was a practical political goal, based on current Russian interests in trade relations with Spain and her colonies.[62] Thus, like Ber, Pokrovskii linked the expedition with Peter the Great's trade ambitions. His Spanish theory, however, did not win many supporters.

After World War 2, Soviet scholars advanced more theories about the expedition's ultimate purpose. Aleksei Efimov, an outstanding specialist on Russian cartography, suggested in 1950, perhaps under influence of the cold war atmosphere, that Peter's chief concern was for security and the defence of Russia's east border.[63] In 1976 Evgenii Kushnarev – author of the most thorough Soviet monograph on the First Kamchatka Expedition, with extensive use of archival sources – rejected Efimov's security theory.[64] Kushnarev argued that at the beginning of the eighteenth century Northwest America was not only unclaimed by Europeans – they had not even discovered it yet. The most sensational of these theories was put forth by Boris Polevoi in 1964, in a remote geographical journal published in Kamchatka.[65] Polevoi argued that the obscure second paragraph of Peter's instructions made sense, on the assumption that the emperor was referring to the Homann map of Kamchatka (reproduced on p. 264 of the present volume). According to Polevoi, Peter wanted Bering to sail east to the land just opposite Kamchatka on Homann's map, and follow its coast south, to the nearest European settlement in America, or until he met a European ship. The real meaning of this would be to take the first step towards further Russian eastward expansion, that is, to claim overseas American territory that hopefully would yield an increase in Russia's fur income.

Fisher agreed with Polevoi on the relevance of the Homann map for the interpretation of Peter's instructions, but offered his own detailed explanation of how Bering had arrived at his misinterpretation of the instructions by sailing north instead of east.[66] Many scholars in the field reject or are skeptical about the Homann thesis of Polevoi and Fisher, and its implications. Nevertheless, Fisher's book is an outstanding contribution to the study of Bering's voyages as a whole, and the first voyage in particular. His argument is admirably clear, and his command of the literature in the main languages, including Russian, is most impressive.

Another remarkable American contribution is Carol Urness's dissertation *Bering's First Expedition* from 1987, which, as the author states in her introduction, "could not have been undertaken without the pioneering work of Fisher and the Soviet scholars of the Bering voyages."[67] It is a re-examination of the expedition's purpose and results based on eighteenth-century books, maps, and manuscripts. It demonstrates how the early transmission of information about the expedition affected the view of its purpose and results. Urness accepts the Homann thesis, but does not agree

with Polevoi and Fisher that Bering acted against his instructions. On the contrary, she concludes, "It was Bering's misfortune that he tried to follow Peter's orders about the unknown land on Homann's map *exactly*. By sailing as far east as he had, Bering and his officers were convinced that they had sailed around the unknown land and had discovered that it was not joined to America. Bering therefore was later criticized for *not* doing what he was *not* instructed to do [...] Bering had no instructions to go to America, unless the unknown land on the Homann map *joined* to America."[68]

Some short references
Special aspects of the First Kamchatka Expedition are scrutinized in several works listed in the reference section of the present volume. Details about the construction and outward appearance of the decked boat *Holy Gabriel* and the voyages she made, during the First Kamchatka Expedition and later, may be found in Pshenichnyi 1993 and 1995. The provisioning and logistical problems of the expedition are discussed in Gibson 1992. Biographies of the leading officers include a) On Bering: Lauridsen 1885 and 1889; Ostrovskii 1939; Lind & Møller 1997; Frost 2003; Okhotina-Lind 2004; Møller & Lind 2008. b) On Spangberg: Fedorova et al. 1999 and 2002. c) On Chirikov: Divin 1953 and 1993. The cartography of the expedition is treated in Efimov 1950, 1964, 1971, in Fel' 1960, and in several articles: Björkbom 1941; Bagrow 1948; Navrot 1971, Kejlbo 1993.

Notes

THE EDITORS' INTRODUCTION

1   The assertion of A.A. Sopotsko (Sopotsko, p. 18) that the logbooks of the *Holy Gabriel* had been lost and that he found them in 1973 disagrees with these facts.

2   RGAVMF, fund 176, inv. 1, unit 106, folio 30.

3   *ibid.*

4   RGAVMF, fund 176, inv. 1, unit 115, folio 619.

5   RGAVMF, fund 315, inv. 1, unit 693, folio 286.

6   *Russkie ekspeditsii*, p. 66.

7   Cf. the present edition, folio 36, p. 88.

8   Cf. the present edition, folio 70v, p. 232.

9   Veselago 1885-1894, vol. 2, pp. 469-470.

10 *Russkie ekspeditsii*, p. 68.

11 *Russkie ekspeditsii*, p. 88.

12 The form *Spangsberg,* with an *s* in the middle, used in the biography of Bering's associate (*Martin Spangsberg* s.a.), lacks documentation. It has never been found in the Kamchatka Expedition files or other Russian navy records. By using it, the authors of the biography seem to suggest that he belonged to the Spangsberg family of the Danish town Esbjerg, a hypothesis that lacks documentation in the local parish register (cf. Møller, Hintzsche 2002).

13 *Kniga ustav morskoi*, pp. 82-83.

CHAPLIN'S JOURNAL

1   "to the Turnaround", in Russian *do vozvrashcheniia*.

2   The abbreviations explained by Chaplin will not be used in our translation of his journal, with the exception of "a.m." and "p.m." The others are derived from the following Russian words in Latin transcription: P from *pravyi* (right), L from *levyi* (left), R from *reka* (river) and D from *derevnia* (village). In our translation, the corresponding English words will be written in full.

3   An *admiralty* in Russia was a composite shipyard, located on the bank of a river or a lake, or on the seacoast. It carried out not only shipbuilding and repairs, but also the complete outfitting of ships. The Admiralty in St. Petersburg was founded in 1704 on the left bank of the Neva River. Peter the Great himself took part in the drawing up of its plan. The original map, with an overview of buildings and slipways, bears his annotations. It is kept in the RGAVMF (fund 223, inv. 1, unit 12, folio 1). From the middle of the 19th century, when the Admiralty had lost its original functions, it housed the central administrative organs of the navy.
In 1727-1738, the architect I.K. Korovin rebuilt the Admiralty, retaining Peter's intentions. In 1806-1823 the new look of the Admiralty, which has been preserved to the present, was created by the architect A.D. Zakharov. Today the St. Petersburg Admiralty is an outstanding architectural monument, one of the symbols of the city.

4   "For the posting station": the manuscript has *v emskuiu* [= iamskuiu] *slobodu*. *Iamskaia sloboda* is the Russian name for a settlement of coachmen (*iamshchiki*) who were obliged to transport mail and to let out horses and carts to travelers. Vakhtin, in his excerpts from Chaplin's journal, misread the passage as "v Elaiskuiu slobodu" (Vakhtin 1890, p. 4). Understandably, he abstained from commenting on the whereabouts of this place.
Many Russian towns had suburban posting stations until the late 19th century. In St. Petersburg, the iamskaia sloboda was founded in 1713 by decree of Peter the Great. It was urgently needed in connection with the compulsory resettlement of workers to build the city, and for communication between the new capital and the rest of the country. (*Ocherki istorii Leningrada* 1955, p. 98). The iamskaia sloboda of St. Petersburg was located in the Moscow Quarter, beyond the Obvodnoi Canal on present day Ligovskii Avenue. Near the posting station evolved present day Rasstannaia ulitsa (Parting Street) where travelers parted with those who saw them off.

5   "by hired sleighs": in the document *[na] nanjatykh podvodakh*. The Russian word *podvoda* (in dictionaries usually translated as *cart* or *waggon*) stands for a hired means of transport, a vehicle, usually including horse and driver or guide. Depending on the time of the year and the specific location, it could be a sleigh, a cart, a boat, or just a horse.

6   Lieutenant Aleksei Il'ich Chirikov (1703-1748) was the son of a nobleman who owned a small estate in the village of Averkievskoe-Luzhnoe in the Tula District. In February 1715, at the age of twelve, he entered the School of Mathematics and Navigation situated at Sukharev's Tower in Moscow. After only one year, the bright boy transferred to the Marine Academy in St. Petersburg. On 2 March 1721, he graduated from the Academy with excellent marks and the rank of sublieutenant, thus bypassing the rank of midshipman, and was assigned to the ship *Piotr*.
From 1722 to 1724 C. taught navigation at the Marine Academy. When personnel were recruited for the first Kamchatka Expedition, Vice-Admiral Sivers and Schoutbijnacht Siniavin found that this expedition would be useful for him (*Russkie ekspeditsii*, p. 33). C. was appointed assistant to the commander of the expedition, Vitus Bering. On 20 January 1725, a few days before his departure on the expedition, C. was promoted lieutenant because of his mastery of the sciences and competent training of 142 naval cadets (*ibid.*, p. 36). During the expedition's passage to Okhotsk, C. was responsible for the delivery of provisions. As the main part of the expedition went ahead, he stayed behind to secure provisions, and did much of the traveling on his own.
In 1728 C. participated in the voyage of the *Holy Gabriel* to the Arctic Ocean. At 67°19' N he proposed to sail on until either the coast line turned left or they were stopped by ice. However, Bering decided to turn around and go back. During the winter of 1728-29, C. played an important role in compiling the total map of the First Kamchatka Expedition, which was presented to the Senate in 1730. According to Kushnarev (1990, p. 153), he "not only had a firsthand part in the compilation of all the maps, but he actually directed the work."
On 23 August C. was promoted "captain-lieutenant", on 16 October "captain of the third rank", and on 18 January, in accordance with the new table of ranks, "captain with the rank of colonel". From 1733 to 1741 C. was assistant to Bering on the Second Kamchatka Expedition. In 1741 he was in command of the packet *St. Paul* on its voyage to America. He reached the north-western coast of America near Cape Bartholomew on Baker Island, having discovered the Alexander Archipelago. Sailing to the north-west along the American continent for 450 km, he inspected and described the coastline. On the home voyage, he mapped a number of the Aleutian Islands and returned to Petropavlovsk, in the Avacha Bay on Kamchatka, on 12 October. In the early summer of 1742

he sailed east again, but went only as far as Attu Island. He was back in Petropavlovsk in July and left for Okhotsk soon after. In November he arrived in Iakutsk. When the Kamchatka Expedition was suspended by Her Majesty's decree of 26 September 1743, C. and his detachment were transferred to Eniseisk.

C. returned to St. Petersburg in 1746 and was appointed director of the Marine Academy. Under his supervision, a group of naval officers prepared summarizing maps based on observations made during the Second Kamchatka Expedition. At the end of 1746, he transferred to Moscow for health reasons. Here he served as head of the Admiralty office. On 5 October 1747, he was promoted captain-commander. "But his health was undermined by scurvy and tuberculosis" (Kushnarev 1990, p. 170), and he died in Moscow on 24 May 1748.

Today a number of places carry C.'s name: A cape and a shoal at the entrance of the Bay of Tauisk in the Sea of Okhotsk; an island in the Gulf of Alaska; a cape on Attu Island; a cape on Baranov Island; a cape in the Gulf of Anadyrsk; an underwater mountain in the Pacific; a mountain in the Archipelago of Spitsbergen.

7   The name of the physician is Filipp Vilim [Wilhelm] Butskovskii. He was a German who had studied medicine in Berlin. According to Martyn Filippovich B., his son, B. had come to Russia from Brandenburg and entered into Russian service on his own request (The Historical Archive of the Museum of the Artillery, the Engineers, and the Signal Corps, fund 2, inv. ShGF, unit 4666, folio 157). B. participated in the voyage of the *Holy Gabriel* and received a pecuniary reward. In 1733 he was promoted senior physician and appointed to the Second Kamchatka Expedition (*Materialy po istorii russkogo flota*, 1879, Vol. VII, p. 518). On his return to St. Petersburg he served as staff-physician (shtab-lekar') in the Baltic Navy. In August 1761, during the Seven Years' War (1756-1763), B. participated in a successful landing operation at Kolberg in Pomerania, under Captain G.A. Spiridov (*Materialy* X, p. 609). In 1769, still a staff-physician in the Baltic Navy, he was in charge of medical preparations for the First Archipelagic Expedition of the Russian Navy, i.e., the expedition of Admiral Spiridov's squadron to the Mediterranean during the Russian-Turkish war 1768-1774. B. was married to M.P. Spangberg's daughter Anna. Their son, Martyn B., entered the military service in 1754. He participated in many military operations and gradually advanced from draftsman (in Russian: *konduktor*) to colonel, before being pensioned off in 1774, in St. Petersburg. He became the founder of a military dynasty. Generations of Butskovskiis served with distinction in the Russian army and fought in several wars, including the Patriotic War of 1812.

8   The name of the geologist is Grigorii Putilov. In Peter the Great's decree of 23 December 1724, he is mentioned among geologists who had been to Siberia and were back again (*Russkie ekspeditsii*, p. 33). P. went with Bering's command all the way to Kamchatka, but did not participate in the sea voyage to the straits in 1728 (*ibid.*, p. 68). Owing to ill-health, he remained at the outpost of Lower Kamchatsk. On the journey back to St. Petersburg, Putilov fell ill again and had to be left at Ilimsk (cf. the present journal, folio 72).

9   This "naval cadet" (in Russian: *gardemarin*) is the author of the journal, Piotr Chaplin. He was promoted midshipman in 1727, during the expedition, cf. the biographical note on p. 12 of the present volume.

10   The name of the quartermaster (*kvartirmejster*) is Ivan Borisov. After the completion of the expedition, he was recommended for promotion.

11   The name of the apprentice river craft and launch builder (in Russian: *botovogo i shljupochnogo dela uchenik*) is Fiodor Fedotovich Kozlov. He came from a family of "boyar's children" (*deti boiarskie*), i.e., petty noblemen in the military service. On 12 November 1710, he entered the School of Mathematics and Navigation. By 1714, when he had already taken geometry, trigonometry (including spheric trigonometry), navigation, astronomy and geography, it was found out that some of the schoolboys, including K., had not been taught arithmetic. They wrote a letter of complaint, saying that "we cannot be without arithmetic, since, without it, it is impossible to make drawings and solve other problems in the higher sciences" (RGAVMF, fund 176, inv. 1, unit 96, folio 817). Evidently, K. wished from the beginning to become a shipwright. The gap was filled, and on 1 March 1714 his name appears on a list of apprentices ready for practical work. When recruitment of personnel for the expedition began, it was necessary to find a shipwright or an apprentice capable of building boats with a deck. The Admiralty College recommended K.: "We have an apprentice launch builder Fiodor Kozlov who can build ships with or without a deck, from drafts". K. was appointed to the expedition, and four carpenters, quartermaster Borisov and 10 seamen were placed under his command.

On 4 April 1728, at Ushki on Kamchatka, he laid the foundation of the *Holy [Archangel] Gabriel* that was launched on 9 June and ready to sail already on 12 July. It was strong and reliable, with fine navigability. It completed several voyages in the Pacific Ocean, including a voyage to Japan in 1739, before it was demolished in 1755.

K. was also a member of the Second Kamchatka Expedition and traveled as far as to Okhotsk. The shipbuilding here, however, was already in the charge of a master launch builder (*shliupochnykh del master*). On Bering's recommendation, K. was then sent to Lake Baikal to build merchants' ships. He arrived in Irkutsk on 10 April 1739, where he made calculations and detailed descriptions for crafts of 55, 46 and 40 feet in length (*ibid.*, fund 216, inv. 1, unit 24, fol.s 243-257). The Irkutsk chancellery entrusted him with finding a convenient place to construct a craft 40 feet long (*ibid.*, unit 49, fol. 86). A craft of this size was completed in 1740 and delivered to the chancellery of the Voevoda of Selenginsk. K. then returned to St. Petersburg to rejoin the crew of the Admiralty on 18 September 1741 (*ibid.*, unit 52, fol.s 536-539). On 23 November 1756, already in retirement, he submitted an application to be enlisted again, but died on 3 December 1756 (*ibid.*, fund 212, inv. 3, unit 410, fol. 81).

12   The name of the apprentice mast maker (in Russian: *Machtmakerskii uchenik pervogo klassa*) is Ivan Endogurov. After the completion of the expedition, he was recommended for promotion.

13   Martin Pedersen Spangberg, in Russian *Martyn Petrovich Shpanberg*, was born on 31 December 1696 on the west coast of the Danish peninsula Jutland, probably near the present-day seaport Esbjerg, which had not yet been founded. On 1 November 1720, he entered the Russian service as lieutenant (*poruchik*), for five years and 2 additional years "at Peter the First's discretion". On 23 February 1721, he arrived in Russia, apparently with his young family, and pledged allegiance to the Russian Tsar. The Great Nordic War was over in August 1721, before Spangberg could join the fighting. On 28 May 1724, at the suggestion of the Admiralty College, he was appointed commander of the frigate *Saint Jacob* (*Sviatoi Iakov*). His two voyages to the German town Lübeck later that year opened regular passenger traffic, freight transportation and mail service between Kronstadt and Lübeck. In late December 1724, Spangberg got a new designation – as assistant to the leader of the first Kamchatka Expedition, Vitus Bering. In 1728, at Ushki on the Kamchatka River, he supervised the building of the seagoing vessel *Holy Gabriel* that sailed through the strait between Asia and America.

In 1733-1743 Spangberg participated in the Second Kamchatka Expedition, once again as one of Bering's assistants. (The second assistant was, as before, Chirikov). In 1738-1739, at the head of a squadron, Spangberg sailed from the north down along the Kuril Islands and reached Honshu, the main Japanese island. This was a remarkable event in the history of geographical discovery. In 1743, when the Second Kamchatka Expedition was suspended,

Spangberg and his detachment transfered to Tomsk. In 1745 he returned to St. Petersburg, where he was arrested and prosecuted for having left Siberia without authorization from the Admiralty College. After two years of investigations, he was sentenced to demotion for three months. However, in December 1747 he was restored in his former rank of captain of the first degree.

In 1749, Spangberg was sent to Arkhangel'sk in order to take the vessel *Varakhail* down to Kronstadt. On June 7, the ship capsized and 28 men drowned. Soon after, Spangberg was arrested, found guilty of the accident, and sentenced to the galleys for life. However, the Admiralty College did not sanction the sentence, and investigations continued for another two and a half years in St. Petersburg. In the end, Spangberg and the other officers were acquitted. The Admiralty College resolved that the shipwreck was "God's will". In December 1752, Spangberg was once again freed from arrest.

On 15 September 1761, Spangberg died in Kronstadt. He was buried with military honors (Fedorova 1998; Fedorova 2007a; Fedorova 2007b; *Martin Spangsberg* s.a.).

14 The two navigators enrolled in the first Kamchatka Expedition were George Morrison (*Dzhorzh Morison, Morisen*) and Richard Angel (*Engel', Enzel'*). Morrison died on 2 February 1727 at Iudoma Cross, where he had been left on the way to Okhotsk owing to ill-health (cf. the present journal, fol. 20 verso). Richard Angel did not participate in the voyage of the *Holy Gabriel*, but Bering recommended him for promotion in recognition of his work during the expedition (*Russkie ekspeditsii*, p. 91).

15 The mapping of the expedition begins here. See the chapters on mapmaking, pp. 270 and on navigation, pp. 276.

16 Chaplin frequently omits the first digit of the year.

17 The name of the chaplain (*ieromonakh*) was Treskin. The authorities in Tobol'sk had also offered to send a deacon (*d'iakon*) and a sexton (*ponomar'*), but Bering had refused (Kushnarev 1976, p. 25). This information was omitted from the American edition of Kushnarev's book (Kushnarev 1990).

18 The name of the commissar was Ivan Durasov. He arrived at Bering's request, to be the representative of the Siberian Governor and the cost accountant of the expedition (Kushnarev 1976, p. 25). This information was omitted from the American edition of Kushnarev's book (Kushnarev 1990). – In the age of Peter the Great, the word "commissar" meant an authorized agent of a state institution. Usually they would be the local agents of the state in remote outposts and surrounding territories. Here they were to a considerable extent their own masters, and acted without clear definitions of their powers and areas of responsibility. The rulers of the ostrogs would often be commissars. Commissar S. Bobrovskii, who had been designated to "manage" (*zavedyvat'*) the outposts of Verkhnekamchatsk (Upper Kamchatsk) and Bol'sheretsk, received in 1720 for the first time an instruction that defined his functions with regard to the administration of the ostrogs and the collection of tribute (Sgibnev 1869b, p. 103-104).

19 Again, Chaplin's abbreviations of the four Russian words will not be applied in our English translation.

20 The navigators of the expedition measured time by sandglass (Imbert 1992, p. 53).

21 The figure 37.67 versts is the dead-reckoning estimate of the straight line (via rhumb) distance traveled since leaving Tobolsk. 41.85 versts is the corrected estimate based on an astronomical observation for latitude. An example of how these estimates are made is given in the essay, "Navigation and Surveying," on pp. 276-278.

22 "Ostiaks", one of the peoples of western Siberia. Ostiaks is a Russian ethnonym. It was used from the 16th century until 1930, when it was officially replaced by the autoethnonym *Khanty*. Bering made the following comment on the Ostiaks in his report on the first Kamchatka Expedition: "Along the course that we followed from Tobolsk to Makovska live the Ostyaks, who were

formerly idolaters but through the labors of the Metropolitan Philophei of Tobolsk were converted to Christianity in 1715" (Golder 1968 /1922, vol. I, p. 12). In the All-Russian Census of 2002, the Khanty numbered 28,678. The Khanty language belongs to the Obsko-Ugrian group of Ural languages and is subdivided into three groups of dialects. In 1989, 60.8% of the ethnos considered the Khanty language their native tongue (Karabulatova 2005, pp. 277, 449).

23 The manuscript has "Thursday", when it should be "Saturday".

24 "helms or rudders", in the document *soptsy ili ruli*.

25 "the Tobol'sk Guberniia Chancellery": in Russian *Tobol'skaia gubernskaia kantseliariia*. From the late 16th to the early 18th century, Tobol'sk was the main administrative center of Siberia. Following the provincial reform of Peter the Great in 1708, Tobol'sk became the capital of the newly established Siberian Guberniia.

26 Chaplin left a space for the number of versts, but did not fill it in.

27 The manuscript has "Thursday" and "2". It should be either "Wednesday" and "2", or "Thursday" and "3".

28 "Rubashkino Reach", in Russian *Rubashkino plioso*. *Plioso* (плёсо), in modern Russian *plios* (плёс), means a straight stretch of a river between two bends, shoals, or islands.

29 One word was erased.

30 "Oslopovo Reach", in Russian *Oslopovo plioso*.

31 Chaplin left a space for the number of versts, but did not fill it in.

32 "The men", *sluzhiteli*.

33 "Gorodishche": the Russian word means a site of ancient settlement.

34 "supplies", in Russian *pripasy*.

35 "the Tobol'sk District Office", *Tobol'skaia zemskaia kontora*.

36 The Makovskii portage (*Makovskii volok*) leads from the Makovskii outpost on the Ket' River to the town of Eniseisk on the Enisei River.

37 Chirikov arrived at Eniseisk some two weeks after Chaplin and stayed there from 26 July to 12 August 1725, but neither of them recorded that at the same time the German naturalist Daniel Gottlieb Messerschmidt was in Eniseisk on his way back from Siberia. Evidently, this was not the kind of information that naval officers were expected to enter into their journals. The meetings between Messerschmidt, on the one hand, and Bering, Martin Spangberg and Filip Butskovskii of the Kamchatka Expedition on the other, are known to us only from the German scholar's diary in the St. Petersburg Branch of the Archives of the Russian Academy of Sciences (PbF ARAN). It has been published (Messerschmidt 1968, pp. 172-193).

38 "a post-horse order", in Russian *podorozhnaia*.

39 "for 2 vehicles with a guide", *na 2 podvody vozhiom* (на 2 подводы вожем).

40 "the Enisei District Office", *Eniseiskaia zemskaia kontora*.

41 "Rapids", in Russian *porog* (i.e., threshold). Bering gave the following explanation in his report on the First Kamchatka Expedition: "On the Tunguska there are three rapids (*poroga*) [...] In the rapids there are large submerged rocks across the whole width of the stream so that a boat can get through in only one or two places" (Golder 1922 /1968, vol. I, p. 12).

42 "Old versts". According to the standard textbook of Russian metrology, two differents versts were used in Russia towards the end of the 17th century: *Versta mezhevaia* (= 1000 sazhens) and *versta putevaia* (= 500 sazhens) (Kamentseva and Ustiugov 1975, p. 89). Since the shorter of the two versts prevailed in the 18th century, it is likely that Chaplin refers to the larger as the old one.

43 "Mur rapids", in Russian *Murskoi porog*.

44 "the stony Kashin shoal", in the document *Kashinu shiveru*. A *shivera* is a stony, shallow stretch of the riverbed. Bering gave the following explanation in his report on the first Kamchatka Expedition: "On the Tunguska there are three rapids [...] and several rocky shoals [...]; the shoals likewise [i.e., like the rapids] have

293

rocks above and below the surface but they are not very large. The shoals differ from the rapids in that the former have little water and continue for a verst or two at a stretch, which causes some trouble in getting over them" (Golder 1922 /1968, vol. I, p. 12).

45   For comparison, see Chirikov's description of Ilimsk, where he arrived on 26 September 1725. He wrote in his journal: "At 9 o'clock, having traveled 3 versts to the SSE, we arrived in the town of Ilimsk, which lies between mountains that are high, but sloping, some of them completely forest clad. The town itself stands on a slope that falls down to the very bank of the river. There are some 90 dwellings in and around the town" (RGAVMF, fund 913, inv. 1, unit 2, folio 107v).

This passage is followed by a detailed description of the Ilim River, the vegetation on its banks, its fish species, and the indigenous peoples that live along the Ilim. On 10 October, during his sojourn in Ilimsk, Chirikov observed an eclipse of the moon: "On this date, in the town of Ilimsk, which lies in latitude 56°37′ N, a lunar eclipse occurred, and at the beginning of it, the angle of the center of the moon was 43°10 ⅓′ on the eastern side of the meridian. Because of the clouds, it was impossible to observe the angle of any of the well-known stars, and so, using this observation, the time of the beginning of the lunar eclipse on the Ilimsk meridian was found to be 11:31:01 p.m., while on the St. Petersburg meridian the same eclipse began at 7:03:13 p.m., as the calendar indicates. From this follows that the difference of longitude from the St. Petersburg meridian to that of Ilimsk is 66°57′ or 4 hours, 27 minutes, 48 seconds, to the east. And according to the correct mercator map, the rhumb from St. Petersburg to Ilimsk is east-by-south 5°52′ to the east. The distance is 2,121 Italian miles (these are equal to the minutes of a terrestrial degree) or 3,694 Russian versts (one degree being equal to 104½ versts), by the shortest geographical distance, 33°52′ or 3,539 of the above-mentioned Russian versts. The angle of location from St. Petersburg to Ilimsk is 65°24′, that is east-north-east 2°6′ to the north". (ibid, folio 108). This was the first eclipse of the moon to be recorded with navigation instruments in Siberia, and the first attempt at a scientific calculation of the distance between St. Petersburg and Ilimsk. On 10 November 1730, less than a year after the return of the expedition, the French astronomer Joseph Nicolas Delisle gave a report to the Academy of Sciences in St. Petersburg on the determination of the longitude of Kamchatka, Tobol'sk, and Ilimsk. He discussed, among other things, Lieutenant Chirikov's calculation of the longitude of Ilimsk, and offered some sceptical comments (Hintzsche 2004, pp. 3-18).

46   "Rafting place", in Russian plotbishche.

47   "3 men as guides", 3-kh chelovek v podvody.

48   "Natives", in Russian inozemtsy (actually "foreigners"!)

49   For comparison, see Chirikov's description of Iakutsk, where he arrived on 16 June 1726. He wrote in his journal: "[…] we saw Iakutsk to NbW½W, and at 12 o'clock we arrived in the town of Iakutsk and took our stand opposite the monastery, where the other ships of our command were already standing, having arrived earlier with the Captain. Iakutsk is situated on the left bank of the Lena River and surrounded by lowlands to all sides for more than a hundred versts in both directions along the river, and across the river for about 30 versts, in some places even 40 or more, and beyond these lowlands stand rocky mountains with ample coniferous forest. The Russians in the town have about 300 dwellings, and near the town, there are 30,000 Iakuts, counting males only, that lead a nomad's life. Near Iakutsk, the Lena River branches out into three channels, thus creating two islands. However, when the water rises, the number of islands increases, since the river often leaves its usual bed and makes a new one by digging out sand. This is what many rivers do, when they pass through low, sandy territory, and they do it especially in the wintertime, under the pressure of ice. They have the following fish: small sturgeons,

sterlets, mouksuns [Salmo muxun], taimens [Hucho], whitefish, pikes, perches […] Ruffs are rare, but tasty.

Beyond Iakutsk further down the Lena River there is a small Russian settlement called Zhigany by the local indigenous population, from whom tribute [in Russian iasak] is collected for the state treasury. It takes 2½ weeks or more to reach it by boat from Iakutsk, and it is situated within the Polar circle, since those who have been there say that in the summer the sun does not go down for several days, and does not rise in the winter. And it takes about two weeks to sail from Zhigany to the mouth of the Lena River, using sails, too, when possible. The mouth of the river lies between N and W from Iakutsk. The banks of the Lena River between Ust-Kut and Iakutsk are not always covered with thicket. There are small mountains, which in some places rise with moderate steepness to a height of 100-150 sazhens, and they are forest-clad: pine, spruce, fir, larch, in some places also cedar, asp, not just birch and willow scrub. Fruit trees: bird cherry trees are rare, rowan, currant, black and red. The indigenous inhabitants are Tunguses and Iakuts, and for about 300 versts down from the Oliokma settlement, there are wandering Tunguses and Iakuts, but below these places there are only Iakuts, and the Iakuts wander up the Lena to and along the Vitim River."

On 17 June Chirikov continued: "Sunshine, strong gale from the west, and gloom due to fires. These are caused by the lack of rain. Generally, it rains very little in Iakutsk. For that reason grass is also scarce, and this summer there was none at all, except in places that had been inundated by the river. Likewise, in the winter, it snows only little, but the frost is fierce. The reason for the rare occurrence of rain and snow demands explanation, since it seems to contradict the climate (RGAVMF, fund 913, inv. 1, unit 2, folios 118v-119).

50   Either the day of the week or the date is wrong.

51   Either the day of the week or the date is wrong.

52   "Lama". The name may mean either Okhotsk or the Sea of Okhotsk. Chaplin explains (folio 13v) that Lama, or Lamo, is the Tungus word for the sea. At this time, the Sea of Okhotsk was known to Russians as Lamskoe more, i.e., the Lama Sea.

53   In June 1720, Aleksei Shestakov was appointed steward (prikazchik) in the Lower Kamchatsk outpost. Together with Commissar S. Bobrovskii he traveled from Iakutsk to Okhotsk. Here they were joined by the geodesists I.M. Evreinov and F.F. Luzhin, who had been sent out by Peter the Great to search for America (Cf. note XXX, NB: to folio 21v). They made it to Kamchatka on a freight vessel (lad'ia) navigated by the seafarer K. Moshkov. Here, however, Evreinov removed Shestakov from his post and made an inventory of his belongings. Shestakov returned to Iakutsk (Sgibnev 1869b, pp. 103-105). On 12 May 1726 Bering informed the chancellery of the Voevoda of Iakutsk that Shestakov was unable to come to assist the expedition, since "charges had been brought against him" (RGAVMF, fund 216, inv. 1, unit 88, folio 85v).

54   "to the chancellery of the Tobol'sk garrison", in the document v kantseliariiu Tobol'skogo gvarnizona.

55   "the boyar's son L'vov": this might be Ivan L'vov, a Iakutsk nobleman, the author of a map of the Chukotka Peninsula and Alaska. Following a sketch by the Cossack P.I. Popov from 1711, L.'s map shows Chukotka as "two-horned", America (the Big Land, in Russian Bolshaia zemlia) in the shape of a bent cucumber, and the two Diomedian Islands. Bering may have had this map with him, which would explain his interest in L. (Efimov 1964, map no. 55; Bolkhovitinov 1997, t. I, pp. 47-48, 56. Figure no. 7). Evidently, Bering did not meet L'vov, since there is no further mention of him in the journal.

56   Bering wanted Ivan Grigor'evich Shestakov attached to the expedition as a man "familiar with native customs" (Kushnarev 1990, p. 48). As noted by Chaplin, I.S. arrived in Okhotsk on 19 October 1726, and remained a member of Bering's expedition until

6 November 1726, when he "left for Taui to take up the post of commissary there, as ordered by the Iakutsk chancellery" (folios 14 verso and 15). I.S. was the nephew of the Iakutsk Cossack chief Afanasii Shestakov and eventually joined his uncle's expedition (cf. note 393, p. 305). On 1 September 1729, after Bering and his crew had left Okhotsk on their way back to St. Petersburg, I.S. sailed out from Okhotsk on the *Holy Gabriel* in order to map the rivers that empty into the Sea of Okhotsk and to explore the Kuril Islands. However, stormy weather forced him to anchor in the mouth of the Bol'shaia River on Kamchatka. Although I.S. crossed the Sea of Okhotsk another three times, he never succeeded in accomplishing his original task. On 9 September 1730 in Okhotsk, he surrendered the ship to the navigator Ia. Gens, who was in charge of sea transport for A. Shestakov's expedition.

57 "From [Iudoma] Cross", in the document *ot Kresta*. Chaplin usually abbreviates the name *Iudomskii krest* to *Krest* (the Cross). The name is explained by the fact that a cross had been erected there to indicate the Iudoma-Urak portage on the river route between Iakutsk and Okhotsk.

58 "[tribute] collector", in Russian *sborshchik*.

59 The monk Ignatii, whose worldly name was Ivan Petrovich Kozyrevskii, was the first to explore the Kuril Islands. He descended from a Polish prisoner of war who was exiled to Iakutsk in 1654 and had settled in Siberia. In 1700, Ivan's father had been sent on to Kamchatka, where he was killed by Koriaks in 1704. Shortly after, his two sons, Ivan and Piotr, enlisted as Cossacks. In 1711, K. assisted in the murder of Vladimir Atlasov and joined the insurgent cossacks. Later the same year he made a voyage to the two northernmost Kuril Islands, Shumshu and Paramushir, followed in 1713 by a second, better prepared voyage to the same islands. As a result, the inhabitants of Paramushir (Ainus and runaway Itelmens from Kamchatka) were forced to acknowledge Russian authority and pay tribute. Here he also met a trader from the distant island of Iturup. With the assistance of a translator K. was able to get information from him on nearly all of the Kuril Islands. He used this information to compile the first ever description of the entire string of islands. The original, however, has not survived, and the description is known only from abbreviated renderings (Polevoj 1982, p. 22). In 1715 the investigation of the murder of cossack chief Atlasov and his two companions was resumed. With the threat of reprisals hanging over his head, K. became a monk in 1717, but continued to be interested in the Kuril Islands. When Bering arrived in Iakutsk in 1726, he was given a letter from the Governor of Siberia, Prince M.V. Dolgorukov. It is likely that, together with this letter, he also received a report from K. himself, containing "A sketch of the Kamchatka Promontory and the islands in the sea" and "A description of the Japanese state" (*Russkie ekspeditsii*, pp. 46-52, 285). In the sketch, there are no images of the islands themselves, since K. did not know their configuration, but they are listed consecutively, with interesting explanations from which it may be inferred that the islands are independent from other nations and could be annexed to Russia. K. tried to interest Bering in the Kuril Islands and asked to join the expedition, but Bering refused. Chaplin delivered Bering's answer to the Governor's letter to the chancellery of the Voevoda of Iakutsk on 24 June 1726. On 4 July Bering wrote to the Governor, explaining that K. had not traveled beyond the first three islands, and that K. had received his information on "the Japanese islands" from shipwrecked Japanese sailors who had been taken into custody on Kamchatka. "And concerning his further statement, we consider that we will have no help from him on our expedition, and we do not ask to have him with us. Besides, Kozyrevskii is ill" (RGAVMF, fund 216, inv. 1, unit 88, folios 90, 94v). In 1727 Kozyrevskii became a member of A. Shestakov's expedition. Its intention was to reach the Kuril Islands directly from Iakutsk, by sailing down the Lena River into the Arctic Ocean and from there into the Pacific. However, his vessel, *Evers*, was crushed by ice on the lower Lena. Untiring, Kozyrevskii continued his struggle for the annexation of the Kuril Islands. Without permission, he traveled through Tobol'sk and Moscow to St. Petersburg, where he met the young historian G.F. Müller. Trying to improve Kozyrevskii's situation, Müller wrote an article on his achievements, which was published in *Kalendar' ili mesiatseslov istoricheskii na 1732 g.* (The Historical Calendar for 1732). But it was all to no avail. In late 1730, the monk was arrested for his connection with the murders in 1711, and in January 1732, he was sentenced to death. His appeal for pardon remained unanswered. On 2 December 1734, Kozyrevskii died in the damp underground prison of the Preobrazhenskii Office, where he was kept in manacles and shackles. For more details, cf. Polevoi 1982.

60 "bursar". The Russian word is *rent-mester* (рент-местер), a term introduced in 1719, when Peter the Great attempted to reorganize local government on the Swedish model. Cf. Hughes 1998, p. 117.

61 "46 servitors were sent", in the document *Prislano [...] sluzhilykh 46 chelovek*. Later in the same passage the same men are referred to as "the arrived servitors", in Russian *prislannym k nam sluzhivym*. This shows that Chaplin does not distinguish between the terms *sluzhilyi* and *sluzhivyi* (both translated as *servitor*).

62 "tribute": the Russian word is *iasak*, derived from the Tatar. It was a tax in goods imposed by the Russian government on the non-Russian peoples of the Volga Region and Siberia. In Siberia, iasak was collected from the 16th to the early 20th century. The size and kind of the tribute was determined seperately for each tribe or nation. Tribes of hunters usually paid in fur. The Iakuts paid according to the number of cattle they owned.

63 "to the provincial center", in the document "v pravintsyiu" (в правинцыю), i.e., most likely, to Irkutsk. Following the provincial reform of 1719, Russia's old provinces (*gubernii*) were divided into 50 smaller provinces (*provintsii*). The Siberian Guberniia was divided into five provinces, including the Irkutsk Province (*Irkutskaia provintsiia*), under which Iakutsk belonged.

64 "servicemen and servitors", in the document *sluzhitelei and sluzhivykh liudei*. The passage illustrates that Chaplin distinguished between these two categories of personnel. Cf. note 61 above.

65 "for the horses", *za podvody*.

66 It has been suggested that in connection with the dispatch of the expedition from Iakutsk, the local authorities paid the Iakuts "much less than previously" (Kushnarev 1990, p. 50).

67 According to Sgibnev, commissary Iakov' Makhnachevskii (or Mokhnachevskii) was a nobleman (*dvorianin*). In 1726 he was instructed to go to Kamchatka to collect tribute and to take charge of the two outposts Upper and Lower Kamchatsk on the Kamchatka River. He was given a clerk by the name Sudakov and 20 cossacks to assist him. Having already set out from Iakutsk, he took 70 packhorses from the Iakuts instead of the prescribed 6. Bering, being in need of horses himself, reported on this, and the Iakutsk chancellery discharged Mokhnachevskii from the mission and appointed the cossack lieutenant (*piatidesiatnik*) Tarabukin in his place (Sgibnev 1869b, p. 111). See also note 79.

68 "from the bursar's store", *ot renternoi*.

69 "Official decrees to the outposts". On Bering's request, the voevoda in Iakutsk issued decrees to the outposts of Okhotsk, Bol'sheretsk, Upper Kamchatsk, Lower Kamchatsk and even Anadyrsk. The local administrators were instructed as follows: "Upon receipt of this, Her Imperial Highness' ukaz [decree], you, the local administrators, upon the request of Navy Captain Bering en route, are to supply him with all available goods and provisions for his departure, with all assistance in building ships, and with everything relating to unwritten amendments to his instructions, so that he may set out more conveniently and quickly... Harsh punishment and fines may be anticipated for anyone not carrying out the provisions of this ukaz" (Kushnarev 1990, p. 52).

70 "A man knowledgable about rivers". On Bering's request, the boyar's son Timofei Antipin, who knew the settlements along

the water route from Iakutsk to Okhotsk, was ordered to bring 120 horses to a place that Spangberg could reach by water. The cargo could then "be transferred from there to Okhotsk on these horses" (Kushnarev 1990, p. 52). The place chosen was the Amga River, cf. Chaplin's entry for 15 August 1726.

71 "tribal princeling", in Russian *kniaziok* (князёк).

72 "the distinguished princeling Nirgai", in the document *k lutchemu kniaz'ku Nirgaiu* (к лутчему князьку Ниргаю).

73 "built a corduroy road": in Russian *gatili gat'*.

74 "horsetail": the Russian name of the plant is *khvoshch* (хвощ), its Latin name *Equisetum*.

75 "with a census list": in Russian *s skazkoiu podushnoiu*.

76 "26 workers", *rabotnikov 26 chelovek*.

77 "Koshka": The spit in Okhotsk harbour. The word has been used in Northern Russia, in Siberia and on Kamchatka to designate a bank of sand and pebble; or a flat littoral at the foot of a mountain; or a tongue of land between the sea and a river running parallel to the shore, cf. *Slovar' russkikh narodnykh govorov*, vyp. 15, pp. 149-150. Amusingly, the word is identical with the Russian word for "cat", but its origin is different. The etymologist Max Vasmer suggests it has been borrowed from a Finno-Ugric language.

78 Cf. note 393, p. 305.

79 "Kamchadal", one of the indigenous peoples of Kamchatka. *Kamchadal* is a Russian ethnonym, the corresponding autoethnnonym being *Itelmen*. The "Kamchadal commissary" was a Russian official responsible for collecting tribute from the Kamchadals. Commissary Tarabukin and his command of presumably 20 cossacks had to wait in Okhotsk for almost a year for a shipping opportunity to Kamchatka, where they were to collect tribute. Coinciding with Bering in Okhotsk for this period, they suffered from shortage of provisions and from hard work for the Kamchatka expedition (Sgibnev 1869b, p. 111).

80 Chaplin left an empty space for the number of kopecks, but never filled it in.

81 The *kuklianka* and the *parka* are types of fur garments with a hood used by Siberia's northern natives. Parkas were usually made from reindeer skin, while kukliankas in Kamchatka were mostly made from dog skin.

82 The journey of Spangberg's detachment from Iakutsk to Okhotsk is the most tragic page in the history of the First Kamchatka Expedition. The details are known from Spangberg's later report to Bering (*Russkie ekspeditsii*, pp. 56-59). Spangberg set out from Iakutsk on 7 July 1726 with 13 doshchaniks loaded with provisions and the heaviest equipment (anchors, cannons, sails). He had 203 men with him on the vessels. Sailing along the rivers, they often had to tow the vessels with ropes. Already in August, his men began to desert, and soon desertions became almost daily events. On 2 September the detachment entered the mouth of the Iudoma, a shallow and swift river with many rapids. On the worst stretches, it took the crews of four ships to haul one ship upstream. They proceeded in this way until 13 September, when they could not advance any further: The river was getting increasing shoaly and carried pieces of ice. Spangberg sent 14 sick men back to Iakutsk on a small boat and then ordered the reloading of two ships with the bulky equipment that could not possibly be transported over land on pack horses, and another five with other necessary equipment. His plan was to push on with these seven ships as far as possible, and leave the larger doshchaniks with most of the provisions on the Iudoma, guarded by the navigator Morison. Spangberg himself proceeded with the two ships and the heavy equipment and made it as far as to the Gorbeia River, where he arrived on 22 September. Eventually it became necessary to leave also these two ships and parts of the cargo. The journey continued by sleds. By 4 November, the men had made 100 birch wood sleds that were pulled by the men themselves. Snowstorms and hard frost set in, and provisions were running short, the men fell sick, ran away, began to die. On 25 October, 40 sleds were left behind at the Povorotnaia River. On that date, Spangberg sent a man ahead to Bering with a report on the condition of the detachment and with a request for help. On December 1, they ran out of provisions, and the Lieutenant distributed his own supplies of wheat flour, meat, peas, and groats among the men, but to little avail. By 19 December, there were only 59 reasonably healthy crew members left. On 19 January Spangberg wrote in his report: "Until the 29th [of December] we proceeded with considerable privation, in a fierce freeze, with no provisions, so on the way we ate whatever we came across – dead horses and every bit of leather." (*ibid.*, p. 59; Kushnarev 1990, p. 62). The first help arrived on 31 December, but it took until 16 January for the last men in Spangberg's detachment to reach Okhotsk.

83 "fish flour", in Russian *porsa*. In Eastern Siberia, it was produced by pounding dried fish (*Slovar' russkikh narodnykh govorov*, vyp. 30, p. 89).

84 "state monies", in the document *denezhnuiu kaznu*.

85 "the chaplain": in Russian, *ieromonakh*, i.e., a celibate Orthodox priest.

86 "727": in the manuscript *726*, by an obvious slip of the pen.

87 "orderly": in Russian *denshchik*.

88 "Articles of War": in Russian *artikul*. This was the commonly used short name for Peter the Great's Military Statute of 1716. The part of it read aloud during the review at Iudoma Cross is likely to have included article 29, which states that "it is an officer's job to command and the subordinate's to be obedient" (Hughes 1998: 77).

89 "at the crosses of Bobrovskii and Shestakov", in Russian *u krestov Bobrovskago i Shestakova*. Cf. note 53, p. 294.

90 Chaplin placed the last part of the period in brackets. It was only the following day that his detachment reached the sick men, cf. his entry for Sunday, 12 March.

91 Fiodor Fiodorovich Luzhin (1695-1727), a geodesist, descended from the family of a clergyman. On 12 March 1710 he entered the School of Mathematics and Navigation. He graduated in 1714 and transferred to the Marine Academy. In 1718, when navigators were wanted "with a good knowledge of geography, and of map making to describe the territories of Siberia", Luzhin was chosen to carry out Peter the Great's secret instruction, together with I.M. Evreinov, who had gone through the same education. They were to "travel to Kamchatka and further, as shown to you, to describe these places: Do America and Asia come together?" (*Russkie ekspeditsii*, p. 30). The vague formulation of the instructions still generates discussions over the real purpose and tasks of the mission, cf. *ibid.*, p. 284; Fisher 1977, pp. 57-62.
Evreinov's and Luzhin's expedition left from Bol'sheretsk on Kamchatka on 22 May 1721 on the *lod'ia* (a type of cargo boat) *East* (*Vostok*) and headed for the Kuril Islands. They had reached the fifth island (or the sixth, according to some sources), when the vessel lost its anchor. With fair wind and a torn sail, the travelers made it back to the mouth of the Bolshaia River. As a result of the voyage, the geodesists produced a map of Kamchatka and the Kuril Islands, with an explanatory catalogue. This was the first representation of the Kuriles based on instruments and mathematical calculations.
In 1722 Luzhin served in Tobol'sk. In 1723-1724 he made a description of the territories of the Irkutsk Province. At Bering's invitation, he joined the First Kamchatka Expedition. As a member of Spangberg's crew, he helped to transport supplies from Iakutsk to Okhotsk. On the way he fell ill and was left behind at Iudoma Cross, where he died on 11 March 1727.

92 "Her Majesty's property", in Russian *kazna*.

93 Turchaninov's denunciation of Bering and subsequent arrest illustrates how the system of secret political investigations worked in 18th-century Russia. If a person knew of a crime against the tsar, he was obliged, under the threat of capital punishment, to inform the authorities about it. He could start a legal procedure

by uttering the formula "the sovereign's word and deed" (*gos-udarevo slovo i delo*), or something equivalent, in the presence of a witness. The formula implied that the speaker wanted to bring a charge of high treason against someone. As described by Chaplin, Turchaninov reported to Lieutenant Spanberch in the presence of a witness that he "knew of a grave matter concerning the Captain", that is, he claimed knowledge of a serious crime committed by Bering. In such situations, the authorities were to arrest the informer and without further interrogation send him on to the Preobrazhenskii Office in St. Petersburg, which was until 1729 the institution authorized to investigate high treason. Spanberch reported to Bering on the event and dispatched Turchaninov to St. Petersburg, guarded by two soldiers (cf. Chaplin's entries for 22, 26 April and 20 July 1727, folios 23v, 24 and 28).

On 14 July 1727, Bering reported the event to the Admiralty College. The Captain explained that he had sent a sergeant along with Turchaninov, to make sure the latter did not run away or harm himself on the way, because "I am innocent of high treason, and want to have my innocence of all allegations proved through an investigation" (RGAVMF, fund 216, inv. 1, unit 110, folios 25v-26). What Turchaninov wished to tell the secret chancellery about Bering remains unknown. Kushnarev believes it "pertained to some abuse on Bering's part", and that it might explain the following note in the journal of the Admiralty College, dated 3 December 1728: "An ukaz is to be sent to the Tobol'sk governor, ordering him to have the baggage of Captain Bering, who is with the Siberian Expedition, all his trunks and portmanteaus brought from Iakutsk to Tobol'sk under seal. Once the luggage has arrived at your office, have the fiscal open it and make a list of the contents. When this is done, put the things back into the trunks and portmanteaus, close them again with the seals of the governor and the fiscal, and keep them safe and dry, so that no harm is done to them. But do not return the baggage to the Captain until you receive instructions from the Privy Council or a decree from the Senate". (Kushnarev 1990, p. 68; *Materialy* 1875, Vol. V, pp. 680-681; for a detailed account of the system of political investigations in 18th century Russia, see Anisimov 1999).

94 "all of them [state] servitors", in Russian *iz sluzhivykh*. The term shows that the four artisans were local Siberian workmen, as distinct from the Admiralty men of Bering's own crew.

95 "Her Majesty's property from Tauisk", i.e., the tribute collected by the Tauisk outpost, most likely furs. Cf. note 62, p. 295. Tauisk was some 300 km further up the Siberian east coast from Okhotsk, near present-day Magadan.

96 "(to issue)": in Russian *o vydache*. In the document, Chaplin put these two words in brackets as a substitution for the preceding two words, "to send", in Russian *o posylke*.

97 "among them", in the document *k nim*. The pronoun refers to the men at the mouth of the Urak, cf. Chaplin's entry for the next day, 4 June.

98 On 11 November 1726, thirty horses had been sent from the Okhotsk outpost to the Inia River, where their chances for survival seemed better, cf. Chaplin's entry for that date (folio 15 verso).

99 The sale of the deceased navigator Morrison's property started some three weeks earlier, on May 22, cf. Chaplin's entry for that date, folio 25.

100 "to the supervisor", in Russian *zakashchiku* (закащику). In 18th-century Siberia this word designated the Russian head of an outpost, cf. *Slovar' russkogo jazyka XVIII veka*, vyp. 7, p. 231.

101 "valerian", in the document *mautu* (мауту), probably a misspelling of the genitive singular of the herb name *maun*. Other Russian names for the species *Valeriana officinalis* include *valeriana* and *koshach'ia trava*.

102 "to change hostages", in the document *dlia peremeny amanatov*. The Russians in the Siberian outposts received hostages (*amanaty*) from the surrounding indigenous peoples as a safety measure and a guarantee for the paying of *iasak* tribute. Normally, the hostages were replaced from time to time.

103 "18 pounds of tool steel", in the document *ukladu 18 funtov*. Tool steel (*uklad*) was a type of iron with a reduced content of carbon.

104 "This order was received on the 5th". The manuscript shows that this information was inserted later. It is likely that Chaplin first received an oral order, which was then followed by a written one on 5 July.

105 In 1727 all expedition members were gathered in Okhotsk to get ready for the crossing to Kamchatka. Therefore, it is possible to compare journal entries by Chaplin and Chirikov for the same dates at the same place. Chirikov's entry for 4 July reads: "Dark, wind from between S and E. Soldier Trifonov arrived with cattle, all healthy, except that at my written orders he gave one bull to Corporal Anashkin and the servicemen that went with him. The 5 horses [in Russian, *5 podvod*] given to him also arrived intact, and so did a pair of bags of flour" (RGAVMF, fund 913, inv. 1, unit 2, folio 129r).

106 Chirikov's entry for 5 July reads: "Dark, wind variable and calm" (*ibid.*).

107 Chirikov's entry for 6 July reads: "Dark, and at night rain with thunder. The quartermaster arrived, bringing with him 100 pairs of bags of flour on 120 horses. 3 horses had fallen on the way" (*ibid.*).

108 "SWW": in the document *ZWW*. The English text reproduces in translation the error in writing of the original document (cf. Key to bearings, p. 17).

109 "with the property of Her Imperial Majesty", in the document *s kaznoiu eia imperatorskogo velichestva*. Property refers to the *iasak* tribute, paid in furs by the natives of Kamchatka and now being brought from Bol'sheretsk to Okhotsk by two commissaries. Cf. note 95.

110 The two returning commissaries were Stepan Trifonov, who had been appointed in 1724 to collect tribute on Kamchatka, and one of his assistants, possibly Piotr Kariakin. Leaving Okhotsk in the autumn of 1725, they had strict orders to deliver the tribute in Iakutsk in 1726, but stayed in Kamchatka for an extra year. The absence of their vessel was one of the unfortunate circumstances that forced Bering to winter in Okhotsk 1726-1727. After the commissars' arrival, Bering interrogated them and their seafarers about their long absence (Sgibnev 1869b, pp. 108-111; Sgibnev 1869c, p. 13; *Russkie ekspeditsii*, pp. 62, 289; Kushnarev 1990, pp. 72-73).

111 "An old vessel". The newly arrived vessel was a *lod'ia* (cargo boat). Its keel had been laid in Okhotsk in 1720, but it was finished only in 1723 (A.P. 1851, p. 10; Sgibnev 1869c, pp. 11-14).

112 Chirikov's entry for 10 July reads: "Clear weather with few clouds. Wind variable from S by E and W. In the evening dark. Today a worker, Vasilei Novokreshchenoi [i.e., Vasilei the Newly Baptized], who belongs to the Iakut nobleman Trifonov, arrived. He brought with him 10 pairs of bags of flour that he transported not on the Iakuts' horses [*vmesto iakutskikh podvod*], but on the horses of his master, as agreed with the Iakuts. The said Novokreshchenoi had been sent from Aldan with the soldier Vyrodov" (RGAVMF, fund 913, inv. 1, unit 2, folio 129r).

113 "A Cossack lieutenant", in Russian *piatidesiatnik*, an officer in command of 50 Cossacks.

114 Founded on 11 April 1717 by edict of Peter the Great, the Admiralty College was the supreme collegiate body of the navy, responsible for its military operations, its administration and finances. It consisted of a president, a vice-president, and a number of fellows. An attorney general (*prokuror*), an auditor general (*general-auditor*), and a secretary general (*ober-sekretar'*) were attached to it. Its first president was Count F.M. Apraksin (1717-1728). The vice-president normally conducted day-to-day business. The Admiralty College was subordinate to the Senate. From 1802, it

was an advisory body under the Navy Secretary, and in 1828 it ceased to exist altogether.

Bering sent regular reports to the Admiralty College on the progress of the Kamchatka Expedition, but Chaplin's journal rarely mentions them.

115 "Soldier Vyrodov". Boris Vyrodov, of the Tobol'sk Regiment, had participated in the expedition of Evreinov and Luzhin (cf. note 91). In a letter to the Tobol'sk Guberniia Chancellery of 19 April 1725, Bering requested that Vyrodov be sent to the Kamchatka Expedition (*Russkie ekspeditsii*, p. 44).

116 "Wood blocks and butts", in the document *plakhi i kokory*. A wood block (*plakha*) is a section of the stem split in halves. *Kokora* is a butt section with a bent root.

117 "Attached a wale", in the document *pribivali barkhout*.

118 Chaplin left a space for the number of servicemen, but never filled it in.

119 The four seafarers (*morekhody*) that went with Chirikov were Andrei Bush, Ivan Butin, Kondratii Moshkov, and Nikifor Treska. For more information on Moshkov, see Konstantin Shopotov's article "Kondratii Moshkov: Navigator in the North Pacific", in Frost 1992, pp. 151-157.

120 Chirikov's entry for 21 August reads: "Intermittent sunshine, wind from SE, in the evening heavy wind NWbW and clearing up. The Captain wrote an order to the apprentice mast maker Endogurov, concerning what he should do after our departure, namely: to strive to bring [everything that had been left along the Iudoma] to the Okhotsk outpost, to produce salt and prepare meat as a supplement to the servicemen's provisions, to get to Kamchatka, and other things concerning him." (RGAVMF, fund 913, inv. 1, unit 2, folio 129v).

121 Chirikov's entry for 22 August reads: "Clear weather, heavy wind. At 8 o'clock p.m. our commander, the Captain, went on board the new ship and having cast off, dropped anchor on the Okhota River, and ordered me to embark the old ship for our voyage to Kamchatka, to the mouth of the Bol'shaia River. Therefore, at 9 o'clock I also cast off on the old ship and dropped anchor. At 12 o'clock the Captain and we proceeded from the mouth of the Okhota to SEbE, with the island in the mouth of the river on our left side. We sighted the mouth of the Inia River 7 versts away to NNE. At 4 o'clock we sighted Cape Shalkapskoi to EbN 15 versts away" (*ibid*, folio 130r).

122 "SE¾", in the document *ZO¾*. The English text reproduces in translation the error in writing of the original document (cf. Key to bearings, p. 17).

123 Actually Chaplin used the Latin letter D as a ditto mark. Like the English *do.*, it stands for "the above repeated" and is an abbreviation of the old Italian *ditto*.

124 "storm-clouds", *tuchno*.

125 "Events occurring": in the document *Sluchai prikliuchaiushchiia*.

126 "from 6 o'clock", *s nachala 7-go chasa*.

127 "After 9 o'clock", *V nachale 10-go chasa*.

128 Chaplin uses the symbol *<* as an abbreviation for the Russian word *ugol* (angle, corner, cape, or point).

129 G.W. Steller, who was in Kamchatka 1740-1741 and again 1742-1744, has described the summer dwellings of the Itelmen natives: "All summer long, people live in dwellings the Cossacks call balagans. Each family or head of household has its separate balagan because it is easier to build and maintain than the winter dwellings and does not require lighting or heating [...]. The balagans are polygonal dwellings, built like pyramids with a wide bottom and pointed top, standing on nine to twelve posts secured with thongs. The upper structure consists of poles that are tied together at the top and covered entirely with straw.[...] These balagans are built so close together that a person can get from one to another on bridges or planks. [...] These birdhouses are also occasionally blown over by the wind. People who live in balagans for the first time get dizzy because balagans rock constantly like cradles, especially in strong winds." (Steller 2003, pp. 164-165).

130 "kaiurs": in Russian *kaiury*, sing. *kaiur* or *kaiura*. In Kamchatka and Northeastern Siberia, a dog-team or reindeer driver, as explained in the Glossary. The word Chaplin offers as an explanation, *podvodchik*, means a driver, a coachman or – in this case – a ferryman.

131 "to the habitation of Ga[na]lin", in Russian *do Ga[na]lina zhilishcha*.

132 "in 14 dugouts or boats", in the document *v 14 batakh ili lotkakh*.

133 "a few light clouds", *malosvetlye oblaka*.

134 "the administrator of the outpost": in Russian *zdeshnego astrogu upravitel'*. The name of the administrator of the Bol'sheretsk outpost was Aleksei Eremeev. His proper title was *zakazchik* (Kushnarev 1990, p. 77).

135 "From about 8 o'clock", in the document *chasu z 9-go*.

136 "from the seafarer": that is, from the seafarer who had been sent to the Opala River on 16 Dec. 1727, see folio 37.

137 "toion", the Iakut word for a chieftain, explained by Chaplin as "best man", in Russian *lutchei muzhik*. After the Russian conquest of Siberia, it became the standard designation of native leaders of clans or tribes in northern Siberia, including Kamchatka. The Russians made wide use of the toions in their administration of the native population.

138 "Eb", in the document *Ot*, an incomplete indication of wind direction, cf. Key to bearings, p. 17 in the present volume.

139 The Itelmen language and its dialects were first described by Georg Wilhelm Steller, cf. Steller 2003, pp. 5-6, 161.

140 "after midnight sunshine", i.e., sunshine in the morning and/or before noon. Chaplin was still counting nautical days, from midday to midday.

141 "9 tradespeople's sleds", in the document *9 podvod ot posatskikh*. Tradespeople (*posadskie liudi*) were a category of free townspeople that made a living from trade or crafts.

142 "a natives' outpost", in the document *inozemcheskoi ostrog*. Here the word *outpost/ ostrog* is used about natives' settlements.

143 "the yurt of the toion was very big". In this case, the word *yurt* (in Russian *iurta*) refers to an Itelmen winter dwelling, that is, a large pit dug into the ground and with a roof covered by the excavated dirt, as described in detail by Steller. "In large villages, there are several subterranean winter dwellings, but the one where the *toyon* [headman, leader] lives and guests and travelers are lodged is the largest and best furnished and the one in which everybody gathers on holidays and during winter evenings in order to conserve fuel." (Steller 2003, p. 164).

144 Chaplin and Chirikov sailed from Okhotsk to Bol'sheretsk on the same ship (the old one!), but on Kamchatka their ways again parted for some months, and they arrived at the same places at different times. Chirikov arrived at Lower Kamchatsk on 30 May and made the following entry in his journal: "By 2 o'clock I arrived at the Lower Kamchatsk outpost, and from there I sailed down to Kliuchi, which is situated some 7 versts to SbE. Here our commander, the Captain, and the other servicemen of our crew have their quarters. The Kliuchi settlement has a church devoted to Saint Nikolai and about 20 households for people of all ranks. Gradually, however, all inhabitants of Lower Kamchatsk, which has about 60 Russian dwellings, will move to Kliuchi, because this place is better fit for habitation. The outpost is situated among low grounds, and every year when the water rises, the Kamchatka River floods the whole settlement for two or three weeks. During that time, the inhabitants have to use boats to get to one another or, if necessary, to other places" (RGAVMF, fund 913, inv. 1, unit 2, folio 137v).

145 "iukola", fish, usually salmon, dried in the open air, used widely in Siberia for winter provisions. In Kamchatka, the head and backbone of the fish were often given to sled dogs.

146 "5 poods of cod-liver oil", *5 pud ryb'ego zhiru*.

147 "With plenty of vodka", in the document *vinom dovol'no*. In the 18th century, the Russian word *vino* normally meant *vodka*, and only rarely wine (*Slovar' russkogo iazyka XVIII veka*, vol. 3).

148 A substantial part of the fur tribute collected on Kamchatka was shipped from the Bol'sheretsk outpost to Okhotsk on the mainland. While still in Okhotsk, Chaplin noted on 20 July 1727 the arrival of a boat with fur tribute from Kamchatka (folio 27 verso).

149 "stickleback": in the document *khakhalcha*, which is the local Kamchatkan name for the threespine stickleback (*Gasterosteus aculeatus*), a small fish that was periodically caught in large numbers in the rivers of eastern Kamchatka. The origin of the word is unclear (Vasmer 1953-1958). Steller, however, notes that it is called "*chakal* in Itelmen" and "along the Kamchatka River *chakaltsh*". He named it *obularius* (from a small Greek coin), because it has "two silvery scales like two small silver coins" behind the head on either side. "When these fish are boiled, they make such a tasty, rich broth that it could be mistaken for chicken broth, and it is therefore cooked by the food-loving Cossacks and Itelmen only for the broth" (Steller 2003, pp. 109-110).

150 "For the skilled workers", *dlia masterovykh liudei*.

151 "The place is called Shchioki etc." The Russian word *shchioki* (щёки) means *cheeks*, but in Eastern Siberia it may also denote "steep rocky banks that narrow a river from both sides" (Vasmer).

152 "from the Lieutenants": that is, from Chirikov at Upper Kamchatsk and Spanberch at the ship building site.

153 "Cape Kronovskii": in the document "Kronovskoi ugol". The Kronotsk Peninsula (*Poluostrov Kronotskii*) protrudes some 100 km down the coast from the mouth of the Kamchatka River.

154 Chaplin left an empty space for the number of native boatmen brought by the soldier, but never filled it in.

155 "from about 3 p.m.", *chasu s 4-go popoludni*.

156 Chaplin left an empty space for the date, but never filled it in.

157 "2 packs of nerpa or seal blubber": in the document "2 kupa zhiru nerpich'ego ili tiulenego". By adding "ili tiulenego" ("or seal"), Chaplin is explaining the local Siberian name for seal, *nerpa*, by its more usual Russian synonym *tiulen'*, rather than distinguishing between two species of seal. Some 15 years later, Steller, in his information on Kamchatka, found it necessary to give the same explanation: "The seals, called *nerpi* in Siberian and *tiuleni* in Russian, are frequently found around the rivers where they are caught in large numbers by various means and are very useful." (Steller 2003, p. 80)

158 "2½ buckets of vodka": a bucket is an old Russian measure of capacity (= 12,299 litres).

159 "breechings [?]": The Russian word in the document is partly illegible, but could possibly be "briuki", the plural of *briuk*, a short, thick rope with hooks at the end, for fastening a canon to the shipboard.

160 On 5 July 1728, when Chaplin returned from Kliuchi to Lower Kamchatsk, Bering held a council in Lower Kamchatsk with Spanberg and Chirikov. They discussed a number of problems in connection with the imminent voyage of the *Holy Gabriel*. If the *Fortuna* arrived from Bol'sheretsk in time, should it go with them? The answer was no. Bering explained the decision to go in only one ship with the poor condition of *Fortuna's* rigging and the lack of time to make repairs. Actually, the *Fortuna* arrived on the next day (cf. note 161). They also decided that the attendants, who would be at sea, should be paid in advance. The chaplain was to be sent back to Tobol'sk because of lack of space on board, while the ailing geodesist Putilov was to remain in Lower Kamchatsk. Three soldiers were left behind to safeguard the expedition's materiel and provisions. Significantly, the route that the ship was to follow was not discussed at the council (*Russkie ekspeditsii* 1984, p. 67; Kushnarev 1990, pp. 87-90).

161 The vessel was the *Fortuna*, which had left Bol'sheretsk 20 June (Kushnarev 1990, p. 89).

162 Chaplin left an empty space for the number of poods of flour and of rusks, but never filled it in.

163 Chaplin left an empty space for the number of sazhens, but never filled it in.

164 "the spit or tongue of land", *sredi koshki ili kosy*.

165 "In all": The sum is not indicated.

166 "The cape we have to pass", in the document *ugol zemli, mimo kotorago itit'*. A part of the southwestern coast of the Kamchatsk Peninsula (*Kamchatskii poluostrov*), near the mountain Kamennaia (847 m) (Sopotsko, pp. 60, 62).

167 "Leeway", in the document *sklonenie ot vetra*.

168 Between 7 and 8 p.m., Bering crossed the latitude of Cape Kamchatka (*Mys Kamchatskii*), thus leaving the Kamchatsk Bay (*Kamchatskii zaliv*) and entering the Bering Sea (Sopotsko, p. 60).

169 Throughout the voyage, the longitudinal position of the *Holy Gabriel* was determined as the difference from the longitude of the Lower Kamchatsk outpost, in this case 1°3′ to E, corresponding to 163°33′ E longitude. According to Sopotsko, this particular position of the ship was miscalculated by 19′, its correct longitudinal position being 163°14′ E (Sopotsko, pp. 63, 65).

170 "Newly emerged cape": According to Sopotsko, p. 61, this was Cape Kamchatka (the southernmost point of Kamchatsk Peninsula), sighted at a distance of 8 miles. On the concluding map of the expedition, Cape Kamchatka was correctly placed at 56°N latitude. Here and later in the journal, Chaplin used a symbol in the form of an acute angle with an arc inside as a substitute for the Russian word *ugol*, which means a corner, an angle or, as here, a salient point on the coast, a cape.

171 "A newly appeared [cape]": Cape Nos (*Mys Nos*) on the east coast of the Kamchatsk Peninsula (Sopotsko, pp. 62, 65).

172 "Another new one": Cape Rify (*Mys Rify*) on the east coast of the Kamchatsk Peninsula (Sopotsko, pp. 62, 65).

173 "land, extending to WNW": The coastline of the Ozernoi Peninsula (*Ozernoi poluostrov*), extending from Cape Ozernoi to Cape Nizkii (Sopotsko, pp. 64, 66).

174 "A mountain white with snow": Mount Krysha (*Gora Krysha*), a peak in the Stolovye Mountains, which extend between Cape Ozernoi and Cape Nizkii, about two miles behind the shoreline. Mount Krysha is 669 m high and snow-covered also in the summer time (Sopotsko, pp. 64, 66).

175 "Illustrious place on the shore", in Russian *znamenitoe na beregu mesto*. This is Cape Ozernoi, the eastern extremity of the Ozernoi Peninsula. It may seem "illustrious" because it marks the northern entrance to the Ozernoi Bay and, at the same time, the southwestern entrance to the Karaginskii Bay (Sopotsko, pp. 64, 67).

176 "A hill, where the shore seems to end": According to Sopotsko, but contrary to Berch 1823 (p. 32), this was the Foggy Mountain (*Tumannaia gora*, 872 m) on the southeastern shore of Karaginskii Island. Actually, the mountain does not mark the end of the shore. Since it was sighted at a distance of 66 miles, the lower coastline extending eastwards from the Tumannaia to Cape Rovnyi could not be seen from the ship (Sopotsko, p. 69).

177 "A hill on the shore etc." – the High Mountain (*Gora Vysokaia*) on the Karaginskii Island (Sopotsko, pp. 69-70); the highest peak (912 m) on the island.

178 "[a cape], from which the shore bent by N etc." – Cape Kzan on the east coast of Karaginskii Island (Sopotsko, p. 71), some 40 km up from the southern tip of the island.

179 "A hill that stands out etc." – once again (cf. note 176) Bering's men sighted the Foggy (*Tumannaia*) Mountain, the second highest peak on the Karaginskii Island (Sopotsko, p. 70).

180 "A corner of the land etc." – Cape Rovnyi (*rovnyi* means straight or even) on the east coast of Karaginskii Island (Sopotsko, p. 71).

181 "The same again". Sopotsko argues (p. 71) that the second time the navigator on the *Holy Gabriel* did not see Cape Rovnyi, but Cape Kekurnyi, some 12 km further up the east coast of Karaginskii Island. The reason for the confusion may have been that the first

observation (cf. note 26) was made *before*, the second one *after* sunrise, which took place at 3:15 a.m. At 4 a.m. the latter cape would have been clearly visible. Thus, the navigator regarded the two capes and the relatively short coast between them as one coherent whole.

182 "Once more rising ground": the Ridge of Malinovskii (*Khrebet Malinovskogo*), on the south coast of Goven Peninsula (*Poluostrov Govena*) (Sopotsko, p. 73).

183 The east coast of Goven Peninsula. Bering spent the day mapping in the Oliutorskii Bay (*Oliutorskii zaliv*) (Sopotsko, 74).

184 "The shore [...] extending to NNE": The shore between Cape Kreshchennyi Ogniom and Cape Krasnyi (Sopotsko, p. 75).

185 "A land to ENE": Cape Krasnyi (Sopotsko, p. 76).

186 "A mountain white with snow", probably Mount Kekurnaia (1227 m), which is snow-covered in the summer (Sopotsko, 74).

187 "An easily recognisable mountain", in the document *gora znamenitaia k priznaniiu*. Sopotsko misread *k priznaniiu* in the logbook as *kriviznoi* (curvature) and believed the mountain to be outstanding for its slope. Partly on this basis, he identified it as Sloping Mountain (*Gora Naklonnaia*), the largest peak in the Kautkgyn Mountains (Sopotsko, p. 74). He may be right anyway.

188 "A mountain distinctly different from the others": Mount Poknav (*Gora Poknav*), the highest mountain on the coast of Oliutorskii Bay between 168° and 169° E longitude. By a slip of the pen, Sopotsko has "between parallels 168° and 169° N latitude" (Sopotsko, p. 75).

189 "A point of land jutting out into the sea": The spit in front of the mouth of the Pakhacha River.

190 "A small mountain beyond the bay": Mount Chaachai (889 m), the highest peak in the Pakhachinskii Ridge (*Khrebet Pakhachinskii*).

191 "A mountain on the very seashore", Gray Mountain (*Gora Seraia*, 921 m) on Cape Seraia, on the Oliutorskii Peninsula (Sopotsko, p. 76).

192 "A mountain with 3 peaks", probably the mountain Aliagetkin with three peaks, the highest reaching 795 m. It is part of the Anana ridge on Oliutorskii Peninsula (Sopotsko, p. 77).

193 "the southernmost one (of those that are washed by the sea in the extreme W)": Cape Oliutorskii, the southernmost point of Oliutorskii Peninsula (Sopotsko, p. 78).

194 "A mountain with 6 peaks", in Russian *gora o 6 verkhakh*. Sopotsko misread the logbook entry about the number of peaks (7 instead of 6) and the direction in which it was sighted (70°08′ NW instead of 10°08′ NW). He identified the mountain as present-day Gora Mnogovershinnaia (the many-peaked mountain), which "has 7 peaks and stands out from neighboring mountains by its peculiar appearance" (Sopotsko, pp. 78-79). In addition, he overlooked that this observation and the following one refer to the same mountain (cf. note 195).

195 "The same once more", identified by Sopotsko as a mountain 819 m high on the western shore of Deep Bay (*Buchta Glubokaia*) (Sopotsko, pp. 79-81). Unfortunately, Sopotsko overlooked that this observation and the previous one refer to the same mountain, cf. note 194.

196 "A mountain with 2 peaks like a tent": High Mountain (*Gora Vysokaia*) (Sopotsko, p. 81).

197 "A steep mountain": Even Mountain (*Gora Rovnaia*), a peak in the Snow Range (*Khrebet Snegovoi*) (Sopotsko, pp. 81-82).

198 "At 8:45 a.m.", in the document *do poludnia za 3¼ chasa*.

199 "A mountain, easy to recognize", in Russian *gora udobna k primechaniiu*: Flat Mountain (*Gora Ploskaia*). It stands out by its considerable height (799 m) and its flat top (Sopotsko, p. 82).

200 "A mountain patched with snow", in Russian *piostraia gora ot snega*: Pyramid Mountain (*Gora Piramida*). Its top is partly snow-covered throughout the summer (Sopotsko, p. 82).

201 "The hank of the spanker gaff broke": in the document *porvalsia u gafelia rakstou*.

202 "The lift broke": in the document *porvalsia toponant*.

203 "Same motley-looking mountain with snow", in the document *Ta zhe pestrovidnaia gora ot snega*.

204 "A mountain standing apart behind a lowland": Sopotsko identified it as the mountain Telileut (or Konus), 460 m high, 13 miles NE of the mouth of the Khatyrka River. A truncated peak characterizes this mountain. However, S. partly misread the logbook entry, seeing *chrez vershinu* (through/by its peak) instead of *chrez nizkost′* (behind/on the other side of a lowland) (Sopotsko, p. 83).

205 "Another one, similar": the mountain Zubets, 1070 m. Both Telileut and Zubets are obvious landmarks when sailing from Khatyrka River towards Cape Navarin (Sopotsko, p. 83).

206 "A bay to the NW½N of us": The mouth of the Khatyrka River (Sopotsko, pp. 83-84).

207 "A high sharp-pointed mountain", in Russian *gora vysokaia ostra*. The mountain, 592 m high, is part of the Etyret Range (*Khrebet Etyret*) (Sopotsko, p. 83).

208 "The land extends parallel to our route in a curve", in Russian *zemlia prostiraetsia v parallel′ puti nashego s pogibom*: Between Cape Khatyrka and Cape Navarin the coastline forms a curve (Sopotsko, p. 84).

209 "A bay was from us to NEbN": The modern name of this inlet, discovered by the expedition, is Pekulveem Bay (*Zaliv Pekulveem*/Пэкулвээм). The same inlet was observed at 5 p.m., cf. note 56XXX (Sopotsko, pp. 84-85).

210 "Land ahead on our course": The mountains of the Etyret Range (*Khrebet Etyret*). The *Holy Gabriel* was heading straight towards its highest peak (592 m) and then turned east along the coast (Sopotsko, p. 85).

211 Pekulveem Bay. Several rivers empty into the bay, the largest of them being the Pekulveem River (Sopotsko, p. 85).

212 "At 6:30 land was from us 7 miles to NbE": Probably Round Mountain (*Gora Kruglaia*, 856 m), part of the Ukvushvuinen/Уквушвуйнэн Range (Sopotsko, p. 85).

213 "A land to WNW, 12 miles away": Cape Navarin, see note 216 (Sopotsko, p. 85).

214 "A bay from which etc.": Gabriel's Bay (*Bukhta Gavriila*). In 1835 Litke named it the Bay of the Archangel Gabriel (*Guba Arkhangela Gavriila*) after Bering's ship. Sopotsko (p. 89) misread the bearing in Chaplin's logbook as WNW instead of the correct WSW.

215 "Conspicuous land": Probably the mountain Stantsionnaia. Like Kruglaia (see note 212), it is part of the Ukvushvuinen Range (Sopotsko, p. 85).

216 "A point jutting out into the sea, land behind it not visible". Present-day Cape Navarin (*Mys Navarin*), named by Litke, at the southern entrance of the Bay of Anadyr′ (Sopotsko, pp. 85-87).

217 "A new point of land". Chirikov has "a newly appeared point of land" (*vnov′ pokazavsheisia ugol zemli*, folio 142 verso). Cape Faddei (*Mys Faddeia*). Bering named it St. Fadei (S. Fadeia) on the return voyage, 22 August, see folio 55. As discussed by Sopotsko (pp. 87-88), the cape was misplaced on the Final Map of the expedition. The mistake was corrected by Litke in 1835.

218 "variegated skins", *kozha piostraia*.

219 "From 4 o'clock to 9", *s 5-go chasa do 9*.

220 "Land was seen from us to WSW": Probably a stretch of the coast from Cape Barykov (*Mys Barykova*) to Cape Ginter (*Mys Gintera*) (Sopotsko, p. 90).

221 "A part of the land [...] between SW and NW": The crew saw individual landmarks on the coastline between Cape Barykov and the Anadyr′ Estuary (*Anadyrskii liman*) (Sopotsko, p. 90).

222 "Once more the same newly appeared point": Sopotsko (p. 90) read *krutoi* (steep) instead of the correct *V drugoi* (once more) and therefore missed that this bearing is to the same "conspicuous place" (No. 31) as the previous bearing, taken at 9:12 a.m. He suggests that the point observed at 5 p.m. is present-day Cape Barykov (63°03′ N latitude, 179°26′ E longitude), the northern entrance point to Coal Bay (*bukhta Ugol′naia*).

223 "A high steep mountain by the sea": A mountain, 430 m, on Cape Barykov (Sopotsko, p. 90).

224 "The land was low near the shore [etc.]": Sopotsko (pp. 91-92) believes the land observed from the ship was a section of the west coast of the Bay of Anadyr' between the rivers Chimchengeiveem and Tumanskaia. "This log book entry provides an absolutely correct description of the western coast of the Bay of Anadyr', [which] may indeed be divided into two parts: the first one from Cape Navarin to Cape Ginter and the second from Cape Ginter to Cape Geka." The first part is generally "high, jagged, and rocky"; the second is "even and low".

225 Sopotsko read (p. 91) Pri more gora krutaia (A steep mountain by the sea) instead of the correct Pri more gora v drugoi (The mountain by the sea a second time), thus failing to notice that this bearing is to the same "conspicuous place" (No. 32) as the one taken at 5 p.m. the previous day.

226 "A mountain ahead" (gora vperedi) and "A mountain like a haystack" (gora stoga podobna). Sopotsko (p. 91) identified them as the mountains Bol'shaia (134 m) and Skal'naia (646 m), respectively. However, he made several mistakes in his reading of the logbook entry concerning the two places (No. 33 and No. 34).

227 Sopotsko believes the anchorage was near the joint entrance to the four lagoons Chymchengejkuim, Sredniaia, Glubokaia, and Kaingu-Pil'gyn in the western part of the Bay of Anadyr' (Sopotsko, p. 93).

228 "A mountain appeared to WNW½N": the mountain Primetnaia (conspicuous) on the northern coast of the Anadyr' estuary. All black, it stands out against the background of the Golden Range (Zolotoi khrebet) (Sopotsko, p. 94).

229 Because of the low visibility during the crossing of the Anadyr' Estuary, Bering and his men failed to observe the mouth of the Anadyr' River. Later they had to question the Chukchi about its location (Sopotsko, p. 94). Cf. also note 260.

230 "We ran close-hauled", in the document poshli bejdevint.

231 "A small hill on the lowland", in the document Na niskoj zemle kholmok. The hill Pologaia (75m) (Sopotsko, p. 92).

232 "The shore was near": that is, the north shore of the Bay of Anadyr' (Sopotsko, p. 95).

233 "We saw a land on the left": The island Meechken Spit (Kosa Meechken), described and mapped by Litke in 1828 (Sopotsko, pp. 95, 228-229).

234 "We turned bow to the wind", in the document povorotili na druguiu storonu protiv vetra.

235 "After 5 o'clock", v 6-om chasu.

236 "A shore with high mountains". Bering and his men had found a bay. They named it the Bay of the Holy Cross (zaliv Sv. Kresta, often abbreviated zaliv Kresta), since, on 1 August, the Russian Orthodox Church celebrates the Life-giving Cross of the Lord (zhivotvoriashchii krest gospoden'). Litke established that the coast mentioned by Bering was the east coast of that bay. The coast itself is low, but behind it in the indicated direction the crew of the Holy Gabriel could see two peaks presently called Linglingei (in Russian Serdtse-Kamen', i.e. Heart-Stone, 378 m) and Miliutngei (in Russian Zaiachii Kamen', i.e. Hare-Stone) (Sopotsko, p. 96).

237 "We stood at the same place": that is, in the Bay of the Holy Cross. The improved visibility and afternoon calm gave Bering's navigators an opportunity to take a good look at the bay, which eventually was entered with remarkable precision on the Final Map of the expedition (Sopotsko, p. 96).

238 "Land from us to ENE 5 miles away, extending to E": Again the Meechken Spit (cf. note 233). Probably, the observation also includes the section of the north coast of the Bay of Anadyr' that runs parallel to the low Meechken Spit (Sopotsko, pp. 97-98).

239 "NWbN": The Holy Gabriel turned around and headed back to the Bay of the Holy Cross. According to Chaplin, this happened "in order to find a convenient place to get fresh water" (cf. folio 48, continuation, p. 128).

240 "We [...] ran from the bay": The attempt to get fresh water in the Bay of the Holy Cross was given up, apparently because of the fog.

241 "The land to E½S which [we saw] on the second day of this month": Approaching the outlet from the Bay of the Cross, Bering sighted the Meechken Spit once again.

242 "current from the shore to SbW": The ebb-tide current in the Bay of the Cross. As correctly noted by Chaplin, the direction of the current is from N to S (Sopotsko, p. 99).

243 Thus in the document.

244 "very calm", zelo tikho.

245 "A land with high mountains…" The north coast of the Bay of Anadyr' (Sopotsko, p. 99).

246 "Stone mountains about 4 miles from the shore": Mountains on the Chukhotsk Peninsula (Sopotsko, p. 100).

247 "A high land to 75° from N by E": The southern coast of the Chukhotsk Peninsula (Russkie ekspeditsii 1984, p. 70) or, in other words, the east coast of the Bay of Anadyr' (Sopotsko, p. 100).

248 "At 7 o'clock land was seen to 85° from S by E": Sopotsko (pp. 100-101) suggests that Chaplin sighted present-day Cape Achchen (Mys Achchen). However, Sopotsko misread the number of degrees in Chaplin's entry (75° instead of 85°).

249 "And forms a bay", i.e., present-day Rudder Bay (Russkie ekspeditsii 1984, p. 70).

250 "We reckon the return of the shore to S is 12 miles away": Sopotsko points out (p. 102) that from Rudder Bay to Cape Bering the coastline turns sharply south. He argues that at 9 o'clock in the evening the crew of the Holy Gabriel saw the entire northeastern coast of the Bay of Anadyr' from the lagoon Cheutakan to Cape Bering.

251 "At 6 o'clock we drew near a point of rocky mountains…": This was present-day Cape Bering, named in his honor by Litke in 1828 (Sopotsko, pp. 102-103).

252 "The mountains stretched to E by compass [etc]": Chaplin describes the coast from Cape Bering to Transfiguration Bay (Sopotsko, pp. 103).

253 The inlet was named Transfiguration Bay (Zaliv Preobrazheniia Gospodnia), in honor of the feast day (see folio 52 verso, continuation; Russkie ekspeditsii 1984, p. 71; Kushnarev 1990, p. 96). The Orthodox Church celebrates the transfiguration of our Lord on 6 August, according to the Julian calendar.

254 The drawing of the bay, made by members of Bering's expedition, seems to have been lost (Sopotsko, p. 104).

255 "stones, not very large, and broken slabs", in Russian kamen' ne ves'ma velikoi i plitnoi driazg. Sopotsko (p. 104) misread Chaplin's description of the bottom.

256 On 7 August, Chaplin was busy exploring Transfiguration Bay and fetching water, and made no entries in the usual columns of his logbook. Onboard the Holy Gabriel Chirikov recorded the changing winds during the day (RGAVMF, fund 913, inv. 1, unit 2, folio 145ob).

257 "At 1:30 o'clock we observed that the shore extended to EbS": The coastline from Cape Achchen to Cape Skalistyi (i.e., "cliffy"). The Holy Gabriel passed Cape Achchen at about 2 p.m. (Sopotsko, p. 106).

258 "At 7 o'clock we were in front of a bay 9 miles wide…": Bering saw the bay Bezymiannaia (i.e., nameless), which is 9.5 miles wide between its extreme points, Cape Skalistyi to W and Cape Spanberg to E., and also Lake Achchen just behind the coast of the bay (Sopotsko, pp. 107-108).

259 "The shore was 3 miles from us to N": Bering had sighted present-day Cape Ulakhpen.

260 The meeting with the Chukchi seems to have taken place between the two capes Iakun and Ching-An, approximately in 64°32' northern latitude (Kushnarev 1990, p. 99). An identical record of the meeting appears in Chirikov's journal (RGAVMF, fund 913, inv. 1, unit 2, folio 145ob). A more detailed account of the six questions that were put to the Chukchi, and of their answers, is

given in a document signed by Bering, Chirikov, and Spangberg, in the expedition's "Journal of incoming documents". It has been published in *Russkaia tikhookeanskaia epopeia* 1979, pp. 147-148, and *Russkie ekspeditsii* 1984, p. 84, and cited in English translation in Kushnarev 1990, pp. 97-98). It also provides the names of the two interpreters: "the servitor Ivan Pankarin and the newly baptized Iakov Povirka". The questions and answers read as follows:
"*1. What is the name of your people?*
Chukchi
2. Where is the Anadar [Anadyr'] River, and is it far from here?
You have passed the Anadar River, and it is far behind. How did you get as far as this? No ships have ever come here before.
3. Do you know the Kolyma River?
We do not know the Kolyma River, but we have heard from the reindeer Chukchi that they go by land to a river and they say that Russian people live on that river, but we do not know if this river is the Kolyma or some other.
4. Do you have any forest land, and are there any big rivers that flow from the land into the sea? To where does your land extend, and is it far?
We have no forest anywhere, and no large rivers in our land that empty into the sea. Any rivers that do are small. Almost from here our land turns to the left and extends far, and those who live on it are all our Chukchi.
5. Is there any promontory that extends from your land into the sea?
There is no promontory that extends from our land into the sea, all our land is level.
6. Are there not any islands or land in the sea?
There is an island not far from land and when it is not foggy, one can see it. And there are people on that island, but we do not know about any more lands, only all of our Chukchi land."
Bering included a short account of this meeting with the Chukchi in his final report on the expedition: "On August 8 when we were in latitude 64°18' N., eight men who claimed to be Chukchi (a people known for a long time to the Russians of the country) rowed to us from the shore in a leathern boat and, when near, asked who we were and why we came. On being invited on board, they put one man over, who, with the help of large inflated seal bladders, swam over to have a talk with us. A little later the boat moved up to us and the men in it told us that large numbers of Chukchi live along the shore, that a short distance from there the coast turns to the west, and that not far ahead of us is an island. We located this island, which we named St. Lawrence, in honor of the day, and found on it a few huts but no people, although I twice sent the midshipman to look for them" (Golder 1968, p. 18).

261 "A mountain near the sea…": The mountain Ivlychyn (also named *gora Bol'shaia*, 711 m), located 2.5 miles from the shore. The two bearings were taken at a distance of 38 and 33 nautical miles, respectively (Sopotsko, p. 107).

262 "A cape stretching out into the sea": Cape Centenary (Mys Stoletiia), named so by Litke, who arrived here on 10 August 1828, a hundred years after Bering (Sopotsko, p. 107; Litke, p. 217).

263 "At 7:30 o'clock we had land to ENE in 3 miles": Sopotsko suggests (p. 111) that the land sighted was Cape Bald Head (*mys Lysaia Golova*). However, he based his calculation partially on a misreading of Chaplin's entry (8 miles instead of the correct 3).

264 Leaving the Bay of Anadyr', Bering turned his ship to the south at nightfall in order to reach a safer distance from the unknown shore. At 6 a.m. Bering turned east and at 7 a.m. northeast, thus approaching the shore again. He resumed the search for the turn of the coastline as well as for the island that the Chukchi had talked about on 8 August (Sopotsko, p. 113).

265 "At 9 a.m. we sighted…": At about the same time, the *Holy Gabriel* passed present-day Cape Chukotsk (*Mys Chukotskii*), the southernmost point of the Chukchi Peninsula, at a distance of 10 miles, without sighting it (Sopotsko, p. 113).

266 "From noon to 9 o'clock we maneuvered off the shore…": From this entry Sopotsko concludes (p. 113) that by noon on 10 August Bering was convinced he had reached the land to the east where the coastline turned left (that is, to the north). However, the captain had still not been able to determine the southernmost point of this land and therefore continued maneuverings along this shore.

267 "A point of land by N": After some searching, Bering had finally sighted Cape Chukotsk. He put it on the Final Map of the expedition as *Ugol Chukotskoi*, at latitude 64°25'N (Sopotsko, p. 114). Captain James Cook sighted the cape on 4 September 1778 and wrote in his journal: "I take this to be the point which Capt. Behring calls the East Point of Suchotski or Cape Tchuktschki, probably from some of that Nation coming off to him here. I make its latitude to be 64°13'N, Longitude 186°36'E" (Cook, p. 433).

268 "we saw a land […] which we believed was an island": Bering discovered St. Lawrence Island (*Ostrov sv. Lavrentiia*) on 10 August (11 August by the navy's special count of days at sea). The Russian Church Calendar prompted his choice of a name for it: 10 August is the feast of the Roman martyr Laurentius. On 4 September 1778, Captain Cook found himself near Cape Chukotsk and decided to look at the island. "I did not follow the direction of the Coast as I found it took a Westerly direction towards the Gulph of Anidar [Bay of Anadyr'], into which I had no inducement to go, but steered to the Southward in order to get a sight of the island of St. Lawrence discovered by Captain Behring". Like Bering, Cook did not realize the full extent of the island. On his way to the Bering Strait in March 1778, he got a sight of its easternmost part, but thought it was a separate island. He named it Anderson's Island in memory of his deceased surgeon (Cook, pp. 443, 406). Bering thought the small northwestern jut of the island was the whole island (Sopotsko, p. 115).

269 "and wet fog": *i ot tumanu shla vlaga.*

270 "S point […] E point of the […] island": Bering took the newly discovered St. Lawrence Island to be much smaller than it actually is. Just how small is revealed by Chaplin's observations of what he thought to be the S and E points of the island. According to Sopotsko (p. 116) the two points are, respectively, Cape Agsit on the west coast and an unnamed protrusion between Cape Chibukak and Cape Nuvulak. Sopotsko, however, misread Chaplin's entry about the second observation of these two points. Reading *drugoi* (another) instead of *v drugoi* (a second time), he believed the observations carried out at 3:30 p.m. were to another two points.

271 "At 1 o'clock", in the document *v yskhode 1 chasa.*

272 "A high land behind us", *pozadi sebia vysokuiu zemliu.* The mountains on Cape Uelen (Mys Uelen, by Sopotsko referred to as Mys Kekurnyi), the northeastern extremity of Asia. The Chukchi Peninsula ends to the east in a smaller peninsula which has since 1973 been named Daurkin Peninsula (*Poluostrov Daurkina*), earlier referred to as Dezhnev Peninsula (Poluostrov Dezhniova) or Eastern Cape (Mys Vostochnyi). The coastline of Daurkin Peninsula extends from Cape Uelen in the north to Cape Dezhnev in the east and down to Cape Peek in the south (Sopotsko, pp. 125, 230).

273 "High mountains, probably on the big land", *vysokie gory, kotorye chaem byt' na bol'shoi zemle.* In Sopotsko's interpretation, pp. 125-126, Bering saw Cape Ikigur (*Mys Ikigur*) to WbS and Cape Serdtse-Kamen' (in translation, Cape Heart-Rock) to *WSW* (sic – WSW is most likely a misreading of Chaplin's WNW). Cook visited the same stretch of the north-coast of the Chukchi Peninsula on 1 September 1778: "The Coast seemed to form several rocky points, connected to one another by a low shore without the least appearance of a harbour […]. I was now well assured that this was the Coast of Tchuktschi, or the NE coast of Asia, and that thus far Captain Behring proceeded in 1728, that is to this head which Mr Muller says is called *Serdze Kamen*, on account of a rock upon it in the shape of a heart […]; it is a pretty lofty promontory with a

steep rocky cliff facing the Sea and lies in the Latitude of 67°03′ N, Longitude 187°11′ E." (Cook, p. 429). J.C. Beaglehole, editor of Cook's journal, argues, "Bering left the land at Cape Dezhneva (East Cape), the north-eastern extremity of the Asian continent. Nevertheless Cook found a cape somewhere in the neighbourhood of lat. 67°18′N [the latitude of Bering's turnaround], and going on the geographical reading he had (Müller and Harris), was justified in making the identification he did. The modern position for the cape is lat. 66°57′ N, long. 172°38′ W (187°22′ E)" (Cook, pp. 429-30). Although Bering did not proceed along the coast as far as to Cape Serdtse-Kamen, Chaplin's record shows that Bering also saw land after having passed through the Bering Strait into the Chukchi Sea. Sopotsko goes as far as to claim that the cape, which Cook found and named Serdtse-Kamen′, was first sighted by Bering. He even suggests that Cook may have had a copy of Chaplin's journal with him (Sopotsko, p. 231, note 56). It would seem that Chaplin's entry about "high mountains" observed "between WbS and WNW" does not quite prove that Bering saw present-day Cape Serdtse-Kamen′ – whether to WSW or at all.

274 "that is until 3 o'clock p.m.", in the document *a imianno do 4 chasa popoludni*.

275 "With addition". The number of miles covered on 15 August is only 60.15. The indicated sum total 66.15 includes an addition of 6 miles, for the first hours of 16 August, before the turnaround. There seems to be a small arithmetical error here. The sum total for 16 August is 121.45 miles, but Chaplin indicates only 114.45, having transferred 7 miles (for the three hours before the turnaround) to 15 August (see folio 51 v). Most likely, the sum total for August 15 should have been 67.15 instead of 66.15. The corresponding figures in Chirikov's diary are identical with those of Chaplin (RGAVMF, fund 913, inv. 1, unit 2, folio 147-147 verso).

276 Before making the decision to turn around and return to Kamchatka, Bering had summoned his lieutenants Chirikov and Spangberg, on 13 August, and read to them once again His Majesty's decree and also the recent answers of the Chukchi (see note 260). In view of their present location and the time of the year, he wanted his lieutenants' advice. He asked for their written opinion on "what would be the best thing to do in the interest of the state [*dlia interesu gosudarstvennogo*] for the safety of the ship and the men, considering the decree given to me, as well as the condition of the ship" (*Russkie ekspeditsii* 1984, p. 86). Chirikov submitted his opinion the same day. He argued that in order to find out for sure if Asia and America were separated by the sea, the ship would have to proceed either to the Kolyma River or until it met ice. His advice was to continue along the shore until the ice prevented further progress, or until the shoreline turned west, towards the mouth of the Kolyma River. If the land continued to extend to the north, they should start looking for a place to winter no later than 25 August. However, the *Holy Gabriel* was likely to reach ice before that date, and then it would be unnecessary to sail to Kolyma or search for a winter harbor.
Spangberg's opinion, submitted on 14 August, was quite different. He suggested that they continue to the north until 16 August, and then return to Kamchatka (*Russkaia tikhookeanskaia epopeia* 1979, pp. 148-149; *Russkie ekspeditsii* 1984, p. 85). Having received his officers' advice, Bering supported Spangberg's view. For a detailed, if not unbiased discussion of the opinions of Chirikov and Spangberg, see Kushnarev 1990, pp. 101-108.

277 "At 12 o'clock the land […] 13 miles distant" etc. The *Holy Gabriel* sailed off the northern coast of Cape Dezhnev, the easternmost point of Asia (Sopotsko, p. 131). There is, however, a mistake in Sopotsko's quotation from Chaplin: *3 miles distant*, instead of the correct *13 miles distant*.

278 Cf. note 275.

279 "A mountain, on which Chukchi live", a mountain 650m high, 2 miles from Cape Uelen (Sopotsko, p. 130).

280 "High mountains on the right side", two mountains on Cape Dezhnev. The cape itself is formed by the slope of a mountain 568m high (Sopotsko, p. 130).

281 "Presumed an island": The island sighted is present-day Ratmanov Island (one of the two Diomede Islands) in the Bering Strait. Bering saw only one of the islands and named it St. Diomede (Sopotsko, p. 136), based on the Russian orthodox calendar of feasts. The 2nd century martyr St. Diomede is commemorated on 16 August.

282 "in 2 places their dwellings", possibly the location of the present-day village of Nuukan, less than one mile from Cape Peek (Sopotsko, p. 134).

283 "the end of the mountains etc.", the shore of Cape Peek, made up from the slopes of a mountain 636m high (Sopotsko, p. 135).

284 "a high land was seen to WbN etc.", mountains in the vicinity of Cape Leimin (Sopotsko, p. 138).

285 "a high mountain to WtN½W […] with a small bay beneath", Mt. Enmyngai, 353m, near the northeastern entrance of St. Lawrence Bay (*Zaliv Lavrentiia*), cf. Sopotsko, pp. 138-139.

286 "land to SbW, 1½ miles distant", Mys Nygchigen, at the southwestern exit from Mechigmenskii Bay (Sopotsko, p. 145).

287 "a bay on the right hand", the northern entrance to the Seniavin Sound (*Proliv Seniavina*), between the capes Ngeegchen and Kygynin (the easternmost point of the island Arakamchechen). Bering crossed the entrance without realizing that what seemed to be a bay was actually a sound. This discovery remained to be made – by F.P. Litke in 1835 (Sopotsko, pp. 146-147, 198).

288 Cf. note 282.

289 Cf. note 285.

290 Cf. note 287.

291 "a great number", in Russian *premnozhestvo*.

292 "a bay or the mouth of a river", Tkachen Bay (*Zaliv Tkachen*) (Sopotsko, pp. 147-148).

293 "columns of light in the air", *na vozdukhe byli svetlye stolby*, northern lights.

294 Bering discovered St. Lawrence Island on 10 August 1728, cf. folio 50, continuation (p. 137).

295 Chaplin left a space for the sum total, but never filled it in. Chirikov's journal provides the missing figure: 72.1 miles (RGAVMF, fund 913, inv. 1, unit 2, folio 148).

296 "A point of land etc.", Mys Sivolkut, the northeastern entrance point of Tkachen Bay (Sopotsko, pp. 147-148).

297 "Left side-keel", in Russian *shverets na levoi storone*.

298 Chaplin left a space for the sum total, but never filled it in. Chirikov's journal provides the missing figure: 70.2 miles. (RGAVMF, fund 913, inv. 1, unit 2, folio 148).

299 "4 boats", *4 lotki*.

300 "People of our kin", in Russian *liudi nashego roda*.

301 The second conversation with the Chukchi also seems to have taken place near Cape Iakun, at 64°25′ northern latitude. A record of the three questions that were put to the Chukchi, and of their answers, is given in a document signed by Bering, Spangberg, and Chirikov (published in *Russkaia tikhookeanskaia epopeia* 1979, pp. 149-150, in *Russkie ekspeditsii* 1984, p. 86, and cited in English translation in Kushnarev 1990, p. 114). The questions and answers read as follows:
"1. Where is the Anadyr′ River, and is it far?
The Anadyr′ River is to the south from here, and not near. I have been to the Anadyrskii Ostrog to sell walrus tusks, and have known of the Russians for a long time.
2. Do you know the Kolyma River, and is there a sea route from here to the Kolyma?
I know the Kolyma River and have gone there overland with reindeer. The sea is shallow off the mouth of the Kolyma and there is always ice there in the sea. We have never gone by sea from here to the mouth of the Kolyma, but the people who live along the coast from here to the distant Kolyma are all our kin.

3. Are there islands or is there land in the sea opposite your land? To this question, they answered the same as the Chukchi we met before."

Bering gave the following account of this meeting with the Chukchi in his final report on the expedition: "On August 20 there came to our ship four boats containing 40 Chukchi like those who had visited us before. They offered for sale meat, fish, water, about 15 red and white fox skins, four walrus tusks – all of which they disposed of to the crew for needles and such like articles. They told us that their relatives go to the Kolyma on deer and not by boat, that farther along the coast live some of their people, that they had known the Russians for a long time, and that one of their number had been at Anadyrsk Post to trade. The rest of their conversation did not differ greatly from what was said by those who had been to see us before." (Golder 1968, pp. 19-20).

302 "The Bay of the Transfiguration of our Lord", in Russian *Zaliv preobrazheniia gospodnia*. On 6 August, during the outward voyage, Chaplin had been sent ashore here with six men to fill water casks, see folio 49 (p. 131).

303 "to change bad gaskets", in the document *dlia peremennykh i khudykh rebontov*.

304 "Cape of the Holy Apostle Faddei", in the document *Ugol sv. apostola Fadeia*. Once again, Bering resorted to the orthodox church calendar, when it came to naming a new geographical location. The apostle Faddei is commemorated on 21 August of the Julian calendar. In the early cartography of the region there has been some confusion of Cape Faddei and the more southern Cape Navarin, see Sopotsko, pp. 87-88. Kushnarev believed, as did some of the early map makers, that the two capes were identical (Kushnarev 1990, p. 115).

305 "A steep corner of land": Present-day Cape Navarin (*Mys Navarin*), discovered on the outward voyage, 27 July, see folio 46 verso.

306 "Behind, as far as the sight could reach", Mys Kinga, the northern entrance point to Ushakov Bay (Sopotsko, p. 152, 213).

307 "Yards", in the document *rei (рей)*, the plural of *reia* or *rei (рея, рей)*. In nautical terminology, a yard is a long cylindrical spar, slung crosswise to a mast and suspending a sail.

308 Chaplin left a space for the sum total, but never filled it in.

309 "We saw the shore", that is, the coast between present-day Mys Rubikon and the mouth of Khatyrka River. Its highest point is Pyramid Mountain (*Gora Piramida*), which Chaplin had already seen on the outward voyage, on 23 July, and described as "a mountain patched with snow" (see folio 45 verso; Sopotsko, p. 153).

310 "Again we saw the shore", probably once again Pyramid Mountain (Sopotsko, p. 153).

311 "By sand clock", in the document *po skliankam*.

312 See note 307.

313 Chaplin put his explanation about the location of this "part of the land" in brackets. The *Holy Gabriel* was (too) near the east coast of Kamchatsk Peninsula (*Kamchatskii poluostrov*) at Cape Rify (*Mys Rify*), see Sopotsko, pp. 154-155. To get to the mouth of the Kamchatka River, the ship had to round the southernmost point of the peninsula. Bering had observed Cape Rify on 16 July, on the outward voyage, see folio 43 verso, continuation, and note 172.

314 "till 10 p.m.", *do desiatogo chasa popoludni*.

315 "A point of land etc.", Cape Kamchatsk, *Mys Kamchatskii* (Sopotsko, p. 156).

316 See folios 41 and 43.

317 Chaplin left spaces for the quantity of rusks and barley groats, but never filled them in.

318 Calculating the amount of flour that was handed over to local servitors, Chaplin made a slight arithmetical error. He got the number of bags right (305 = 210 + 38 + 57), but their total weight should be 800 poods (546 + 100 + 154), rather than 790.

319 See folio 42 verso.

320 Catherine I (*Ekaterina Alekseevna*) was the second wife of Peter the Great and became his successor to the throne at the insistence of the Guards regiments. Born in 1684, she ruled from 28 January 1725 to her death, 6 May 1727. However, the political power passed to Prince A.D. Men'shikov and the Supreme Privy Council (*Verkhovnyj tainyi sovet*). It took a year and 5 months for the news of her demise to reach Bering's expedition in Kamchatka. A few days before her death, Catherine signed a testament, appointing the young Peter (*Piotr Alekseevich*, 1715-1730, son of Prince Aleksei and grandson of Peter the Great) heir to the throne. The short rule of Peter II became a spell of reaction against Peter's reforms. He died of smallpox shortly before Bering's return to St. Petersburg. The news of his death reached the expedition at Velikii Ustiug, on 13 February 1730 (see folio 74).

321 Chaplin bracketed the incorrect *cloudy (oblachno)* and added the correct *sunshine (siianie)*.

322 "For his own needs", in Russian *dlia ego nuzhd*.

323 "On the name day of Her Sovereign Majesty", in Russian *dlia tezoimenitstva gosudaryni tsesarevny*. Chaplin refers to the eldest daughter of Peter the Great, Anna Petrovna, born 1708. Her name day was 3 February. Clearly, the news of her death on 4 March 1728 had not yet reached Kamchatka.

324 "The same as in January". This observation seems to refer to the sick in the following line.

325 "5 old reindeer beddings", in the document *5 postel' alennykh starykh*.

326 Chaplin left two spaces for the weight of the canon powder, but did not fill them in.

327 "On 3 ferries", in Russian *na 3-kh poromakh*.

328 "Aboard the ship", in the document *na botu*, that is, on the *Holy Gabriel*.

329 "1 The Captain", in the document *Gospodin kapitan 1*.

330 "Aboard the other vessel", that is, on the *Fortuna*.

331 "assistant skipper", in Russian *podshturman*.

332 Chaplin corrected himself by bracketing the four words he had repeated by mistake.

333 "The eastern point of Kamchatka land", *vostochnoi ugol Kamchatskoi zemli*. Probably Cape Africa (*Mys Afrika*), the easternmost point of Kamchatsk Peninsula (Sopotsko, p. 158).

334 "a land to WNW, 10 minutes distant", Cape Kozlov (*Mys Kozlova*) on Kronotsk Peninsula (Sopotsko, p. 160).

335 "At noon […] the land was 9 minutes to WNW", Cape Olga (*Mys Ol'ga*), ibid.

336 "the land extends back as far as […] and ahead etc.", probably the southern coast of Kronotsk Peninsula, from Cape Kozlov *back* to Cape Kronotsk (*Mys Kronotskii*) and *ahead* to Cape Olga. A further part of Sopotsko's identification, that the land also includes the coast of Kronotsk Bay (*Kronotskii zaliv*) from Cape Olga to Cape Bol'shoi, is based on his misreading of this passage in Chaplin's journal. Instead of *nazad kak*, "back as far as", he reads *ot ziuida k W*, "from south to W", ibid.

337 "Leeway", in the document *sklonenie bota ot vetra*.

338 "high rocks", *vysokoe kamen'e*. Sopotsko believes the two words summarize a general impression of the coast of Kronotsk Bay, from the mouth of Olga River to Cape Kozlov, ibid.

339 "a high mountain to NWbN", the Krasheninnikov Volcano, *Vulkan Krasheninnikova*, 1856 m (Sopotsko, p. 161).

340 "Land from us to W […] and extending […]" – Cape Shipunskii and the coast of Avachinskii zaliv, from Cape Nalychev (*Mys Nalycheva*) to Cape Maiachnyi (Sopotsko, p. 161).

341 "the land was from us NWbW½N", Cape Nalychev, see Sopotsko, p. 162.

342 "A mountain in Kronoki", Kronotsk Volcano, *Sopka Kronotskaia*, 3521 m (Sopotsko, p. 161).

343 "A mountain on Zhupanova", Zhupanovskaia Volcano, *Sopka Zhupanovskaia*, 2923 m (ibid.).

344 "A mountain on Avacha", Avacha Volcano, *Sopka Avachinskaia*, 2741 m (*ibid.*).

345 "along the shore described above", the coast of Avanchinskii zaliv (Sopotsko, pp. 162-163).

346 "ahead a high mountain to WbS¼W", *Gora Iushinskaia*, 815 m (Sopotsko, pp. 163, 203).

347 "With rare glimpses of sun through the dark", *malo prosiiavalo solntse skvoz' mrak.*

348 From noon on 13 June to 15 June, the *Holy Gabriel* was generally northward bound (Sopotsko, p. 163).

349 "After 8 o'clock", in the document *po 8 chasekh.*

350 "Land was not seen to any side". Sopotsko points out (p. 164) that the sailors were looking for land not only on the left, in the direction of Kamchatka, but also on the right. "This logbook entry, as always taciturn and precise, communicates the atmosphere onboard the small ship, where the brave crew was engaged in removing white spots from the map of the world, and proving that there was no Company Land or other lands in the Pacific to the east of Kamchatka".

351 "The Kamchatka shore appeared etc." – the coast of Avachinskii zaliv from Cape Maiachnyi to Cape Shipunskii (*ibid.*).

352 "the shore to NW, 25 minutes distant", Cape Nalycheva (Sopotsko, p. 165).

353 "Kronovskaia mountain", that is, Kronotsk Volcano.

354 "And [got] higher", in Russian *i vyshe*. Approaching Kronotsk Bay for the second time, now in clear weather, Bering and his men could see the mountainous eastern and southeastern shore of the Kronotsk Peninsula, from Cape Kamennyi and Cape Kronotsk to Cape Kozlov (Sopotsko, p. 166).

355 "18 minutes away", in Russian *v 18 minutakh*, i.e., 18 nautical miles away. The land was still the shore of Kronotsk Peninsula, between Cape Kronotsk and Cape Kozlov (Sopotsko 1983, p. 166).

356 "The land [...] extended to SSW and NEbN", that is, the coast line from Cape Zhupanova to Olga Bay, and from Cape Zhupanova to Cape Shipunskii (*ibid.*).

357 "land by S, which disappeared by SSW½W", Cape Shipunskii at the southern end of Kronotsk Bay (*ibid.*).

358 "the land was to SW½W", again Cape Shipunskii (*ibid.*).

359 Cape Shipunskii (*ibid.*).

360 The two mountains are the Beriozovaia Volcano (*Beriozovaia sopka*, 1131 m) and the Srezannaia Mountain (Sopotsko, pp. 167, 205). On modern maps, Srezannaia Mountain is called Malyi Semiachik Volcano (1563 m).

361 "The aforementioned mountains", that is, Beriozovaia and Malyi Semiachik volcanoes.

362 Sopotsko writes (p. 167) that the difference in longitude was 1°18′ "to the east" (*k vostoku*). However, the logbook entry reads "to the west" (*W*).

363 On 28 June, the search for new lands in the Pacific between 52° and 53° northern latitude continued (*ibid.*).

364 Sopotsko (*ibid.*) suggests that the navigator took bearing of Cape Sarannyi, the northern entrance point of the Sarannaia Bay. Thus, the logbook entry marks the beginning of the expedition's description of the coast of Kamchatka south of Avacha Bay (*Avachinskaia guba*).

365 "The land was in sight on our right side", probably the mountainous coast south of Cape Bezymiannyi (Sopotsko, p. 168).

366 The indicated direction of the coastline down from Avacha Bay corresponds to the line from Cape Bezymiannyi to Cape Sarannyi. The stretch between these two points matches Chaplin's description: the coast is steep, with mountains of considerable height close to the shore (Sopotsko, p. 167).

367 "Flat mountain with small mountain on top", Avacha Volcano – and, possibly, the nearby Kozel'skaia Volcano (Sopotsko, pp. 168, 165, 166).

368 "A high land", Cape Povorotnyi, the southwestern entrance point to Avachinskii zaliv (Sopotsko, p. 168).

369 "judged by eye", in the document *na antrent.*

370 "the land was [...] 13 minutes distant to WbN etc.", the high rocky shores of Cape Khodzhelaika (Sopotsko, p. 169).

371 "A high mountain by S", *gora vysokaia to Z*, Mutnovskaia Volcano, 2324 m (Sopotsko, p. 168).

372 "Another mountain, small", *gora drugaia nebol'shaia.* Sopotsko's identification of this place as "a mountain 938 m high" (*ibid.*) is partly based on a misreading of Chaplin's manuscript: *krutaia* (steep) instead of the correct *drugaia* (another).

373 "On the land [...] low stone mountains, and the seashore was steep", the coast of southeastern Kamchatka between Cape Three Sisters (*Mys tri sestry*) and Cape Triokhpolosnyi (Sopotsko, p. 170).

374 "The land was low etc." – the coast of southeastern Kamchatka from Cape Three Sisters to Cape Lopatka (Sopotsko, p. 171).

375 "The S point of the land of Kamchatka", in the document *Z ugol zemli Kamchatskoi*, present day Cape Lopatka. Based on Chaplin's logbook, Sopotsko calculated the following geographical coordinates of Cape Lopatka: 51°10′ northern latitude and 156°11′ eastern longitude. Modern maps have Cape Lopatka at 50°54′ northern latitude and 156°40′ eastern longitude. Thus, Bering's mistake was 16′ on the latitude and 29′ on longitude. Later explorers such as Krusenstern, Sarychev and King made mistakes of similar dimensions when determining the location of Cape Lopatka (*ibid.*, pp. 171-172).

376 The island sighted here is Shumshu, the northernmost of the Kuril Islands, the chain of islands extending from the southern tip of Kamchatka to northern Japan. The *Holy Gabriel* was passing from the Pacific into the Sea of Okhotsk through the strait later named the First Kuril Strait (*Pervyi Kamchatskii proliv*), between Cape Lopatka and Shumshu (Sopotsko, pp. 172-174).

377 Actually the sailors observed two islands, see the table "Conspicuous places" on folio 67, further down.

378 The mountain Moshkovskaia on Cape Kambal'nyi (Sopotsko, p. 176).

379 The island Paramushir (Sopotsko, p. 175).

380 The < (*ibid.*).

381 "W point of the 1st island" – Sopotsko notes that Bering seems to have believed he saw "the eastern point" of Atlasov Island to SW at 68°26′ (*ibid.*), which would be unlikely. Actually, Sopotsko misread the logbook entry that gives the bearing to the *western* point of "the 1st island", i.e., Paramushir.

382 "The first mate", *podshkhiper.*

383 "Mount Opal'skaia", in the document *Apal'skaia gora*, the Opala Volcano (*Sopka Opala*, 2475 m).

384 "A high mountain to 62°30′ from S by E", present day Bol'shaia Ipel'ka, 1139 m (Sopotsko, p. 180).

385 "To the commissary of the Kamchadal outposts", in the document *kamisaru kamchadal'skikh astrogov.* The adjective Kamchadal usually refers to the Itelmen natives of Kamchatka, but it may also refer to the land of Kamchatka, as here.

386 "Skins of Russia leather 5", in the document *kozh iuftenykh 5.*

387 "from 7 to 8 o'clock we drifted without sails", *vos'moi chas lezhali bez parusov.*

388 "Per day", in Russian *v sutki.*

389 "The navigator", in Russian *shtiurman.*

390 "We waved a flag", in the document *zdelali flagshou.*

391 The hour not recorded.

392 "to arrange for horses", *dlia vysylki podvod.*

393 The Cossack chief of Iakutsk was Afanasii Fedotovich (or Fiodorovich) Shestakov. S. had recently returned from St. Petersburg, where he had presented his proposal for an expedition to the northeast of Siberia. The Cossack chief arrived in the capital in 1725. He was able to meet with the commander-in-chief of Kronstadt, Admiral P.I. Sivers, and with the powerful Prince A.D. Men'shikov, and to convince them of the necessity of the proposed expedition. On 23 March the Privy Council (*Verkhovnyi tainyi*

sovet) issued a decree to the Senate for the organization of an expedition under Shestakov's command. The expedition was to explore and annex new territories, to subdue the inhabitants of Chukotka and Kamchatka, and to turn them into tribute-paying subjects of the Russian crown. In June 1727, he returned to Siberia with the title of commander-in-chief of the north-eastern region and as head of a military detachment. In the fall of 1729 he set out from Okhotsk on the newly built vessel the *Eastern Gabriel* (*Vostochnyi Gavriil*) to the Tauisk outpost, advancing further overland and collecting tribute on his way. On 14 March 1730, the Chukchi killed him on the Egach River. For more details, cf. Sgibnev 1869a, pp. 1-34; Sgibnev 1869b, pp. 129-130; *Russkaia tikhookeanskaia* 1979, pp. 134-139, 281; *Russkie ekspeditsii* 1984, pp. 88, 91, 92, 94. In view of their common interest in Chukotka and Kamchatka, Bering and Shestakov must have had a lot to talk about. However, their only meeting, on 30 July 1729, near Okhotsk, was short. Bering was already on his way back to St. Petersburg, and the Cossack chief on his way to Okhotsk.

394   "Ridge", in Russian *khrebet*.

395   "Mountain", in Russian *gora*.

396   "to make rafts", in the document *ploty delat'*.

397   "a rowboat", in the document *lotku*. By the 18th century, a *lodka* was normally a small rowboat (*Slovar' russkogo iazyka XVIII veka*, vol. 11, p. 216). Locally, the word could also mean a type of cargo vessel for hauling freight on the rivers (*Slovar' russkikh narodnykh govorov*, vol. 17, pp. 105-106), a wherry (Gibson 1969, p. 75).

398   "Just like a man-made wall", in the document *vlasno kak narochno kladena stena*.

399   See the description of the meeting with "the best Iakut" on the expedition's outward journey, folio 11.

400   "Ahead of schedule", in Russian *do vakantsii*.

401   "Government tobacco", in the document *kazionnoi tabak*.

402   "Kaiuk", a large cargo vessel with a gable roof and a pointed bow (Gibson 1969, p. 74).

403   "Took up autumn quarters", in the document *stali po kvarteram osenovat'*. In Peledui Bering and his men awaited winter travel conditions.

404   "The workers", in Russian *rabotnye liudi*.

405   Vasilii Ivanovich Kazantsov was admitted to the School of Mathematical and Navigational Sciences in Moscow, and after four years sent to England for further education. Until 1713, he participated in several ocean voyages. In 1713-1725, he served in the Baltic Fleet, on various ships. In January 1724, he was promoted captain-lieutenant. In 1727 he was arrested for using "indecent [*nepristoinye*] words" in defence of Prince A.D. Men'shikov, who had fallen into disgrace. By decree of Peter II from 5 January 1728, Kazantsev was exiled to Siberia and appointed to the Kamchatka Expedition. On 23 January 1730, in Tobol'sk, he was dismissed again from the expedition and in 1731 sent to Kamchatka to make descriptions of the land and its forts. Having learned more about Bering's activities in Siberia, Kazantsev arrived at the conclusion that Bering's second expedition (from 1733) was the cause "of considerable, but useless state spending and loss", and should be stopped the sooner the better. In the following years, he wrote numerous denunciations against Bering, trying to prove to the Admiralty College, the Senate, and the Academy of Sciences his own rightfulness. To the Senate he presented his own geographic and ethnographic description of the Okhotsk area and Kamchatka, including 4 maps. He was arrested several times and in 1740 transferred to Moscow under guard. However, his writings were set aside as being "unjust" and containing nothing new. By Senate decree of 6 October 1743, he was allowed to go and live at a monastery, after having signed a promise never to address himself to the Senate again. Instead, Kazantsev addressed a petition to Empress Elisabeth, but again his ideas met with no response. Ailing, destitute, and unable to find a monastery that would admit him, Kazantsev continued to write denunciations – and receive

denials. The last known denial dates from 1747. His further fate is unknown. For more details, see Veselago 1885, pp. 162-163; *Russkie ekspeditsii* 1984, pp. 298-299; Fedorova 2003.

406   "without sword", *bez shpagi*. As an exiled convict, Kazantsev did not have the right to wear a sword.

407   "On 13 sledges", in the document *na 13 podvodakh*. Actually, the Russian word *podvoda* refers more broadly to horse-drawn vehicles, and often, as here, to vehicles that travelers could hire at the posting stations: carts for summer travel, sledges for winter travel. The word could also refer to horses, including draught horses and packhorses.

408   "squatter's holding", in Russian *zaimka*.

409   "changed sledges", in Russian *peremenia podvody*. This phrase, frequently used in Chaplin's account of the return journey, will be consistently translated as "changed sledges". The reader, however, should keep in mind that due to the multiple meanings of the word *podvoda* (see note 407), it may indicate a change of horses only.

410   "to fill up the quarters along the route ahead", in the document *dlia utesneniia po doroge vperedi kvartir*.

411   "changing of horses", in the document *peremena loshadei*.

412   "To the yurts of the Cossack captain", in the document *v iurty k iasaulu*.

413   "Parish", in Russian *pogost*, a small village, basically a country church together with a cemetery and adjacent buildings.

414   "From the Kazakh Horde", in the document *ot kazach'ei ordy*. The Kazakh Khanate, situated approximately in the territory of present-day Kazakhstan, was divided into three "hordes". At this time (December 1729), the Kazakhs were still independent of Russia. However, between 1731 and the 1820s the three hordes were incorporated into the Russian Empire one by one.

415   "Always to a Tatar", in Russian *a vsio tataru*.

416   "Only compulsory horse service", in the document *vsio mezhdvornye*.

417   The Province of Siberia (*Sibirskaia guberniia*) was established in 1708, with Tobol'sk as its administrative center. Probably at the same time an internal customs administration was set up here, for inspecting the baggage of travelers from Siberia and for imposing customs duty. To assist the state authorities in this work, special officials, so-called *tseloval'niki* (from the verb *tselovat'*, to kiss), were appointed. *Tseloval'niki* were sworn in by kissing the cross (hence the Russian name) and formed a stratum of low-ranking elected assistants to the officials that performed various small administrative and economic tasks in the local districts of Siberia, from inn keeping to customs inspection. The title of *tseloval'nik* was abolished by the provincial reform of 1719, but nevertheless it occurs in documents throughout the first half of the 18th century (*Gosudarstvennost' Rossii*, vol. 5:2, pp. 455-456). The internal customs were abolished by imperial decree of 20 December 1753 (*ibid.*, vol. 3, p. 332).

418   "post-horse order", in Russian *podorozhnaia*.

419   "Schlüsselburg", in the document *Shliutenburch*.

VITUS JONASSEN BERING AND THE FIRST KAMCHATKA EXPEDITION

1   Lind & Møller 1997; Okhotina-Lind & Mëller 2001; Møller & Lind 2003; Okhotina-Lind 2004; Møller & Lind 2008.

2   "scoot": in Russian *shkut* (from Dutch *schuit*).

3   "snow": in Russian *shniava* (from Dutch *snauw*).

4   Instruction issued to G. Simson, captain of the ship *Lastka*. RGAVMF, fund 233, inv. 1, unit 11, folio 188-191; Elagin 1864, p. 138.

5   RGAVMF, fund 233, inv. 1, unit 18, folio 746 verso.

6   Okhotina-Lind & Mëller 2001, p. 34; Møller & Lind 2008, pp. 42-43.

7   RGAVMF, fund 212, inv. 11, unit 338, folio 85.

8   *Ibid.*, folio 85 verso.

9 "and do not expect for myself any better application", in Russian *ne ozhidaiu sebe luchshego ankurazhmentu. Ibid.,* folio 81.
10 *Ibid.,* folio 84.
11 RGAVMF, fund 223, inv. 1, unit 29, folio 110-111.
12 Published in English in Golder 1968/1922, Vol. I, pp. 5-8.
13 "...Bering has been in the East Indies etc.", in Russian: *Bering v Ost-Indii byl i obkhozhdenie znaet, a fon Verd byl shturmanom* (*Russkie ekspeditsii,* p. 33).
14 Kushnarev 1990, p. 182. On Bering's wife and in-laws in Vyborg, cf. Møller & Lind 2008, pp. 40-47.
15 RGAVMF, fund 216, inv. 1, unit 88, folio 12 verso.
16 RGAVMF, fund 212, inv. 11, unit 212, folio 107 verso.
17 *Russkie ekspeditsii,* pp. 36-37.
18 *Ibid.,* p. 40.
19 *Ibid.,* p. 43.
20 *Ibid.,* p. 44.
21 *Ibid.,* p. 40.
22 *Ibid.,* p. 41.
23 Novlianskaia 1970, p. 125.
24 *Ibid.,* p. 127.
25 *Ibid.,* p. 128.
26 *Ibid.*
27 *Ibid.,* p. 130.
28 *Russkie ekspeditsii,* p. 42.
29 *Ibid.,* pp. 45-46; RGAVMF, fund 216, inv. 1, unit 88, folio 49-52.
30 *Russkie ekspeditsii,* p. 45.
31 *Ibid.,* p. 46; as translated in Kushnarev 1990, p. 42.
32 Polonskij 1850, pp. 548-549.
33 Kushnarev 1990, p. 42.
34 *Russkie ekspeditsii,* p. 46.
35 Sgibnev 1868; *Russkie ekspeditsii,* pp. 28-30, 283-284.
36 RGADA, fund 9, section II, unit 43, folio 374; Efimov 1964, map no. 56.
37 RGAVMF, fund 216, inv. 1, unit 88, folio 58.
38 *Ibid.,* folio 67 verso.
39 Sgibnev 1869a; Sgibnev 1869b, pp. 129-130; *Russkie ekspeditsii,* pp. 55, 59-61, 287-288.
40 RGAVMF, fund 913, inv. 1, unit 2, folio 8 verso.
41 RGAVMF, fund 216, inv. 1, unit 88, folio 101v-102.
42 *Russkie ekspeditsii,* p. 54.
43 RGAVMF, fund 216, inv. 1, unit 88, folio 108; fund 913, inv. 1, unit 2, folio 11, 119v.
44 RGAVMF, fund 216, inv. 1, unit 88, folio 111v.-112; *Russkie ekspeditsii,* p. 55.
45 RGAVMF, fund 216, inv. 1, unit 88, folio 112.
46 RGAVMF, fund 913, inv. 1, unit 2, folio 14.
47 RGAVMF, fund 216, inv. 1, unit 88, folio 113.
48 *Ibid.,* folio 115.
49 *Ibid.,* folio 118.
50 *Ibid.,* folio 119 verso; *Russkie ekspeditsii,* pp. 56-59.
51 RGAVMF, fund 216, inv. 1, unit 88, folio 100.
52 RGAVMF, fund 216, inv. 1, unit 110, folio 12.
53 *Ibid.,* folio 21 verso.
54 *Russkie ekspeditsii,* p. 66.
55 *Ibid.,* p. 63.
56 *Ibid.,* p. 66.
57 RGAVMF, fund 216, inv. 1, unit 110, folio 40.
58 *Ibid.,* folio 41.
59 *Ibid.,* folio 41 verso.
60 *Ibid.,* folio 42 verso.
61 *Ibid.*
62 *Ibid.,* folio 43.
63 *Ibid.,* folio 45.
64 *Ibid.,* folio 45 verso.
65 *Ibid.*
66 Cf. the present edition, folio 40 verso.

67 RGAVMF, fund 216, inv. 1, unit 88, folio 225; *Russkie ekspeditsii,* p. 67.
68 RGAVMF, fund 216, inv. 1, unit 110, folio 60; *Russkie ekspeditsii,* p. 69.
69 Pshenichnyi 1993, p. 7.
70 *Ibid.,* pp. 8-9.
71 Polonskii 1850, p. 535; Berg 1946, pp. 88-89; Kushnarev 1976, pp. 8-11; Kushnarev 1990, pp. 9-14; Pasetskij 1982, p. 16; *Russkie ekspeditsii.*
72 Belov 1956, p. 258.
73 In Russian *razvedat' put' v Ameriku, primykaiushchuiu k Azii, i vyiasnit', kto iavliaetsia sosedom Rossii na etom materike.* Grekov 1960, pp. 20-21.
74 Pokrovskii 1941, p. 25; Andreev 1943, p. 31; Lebedev 1950, p. 94.
75 Polevoj 1975, p. 30.
76 *Russkie ekspeditsii,* p. 35.
77 *Ibid.,* p. 290.
78 Berg 1946, pp. 50-54; *Russkie ekspeditsii,* p. 290.
79 Miller 1758, p. 104.
80 Cf. the present edition, folio 49 verso.
81 Cf. the present edition, note 260, pp. 301-302.
82 Cf. the present edition, folio 50.
83 RGAVMF, fund 216, inv. 1, unit 87, folio 228; *Russkie ekspeditsii,* p. 85; Kushnarev 1990, p. 101.
84 RGAVMF, fund 216, inv. 1, unit 87, folio 228; *Russkie ekspeditsii,* p. 85; Kushnarev 1990, p. 102.
85 RGAVMF, fund 216, inv. 1, unit 87, folio 228; *Russkie ekspeditsii,* p. 85; Kushnarev 1990, pp. 105-106.
86 *Russkie ekspeditsii,* p. 86; Kushnarev 1990, p. 107.
87 Cf. the present edition, folio 51 verso.
88 RGAVMF, fund 216, inv. 1, unit 14, folio 158.
89 Cf. the present edition, folio 59.
90 RGAVMF, fund 216, inv. 1, unit 110, folio 99; *Russkie ekspeditsii,* p. 88.
91 Cf. the present edition, folio 61.
92 RGAVMF, fund 216, inv. 1, unit 110, folio 99; *Russkie ekspeditsii,* p. 88.
93 Cf. the present edition, folio 74.
94 *Russkie ekspeditsii,* p. 88.
95 Quoted from the English translation in Fisher 1977, p. 12.
96 Vozgrin 1975, pp. 34-35; *Russkie ekspeditsii,* p. 290.
97 RGIA, fund 1329, inv. 1, unit 35, folio 283-288; *Russkie ekspeditsii,* pp. 94-96.
98 *Ibid.,* p. 96.
99 RGIA, fund 1329, inv. 1, unit 35, folio 289-291; *Russkie ekspeditsii,* p. 97; in English translation, Fisher 1977, pp. 112-113.
100 RGADA, fund 248, inv. 17, unit 1089, folios 788-788 verso.
101 *Ibid.,* folio 789.
102 RGAVMF, fund 212, inv. 3, unit 129, folio 392 verso.
103 RGAVMF, fund 216, inv. 1, unit 1, folio 622; *Russkie ekspeditsii,* p. 133.
104 *Ibid.*
105 RGAVMF, fund 216, inv. 1, unit 29, folio 233 verso.
106 Pokrovskij 1941, p. 332.

THE RUSSIAN NAVY AND MAPPING

1 Deane, p. 47.
2 Phillips, p. 27.
3 Phillips, pp. 24-25.
4 Hughes, p. 51.
5 Hughes, p. 13.
6 Phillips, p. 33.
7 Phillips, p. 34.
8 Phillips, p. 39.
9 Phillips, p. 43.
10 Deane, p. 4.

11 Vucinich, pp. 48-50.
12 Okhuizen, Edwin, see p. 102.
13 Vucinich, pp. 55-60.
14 Vucinich, pp. 60-61.
15 Okhuizen, p. 106.
16 Phillips, pp. 50-51.
17 Kendrick, p. 89.
18 Jones, p. 193.
19 Jones, pp. 196-97.
20 Vucinich, p. 66.
21 Vucinich, p. 70.
22 Urness 1993, p. 24.
23 Konvitz, Josef, Cartography in France, 1660-1848: Science, Engineering, and Statecraft. Chicago: University of Chicago Press, 1987, pp. 4-68.
24 Howse, p. 16.
25 Kushnarev 1990, p. 6. The author states that this was the last of the old, poorly organized expeditions. The expedition of Evreinov and Luzhin was the first of the scientific expeditions.
26 Fisher 1977, p. 57. Note also the author's commentary on the translation of these orders.
27 Kushnarev 1990, p. 6.
28 Fisher 1977, p. 59.
29 Deane, pp. 56, 82.
30 This is the thesis of Fisher's book, Bering's Voyages, 1977.
31 Carol Urness 2003, p. 26.
32 Kushnarev 1990, pp. 9-10.
33 Fisher 1977, p. 85.
34 Frost 2003, p. 55.
35 Frost 2003, p. 56.
36 Vucinich, p. 71.
37 Vucinich, 76-77
38 This same newspaper article appeared in the Danish newspapers and Strahlenberg, a Swede who had been in Russia for many years, reported seeing it in "the common newspapers" in Sweden. Translated by Paul Brashear from the German edition, St. Peterburgische Zeitung.
39 Golder 1971, frontispiece.
40 Müller 1986, p. 56.
41 Müller 1986, p. 56.
42 Gibson, James R., Feeding the Russian Fur Trade: Provisionment of the Okhotsk Seaboard and the Kamchatka Peninsula, 1639-1856. Madison: University of Wisconsin Press, 1969, is the outstanding work on this subject.
43 Frost, Bering, has a fine description of the journey from St. Petersburg to Okhotsk on pages 29-47.

NAVIGATION AND SURVEYING

1 Imbert, p. 57.
2 Kushnarev 1990, p. 154.
3 Kushnarev 1990, p. 155, referring to Cook, James and J. King, A Voyage to the Pacific Ocean, vol. II, London, 1785, p. 473.
4 Pannekoek, A., A History of Astronomy, London: Allen and Unwin, 1961, Dover Edition, 1989, p. 289-90.
5 Forbes and Wilson, pp. 55-69.
6 Brown, pp. 221-22.
7 Smith, p. 183.
8 Kushnarev 1990, p. 39.
9 Imbert, p. 57.
10 Cross, Anthony G., "Shipbuilders and officers in the Russian navy," in ejusdem: By the Banks of the Neva: Chapters from the lives and careers in eighteenth-century Russia. Cambridge: Cambridge University Press, 1997, pp. 159-223, see p. 174.
11 Cross 1980, p. 225.
12 Hughes 1998, p. 54.
13 Hughes 1998, p. 302.
14 Hughes 1998, p. 303.
15 Bourne, p. xiii.
16 Bourne, p. 170.
17 Bourne, p. 1.
18 Taylor, p. 201.
19 Newton, p. 4.
20 Newton, p. 80.
21 Newton, p. 159.
22 Seller, p. 1.
23 Seller, p. 2.
24 Descriptions are from Seller, Taylor, and Waters.
25 Seller, p. [v], signature a.
26 Taylor, p. 121.
27 Divin 1993, p. 30.
28 Fisher 1992, pp. 28-29.
29 Imbert, p. 53.
30 Imbert, pp. 51-74.
31 Moore 1799; Lee 1853.
32 Bretagnon and Simon.

A SURVEY OF LITERATURE ON THE FIRST KAMCHATKA EXPEDITION

1 Berkh 1823, pp. II-III.
2 Ibid., pp. 2, 6-7.
3 Ibid., pp. 13, 16.
4 Ibid., pp. 28-29.
5 Ibid., pp. 35, 44.
6 Ibid., pp. 41, 49-50.
7 Ibid., pp. 56-57.
8 Ibid., p. 76.
9 Russkie ekspeditsii, pp. 70-84.
10 Dall 1890b, pp. 761-771
11 Bering 1847. Republished in Russian in Vakhtin 1890, pp. 86-96; Pokrovskii 1941, pp. 59-68. The first English translation of the printed Russian text appeared in Dall 1890a, pp. 135-143. More recent English translations in Golder 1922/1968, vol. I, pp. 9-20, and Dmytryshyn 1988, pp. 79-86 (incomplete). Manuscript copies of the original report are in the Foreign Policy Archives of the Russian Empire (AVPRI, fund 130, inv. 130/1, unit 1, pp. 1-10) and the Russian State Archives of Military History (RGVIA, fund 846, unit 23471), both in Moscow. The latter manuscript copy is the one Pokrovskii used.
12 Dmytryshyn 1988, pp. 85-86. Immediately after the passage cited here, a whole page of the text, covering Bering's return voyage from the Arctic Ocean to Lower Kamchatsk, is missing in Dmytryshyn's translation, clearly by accident.
13 The more recent English translations of the "Short Account" (Golder 1922/1968, Dmytryshyn 1988) omit the appended schedules. Dall 1890a reproduced the "Catalogue of towns and notable places" (p. 144), but omitted the "Table showing distances etc."
14 Dmytryshyn 1988, p. 82.
15 The precise time of the dispatch of the map is disputed. Kushnarev insists that Bering sent the map from Okhotsk the day before he put out to sea, 21 August 1727 (Kushnarev 1990, p. 193).
16 One map is in the Russian State Archives of Military History (RGVIA). First published in Efimov 1964 as map no. 64. The second one is in the Russian State Archives of Ancient Documents (RGADA). First published in Efimov 1971, between pp. 244-245.
17 Urness 1987 reproduces five eighteenth-century printings of Bering's "Short Account", in French and English, pp. 261-336.
18 Urness 1987, pp. 179-183; Kushnarev 1991, p. 158.
19 Okhotina-Lind & Møller 2001, pp. 415-418.
20 Bagrow 1948, pp. 35-37, lists 12+2 manuscript copies of the "Final Map"; Kejlbo 1993 adds two maps to Bagrow's list; Kushnarev 1990 states, with reference to Efimov 1964, that "in all there are seventeen known copies". However, none of the lists includes the

so-called "Prince of Liechtenstein copy" from the James Ford Bell Library of the University of Minnesota (cf. plate XXX). A copy with ethnographic sketches, in the State Historical Museum (GIM) in Moscow, briefly mentioned in Efimov 1964 (no. 66), was more thoroughly described in Navrot 1971. After thorough restoration it was displayed at the GIM in 1997 at the exhibition "Relics from the History of the Russian State, from the eleventh to the twentieth century" (*Relikvii istorii Gosudarstva Rossiiskogo XI-XIX vv.*).

21 The English quotations are from R. Fisher's translation of the article (Fisher 1977, pp. 12-13).

22 Anon. [G.F. Müller?] 1730.

23 Lauridsen 1889, p. 36.

24 Fisher 1977, pp. 180-183.

25 *Russkie ekspeditsii* 1984, Nos. 57 and 59, pp. 87-90.

26 Bering's letter was originally published in Hofman 1755, pp. 249-250. Republished, in the original Danish and in Russian translation, in Okhotina-Lind & Møller 2001, pp. 30-35. The manuscript seems to have been lost.

27 In Danish: "[Jeg] har været nogle 1000 Miile igiennem Øster-Tartariet, saa vidt, som Land var at finde, forbi Chamsiatke; og endnu nogle 100 Miile længere, som kand sees af Land-Korterne, nemlig den Asiatiske Part, som man ellers faaer fra Nørrenberg, jeg maa tilstaae, at, eftersom jeg havde Lyst at reyse i min Ungdom, at jeg hidtil har havt min Deel; thi denne Reyse har været forbi China og Japan, og kommer ey derved nogen Ostindiske Reyse, saavel til Lands som til Vands".

28 The text of Delisle's report was published in Hintzsche 2004, no. 1, pp. 3-18, in the original French and in German translation. The protocol entry is quoted on p. 16, in the original Latin and in German translation.

29 The decree was published in Russian in Gnučeva 1940, p. 40, and in German translation in Hintzsche 2004, no. 4, pp. 26-29.

30 Delisle's instructions have been published in Hintzsche 2004, nos. 18 and 19, pp. 73-120.

31 Delisle's memoir was recently published in Hintzsche 2004, no. 14, pp. 46-67, in the original French and in German translation. For an English translation, cf. Golder 1914/1971, pp. 303-313. A 1733 copy of the map, entitled "Carte de la Tartarie Orientale iusqaux terres les plus voisines de l'Amerique…" is reproduced in the appendix to Hintzsche 2004.

32 Müller 1754, p. 64.

33 *Ibid.*, p. 65-67; Breitfuss 1939, p. 93.

34 Müller 1754, pp. 63-64.

35 Urness 1987, pp. 221-223.

36 *Ibid.*, p. 228.

37 Müller 1754, p. 12.

38 Müller 1758a and 1758b.

39 Müller 1761, Müller 1766, and Müller 1784. Müller 1986 is a modern English edition by Carol Urness, with a most informative introductory essay.

40 Müller 1758a, pp. 116-119.

41 Cook 1967, 1, p. 433. Cook left an unfilled space for page reference to "Harris's Collection".

42 Muller/ Müller 1761.

43 Harris 1764, p. 1021. "Behring's original journal" could be either Chaplin's Journal or Bering's report to the Admiralty College of March 10, 1730. Both documents include the additional information found in Campbell's paraphrase. For a detailed discussion of the Bering material in the Harris/ Campbell volume and its relation to Du Halde, cf. Urness 1987, pp. 186-190, 302-319).

44 Litke 1835, pp. 230-235.

45 Sopotsko 1983, pp. 187-222.

46 *Ibid.*, p. 186.

47 Møller 2003, pp. 87-90.

48 A.P. 1850; [A.S. Polonskii] 1851.

49 Kushnarev 1976 and 1990.

50 [A.S. Polonskii] 1851, p. 19.

51 Ber 1849a, pp. 252-253.

52 Ber 1849a.

53 Sokolov 1851.

54 Sokolov 1849, p. 396.

55 Ber 1849b. Looking back at the controversy 23 years later, Ber wrote, in the preface to the German version of his treatise, that his lecture in the Geographical Society not only stirred sympathy for Bering, but also, quite unintentionally, provoked spiteful Russian patriotism (Ber 1872, p. IV).

56 Perevalov 1949, p. 84.

57 Divin 1950, p. 3.

58 Fisher 1992, pp. 39, 41, 48.

59 *Ibid.*, pp. 40-41.

60 Ber 1872, p. 234; Ber 1850, p. 283.

61 Fisher 1977, p. 8.

62 Pokrovskii 1941, pp. 21-26.

63 Efimov 1950, pp. 23-26, 230-236.

64 Kushnarev 1976, p. 11; Kushnarev 1990, p. 14.

65 Polevoi 1964.

66 Fisher 1977, pp. 76-107.

67 Urness 1987, p. VI.

68 ibid., pp. 243-244.

References

Andreev, A. I. (1943) "Ekspeditsii V. Beringa", *Izvestiia Vsesoiuznogo geograficheskogo obshchestva*, 75, no. 2 (March-April), pp. 3-44.

Andriushchenko, N.S. (2006) *Polnaia morskaia entsiklopediia*. Moscow: AST, Astrel'.

Anisimov, Evgenii (1999) *Dyba i knut. Politicheskii sysk i russkoe obshchestvo v XVIII veke*. Moscow: Novoe literaturnoe obozrenie.

Anon. [Sokolov, A.P.] (1850) "Pervaia kamchatskaia ekspeditsiia Beringa, 1725-29 goda", *Zapiski gidrograficheskogo departamenta Morskogo ministerstva*, vol. VIII. St. Petersburg. Section IV, Smes' [Varia], pp. 1-24.

Anon. [G.F. Müller?] (1730) "Udi Aaret 1725 den 5. Febr. er Søe-Capitrin Bering ..." *Nye Tidender om Lærde og curieuse Sager*. No. 16, 20 April, pp. 254-256.

A.P. [Polonskii, A.S.] (1851) "Pervaia kamchatskaia ekspeditsiia Beringa 1725-1729 goda", *Otechestvennye zapiski*, vol. LXXV, 3-4. St. Petersburg. Section VIII, Smes' [Varia], pp. 1-24.

Bagrow, L. (1948) »The Vitus Bering first voyage maps«, *Geografisk Tidsskrift*, vol. XLIX. Copenhagen, pp. 32-40.

Belov, M.I. (1956) *Arkticheskoe moreplavanie s drevnejshikh vremion do serediny XIX veka* (= Istoriia otkrytiia i osvoeniia severnogo morskogo puti, 1), Moscow: Morskoi transport.

Ber, K.M. (1849a) "Zaslugi Petra Velikogo po chasti rasprostraneniia geograficheskikh poznanii. Chast' pervaia", *Zapiski russkogo geograficheskogo obshchestva*. St. Petersburg. Kn.3, pp. 217-253.

Ber, K.M. (1849b) "Bering i Chirikov", *Russkij invalid,* no. 121-123.

Ber, K. M. (1850) »Zaslugi Petra Velikogo po chasti rasprostraneniia geogr. poznanii. Chast' vtoraia«, *Zapiski Russkogo geograficheskogo obshchestva*. St. Petersburg. Kn. 4, pp. 260-283.

Ber, K.M. (1872) [Karl E. von Baer] *Peters des Großen Verdienste um die Erweiterung der geographischen Kenntnisse*. St. Petersburg: Die Kaiserliche Akademie der Wissenschaften. (= Beiträge zur Kenntnis des russischen Reiches und der angrenzenden Länder Asiens, 16. Bd.).

Berg, L.S. (1946) *Otkrytie Kamchatki i ekspeditsii Beringa. 1725-1742,* Moscow: Izd-vo Akademii Nauk SSSR.

Bering, Vitus (1847) "Donesenie flota kapitana Beringa ob ekspeditsii ego k vostochnym beregam Sibiri", *Zapiski voenno-topograficheskogo depo,* chast' X, St. Petersburg, pp. 69-79.

Berkh, Vasilii (1823) *Pervoe morskoe puteshestvie rossiian, predpriniatoe dlia resheniia geograficheskoi zadachi: Soediniaetsia li Aziia s Amerikoiu? i sovershennoe v 1727, 1728 i 1729 godakh pod nachal'stvom flota Kapitana 1-go ranga Vitusa Beringa. S prisovokupleniem kratkogo biograficheskogo svedeniia o Kapitane Beringe i byvshikh s nim ofitserakh*. St. Petersburg: The Imperial Academy of Sciences, 1823.

Berkh, Vasilii (1833) "Zhizneopisanie Kapitana Komandora Vitusa Bering", in ejusdem: *Zhizneopisaniia pervykh rossiiskikh admiralov ili Opyt istorii rossiiskogo flota*. Vol. 2. St. Petersburg: Morskaia Tipografiia, pp. 202-234.

Björkbom, Carl (1941) "Two Bering maps in the Royal Library at Stockholm, *Ethnos*, Vol. 6, July-December, Nos. 3-4., pp. 128-134.

Bourne, William (1963) *A Regiment for the Sea and other writings on navigation*. Edited by E.G.R. Taylor. Cambridge: Hakluyt Society.

Breitfuss, L. (1939) "Early Maps of North-Eastern Asia and of the Lands around the North Pacific. Controversy between G.F. Müller and N. Delisle", *Imago Mundi*, Vol. 3, pp. 87-99.

Bretagnon, P., and Simon, J-L (1986) *Planetary Programs and Tables from -4000 to +2800*. Richmond, VA: Willman-Bell.

Brown, L. (1949) *The Story of Maps*. Boston: Little, Brown and Company. Dover Press edition, 1979.

Cook, James (1967) *The Journals of Captain James Cook on his voyages of discovery*. Edited from the original manuscripts by J.C. Beaglehole, Vol. 3, Part 1 and 2, Cambridge University Press.

Cross, Anthony G. (1980) *"By the Banks of the Thames": Russians in Eighteenth Century Britain*. Newtonville, Mass: Oriental Research Partners.

Cross, Anthony G. (1997) *By the Banks of the Neva: Chapters from the lives and careers in eighteenth-century Russia*. Cambridge: Cambridge University Press.

Dall, William Healey (1890a) "A critical review of Bering's First Expedition, 1725-30, together with a translation of his original report upon It. With a map", *The National Geographic Magazine*, Washington D.C., vol. 2, pp. 111-167.

Dall, William Healey (1890b) "Notes on an original manuscript chart of Bering's expedition of 1725-1730, and on an original manuscript chart of his second expedition; together with a summary of a journal of the first expedition, kept by Peter Chaplin, and now first rendered into English from Bergh's Russian version", *Report of the Superintendent of the Coast and Geodetic Survey*, Appendix No. 19, pp. 759-774.

[Deane, John] (1899), *History of the Russian Fleet during the Reign of Peter the Great*. London: Navy Records Society (= Navy Records Society Publications, no. 15).

Divin, Vasilii A. (1950) *A.I. Chirikov – zamechatel'nyi russkii moreplavatel' i uchionyi*. Moscow: Vsesoiuznoe obshchestvo po rasprostraneniiu politicheskikh i nauchnykh znanii.

Divin, Vasilii A. (1953) *Velikii russkii moreplavatel' A.I. Chirikov*. Moscow: Gos. izd-vo geograficheskoi literatury.

Divin, Vasilii A. (1993) *The Great Russian Navigator, A.I. Chirikov*, translated and edited by Raymond H. Fisher. Fairbanks: University of Alaska Press. [English translation of Divin 1953]

Dmytryshyn, Basil et al. (eds.) (1988) *Russian Penetration of the North Pacific Ocean, 1700-1797*. Volume two: *To Siberia and Russian America*, Portland, Oregon: Oregon Historical Society Press.

Du Halde, Jean Baptiste (1735) *Description géographique, historique, chronologique, politique et physique de l'empire de la Chine et de la Tartarie chinoise*. 4 vols. Paris: P.G. Mercier.

Efimov, A.V. (1950) *Iz istorii velikikh russkikh geograficheskikh otkrytii v Severnom Ledovitom i Tikhom okeanakh. XVII - pervaja polovina XVIII v*. Moscow: Gos. izd-vo geograficheskoi literatury.

Efimov, A.V. (ed) (1964) *Atlas geograficheskikh otkrytii v Sibiri i v severo-zapadnoi Amerike XVII-XVIII vv*. Moscow: Nauka.

Efimov, A.V. (1971) *Iz istorii velikikh russkikh geograficheskikh otkrytii*. Moscow: Nauka.

Elagin, Sergei (1864) *Istoriia russkogo flota. Period Azovskii*. St. Peterburg: Tipografiia Gogenfel'dena i Ko.

Enlightenment and Exploration in the North Pacific, 1741-1805 (1997) edited by Stephen Haycox, James Barnett, and Caedmon Liburd. Seattle: University of Washington Press.

Fedorova, T.S. (1998) "...I khodit' do Liubeka, a v Liubeke ozhidat' passazhirov..." *Gangut,* vyp. 17, St. Petersburg, pp. 84-90.

Fedorova, T. S. [Tatjana Fjodorova] et al. (1999) *Martin Spangsberg. En dansk opdagelsesrejsende i russisk tjeneste*. Esbjerg: Fiskeri-og Søfartsmuseet.

Fedorova, T. S. [Tatjana Fjodorova] et al. (s.a. [2002]). *Martin Spangsberg. A Danish Explorer in Russian Service*. Esbjerg: Fiskeri og Søfartsmuseet.

Fedorova, T.S. (2003) "Donosy na Beringa kak istochnik dlia izucheniia bytovoi zhizni Vtoroi Kamchatskoi ekspeditsii", in: Møller and Lind (eds.) 2003, pp. 33-49.

Fedorova, T.S. (2007a) "Martyn Petrovich Shpanberg", in: A.R. Artem'ev (ed) *Russkie pervoprokhodtsy na Dal'nem Vostoke v XVII XIX vv.* (= Istoriko-arkheologicheskie issledovaniia), Vol. 5, Part I, Vladivostok: Dal'nauka, pp. 318-333.

Fedorova, T.S. (2007b) "Pervoe plavanie rossiian v Iaponiiu", in: V.P. Leonov (ed) *Rossiia i Iaponiia. Sbornik nauchnykh trudov.* St. Petersburg: Izd-vo Al'faret, pp. 21-27.

Fel', Sergej E. (1960) *Kartografiia Rossii XVIII veka,* Moscow: Izd-vo geodezicheskoi literatury.

Fisher, Raymond H. (1977) *Bering's Voyages: Whither and Why.* Seattle and London: University of Washington Press.

Fisher, Raymond H. (1984) "The Early Cartography of the Bering Strait Region", *Arctic,* Vol. 37, No. 4 (December), pp. 574-589.

Fisher, Raymond H. (1992) "To Give Chirikov His Due," in: *Bering and Chirikov: The American Voyages and Their Impact,* edited by O.W. Frost. Anchorage: Alaska Historical Society, pp. 37-50.

Forbes, E., and Wilson, C. (1995) "The Solar Tables of Lacaille and the Lunar Tables of Mayer", in: *Planetary Astronomy from the Renaissance to the Rise of Astrophysics,* Volume 2 Part B, R. Taton and C. Wilson (eds.) Cambridge: Cambridge University Press, pp. 55-69.

Frost, O.W. (ed) (1992) *Bering and Chirikov. The American Voyages and Their Impact.* Anchorage, Alaska: Alaska Historical Society.

Frost, Orcutt (2003) *Bering: The Russian Discovery of America.* New Haven: Yale University Press.

Gibson, James R. (1969) *Feeding the Russian Fur Trade. Provisionment of the Okhotsk Seaboard and the Kamchatka Peninsula 1639-1856.* Madison, Milwaukee, and London: The U. of Wisconsin Press.

Gibson, James R. (1992) "Supplying the Kamchatka Expeditions 1725-30 and 1733-1742, in: Frost, O.W. (ed) (1992) *Bering and Chirikov. The American Voyages and Their Impact.* Anchorage, Alaska: Alaska Historical Society, pp. 90-116.

Gnucheva, V.F. (ed.) (1940) *Materialy dlia istorii ekspeditsii Akademii nauk v XVIII i XIX vekakh.* Moscow & Leningrad: Izd-vo Akademii nauk SSSR.

Golder, F.A. (1922/1968) *Bering's Voyages. An Account of the Efforts of the Russians to Determine the Relation of Asia and America.* Volume I: The Log Books and Official Reports of the First and Second Expeditions 1725-1730 and 1733-1742. New York: Octagon Books, Inc. (Reprint, orig. pub. 1922).

Golder, Frank A. (1914/1971) *Russian Expansion on the Pacific, 1641-1850.* New York: Paragon Book Reprint Corp. (Reprint, orig. pub. 1914).

Gosudarstvennost' Rossii. Slovar'-spravochnik (1996-2005) Kniga 1-5:2. (O.F. Kozlov et al., eds.) Moscow: Nauka.

Grekov, Vadim I. (1960) *Ocherki iz istorii russkikh geograficheskikh issledovanii v 1725-65 gg.* Moscow: Izd-vo Akademii nauk SSSR.

Harris, John (ed.) (1764) *Navigantium atque Itenerantium Bibliotheca, or a complete collection of voyages and travels. Now carefully revised, with large additions, and continued down to the present time.* Vol. II, London [revised by John Campbell].

Hintzsche, Wieland (ed.) *Dokumente zur 2. Kamčatkaexpedition 1730-1733. Akademiegruppe* (2004) Bearbeitet von Wieland Hintzsche in Zusammenarbeit mit Natasha Ochotina Lind und Peter Ulf Møller. (= Quellen zur Geschichte Sibiriens und Alaskas aus russischen Archiven, Band IV.2). Halle: Verlag der Franckeschen Stiftungen zu Halle.

Hofman, Hans de (1755) *Samlinger af publique og private Stiftelser, Fundationer og Gavebreve,* Tome II. Copenhagen: Henrich Lillies enke.

Howse, Derek (1980) *Greenwich Time and the Discovery of the Longitude.* Oxford: Oxford University Press.

Hughes, Lindsey (1998) *Russia in the Age of Peter the Great.* New Haven and London: Yale UP.

Imbert, Bertrand (1992) "Bering and Chirikov: Pioneers of Siberian and North Pacific Geography", in: Frost, O.W. (ed) *Bering and Chirikov. The American Voyages and their Impact.* Anchorage, Alaska: Alaska Historical Society, pp. 51-74.

Jones, Robert E., "Why St Petersburg?" (2001) in: Lindsey Hughes (ed) *Peter the Great and the West: New Perspectives.* London: Palgrave, pp. 189-205.

Kamentseva, E. and N. Ustiugov (1975) *Russkaia metrologiia.* Moscow: Vysshaia shkola, 2nd edition.

Karabulatova, I.S., et al. (2005) *Malaia entsiklopediia narodov Tiumenskoi oblasti.* Tiumen': Izd-vo "Vektor Buk".

Kejlbo, Ib Rønne (1993) "Two previously unknown Vitus Bering maps", in: *Vitus Bering 1741-1991,* edited by N. Kingo Jacobsen. Copenhagen (= *Kulturgeografiske Skrifter* Bd. 13.2, English edition), pp. 41-64.

Kendrick, John (1997) "The Evolution of Shipbuilding in the Eighteenth Century," in: *Enlightenment and Exploration in the North Pacific, 1741-1805,* edited by Stephen Haycox, James Barnett, and Caedmon Liburd. Seattle: University of Washington Press, pp. 88-108.

Kniga ustav morskoi o vsiom chto kasaetsia dobromu upravleniiu v bytnosti flota na more (1993, reprint 1763/ 1720). Izdatel' K.V. Krenov. Moscow: "Novator".

Konvitz, Josef (1987) *Cartography in France, 1660-1848: Science, Engineering, and Statecraft.* Chicago: University of Chicago Press.

Kushnarev, Evgenii G. (1964) "Nereshionnye voprosy istorii pervoi kamchatskoi ekspeditsii", in: M.I. Belov (ed.) *Russkie arkticheskie ekspeditsii.* Leningrad: Gidrometeorologicheskoe izdatel'stvo, pp. 5-15.

Kushnarev, Evgenii G. (1976) *V poiskakh proliva.* Leningrad: Gidrometeoizdat.

Kushnarev, Evgenii G. (1990) *Bering's Search for the Strait. The First Kamchatka Expedition 1725-1730.* Edited and translated by E.A.P. Crownhart-Vaughan. Portland, Oregon: Oregon Historical Society Press.

Kušnarev, E. G. [Kushnarev] (1981) *På jagt efter strædet: Første Kamčatka-ekspedition,* Horsens. [Danish translation of Kushnarev 1976 by Kirsten Marie Møller-Sørensen].

Lauridsen, Peter (1885) *Vitus J. Bering og de russiske Opdagelsesrejser fra 1725-43.* Copenhagen: Gyldendalske Boghandels Forlag.

Lauridsen, Peter (1889) *Vitus Bering. The Discoverer of Bering Strait* Revised by the author and translated from the Danish by Julius E. Olson. Chicago: S.C. Griggs Company.

Lebedev, D.M. (1950) *Geografiia v Rossii Petrovskogo vremeni.* M-L: Izd-vo Akademii nauk SSSR.

Lee, T.J. (1853) *A Collection of Tables and Formulae Useful in Surveying, Geodesy, and Practical Astronomy Including Elements for the Projection of Maps,* 2nd edition. U.S. Corps of Topographical Engineers, Washington DC.

Lind, Natasha Okhotina and Peter Ulf Møller (1997) *Kommandøren og konen. Arkivfund om danske deltagere i Vitus Berings ekspeditioner.* Copenhagen: Gyldendal.

Litke, F. (1835) *Puteshestvie vokrug sveta, sovershennoe po poveleniiu Imperatora Nikolaia I, na voennom shliupe Seniavine, v 1826, 1827, 1828 i 1829 godakh.* St. Petersburg: v tipografii Kh. Gintse.

Messerschmidt, Daniel Gottlieb (1968) *Forschungsreise durch Sibirien 1720-1727,* Teil 4. Edited by E. Winter, G. Uschmann und G. Jarosch. Berlin: Akademie-Verlag.

Materialy po istorii russkogo flota, Vol. V (1875) St. Petersburg: Tipografiia Morskogo ministerstva.

Materialy po istorii russkogo flota, Vol. VII (1879) St. Petersburg: Tipografiia Morskogo ministerstva.

Materialy po istorii russkogo flota, Vol. × (1883) St. Petersburg: Tipografiia Morskogo ministerstva.

Moore, Sir Jonas (1681) *A New Systeme of the Mathematicks.* London: A. Godbid, 1681.

Moore, J.H. (1799) *The New Practical Navigator,* First American Edition, from 13th English edition. Newburyport MA: E.M. Blunt.

Morskoi entsiklopedicheskii slovar', 1-3 (1991-1994) Edited by V.V. Dmitriev, Leningrad/ St. Petersburg: Sudostroenie.

[Müller, G.F.] (1754) *A Letter from a Russian Sea-Officer,* London: A. Linde.

Müller, Gerhard Friedrich (1758a) *Nachrichten von Seereisen, und zur See gemachten Entdeckungen, die von Russland aus längst den Küsten des Eismeeres und auf dem östlichen Weltmeere gegen Japon und America geschehen sind,* St. Petersburg (= Sammlung russischer Geschichte, III).

Miller [Müller, G.F.] (1758b) „Opisanie morskikh puteshestvii po ledovitomu i po vostochnomu moriu s rossiiskoi storony uchinionnykh", *Sochineniia i perevody, k pol'ze i uveseleniu sluzhashchie,* VII (janvar'), 3-27; (fevral'), 99-120; (mart), 195-212; (aprel'), 291-325; (mai), 387-409; VIII (iiul'), 9-32; (avgust), 99-129; (sentiabr'), 195-232; (oktiabr'), 309-336; (noiabr'), 394-424.

Muller, S. [Müller, G.F.] (1761) *Voyages from Asia to America, For Completing the Discoveries of the North West Coast of America.* By Thomas Jefferys, Geographer to his Majesty, London: Printed for T. Jefferys, the Corner of St. Martin's Lane, Charing Cross. [Translation from the German edition, Müller 1758a]

Müller, Gerhard Friedrich (1766) *Voyages et découvertes faites par les Russes le long des côtes de la mer Glaciale & sur l'ocean Oriental, tant vers le Japon que vers l'Amerique,* 2 vols., Amsterdam.

Müller, Gerhard Friedrich (1784) "Efterretninger om Søe-Reiser og til Søes gjorte Opdagelser som ere foretagne fra Rusland af langs med Kysterne af Iishavet og fornemmelig i det Østlige Ocean, imod Japon og Amerika", in: Hallager, M. [translator and publisher] *Udførlige og troeværdige Efterretninger* [...], Copenhagen, pp. 1-248.

Müller, G.F. (1967) *Voyages from Asia to America, For Completing the Discoveries of the North West Coast of America.* Bibliotheca Australiana 26. Amsterdam: N. Israel & New York: Da Capo Press. [Photo mechanic reprint of Müller 1761].

Müller, Gerhard Friedrich (1986) *Bering's Voyages: The Reports from Russia.* Translated, with commentary by Carol Urness (= The Rasmuson Library. Historical Translation Series, Volume III). Fairbanks: University of Alaska Press.

Møller, Peter Ulf and Wieland Hintzsche (2003) "Hvornår og hvor blev Morten Spangberg født?" [When and where was M.Spangberg born?], *Personalhistorisk Tidsskrift* 2003:1, pp. 1-12.

Møller, Peter Ulf (2003) "The Changing Images of Vitus Bering: A Critical Study in the Russian and Danish Historiography of his Expeditions", in: Møller, Peter Ulf and Natasha Okhotina Lind (eds.) (2003) *Under Vitus Bering's Command: New Perspectives on the Russian Kamchatka Expeditions* (= Beringiana, vol. 1). Århus: Aarhus University Press, pp. 83-111.

Møller, Peter Ulf and Natasha Okhotina Lind (eds.) (2003) *Under Vitus Bering's Command: New Perspectives on the Russian Kamchatka Expeditions* (= Beringiana, vol. 1). Århus: Aarhus University Press.

Møller, Peter Ulf and Natasha Okhotina Lind (2008) *Until Death Do Us Part. The Letters and Travels of Anna and Vitus Bering.* Translated by Anna Halager (= Historical Translation Series, Vol. 14). Fairbanks, Alaska: University of Alaska Press.

Navrot, M.I. (1971) "Novyi variant itogovoi karty pervoi Kamchatskoi ekspeditsii", *Letopis' severa,* V, Moscow, pp. 173-179.

Newton, Samuel (1695) *An Idea of Geography and Navigation.* London: Christopher Hussey.

Novlianskaia, M.G. (1970) *Daniil Gotlib Messershmidt i ego raboty po issledovaniiu Sibiri.* Leningrad: Nauka.

Ocherki istorii Leningrada (1955), edited by M.P. Viatkin.Vol. I. Moscow-Leningrad: Izd-vo Akademii nauk SSSR.

Okhotina-Lind, Natal'ia (2004) "'Ia i moj Bering...' Chastnye pis'ma Vitusa Beringa i ego sem'i iz Okhotska v fevrale 1740 g." *Rossiia v XVIII stoletii.* Vypusk II, edited by E.E. Rychalovskii. Moscow: Jazyki slavianskoi kul'tury, pp. 177-220.

Okhotina-Lind, Natal'ia & Peter Ul'f Mëller [Møller] (eds.) (2001) *Vtoraia kamchatskaia ekspeditsiia. Dokumenty 1730-1733.* Chast' 1. *Morskie otriady.* Moscow: Pamiatniki istoricheskoi mysli.

Okhuizen, Edwin (1993) "The Dutch contribution to the cartography of Russia during the 16th-18th centuries," in: *Russians and Dutchmen: Proceedings of the Conference on the Relations between Russia and the Netherlands from the 16th to the 20th century held at the Rijks-*

museum Amsterdam, June 1989, edited by J. Braat, A.H. Huussen, jr., B. Naarden, and C.A.L.M. Willemsen. Groningen: Instituut voor Noord-en Oosteuropese Studies, pp. 71-115.

Pannekoek, A. (1989) *A History of Astronomy.* Dover Publications, 1989 [English edition first published in 1961, Dutch original in 1951].

Pasetskii, V.M. (1982) *Vitus Bering.* Moscow: Nauka.

Perevalov, V.A. (1949) *Lomonosov i Arktika: iz istorii geograficheskoi nauki i geograficheskikh otkrytii,* Moscow: Izdatel'stvo Glavsevmorputi.

Phillips, Edward J. (1995) *The Founding of Russia's Navy: Peter the Great and the Azov Fleet,* 1688-1714. Westport: Greenwood Press.

Pokrovskii, A. (ed) (1941) *Ekspeditsiia Beringa: sbornik dokumentov,* Moscow: Glavnoe arkhivnoe upravlenie NKVD SSSR.

Polevoi, B.P. (1964) "Glavnaia zadacha pervoi kamchatskoi ekspeditsii po zamyslu Petra I. (O novoi interpretatsii instruktsii Vitusu Beringu 1725 g.)" [The principal task of the First Kamchatka Expedition according to the intent of Peter the Great. (A new interpretation of the instruction of 1725 to Vitus Bering)], *Voprosy geografii Kamchatki.* Petropavlovsk-Kamchatskii. No. 2, pp. 88-94.

Polevoi, B.P. (1975) "Piotr Pervyi, Nikolai Vitsen i problema 'soshlasia li Amerika s Asiej'", *Strany i narody vostoka,* vyp. XVII, kn. 3.

Polevoi, B.P. (1982) *Pervootkryvateli Kuril'skikh ostrovov.* Iuzhno-Sakhalinsk: Dal'nevostochnoe.

Polonskii, A.S. (1850) "Pervaia Kamchatskaia ekspeditsiia 1725-1729", *Zapiski Gidrograficheskogo departamenta Morskogo ministerstva.* Chast' VIII, pp. 535-556.

Pshenichnyi, I.P. (1993) "Bot 'Sv. Gavriil'", *Gangut,* No. 4, pp. 4-10.

Pshenichnyi, I.P. (1995) "Bot 'Sv. Gavriil'", *Gangut,* No. 6, pp. 90-97.

Russkaia tikhookeanskaia epopeia (1979) Edited by V.A. Divin et al. Khabarovsk: Khabarovskoe knizhnoe izdatel'stvo.

Russkie ekspeditsii po izucheniiu severnoi chasti Tikhogo okeana v pervoi polovine XVIII v. Sbornik dokumentov (1984) Edited by T.S. Fedorova et al. (= Issledovaniia russkikh na Tikhom okeane v XVIII-pervoi polovine XIX v.). Moscow: Nauka.

Seller, John (1694) *Practical Navigator,* 7th edition. London: J.D. for the Author...and Richard Mount.

Sgibnev, A.S. (1868) "Bol'shoi Kamchatskii nariad", *Morskoi sbornik,* no. 12. Neofitsial'nyi otdel, pp. 131-139.

Sgibnev, A.S. (1869a) "Ekspeditsiia Shestakova", *Morskoi sbornik,* no. 2. Neofitsial'nyi otdel, pp. 1-34.

Sgibnev, A.S. (1869b) "Istoricheskii ocherk glavneishikh sobytii v Kamchatke. 1. 1650 g. – 1742 g." *Morskoi sbornik,* vol. CI, no. 4 (April). Neofitsial'nyi otdel, pp. 65-142.

Sgibnev, A.S. (1869c) "Okhotskii port s 1649 po 1852 g. (Istoricheskii ocherk)." *Morskoi sbornik,* vol. CV, no. 11 (November). Neofitsial'nyi otdel, pp. 1-63.

Shishkov, A.S. (1832) *Morskoi slovar' soderzhashchii ob''iasnenie vsekh nazvanii upotrebliaemykh v morskom iskusstve.* Dopolnen i izdan Uchionym komitetom Glavnogo morskogo shtaba Ego Imperatorskogo Velichestva, St. Petersburg: V tipografii Imperatorskoi Rossiiskoi Akademii. [Shipbuilding dictionary]

Shishkov, A.S. (1835) *Morskoi slovar' soderzhashchii ob''iasnenie vsekh nazvanii upotrebliaemykh v morskom iskusstve.* Dopolnen i izdan Uchionym komitetom Glavnogo morskogo shtaba Ego Imperatorskogo Velichestva, St. Petersburg: V tipografii Imperatorskoi Rossiiskoi Akademii. [Navigation dictionary]

Slovar' russkikh narodnykh govorov, 40 vols. (more forthcoming) (1965-2006). Edited by F.P. Filin, F.P. Sorokoletov et al. Leningrad/ St. Petersburg: Nauka.

Slovar' russkogo iazyka XI-XVII vv., 27 vols. (more forthcoming) (1975-2006). Edited by S.G. Barkhudarov et al. Moscow: Nauka.

Slovar' russkogo iazyka XVIII veka, 17 vols. (more forthcoming) (1984-2007). Edited by L.L. Kutina, Iu.S. Sorokin et al. Leningrad/ St. Petersburg: Nauka.

Smith, J. (1986) *From Plane to Spheroid: Determining the Figure of the Earth from 3000 B.C. to the 18th Century Lapland and Peruvian*

Society Expeditions. Rancho Cordovo, California: Landmark En-
terprises.

Sokolov, A.P. (1849) "Bering i Chirikov", *Severnaia pchela*, no. 98, 5
May, pp. 391-392; no. 99, 6 May, pp. 395-396.

Sokolov, A.P. (1851) "Severnaia ekspeditsiia 1733-1743 goda", *Zapiski
gidrograficheskogo departamenta morskogo ministerstva*, chast'
IX, pp. 190-469.

Sopotsko, A.A. (1983) *Istoriia plavaniia V. Beringa na bote "Sv. Gavriil"
v Severnyj Ledovityj okean*. Moscow: Nauka.

Steller, Georg Wilhelm (2003) *Steller's History of Kamchatka: Collected
Information Concerning the History of Kamchatka, Its Peoples,
Their Manners, Names, Lifestyle, and Various Customary Practices.*
Edited by Marvin W. Falk. Translated by Margritt Engel and Karen
Willmore (= Rasmuson Library Historical Translation Series, Vol.
12). Fairbanks, Alaska: University of Alaska Press.

Taylor, E.G.R. (1958) *The Haven-Finding Art: A History or Navigation
from Odysseus to Captain Cook*. London: Hollis & Carter.

Urness, Carol L. (1987) *Bering's First Expedition. A Re-examination
Based on Eighteenth-Century Books, Maps, and Manuscripts*. New
York and London: Garland Publishing, Inc.

Urness, Carol L. (1993) "Rybakov on the Delisle Map of 1706," in *New
Perspectives on Muscovite History: Selected Papers from the Fourth
World Congress for Soviet and East European Studies, Harrogate,
1990*. Edited by Lindsey Hughes. New York: St. Martin's Press,
pp. 24-34.

Urness, Carol L. (2003) "The First Kamchatka Expedition in Focus," in
*Under Vitus Bering's Command: New Perspectives on the Russian
Kamchatka Expeditions*. Edited by Peter Ulf Møller and Natasha
Okhotina Lind. Århus: Aarhus University Press, pp. 17-31.

Vakhtin, V. (1890) *Russkie truzheniki moria. Pervaia morskaia ekspeditsiia Beringa dlia resheniia voprosa soediniaetsia li Aziia s Amerikoi.*
St. Petersburg: Tipografiia Morskogo ministerstva.

Vasmer, Max (1953-58) *Russisches etymologisches Wörterbuch*, 1-3.
Heidelberg: Carl Winter. Universitätsverlag.

Veselago, F.F., ed. (1885-94) *Obshchii morskoi spisok*. Vols. 1-2. St.
Petersburg: Tipografiia V. Demakova.

Vozgrin, V.E. (1975) "Vitus Jonassen Bering: Obzor zarubezhnoi literatury", *Strany i narody Vostoka*, vyp. XVII, kn. 3, pp. 34-35.

Vucinich, Alexander (1965) *Science in Russian Culture: A History to
1860*. London: Peter Owen.

Waters, David W. (1958) *The Art of Navigation in England in Elizabe-
than and Early Stuart Times*. London: Hollis and Carter.

Notes on the Contributors

Gary A. Davis is a Professor in the Department of Civil Engineering
at the University of Minnesota. In addition to research in transportation engineering and traffic safety, he has also studied the astronomical methods used by 18th and 19th century explorers, such as David
Thompson and Joseph Nicollet. His paper "David Thompson and the
Source of the Mississippi," appeared in *Terrae Incognitae*, 21, 2009, 1-20.

Tatiana Sergeevna Fedorova is Senior Research Fellow and former
Deputy Director at the Russian State Naval Archives in St. Petersburg. A
native of Leningrad and a 1954 graduate from the History Department
of Leningrad State University, she has devoted her entire working life
to the Naval Archives. Her numerous scholarly publications include a
co-edited multi-volume anthology of archival documents titled *Russkie
ekspeditsii po izucheniiu severnoj chasti Tikhogo okeana* (Moscow 1984-
2007) on the Russian Expeditions for the Exploration of the Northern
Pacific Ocean. Tatiana Fedorova is also co-author of *Martin Spangsberg.
A Danish Explorer in Russian Service*, Esbjerg 2002.

Peter Ulf Møller held the chair of Slavic Studies at the University of
Aarhus from 1999 to 2007. He is now Honorary Professor at the Depart-
ment of Cross-Cultural and Regional Studies at Copenhagen University.
For more than a decade, he has been engaged in publishing archival
documents from Vitus Bering's Kamchatka expeditions. Together with
Natasha Lind, he is co-editor of an extensive edition in Russian of
source material from the Second Kamchatka Expedition: *Vtoraia Ka-
mchatskaia Ekspeditsiia* (2001 and 2009), and co-author of *Until Death
Do Us Part: The Letters and Travels of Anna and Vitus Bering* (2008).
Other research interests include travel writing and Russian literature.

Viktor Georgievich Sedov, Captain, now retired. As former Deputy
Head of the Soviet Atlantic Oceanographic Expedition, he partici-
pated in the exploration of the Arctic, Atlantic and Indian oceans. As
Deputy Chief Editor (on science) of the Atlas of the Oceans, he took
part in compilation and publication of the Atlantic and Arctic Oceans
Atlases. As Senior Assistant of the Secretary of the Intergovernmental
Oceanographic Commission (UNESCO), he was responsible for UN
Ocean mapping activities. Now he works as Senior Researcher in the
State Hydrological Institute in St. Petersburg, on the study of inner
water bodies of Russia.

Carol Louise Urness is former Curator and Professor of the James
Ford Bell Library in Minneapolis, MN. Her PhD thesis, *Bering's First
Expedition. A Re-examination Based on Eighteenth-Century Books,
Maps, and Manuscripts* (published 1987) is an important contribu-
tion to understanding the purpose of the First Kamchatka Expedition.
Other publications include *A Naturalist in Russia: Letters of Peter Simon
Pallas to Thomas Pennant* (1967), *Bering's Voyages: The Reports from
Russia. A translation and edition of the writings of Gerhard Friedrich
Müller* (1986), and articles for *Terrae Incognitae* and *Mercator's World*.
In 2007, Carol Urness was named Fellow of the Society for the History
of Discoveries.

List of Illustrations

Index